General Motors

Cadillac Eldorado and Seville
Oldsmobile Toronado
Buick Riviera

Automotive Repair Manual

by Mike Stubblefield
and John H Haynes
Member of the Guild of Motoring Writers

Models covered:
Cadillac Eldorado (1971 thru 1985)
Cadillac Seville (1980 thru 1985)
Oldsmobile Toronado (1971 thru 1985)
Buick Riviera (1979 thru 1985)
Does not include diesel engine information

(38030-8B3)

Haynes Group Limited
Haynes North America, Inc.
www.haynes.com

Disclaimer

There are risks associated with automotive repairs. The ability to make repairs depends on the individual's skill, experience and proper tools. Individuals should act with due care and acknowledge and assume the risk of performing automotive repairs.

The purpose of this manual is to provide comprehensive, useful and accessible automotive repair information, to help you get the best value from your vehicle. However, this manual is not a substitute for a professional certified technician or mechanic.

This repair manual is produced by a third party and is not associated with an individual vehicle manufacturer. If there is any doubt or discrepancy between this manual and the owner's manual or the factory service manual, please refer to the factory service manual or seek assistance from a professional certified technician or mechanic.

Even though we have prepared this manual with extreme care and every attempt is made to ensure that the information in this manual is correct, neither the publisher nor the author can accept responsibility for loss, damage or injury caused by any errors in, or omissions from, the information given.

About this manual

Its purpose

The purpose of this manual is to help you get the best value from your vehicle. It can do so in several ways. It can help you decide what work must be done, even if you choose to have it done by a dealer service department or a repair shop; it provides information and procedures for routine maintenance and servicing; and it offers diagnostic and repair procedures to follow when trouble occurs.

We hope you use the manual to tackle the work yourself. For many simpler jobs, doing it yourself may be quicker than arranging an appointment to get the vehicle into a shop and making the trips to leave it and pick it up. More importantly, a lot of money can be saved by avoiding the expense the shop must pass on to you to cover its labor and overhead costs. An added benefit is the sense of satisfaction and accomplishment that you feel after doing the job yourself.

Using the manual

The manual is divided into Chapters. Each Chapter is divided into numbered Sections, which are headed in bold type between horizontal lines. Each Section consists of consecutively numbered paragraphs.

At the beginning of each numbered Section you will be referred to any illustrations which apply to the procedures in that Section. The reference numbers used in illustration captions pinpoint the pertinent Section and the Step within that Section. That is, illustration 3.2 means the illustration refers to Section 3 and Step (or paragraph) 2 within that Section.

Procedures, once described in the text, are not normally repeated. When it's necessary to refer to another Chapter, the reference will be given as Chapter and Section number. Cross references given without use of the word "Chapter" apply to Sections and/or paragraphs in the same Chapter. For example, "see Section 8" means in the same Chapter.

References to the left or right side of the vehicle assume you are sitting in the driver's seat, facing forward.

Even though we have prepared this manual with extreme care, neither the publisher nor the author can accept responsibility for any errors in, or omissions from, the information given.

NOTE

A **Note** provides information necessary to properly complete a procedure or information which will make the procedure easier to understand.

CAUTION

A **Caution** provides a special procedure or special steps which must be taken while completing the procedure where the Caution is found. Not heeding a Caution can result in damage to the assembly being worked on.

WARNING

A **Warning** provides a special procedure or special steps which must be taken while completing the procedure where the Warning is found. Not heeding a Warning can result in personal injury.

Acknowledgements

Wiring diagrams produced exclusively for Haynes North America, Inc. by Valley Forge Technical Communications. Technical writers who contributed to this project include Rob Maddox, Jay Storer and Jeff Kibler.

A book in the Haynes Automotive Repair Manual Series

ISBN-10: 1-56392-231-2
ISBN-13: 978-1-56392-231-2

Library of Congress Catalog Card Number 96-78093

99-320

Contents

Haynes author, mechanic and photographer with 1983 Cadillac Eldorado

Introduction to the Cadillac Eldorado and Seville, Oldsmobile Toronado and Buick Riviera

The Cadillac Eldorado, Oldsmobile Toronado and Buick Riviera models are available in a two-door coupe body style only. The Cadillac Seville is available in only a four-door sedan body style.

Both V6 and V8 engines are used in these vehicles. Oldsmobile and Buick models use carburetors, while early Cadillac models use carburetors and later Cadillac models are equipped with Multi-Port Fuel Injection (MPFI) or Throttle Body Injection (TBI).

The engine drives the front wheels through either a three- or four-speed automatic transmission via a separate final drive unit and driveaxles.

The front suspension is composed of upper and lower control arms, torsion bars and a stabilizer bar. The rear suspension on 1978 and earlier models consists of a solid axle with trailing arms, coil springs and shock absorber units. 1979 and later models are equipped with independent rear suspension, consisting of lower control arms, coil springs, shock absorber units and a rear stabilizer bar. Electronic level control is optional on all models. Power assisted steering is standard on all models.

The brakes are either four wheel disc or disc on the front and drum on the rear wheels, depending on model. Power assisted brakes are standard on all models.

Vehicle identification numbers

The Vehicle Identification Number (VIN) is visible through the driver's side of the windshield

Modifications are a continuing and unpublicized part of vehicle manufacturing. Since spare parts manuals and lists are compiled on a numerical basis, the individual vehicle numbers are essential to correctly identify the component required.

The body identification plate is normally found on the upper surface of the engine compartment firewall

Vehicle Identification Number (VIN)

This very important identification number is stamped on a plate attached to the left side of the dashboard and is visible through the driver's side of the windshield **(see illustration)**. The VIN also appears on the Vehicle Certificate of Title and Registration. It contains valuable information such as where and when the vehicle was manufactured, the model year and the body style.

Body identification plate

The body identification plate is normally located in the engine compartment on the right upper surface of the firewall **(see illustration)**. Like the VIN it contains valuable information about the manufacture of the vehicle, as well as information on the options with which it is equipped. This plate is especially useful for matching the color and type of paint for repair work.

VIN engine and model year codes

Two particularly important pieces of information found in the VIN are the engine code and the model year code. Counting from the left, on 1980 and earlier models the engine code letter designation is the 5th digit and the model year code letter designation is the 6th digit. On 1981 and later models, the engine code letter designation is the 8th digit and the model year code letter designation is the 10th digit.

On the models covered by this manual the engine codes are:

1971	
S (Oldsmobile)	455 cu in (7.5L) V8
S (Cadillac)	500 cu in (8.2L) V8
1972 through 1975	
W (Oldsmobile)	455 cu in (7.5L) V8
S (Cadillac)	500 cu in (8.2L) V8
1976	
S (Oldsmobile)	455 cu in (7.5L) V8
S (Cadillac)	500 cu in (8.2L) V8
1977 and 1978	
K (Oldsmobile)	403 cu in (6.6L) V8
S (Cadillac)	425 cu in (7.0L) V8 carbureted
T (Cadillac)	425 cu in (7.0L) V8 EFI
1979	
3 (Buick)	231 cu in (3.8L) turbo V6
R (Buick, Oldsmobile)	350 cu in (5.7L) V8
B (Cadillac)	350 cu in (5.7L) V8 (EFI)
1980	
3 (Buick)	231 cu in (3.8L) turbo V6
Y (Buick, Oldsmobile)	307 cu in (5.0L) V8 carbureted
R (Buick, Oldsmobile)	350 cu in (5.7L) V8 carbureted
8 (Cadillac)	350 cu in (5.7L) V8 EFI
9 (Cadillac)	368 cu in (6.0L) V8 DEFI
1981	
3 (Buick)	231 cu in (3.8L) turbo V6
4 (Buick, Cadillac, Oldsmobile)	252 cu in (4.1L) V6 carbureted
Y (Buick, Oldsmobile)	307 cu in (5.0L) V8 carbureted
9 (Cadillac)	368 cu in (6.0L) V8 DEFI
1982	
3 (Buick)	231 cu in (3.8L) turbo V6
4 (Buick, Cadillac, Oldsmobile)	252 cu in (4.1L) V6 carbureted
8 (Cadillac)	HT4100 (4.1L) V8 DFI
Y (Buick, Oldsmobile)	307 cu in (5.0L) V8 carbureted

Engine codes:

1983	
8 (Buick)	231 cu in (3.8L) turbo V6
4 (Buick, Oldsmobile)	252 cu in (4.1L) V6 carbureted
8 (Cadillac)	HT4100 (4.1L) V8 DFI
Y (Buick, Oldsmobile)	307 cu in (5.0L) V8 carbureted
1984	
4 (Buick, Oldsmobile)	252 cu in (4.1L) V6 carbureted
8 (Cadillac)	HT4100 (4.1L) V8 DFI
Y (Buick, Oldsmobile)	307 cu in (5.0L) V8 carbureted
1985	
4 (Buick)	252 cu in (4.1L) V6 carbureted
8 (Cadillac)	HT4100 (4.1L) V8 DFI
Y (Buick, Oldsmobile)	307 cu in (5.0L) V8 carbureted

On the models covered by this manual the model year codes are:

Code	Year
1	1971
2	1972
3	1973
4	1974
5	1975
6	1976
7	1977
8	1978
9	1979
A	1980
B	1981
C	1982
D	1983
E	1984
F	1985

Location of the engine identification number - V6 and HT4100 V8 engines

Location of the engine identification number - 307 and 350 cu in V8 engines

Engine identification numbers

On 231 cu in (3.8L) turbo V6, 252 (4.1L) V6 and HT-4100 V8 engines, the number is on the left (driver's side) of the block at the rear, just above the oil pan **(see illustration)**.

On the 307 cu in (5.0L) and 350 cu in (5.7L) V8 engines, the identification number is found on the front side of the block below the cylinder head **(see illustration)**.

The 368 cu in (6.0L), 425 cu (7.0L) and 500 cu in (8.2L) V8 engine number is located on the top of the block behind the intake manifold **(see illustration)**.

The 403 cu in (6.6L) V8 engine number is taped to the oil filler tube and left valve cover. On the 455 cu in (7.5L) engine, the number is taped to the oil filler tube as well.

Location of the engine identification number - 368, 425 and 500 cu in V8 engines

Location of the transmission identification number

Transmission identification number

The nameplate/ID number on the transmission can be found on the left side of the torque converter case **(see illustration)**.

Vehicle Emissions Control Information label

This label is found in the engine compartment. See Chapter 6 for more information on this label.

Buying parts

Replacement parts are available from many sources, which generally fall into one of two categories - authorized dealer parts departments and independent retail auto parts stores. Our advice concerning these parts is as follows:

Retail auto parts stores: Good auto parts stores will stock frequently needed components which wear out relatively fast, such as clutch components, exhaust systems, brake parts, tune-up parts, etc. These stores often supply new or reconditioned parts on an exchange basis, which can save a considerable amount of money. Discount auto parts stores are often very good places to buy materials and parts needed for general vehicle maintenance such as oil, grease, filters, spark plugs, belts, touch-up paint, bulbs, etc. They also usually sell tools and general accessories, have convenient hours, charge lower prices and can often be found not far from home.

Authorized dealer parts department: This is the best source for parts which are unique to the vehicle and not generally available elsewhere (such as major engine parts, transmission parts, trim pieces, etc.).

Warranty information: If the vehicle is still covered under warranty, be sure that any replacement parts purchased - regardless of the source - do not invalidate the warranty!

To be sure of obtaining the correct parts, have engine and chassis numbers available and, if possible, take the old parts along for positive identification.

Maintenance techniques, tools and working facilities

Maintenance techniques

There are a number of techniques involved in maintenance and repair that will be referred to throughout this manual. Application of these techniques will enable the home mechanic to be more efficient, better organized and capable of performing the various tasks properly, which will ensure that the repair job is thorough and complete.

Fasteners

Fasteners are nuts, bolts, studs and screws used to hold two or more parts together. There are a few things to keep in mind when working with fasteners. Almost all of them use a locking device of some type, either a lockwasher, locknut, locking tab or thread adhesive. All threaded fasteners should be clean and straight, with undamaged threads and undamaged corners on the hex head where the wrench fits. Develop the habit of replacing all damaged nuts and bolts with new ones. Special locknuts with nylon or fiber inserts can only be used once. If they are removed, they lose their locking ability and must be replaced with new ones.

Rusted nuts and bolts should be treated with a penetrating fluid to ease removal and prevent breakage. Some mechanics use turpentine in a spout-type oil can, which works quite well. After applying the rust penetrant, let it work for a few minutes before trying to loosen the nut or bolt. Badly rusted fasteners may have to be chiseled or sawed off or removed with a special nut breaker, available at tool stores.

If a bolt or stud breaks off in an assembly, it can be drilled and removed with a special tool commonly available for this purpose. Most automotive machine shops can perform this task, as well as other repair procedures, such as the repair of threaded holes that have been stripped out.

Flat washers and lockwashers, when removed from an assembly, should always be replaced exactly as removed. Replace any damaged washers with new ones. Never use a lockwasher on any soft metal surface (such as aluminum), thin sheet metal or plastic.

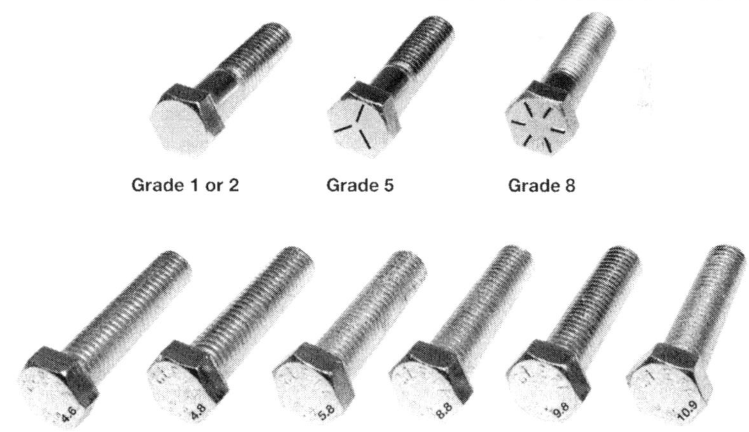

Bolt strength marking (standard/SAE/USS; bottom - metric)

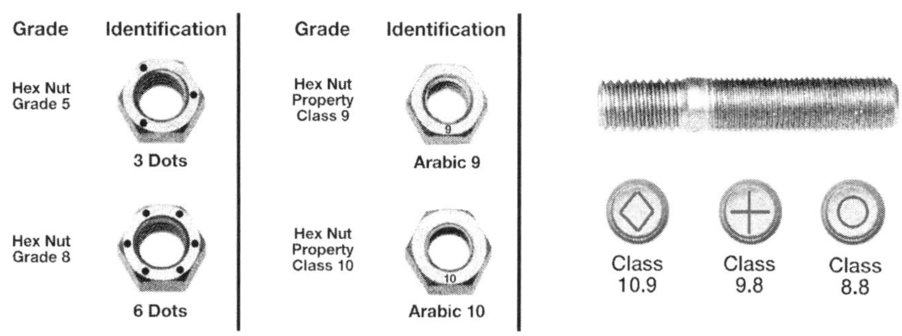

Standard hex nut strength markings

Metric hex nut strength markings

Metric stud strength markings

00-1 HAYNES

Fastener sizes

For a number of reasons, automobile manufacturers are making wider and wider use of metric fasteners. Therefore, it is important to be able to tell the difference between standard (sometimes called U.S. or SAE) and metric hardware, since they cannot be interchanged.

All bolts, whether standard or metric, are sized according to diameter, thread pitch and length. For example, a standard 1/2 - 13 x 1 bolt is 1/2 inch in diameter, has 13 threads per inch and is 1 inch long. An M12 - 1.75 x 25 metric bolt is 12 mm in diameter, has a thread pitch of 1.75 mm (the distance between threads) and is 25 mm long. The two bolts are nearly identical, and easily confused, but they are not interchangeable.

In addition to the differences in diameter, thread pitch and length, metric and standard bolts can also be distinguished by examining the bolt heads. To begin with, the distance across the flats on a standard bolt head is measured in inches, while the same dimension on a metric bolt is sized in millimeters (the same is true for nuts). As a result, a standard wrench should not be used on a metric bolt and a metric wrench should not be used on a standard bolt. Also, most standard bolts have slashes radiating out from the center of the head to denote the grade or strength of the bolt, which is an indication of the amount of torque that can be applied to it. The greater the number of slashes, the greater the strength of the bolt. Grades 0 through 5 are commonly used on automobiles. Metric bolts have a property class (grade) number, rather than a slash, molded into their heads to indicate bolt strength. In this case, the higher the number, the stronger the bolt. Property class numbers 8.8, 9.8 and 10.9 are commonly used on automobiles.

Strength markings can also be used to distinguish standard hex nuts from metric hex nuts. Many standard nuts have dots stamped into one side, while metric nuts are marked with a number. The greater the number of dots, or the higher the number, the greater the strength of the nut.

Metric studs are also marked on their ends according to property class (grade). Larger studs are numbered (the same as metric bolts), while smaller studs carry a geometric code to denote grade.

It should be noted that many fasteners, especially Grades 0 through 2, have no distinguishing marks on them. When such is the case, the only way to determine whether it is standard or metric is to measure the thread pitch or compare it to a known fastener of the same size.

Standard fasteners are often referred to as SAE, as opposed to metric. However, it should be noted that SAE technically refers to a non-metric fine thread fastener only. Coarse thread non-metric fasteners are referred to as USS sizes.

Since fasteners of the same size (both standard and metric) may have different strength ratings, be sure to reinstall any bolts, studs or nuts removed from your vehicle in their original locations. Also, when replacing a fastener with a new one, make sure that the new one has a strength rating equal to or greater than the original.

Metric thread sizes	Ft-lbs	Nm
M-6	6 to 9	9 to 12
M-8	14 to 21	19 to 28
M-10	28 to 40	38 to 54
M-12	50 to 71	68 to 96
M-14	80 to 140	109 to 154
Pipe thread sizes		
1/8	5 to 8	7 to 10
1/4	12 to 18	17 to 24
3/8	22 to 33	30 to 44
1/2	25 to 35	34 to 47
U.S. thread sizes		
1/4 - 20	6 to 9	9 to 12
5/16 - 18	12 to 18	17 to 24
5/16 - 24	14 to 20	19 to 27
3/8 - 16	22 to 32	30 to 43
3/8 - 24	27 to 38	37 to 51
7/16 - 14	40 to 55	55 to 74
7/16 - 20	40 to 60	55 to 81
1/2 - 13	55 to 80	75 to 108

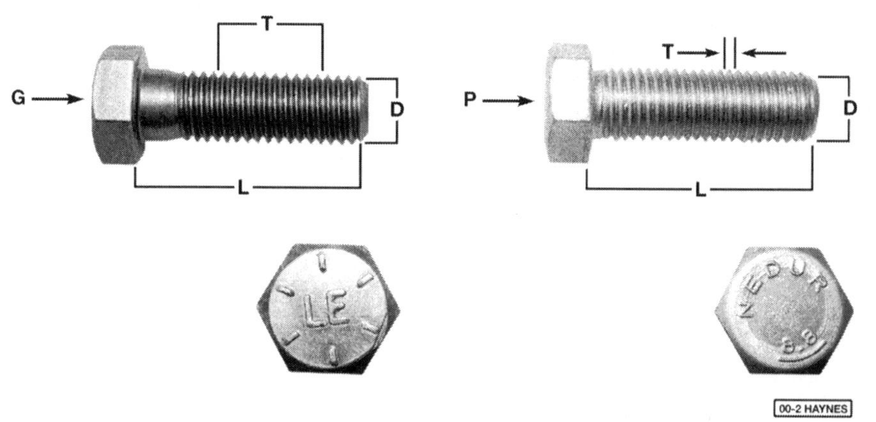

Standard (SAE and USS) bolt dimensions/grade marks

- G *Grade marks (bolt strength)*
- L *Length (in inches)*
- T *Thread pitch (number of threads per inch)*
- D *Nominal diameter (in inches)*

Metric bolt dimensions/grade marks

- P *Property class (bolt strength)*
- L *Length (in millimeters)*
- T *Thread pitch (distance between threads in millimeters)*
- D *Diameter*

Tightening sequences and procedures

Most threaded fasteners should be tightened to a specific torque value (torque is the twisting force applied to a threaded component such as a nut or bolt). Overtightening the fastener can weaken it and cause it to break, while undertightening can cause it to eventually come loose. Bolts, screws and studs, depending on the material they are made of and their thread diameters, have specific torque values, many of which are noted in the Specifications at the beginning of each Chapter. Be sure to follow the torque recommendations closely. For fasteners not assigned a specific torque, a general torque value chart is presented here as a guide. These torque values are for dry (unlubricated) fasteners threaded into steel or cast iron (not aluminum). As was previously mentioned, the size and grade of a fastener determine the amount of torque that can safely be applied to it. The figures listed here are approximate for Grade 2 and Grade 3 fasteners. Higher grades can tolerate higher torque values.

Fasteners laid out in a pattern, such as cylinder head bolts, oil pan bolts, differential cover bolts, etc., must be loosened or tightened in sequence to avoid warping the com-

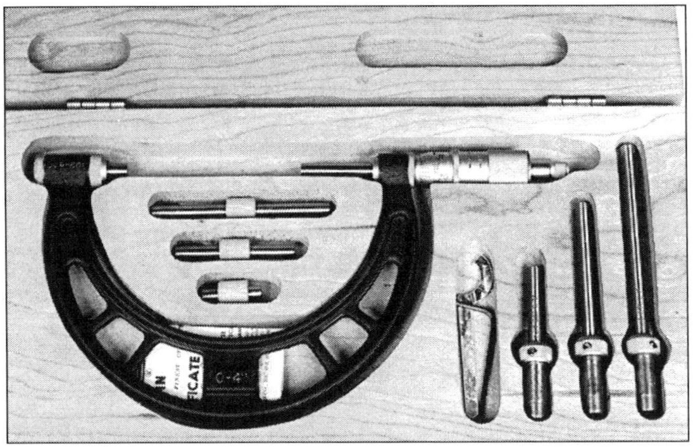

Micrometer set

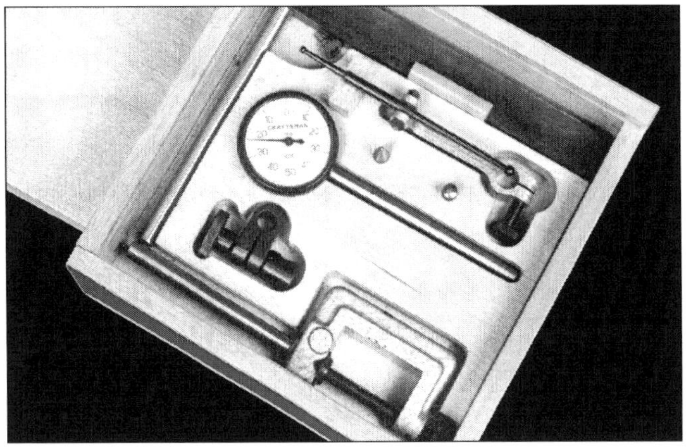

Dial indicator set

ponent. This sequence will normally be shown in the appropriate Chapter. If a specific pattern is not given, the following procedures can be used to prevent warping.

Initially, the bolts or nuts should be assembled finger-tight only. Next, they should be tightened one full turn each, in a criss-cross or diagonal pattern. After each one has been tightened one full turn, return to the first one and tighten them all one-half turn, following the same pattern. Finally, tighten each of them one-quarter turn at a time until each fastener has been tightened to the proper torque. To loosen and remove the fasteners, the procedure would be reversed.

Component disassembly

Component disassembly should be done with care and purpose to help ensure that the parts go back together properly. Always keep track of the sequence in which parts are removed. Make note of special characteristics or marks on parts that can be installed more than one way, such as a grooved thrust washer on a shaft. It is a good idea to lay the disassembled parts out on a clean surface in the order that they were removed. It may also be helpful to make sketches or take instant photos of components before removal.

When removing fasteners from a component, keep track of their locations. Sometimes threading a bolt back in a part, or putting the washers and nut back on a stud, can prevent mix-ups later. If nuts and bolts cannot be returned to their original locations, they should be kept in a compartmented box or a series of small boxes. A cupcake or muffin tin is ideal for this purpose, since each cavity can hold the bolts and nuts from a particular area (i.e. oil pan bolts, valve cover bolts, engine mount bolts, etc.). A pan of this type is especially helpful when working on assemblies with very small parts, such as the carburetor, alternator, valve train or interior dash and trim pieces. The cavities can be marked with paint or tape to identify the contents.

Whenever wiring looms, harnesses or connectors are separated, it is a good idea to identify the two halves with numbered pieces of masking tape so they can be easily reconnected.

Gasket sealing surfaces

Throughout any vehicle, gaskets are used to seal the mating surfaces between two parts and keep lubricants, fluids, vacuum or pressure contained in an assembly.

Many times these gaskets are coated with a liquid or paste-type gasket sealing compound before assembly. Age, heat and pressure can sometimes cause the two parts to stick together so tightly that they are very difficult to separate. Often, the assembly can be loosened by striking it with a soft-face hammer near the mating surfaces. A regular hammer can be used if a block of wood is placed between the hammer and the part. Do not hammer on cast parts or parts that could be easily damaged. With any particularly stubborn part, always recheck to make sure that every fastener has been removed.

Avoid using a screwdriver or bar to pry apart an assembly, as they can easily mar the gasket sealing surfaces of the parts, which must remain smooth. If prying is absolutely necessary, use an old broom handle, but keep in mind that extra clean up will be necessary if the wood splinters.

After the parts are separated, the old gasket must be carefully scraped off and the gasket surfaces cleaned. Stubborn gasket material can be soaked with rust penetrant or treated with a special chemical to soften it so it can be easily scraped off. A scraper can be fashioned from a piece of copper tubing by flattening and sharpening one end. Copper is recommended because it is usually softer than the surfaces to be scraped, which reduces the chance of gouging the part. Some gaskets can be removed with a wire brush, but regardless of the method used, the mating surfaces must be left clean and smooth. If for some reason the gasket surface is gouged, then a gasket sealer thick enough to fill scratches will have to be used during reassembly of the components. For most applications, a non-drying (or semi-drying) gasket sealer should be used.

Hose removal tips

Warning: *If the vehicle is equipped with air conditioning, do not disconnect any of the A/C hoses without first having the system depressurized by a dealer service department or a service station.*

Hose removal precautions closely parallel gasket removal precautions. Avoid scratching or gouging the surface that the hose mates against or the connection may leak. This is especially true for radiator hoses. Because of various chemical reactions, the rubber in hoses can bond itself to the metal spigot that the hose fits over. To remove a hose, first loosen the hose clamps that secure it to the spigot. Then, with slip-joint pliers, grab the hose at the clamp and rotate it around the spigot. Work it back and forth until it is completely free, then pull it off. Silicone or other lubricants will ease removal if they can be applied between the hose and the outside of the spigot. Apply the same lubricant to the inside of the hose and the outside of the spigot to simplify installation.

As a last resort (and if the hose is to be replaced with a new one anyway), the rubber can be slit with a knife and the hose peeled from the spigot. If this must be done, be careful that the metal connection is not damaged.

If a hose clamp is broken or damaged, do not reuse it. Wire-type clamps usually weaken with age, so it is a good idea to replace them with screw-type clamps whenever a hose is removed.

Tools

A selection of good tools is a basic requirement for anyone who plans to maintain and repair his or her own vehicle. For the owner who has few tools, the initial investment might seem high, but when compared to the spiraling costs of professional auto maintenance and repair, it is a wise one.

To help the owner decide which tools are needed to perform the tasks detailed in this manual, the following tool lists are offered: *Maintenance and minor repair*, *Repair/overhaul* and *Special*.

The newcomer to practical mechanics

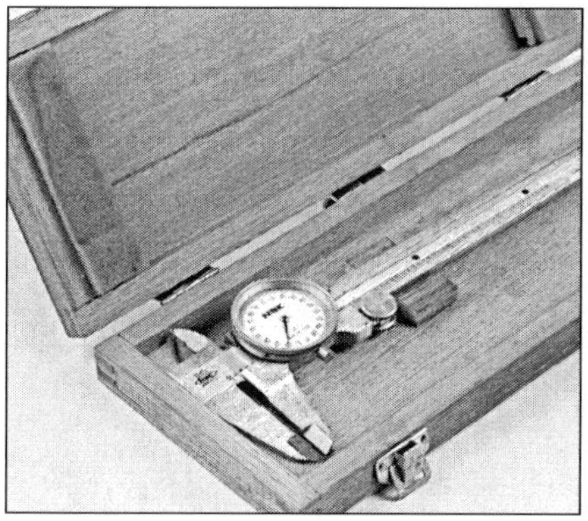
Dial caliper

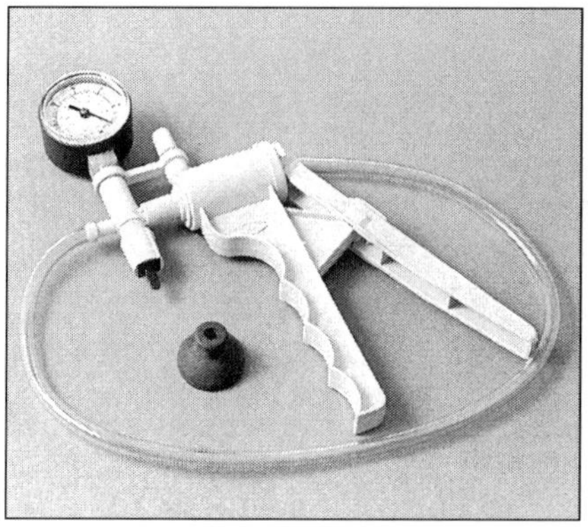
Hand-operated vacuum pump

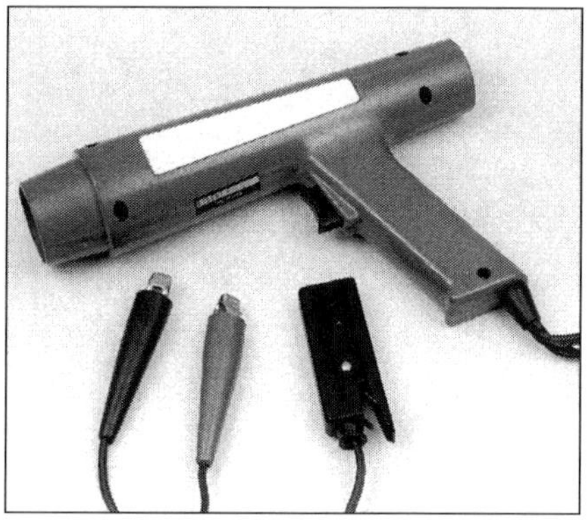
Timing light

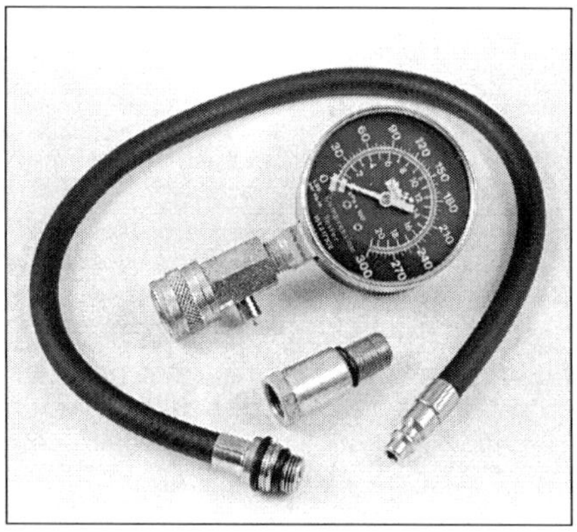
Compression gauge with spark plug hole adapter

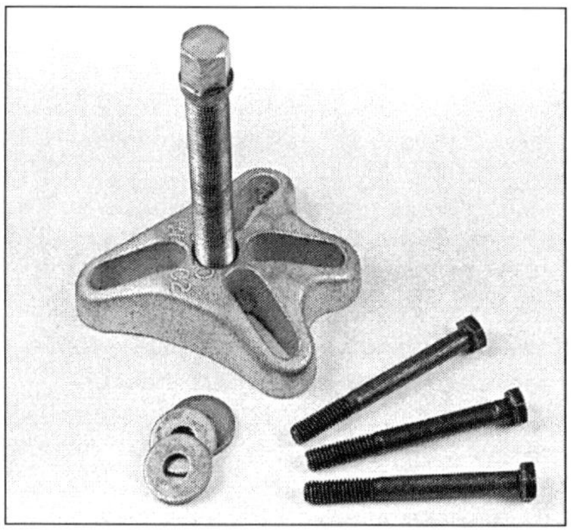
Damper/steering wheel puller

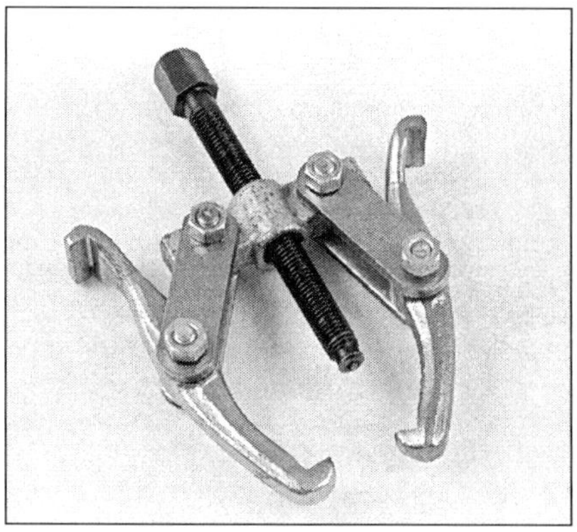
General purpose puller

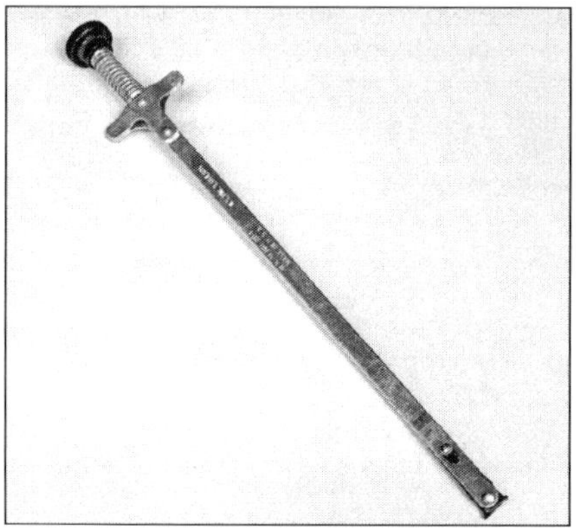
Hydraulic lifter removal tool

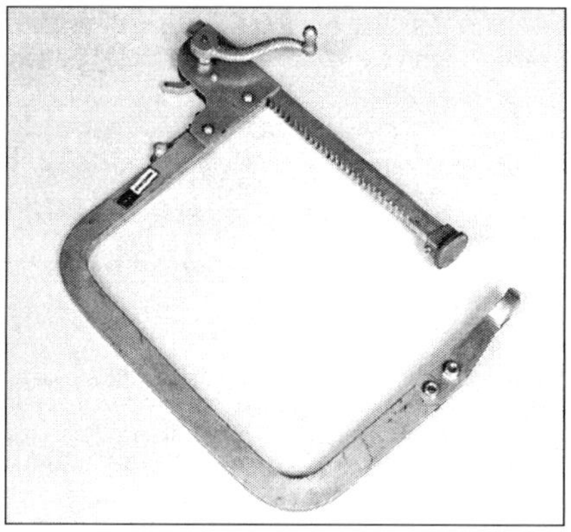
Valve spring compressor

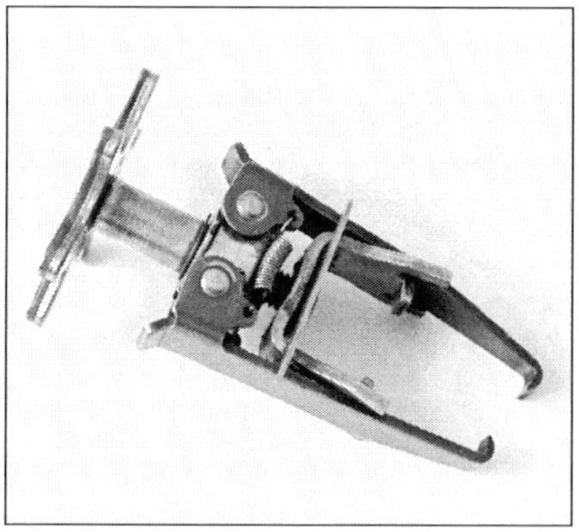
Valve spring compressor

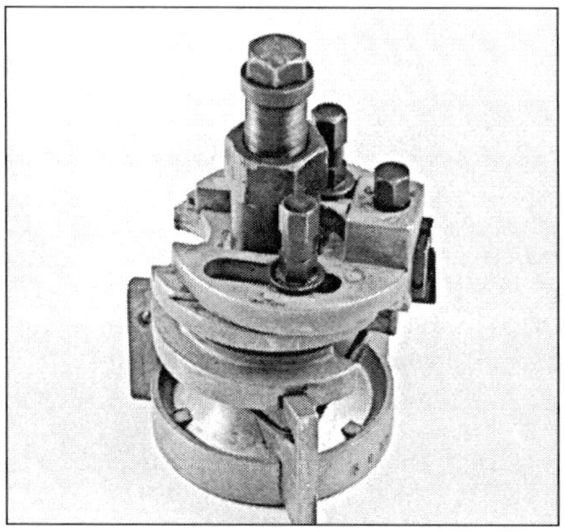
Ridge reamer

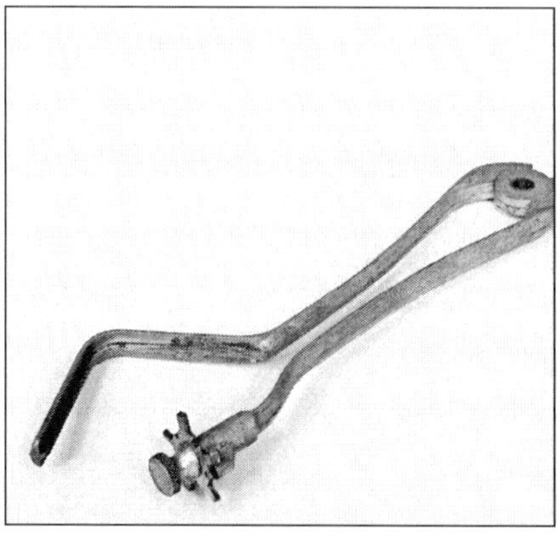
Piston ring groove cleaning tool

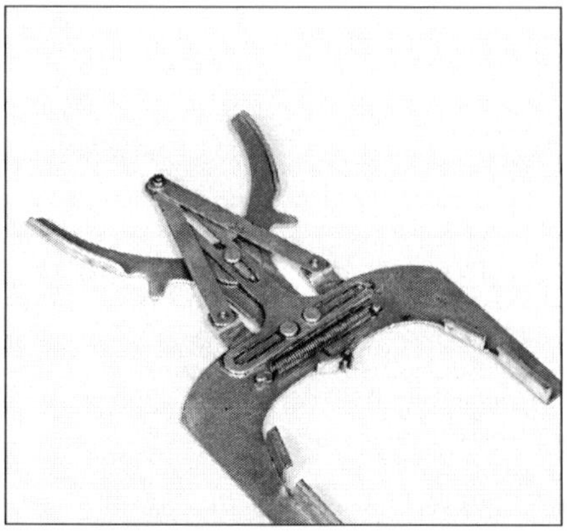
Ring removal/installation tool

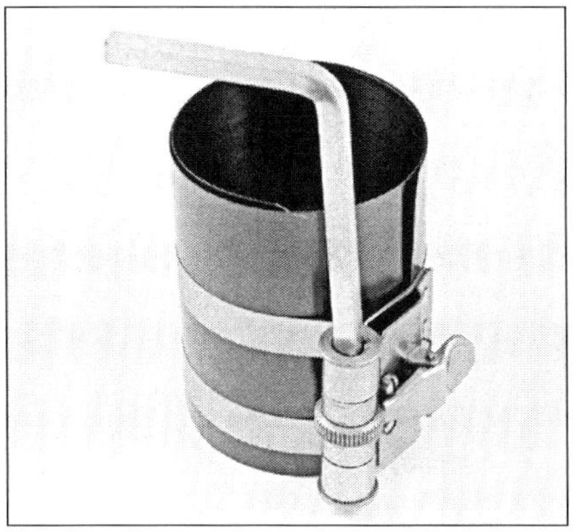

Ring compressor

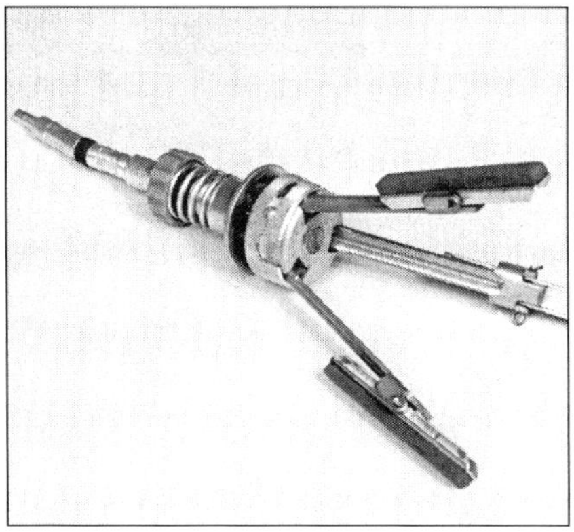

Cylinder hone

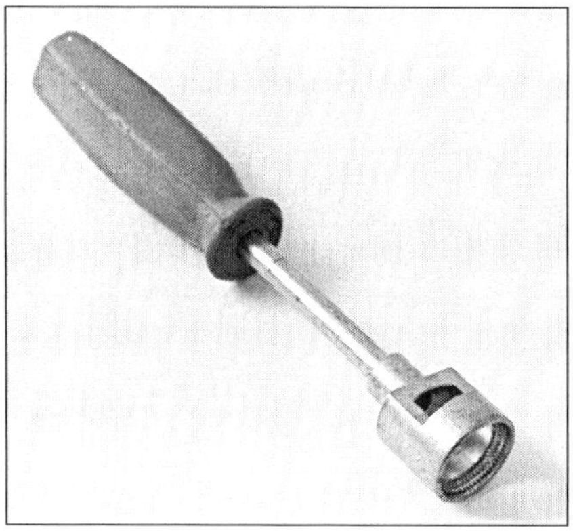

Brake hold-down spring tool

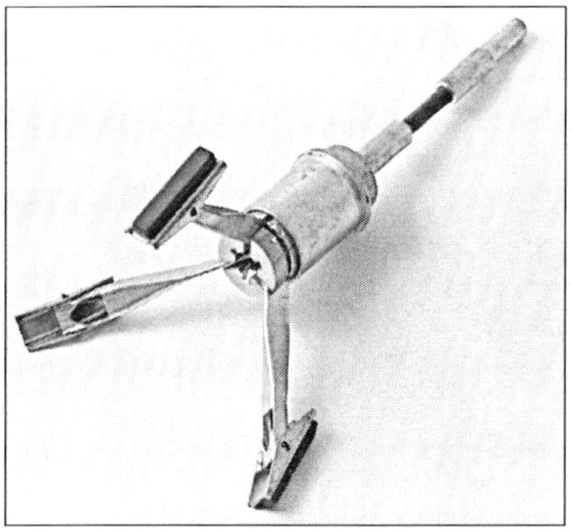

Brake cylinder hone

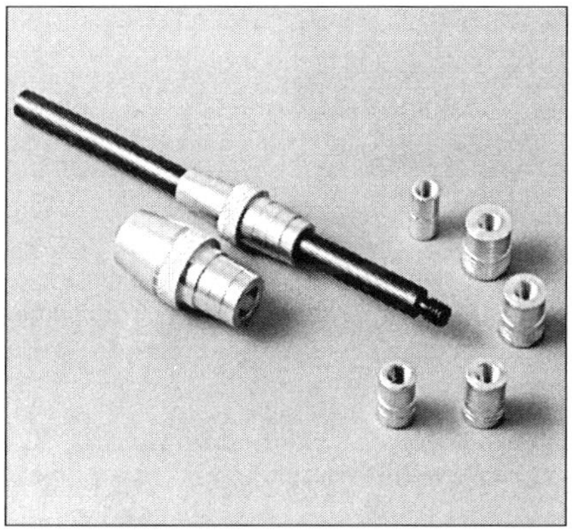

Clutch plate alignment tool

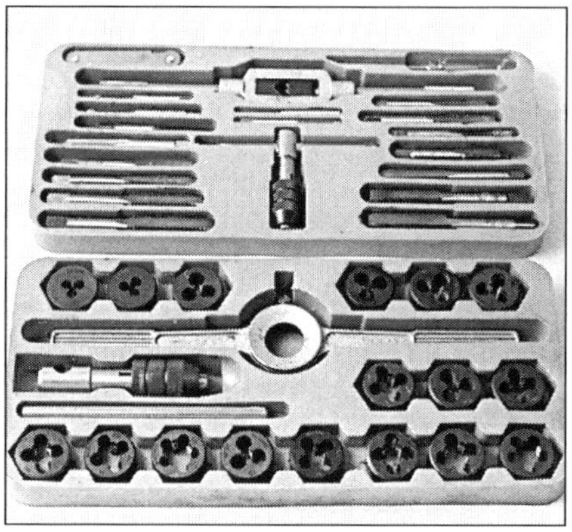

Tap and die set

should start off with the *maintenance and minor repair* tool kit, which is adequate for the simpler jobs performed on a vehicle. Then, as confidence and experience grow, the owner can tackle more difficult tasks, buying additional tools as they are needed. Eventually the basic kit will be expanded into the *repair and overhaul* tool set. Over a period of time, the experienced do-it-yourselfer will assemble a tool set complete enough for most repair and overhaul procedures and will add tools from the special category when it is felt that the expense is justified by the frequency of use.

Maintenance and minor repair tool kit

The tools in this list should be considered the minimum required for performance of routine maintenance, servicing and minor repair work. We recommend the purchase of combination wrenches (box-end and open-end combined in one wrench). While more expensive than open end wrenches, they offer the advantages of both types of wrench.

Combination wrench set (1/4-inch to 1 inch or 6 mm to 19 mm)
Adjustable wrench, 8 inch
Spark plug wrench with rubber insert
Spark plug gap adjusting tool
Feeler gauge set
Brake bleeder wrench
Standard screwdriver (5/16-inch x 6 inch)
Phillips screwdriver (No. 2 x 6 inch)
Combination pliers - 6 inch
Hacksaw and assortment of blades
Tire pressure gauge
Grease gun
Oil can
Fine emery cloth
Wire brush
Battery post and cable cleaning tool
Oil filter wrench
Funnel (medium size)
Safety goggles
Jackstands (2)
Drain pan

Note: *If basic tune-ups are going to be part of routine maintenance, it will be necessary to purchase a good quality stroboscopic timing light and combination tachometer/dwell meter. Although they are included in the list of special tools, it is mentioned here because they are absolutely necessary for tuning most vehicles properly.*

Repair and overhaul tool set

These tools are essential for anyone who plans to perform major repairs and are in addition to those in the maintenance and minor repair tool kit. Included is a comprehensive set of sockets which, though expensive, are invaluable because of their versatility, especially when various extensions and drives are available. We recommend the 1/2-inch drive over the 3/8-inch drive. Although the larger drive is bulky and more expensive, it has the capacity of accepting a very wide range of large sockets. Ideally, however, the mechanic should have a 3/8-inch drive set and a 1/2-inch drive set.

Socket set(s)
Reversible ratchet
Extension - 10 inch
Universal joint
Torque wrench (same size drive as sockets)
Ball peen hammer - 8 ounce
Soft-face hammer (plastic/rubber)
Standard screwdriver (1/4-inch x 6 inch)
Standard screwdriver (stubby - 5/16-inch)
Phillips screwdriver (No. 3 x 8 inch)
Phillips screwdriver (stubby - No. 2)
Pliers - vise grip
Pliers - lineman's
Pliers - needle nose
Pliers - snap-ring (internal and external)
Cold chisel - 1/2-inch
Scribe
Scraper (made from flattened copper tubing)
Centerpunch
Pin punches (1/16, 1/8, 3/16-inch)
Steel rule/straightedge - 12 inch

Allen wrench set (1/8 to 3/8-inch or 4 mm to 10 mm)
A selection of files
Wire brush (large)
Jackstands (second set)
Jack (scissor or hydraulic type)

Note: *Another tool which is often useful is an electric drill with a chuck capacity of 3/8-inch and a set of good quality drill bits.*

Special tools

The tools in this list include those which are not used regularly, are expensive to buy, or which need to be used in accordance with their manufacturer's instructions. Unless these tools will be used frequently, it is not very economical to purchase many of them. A consideration would be to split the cost and use between yourself and a friend or friends. In addition, most of these tools can be obtained from a tool rental shop on a temporary basis.

This list primarily contains only those tools and instruments widely available to the public, and not those special tools produced by the vehicle manufacturer for distribution to dealer service departments. Occasionally, references to the manufacturer's special tools are included in the text of this manual. Generally, an alternative method of doing the job without the special tool is offered. However, sometimes there is no alternative to their use. Where this is the case, and the tool cannot be purchased or borrowed, the work should be turned over to the dealer service department or an automotive repair shop.

Valve spring compressor
Piston ring groove cleaning tool
Piston ring compressor
Piston ring installation tool
Cylinder compression gauge
Cylinder ridge reamer
Cylinder surfacing hone
Cylinder bore gauge
Micrometers and/or dial calipers
Hydraulic lifter removal tool
Balljoint separator
Universal-type puller
Impact screwdriver
Dial indicator set
Stroboscopic timing light (inductive pick-up)
Hand operated vacuum/pressure pump
Tachometer/dwell meter
Universal electrical multimeter
Cable hoist
Brake spring removal and installation tools
Floor jack

Buying tools

For the do-it-yourselfer who is just starting to get involved in vehicle maintenance and repair, there are a number of options available when purchasing tools. If maintenance and minor repair is the extent of the work to be done, the purchase of individual tools is satisfactory. If, on the other hand, extensive work is planned, it would be a good idea to purchase a modest tool set from one of the large retail chain stores. A set can usually be bought at a substantial savings over the individual tool prices, and they often come with a tool box. As additional tools are needed, add-on sets, individual tools and a larger tool box can be purchased to expand the tool selection. Building a tool set gradually allows the cost of the tools to be spread over a longer period of time and gives the mechanic the freedom to choose only those tools that will actually be used.

Tool stores will often be the only source of some of the special tools that are needed, but regardless of where tools are bought, try to avoid cheap ones, especially when buying screwdrivers and sockets, because they won't last very long. The expense involved in replacing cheap tools will eventually be greater than the initial cost of quality tools.

Care and maintenance of tools

Good tools are expensive, so it makes sense to treat them with respect. Keep them clean and in usable condition and store them properly when not in use. Always wipe off any dirt, grease or metal chips before putting them away. Never leave tools lying around in the work area. Upon completion of a job, always check closely under the hood for tools that may have been left there so they won't get lost during a test drive.

Some tools, such as screwdrivers, pliers, wrenches and sockets, can be hung on a panel mounted on the garage or workshop wall, while others should be kept in a tool box or tray. Measuring instruments, gauges, meters, etc. must be carefully stored where they cannot be damaged by weather or impact from other tools.

When tools are used with care and stored properly, they will last a very long time. Even with the best of care, though, tools will wear out if used frequently. When a tool is damaged or worn out, replace it. Subsequent jobs will be safer and more enjoyable if you do.

How to repair damaged threads

Sometimes, the internal threads of a nut or bolt hole can become stripped, usually from overtightening. Stripping threads is an all-too-common occurrence, especially when working with aluminum parts, because aluminum is so soft that it easily strips out.

Usually, external or internal threads are only partially stripped. After they've been cleaned up with a tap or die, they'll still work. Sometimes, however, threads are badly damaged. When this happens, you've got three choices:

1) *Drill and tap the hole to the next suitable oversize and install a larger diameter bolt, screw or stud.*
2) *Drill and tap the hole to accept a threaded plug, then drill and tap the plug to the original screw size. You can also buy a plug already threaded to the original size. Then you simply drill a hole to the specified size, then run the threaded plug into the hole with a bolt and jam nut. Once the plug is fully seated, remove the jam nut and bolt.*
3) *The third method uses a patented thread repair kit like Heli-Coil or Slimsert. These easy-to-use kits are designed to repair damaged threads in straight-through holes and blind holes. Both are available as kits which can handle a variety of sizes and thread patterns. Drill the hole, then tap it with the special included tap. Install the Heli-Coil and the hole is back to its original diameter and thread pitch.*

Regardless of which method you use, be sure to proceed calmly and carefully. A little impatience or carelessness during one of these relatively simple procedures can ruin your whole day's work and cost you a bundle if you wreck an expensive part.

Working facilities

Not to be overlooked when discussing tools is the workshop. If anything more than routine maintenance is to be carried out, some sort of suitable work area is essential.

It is understood, and appreciated, that many home mechanics do not have a good workshop or garage available, and end up removing an engine or doing major repairs outside. It is recommended, however, that the overhaul or repair be completed under the cover of a roof.

A clean, flat workbench or table of comfortable working height is an absolute necessity. The workbench should be equipped with a vise that has a jaw opening of at least four inches.

As mentioned previously, some clean, dry storage space is also required for tools, as well as the lubricants, fluids, cleaning solvents, etc. which soon become necessary.

Sometimes waste oil and fluids, drained from the engine or cooling system during normal maintenance or repairs, present a disposal problem. To avoid pouring them on the ground or into a sewage system, pour the used fluids into large containers, seal them with caps and take them to an authorized disposal site or recycling center. Plastic jugs, such as old antifreeze containers, are ideal for this purpose.

Always keep a supply of old newspapers and clean rags available. Old towels are excellent for mopping up spills. Many mechanics use rolls of paper towels for most work because they are readily available and disposable. To help keep the area under the vehicle clean, a large cardboard box can be cut open and flattened to protect the garage or shop floor.

Whenever working over a painted surface, such as when leaning over a fender to service something under the hood, always cover it with an old blanket or bedspread to protect the finish. Vinyl covered pads, made especially for this purpose, are available at auto parts stores.

Jacking and towing

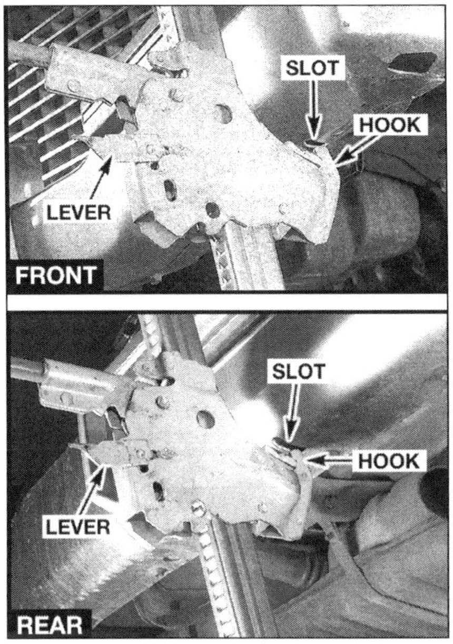

On earlier models, a bumper jack is used to raise the vehicle - it either fits into a slot in the bumper, as shown, or hooks onto the lower edge of the bumper at a specific location (see the owner's manual for the location)

Jacking

Warning: *The jack supplied with the vehicle should only be used for raising the vehicle when changing a tire or placing jackstands under the frame. Never work under the vehicle or start the engine while the jack is being used as the only means of support.*

The vehicle must be on a level surface with the wheels blocked and the transmission in Park. Apply the parking brake if the front of the vehicle must be raised. Make sure no one is in the vehicle as it's being raised with the jack.

Remove the jack, lug nut wrench and spare tire from the trunk compartment. To replace the tire, use the tapered end of the lug wrench to pry loose the wheel cover. Loosen the lug nuts one-half turn, but leave them in place until the tire is raised off the ground.

With the lever on the jack in the "Up" position, locate the load rest bracket or hook (depending on the design) to the bumper **(see illustrations)**. Using the lug wrench as a jack handle, raise the vehicle until the tire clears the ground. Remove the lug nuts and pull the tire off. Clean the mating surfaces of the hub and wheel, then install the spare. Replace the lug nuts with the beveled edges facing in and tighten them snugly. Don't attempt to tighten them completely until the vehicle is lowered or it could slip off the jack.

Lower the vehicle. Remove the jack and tighten the lug nuts in a criss-cross pattern. If possible, tighten the nuts with a torque wrench (see Chapter 1 for the torque specifications). If you don't have access to a torque wrench, have the nuts checked by a service station or repair shop as soon as possible. **Caution:** *The compact spare included with some of these models is intended for temporary use only. Have the flat tire repaired at the earliest opportunity and install it on the vehicle and don't exceed 50 mph with the spare on the car.*

Install the wheel cover, then stow the tire, jack and wrench and unblock the wheels.

Towing

We recommend these vehicles be towed from the front, with the front wheels off the ground. If it's absolutely necessary, these vehicles can be towed from the front with the front wheels on the ground, provided that speeds don't exceed 35 mph and the distance is less than 50 miles; the transmission can be damaged if these mileage/speed limitations are exceeded.

Later model jacking details

Equipment specifically designed for towing should be used. It must be attached to the main structural members of the vehicle, not the bumpers or brackets.

Safety is a major consideration when towing and all applicable state and local laws must be obeyed. A safety chain must be used at all times.

The parking brake must be released and the transmission must be in Neutral. The steering must be unlocked (ignition switch in the Off position). Remember that power steering and power brakes won't work with the engine off.

Booster battery (jump) starting

Observe these precautions when using a booster battery to start a vehicle:

a) *Before connecting the booster battery, make sure the ignition switch is in the Off position.*
b) *Turn off the lights, heater and other electrical loads.*
c) *Your eyes should be shielded. Safety goggles are a good idea.*
d) *Make sure the booster battery is the same voltage as the dead one in the vehicle.*
e) *The two vehicles MUST NOT TOUCH each other!*
f) *Make sure the transaxle is in Neutral (manual) or Park (automatic).*
g) *If the booster battery is not a maintenance-free type, remove the vent caps and lay a cloth over the vent holes.*

Connect the red jumper cable to the positive (+) terminals of each battery **(see illustration)**.

Connect one end of the black jumper cable to the negative (-) terminal of the booster battery. The other end of this cable should be connected to a good ground on the vehicle to be started, such as a bolt or bracket on the body.

Start the engine using the booster battery, then, with the engine running at idle speed, disconnect the jumper cables in the reverse order of connection.

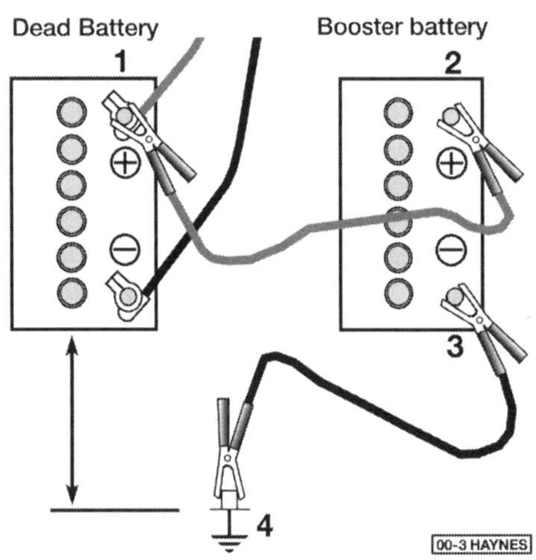

Make the booster battery cable connections in the numerical order shown (note that the negative cable of the booster battery is NOT attached to the negative terminal of the dead battery)

Automotive chemicals and lubricants

A number of automotive chemicals and lubricants are available for use during vehicle maintenance and repair. They include a wide variety of products ranging from cleaning solvents and degreasers to lubricants and protective sprays for rubber, plastic and vinyl.

Cleaners

Carburetor cleaner and choke cleaner is a strong solvent for gum, varnish and carbon. Most carburetor cleaners leave a dry-type lubricant film which will not harden or gum up. Because of this film it is not recommended for use on electrical components.

Brake system cleaner is used to remove grease and brake fluid from the brake system, where clean surfaces are absolutely necessary. It leaves no residue and often eliminates brake squeal caused by contaminants.

Electrical cleaner removes oxidation, corrosion and carbon deposits from electrical contacts, restoring full current flow. It can also be used to clean spark plugs, carburetor jets, voltage regulators and other parts where an oil-free surface is desired.

Demoisturants remove water and moisture from electrical components such as alternators, voltage regulators, electrical connectors and fuse blocks. They are non-conductive, non-corrosive and non-flammable.

Degreasers are heavy-duty solvents used to remove grease from the outside of the engine and from chassis components. They can be sprayed or brushed on and, depending on the type, are rinsed off either with water or solvent.

Lubricants

Motor oil is the lubricant formulated for use in engines. It normally contains a wide variety of additives to prevent corrosion and reduce foaming and wear. Motor oil comes in various weights (viscosity ratings) from 5 to 80. The recommended weight of the oil depends on the season, temperature and the demands on the engine. Light oil is used in cold climates and under light load conditions. Heavy oil is used in hot climates and where high loads are encountered. Multi-viscosity oils are designed to have characteristics of both light and heavy oils and are available in a number of weights from 5W-20 to 20W-50.

Gear oil is designed to be used in differentials, manual transmissions and other areas where high-temperature lubrication is required.

Chassis and wheel bearing grease is a heavy grease used where increased loads and friction are encountered, such as for wheel bearings, balljoints, tie-rod ends and universal joints.

High-temperature wheel bearing grease is designed to withstand the extreme temperatures encountered by wheel bearings in disc brake equipped vehicles. It usually contains molybdenum disulfide (moly), which is a dry-type lubricant.

White grease is a heavy grease for metal-to-metal applications where water is a problem. White grease stays soft under both low and high temperatures (usually from -100 to +190-degrees F), and will not wash off or dilute in the presence of water.

Assembly lube is a special extreme pressure lubricant, usually containing moly, used to lubricate high-load parts (such as main and rod bearings and cam lobes) for initial start-up of a new engine. The assembly lube lubricates the parts without being squeezed out or washed away until the engine oiling system begins to function.

Silicone lubricants are used to protect rubber, plastic, vinyl and nylon parts.

Graphite lubricants are used where oils cannot be used due to contamination problems, such as in locks. The dry graphite will lubricate metal parts while remaining uncontaminated by dirt, water, oil or acids. It is electrically conductive and will not foul electrical contacts in locks such as the ignition switch.

Moly penetrants loosen and lubricate frozen, rusted and corroded fasteners and prevent future rusting or freezing.

Heat-sink grease is a special electrically non-conductive grease that is used for mounting electronic ignition modules where it is essential that heat is transferred away from the module.

Sealants

RTV sealant is one of the most widely used gasket compounds. Made from silicone, RTV is air curing, it seals, bonds, waterproofs, fills surface irregularities, remains flexible, doesn't shrink, is relatively easy to remove, and is used as a supplementary sealer with almost all low and medium temperature gaskets.

Anaerobic sealant is much like RTV in that it can be used either to seal gaskets or to form gaskets by itself. It remains flexible, is solvent resistant and fills surface imperfections. The difference between an anaerobic sealant and an RTV-type sealant is in the curing. RTV cures when exposed to air, while an anaerobic sealant cures only in the absence of air. This means that an anaerobic sealant cures only after the assembly of parts, sealing them together.

Thread and pipe sealant is used for sealing hydraulic and pneumatic fittings and vacuum lines. It is usually made from a Teflon compound, and comes in a spray, a paint-on liquid and as a wrap-around tape.

Chemicals

Anti-seize compound prevents seizing, galling, cold welding, rust and corrosion in fasteners. High-temperature ant-seize, usually made with copper and graphite lubricants, is used for exhaust system and exhaust manifold bolts.

Anaerobic locking compounds are used to keep fasteners from vibrating or working loose and cure only after installation, in the absence of air. Medium strength locking compound is used for small nuts, bolts and screws that may be removed later. High-strength locking compound is for large nuts, bolts and studs which aren't removed on a regular basis.

Oil additives range from viscosity index improvers to chemical treatments that claim to reduce internal engine friction. It should be noted that most oil manufacturers caution against using additives with their oils.

Gas additives perform several functions, depending on their chemical makeup. They usually contain solvents that help dissolve gum and varnish that build up on carburetor, fuel injection and intake parts. They also serve to break down carbon deposits that form on the inside surfaces of the combustion chambers. Some additives contain upper cylinder lubricants for valves and piston rings, and others contain chemicals to remove condensation from the gas tank.

Miscellaneous

Brake fluid is specially formulated hydraulic fluid that can withstand the heat and pressure encountered in brake systems. Care must be taken so this fluid does not come in contact with painted surfaces or plastics. An opened container should always be resealed to prevent contamination by water or dirt.

Weatherstrip adhesive is used to bond weatherstripping around doors, windows and trunk lids. It is sometimes used to attach trim pieces.

Undercoating is a petroleum-based, tar-like substance that is designed to protect metal surfaces on the underside of the vehicle from corrosion. It also acts as a sound-deadening agent by insulating the bottom of the vehicle.

Waxes and polishes are used to help protect painted and plated surfaces from the weather. Different types of paint may require the use of different types of wax and polish. Some polishes utilize a chemical or abrasive cleaner to help remove the top layer of oxidized (dull) paint on older vehicles. In recent years many non-wax polishes that contain a wide variety of chemicals such as polymers and silicones have been introduced. These non-wax polishes are usually easier to apply and last longer than conventional waxes and polishes.

Conversion factors

Length (distance)					
Inches (in)	X 25.4	= Millimetres (mm)	X	0.0394	= Inches (in)
Feet (ft)	X 0.305	= Metres (m)	X	3.281	= Feet (ft)
Miles	X 1.609	= Kilometres (km)	X	0.621	= Miles
Volume (capacity)					
Cubic inches (cu in; in^3)	X 16.387	= Cubic centimetres (cc; cm^3)	X	0.061	= Cubic inches (cu in; in^3)
Imperial pints (Imp pt)	X 0.568	= Litres (l)	X	1.76	= Imperial pints (Imp pt)
Imperial quarts (Imp qt)	X 1.137	= Litres (l)	X	0.88	= Imperial quarts (Imp qt)
Imperial quarts (Imp qt)	X 1.201	= US quarts (US qt)	X	0.833	= Imperial quarts (Imp qt)
US quarts (US qt)	X 0.946	= Litres (l)	X	1.057	= US quarts (US qt)
Imperial gallons (Imp gal)	X 4.546	= Litres (l)	X	0.22	= Imperial gallons (Imp gal)
Imperial gallons (Imp gal)	X 1.201	= US gallons (US gal)	X	0.833	= Imperial gallons (Imp gal)
US gallons (US gal)	X 3.785	= Litres (l)	X	0.264	= US gallons (US gal)
Mass (weight)					
Ounces (oz)	X 28.35	= Grams (g)	X	0.035	= Ounces (oz)
Pounds (lb)	X 0.454	= Kilograms (kg)	X	2.205	= Pounds (lb)
Force					
Ounces-force (ozf; oz)	X 0.278	= Newtons (N)	X	3.6	= Ounces-force (ozf; oz)
Pounds-force (lbf; lb)	X 4.448	= Newtons (N)	X	0.225	= Pounds-force (lbf; lb)
Newtons (N)	X 0.1	= Kilograms-force (kgf; kg)	X	9.81	= Newtons (N)
Pressure					
Pounds-force per square inch (psi; lbf/in^2; lb/in^2)	X 0.070	= Kilograms-force per square centimetre (kgf/cm^2; kg/cm^2)	X	14.223	= Pounds-force per square inch (psi; lbf/in^2; lb/in^2)
Pounds-force per square inch (psi; lbf/in^2; lb/in^2)	X 0.068	= Atmospheres (atm)	X	14.696	= Pounds-force per square inch (psi; lbf/in^2; lb/in^2)
Pounds-force per square inch (psi; lbf/in^2; lb/in^2)	X 0.069	= Bars	X	14.5	= Pounds-force per square inch (psi; lbf/in^2; lb/in^2)
Pounds-force per square inch (psi; lbf/in^2; lb/in^2)	X 6.895	= Kilopascals (kPa)	X	0.145	= Pounds-force per square inch (psi; lbf/in^2; lb/in^2)
Kilopascals (kPa)	X 0.01	= Kilograms-force per square centimetre (kgf/cm^2; kg/cm^2)	X	98.1	= Kilopascals (kPa)
Torque (moment of force)					
Pounds-force inches (lbf in; lb in)	X 1.152	= Kilograms-force centimetre (kgf cm; kg cm)	X	0.868	= Pounds-force inches (lbf in; lb in)
Pounds-force inches (lbf in; lb in)	X 0.113	= Newton metres (Nm)	X	8.85	= Pounds-force inches (lbf in; lb in)
Pounds-force inches (lbf in; lb in)	X 0.083	= Pounds-force feet (lbf ft; lb ft)	X	12	= Pounds-force inches (lbf in; lb in)
Pounds-force feet (lbf ft; lb ft)	X 0.138	= Kilograms-force metres (kgf m; kg m)	X	7.233	= Pounds-force feet (lbf ft; lb ft)
Pounds-force feet (lbf ft; lb ft)	X 1.356	= Newton metres (Nm)	X	0.738	= Pounds-force feet (lbf ft; lb ft)
Newton metres (Nm)	X 0.102	= Kilograms-force metres (kgf m; kg m)	X	9.804	= Newton metres (Nm)
Vacuum					
Inches mercury (in. Hg)	X 3.377	= Kilopascals (kPa)	X	0.2961	= Inches mercury
Inches mercury (in. Hg)	X 25.4	= Millimeters mercury (mm Hg)	X	0.0394	= Inches mercury
Power					
Horsepower (hp)	X 745.7	= Watts (W)	X	0.0013	= Horsepower (hp)
Velocity (speed)					
Miles per hour (miles/hr; mph)	X 1.609	= Kilometres per hour (km/hr; kph)	X	0.621	= Miles per hour (miles/hr; mph)
Fuel consumption*					
Miles per gallon, Imperial (mpg)	X 0.354	= Kilometres per litre (km/l)	X	2.825	= Miles per gallon, Imperial (mpg)
Miles per gallon, US (mpg)	X 0.425	= Kilometres per litre (km/l)	X	2.352	= Miles per gallon, US (mpg)

Temperature

Degrees Fahrenheit = (°C x 1.8) + 32

Degrees Celsius (Degrees Centigrade; °C) = (°F - 32) x 0.56

**It is common practice to convert from miles per gallon (mpg) to litres/100 kilometres (l/100km), where mpg (Imperial) x l/100 km = 282 and mpg (US) x l/100 km = 235*

Safety first!

Regardless of how enthusiastic you may be about getting on with the job at hand, take the time to ensure that your safety is not jeopardized. A moment's lack of attention can result in an accident, as can failure to observe certain simple safety precautions. The possibility of an accident will always exist, and the following points should not be considered a comprehensive list of all dangers. Rather, they are intended to make you aware of the risks and to encourage a safety conscious approach to all work you carry out on your vehicle.

Essential DOs and DON'Ts

DON'T rely on a jack when working under the vehicle. Always use approved jackstands to support the weight of the vehicle and place them under the recommended lift or support points.

DON'T attempt to loosen extremely tight fasteners (i.e. wheel lug nuts) while the vehicle is on a jack - it may fall.

DON'T start the engine without first making sure that the transmission is in Neutral (or Park where applicable) and the parking brake is set.

DON'T remove the radiator cap from a hot cooling system - let it cool or cover it with a cloth and release the pressure gradually.

DON'T attempt to drain the engine oil until you are sure it has cooled to the point that it will not burn you.

DON'T touch any part of the engine or exhaust system until it has cooled sufficiently to avoid burns.

DON'T siphon toxic liquids such as gasoline, antifreeze and brake fluid by mouth, or allow them to remain on your skin.

DON'T inhale brake lining dust - it is potentially hazardous (see *Asbestos* below).

DON'T allow spilled oil or grease to remain on the floor - wipe it up before someone slips on it.

DON'T use loose fitting wrenches or other tools which may slip and cause injury.

DON'T push on wrenches when loosening or tightening nuts or bolts. Always try to pull the wrench toward you. If the situation calls for pushing the wrench away, push with an open hand to avoid scraped knuckles if the wrench should slip.

DON'T attempt to lift a heavy component alone - get someone to help you.

DON'T rush or take unsafe shortcuts to finish a job.

DON'T allow children or animals in or around the vehicle while you are working on it.

DO wear eye protection when using power tools such as a drill, sander, bench grinder, etc. and when working under a vehicle.

DO keep loose clothing and long hair well out of the way of moving parts.

DO make sure that any hoist used has a safe working load rating adequate for the job.

DO get someone to check on you periodically when working alone on a vehicle.

DO carry out work in a logical sequence and make sure that everything is correctly assembled and tightened.

DO keep chemicals and fluids tightly capped and out of the reach of children and pets.

DO remember that your vehicle's safety affects that of yourself and others. If in doubt on any point, get professional advice.

Asbestos

Certain friction, insulating, sealing, and other products - such as brake linings, brake bands, clutch linings, torque converters, gaskets, etc. - may contain asbestos. Extreme care must be taken to avoid inhalation of dust from such products, since it is hazardous to health. If in doubt, assume that they do contain asbestos.

Fire

Remember at all times that gasoline is highly flammable. Never smoke or have any kind of open flame around when working on a vehicle. But the risk does not end there. A spark caused by an electrical short circuit, by two metal surfaces contacting each other, or even by static electricity built up in your body under certain conditions, can ignite gasoline vapors, which in a confined space are highly explosive. Do not, under any circumstances, use gasoline for cleaning parts. Use an approved safety solvent.

Always disconnect the battery ground (-) cable at the battery before working on any part of the fuel system or electrical system. Never risk spilling fuel on a hot engine or exhaust component. It is strongly recommended that a fire extinguisher suitable for use on fuel and electrical fires be kept handy in the garage or workshop at all times. Never try to extinguish a fuel or electrical fire with water.

Fumes

Certain fumes are highly toxic and can quickly cause unconsciousness and even death if inhaled to any extent. Gasoline vapor falls into this category, as do the vapors from some cleaning solvents. Any draining or pouring of such volatile fluids should be done in a well ventilated area.

When using cleaning fluids and solvents, read the instructions on the container carefully. Never use materials from unmarked containers.

Never run the engine in an enclosed space, such as a garage. Exhaust fumes contain carbon monoxide, which is extremely poisonous. If you need to run the engine, always do so in the open air, or at least have the rear of the vehicle outside the work area.

If you are fortunate enough to have the use of an inspection pit, never drain or pour gasoline and never run the engine while the vehicle is over the pit. The fumes, being heavier than air, will concentrate in the pit with possibly lethal results.

The battery

Never create a spark or allow a bare light bulb near a battery. They normally give off a certain amount of hydrogen gas, which is highly explosive.

Always disconnect the battery ground (-) cable at the battery before working on the fuel or electrical systems.

If possible, loosen the filler caps or cover when charging the battery from an external source (this does not apply to sealed or maintenance-free batteries). Do not charge at an excessive rate or the battery may burst.

Take care when adding water to a non maintenance-free battery and when carrying a battery. The electrolyte, even when diluted, is very corrosive and should not be allowed to contact clothing or skin.

Always wear eye protection when cleaning the battery to prevent the caustic deposits from entering your eyes.

Household current

When using an electric power tool, inspection light, etc., which operates on household current, always make sure that the tool is correctly connected to its plug and that, where necessary, it is properly grounded. Do not use such items in damp conditions and, again, do not create a spark or apply excessive heat in the vicinity of fuel or fuel vapor.

Secondary ignition system voltage

A severe electric shock can result from touching certain parts of the ignition system (such as the spark plug wires) when the engine is running or being cranked, particularly if components are damp or the insulation is defective. In the case of an electronic ignition system, the secondary system voltage is much higher and could prove fatal.

Troubleshooting

Contents

This section provides an easy reference guide to the more common problems which may occur during the operation of the vehicle. These problems and possible causes are grouped under various components or systems, such as Engine, Cooling system, etc., and also refer to the Chapter and/or Section which deals with the problem.

Remember that successful troubleshooting is not a mysterious art practiced only by professional mechanics. It's simply the result of a bit of knowledge combined with an intelligent, systematic approach to the problem. Always work by a process of elimination, starting with the simplest solution and working through to the most complex - and never overlook the obvious. Anyone can forget to fill the gas tank or leave the lights on overnight, so don't assume you are exempt from such oversights.

Finally, always get clear in your mind why a problem has occurred and take steps to ensure that it doesn't happen again. If the electrical system fails because of a poor connection, check all other connections in the system to make sure that they don't fail as well. If a particular fuse continues to blow, find out why - don't just go on replacing fuses. Remember, failure of a small component can often be indicative of potential failure or incorrect functioning of a more important component or system.

Engine

1 Engine will not rotate when attempting to start

1 Battery terminal connections loose or corroded. Check the cable terminals at the battery. Tighten the cable or remove corrosion as necessary.
2 Battery discharged or faulty. If the cable connections are clean and tight on the battery posts, turn the key to the On position and switch on the headlights and/or windshield wipers. If they fail to function, the battery is discharged.
3 Automatic transmission not completely engaged in Park or neutral start switch defective or misadjusted (Chapter 7).
4 Broken, loose or disconnected wiring in the starting circuit. Inspect all wiring and connectors at the battery, starter solenoid and ignition switch.
5 Starter motor pinion jammed in flywheel ring gear. Remove the starter and inspect the pinion and flywheel at earliest convenience.
6 Starter solenoid faulty (Chapter 5).
7 Starter motor faulty (Chapter 5).
8 Ignition switch faulty (Chapter 12).

2 Engine rotates but will not start

1 Fuel tank empty.
2 Battery discharged (engine rotates slowly). Check the operation of electrical components as described in previous Section.
3 Battery terminal connections loose or corroded. See previous Section.
4 Carburetor flooded and/or fuel level in carburetor incorrect. This will usually be accompanied by a strong fuel odor from under the hood. Wait a few minutes, depress the accelerator pedal all the way to the floor and attempt to start the engine.
5 Choke control inoperative (Chapter 1).
6 Fuel not reaching carburetor or fuel injectors. With the ignition switch in the Off position, open the hood, remove the top plate of the air cleaner assembly and observe the top of the carburetor (manually move the choke plate back if necessary). Have an assistant depress the accelerator pedal and check that fuel spurts into the carburetor. If not, check the fuel filter (Chapter 1), fuel lines and fuel pump (Chapter 4).
7 Fuel injector or fuel pump faulty (fuel injected vehicles) (Chapter 4).
8 No power to the fuel pump (Chapter 4).
9 Worn, faulty or incorrectly gapped spark plugs (Chapter 1).
10 Damaged distributor cap or rotor (Chapter 1).
11 Broken, loose or disconnected wiring in the starting circuit (see previous Section).
12 Distributor loose, causing ignition timing to change. Turn the distributor as necessary to start the engine, then set the ignition timing as soon as possible (Chapter 1).
13 Broken, loose or disconnected wires at the ignition coil or faulty coil (Chapter 5).
14 Faulty ignition module or pick-up coil (Chapter 5).

3 Starter motor operates without rotating engine

1 Starter pinion sticking. Remove the starter (Chapter 5) and inspect.
2 Starter pinion or flywheel teeth worn or broken. Remove the cover at the rear of the engine and inspect.

4 Engine hard to start when cold

1 Battery discharged or low. Check as described in Section 1.
2 Choke control inoperative or out of adjustment (Chapter 4).
3 Carburetor flooded or in need of overhaul (see Section 2).
4 Fuel supply not reaching the carburetor or fuel injection system (see Section 2).
5 Fuel injection system malfunction (Chapter 4).
6 Engine coolant temperature sensor, circuit or ECM defective (fuel injected models) (Chapter 6).
7 Distributor cap or rotor cracked, corroded or carbon tracked (Chapter 5).

5 Engine hard to start when hot

1 Air filter clogged (Chapter 1).
2 Fuel not reaching the carburetor of fuel injectors (see Section 2).
3 Corroded electrical leads at the battery (Chapter 1).
4 Bad engine ground (Chapter 1).
5 Starter worn (Chapter 5).
6 Fuel injection system malfunction (Chapter 4).
7 Engine coolant temperature sensor, circuit or ECM defective (fuel injected models) (Chapter 6).

6 Starter motor noisy or excessively rough in engagement

1 Pinion or flywheel gear teeth worn or broken. Remove the cover at the rear of the engine (if so equipped) and inspect.
2 Starter motor mounting bolts loose or missing.

7 Engine starts but stops immediately

1 Loose or faulty electrical connections at distributor, coil or alternator.
2 Insufficient fuel reaching the carburetor or fuel injectors (Chapter 4).
3 Problem with the fuel injection or engine management system (Chapter 4 or 6).
4 Vacuum leak at the gasket surfaces of the carburetor or throttle body. Make sure that all mounting bolts/nuts are tightened securely and that all vacuum hoses connected to the carburetor or fuel injection unit and manifold are positioned properly and in good condition.

8 Engine lopes while idling or idles erratically

1 Vacuum leakage. Check mounting bolts/nuts at the carburetor/throttle body and intake manifold for tightness. Make sure that all vacuum hoses are connected and in good condition. Use a stethoscope or a length of fuel hose held against your ear to listen for vacuum leaks while the engine is running. A hissing sound will be heard. Check the carburetor/fuel injector and intake manifold gasket surfaces.
2 Leaking EGR valve or plugged PCV valve (see Chapters 1 and 6).
3 Air filter clogged (Chapter 1).
4 Fuel pump not delivering sufficient fuel to the carburetor or fuel injectors (see Section 7).
5 Carburetor out of adjustment (Chapter 4).
6 Problem with the idle control system (fuel injected models) (Chapter 6).
7 Leaking head gasket. If this is suspected, take the vehicle to a repair shop or dealer where the engine can be pressure checked.
8 Timing chain and/or gears worn (Chapter 2).
9 Camshaft lobes worn (Chapter 2).

9 Engine misses at idle speed

1 Spark plugs worn or not gapped properly (or improper spark plugs installed) (Chapter 1).
2 Faulty spark plug wires, distributor cap or rotor (Chapter 1).
3 Choke not operating properly (Chapter 1).
4 Faulty emissions system components (Chapter 6).
5 Clogged fuel filter and/or foreign matter in fuel. Remove the fuel filter (Chapter 1) and inspect.
6 Problem with the fuel injection or engine management system (Chapter 4 or 6).
7 Vacuum leaks at the intake manifold or at hose connections. Check as described in Section 8.
8 Incorrect idle speed or idle mixture (Chapter 1).
9 Incorrect ignition timing (Chapter 1).
10 Uneven or low cylinder compression. Check compression as described in Chapter 1.
11 Faulty fuel injectors

10 Engine misses throughout driving speed range

1 Fuel filter clogged and/or impurities in the fuel system (Chapter 1). Also check fuel output at the carburetor/fuel injector (see Section 7).
2 Faulty or incorrectly gapped spark plugs (or improper plugs installed) (Chapter 1).
3 Incorrect ignition timing (Chapter 1).
4 Cracked distributor cap, disconnected distributor wires or damaged distributor components (Chapter 1).
5 Defective spark plug wires (Chapter 1).
6 Faulty emissions system components (Chapter 6).
7 Problem with the fuel injection or engine management system (Chapter 4 or 6).
8 Low or uneven cylinder compression pressures. Remove the spark plugs and test the compression with gauge (Chapter 1).
9 Weak or faulty ignition system (Chapter 5).
10 Vacuum leaks at the carburetor/throttle body or vacuum hoses (see Section 8).

11 Engine stalls

1 Idle speed incorrect (Chapter 1).
2 Fuel filter clogged and/or water and impurities in the fuel system (Chapter 1).
3 Choke improperly adjusted or sticking (Chapter 1).
4 Distributor components damp or damaged (Chapter 5).
5 Faulty emissions system components (Chapter 6).
6 Problem with the fuel injection or engine management system (Chapter 4 or 6).
7 Faulty or incorrectly gapped spark plugs (Chapter 1). Also check spark plug wires (Chapter 1).
8 Vacuum leak at the carburetor/throttle body or vacuum hoses. Check as described in Section 8.

12 Engine lacks power

1 Incorrect ignition timing (Chapter 1).
2 Excessive play in distributor shaft. At the same time, check for worn rotor, faulty distributor cap, wires, etc. (Chapters 1 and 5).
3 Faulty or incorrectly gapped spark plugs (or improper plugs installed) (Chapter 1).
4 Problem with the fuel injection or engine management system (Chapter 4 or 6).
5 Faulty coil (Chapter 5).
6 Brakes binding (Chapter 1).
7 Automatic transmission fluid level incorrect (Chapter 1).
8 Fuel filter clogged and/or impurities in the fuel system (Chapter 1).
9 Emissions control system not functioning properly (Chapter 6).
10 Use of substandard fuel. Fill tank with proper octane fuel.
11 Low or uneven cylinder compression pressures. Test with compression tester, which will detect leaking valves and/or blown head gasket (Chapter 2C).
12 Plugged catalytic converter or exhaust system.

13 Engine backfires

1 Emissions system not functioning properly (Chapter 6).
2 Ignition timing incorrect (Chapter 1).
3 Faulty secondary ignition system (cracked spark plug insulator, faulty plug wires, distributor cap and/or rotor) (Chapters 1 and 5).
4 Problem with the carburetor, fuel injection system or engine management system (Chapter 4 or 6).
5 Vacuum leak at the throttle body or vacuum hoses. Check as described in Section 8.
6 Burned valve or valves sticking in guides (Chapter 2).
7 Crossed plug wires (Chapter 1).

14 Pinging or knocking engine sounds during acceleration or uphill

1 Incorrect grade of fuel. Fill tank with fuel of the proper octane rating.
2 Ignition timing incorrect (Chapter 1).
3 Problem with the carburetor, fuel injection or engine management system (Chapter 4 or 6).
4 Malfunctioning electronic spark timing system.
5 Improper spark plugs. Check plug type against the Vehicle Emissions Control Information label located in engine compartment. Also check plugs and wires for damage (Chapter 1).
6 Worn or damaged distributor components (Chapter 5).
7 Faulty emissions system (Chapter 6).
8 Vacuum leak. Check as described in Section 8.
9 Carbon build-up in cylinders (Chapter 2).

15 Engine diesels (continues to run) after switching off

1 Idle speed too high (Chapter 1).
2 Ignition timing incorrectly adjusted (Chapter 1).
3 Thermo-controlled air cleaner heat valve not operating properly (Chapter 6).
4 Excessive engine operating temperature. Probable causes of this are malfunctioning thermostat, clogged radiator, faulty water pump (Chapter 3).
5 Excessive carbon build-up in combustion chambers.
6 Incorrect grade of fuel. Fill tank with fuel of the proper octane rating.

Engine electrical system

16 Battery will not hold a charge

1 Alternator drivebelt defective or not adjusted properly (Chapter 1).
2 Electrolyte level low or battery discharged (Chapter 1).
3 Battery terminals loose or corroded (Chapter 1).
4 Alternator not charging properly (Chapter 5).
5 Loose, broken or faulty wiring in the charging circuit (Chapter 5).
6 Short in the vehicle wiring causing a continual drain on the battery.
7 Battery defective internally.

17 Ignition light fails to go out

1 Fault in alternator or charging circuit (Chapter 5).
2 Alternator drivebelt defective or not properly adjusted (Chapter 1).

18 Ignition light fails to come on when key is turned on

1 **Warning** light bulb defective (Chapter 12).
2 Alternator faulty (Chapter 5).
3 Fault in the printed circuit, dash wiring or bulb holder (Chapter 12).

19 "Check engine" light comes on

See Chapter 6

Fuel system

20 Excessive fuel consumption

1 Dirty or clogged air filter element (Chapter 1).
2 Incorrectly set ignition timing (Chapter 1).
3 Choke sticking or improperly adjusted (Chapter 1).
4 Emissions system not functioning properly (Chapter 6).
5 Carburetor idle speed and/or mixture not adjusted properly (Chapter 1).
6 Carburetor, fuel injection system or engine management system malfunctioning (Chapter 5 or 6).
7 Low tire pressure or incorrect tire size (Chapter 1).

21 Fuel leakage and/or fuel odor

1 Leak in a fuel feed or vent line (Chapter 4).

2 Tank overfilled. Fill only to automatic shut-off.
3 Emissions system filter clogged (Chapter 1).
4 Vapor leaks from system lines (Chapter 4).
5 Leak in a carburetor or fuel injection system component (Chapter 5).

Cooling system

22 Overheating

1 Insufficient coolant in system (Chapter 1).
2 Water pump drivebelt defective or not adjusted properly (Chapter 1).
3 Radiator core blocked or radiator grille dirty and restricted (Chapter 3).
4 Thermostat faulty (Chapter 3).
5 Fan blades broken or cracked (Chapter 3).
6 Radiator cap not maintaining proper pressure. Have cap pressure tested by a service station or repair shop.
7 Ignition timing incorrect (Chapter 1).
8 Cylinder head gasket leaking combustion into cooling system (Chapter 2).

23 Overcooling

1 Thermostat faulty (Chapter 3).
2 Inaccurate temperature gauge (Chapter 12)

24 External coolant leakage

1 Deteriorated or damaged hoses or loose clamps. Replace hoses and/or tighten clamps at hose connections (Chapter 1).
2 Water pump seals defective. If this is the case, water will drip from the weep hole in the water pump body (Chapter 1).
3 Leakage from radiator core or header tank. This will require the radiator to be professionally repaired (see Chapter 3 for removal procedures).
4 Engine gasket, drain plugs or water jacket core plugs leaking (Chapter 2).

25 Internal coolant leakage

Note: *Internal coolant leaks can usually be detected by examining the oil. Check the dipstick and inside of the rocker arm cover for water deposits and milky oil.*
1 Leaking intake manifold gasket or cylinder head gasket. Have the cooling system pressure tested.
2 Cracked cylinder bore or cylinder head. Dismantle engine and inspect (Chapter 2).

26 Coolant loss

1 Too much coolant in system (Chapter 1).
2 Coolant boiling away due to overheating (see Section 16).
3 Internal or external leakage (see Sections 26 and 27).
4 Faulty radiator cap. Have the cap pressure tested.

27 Poor coolant circulation

1 Inoperative water pump. A quick test is to pinch the top radiator hose closed with your hand while the engine is idling, then let it loose. You should feel the surge of coolant if the pump is working properly (Chapter 1).
2 Restriction in cooling system. Drain, flush and refill the system (Chapter 1). If necessary, remove the radiator (Chapter 3) and have it reverse flushed.
3 Water pump drivebelt defective or not adjusted properly (Chapter 1).
4 Thermostat sticking (Chapter 3).

Automatic transmission

Note: *Due to the complexity of the automatic transmission, it is difficult for the home mechanic to properly diagnose and service this component. For problems other than the following, the vehicle should be taken to a dealer service department or reputable repair shop.*

28 General shift mechanism problems

1 Chapter 7 deals with checking and adjusting the shift linkage on automatic transmissions. Common problems which may be attributed to poorly adjusted linkage are:

Engine starting in gears other than Park or Neutral.

Indicator on shifter pointing to a gear other than the one actually being used.

Vehicle moves when in Park.

2 Refer to Chapter 7 to adjust the linkage.

29 Transmission will not downshift with accelerator pedal pressed to the floor

Chapter 7 deals with adjusting the downshift switch or TV cable to enable the transmission to downshift properly.

30 Transmission slips, shifts rough, is noisy or has no drive in forward or reverse gears

1 There are many probable causes for the above problems, but the home mechanic should be concerned with only one possibility - fluid level.
2 Before taking the vehicle to a repair shop, check the level and condition of the fluid as described in Chapter 1. Correct fluid level as necessary
or change the fluid and filter if needed. If the problem persists, have a professional diagnose the probable cause.

31 Fluid leakage

1 Automatic transmission fluid is a deep red color. Fluid leaks should not be confused with engine oil, which can easily be blown by air flow to the transmission.
2 To pinpoint a leak, first remove all built-up dirt and grime from around the transmission. Degreasing agents and/or steam cleaning will achieve this. With the underside clean, drive the vehicle at low speeds so air flow will not blow the leak far from its source. Raise the vehicle and determine where the leak is coming from. Common areas of leakage are:

a) ***Pan:*** *Tighten mounting bolts and/or replace pan gasket as necessary* (see Chapters 1 and 7).
b) ***Filler pipe:*** *Replace the rubber seal where pipe enters transmission case.*
c) ***Transmission oil lines:*** *Tighten connectors where lines enter transmission case and/or replace lines.*
d) ***Vent pipe:*** *Transmission overfilled and/or water in fluid* (see checking procedures, Chapter 1).
e) ***Speedometer connector:*** *Replace the O-ring where speedometer cable enters transmission case* (Chapter 7).
f) ***Vacuum modulator:*** *Remove the modulator and replace the O-ring* (Chapter 7).

Driveaxles

32 Oil leak at inner end of driveaxle

Defective differential seal. See Chapter 7 for replacement procedures. While this is done, check the driveaxle boots for cracks, leaks or loose clamps.

33 Knock or clunk when the transmission is under initial load (just after transmission is put into gear)

1 Loose or disconnected front suspension components. Check all mounting bolts, nuts and bushings (Chapter 10).
2 Damaged inner or outer CV joints.

34 Clicking sound when turning

Worn or damaged CV joints. Check as described in Chapter 8.

35 Vibration

Note: *Before assuming that the driveaxles are at fault, make sure the tires are perfectly balanced and perform the following test.*

1 Worn CV joint bearings. Inspect and replace as necessary (Chapters 1 and 8).
2 Check the front balljoints for wear or damage (Chapters 1 and 10).
3 Worn or leaking shock absorbers. Inspect and replace as necessary (Chapters 1 and 10).

Rear axle

36 Noise

1 Road noise. No corrective procedures available.
2 Tire noise. Inspect the tires and check tire pressures (see Chapter 1).
3 Rear wheel bearings loose, worn or damaged (Chapter 10).

37 Vibration

Check the rear wheel bearings by raising the rear of the vehicle and spinning the wheels by hand. Listen for evidence of rough (noisy) bearings. Remove and inspect (Chapter 8).

38 Grease leakage

1 Rear wheel bearing seals damaged (Chapter 8).

Brakes

Note: *Before assuming that a brake problem exists, make sure that the tires are in good condition and inflated properly* (see Chapter 1), *that the front end alignment is correct and that the vehicle is not loaded with weight in an unequal manner.*

39 Vehicle pulls to one side during braking

1 Defective, damaged or oil contaminated brake pads or shoes on one side. Inspect as described in Chapter 9.
2 Excessive wear of brake shoe or pad material or drum/disc on one side. Inspect and correct as necessary.
3 Loose or disconnected front suspension components. Inspect and tighten all bolts to the specified torque (Chapter 10).
4 Defective drum brake or caliper assembly. Remove the drum or caliper and inspect for a stuck piston or other damage (Chapter 9).

40 Noise (high-pitched squeal with the brakes applied)

Disc brake pads worn out. The noise comes from the wear sensor rubbing against the disc (does not apply to all vehicles). Replace the pads with new ones immediately (Chapter 9).

41 Excessive brake pedal travel

1 Partial brake system failure. Inspect the entire system (Chapter 9) and correct as required.
2 Insufficient fluid in the master cylinder. Check (Chapter 1), add fluid and bleed the system if necessary (Chapter 9).
3 Brakes not adjusting properly. Make a series of starts and stops with the vehicle is in Reverse. If this does not correct the situation, remove the drums and inspect the self-adjusters (Chapter 9).

42 Brake pedal feels spongy when depressed

1 Air in the hydraulic lines. Bleed the brake system (Chapter 9).
2 Faulty flexible hoses. Inspect all system hoses and lines. Replace parts as necessary.
3 Master cylinder mounting bolts/nuts loose.
4 Master cylinder defective (Chapter 9).

43 Excessive effort required to stop vehicle

1 Power brake booster not operating properly (Chapter 9).
2 Excessively worn linings or pads. Inspect and replace if necessary (Chapter 9).
3 One or more caliper pistons or wheel cylinders seized or sticking. Inspect and rebuild as required (Chapter 9).
4 Brake linings or pads contaminated with oil or grease. Inspect and replace as required (Chapter 9).
5 New pads or shoes installed and not yet seated. It will take a while for the new material to seat against the drum (or disc).

44 Pedal travels to the floor with little resistance

Little or no fluid in the master cylinder reservoir caused by leaking wheel cylinder(s), leaking caliper piston(s), loose, damaged or disconnected brake lines. Inspect the entire system and correct as necessary.

45 Brake pedal pulsates during brake application

1 Wheel bearings not adjusted properly or in need of replacement (Chapter 1).
2 Caliper not sliding properly due to improper installation or obstructions. Remove and inspect (Chapter 9).
3 Rotor or drum defective. Remove the rotor or drum (Chapter 9) and check for excessive lateral runout, out of round and parallelism. Have the drum or rotor resurfaced or replace it with a new one.

Suspension and steering systems

46 Vehicle pulls to one side

1 Tire pressures uneven (Chapter 1).
2 Defective tire (Chapter 1).
3 Excessive wear in suspension or steering components (Chapter 10).
4 Front end in need of alignment.
5 Front brakes dragging. Inspect the brakes as described in Chapter 9.

47 Shimmy, shake or vibration

1 Tire or wheel out-of-balance or out-of-round. Have professionally balanced.
2 Loose, worn or out-of-adjustment wheel bearings (Chapters 1 and 8).
3 Shock absorbers and/or suspension components worn or damaged (Chapter 10).

48 Excessive pitching and/or rolling around corners or during braking

1 Defective shock absorbers. Replace as a set (Chapter 10).
2 Broken or weak springs and/or suspension components. Inspect as described in Chapter 10.

49 Excessively stiff steering

1 Lack of fluid in power steering fluid reservoir (Chapter 1).
2 Incorrect tire pressures (Chapter 1).
3 Lack of lubrication at steering joints (Chapter 1).
4 Front end out of alignment.
5 See also section titled *Lack of power assistance.*

50 Excessive play in steering

1 Loose front wheel bearings (Chapter 8).
2 Excessive wear in suspension or steering components (Chapter 10).
3 Steering gearbox out of adjustment (Chapter 10).

51 Lack of power assistance

1 Steering pump drivebelt faulty or not adjusted properly (Chapter 1).
2 Fluid level low (Chapter 1).
3 Hoses or lines restricted. Inspect and replace parts as necessary.
4 Air in power steering system. Bleed the system (Chapter 10).

52 Excessive tire wear (not specific to one area)

1 Incorrect tire pressures (Chapter 1).
2 Tires out of balance. Have professionally balanced.
3 Wheels damaged. Inspect and replace as necessary.
4 Suspension or steering components excessively worn (Chapter 10).

53 Excessive tire wear on outside edge

1 Inflation pressures incorrect (Chapter 1).
2 Excessive speed in turns.
3 Front end alignment incorrect. Have professionally aligned.
4 Suspension arm bent or twisted (Chapter 10).

54 Excessive tire wear on inside edge

1 Inflation pressures incorrect (Chapter 1).
2 Front end alignment incorrect. Have professionally aligned.
3 Loose or damaged steering components (Chapter 10).

55 Tire tread worn in one place

1 Tires out of balance.
2 Damaged or buckled wheel. Inspect and replace if necessary.
3 Defective tire (Chapter 1).

Chapter 1
Tune-up and routine maintenance

Contents

Specifications

Recommended lubricants and fluids

Note: *Listed here are manufacturer recommendations at the time this manual was written. Manufacturers occasionally upgrade their fluid and lubricant specifications, so check with your local auto parts store for current recommendations.*

Engine oil	
Type	API grade SF, SF/CC or SF/CD multigrade and fuel-efficient oil
Viscosity	See accompanying chart
Automatic transmission fluid	Dexron II, IIE or III
Engine coolant	50/50 mixture of water and the specified ethylene glycol-based coolant
Differential fluid	SAE 80W or SAE 80-90 GL-5
Brake fluid	DOT 3 fluid
Power steering fluid	GM power steering fluid or equivalent

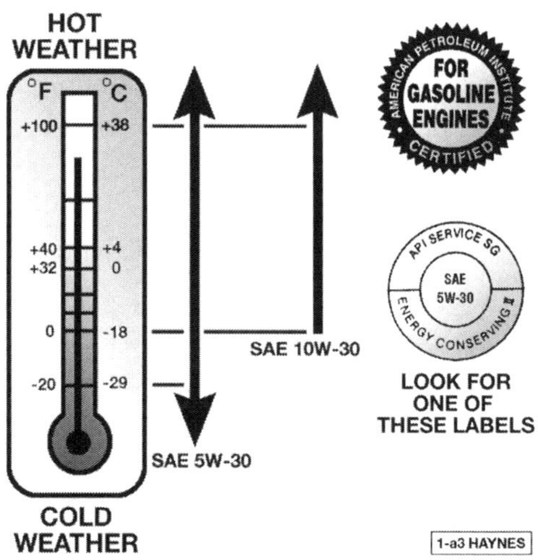

Engine oil viscosity chart - For best fuel economy and cold starting, select the lowest SAE viscosity grade for the expected temperature range

Capacities*

Engine oil (with filter change)	
V6	
231 (3.8L turbo)	5.0 qts
231 (3.8L turbo) (1982 Riviera ONLY)	6.0 qts
252 (4.1L)	5.0 qts
V8	
HT4100 (4.1L)	5.0 qts
307 (5.0L)	5.0 qts
350 (5.7L)	5.0 qts
350 (5.7L) (1979 Toronado ONLY)	6.0 qts
368 (6.0L DFI)	6.0 qts
403 (6.6L)	6.0 qts
425 (7.0L)	6.0 qts
455 (7.5L)	6.0. qts
500 (8.2L)	6.0 qts
Cooling system	
V6	14 qts
V8	
HT4100 (4.1L)	16 qts
307 (5.0L)	16 qts
350 (5.7L)	16 qts
368 (6.0L DFI)	21 qts
403 (6.6L)	18 qts
425 (7.0L)	26 qts
455 (7.5L)	21 qts
500 (8.2L)	23 qts
Automatic transmission (fluid and filter replacement)	
1971 thru 1978	5.0 qts
1979 thru 1981	4.5 qts
1982	4.3 qts
1983 thru 1985	5.3 qts

Note: *All capacities approximate. Add as necessary to bring to appropriate level.*

General

Radiator cap pressure rating	15 psi
Brake pad wear limit	1/8 inch

Ignition system

Spark plug type and gap

V6

1979	
231 (3.8L turbo)	
Type	AC R44TS or equivalent
Gap	0.040 inch
1980 and 1981	
231 (3.8L turbo)	
Type	AC R45TS or equivalent
Gap	0.040 inch
252 (4.1L)	
Type	AC R45TS8 or equivalent
Gap	0.080 inch
1982 and 1983	
231 (3.8L turbo)	
Type	AC R45TSX or equivalent
Gap	0.060 inch
252 (4.1L)	
Type	AC R45TS8 or equivalent
Gap	0.080 inch
1984 and 1985	
252 (4.1L)	
Type	AC R45TS8 or equivalent
Gap	0.080 inch

V8

1971 thru 1976	
455 (7.5L) (without HEI)	
Type	AC 46S or equivalent
Gap	0.040 inch

455 (7.5L) (with HEI)	
Type	AC 46SX or equivalent
Gap	0.080 inch
500 (8.2L) (without HEI)	
Type	AC R44XLS or equivalent
Gap	0.035 inch
500 (8.2L) (with HEI)	
Type	AC R45XLS6 or equivalent
Gap	0.060 inch
1977 and 1978	
403 (6.6L)	
Type	AC R46SZ or equivalent
Gap	0.060 inch
425 (7.0L)	
Type	AC R45XLS6 or equivalent
Gap	0.060 inch
1979	
350 (5.7L) (Carb and EFI)	
Type	AC R46SZ or equivalent
Gap	0.060 inch
1980 and 1981	
307 (5.0L) and 350 (5.7L) (Carb)	
Type	AC R46SX or equivalent
Gap	0.080 inch
350 (5.7L) (EFI)	
Type	AC R46SZ or equivalent
Gap	0.060 inch
368 (6.0L)	
Type	AC R45XLS6 or equivalent
Gap	0.060 inch
1982 thru 1984	
307 (5.0L)	
Type	AC R46SX or equivalent
Gap	0.080 inch
HT4100 (4.1L)	
Type	AC R43NTS6 or equivalent
Gap	0.060 inch
1985	
307 (5.0L)	
Type	AC FR3LS6 or equivalent
Gap	0.060 inch
HT4100 (4.1L)	
Type	AC R44LTS6 or equivalent
Gap	0.060 inch

Distributor ignition points

Point gap	0.016 inch
Dwell angle	30 degrees

Ignition timing and idle speed

V6	
1979 thru 1980	
Timing	15 degrees BTDC @ 650 rpm*
Idle speed	650 rpm in Drive
1981 thru 1984	
231 (3.8L turbo)	
Timing	15 degrees BTDC @ 650 rpm**
Idle speed	non adjustable
252 (4.1L)	
Timing	15 degrees BTDC in Park**
Idle speed	
1981	550 rpm in Drive
1982 thru 1985	non adjustable
V8	
1971 thru 1973	
455 (7.5L)	
Timing	8 degrees BTDC @ 1100 rpm*
Idle speed	550 rpm in Drive
500 (8.2L)	
Timing	8 degrees BTDC @ 600 rpm*
Idle speed	600 rpm in Drive

Ignition timing and idle speed (continued)

1974
- 455 (7.5L)
  - Timing .... 10 degrees BTDC @ 1100 rpm*
  - Idle speed .... 550 rpm in Drive
- 500 (8.2L)
  - Timing .... 10 degrees BTDC @ 600 in Drive*
  - Idle speed .... 600 in Drive

1975
- 455 (7.5L)
  - Timing
    - Federal .... 12 degrees BTDC @ 1100 rpm*
    - California .... 12 degrees BTDC @ 1100 rpm*
  - Idle speed
    - Federal .... 550 rpm in Drive
    - California .... 600 rpm in Drive
- 500 (8.2L)
  - Timing
    - Carb .... 6 degrees BTDC @ 600 in Drive*
    - EFI .... 12 degrees BTDC @ 600 in Drive*
  - Idle speed .... 600 in Drive

1976
- 455 (7.5L)
  - Timing
    - Federal .... 14 degrees BTDC @ 1100 rpm*
    - California .... 12 degrees BTDC @ 1100 rpm*
  - Idle speed
    - Federal .... 550 rpm in Drive
    - California .... 600 rpm in Drive
- 500 (8.2L)
  - Timing
    - Carb .... 6 degrees BTDC @ 600 in Drive*
    - EFI .... 12 degrees BTDC @ 600 in Drive*
  - Idle speed .... 600 in Drive

1977
- 403 (6.6L)
  - Timing .... 20 degrees BTDC in Park***
  - Idle speed .... 600 rpm in Drive
- 425 (7.0L)
  - Timing
    - Federal .... 18 degrees BTDC @ 1400 rpm*
    - California .... 18 degrees BTDC @ 1600 rpm*
  - Idle speed .... 650 rpm in Drive

1978
- 403 (6.6L)
  - Timing
    - Federal .... 20 degrees BTDC @ 1100 rpm***
    - California .... 22 degrees BTDC @ 1100 rpm***
  - Idle speed .... 600 rpm in Drive
- 425 (7.0L)
  - Timing
    - Federal .... 18 degrees BTDC @ 1400 rpm*
    - California .... 18 degrees BTDC @ 1600 rpm*
  - Idle speed .... 650 rpm in Drive

1979
- 350 (5.7L)
  - Eldorado and Seville
    - Timing .... 10 degrees BTDC @ 600 rpm*
    - Idle speed .... 600 rpm in Drive
  - Riviera and Toronado
    - Timing
      - Federal .... 20 degrees BTDC @ 1100 rpm*
      - California .... 20 degrees BTDC @ 1100 rpm*
    - Idle speed
      - Federal .... 550 rpm in Drive
      - California .... 500 rpm in Drive

1980
- 307 (5.0L)
  - Timing .... 20 degrees BTDC @ 1100 rpm*
  - Idle speed .... 500 rpm in Drive

350 (5.7L)	
Eldorado and Seville	
Timing	10 degrees BTDC @ 600 rpm*
Idle speed	600 rpm in Drive
Riviera and Toronado	
Timing	
Federal	18 degrees BTDC @ 1100 rpm*
California	16 degrees BTDC @ 1100 rpm*
Idle speed	
Federal	500 rpm in Drive
California	550 rpm in Drive
368 (6.0L DFI)	
Timing	10 degrees BTDC @ 600 rpm***
Idle speed	non adjustable
1981	
307 (5.0L)	
Timing	15 degrees BTDC @ 1100 rpm****
Idle speed	non adjustable
368 (6.0L DFI)	
Timing	10 degrees BTDC @ 600 rpm***
Idle speed	non adjustable
1982 thru 1985	
HT4100 (4.1L)	
Timing	10 degrees BTDC in Park***
Idle speed	non adjustable
307 (5.0L)	
Timing	20 degrees BTDC @ 1100 rpm****
Idle speed	non adjustable

**With vacuum advance, EGR (if equipped) and ride control disconnected*
***With four pin distributor connector disconnected*
****With set timing terminal grounded*
*****With ALDL test lead grounded*

Note: *Use the information printed on the Vehicle Emissions Control Information label, if different than the Specifications listed here.*

Firing order and distributor rotation

V6	
Firing order	1-6-5-4-3-2
Distributor rotation	clockwise
V8	
368 (6.0L),425 (7.0L) and 500 (8.2L) engines	
Firing order	1-5-6-3-4-2-7-8
Distributor rotation	clockwise
All other engines	
Firing order	1-8-4-3-6-5-7-2
Distributor rotation	counterclockwise

Cylinder location and distributor rotation

The blackened terminal shown on the distributor cap indicates the Number One spark plug wire position

V6 engines

Torque specifications

	Ft-lbs
Spark plugs	
V6	15
V8	25
Engine oil drain plug	15 to 20
Automatic transmission pan bolts	7 to 10
Wheel lug nuts	
1971 thru 1976	100 to 130
1977 thru 1985	90 to 100

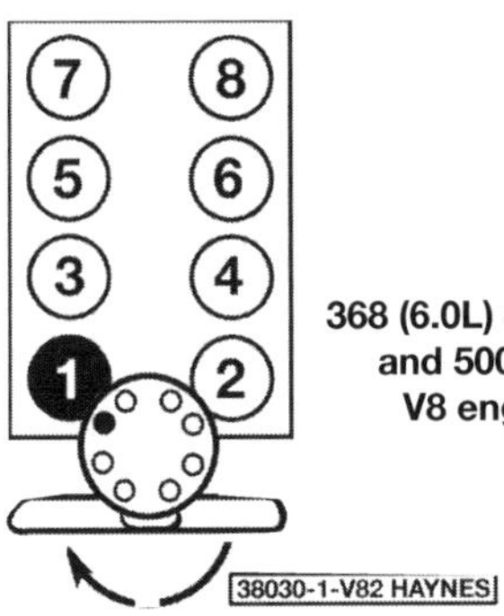

368 (6.0L) 425 (7.0L) and 500 (8.2L) V8 engines

Oldsmobile 455 V8 engine (with points-type ignition)

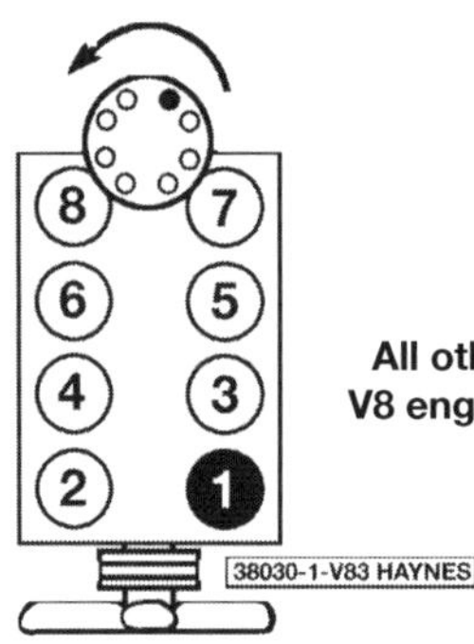

All other V8 engines

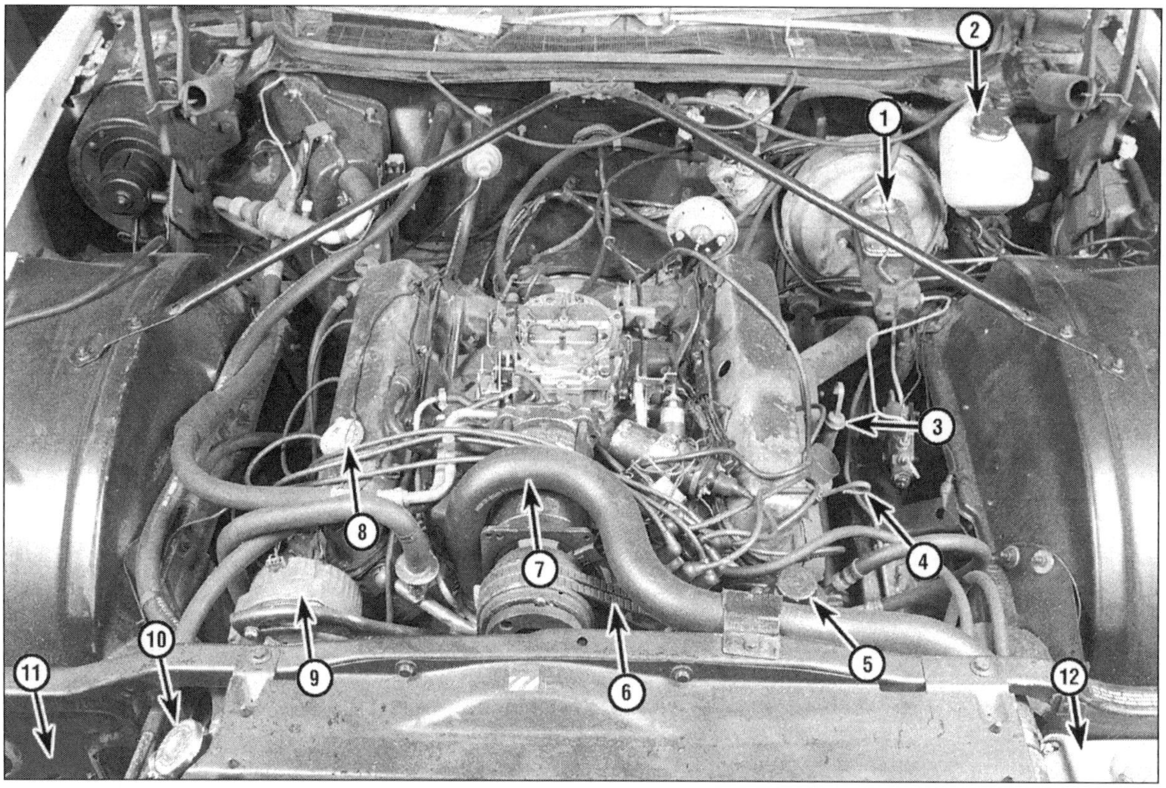

Typical 500 (8.2L) V8 engine compartment layout

1. *Brake master cylinder reservoir*
2. *Windshield washer fluid reservoir*
3. *Automatic transmission dipstick*
4. *Engine oil dipstick*
5. *Power steering fluid reservoir*
6. *Drivebelts*
7. *Upper radiator hose*
8. *Engine oil filler cap*
9. *Alternator*
10. *Radiator cap*
11. *Battery*
12. *Engine coolant reservoir*

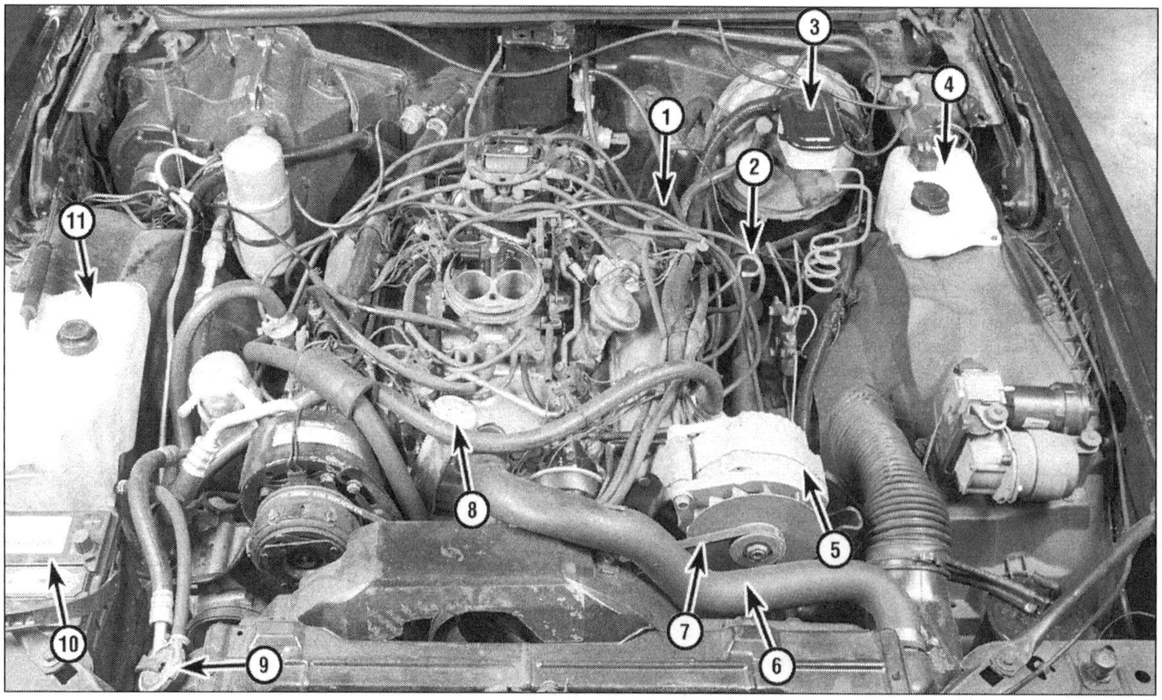

Typical 350 (5.7L) V8 engine compartment layout

1. *Automatic transmission dipstick*
2. *Engine oil dipstick*
3. *Brake master cylinder reservoir*
4. *Windshield washer fluid reservoir*
5. *Alternator*
6. *Upper radiator hose*
7. *Drivebelt*
8. *Engine oil filler cap*
9. *Radiator cap*
10. *Battery*
11. *Engine coolant reservoir*

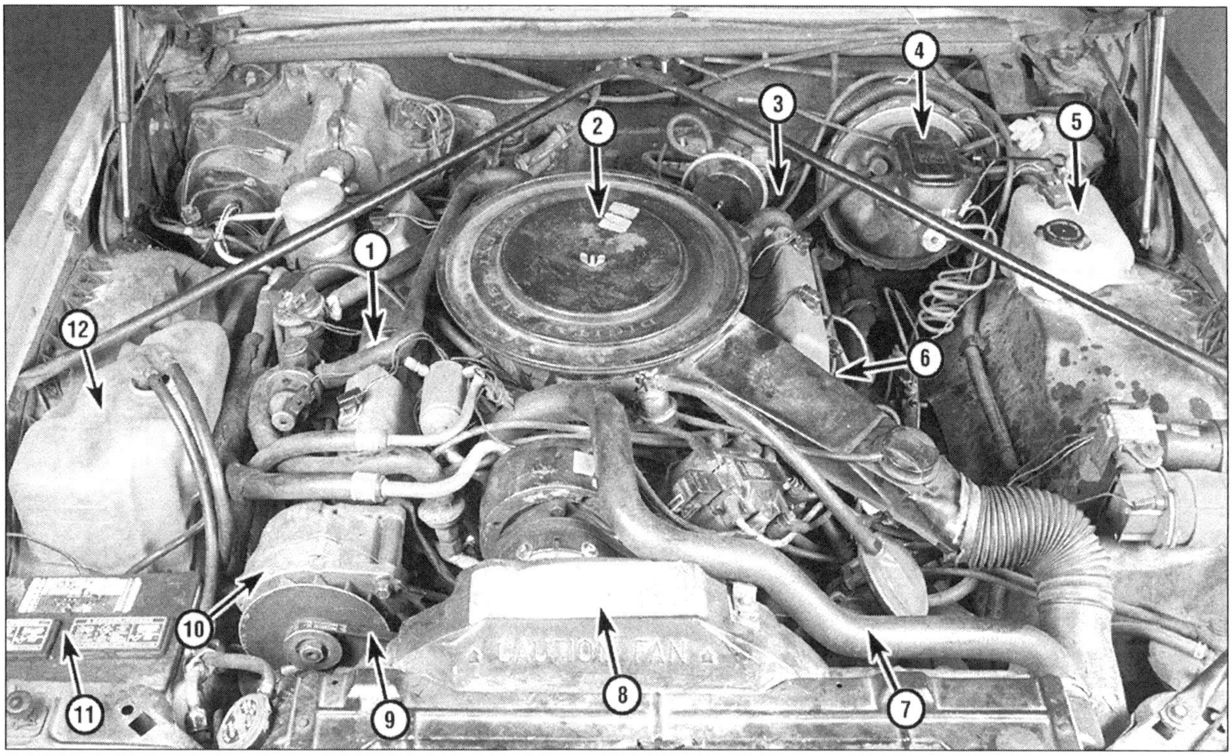

Typical 368 (6.0L) V8 engine compartment layout

1 *Engine oil filler cap*
2 *Air cleaner housing*
3 *Automatic transmission dipstick*
4 *Brake master cylinder reservoir*
5 *Windshield washer fluid reservoir*
6 *Engine oil dipstick*
7 *Upper radiator hose*
8 *Vehicle Emission Control Information label*
9 *Drivebelt*
10 *Alternator*
11 *Battery*
12 *Engine coolant reservoir*

Typical HT4100 (4.1L) V8 engine compartment layout

1 *Air cleaner housing*
2 *Engine oil filler cap*
3 *Automatic transmission dipstick*
4 *Engine oil dipstick*
5 *Brake master cylinder reservoir*
6 *Windshield washer fluid reservoir*
7 *Power steering fluid reservoir*
8 *Upper radiator hose*
9 *Vehicle emissions label*
10 *Drivebelt*
11 *Alternator*
12 *Battery*
13 *Engine coolant reservoir*

Typical V8 engine compartment underside components (Early models)

1. *Front brake caliper*
2. *lower radiator hose*
3. *Engine oil filter*
4. *Fuel pump*
5. *Differential cover*
6. *Radiator drain*
7. *Drive axle*
8. *Shock absorber*
9. *Automatic transmission fluid pan*
10. *Exhaust system*
11. *Engine oil drain plug*
12. *Starter motor*
13. *Brake rotor*

Typical V8 engine compartment underside components (Later models)

1. *Front brake caliper*
2. *Differential cover*
3. *Automatic transmission fluid pan*
4. *Catalytic converter*
5. *Engine oil drain plug*
6. *Starter motor*
7. *Engine oil filter*
8. *Drive axle*
9. *Engine mount*

Typical rear underside components (Early models)

1 *Control arm bushing*
2 *Muffler*
3 *Shock absorber*
4 *Rear brake*
5 *Coil spring*
6 *Fuel tank*
7 *Exhaust pipe*
8 *Exhaust resonator*
9 *Parking brake cable*

Typical rear underside components (Later models)

1 *Fuel tank*
2 *Control arm bushing*
3 *Tail pipe*
4 *Rear brake assembly*
5 *Shock absorber*
6 *Coil spring*
7 *Muffler*
8 *Fuel filter*
9 *Fuel pump*
10 *Parking brake cable*

1 Maintenance schedule

The following maintenance intervals are based on the assumption that the vehicle owner will be doing the maintenance or service work, as opposed to having a dealer service department do the work. Although the time/mileage intervals are loosely based on factory recommendations, most have been shortened to ensure, for example, that such items as lubricants and fluids are checked/changed at intervals that promote maximum engine/driveline service life. Also, subject to the preference of the individual owner interested in keeping his or her vehicle in peak condition at all times, and with the vehicle's ultimate resale in mind, many of the maintenance procedures may be performed more often than recommended in the following schedule. We encourage such owner initiative.

When the vehicle is new it should be serviced initially by a factory authorized dealer service department to protect the factory warranty. In many cases the initial maintenance check is done at no cost to the owner (check with your dealer service department for more information).

Every 250 miles or weekly, whichever comes first

Check the engine oil level (Section 4)
Check the engine coolant level (Section 4)
Check the windshield washer fluid level (Section 4)
Check the brake fluid level (Section 4)
Check the tires and tire pressures (Section 5)

Every 3000 miles or 3 months, whichever comes first

All items listed above plus:

Check the automatic transmission fluid level (Section 6)
Check the power steering fluid level (Section 7)
Change the engine oil and filter (Section 8)

Every 7500 miles or 6 months, whichever comes first

All items listed above plus:

Check and service the battery (Section 9)
Check the cooling system (Section 10)
Inspect and replace, if necessary, all underhood hoses (Section 11)
Inspect and replace, if necessary, the windshield wiper blades (Section 12)
Lubricate the chassis (Section 13)
Inspect the suspension and steering components (Section 14)
Inspect the exhaust system (Section 15)
Inspect and rotate the tires (Section 16)
Inspect the seat belts (Section 17)
Check the starter safety switch (Section 18)

Every 15,000 miles or 12 months, whichever comes first

Inspect and replace ignition points (1974 and earlier models) (Section 19)
Check the ignition timing (Section 20)
Check the idle speed adjustment (Section 21)
Inspect the air cleaner thermostatic control valve (Section 22)
Check the carburetor choke operation (Section 23)
Check the carburetor/throttle body mounting nut torque (Section 24)
Check the EFE (heat riser) system (Section 25)
Check the brakes (Section 26)*
Check the differential lubricant level (Section 27)
Inspect the fuel system (Section 28)
Replace the oxygen sensor (1980 Eldorado and Seville models only) (see Chapter 6 for oxygen sensor replacement and Section 41 of this Chapter for emissions indicator resetting)

Every 30,000 miles or 24 months, whichever comes first

All items listed above plus:

Replace the air filter (Section 29)
Replace the fuel filter (Section 30)
Check the engine drivebelts (Section 31)
Inspect and repack the rear wheel bearings (1978 and earlier models only) (Section 32)
Change the automatic transmission fluid and filter (Section 33)**
Change the differential lubricant (Section 34)
Service the cooling system (drain, flush and refill) (Section 35)
Inspect and replace, if necessary, the PCV valve (Section 36)
Inspect the evaporative emissions control system (Section 37)
Check the EGR valve (Section 38)
Inspect and replace the spark plugs (Section 39)
Inspect the spark plug wires, distributor cap and rotor (Section 40)

** If the vehicle frequently tows a trailer or is operated primarily in stop-and-go conditions or its brakes receive severe usage for any other reason, check the brakes every 3000 miles or three months.*

***If operated under one or more of the following conditions, change the automatic transmission fluid every 15,000 miles:*

In heavy city traffic where the outside temperature regularly reaches 90-degrees F (32-degrees C) or higher
In hilly or mountainous terrain
Frequent trailer pulling

2 Introduction

This Chapter is designed to help the home mechanic maintain General Motors full-size front wheel drive models with the goals of maximum performance, economy, safety and reliability in mind.

Included is a master maintenance schedule, followed by procedures dealing specifically with each item on the schedule. Visual checks, adjustments, component replacement and other helpful items are included. Refer to the **accompanying illustrations** of the engine compartment and the underside of the vehicle for the locations of various components.

Servicing your vehicle in accordance with the mileage/time maintenance schedule and the step-by-step procedures will result in a planned maintenance program that should produce a long and reliable service life. Keep in mind that it's a comprehensive plan, so maintaining some items but not others at the specified intervals will not produce the same results.

As you service your vehicle, you'll discover that many of the procedures can - and should - be grouped together because of the nature of the particular procedure you're performing or because of the close proximity of two otherwise unrelated components to one another.

For example, if the vehicle is raised, you should inspect the exhaust, suspension, steering and fuel systems while you're under the vehicle. When you're rotating the tires, it makes good sense to check the brakes since the wheels are already removed. Finally, let's suppose you have to borrow or rent a torque wrench. Even if you only need it to tighten the spark plugs, you might as well check the torque of as many critical fasteners as time allows.

The first step in this maintenance program is to prepare yourself before the actual work begins. Read through all the procedures you're planning to do, then gather up all the parts and tools needed. If it looks like you might run into problems during a particular job, seek advice from a mechanic or an experienced do-it-yourselfer.

3 Tune-up general information

The term tune-up is used in this manual to represent a combination of individual operations rather than one specific procedure.

If, from the time the vehicle is new, the routine maintenance schedule is followed closely and frequent checks are made of fluid levels and high wear items, as suggested throughout this manual, the engine will be kept in relatively good running condition and the need for additional work will be minimized due to lack of regular maintenance. This is even more likely if a used vehicle, which has not received regular and frequent maintenance checks, is purchased. In such cases, an engine tune-up will be needed outside of the regular routine maintenance intervals.

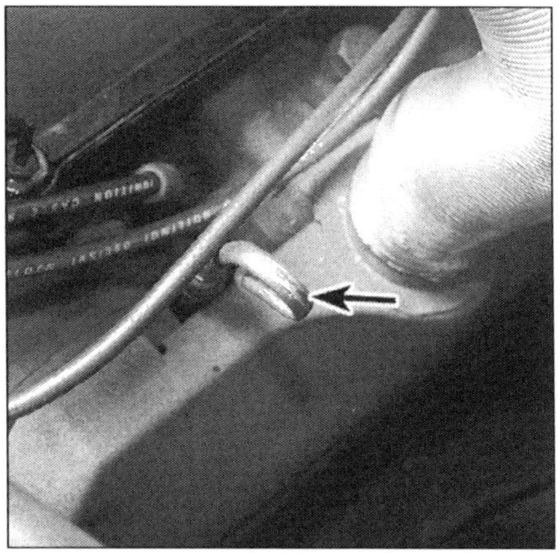

4.2 The engine oil dipstick on most models is located on the left side of the engine, toward the front (arrow)

The first step in any tune-up or diagnostic procedure to help correct a poor running engine is a cylinder compression check. A compression check (see Chapter 2, Part C) will help determine the condition of internal engine components and should be used as a guide for tune-up and repair procedures. If, for instance, a compression check indicates serious internal engine wear, a conventional tune-up won't improve the performance of the engine and would be a waste of time and money. Because of its importance, the compression check should be done by someone with the right equipment and the knowledge to use it properly.

The following procedures are those most often needed to bring a generally poor running engine back into a proper state of tune.

Minor tune-up

Check all engine related fluids (Section 4)
Clean, inspect and test the battery (Section 9)
Check the cooling system (Section 10)
Check all underhood hoses (Section 11)
Check the air filter (Section 29)
Check and adjust the ignition timing (Section 20)
Check and adjust the idle speed (Section 21)
Check and adjust the drivebelts (Section 31)
Check the PCV valve (Section 36)
Replace the spark plugs (Section 39)
Inspect the spark plug wires (Section 40)

Major tune-up

All items listed under Minor tune-up plus . . .

Check the fuel system (Section 28)
Check the EGR system (Section 38)
Replace the air filter (Section 29)
Replace the PCV valve (Section 36)
Replace the spark plug wires (Section 39)

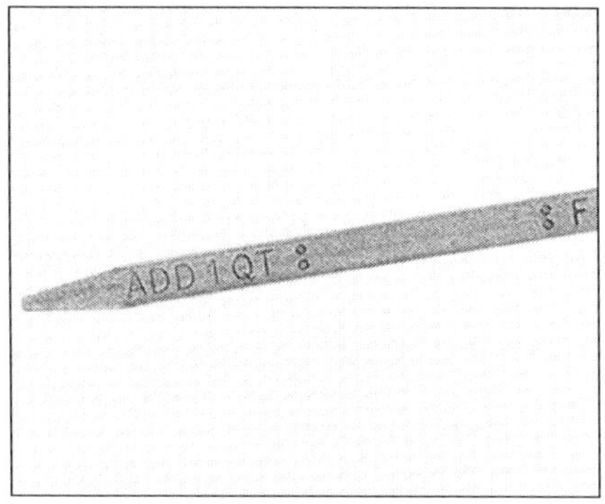

4.4 The oil level must maintained between the marks at all times-it takes one quart of oil to raise the level from the ADD mark to the FULL mark

Replace the ignition points and adjust the dwell (1974 and earlier models) (Section 19)
Check the charging system (Chapter 5)
Check the EGR system (Chapter 6)
Replace the distributor cap, rotor and spark plug wires (Section 40)

4 Fluid level checks (every 250 miles or weekly)

Note: *The following are fluid level checks to be done on a 250 mile or weekly basis. Additional fluid level checks can be found in specific maintenance procedures which follow. Regardless of intervals, be alert to fluid leaks under the vehicle which would indicate a problem to be corrected immediately.*

1 Fluids are an essential part of the lubrication, cooling, brake and windshield washer systems. Because the fluids gradually become depleted and/or contaminated during normal operation of the vehicle, they must be periodically replenished. See Recommended lubricants and fluids at the beginning of this Chapter before adding fluid to any of the following components. **Note:** *The vehicle must be on level ground when fluid levels are checked.*

Engine oil

Refer to illustrations 4.2, 4.4, 4.6a, and 4.6b

2 The engine oil level is checked with a dipstick **(see illustration)**. The dipstick extends through a metal tube down into the oil pan.

3 The oil level should be checked before the vehicle has been driven, or about 15 minutes after the engine has been shut off. If the oil is checked immediately after driving the vehicle, some of the oil will remain in the upper part of the engine, resulting in an inaccurate reading on the dipstick.

4 Pull the dipstick from the tube and wipe all the oil from the end with a clean rag or paper towel. Insert the clean dipstick all the way back into the tube and pull it out again. Note the oil at the end of the dipstick. Add oil as necessary to keep the level above the

4.6a **Oil is added to the engine after removing the twist off cap (arrow) located on the valve cover**

4.6b **On 350 (5.7L) and 307 (5.0L) engines the oil filler tube (arrow) is located at the front of the engine**

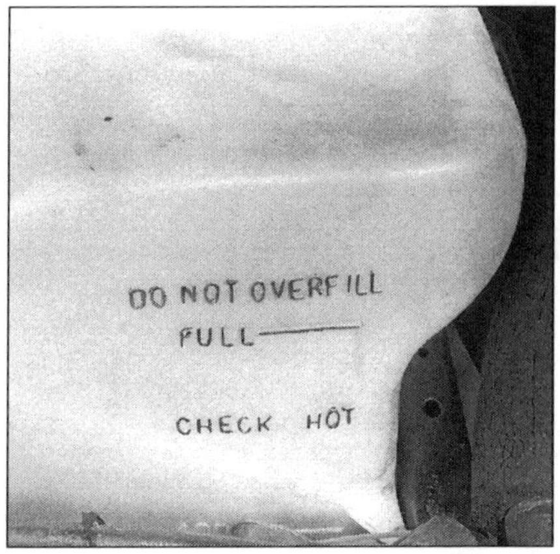

4.9a **Check the coolant level with the engine hot - it should be visible through the translucent reservoir**

ADD mark and below the FULL mark on the dipstick **(see illustration)**.

5 Do not overfill the engine by adding too much oil since this may result in oil fouled spark plugs, oil leaks or oil seal failures.

6 Oil is added to the engine after removing a twist-off cap located on the engine **(see illustrations)**. A funnel may help to reduce spills.

7 Checking the oil level is an important preventive maintenance step. A consistently low oil level indicates oil leakage through damaged seals, defective gaskets or past worn rings or valve guides. If the oil looks milky in color or has water droplets in it, the cylinder head gasket may be blown or the head or block may be cracked. The engine should be checked immediately. The condition of the oil should also be checked. Whenever you check the oil level, slide your thumb and index finger up the dipstick before wiping off the oil. If you see small dirt or metal particles clinging to the dipstick, the oil should be changed (see Section 8).

Engine coolant

Refer to illustrations 4.9a and 4.9b

Warning: *Do not allow antifreeze to come in contact with your skin or painted surfaces of the vehicle. Flush contaminated areas immediately with plenty of water. Do not store new coolant or leave old coolant lying around where it's accessible to children or pets - they're attracted by its sweet smell. Ingestion of even a small amount of coolant can be fatal! Wipe up garage floor and drip pan coolant spills immediately. Keep antifreeze containers covered and repair leaks in the cooling system immediately.*

8 All vehicles covered by this manual are equipped with a pressurized coolant recovery system. A plastic coolant reservoir located at the front of the engine compartment is connected by a hose to the radiator filler neck. As the engine warms up and the coolant expands, it escapes through a valve in the radiator cap and travels through the hose into the reservoir. As the engine cools, the coolant is automatically drawn back into the cooling system to maintain the correct level.

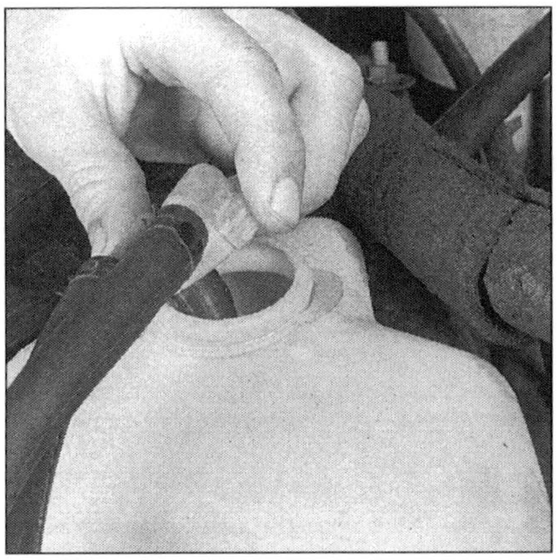

4.9b **To add coolant, unscrew or pop the top off the reservoir**

9 The coolant level in the reservoir should be checked regularly. Unscrew the coolant reservoir cap and withdraw the dipstick to check the coolant level **(see illustrations)**. **Warning:** *Do not remove the radiator cap to check the coolant level when the engine is warm.* The level in the reservoir varies with the temperature of the engine. When the engine is cold, the coolant level should be at or slightly above the FULL COLD mark on the reservoir. Once the engine has warmed up, the level should be at or near the FULL HOT mark **(see illustrations)**. If it isn't, allow the engine to cool, then unscrew the cap from the reservoir and add a 50/50 mixture of ethylene glycol based antifreeze and water.

10 Drive the vehicle and recheck the coolant level. If only a small amount of coolant is required to bring the system up to the proper level, water can be used. However, repeated additions of water will dilute the antifreeze and water solution. In order to maintain the proper ratio of antifreeze and water, always top up the coolant level with the correct mixture. An empty plastic milk jug or bleach bottle makes an excellent container for mixing coolant. Do not use rust inhibitors or additives.

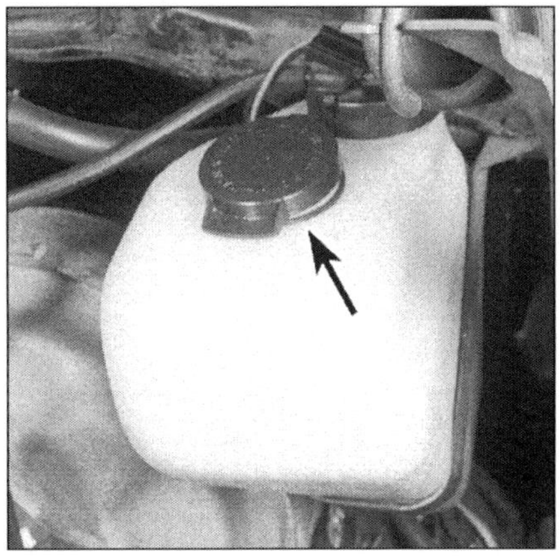

4.14 **Flip up the windshield washer fluid cap (arrow) up to add fluid**

11 If the coolant level drops consistently, there may be a leak in the system. Inspect the radiator, hoses, filler cap, drain plugs and water pump (see Section 10). If no leaks are noted, have the radiator cap pressure tested by a service station.

12 If you have to remove the radiator cap, wait until the engine has cooled completely, then wrap a thick cloth around the cap and turn it to the first stop. If coolant or steam escapes, let the engine cool down longer, then remove the cap.

13 Check the condition of the coolant as well. It should be relatively clear. If it is brown or rust colored, the system should be drained, flushed and refilled. Even if the coolant appears to be normal, the corrosion inhibitors wear out, so it must be replaced at the specified intervals.

Windshield washer fluid

Refer to illustration 4.14

14 Fluid for the windshield washer system is located in a plastic reservoir on the left side of the engine compartment **(see illustration)**. In milder climates, plain water can be used in the reservoir, but it should be kept no more than two-thirds full to allow for expansion if

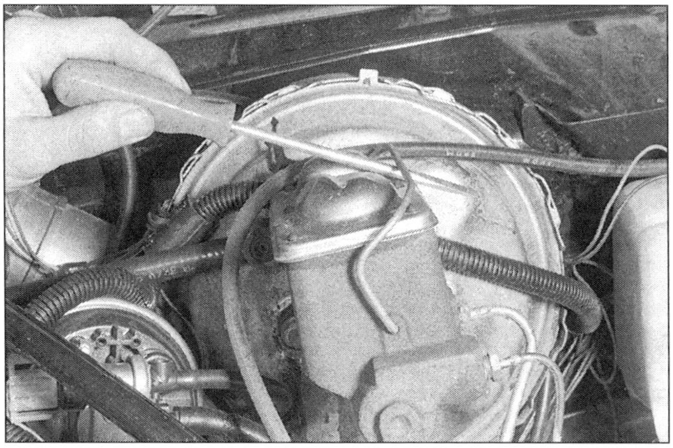

4.17a Early models have a cast iron brake master cylinder with a cover which must be removed to check the fluid level - use a screwdriver to unsnap the retainer

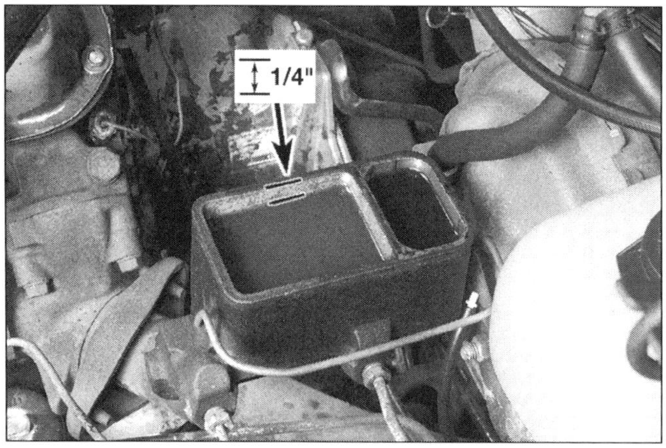

4.17b On early models, maintain the brake fluid level 1/4-inch below the top edge (arrow)

the water freezes. In colder climates, use windshield washer system antifreeze, available at any auto parts store, to lower the freezing point of the fluid. Mix the antifreeze with water in accordance with the manufacturer's directions on the container. **Caution:** *Do not use cooling system antifreeze - it will damage the vehicle's paint.*

15 To help prevent icing in cold weather, warm the windshield with the defroster before using the washer.

Battery electrolyte

16 Most vehicles covered by this manual are equipped with a battery which is permanently sealed (except for vent holes) and has no filler caps. Water does not have to be added to these batteries at any time; however, if a maintenance-type battery has been installed on the vehicle since it was new, remove all the cell caps on top of the battery (usually there are two caps that cover three cells each). If the electrolyte level is low, add distilled water until the level is above the plates. There is usually a split-ring indicator in each cell to help you judge when enough water has been added. Add water until the electrolyte level is just up to the bottom of the split ring indicator. Do not overfill the battery or it will spew out electrolyte when it is charging.

Brake fluid

Refer to illustrations 4.17a, 4.17b and 4.18

17 The brake master cylinder is located on the front of the power booster unit in the engine compartment **(see illustrations)**.

18 On later models the brake reservoir can be checked visually from the outside to make sure the level is above the minimum specified level **(see illustration)**.

19 When adding fluid, pour it carefully into the reservoir to avoid spilling it on surrounding painted surfaces. Be sure the specified fluid is used, since mixing a different type of brake fluid can cause damage to the system. See *Recommended lubricants and fluids* at the front of this Chapter or your owner's

4.18 On later models, the fluid level inside the brake reservoir can easily be checked by observing the level from the outside - fluid can be added to the reservoir after the cover is removed by prying up on the tabs

manual. **Warning:** *Brake fluid can harm your eyes and damage painted surfaces, so use extreme caution when handling or pouring it. Do not use brake fluid that has been standing open or is more than one year old. Brake fluid absorbs moisture from the air. Excess moisture can cause a dangerous loss of braking effectiveness.*

20 At this time the fluid and master cylinder can be inspected for contamination. The system should be drained and refilled if deposits, dirt particles or water droplets are seen in the fluid.

21 After filling the reservoir to the proper level, make sure the cap is on tight to prevent fluid leakage.

22 The brake fluid level in the master cylinder will drop slightly as the pads at each wheel wear down during normal operation. If the master cylinder requires repeated replenishing to keep it at the proper level, this is an indication of leakage in the brake system, which should be corrected immediately. Check all brake lines and connections (see

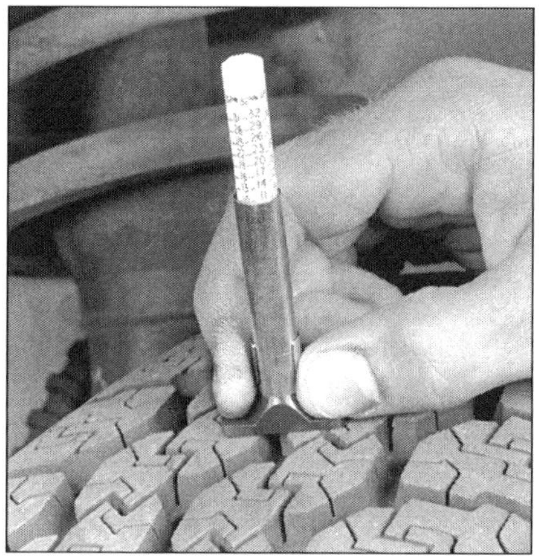

5.2 Use a tire tread depth gauge to monitor tire wear - they are available at auto parts stores and service stations and cost very little

Section 26 for more information).

23 If, when checking the master cylinder fluid level, you discover one or both reservoirs empty or nearly empty, the brake system should be bled (see Chapter 9).

5 Tire and tire pressure checks (every 250 miles or weekly)

Refer to illustrations 5.2, 5.3, 5.4a, 5.4b and 5.8

1 Periodic inspection of the tires may spare you the inconvenience of being stranded with a flat tire. It can also provide you with vital information regarding possible problems in the steering and suspension systems before major damage occurs.

2 The original tires on this vehicle are equipped with 1/2-inch wide bands that appear when tread depth reaches 1/16-inch, indicating the tires are worn out. Tread wear can be monitored with a simple, inexpensive device known as a tread depth indicator **(see illustration)**.

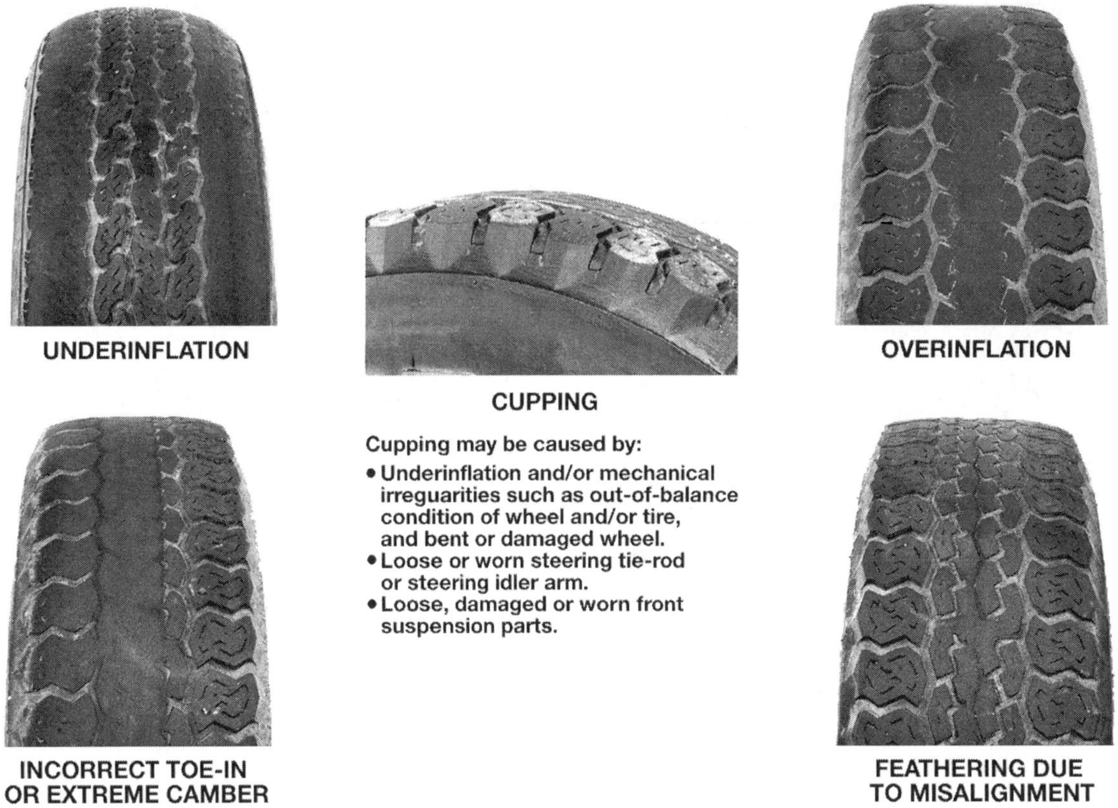

5.3 This chart will help you determine the condition of the tires, the probable cause of abnormal wear and the corrective action necessary

3 Note any abnormal tread wear **(see illustration)**. Tread pattern irregularities such as cupping, flat spots and more wear on one side than the other are indications of front end alignment and/or balance problems. If any of these conditions are noted, take the vehicle to a tire shop or service station to correct the problem.

4 Look closely for cuts, punctures and embedded nails or tacks. Sometimes a tire will hold air pressure for short time or leak down very slowly after a nail has embedded itself in the tread. If a slow leak persists, check the valve stem core to make sure it's tight **(see illustration)**. Examine the tread for an object that may have embedded itself in the tire or for a "plug" that may have begun to leak (radial tire punctures are repaired with a plug that's installed in a puncture). If a puncture is suspected, it can be easily verified by spraying a solution of soapy water onto the suspected area **(see illustration)**. The soapy solution will bubble if there's a leak. Unless the puncture is unusually large, a tire shop or service station can usually repair the tire.

5 Carefully inspect the inner sidewall of each tire for evidence of brake fluid. If you see any, inspect the brakes immediately.

6 Correct air pressure adds miles to the lifespan of the tires, improves mileage and enhances overall ride quality. Tire pressure cannot be accurately estimated by looking at a tire, especially if it's a radial. A tire pressure gauge is essential. Keep an accurate gauge in the vehicle. The pressure gauges attached to the nozzles of air hoses at gas stations are

5.4a If a tire looses air on a steady basis, check the valve core first to make sure it's snug (special inexpensive wrenches are commonly available at auto parts stores)

5.4b If the valve core is tight, raise the corner of the vehicle with the low tire and spray a soapy water solution onto the tread as the tire is turned slowly - leaks will cause small bubbles to appear

5.8 To extend the life of the tires, check the air pressure at least once a week with an accurate gauge (don't forget the spare)

6.3 The automatic transmission fluid dipstick (arrow) is located at the rear of the engine compartment

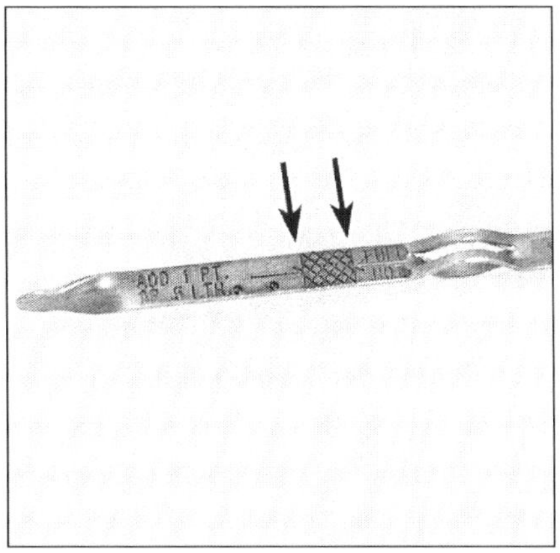

6.5 The automatic transmission fluid level must be maintained between the ADD mark and the FULL mark (arrows) with the engine idling at operating temperature

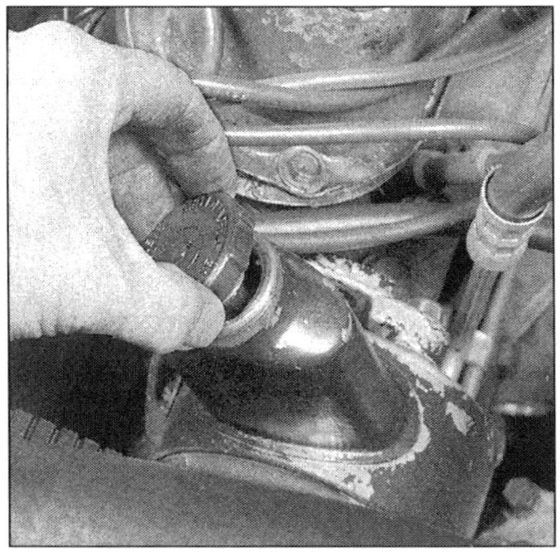

7.2 The power steering fluid reservoir is located on the left (driver's side) of the engine compartment; turn the cap counterclockwise for removal

often inaccurate.

7 Always check tire pressure when the tires are cold. Cold, in this case, means the vehicle has not been driven over a mile in the three hours preceding a tire pressure check. A pressure rise of four to eight pounds is not uncommon once the tires are warm.

8 Unscrew the valve cap protruding from the wheel or hubcap and push the gauge firmly onto the valve stem **(see illustration)**. Note the reading on the gauge and compare the figure to the recommended tire pressure shown on the label attached to the inside of the glove compartment door. Be sure to reinstall the valve cap to keep dirt and moisture out of the valve stem mechanism. Check all four tires and, if necessary, add enough air to bring them up to the recommended pressure.

9 Don't forget to keep the spare tire inflated to the specified pressure (refer to your owner's manual or the tire sidewall).

6 Transmission fluid level check (every 3000 miles or 3 months)

Refer to illustrations 6.3 and 6.5

1 The automatic transmission fluid level should be carefully maintained. Low fluid level can lead to slipping or loss of drive, while overfilling can cause foaming and loss of fluid.

2 With the parking brake set, start the engine, then move the shift lever through all the gear ranges, ending in Park. The fluid level must be checked with the vehicle level and the engine running at idle. **Note:** *Incorrect fluid level readings will result if the vehicle has just been driven at high speeds for an extended period, in hot weather in city traffic, or if it has been pulling a trailer. If any of these conditions apply, wait until the fluid has cooled (about 30 minutes).*

3 With the transmission at normal operating temperature, remove the dipstick from the filler tube. The dipstick is located at the rear of the engine compartment on the drivers side **(see illustration)**.

4 Carefully touch the fluid at the end of the dipstick to determine that the fluid is hot. Wipe the fluid from the dipstick with a clean rag and push it back into the filler tube until the cap seats.

5 Pull the dipstick out again and note the fluid level. It should be above the ADD and below the FULL marks **(see illustration)**.

6 If additional fluid is required, pour it directly into the tube using a funnel. It takes about one pint to raise the level from the lower mark to the upper mark with a hot transmission, so add the fluid a little at a time and keep checking the level until it's correct.

7 The condition of the fluid should also be checked along with the level. If the fluid at the end of the dipstick is a dark reddish-brown color, or if the fluid has a burned smell, the fluid should be changed. If you're in doubt about the condition of the fluid, purchase some new fluid and compare the two for color and smell.

7 Power steering fluid level check (every 3000 miles or 3 months)

Refer to illustrations 7.2 and 7.6

1 The power steering system relies on fluid which may, over a period of time, require replenishing.

2 The fluid reservoir for the power steering pump is located at the front of the engine on the drivers side **(see illustration)**. **Note:** *On some later models the fluid reservoir is mounted to the fan shroud on the drivers side.*

3 For the check, the front wheels should be pointed straight ahead and the engine should be off.

4 Use a clean rag to wipe off the reservoir cap and the area around the cap. This will help prevent any foreign matter from entering the reservoir during the check.

5 Twist off the cap and check the temperature of the fluid at the end of the dipstick with your finger.

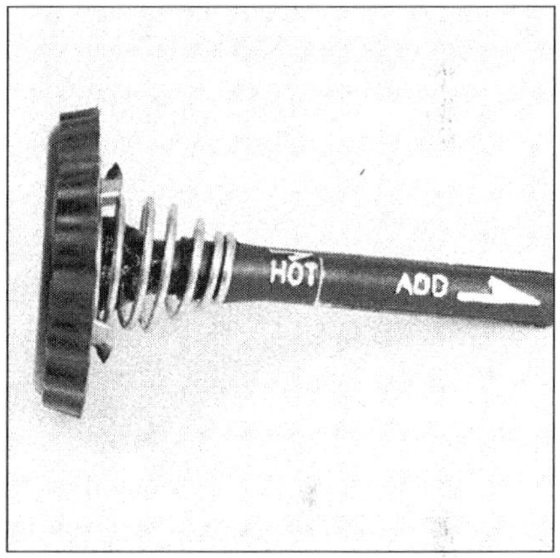

7.6 The marks on the dipstick indicate the safe fluid range

6 Wipe off the fluid with a clean rag, reinsert it, then withdraw it and read the fluid level. The level should be at the HOT mark if the fluid was hot to the touch **(see illustration)**. It should be at the COLD mark if the fluid was cool to the touch.

7 If additional fluid is required, pour the specified type directly into the reservoir, using a funnel to prevent spills.

8 If the reservoir requires frequent fluid additions, all power steering hoses, hose connections, the power steering pump and the rack and pinion assembly should be carefully checked for leaks.

8 Engine oil and filter change (every 3000 miles or 3 months)

Refer to illustrations 8.2, 8.7, 8.12 and 8.14

1 Frequent oil changes are the best preventive maintenance the home mechanic can give the engine, because aging oil becomes diluted and contaminated, which leads to premature engine wear.

2 Make sure you have all the necessary

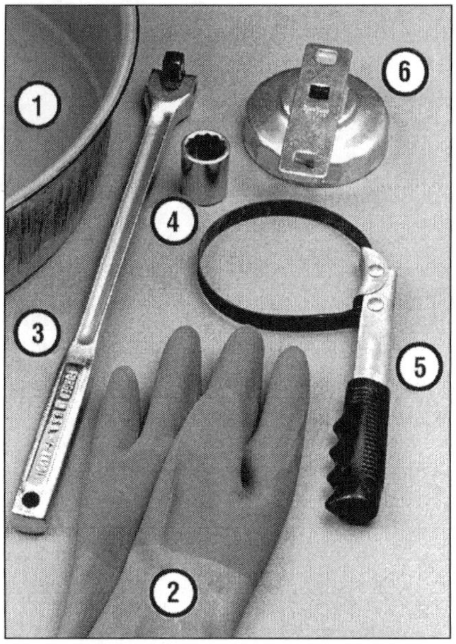

8.2 These tools are required when changing the engine oil and filter

1. ***Drain pan*** *- It should be fairly shallow in depth, but wide to prevent spills*
2. ***Rubber gloves*** *- When removing the drain plug and filter, you will get oil on your hands (the gloves will prevent burns)*
3. ***Breaker bar*** *- Sometimes the oil drain plug is tight, and a long breaker bar is needed to loosen it*
4. ***Socket*** *- To be used with the breaker bar or a ratchet (must be the correct size to fit the drain plug)*
5. ***Filter wrench*** *- This is a metal band-type wrench, which requires clearance around the filter to be effective*
6. ***Filter wrench*** *- This type fits on the bottom of the filter and can be turned with a ratchet or breaker bar (different-size wrenches are available for different type of filters)*

tools before you begin this procedure **(see illustration)**. You should also have plenty of rags or newspapers handy for mopping up any spills.

3 Access to the underside of the vehicle is greatly improved if the vehicle can be lifted on a hoist, driven onto ramps or supported by jackstands. **Warning:** *Do not work under a vehicle which is supported only by a hydraulic or scissors-type jack.*

4 If this is your first oil change, get under the vehicle and familiarize yourself with the locations of the oil drain plug and the oil filter. The engine and exhaust components will be warm during the actual work, so try to anticipate any potential problems before the engine and accessories are hot.

5 Park the vehicle on a level spot. Start the engine and allow it to reach its normal operating temperature. Warm oil and sludge will flow out more easily. Turn off the engine when it's warmed up. Remove the filler cap from the valve cover.

6 Raise the vehicle and support it securely on jackstands. **Warning:** *Never get beneath the vehicle when it is supported only by a jack. The jack provided with your vehicle is designed solely for raising the vehicle to remove and replace the wheels. Always use jackstands to support the vehicle when it becomes necessary to place your body underneath the vehicle.*

7 Being careful not to touch the hot exhaust components, place the drain pan under the drain plug in the bottom of the pan and remove the plug **(see illustration)**. You may want to wear gloves while unscrewing the plug the final few turns if the engine is hot.

8 Allow the old oil to drain into the pan. It may be necessary to move the pan farther under the engine as the oil flow slows to a trickle. Inspect the old oil for the presence of metal shavings and chips.

9 After all the oil has drained, wipe off the drain plug with a clean rag. Even minute metal particles clinging to the plug would immediately contaminate the new oil.

10 Clean the area around the drain plug opening, reinstall the plug and tighten it securely, but do not strip the threads.

11 Move the drain pan into position under the oil filter.

12 Loosen the oil filter **(see illustration)** by turning it counterclockwise with the filter wrench. Any standard filter wrench will work. Sometimes the oil filter is screwed on so tightly that it cannot be loosened. If this situation occurs, punch a metal bar or long screwdriver directly through the side of the canister and use it as a T-bar to turn the filter. Be prepared for oil to spurt out of the canister as it is punctured. Once the filter is loose, use your hands to unscrew it from the block. Just as the filter is detached from the block, immediately tilt the open end up to prevent the oil inside the filter from spilling out. **Warning:** *The exhaust system may still be hot, so be careful.*

13 With a clean rag, wipe off the mounting surface on the block. If a residue of old oil is allowed to remain, it will smoke when the block is heated up. Also make sure that none of the old gasket remains stuck to the mounting surface. It can be removed with a scraper if necessary.

14 Compare the old filter with the new one to make sure they are the same type. Smear some clean engine oil on the rubber gasket of the new filter and screw it into place **(see illustration)**. Because overtightening the filter will damage the gasket, do not use a filter wrench to tighten the filter. Tighten it by hand until the gasket contacts the seating surface. Then seat the filter by giving it an additional 3/4-turn.

15 Remove all tools, rags, etc. from under the vehicle, being careful not to spill the oil in the drain pan, then lower the vehicle.

16 Add new oil to the engine through the oil filler cap in the valve cover. Use a funnel, if necessary, to prevent oil from spilling onto the top of the engine. Pour three quarts of fresh oil into the engine. Wait a few minutes

8.7 The engine oil drain plug is located on the bottom of the oil pan - it is usually very tight, so use a box-end wrench to avoid rounding off the hex. Some older models have two drain plugs (arrows)

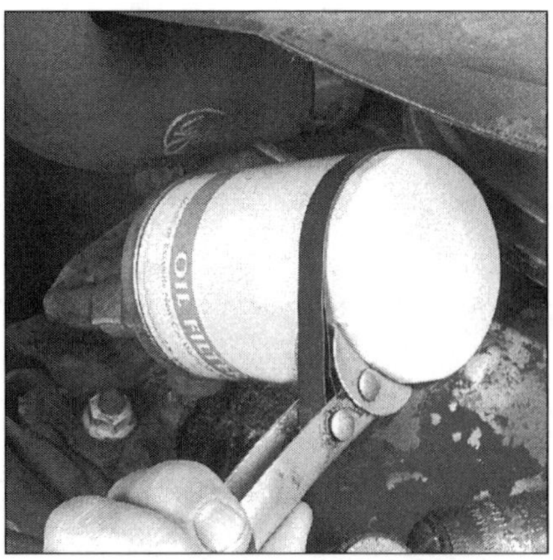

8.12 The oil filter is usually on very tight and will require a special wrench for removal - DO NOT use the wrench to tighten the new filter!

8.14 Lubricate the oil filter gasket with clean engine oil before installing the filter on the engine

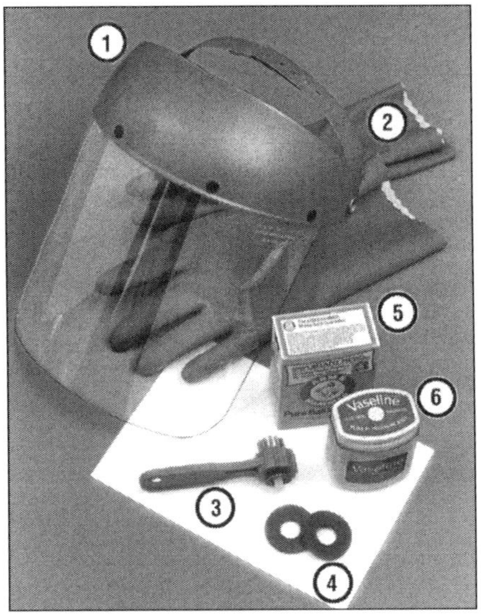

9.1 Tools and materials required for battery maintenance

1. ***Face shield/safety goggles*** - *When removing corrosion with a brush, the acidic particles can easily fly up into your eyes*
2. ***Rubber gloves*** - *Another safety item to consider when servicing the battery - remember that's acid inside the battery!*
3. ***Battery terminal/cable cleaner*** - *This wire brush cleaning tool will remove all traces of corrosion from the battery and cable*
4. ***Treated felt washers*** - *Placing one of these on each terminal, directly under the cable end, will help prevent corrosion (be sure to get the correct type for side-terminal batteries)*
5. ***Baking soda*** - *A solution of baking soda and water can be used to neutralize corrosion*
6. ***Petroleum jelly*** - *A layer of this on the battery terminal bolts will help prevent corrosion*

9.4 Check the tightness of the battery cable terminal bolts

9.5a A tool like this one (available at auto parts stores) is used to clean the side terminal type battery contact area

9.5b Use the brush to finish the cleaning job

9.5c When cleaning the cable clamps, all corrosion must be removed (on top post batteries the inside of the clamp is tapered to match the taper on the post, so don't remove too much material)

to allow the oil to drain into the pan, then check the level on the oil dipstick (see Section 4 if necessary). If the oil level is at or near the upper hole on the dipstick, install the filler cap hand tight, start the engine and allow the new oil to circulate.

17 Allow the engine to run for about a minute. While the engine is running, look under the vehicle and check for leaks at the oil pan drain plug and around the oil filter. If either is leaking, stop the engine and tighten the plug or filter.

18 Wait a few minutes to allow the oil to trickle down into the pan, then recheck the level on the dipstick and, if necessary, add enough oil to bring the level to the upper hole.

19 During the first few trips after an oil change, make it a point to check frequently for leaks and proper oil level.

20 The old oil drained from the engine cannot be re-used in its present state and should be discarded. Check with your local refuse disposal company, disposal facility or environmental agency to see whether they will accept the oil for recycling. Don't pour used oil into drains or onto the ground. After the oil has cooled, it can be drained into a suitable container (capped plastic jugs, topped bottles, milk cartons, etc.) for transport to one of these disposal sites.

9 Battery check, maintenance and charging (every 7500 miles or 6 months)

Refer to illustrations 9.1, 9.4, 9.5a, 9.5b, 9.5c, 9.5d and 9.6

Warning: *Hydrogen gas is produced by the battery, so keep open flames and lighted tobacco away from it at all times. Always wear eye protection when working around the battery. Rinse off spilled electrolyte immediately with large amounts of water. When removing the battery cables, always detach the negative cable first and hook it up last!*

1 Battery maintenance is an important procedure which will help ensure you aren't stranded because of a dead battery. Several tools are required for this procedure **(see illustration)**.

2 A sealed battery is standard equipment on most vehicles covered by this manual. This type of battery never requires any water and has many advantages over the older, capped cell type, which requires the addition of water frequently. Both types of batteries should still be routinely maintained according to the procedures which follow.

Check

3 The battery is located in the right front corner of the engine compartment. The exterior of the battery should be inspected periodically for damage such as a cracked case or cover.

4 Check the tightness of the battery cable terminals and connections to ensure good electrical connections and check the entire length of each cable for cracks and frayed conductors **(see illustration)**.

5 If corrosion (visible as white, fluffy deposits) is evident, remove the cables from the terminals, clean them with a battery brush and reinstall the cables **(see illustrations)**. Corrosion can be kept to a minimum by using special treated fiber washers available at auto parts stores or by applying a layer of

9.5d Regardless of the type of tool used on the battery posts, a clean, shiny surface should be the result

9.6 Remove the cell caps to check the water level in the battery - if the level is to low, add distilled water only

petroleum jelly to the terminals and cables after they are assembled.

6 On older capped cell-type batteries remove the caps and check the electrolyte level in each of the battery cells **(see illustration)**. It must be above the plates. There's usually a split ring indicator in each cell to indicate the correct level. If the level is to low, add distilled water only, then reinstall the cell caps. **Caution:** *Overfilling the cells may cause the electrolyte to spill over during periods of heavy charging, causing corrosion and damage to nearby components*

7 Make sure that the battery tray is in good condition and the hold-down clamp bolt is tight. If the battery is removed from the tray, make sure no parts remain in the bottom of the tray when the battery is reinstalled. When reinstalling the hold-down clamp bolt, do not over-tighten it.

8 Information on removing and installing the battery can be found in Chapter 5. Information on jump starting can be found at the front of this manual. For more detailed battery checking procedures, refer to the Haynes *Automotive Electrical Manual*.

Cleaning

9 Corrosion on the hold-down components, battery case and surrounding areas can be removed with a solution of water and baking soda. Thoroughly rinse all cleaned areas with plain water.

10 Any metal parts of the vehicle damaged by corrosion should be covered with a zinc-based primer, then painted.

Charging

Warning: *When batteries are being charged, hydrogen gas, which is very explosive and flammable, is produced. Do not smoke or allow open flames near a charging or a recently charged battery. Wear eye protection when near the battery during charging. Also, make sure the charger is unplugged before connecting or disconnecting the battery from the charger.*

11 Slow-rate charging is the best way to restore a battery that's discharged to the point where it will not start the engine. It's also a good way to maintain the battery charge in a vehicle that's only driven a few miles between starts. Maintaining the battery charge is particularly important in the winter when the battery must work harder to start the engine and electrical accessories that drain the battery are in greater use.

12 It's best to use a one or two-amp battery charger (sometimes called a "trickle" charger). They are the safest and put the least strain on the battery. They are also the least expensive. For a faster charge, you can use a higher amperage charger, but don't use one rated more than 1/10 the amp/hour rating of the battery. Rapid boost charges that claim to restore the power of the battery in one to two hours are hardest on the battery and can damage batteries that aren't in good condition. This type of charging should only be used in emergency situations.

13 The average time necessary to charge a battery should be listed in the instructions that come with the charger. As a general rule, a trickle charger will charge a battery in 12 to 16 hours.

14 Remove all of the cell caps (if equipped) and cover the holes with a clean cloth to prevent spattering electrolyte. Disconnect the negative battery cable and hook the battery charger leads to the battery posts (positive to positive, negative to negative), then plug in the charger. Make sure it is set at 12-volts if it has a selector switch.

15 If you're using a charger with a rate higher than two amps, check the battery regularly during charging to make sure it doesn't overheat. If you're using a trickle charger, you can safely let the battery charge overnight after you've checked it regularly for the first couple of hours.

16 If the battery has removable cell caps, measure the specific gravity with a hydrometer every hour during the last few hours of the charging cycle. Hydrometers are available inexpensively from auto parts stores - follow the instructions that come with the hydrometer. Consider the battery charged when there's no change in the specific gravity reading for two hours and the electrolyte in the cells is gassing (bubbling) freely. The specific gravity reading from each cell should be very close to the others. If not, the battery probably has a bad cell(s).

17 Some batteries with sealed tops have built-in hydrometers on the top that indicate the state of charge by the color displayed in the hydrometer window. Normally, a bright-colored hydrometer indicates a full charge and a dark hydrometer indicates the battery still needs charging. Check the battery manufacturer's instructions to be sure you know what the colors mean.

18 If the battery has a sealed top and no built-in hydrometer, you can hook up a digital voltmeter across the battery terminals to check the charge. A fully charged battery should read 12.5-volts or higher.

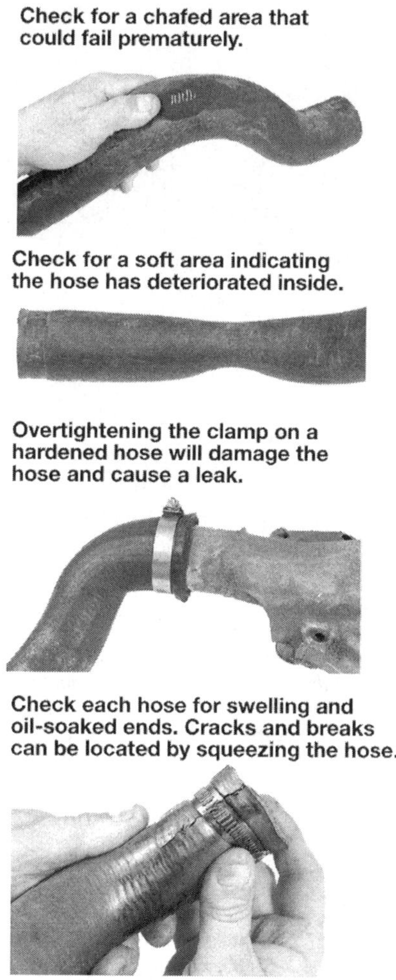

10.4a Hoses, like drivebelts, have a habit of failing at the worst possible time - to prevent the inconvenience of a blown radiator or heater hose, inspect them carefully as shown here

10 Cooling system check (every 7500 miles or 6 months)

Refer to illustrations 10.4a and 10.4b

1 Many major engine failures can be

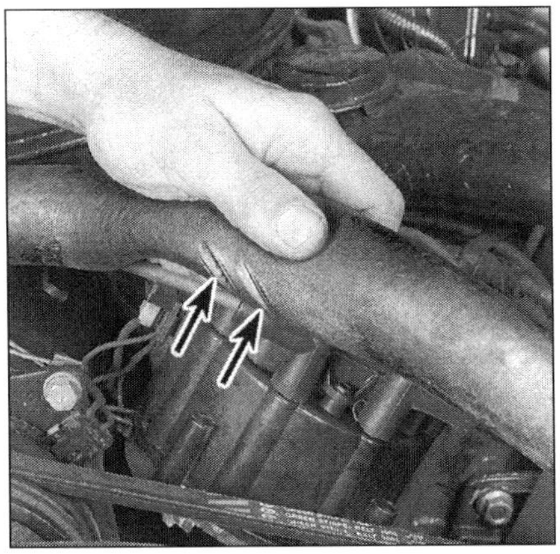

10.4b Be sure to check the underside of each hose; chafing like this, caused by contact with the air conditioning belt, is a common problem on the upper radiator hose - this hose should be replaced immediately

attributed to a faulty cooling system. If the vehicle is equipped with an automatic transmission, the cooling system also cools the transmission fluid and plays an important role in prolonging transmission life.

2 The cooling system should be checked with the engine cold. Do this before the vehicle is driven for the day or after the engine has been shut off for at least three hours.

3 Remove the radiator cap by turning it to the left until it reaches a stop. If you hear any hissing sounds (indicating there is still pressure in the system), wait until it stops. Now press down on the cap with the palm of your hand and continue turning to the left until the cap can be removed. Thoroughly clean the cap, inside and out, with clean water. Also clean the filler neck on the radiator. All traces of corrosion should be removed. The coolant inside the radiator should be relatively transparent. If it is rust colored, the system should be drained and refilled (see Section 35). If the coolant level is not up to the top, add additional antifreeze/coolant mixture (see Section 4).

4 Carefully check the large upper and lower radiator hoses along with any smaller diameter heater hoses which run from the engine to the firewall. Inspect each hose along its entire length, replacing any hose which is cracked, swollen or shows signs of deterioration. Cracks may become more apparent if the hose is squeezed **(see illustrations)**.

5 Make sure all hose connections are tight. A leak in the cooling system will usually show up as white or rust colored deposits on the areas adjoining the leak. If wire-type clamps are used at the ends of the hoses, it may be wise to replace them with more secure screw-type clamps.

6 Use compressed air or a soft brush to remove bugs, leaves, etc. from the front of the radiator or air conditioning condenser. Be careful not to damage the delicate cooling fins or cut yourself on them.

7 Every other inspection, or at the first indication of cooling system problems, have the cap and system pressure tested. If you don't have a pressure tester, most gas stations and repair shops will do this for a minimal charge.

11 Underhood hose check and replacement (every 7500 miles or 6 months)

General

1 High temperatures under the hood can cause the deterioration of the rubber and plastic hoses used for engine, accessory and emission systems operation. Periodic inspection should be made for cracks, loose clamps, material hardening and leaks. Information specific to the cooling system hoses can be found in (Section 10). **Warning:** *Replacement of air conditioning hoses must be left to a dealer service department or air conditioning shop that has the equipment to depressurize the system safely. Never remove air conditioning components or hoses until the system has been depressurized.*

2 Some, but not all, hoses are secured to the fittings with clamps. Where clamps are used, check to be sure they haven't lost their tension, allowing the hose to leak. If clamps aren't used, make sure the hose hasn't expanded and/or hardened where it slips over the fitting, allowing it to leak.

Vacuum hoses

3 It's quite common for vacuum hoses, especially those in the emissions system, to be color coded or identified by colored stripes molded into each hose. Various systems require hoses with different wall thickness, collapse resistance and temperature resistance. When replacing hoses, be sure the new ones are made of the same material.

4 Often the only effective way to check a hose is to remove it completely from the vehicle. If more than one hose is removed, be sure to label the hoses and fittings to ensure correct installation.

5 When checking vacuum hoses, be sure to include any plastic T-fittings in the check. Inspect the fittings for cracks and the hose where it fits over the fitting for distortion, which could cause leakage.

6 A small piece of vacuum hose (1/4-inch inside diameter) can be used as a stethoscope to detect vacuum leaks. Hold one end of the hose to your ear and probe around vacuum hoses and fittings, listening for the "hissing" sound characteristic of a vacuum leak. **Warning:** *When probing with the vacuum hose stethoscope, be careful not to allow your body or the hose to come into contact with moving engine components such as the drivebelt, cooling fan, etc.*

Fuel hose

Warning: *Gasoline is extremely flammable, so take extra precautions when you work on any part of the fuel system. Don't smoke or allow open flames or bare light bulbs near the work area, and don't work in a garage where a natural gas-type appliance (such as a water heater or clothes dryer) with a pilot light is present. If you spill any fuel on your skin, rinse it off immediately with soap and water. When you perform any kind of work on the fuel system, wear safety glasses and have a Class B type fire extinguisher on hand. The fuel system is under pressure, so if any lines must be disconnected, the pressure in the system must be relieved first* (see Chapter 4 for more information).

7 Check all rubber fuel lines for deterioration and chafing. Check especially for cracks in areas where the hose bends and just before fittings, such as where a hose attaches to the fuel filter and carburetor or fuel injection unit.

8 High quality fuel line, usually identified by the word Fluoroelastomer printed on the hose, should be used for fuel line replacement. Never, under any circumstances, use unreinforced vacuum line, clear plastic tubing or water hose for fuel lines.

9 Spring-type clamps are commonly used on fuel lines. These clamps often lose their tension over a period of time, and can be "sprung" during the removal process. As a result spring-type clamps should be replaced with screw-type clamps whenever a hose is replaced.

Metal lines

10 Sections of steel tubing often used for fuel line between the fuel pump and carburetor or fuel injection system. Check carefully for cracks, kinks and flat spots in the line.

11 If a section of metal fuel line must be replaced, only seamless steel tubing should be used, since copper and aluminum tubing do not have the strength necessary to withstand normal engine vibration.

12 Check the metal brake lines where they enter the master cylinder and brake proportioning unit (if used) for cracks in the lines and loose fittings. Any sign of brake fluid leakage calls for an immediate thorough inspection of the brake system.

12 Wiper blade inspection and replacement (every 7500 miles or 6 months)

Refer to illustrations 12.6 and 12.7

1 The windshield wiper and blade assemblies should be inspected periodically for damage, loose components and cracked or worn blade elements.

2 Road film can build up on the wiper blades and affect their efficiency, so they should be washed regularly with a mild detergent solution.

3 The action of the wiping mechanism can loosen the bolts, nuts and fasteners, so they should be checked and tightened, as necessary, at the same time the wiper blades are checked.

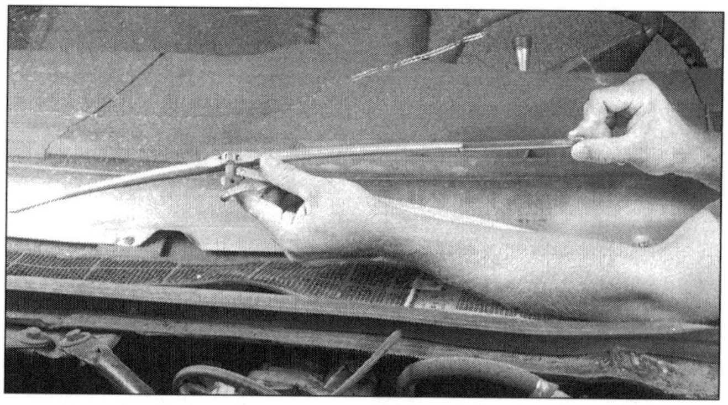

12.6 Squeeze the end of the wiper element to free it from the bridge claw, then slide the element out

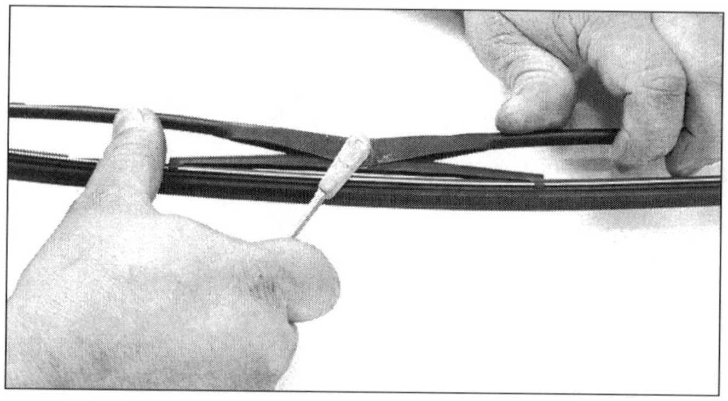

12.7 Detach the blade assembly from the wiper arm pin

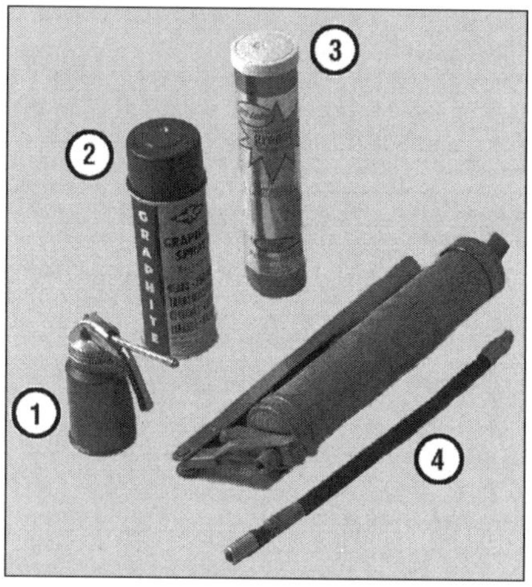

13.1 Materials required for chassis and body lubrication

1. ***Engine oil*** *- Light engine oil in a can like this can be used for door and hood hinges*
2. ***Graphite spray*** *- Used to lubricate lock cylinders*
3. ***Grease*** *- Grease, in a variety of types and weights, is available for use in a grease gun. Check the Specifications for your requirements*
4. ***Grease gun*** *- A common grease gun, shown here with a detachable hose and nozzle, is needed for chassis lubrication. After use, clean it thoroughly*

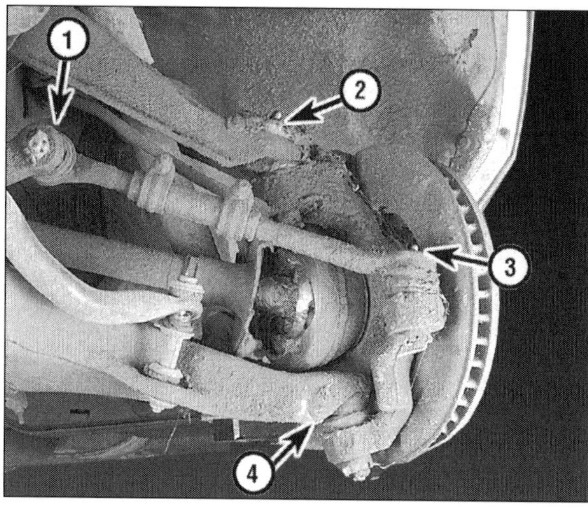

13.6 Grease fittings are located on both sides of the front end to lubricate suspension components

1. *Inner tie rod end grease fitting*
2. *Upper ball joint grease fitting*
3. *Outer tie rod end grease fitting*
4. *Lower ball joint grease fitting*

4 If the wiper blade elements (sometimes called inserts) are cracked, worn or warped, they should be replaced with new ones.

5 The wiper refill as it is sometimes called can be replaced without removing or disassembling the wiper mechanism.

6 Pull the wiper blade/arm assembly away from the glass, then grasp the middle of the wiper bridge securely with one hand and the element with the other. Detach the end of the element from the bridge claw and slide to free it, then slide the element out **(see illustration)**.

7 Often the blade assembly gets bent or it does not enable the element to contact the window evenly and its necessary to replace the complete blade assembly. When this situation occurs use a screwdriver to separate the blade assembly from the wiper arm pin **(see illustration)**.

8 Compare the new element or blade assembly with the old one for length, design, etc.

9 When replacing the element only, slide the new element into the claw, notched end last and secure the claw into the notches.

10 When replacing the complete blade assembly, snap the blade assembly on the wiper arm pin.

11 Wet the windshield and test for proper operation.

13 Chassis lubrication (every 7500 miles or 6 months)

Refer to illustrations 13.1 and 13.6

1 Refer to *Recommended lubricants and fluids* at the front of this Chapter to obtain the necessary grease, etc. You'll also need a grease gun **(see illustration)**. Occasionally plugs will be installed rather than grease fittings. If so, grease fittings will have to be purchased and installed.

2 Look under the vehicle and see if grease fittings or plugs are installed. If there are plugs, remove them and buy grease fittings, which will thread into the component. A dealer or auto parts store will be able to supply the correct fittings. Straight, as well as angled, fittings are available.

3 For easier access under the vehicle, raise it with a jack and place jackstands under the frame. Make sure it's safely supported by the stands. If the wheels are to be removed at this interval for tire rotation or brake inspection, loosen the lug nuts slightly while the vehicle is still on the ground.

4 Before beginning, force a little grease out of the nozzle to remove any dirt from the end of the gun. Wipe the nozzle clean with a rag.

5 With the grease gun and plenty of clean rags, crawl under the vehicle and begin lubricating the components.

6 Wipe one of the grease fittings clean and push the nozzle firmly over it **(see illustration)**. Pump the gun until the balljoint rubber seal is firm to the touch. Do not pump too much grease into the fitting as it could rupture the seal.

7 Wipe the excess grease from the components and the grease fitting. Repeat the procedure for the remaining fittings.

8 Clean and lubricate the parking brake cable, along with the cable guides and levers. This can be done by smearing some of the chassis grease onto the cable and its related parts with your fingers.

9 Open the hood and smear a little chassis grease on the hood latch mechanism.

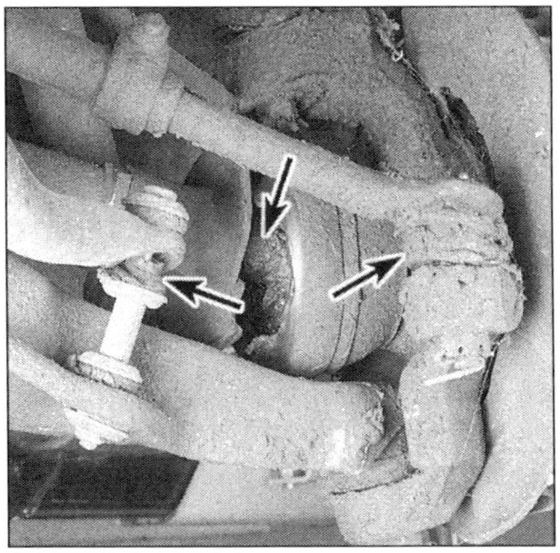

14.4 Inspect the inner and outer drive axle boots on both sides of the car as well as the stabilizer link bushings and the ball joint grease boots

Have an assistant pull the hood release lever from inside the vehicle as you lubricate the cable at the latch.

10 Lubricate all the hinges (door, hood, etc.) with engine oil to keep them in proper working order.

11 The key lock cylinders can be lubricated with spray graphite or silicone lubricant, which is available at auto parts stores.

12 Lubricate the door weatherstripping with silicone spray. This will reduce chafing and retard wear.

14 Suspension and steering check (every 7500 miles or 6 months)

Refer to illustrations 14.4 and 14.5

1 Indications of a fault in these systems are excessive play in the steering wheel before the front wheels react, excessive sway around corners, body movement over rough roads or binding at some point as the steering wheel is turned.

2 Raise the front of the vehicle periodically and visually check the suspension and steering components for wear. Because of the work to be done, make sure the vehicle cannot fall from the stands.

3 Check the wheel bearings. Do this by spinning the rear wheels. Listen for any abnormal noises and watch to make sure the wheel spins true (doesn't wobble). Grab the top and bottom of the tire and pull in-and-out on it. Notice any movement which would indicate a loose wheel bearing assembly. If the bearings are suspect, refer to Chapter 10 for more information.

4 From under the vehicle check for loose bolts, broken or disconnected parts and deteriorated rubber bushings on all suspension and steering components. Check the driveaxle boots for damage or leaking grease **(see illustration)**. Check the power steering hoses and connections for leaks.

5 Check the shock absorbers or leaking fluid or damaged bushings **(see illustration)**.

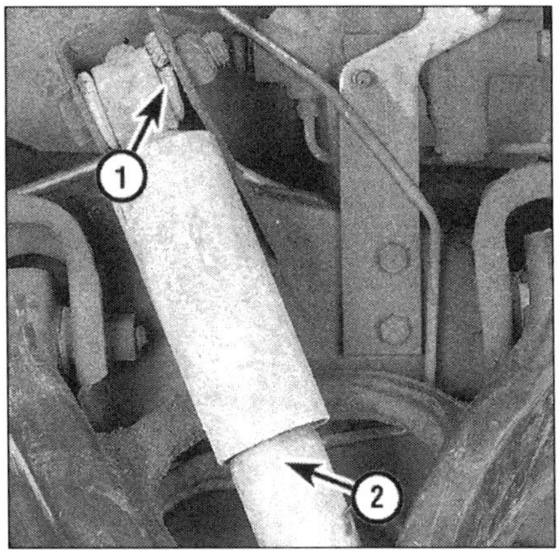

14.5 Check the shock absorbers for signs of wear in two places

1 *Worn bushings at each end of the shock absorber*
2 *Oil leaks in this area*

6 Have an assistant turn the steering wheel from side-to-side and check the steering components for free movement, chafing and binding. If the steering doesn't react with the movement of the steering wheel, try to determine where the slack is located.

15 Exhaust system check (every 7500 miles or 6 months)

Refer to illustration 15.2

1 With the engine cold (at least three hours after the vehicle has been driven), check the complete exhaust system from the engine to the end of the tailpipe. Ideally, the inspection should be done with the vehicle on a hoist to permit unrestricted access. If a hoist is not available, raise the vehicle and support it securely on jackstands.

2 Check the exhaust pipes and connections for evidence of leaks, severe corrosion and damage. Make sure that all brackets and hangers are in good condition and tight **(see illustration)**.

3 At the same time, inspect the underside of the body for holes, corrosion, open seams, etc. which may allow exhaust gases to enter the interior. Seal all body openings with silicone or body putty.

4 Rattles and other noises can often be traced to the exhaust system, especially the mounts and hangers. Try to move the pipes, muffler and catalytic converter. If the components can come in contact with the body or suspension parts, secure the exhaust system with new mounts.

16 Tire rotation (every 7500 miles or 6 months)

Refer to illustration 16.2

1 The tires should be rotated at the specified intervals and whenever uneven wear is noticed.

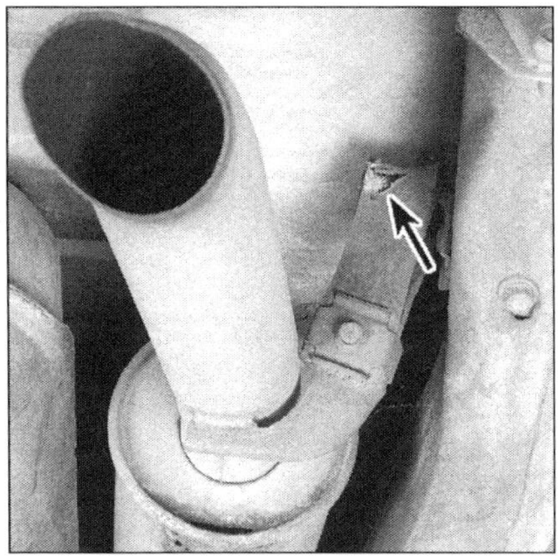

15.2 Check the exhaust system rubber hangers for cracks and damage (arrow)

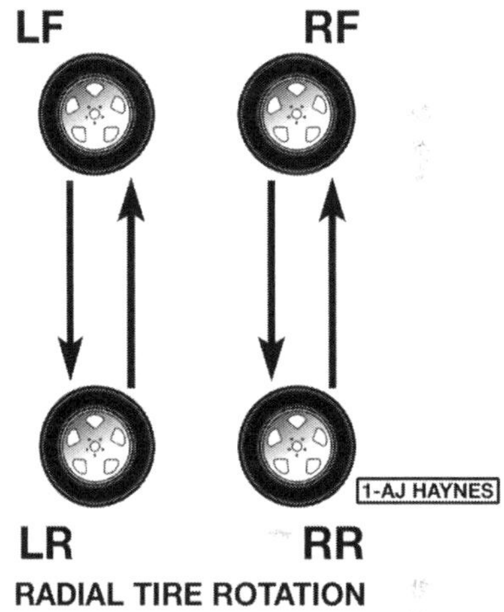

16.2 Tire rotation diagram

2 Front wheel drive vehicles require a special tire rotation pattern **(see illustration)**.

3 Refer to the information in *Jacking and towing* at the front of this manual for the proper procedures to follow when raising the vehicle and changing a tire. If the brakes are going to be checked, don't apply the parking brake as stated. Make sure the tires are blocked to prevent the vehicle from rolling as it's raised.

4 The entire vehicle should be raised at the same time. This can be done on a hoist or by jacking up each corner and then lowering the vehicle onto jackstands placed under the frame rails. Always use four jackstands and make sure the vehicle is safely supported.

5 After rotation, check and adjust the tire pressures as necessary and be sure to check the lug nut tightness.

17 Seat belt check (every 7500 miles or 6 months)

1 Check the seat belts, buckles, latch plates and guide loops for obvious damage and signs of wear.

2 See if the seat belt reminder light comes

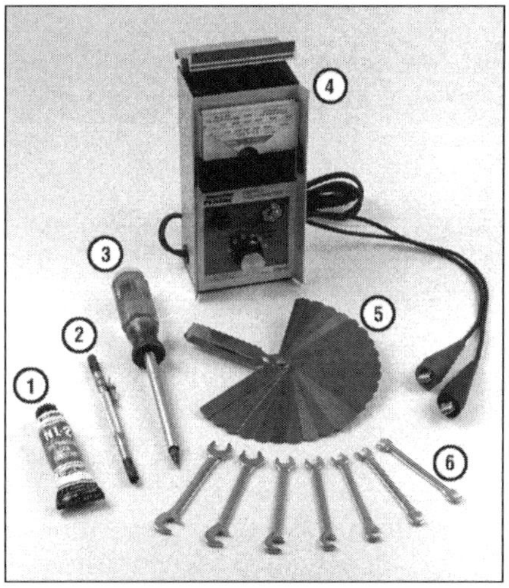

19.1 Tools and materials needed for contact point replacement and dwell angle adjustment

1 ***Distributor cam lube*** *- Sometimes this special lubricant comes with the new points; however, it's a good idea to buy a tube and have it on hand*
2 ***Screw starter*** *- This tool has special claws which hold the screw securely as it's started, which helps prevent accidental dropping of the screw*
3 ***Magnetic screwdriver*** *- Serves the same purpose as 2 above. If you don't have one of these special screwdrivers, you risk dropping the point mounting screws down into the distributor body*
4 ***Dwell meter*** *- A dwell meter is the only accurate way to determine the point setting (gap). Connect the meter according to the instructions supplied with it.*
5 ***Blade-type feeler gauges*** *- These are required to set the initial point gap (space between the points when they are open)*
6 ***Ignition wrenches*** *- These special wrenches are made to work within the tight confines of the distributor. Specifically, they are needed to loosen the nut/bolt which secures the leads to the points*

on when the key is turned to the Run or Start position. A chime should also sound.

3 The seat belts are designed to lock up during a sudden stop or impact, yet allow free movement during normal driving. Make sure the retractors return the belt against your chest while driving and rewind the belt fully when the buckle is unlatched.

4 If any of the above checks reveal problems with the seat belt system, replace parts as necessary.

18 Neutral start switch check (every 7500 miles or 6 months)

Warning: *During the following checks there's a chance the vehicle could lunge forward, possibly causing damage or injuries. Allow plenty of room around the vehicle, apply the parking brake and hold down the regular brake pedal during the checks.*

19.2 Although it is possible to restore ignition points that are pitted, burned and corroded (as shown here), they should be replaced

1 Try to start the engine in each gear. The engine should crank only in Park or Neutral.

2 Make sure the steering column lock allows the key to go into the Lock position only when the shift lever is in Park.

3 The ignition key should come out only in the Lock position.

19 Ignition point replacement (1974 and earlier models) (every 15,000 miles or 12 months)

Refer to illustrations 19.1, 19.2, 19.7, 19.9, 19.16, 19.17 and 19.29

1 The ignition points must be replaced at regular intervals on vehicles not equipped with electronic ignition. Occasionally the rubbing block will wear enough to require adjustment of the points. It's also possible to clean and dress them with a fine file, but replacement is recommended since they are relatively accessible and very inexpensive. Several special tools are required for this procedure **(see illustration)**.

2 After removing the distributor cap and rotor (see Section 40), the ignition points are plainly visible. They can be examined by gently prying them open to reveal the condition of the contact surfaces **(see illustration)**. If they're rough, pitted, covered with oil or burned, they should be replaced, along with the condenser. **Caution:** *This procedure requires the removal of small screws which can easily fall down into the distributor. To retrieve them, the distributor would have to be removed and disassembled. Use a magnetic or spring-loaded screwdriver and be extra careful.*

3 If not already done, remove the distributor cap by positioning a screwdriver in the

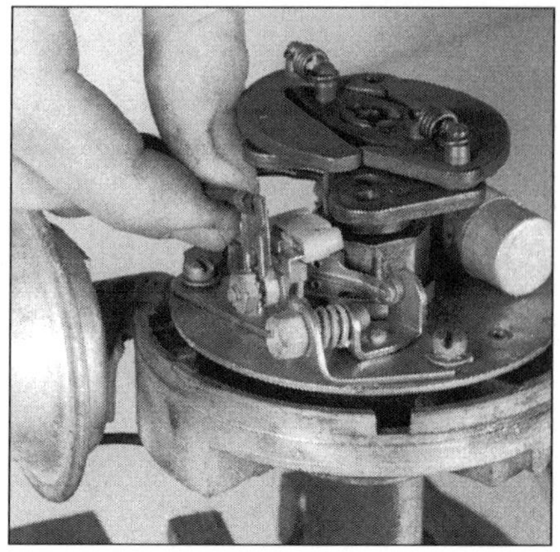

19.7 Loosen the nut and disconnect the primary and condenser wires from the points - note the ignition point mounting screws (arrows)

19.9 The condenser is attached to the breaker plate by a single screw

slotted head of each latch. Press down on the latch and rotate it 1/2-turn to release the cap from the distributor body (see Section 40).

4 Position the cap (with the spark plug wires still attached) out of the way. Use a length of wire to hold it out of the way, if necessary.

5 Remove the rotor, which is held in place with two screws.

6 If equipped with a radio frequency interference shield (RFI), remove the mounting screws and the two-piece shield to gain access to the ignition points.

7 Note how they are routed, then disconnect the primary and condenser wire leads from the points **(see illustration)**. The wires may be attached with a small nut (which should be loosened, but not removed), a small screw or by a spring-loaded terminal. **Note:** *Some models are equipped with ignition points which include the condenser as an integral part of the point assembly. If your vehicle has this type, the condenser removal procedure below will not apply and there will be only one wire to detach from the points, rather than the two used with a separate con-*

19.16 Before adjusting the point gap, the rubbing block must be resting on one of the cam lobes (which will open the points)

19.17 With the points open, insert a 0.016-inch thick feeler gauge and turn the adjustment screw with a 1/8-inch Allen wrench

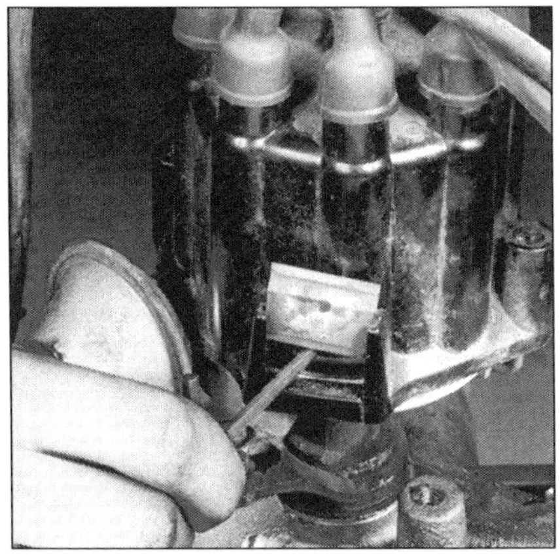

19.29 With the door open, an Allen wrench can be inserted into the adjustment screw socket and turned to adjust the point dwell

denser assembly.

8 Loosen the two screws which secure the ignition points to the breaker plate, but don't completely remove the screws (most ignition point sets have slots at these locations). Slide the points out of the distributor.

9 The condenser can now be removed from the breaker plate. Loosen the mounting strap screw and slide the condenser out or completely remove the condenser and strap **(see illustration)**. If you remove both the condenser and strap, be careful not to drop the mounting screw down into the distributor body.

10 Before installing the new points and condenser, clean the breaker plate and the cam on the distributor shaft to remove all dirt, dust and oil.

11 Apply a small amount of distributor cam lube (usually supplied with the new points, but also available separately) to the cam lobes.

12 Position the new condenser and tighten the mounting strap screw securely.

13 Slide the new point set under the mounting screw heads and make sure the protrusions on the breaker plate fit into the holes in the point base (to properly position the point set), then tighten the screws securely.

14 Attach the primary and condenser wires to the new points. Make sure the wires are routed so they don't interfere with breaker plate or advance weight movement.

15 Although the dwell angle will be adjusted later, make the initial gap adjustment now, which will allow the engine to be started.

16 Make sure that the point rubbing block is resting on one of the high points of the cam **(see illustration)**. If it isn't, turn the ignition switch to Start in short bursts to reposition the cam. You can also turn the crankshaft with a breaker bar and socket attached to the large bolt that holds the vibration damper in place.

17 With the rubbing block on a cam high point (points open), insert a 0.016-inch feeler gauge between the contact surfaces and use an Allen wrench to turn the adjustment screw until the point gap is equal to the thickness of the feeler gauge **(see illustration)**. The gap is correct when a slight amount of drag is felt as the feeler gauge is withdrawn.

18 If equipped, install the RFI shield.

19 Before installing the rotor, check it as described in Section 40.

20 Install the rotor. The rotor is indexed with a square peg underneath on one side and a round peg on the other side, so it will fit on the advance mechanism only one way. Tighten the rotor mounting screws securely.

21 Before installing the distributor cap, inspect it as described in Section 40.

22 Install the distributor cap and lock the latches under the distributor body by depressing and turning them with a screwdriver.

23 Start the engine and check the dwell angle and ignition timing.

24 Whenever new ignition points are installed or the original points are cleaned, the dwell angle must be checked and adjusted.

25 Precise adjustment of the dwell angle requires an instrument called a dwell meter. Combination tach/dwell meters are commonly available at reasonable cost from auto parts stores. An approximate setting can be obtained if a meter isn't available.

26 If a dwell meter is available, hook it up following the manufacturer's instructions.

27 Start the engine and allow it to run at idle until normal operating temperature is reached (the engine must be warm to obtain an accurate reading). Turn off the engine.

28 Raise the metal door in the distributor cap. Hold it in the open position with tape if necessary.

29 Just inside the opening is the ignition point adjustment screw. Insert a 1/8-inch Allen wrench into the adjustment screw socket **(see illustration)**.

30 Start the engine and turn the adjustment screw as required to obtain the specified dwell reading on the meter. Dwell angle specifications can be found at the beginning of this Chapter and on the VECI label or tune-up decal in the engine compartment. If there's a discrepancy between the two, assume the VECI label or tune-up decal is correct. **Note:** *When adjusting the dwell, aim for the lower end of the dwell specification range. Then, as the points wear, the dwell will remain within the specified range over a longer period of time.*

31 Remove the Allen wrench and close the door on the distributor. Turn off the engine and disconnect the dwell meter, then check the ignition timing (see Section 20).

20 Ignition timing check and adjustment (every 15,000 miles or 12 months)

Refer to illustrations 20.3, and 20.6

Note: *It is imperative that the procedures included on the tune-up or Vehicle Emissions Control Information (VECI) label be followed when adjusting the ignition timing. The label will include all information concerning preliminary steps to be performed before adjusting the timing, as well as the timing specifications. If no VECI label is found* refer to the specifications chart at the beginning of this Chapter.

1 At the specified maintenance intervals, whenever the ignition points have been replaced or the distributor removed, the ignition timing should be checked and adjusted.

2 Various procedures (depending on make and model of the vehicle) must be performed to disable the distributor or computer advance mechanism before attempting to check the timing. Locate the Tune-up or VECI label under the hood and read through and perform all preliminary instructions concerning ignition timing. If no VECI label is found refer to the specifications section at the beginning of this Chapter.

3 Before attempting to check the timing

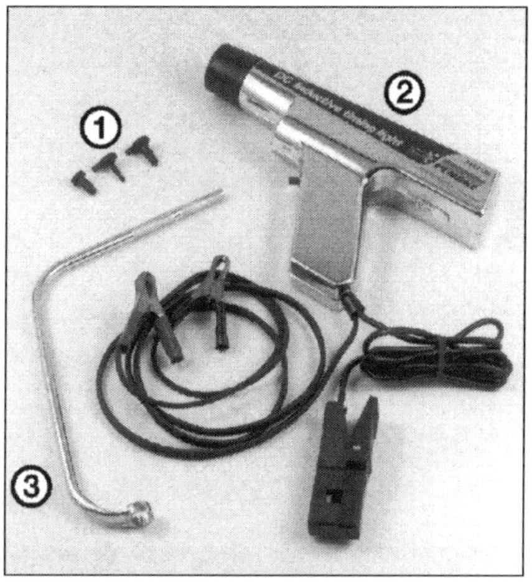

20.3 Tools needed to check and adjust the ignition timing

1 ***Vacuum plugs*** - *Vacuum hoses will, in most cases, have to be disconnected and plugged. Molded plugs in various shapes and sizes are available for this*

2 ***Inductive pick-up timing light*** - *Flashes a bright, concentrated beam of light when the number one spark plug fires. Connect the leads according to the instructions supplied with the light*

3 ***Distributor wrench*** - *On some models, the hold-down bolt for the distributor is difficult to reach and turn with conventional wrenches or sockets. A special wrench like this must be used*

some special tools will be needed for this procedure **(see illustration)**.

4 Check that the idle speed is as specified (Section 21). On pre-1975 vehicles make sure the ignition point dwell angle is correct (see Section 19).

5 Connect a timing light in accordance with the manufacturer's instructions. Generally, the light will be connected to power and ground sources and to the number one spark plug wire (refer to the cylinder location diagram at the beginning of this Chapter).

6 Locate the numbered timing tag on the front cover of the engine **(see illustration)**. It's located just behind the lower crankshaft pulley. Clean it off with solvent if necessary to read the printing and small grooves.

7 Use chalk or paint to mark the groove in the crankshaft pulley.

8 Put a mark on the timing tab in accordance with the number of degrees called for on the VECI label or the tune-up label in the engine compartment. Each peak or notch on the timing tab represents two degrees. The word Before or the letter A indicates advance and the letter O indicates Top Dead Center (TDC). As an example, if your vehicle specifications call for eight degrees BTDC (Before Top Dead Center), you will make a mark on the timing tab four notches before the O.

9 Check that the wiring for the timing light is clear of all moving engine components, then start the engine and warm it up to normal operating temperature.

20.6 The ignition timing indicator is located at the front of the engine behind the crankshaft pulley

10 Aim the flashing timing light at the timing mark by the crankshaft pulley, again being careful not to come in contact with moving parts. The marks should appear to be stationary. If the marks are in alignment, the timing is correct.

11 If the notch is not lining up with the correct mark, loosen the distributor hold-down bolt and rotate the distributor until the notch is lined up with the correct timing mark. **Note:** *On the 1977 Oldsmobile Toronado the ignition timing is adjusted by the adjust timing bolt on the crank sensor located on the lower left front of the block (DO NOT turn the distributor to adjust the timing on this model).*

12 Retighten the hold-down bolt and recheck the timing.

13 Turn off the engine and disconnect the timing light. Reconnect the vacuum advance hose, if removed, and any other components which were disconnected. **Note:** *If the check engine light comes on after performing the timing procedure* (see Chapter 6) *for the procedure to clear trouble codes.*

21 Idle speed check and adjustment (15,000 miles or 12 months)

Refer to illustration 21.4

Note: *This Section pertains only to carbureted models without an Idle Speed Control motor (ISC). For models equipped with an ISC, see Chapter 4A.*

1 Engine idle speed is the speed at which the engine operates when no accelerator pedal pressure is applied. On later models this speed is governed by the ECM, while on earlier models the idle speed can be adjusted. The idle speed is critical to the performance of the engine itself, as well as many engine sub-systems.

2 A hand-held tachometer must be used when adjusting idle speed to get an accurate reading. The exact hook-up for these meters varies with the manufacturer, so follow the particular directions included with the instrument.

21.4 The idle speed on earlier models can be adjusted with a screw (arrow) that's on the left side of the carburetor

3 Since the manufacturer recommended many different adjustment procedures over the time period covered by this manual, it would be impractical to cover all types in this Section. Most models have a tune-up decal or Vehicle Emission Control Information (VECI) label located in the engine compartment with instructions for setting idle speed. If no VECI label is found refer to the specifications section at the beginning of this Chapter.

4 For most applications, the idle speed is set by turning an adjustment screw located on the left side of the carburetor. This screw changes the amount the throttle plate is held open by the throttle linkage. The screw may be on the linkage itself **(see illustration)** or may be part of a device such as an idle speed solenoid.

5 Once you have found the idle screw, experiment with different length screwdrivers until the adjustment can be easily made without coming into contact with hot or moving engine components.

6 Follow the instructions on the tune-up decal or Vehicle Emission Control Information label, which will probably include disconnecting certain vacuum or electrical connections. To plug a vacuum hose after disconnecting, insert a suitable size metal rod into the opening, or thoroughly wrap the open end with tape to prevent any vacuum loss through the hose.

7 If the air cleaner is removed, the vacuum hose to the snorkel should be plugged.

8 Make sure the parking brake is firmly set and the wheels blocked to prevent the vehicle from rolling. This is especially true if the specifications require the transmission to be in Drive. An assistant inside the vehicle pressing on the brake pedal is the safest method.

9 For all applications, the engine must be completely warmed up to operating temperature, which will automatically render the choke fast idle inoperative.

23.3 The carburetor choke plate (arrow) is visible after removing the air cleaner top plate

24.4 Evenly tighten the carburetor or throttle body mounting bolts (arrows) located at each corner

22 Thermostatically controlled air cleaner check (15,000 miles or 12 months)

1 Some engines are equipped with a thermostatically controlled air cleaner which draws air to the carburetor from different locations, depending upon engine temperature.

2 This is a visual check. If access is limited, a small mirror may have to be used.

3 Open the hood and locate the damper door inside the air cleaner assembly. It is inside the long snorkel of the metal air cleaner housing.

4 If there is a flexible air duct attached to the end of the snorkel, leading to an area behind the grille, disconnect it at the snorkel. This will enable you to look through the end of the snorkel and see the damper inside.

5 The check should be done when the engine is cold. Start the engine and look through the snorkel at the damper, which should move to a closed position. With the damper closed, air cannot enter through the end of the snorkel, but instead enters the air cleaner through the flexible duct attached to the exhaust manifold and the heat stove passage. **Note:** *If you have trouble seeing the damper door inside the snorkel lift the air cleaner housing with out disconnecting any vacuum lines, then have an assistant start the engine.*

6 As the engine warms up to operating temperature, the damper should open to allow air through the snorkel end. Depending on outside temperature, this may take 10 to 15 minutes. To speed up this check you can reconnect the snorkel air duct, drive the vehicle, then check to see if the damper is completely open.

23 Carburetor choke check (15,000 miles or 12 months)

Refer to illustration 23.3

1 The choke operates when the engine is cold, and thus this check can only be performed before the vehicle has been started for the day.

2 Open the hood and remove the top plate of the air cleaner assembly. It is usually held in place by a wing nut at the center. If any vacuum hoses must be disconnected, make sure you tag the hoses for reinstallation in their original positions. Place the top plate and wing nut aside, out of the way of moving engine components.

3 Look at the center of the air cleaner housing. You will notice a flat plate (arrow) at the carburetor opening **(see illustration)**.

4 Press the accelerator pedal to the floor. The plate should close completely. Start the engine while you watch the plate at the carburetor. Do not position your face directly over the carburetor, as the engine could backfire, causing serious burns. When the engine starts, the choke plate should open slightly.

5 Allow the engine to continue running at an idle speed. As the engine warms up to operating temperature, the plate should slowly open, allowing more cold air to enter through the top of the carburetor.

6 After a few minutes, the choke plate should be fully open to the vertical position. Press quickly on the accelerator to make sure the fast idle cam disengages.

7 You will notice that the engine speed corresponds with the plate opening. With the plate fully closed, the engine should run at a fast idle speed. As the plate opens and the throttle is moved to disengage the fast idle cam, the engine speed will decrease.

24 Carburetor/throttle body mounting nut torque check (15,000 miles or 12 months)

Refer to illustration 24.4

1 The carburetor or throttle body unit is attached to the top of the intake manifold by several bolts or nuts. These fasteners can sometimes work loose from vibration and temperature changes during normal engine operation and cause a vacuum leak.

2 If you suspect that a vacuum leak exists at the bottom of the carburetor or throttle body, obtain a length of hose about the diameter of fuel hose. Start the engine and place one end of the hose next to your ear as you probe around the base with the other end. You will hear a hissing sound if a leak exists (be careful of hot or moving engine components).

3 Remove the air cleaner assembly, tagging each hose to be disconnected with a piece of numbered tape to make reassembly easier.

4 Locate the mounting nuts or bolts at the base of the carburetor or throttle body **(see illustration)**. Decide what special tools or adapters will be necessary, if any, to tighten the fasteners.

5 Tighten the nuts or bolts securely and evenly. Do not overtighten them, as the threads could strip.

6 If, after the nuts or bolts are properly tightened, a vacuum leak still exists, the carburetor or throttle body must be removed and a new gasket installed. See Chapter 4A for more information.

7 After tightening the fasteners, reinstall the air cleaner and return all hoses to their original positions.

25 EFE (heat riser) system check (15,000 miles or 12 months)

Refer to illustration 25.5

1 The heat riser and the Early Fuel Evaporation (EFE) system both perform the same job, but each functions in a slightly different manner.

2 The heat riser is a valve inside the exhaust pipe, near the junction between the exhaust manifold and exhaust pipe. The heat riser valve used on early models can be identified by an external weight and spring.

3 With the engine and exhaust pipe cold, try moving the weight by hand. It should move freely.

4 Again with the engine cold, start the engine and watch the heat riser. Upon starting, the weight should move to the closed position. As the engine warms to normal operating temperature, the weight should

25.5 On later models, the EFE valve actuator and rod assembly (arrow) is vacuum operated

move the valve to the open position, allowing a free flow of exhaust through the tailpipe. Since it could take several minutes for the system to heat up, you could mark the cold weight position, drive the vehicle, and then check the weight.

5 The EFE system also blocks off exhaust flow when the engine is cold. However, this system uses more precise temperature sensors and vacuum to open and close the exhaust pipe valve **(see illustration)**.

6 Locate the EFE actuator, which is bolted to a bracket on the side of the engine. It will have an actuating rod attached to it which will lead down to the valve inside the pipe. In some cases the entire mechanism, including actuator, will be located at the exhaust pipe-to-manifold junction.

7 With the engine cold, have an assistant start the engine as you watch the actuating rod. It should immediately move to close off the valve as the engine warms. This process may take some time, so you might want to mark the position of the rod when the valve is closed, drive the vehicle to reach normal operating temperature, then open the hood and check that the rod has moved to the open position.

26 Brake check (every 15,000 miles or 12 months)

Warning: *Brake system dust may contain asbestos, which is hazardous to your health. DO NOT blow it out with compressed air or inhale it. DO NOT use gasoline or solvents to remove the dust. Use brake system cleaner or denatured alcohol only.*

Note: *For detailed photographs of the brake system,* see Chapter 9.

1 In addition to the specified intervals, the brakes should be inspected every time the wheels are removed or whenever a defect is suspected. Raise the vehicle and place it securely on jackstands. Remove the wheels (see *Jacking and towing* at the front of this manual, if necessary).

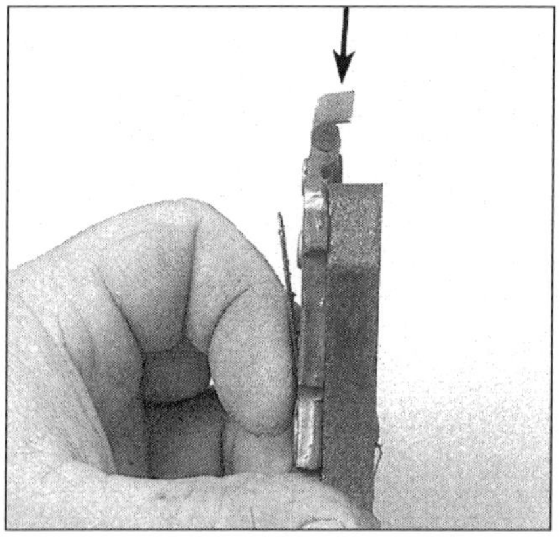

26.3 The disc brake pads have a built in wear indicator that contacts the rotor and makes a squealing sound when the pad has worn to its limit

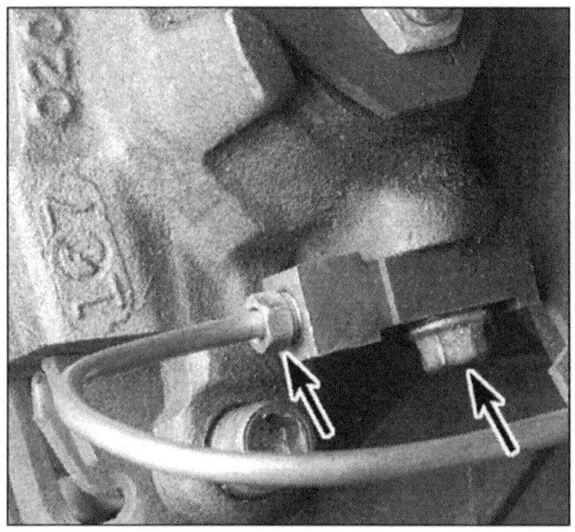

26.7 Check for any sign of brake fluid leakage at the line fittings and the brake hoses

Disc brakes

Refer to illustrations 26.3, 26.5 and 26.7

2 Disc brakes can be checked without removing any parts except the wheels. Extensive disc damage can occur if the pads are not replaced when needed.

3 The disc brake pads have built-in wear indicators **(see illustration)** which make a high-pitched squealing sound when the pads are worn. **Caution:** *Expensive damage to the disc can result if the pads are not replaced soon after the wear indicators start squealing.*

4 The disc brake calipers, which contain the brake pads, have an inner pad and outer pad in each caliper. All pads should be inspected.

5 Each caliper has a "window" to inspect the pads **(see illustration)**. If the pad material has worn to about 1/8-inch thick or less, the pads should be replaced.

6 If you're unsure about the exact thickness of the remaining lining material, remove the pads for further inspection or replacement (see Chapter 9).

7 Before installing the wheels, check for leakage and/or damage at the brake hoses and connections **(see illustration)**. Replace the hose or fittings as necessary, (see Chapter 9).

26.5 With the wheels removed, the brake pad lining can be inspected through the caliper window (arrow) and at each end of the caliper

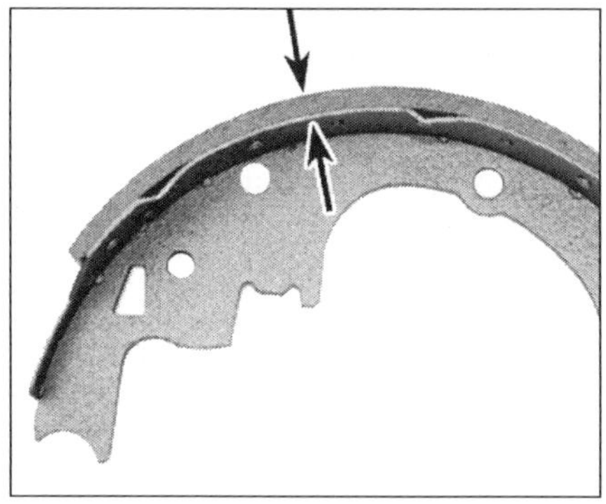

26.14 If the lining is bonded to the brake shoe, measure the lining thickness from the outer surface to the metal shoe, as shown here; if the lining is riveted to the shoe, measure from the lining outer surface to the rivet head

8 Check the condition of the brake rotor. Look for score marks, deep scratches and overheated areas (they will appear blue or discolored). If damage or wear is noted, the disc can be removed and resurfaced by an automotive machine shop or replaced with a new one. See Chapter 9 for more detailed inspection and repair procedures.

Drum brakes

Refer to illustrations 26.14 and 26.16

9 Raise the vehicle and support it securely on jackstands. Block the front tires to prevent the vehicle from rolling; however, don't apply the parking brake or it will lock the drums in place.

10 Remove the wheels, referring to *Jacking and towing* at the front of this manual if necessary.

11 Mark the hub so it can be reinstalled in the same position. Use a scribe, chalk, etc. on the drum, hub and backing plate.

12 Remove the brake drum.

13 With the drum removed, carefully clean the brake assembly with brake system cleaner. **Warning:** *Don't blow the dust out with compressed air and don't inhale any of it (it may contain asbestos, which is harmful to*

26.16 Check for fluid leakage at both ends of the wheel cylinder dust covers (arrow)

your health).

14 Note the thickness of the lining material on both front and rear brake shoes. If the material has worn away to within 1/8-inch of the recessed rivets or metal backing, the shoes should be replaced **(see illustration)**. The shoes should also be replaced if they're cracked, glazed (shiny areas), or covered with brake fluid.

15 Make sure all the brake assembly springs are connected and in good condition.

16 Check the brake components for signs of fluid leakage. With your finger or a small screwdriver, carefully pry back the rubber cups on the wheel cylinder located at the top of the brake shoes **(see illustration)**. Any leakage here is an indication that the wheel cylinders should be overhauled immediately (see Chapter 9). Also, check all hoses and connections for signs of leakage.

17 Wipe the inside of the drum with a clean rag and denatured alcohol or brake cleaner. Again, be careful not to breathe the dangerous asbestos dust.

18 Check the inside of the drum for cracks, score marks, deep scratches and "hard spots" which will appear as small discolored areas. If imperfections cannot be removed with fine emery cloth, the drum must be taken to an automotive machine shop for resurfacing.

19 Repeat the procedure for the remaining wheel. If the inspection reveals that all parts are in good condition, reinstall the brake drums, install the wheels and lower the vehicle to the ground.

Parking brake

20 The parking brake is operated by a foot pedal and locks the rear brake system. The easiest, and perhaps most obvious, method of periodically checking the operation of the parking brake assembly is to park the vehicle on a steep hill with the parking brake set and the transmission in Neutral (be sure to stay in the vehicle during this check!). If the parking brake cannot prevent the vehicle from rolling, it needs service (see Chapter 9).

21 Some models may have a vacuum operated release mechanism which releases the parking brake after the engine has been started and the gear selector is removed from the park position. If the vacuum system becomes inoperable (see Chapter 9) it will be necessary to use the manual over ride lever that is located near the hood release lever

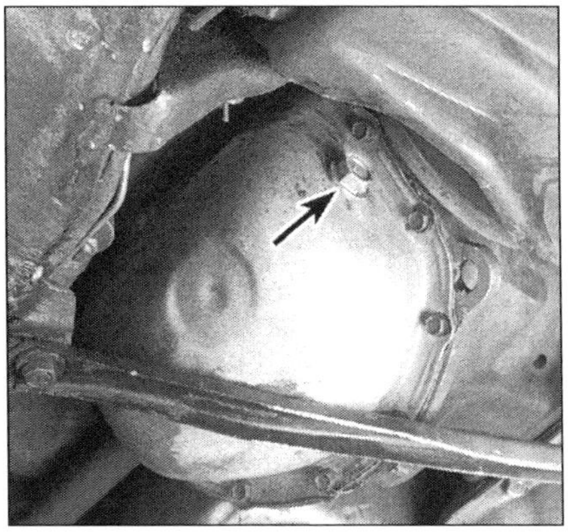

27.2 Differential fill/check plug location (arrow)

27 Differential lubricant level check (every 15,000 miles or 12 months)

Refer to illustration 27.2

1 The differential has a check/fill plug which must be removed to check the lubricant level. If the vehicle is raised to gain access to the plug, be sure to support it safely on jackstands - DO NOT crawl under the vehicle when it's supported only by a jack.

2 Remove the lubricant check/fill plug from the side of the differential **(see illustration)**.

3 The lubricant level should be at the bottom of the plug opening. If not, use a hand pump, syringe or funnel to fill the differential housing with the specified lubricant until it's level with the bottom of the fill plug hole. On some models a tag is located in the area of the plug which gives information regarding lubricant type. If not, refer to the specifications section at the beginning of this Chapter.

4 Install the plug and tighten it securely.

28 Fuel system check (every 15,000 miles or 12 months)

Warning: *Gasoline is extremely flammable, so take extra precautions when you work on any part of the fuel system. Don't smoke or allow open flames or bare light bulbs near the work area, and don't work in a garage where a natural gas-type appliance (such as a water heater or clothes dryer) with a pilot light is present. Since gasoline is carcinogenic, wear latex gloves when there's a possibility of being exposed to fuel, and, if you spill any fuel on your skin, rinse it off immediately with soap and water. Mop up any spills immediately and do not store fuel-soaked rags where they could ignite. The fuel system is under constant pressure, so, if any fuel lines are to be disconnected, the fuel pressure in the system must be relieved first* (see Chapter 4 for more information). *When you perform any kind of work on the fuel system, wear safety glasses and have a Class B type fire extinguisher on hand.*

1 The fuel system is most easily checked with the vehicle raised on a hoist so the components underneath the vehicle are readily visible and accessible.

2 If the smell of gasoline is noticed while driving or after the vehicle has been in the sun, the system should be thoroughly inspected immediately.

3 Remove the gas tank cap and check for damage, corrosion and an unbroken sealing imprint on the gasket. Replace the cap with a new one if necessary.

4 With the vehicle raised, inspect the gas tank and filler neck for cracks and other damage. The connection between the filler neck and tank is especially critical. Sometimes a filler neck will leak due to cracks, problems a home mechanic can't repair. **Warning:** *Do not, under any circumstances, try to repair a fuel tank yourself (except rubber components). A welding torch or any open flame can easily cause the fuel vapors to explode if the proper precautions are not taken.*

5 Carefully check all rubber hoses and metal lines leading away from the fuel tank. Check for loose connections, deteriorated hoses, crimped lines and other damage. Follow the lines to the front of the vehicle, carefully inspecting them all the way. Repair or replace damaged sections as necessary.

29 Air filter and PCV filter replacement (every 30,000 miles or 24 months)

Refer to illustrations 29.2, 29.4 and 29.6

1 At the specified intervals, the air filter and (if equipped) PCV filter should be replaced with new ones. The engine air cleaner also supplies filtered air to the PCV system.

2 The filter is located on top of the carburetor or throttle body and is replaced by

29.2 The first step in removing the air filter is unscrewing the wing nut on the housing

29.4 After setting the top cover aside, the filter element can be lifted out of the housing

29.6 The PCV filter on most models is located in the air cleaner housing

30.6 Two wrenches are required to loosen the carburetor fuel filter fitting

unscrewing the wing nut from the top of the filter housing and lifting off the cover **(see illustration)**.

3 While the top cover is off, be careful not to drop anything down into the carburetor, throttle body or air cleaner assembly.

4 Lift the air filter element out of the housing **(see illustration)** and wipe out the inside of the air cleaner housing with a clean rag.

5 The PCV filter is also located inside the air cleaner housing on most models. Remove the top cover and air filter as previously described, then locate the PCV filter on the inside of the housing.

6 Remove the old filter **(see illustration)**.

7 Install the new PCV filter and the new air filter. Make sure the air filter seats properly in the bottom of the housing.

8 On earlier models, the PCV filter is located in the left rocker arm cover. This type of filter doesn't require replacement; pull it out of the rocker cover and wash it with solvent at the specified intervals.

9 Install the top cover and any hoses which were disconnected.

30 Fuel filter replacement (every 30,000 miles or 24 months)

Warning: *Gasoline is extremely flammable, so take extra precautions when you work on any part of the fuel system. Don't smoke or allow open flames or bare light bulbs near the work area, and don't work in a garage where a natural gas-type appliance (such as a water heater or clothes dryer) with a pilot light is present. Since gasoline is carcinogenic, wear latex gloves when there's a possibility of being exposed to fuel, and, if you spill any fuel on your skin, rinse it off immediately with soap and water. Mop up any spills immediately and do not store fuel-soaked rags where they could ignite. The fuel system is under constant pressure, so, if any fuel lines are to be disconnected, the fuel pressure in the system must be relieved first* (see Chapter 4 for more information). *When you perform any kind of work on the fuel system, wear safety glasses and have a Class B type fire extinguisher on hand.*

Carbureted models

Refer to illustrations 30.6 and 30.8

1 On all carbureted models a fuel filter is located inside the fuel inlet nut at the front of the carburetor. It's made of either pleated paper or porous bronze and cannot be cleaned or reused.

2 The job should be done with the engine cold (after sitting at least three hours). The necessary tools include open-end wrenches to fit the fuel line fitting. Flare nut wrenches (which wrap around the nut) should be used if available. In addition, you have to obtain the replacement filter (make sure it's for your specific vehicle and engine) and some clean rags.

3 Remove the air cleaner assembly (see Chapter 4). If vacuum hoses must be disconnected, be sure to note their positions and/or tag them to ensure that they are reinstalled correctly.

4 Follow the fuel line from the fuel pump to the point where it enters the carburetor. In most cases the fuel line will be metal all the way from the fuel pump to the carburetor.

5 Place some rags under the fuel inlet fittings to catch spilled fuel as the fittings are disconnected.

6 With the proper size wrench, hold the fuel inlet nut immediately next to the carburetor body. Now loosen the fitting at the end of the metal fuel line. Make sure the fuel inlet nut next to the carburetor is held securely while the fuel line is disconnected **(see illustration)**.

7 After the fuel line is disconnected, move it aside for better access to the inlet nut. Don't crimp the fuel line.

8 Unscrew the fuel inlet nut, which was previously held steady. As this fitting is drawn away from the carburetor body, be careful not to lose the thin washer-type gasket on the nut or the spring, located behind the fuel filter. Also pay close attention to how the filter is installed **(see illustration)**.

9 Compare the old filter with the new one to make sure they're the same length and design.

10 Reinstall the spring in the carburetor body.

11 Place the filter in position (a gasket is usually supplied with the new filter) and tighten the nut. Make sure it's not cross-threaded. Tighten it securely, but be careful not to overtighten it as the threads can strip easily, causing fuel leaks. Reconnect the fuel line to the fuel inlet nut, again using caution to avoid cross-threading the nut. Use a back-up wrench on the fuel inlet nut while tightening the fuel line fitting.

12 Start the engine and check carefully for leaks. If the fuel line fitting leaks, disconnect it and check for stripped or damaged threads. If the fuel line fitting has stripped threads, remove the entire line and have a repair shop install a new fitting. If the threads look all right, purchase some thread sealing tape and wrap

30.8 Carbureted fuel filter assembly - Always position the fuel filter inlet hole towards the fuel inlet nut

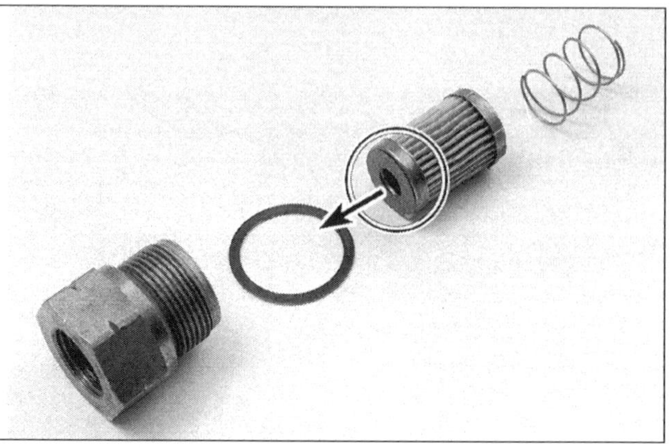

30.17 Unscrew the canister (located underneath the vehicle in front of the left rear tire) counterclockwise for access to the filter element

the threads with it. Inlet nut repair kits are available at most auto parts stores to overcome leaking at the fuel inlet nut.

Fuel injected models

Refer to illustrations 30.17 and 30.19

Warning: *The fuel injection system maintains considerable pressure, even with the engine off. This pressure must be relieved before working on the fuel system. On MPFI systems (1976 through 1979) follow the fuel system pressure relief procedure in Chapter 4B. On TBI systems (1980-on), loosen the fuel tank cap before working on the fuel system. This will allow the system self-bleeding feature to release the pressure.*

13 Two types of filters are used on these models: a canister type on earlier models and an in-line type on later models.

14 Depressurize the fuel system as described above.

15 Raise the vehicle and support it securely on jackstands.

16 Place a container, newspapers or rags under the filter.

17 On canister-type filters, grasp the canister securely, unscrew it, then remove the filter element **(see illustration)**.

18 Place the new filter element in position with the fuel inlet hole facing upward and install the canister.

19 On inline filter-equipped models, use two wrenches (one as a back-up) to disconnect each fuel line, then unbolt the filter from the frame **(see illustration)**. Use flare-nut wrenches, if available, to disconnect the lines,

20 Clean the fuel line fittings, then install the filter with the fuel direction arrow on the side of the filter facing towards the front of the vehicle

31 Drivebelt check and replacement (every 30,000 miles or 24 months)

Check

Refer to illustrations 31.3 and 31.4

1 The drivebelts, or V-belts as they are

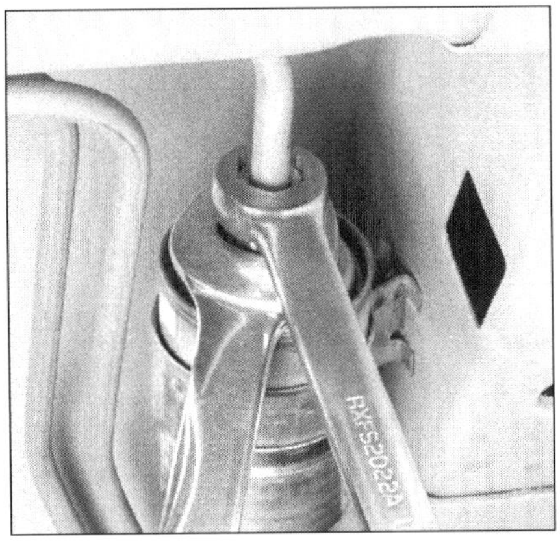

30.19 Use one wrench to steady the filter (located underneath the vehicle in front of the left rear tire), then unscrew the fuel line fitting and remove the filter; if available, use a flare nut wrench on the fuel line fitting

sometimes called, are located at the front of the engine and play an important role in the overall operation of the vehicle and its components. Due to their function and material make-up, the belts are prone to failure after a period of time and should be inspected and adjusted periodically to prevent major engine damage.

2 The number of belts used on a particular vehicle depends on the accessories installed. Drivebelts are used to turn the alternator, power steering pump, water pump and air-conditioning compressor. Depending on the pulley arrangement, more than one of these components may be driven by a single belt.

3 With the engine off, open the hood and locate the various belts at the front of the engine. Using your fingers (and a flashlight, if necessary), move along the belts checking for cracks and separation of the belt plies. Also check for fraying and glazing, which gives the belt a shiny appearance **(see illustration)**. Both sides of each belt should be inspected, which means you will have to twist the belt to check the underside.

4 The tension of each belt is checked by pushing on the belt at a distance halfway between the pulleys. Push firmly with your

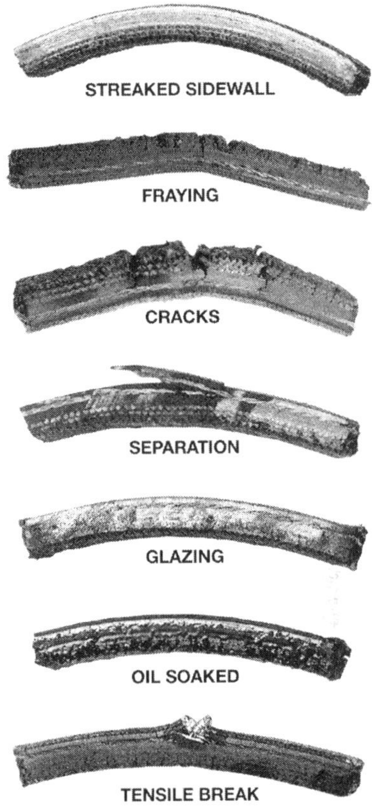

31.3 Here are some of the more common problems associated with drivebelts (check the belts very carefully to prevent an untimely breakdown)

thumb and see how much the belt moves (deflects) **(see illustration)**. A rule of thumb is that if the distance from pulley center-to-pulley center is between 7 and 11 inches, the belt should deflect 1/4-inch. If the belt travels between pulleys spaced 12 to 16 inches apart, the belt should deflect 1/2-inch.

Adjustment

Refer to illustration 31.8

5 If it is necessary to adjust the belt tension, either to make the belt tighter or looser,

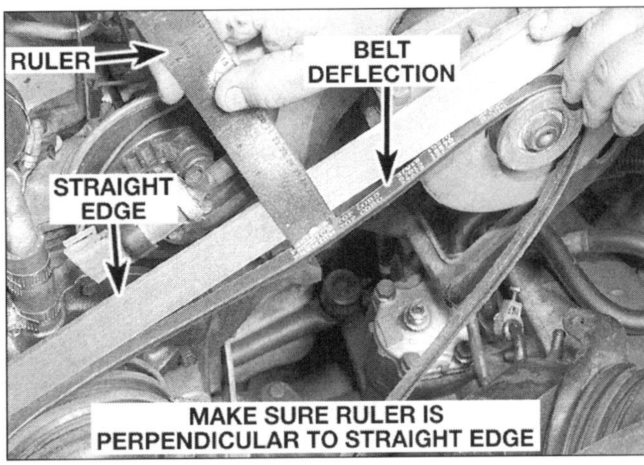

31.4 Measuring drivebelt deflection with a straightedge and ruler

31.8 Insert a 1/2-inch drive ratchet and pry upward to tension the drivebelt

it is done by moving the belt-driven accessory on the bracket.

6 For each component there will be an adjusting bolt and a pivot bolt. Both bolts must be loosened slightly to enable you to move the component.

7 After the two bolts have been loosened, move the component away from the engine to tighten the belt or toward the engine to loosen the belt. Hold the accessory in position and check the belt tension. If it is correct, tighten the two bolts until just snug, then recheck the tension. If the tension is all right, tighten the bolts.

8 To adjust the power steering drivebelt on some later models, loosen the pivot bolt and insert a 1/2-inch drive ratchet to use as a leverage tool to tension the belt **(see illustration)**.

9 It will often be necessary to use some sort of prybar to move the accessory while the belt is adjusted. If this must be done to gain the proper leverage, be very careful not to damage the component being moved or the part being pried against.

Replacement

10 To replace a belt, follow the above procedures for drivebelt adjustment but slip the belt off the pulleys and remove it. Since belts tend to wear out more or less at the same time, it's a good idea to replace all of them at the same time. Mark each belt and the corresponding pulley grooves so the replacement belts can be installed properly.

11 Take the old belts with you when purchasing new ones in order to make a direct comparison for length, width and design.

12 Adjust the belts as described earlier in this Section.

32 Rear wheel bearing check, repack and adjustment (1978 and earlier models) (every 30,000 miles or 24 months)

Note: *On 1979 and later models, the rear wheel bearing/hub assembly is a sealed unit and no maintenance is required. If the hub/bearing assembly requires replacement,* see Chapter 10.

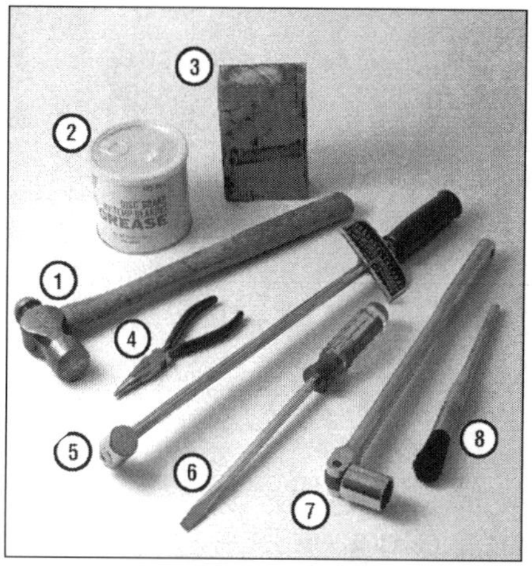

32.1 Tools and materials needed for front wheel bearing maintenance

1 ***Hammer*** *- A common hammer will do just fine*
2 ***Grease*** *- High-temperature grease that is formulated specially for wheel bearings should be used*
3 ***Wood block*** *- If you have a scrap piece of 2x4, it can be used to drive the new seal into the hub*
4 ***Needle-nose pliers*** *- Used to straighten and remove the cotter pin in the spindle*
5 ***Torque wrench*** *- This is very important in this procedure; if the bearing is too tight, the wheel won't turn freely - if it's too loose, the wheel will "wobble" on the spindle. Either way, it could mean extensive damage*
6 ***Screwdriver*** *- Used to remove the seal from the hub (a long screwdriver is preferred)*
7 ***Socket/breaker bar*** *- Needed to loosen the nut on the spindle if it's extremely tight*
8 ***Brush*** *- Together with some clean solvent, this will be used to remove old grease from the hub and spindle*

Check and repack

Refer to illustrations 32.1, 32.7, 32.8a, 32.8b, 32.9, 32.12 and 35.16

1 In most cases the rear wheel bearings will not need servicing until the brake shoes or pads are changed. However, the bearings should be checked whenever the rear of the vehicle is raised for any reason. Several items, including a torque wrench and special grease, are required for this procedure **(see illustration)**.

2 With the vehicle securely supported on jackstands, spin each wheel and check for noise, rolling resistance and freeplay.

3 Grasp the top of each tire with one hand and the bottom with the other. Move the wheel in and out on the spindle. If there's any noticeable movement, the bearings should be checked and then repacked with grease, or replaced if necessary.

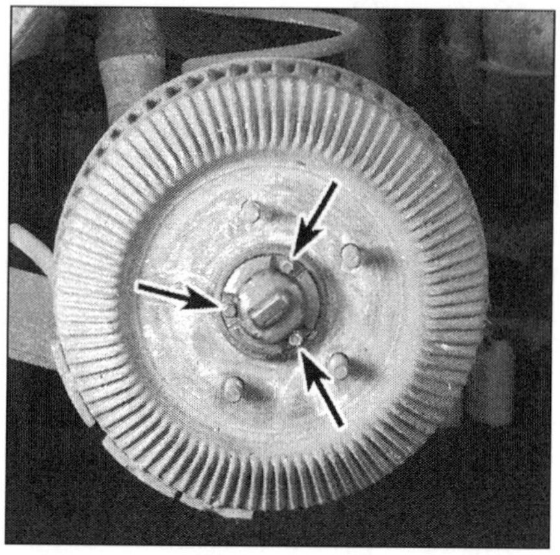

32.7 Remove the dust cap retaining screws (arrows)

32.8a Use a small punch and a hammer to remove the speed sensor drive pin (if equipped)

32.8b Pry off the wheel bearing nut retaining clip

4 Engage the parking brake and remove the wheel.

5 On rear disc brake vehicles fabricate a wood block which can be slid between the brake pads to keep them separated, Remove the caliper (see Chapter 9) and hang it out of the way on a piece of wire.

32.9 Using channel locks, rotate the wheel bearing nut counterclockwise to loosen

32.12 Pry up, in between the hub assembly and the seal lip, to remove the seal

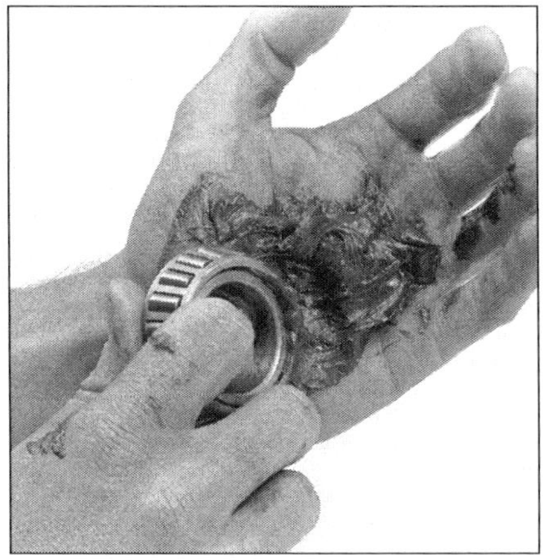

32.16 Work grease into the bearing rollers by pressing it against the palm of your hand

6 Disengage the parking brake and remove the brake drum or rotor (see Chapter 9).
7 Remove the dust cap from the hub assembly. On some early models the dust cap is retained by three screws **(see illustration)**.
8 Detach the insulator pads on each end of the speed sensor drive pin then remove the drive pin (if equipped). Using a screwdriver pry the retaining clip from the wheel bearing nut **(see illustrations).**
9 Remove the wheel bearing nut and washer from the end of the spindle **(see illustration)**.
10 Pull the hub assembly out slightly, then push it back into its original position. This should force the outer bearing off the spindle enough so it can be removed.
11 Pull the hub off the spindle.
12 Use a screwdriver to pry the seal out of the rear of the hub **(see illustration)**. As this is done, note how the seal is installed.
13 Remove the inner wheel bearing from the hub.
14 Use solvent to remove all traces of the old grease from the bearings, hub and spindle. A small brush may prove helpful; however make sure no bristles from the brush embed themselves inside the bearing rollers. Allow the parts to air dry.
15 Carefully inspect the bearings for cracks, heat discoloration, worn rollers, etc. Check the bearing races inside the hub for wear and damage. If the bearing races are defective, the hubs should be taken to a machine shop with the facilities to remove the old races and press new ones in. Note that the bearings and races come as matched sets and old bearings should never be installed on new races.
16 Use high-temperature wheel bearing grease to pack the bearings. Work the grease completely into the bearings, forcing it between the rollers, cone and cage from the back side **(see illustration)**.
17 Apply a thin coat of grease to the spindle at the outer bearing seat, inner bearing seat, shoulder and seal seat.
18 Put a small quantity of grease inboard of each bearing race inside the hub. Using your finger, form a dam at these points to provide extra grease availability and to keep thinned grease from flowing out of the bearing.
19 Place the grease-packed inner bearing into the rear of the hub and put a little more grease outboard of the bearing.
20 Place a new seal over the inner bearing and tap the seal evenly into place with a hammer and block of wood until it's flush with the hub.

Adjustment

21 Carefully place the hub assembly onto the spindle and push the grease-packed outer bearing into position.
22 Install the washer and spindle nut. Tighten the nut only slightly (no more than 12 ft-lbs of torque).
23 Spin the hub in a forward direction to seat the bearings and remove any grease or burrs which could cause excessive bearing play later.
24 Check to see that the tightness of the spindle nut is still approximately 12 ft-lbs.
25 Loosen the spindle nut until it's just loose, no more.
26 Using your hand (not a wrench of any kind), tighten the nut until it's snug. Install the retaining clip through the hole in the spindle and spindle nut. If the nut slots don't line up, loosen the nut slightly until they do. From the hand-tight position, the nut should not be loosened more than one-half flat to install the retaining clip.
27 Install the speed sensor drive pin into the speed sensor (if equipped). Make sure the drive pin is centered within 0.020-inch. then install the insulator pads on each end.
28 Install the dust cap, brake drum and the tire/wheel assembly.
29 Grasp the top and bottom of the tire and check the bearings in the manner described earlier in this Section.
30 Lower the vehicle.

33 Transmission fluid and filter change (every 30,000 miles or 24 months)

Refer to illustrations 33.6, 33.9 and 33.10

1 At the specified intervals, the transmission fluid should be drained and replaced. Since the fluid will remain hot long after driving, perform this procedure only after the engine has cooled down completely.
2 Before beginning work, purchase the specified transmission fluid and a new filter (see *Recommended lubricants and fluids* at the front of this Chapter).
3 Other tools necessary for this job include a floor jack, jackstands to support the vehicle in a raised position, a drain pan capable of holding at least eight pints, newspapers and clean rags.
4 Raise the vehicle and support it securely on jackstands.
5 Place the drain pan underneath the transmission pan. Remove the front and side pan mounting bolts, but only loosen the rear pan bolts approximately four turns.
6 Carefully pry the transmission pan loose with a screwdriver, allowing the fluid to drain **(see illustration)**.

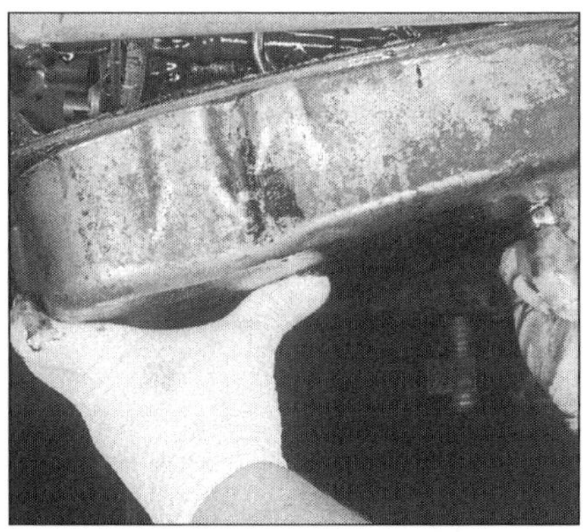

33.6 With the rear bolts in place but loose, pull the front of the pan down to drain the transmission fluid

33.9 Rotate the filter out of the retaining clip, then lower it from the transmission

33.10 Make sure the O-ring on the filter spout comes out with the filter, if it does not reach up into the opening with your finger to retrieve it

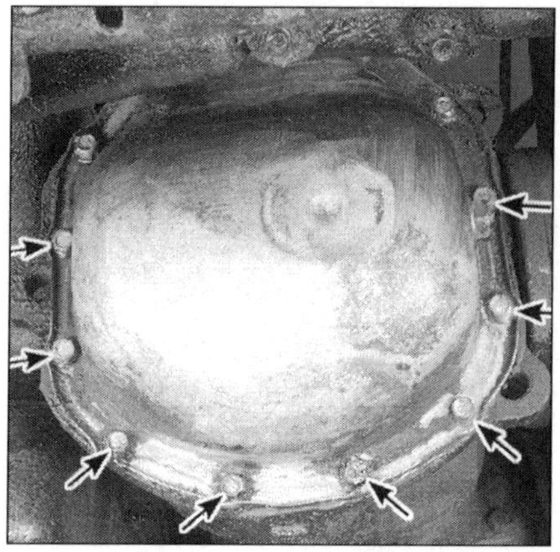

34.5 Remove the bolts (arrows) from the lower edge of the cover

7 Remove the remaining bolts, pan and gasket. Carefully clean the gasket surface of the transmission to remove all traces of the old gasket and sealant.

8 Drain the fluid from the transmission pan, clean it with solvent and dry it with compressed air.

9 Remove the filter from the mount inside the transmission **(see illustration)**.

10 If the seal did not come out with the filter, remove it from the transmission **(see illustration)**. Install a new filter and seal.

11 Make sure the gasket surface on the transmission pan is clean, then install a new gasket on the pan. Put the pan in place against the transmission and, working around the pan, tighten each bolt a little at a time until the final torque figure is reached.

12 Lower the vehicle and add approximately eight pints of the specified type of automatic transmission fluid through the filler tube (Section 6).

13 With the transmission in Park and the parking brake set, run the engine at a fast idle, but don't race it.

14 Move the gear selector through each range and back to Park. Check the fluid level. It will probably be low. Add enough fluid to bring the level up to the COLD FULL range on the dipstick.

15 Check under the vehicle for leaks during the first few trips.

34 Differential lubricant change (every 30,000 miles or 24 months)

Refer to illustrations 34 5 and 34.7

1 It's necessary to remove the cover plate on the differential housing to completely drain the differential lubricant. As an alternative, a hand suction pump can be used to remove the differential lubricant through the filler hole. If you're removing the cover, be sure to obtain a new gasket at the same time the gear lubricant is purchased.

2 Raise the vehicle and support it securely on jackstands. Move a drain pan, rags, newspapers and wrenches under the vehicle.

3 Remove the fill plug from the differential.

4 If a suction pump is being used, insert the flexible hose. Work the hose down to the bottom of the differential housing and pump the lubricant out. Then use a hand pump, syringe or funnel to fill the differential housing with the specified lubricant until it's level with the bottom of the plug hole.

5 If a suction pump is not available remove the bolts on the lower half of the plate **(see illustration)**. Loosen the bolts on the upper half and use them to keep the cover loosely attached. Allow the lubricant to drain into the pan, then completely remove the cover.

6 Using a lint-free rag, clean the inside of the cover and the accessible areas of the differential housing. As this is done, check for chipped gears and metal particles in the lubricant, indicating that the differential should be more thoroughly inspected and/or repaired.

7 Thoroughly clean the gasket mating surfaces of the differential housing and the cover plate. Use a gasket scraper or putty knife to remove all traces of the old gasket **(see illustration)**.

8 Apply a thin layer of RTV sealant to the cover flange and then press a new gasket into position on the cover. Make sure the bolt holes align properly.

9 Place the cover on the differential housing and install the bolts. Tighten the bolts securely.

10 Use a hand pump, syringe or funnel to fill the differential housing with the specified lubricant until it's level with the bottom of the fill plug hole.

11 Install the filler plug and tighten it securely.

35 Cooling system service (draining, flushing and refilling) (every 30,000 miles or 24 months)

Refer to illustrations 35.4 and 3.5

Warning: *Do not allow antifreeze to come in*

34.7 Carefully scrape the old gasket material off to ensure a leak-free seal with the new gasket

contact with your skin or painted surfaces of the vehicle. Rinse off spills immediately with plenty of water. Antifreeze is highly toxic if ingested. Never leave antifreeze lying around in an open container or in puddles on the floor; children and pets are attracted by it's sweet smell and may drink it. Check with local authorities about disposing of used antifreeze. Many communities have collection centers which will see that antifreeze is disposed of safely.

1 Periodically, the cooling system should be drained, flushed and refilled to replenish the antifreeze mixture and prevent formation of rust and corrosion, which can impair the performance of the cooling system and cause engine damage. When the cooling system is serviced, all hoses and the radiator cap should be checked and replaced if necessary.

2 Apply the parking brake and block the wheels. If the vehicle has just been driven, wait several hours to allow the engine to cool down before beginning this procedure.

3 Once the engine is completely cool, remove the radiator cap.

4 Move a large container under the radiator drain fitting to catch the coolant **(see illustration)**. Open the drain fitting and direct

35.4 The radiator drain plug is located at the bottom of the radiator

the coolant into the container, (a pair of pliers may be required to turn it).

5 After the coolant stops flowing out of the radiator, move the container under the engine block drain plugs. Remove the plugs and allow the coolant in the block to drain **(see illustration)**. Engine block drain plugs are generally located on both sides of the block one to two inches above the oil pan rails.

6 While the coolant is draining, check the condition of the radiator hoses, heater hoses and clamps (see Section 10).

7 Replace any damaged clamps or hoses.

8 Once the system is completely drained, flush the radiator with fresh water from a garden hose until it runs clear at the drain. The flushing action of the water will remove sediments from the radiator but will not remove rust and scale from the engine and cooling tube surfaces.

9 These deposits can be removed with a chemical cleaner. Follow the procedure outlined in the manufacturer's instructions. If the radiator is severely corroded, damaged or leaking, it should be removed (see Chapter 3) and taken to a radiator repair shop.

10 Remove the overflow hose from the coolant recovery reservoir. Drain the reservoir and flush it with clean water, then reconnect the hose.

11 Close and tighten the radiator drain. Install and tighten the block drain plugs.

12 Place the heater temperature control in the maximum heat position.

13 The manufacturer recommends adding cooling system sealer any time the coolant is changed. **Note:** *The HT4100 engine requires antifreeze as the special sealer.* Slowly add new coolant (a 50/50 mixture of water and antifreeze) to the radiator until it's full. Add coolant to the reservoir up to the lower mark

14 Leave the radiator cap off and run the engine in a well-ventilated area until the thermostat opens (coolant will begin flowing through the radiator and the upper radiator hose will become hot).

15 Turn the engine off and let it cool. Add more coolant mixture to bring the level back up to the lip on the radiator filler neck.

16 Squeeze the upper radiator hose to

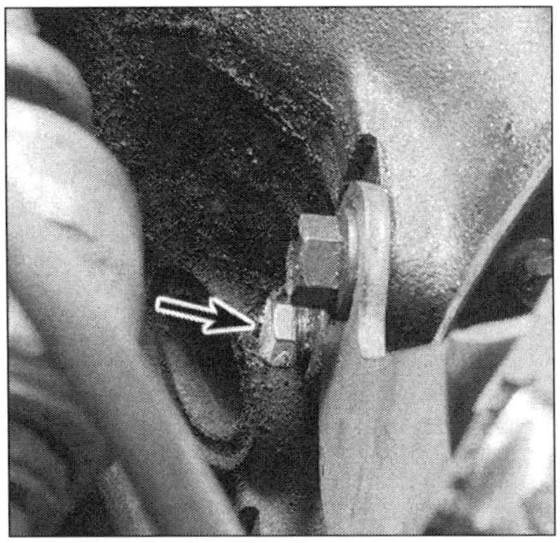

35.5 The block drain plugs (arrow) are generally located about one to two inches above the oil pan rail. There is one on each side of the block

expel air, then add more coolant mixture if necessary. Replace the radiator cap.

17 Start the engine, allow it to reach normal operating temperature and check for leaks.

36 Positive Crankcase Ventilation (PCV) valve check and replacement (every 30,000 miles or 24 months)

Refer to illustrations 36.1 and 36.3

1 The PCV valve is usually located in the valve cover **(see illustration)**. On V6 models the PCV valve is located at the rear of the intake manifold.

2 With the engine idling at normal operating temperature, pull the valve (with hose attached) from the rubber grommet in the cover or manifold.

3 Place your finger over the valve opening **(see illustration)**. If there's no vacuum at the valve, check for a plugged hose, manifold port, or the valve itself. Replace any plugged or deteriorated hoses.

4 Turn off the engine and shake the PCV valve, listening for a rattle. If the valve doesn't rattle, replace it with a new one.

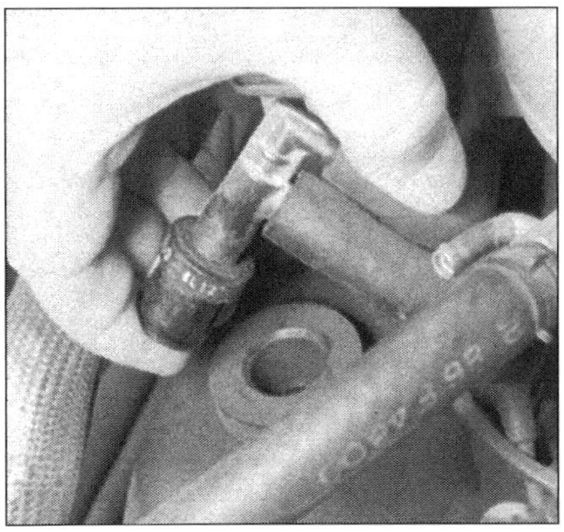

36.3 With the engine running, put your finger over the end of the PCV valve; you should feel vacuum

36.1 On most models the PCV valve is located in the valve cover

5 To replace the valve, pull it from the end of the hose, noting its installed position and direction.

6 When purchasing a replacement PCV valve, make sure it's for your particular vehicle and engine size. Compare the old valve with the new one to make sure they're the same.

7 Push the valve into the end of the hose until it's seated.

8 Inspect the rubber grommet for damage and replace it with a new one if necessary.

9 Push the PCV valve and hose securely into position.

37 Evaporative Emissions Control (EEC) system check (every 30,000 miles or 24 months)

Refer to illustrations 37.2, 37.4 and 37.5

1 The function of the evaporative emissions control system is to draw fuel vapors from the gas tank and fuel system, store them in a charcoal canister and route them to the intake manifold during normal engine operation.

2 The most common symptom of a fault in the evaporative emissions system is a strong fuel odor in the engine compartment. If a fuel

37.2 Check the evaporative emissions control canister for damage and the hose connections for cracks and damage

37.4 Pull the filter element out from the bottom of the canister

odor is detected, inspect the charcoal canister, located in the engine compartment **(see illustration)**. Check the canister and all hoses for damage and deterioration.

3 On earlier models, the filter at the bottom of the canister should be replaced at this time.

4 Remove the retaining bolts, turn the canister upside-down and pull the old filter from the bottom of the canister **(see illustration)**. If you cannot turn the canister enough for this due to the short length of the hoses, mark the hoses to insure correct installation and disconnect them.

5 Push the new filter into the bottom of the canister, making sure it is seated all the way around **(see illustration)**.

6 Install the canister and connect any hoses which were disconnected.

7 The evaporative emissions control system is explained in more detail in Chapter 6.

38 Exhaust Gas Recirculation (EGR) system check (every 30,000 miles or 24 months)

Refer to illustration 38.2

1 The EGR valve is usually located on the intake manifold, adjacent to the carburetor. Most of the time when a problem develops in this emissions system, it's due to a stuck or

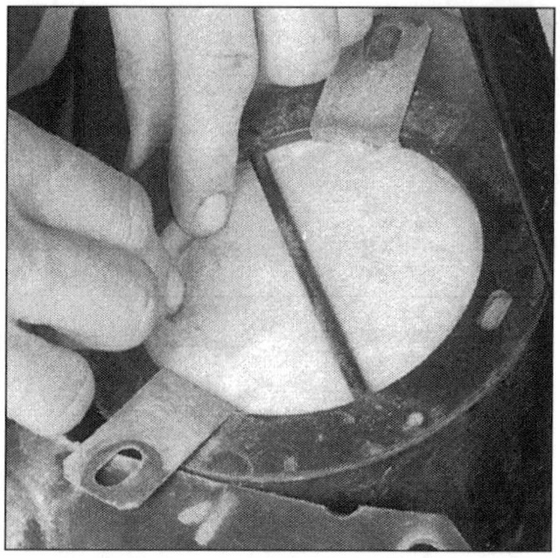

37.5 Make sure the new filter is fully seated all the way around the bottom of the canister

corroded EGR valve.

2 With the engine cold, to prevent burns, push on the EGR valve diaphragm. Using moderate pressure, you should be able to press the diaphragm in and out within the housing **(see illustration)**.

3 If the diaphragm doesn't move or moves only with much effort, replace the EGR valve with a new one. If in doubt about the condition of the valve, compare the free movement of your EGR valve with a new valve.

4 Refer to Chapter 6 for more information on the EGR system.

39 Spark plug replacement (every 30,000 miles or 24 months)

Refer to illustrations 39.2, 39.5a, 39.5b, 39.6a, 39.6b, 39.9 and 39.10

1 The spark plugs are located at the sides of the engine.

2 In most cases, the tools necessary for spark plug replacement include a spark plug socket which fits onto a ratchet (spark plug sockets are padded inside to prevent damage to the porcelain insulators on the new plugs), various extensions and a gap gauge to check and adjust the gap on the new plugs **(see illustration)**. A special plug wire removal tool is available for separating the wire boots from the spark plugs, and is a good idea on

38.2 The diaphragm in the EGR valve (which can be felt by reaching through the hole in the underside of the valve) should move easily with finger pressure

these models because the boots fit very tightly. A torque wrench should be used to tighten the new plugs. It is a good idea to allow the engine to cool before removing or installing the spark plugs.

3 The best approach when replacing the spark plugs is to purchase the new ones in advance, adjust them to the proper gap and replace the plugs one at a time. When buying the new spark plugs, be sure to obtain the correct plug type for your particular engine. The plug type can be found in the Specifications at the front of this Chapter and on the Emission Control Information label located under the hood. If these two sources list different plug type, consider the emission control label correct.

4 Allow the engine to cool completely before attempting to remove any of the plugs. While you are waiting for the engine to cool, check the new plugs for defects and adjust the gap.

5 Check the gap by inserting the proper thickness gauge between the electrodes at the tip of the plug **(see illustration)**. The gap between the electrodes should be the same as the one specified on the Emissions Control Information label. The wire should slide between the electrodes with a slight amount of drag. If the gap is incorrect, use the adjuster on the gauge body to bend the

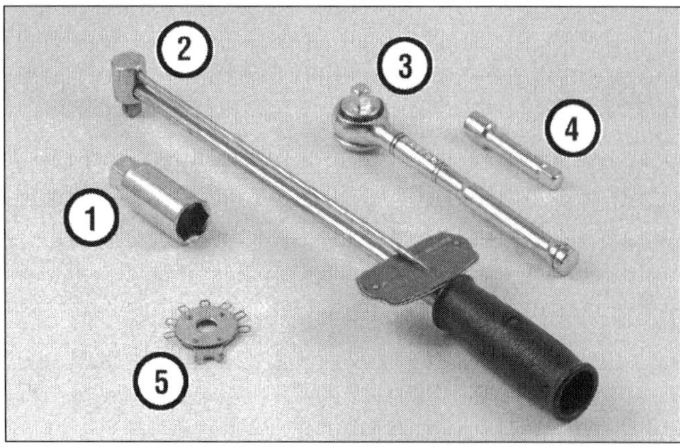

39.2 Tools required for changing spark plugs

1 ***Spark plug socket*** *- This will have special padding inside to protect the spark plug's porcelain insulator*

2 ***Torque wrench*** *- Although not mandatory, using this tool is the best way to ensure the plugs are tightened properly*

3 ***Ratchet*** *- Standard hand tool to fit the spark plug socket*

4 ***Extension*** *- Depending on model and accessories, you may need special extensions and universal joints to reach one or more of the plugs*

5 ***Spark plug gap gauge*** *- This gauge for checking the gap comes in a variety of styles. Make sure the gap for your engine is included*

39.5a Spark plug manufacturers recommend using a wire type gauge when checking the gap - if the wire does not slide between the electrodes with a slight drag, adjustment is required

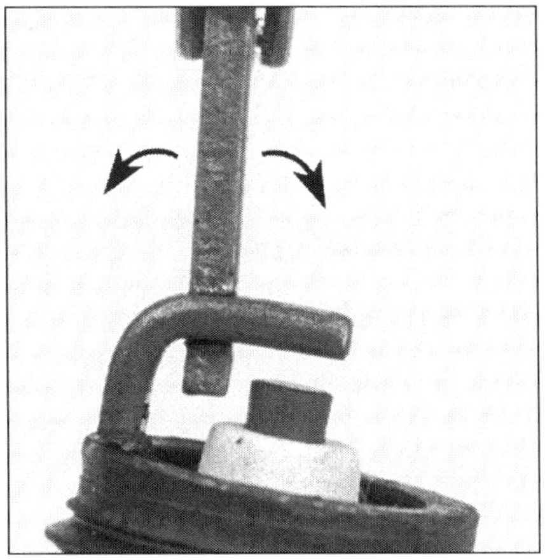

39.5b To change the gap, bend the *side* electrode only, as indicated by the arrows, and be very careful not to crack or chip the porcelain insulator surrounding the center electrode

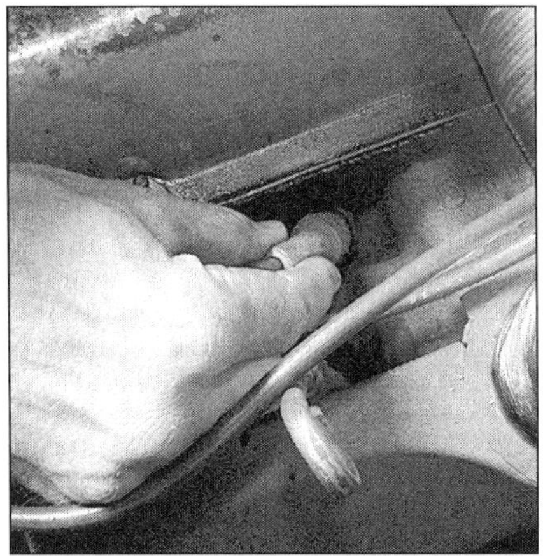

39.6a When removing the spark plug wires, pull only on the boot and use a twisting, pulling motion

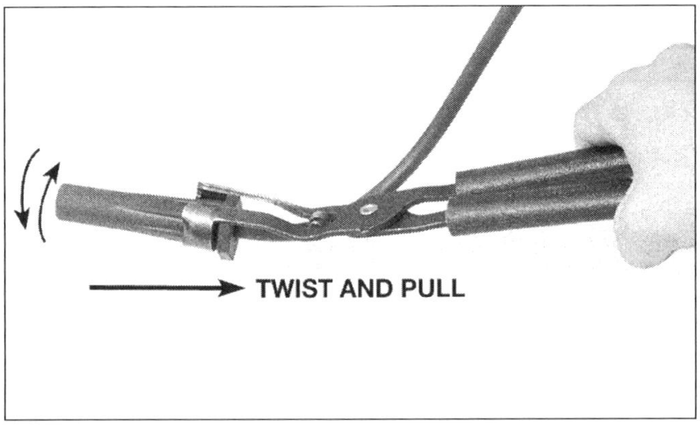

39.6b Using a spark plug boot puller tool like this one will make the job of removing the spark plug boots much easier

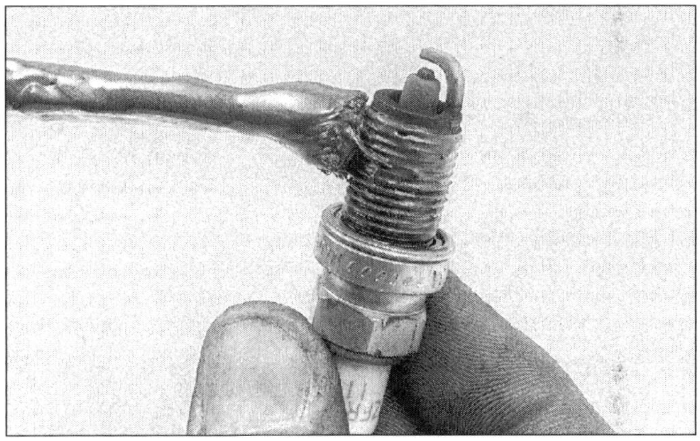

39.9 Apply a thin coat of anti-seize compound to the spark plug threads

curved side electrode slightly until the proper gap is obtained **(see illustration)**. If the side electrode is not exactly over the center electrode, bend it with the adjuster until it is. Check for cracks in the porcelain insulator (if any are found, the plug should not be used).

6 With the engine cool, remove the spark plug wire from one spark plug. Pull only on the boot at the end of the wire - do not pull on the wire **(see illustration)**. A spark plug wire removal tool should be used if available **(see illustration)**.

7 If compressed air is available, use it to blow any dirt or foreign material away from the spark plug hole. A common bicycle pump will also work. The idea here is to eliminate the possibility of debris falling into the cylinder as the spark plug is removed.

8 Place the spark plug socket over the plug and remove it from the engine by turning it in a counterclockwise direction.

9 Compare the spark plug with the chart shown on the inside back cover of this manual to get an indication of the general running condition of the engine. Before installing the new plugs, it is a good idea to apply a thin coat of anti-seize compound to the threads **(see illustration)**.

10 Thread one of the new plugs into the hole until you can no longer turn it with your fingers, then tighten it with a torque wrench (if available) or the ratchet. It's a good idea to slip a short length of rubber hose over the end of the plug to use as a tool to thread it into place **(see illustration)**. The hose will grip the plug well enough to turn it, but will start to slip if the plug begins to cross-thread in the hole - this will prevent damaged threads and the accompanying repair costs.

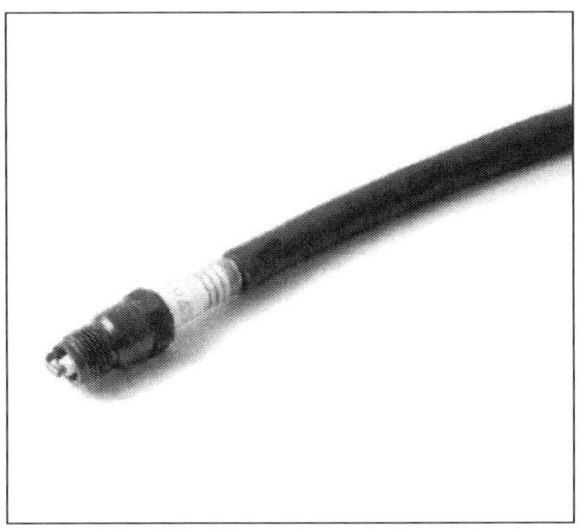

39.10 A length of 3/8-inch rubber hose will save time and prevent damaged threads when installing the spark plugs

11 Before pushing the spark plug wire onto the end of the plug, inspect it following the procedures outlined in Section 40.

12 Attach the plug wire to the new spark plug, again using a twisting motion on the boot until it's seated on the spark plug.

13 Repeat the procedure for the remaining spark plugs, replacing them one at a time to prevent mixing up the spark plug wires.

40 Spark plug wire and distributor cap and rotor check and replacement (every 30,000 miles or 24 months)

Refer to illustrations 40.6a, 40.6b and 40.7

1 The spark plug wires should be checked at the recommended intervals and whenever new spark plugs are installed in the engine.

2 The wires should be inspected one at a

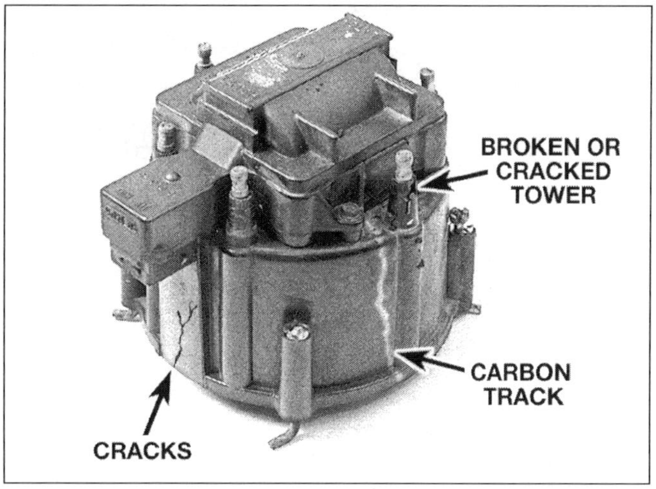

40.6a Look for these common defects when inspecting the outside of the distributor cap

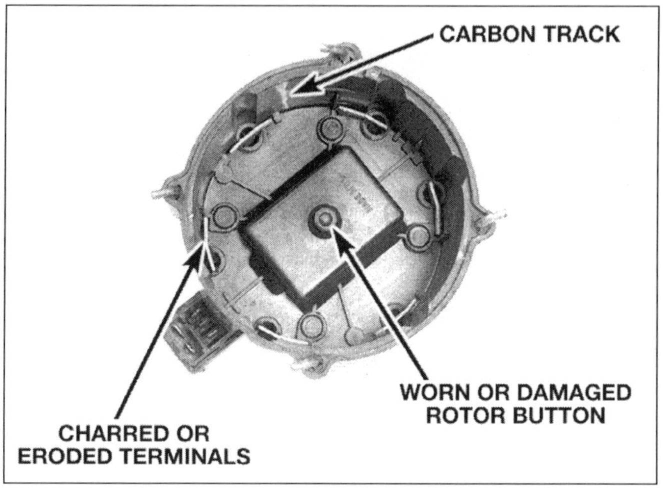

40.6b Check the inside of the distributor cap for these conditions

time to prevent mixing up the order, which is essential for proper engine operation.

3 Disconnect the plug wire from the spark plug. To do this, grab the rubber boot, twist slightly and pull the wire off. Do not pull on the wire itself, only on the rubber boot.

4 Check inside the boot for corrosion, which will look like a white crusty powder. Push the wire and boot back onto the end of the spark plug. It should be a tight fit on the plug. If it isn't, remove the wire and use pliers to carefully crimp the metal connector inside the boot until it fits securely on the end of the spark plug.

5 Using a clean rag, wipe the entire length of the wire to remove any built-up dirt and grease. Once the wire is clean, check for burns, cracks and other damage. Do not bend the wire excessively or pull the wire lengthwise - the conductor inside might break.

6 Detach the clips or loosen the screws and remove the distributor cap. Check the cap for cracks, carbon tracks and worn, burned or loose terminal **(see illustrations)** Check for corrosion and a tight fit in the same manner as the spark plug end. Replace the wire at the coil.

7 Check the distributor rotor for cracks and carbon tracks **(see illustration)**. Make sure the center terminal tension is adequate and look for corrosion and wear on the rotor tip.

8 Check the remaining spark plug wires one at a time, making sure they are securely fastened at the ignition coil and the spark plug when the check is complete.

9 If new spark plug wires are required, purchase a set for your specific engine model. Wire sets are available pre-cut, with the rubber boots already installed. Remove and replace the wires one at a time to avoid mix-ups in the firing order.

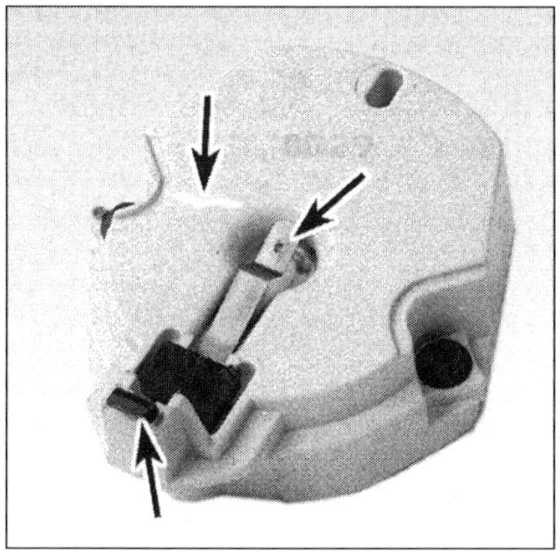

40.7 Check the distributor rotor for carbon tracking, center terminal condition and rotor tip wear (arrows)

41 Emissions maintenance indicator - resetting (every 15,000 miles)

1 On 1980 Eldorado and Seville models, a reminder flag appears in the speedometer face as a reminder to service the oxygen sensor.

2 After the emission service has been completed and the oxygen sensor replaced, reset the flag as follows:

a) Remove the lower steering column cover.

b) Locate the reset cable to the left of the instrument cluster. Pull the cable down lightly (use no more than two-pounds force) to reset the flag.

3 Install the lower steering column cover.

Chapter 2 Part A
V6 Engines

Contents

Specifications

General

Displacement	
3.8L	231 cubic inches
4.1L	252 cubic inches
Cylinder numbers (front-to-rear)	
Left bank (driver's side)	1-3-5
Right bank	2-4-6
Firing order	1-6-5-4-3-2

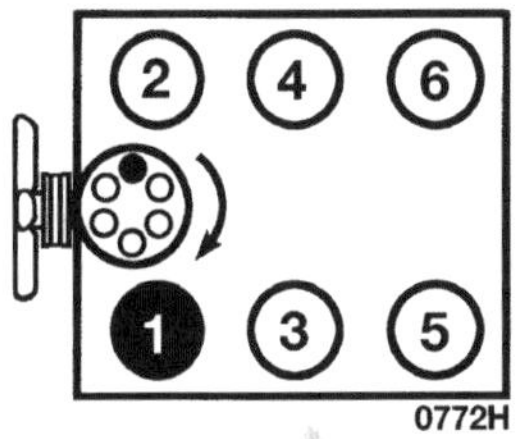

The blackened terminal shown on the distributor cap indicates the Number One spark plug wire position

Cylinder location and distributor rotation

Camshaft

Lobe lift	Compare the readings for each intake and exhaust lobe - replace the camshaft if readings vary more than 0.005 in.
Journal diameter	1.785 to 1.786 in
Journal-to-bearing (oil) clearance	
No. 1 journal	0.005 to 0.0025 in
All others	0.005 to 0.0035 in

Oil pump

Gear tip-to-pump body clearance	0.003 to 0.005 in
End clearance	0.002 to 0.006 in
Gear length	0.872 to 0.874 in
Gear diameter	1.664 to 1.666 in
Depth of pocket	0.8677 to 0.8697 in
Diameter of pocket	1.670 to 1.675 in

Torque specifications

	Ft-lbs (unless otherwise indicated)
Camshaft sprocket bolt	20
Crankshaft pulley-to-vibration damper bolts	20
Cylinder head bolts	80
Exhaust manifold bolts	25
Driveplate bolts	60
Intake manifold-to-cylinder head bolts	45
Motor mount-to-cylinder block bolts	55
Oil pan mounting bolts	168 in-lbs
Oil pump cover-to-front cover bolts	120 in-lbs
Main bearing cap bolts	100
Rocker arm shaft-to-cylinder head bolts	30
Tensioner bracket-to-engine block bolts	180 in-lbs
Oil pump cover-to-front cover bolts	120 in-lbs
Front cover-to-block bolts	30
Timing chain tensioner bolts	156 in-lbs
Vibration damper center bolt	225

1 General information

This Part of Chapter 2 is devoted to in-vehicle repair procedures for the 3.8L and 4.1L V6 engines. The two V6 engines are virtually identical in Specifications and procedures, except that the 4.1L engine has a larger cylinder bore for more displacement. All information concerning engine removal and installation and engine block and cylinder head overhaul can be found in Part C of this Chapter.

The following repair procedures are based on the assumption that the engine is installed in the vehicle. If the engine has been removed from the vehicle and mounted on a stand, many of the steps outlined in this Part of Chapter 2 will not apply.

The specifications included in this Part of Chapter 2 apply only to the procedures contained in this Part. Part C of Chapter 2 contains the specifications necessary for cylinder head and engine block rebuilding.

2 Repair operations possible with the engine in the vehicle

Many major repair operations can be accomplished without removing the engine from the vehicle.

Clean the engine compartment and the exterior of the engine with some type of degreaser before any work is done. It will make the job easier and help keep dirt out of the internal areas of the engine.

Depending on the components involved, it may be helpful to remove the hood to improve access to the engine as repairs are performed (refer to Chapter 11 if necessary). Cover the fenders to prevent damage to the paint. Special pads are available, but an old bedspread or blanket will also work.

If vacuum, exhaust, oil or coolant leaks develop, indicating a need for gasket or seal replacement, the repairs can generally be made with the engine in the vehicle. The intake and exhaust manifold gaskets, timing cover gasket, oil pan gasket, crankshaft oil seals and cylinder head gasket are all accessible with the engine in place.

Exterior engine components, such as the intake and exhaust manifolds, the oil pan (and the oil pump), the water pump, the starter motor, the alternator, the distributor and the fuel system components can be removed for repair with the engine in place.

Since the cylinder heads can be removed without pulling the engine, valve component servicing can also be accomplished with the engine in the vehicle. Replacement of the timing chain, sprockets and camshaft is also possible with the engine in the vehicle.

In extreme cases caused by a lack of necessary equipment, repair or replacement of piston rings, pistons, connecting rods and rod bearings is possible with the engine in the vehicle. However, this practice is not recommended because of the cleaning and preparation work that must be done to the components involved.

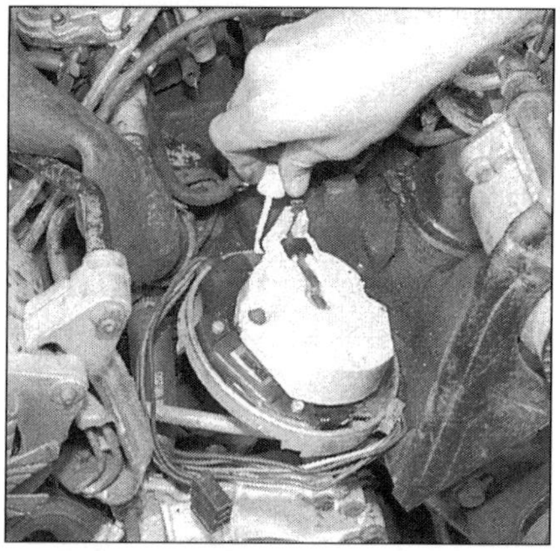

3.4 Mark the distributor body directly below the number one terminal of the distributor cap

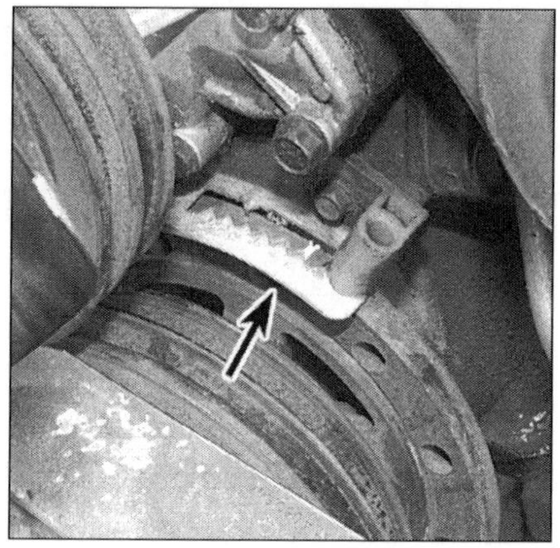

3.6 Turn the crankshaft until the mark on the crankshaft hub aligns with the zero mark on the timing indicator - highlight the marks with white paint

3 Top Dead Center (TDC) for number one piston - locating

Refer to illustrations 3.4 and 3.6

1 Top Dead Center (TDC) is the highest point in the cylinder that each piston reaches as it travels up and down when the crankshaft turns. Each piston reaches TDC on the compression stroke and again on the exhaust stroke, but TDC generally refers to piston position on the compression stroke. The timing marks on the vibration damper installed on the front of the crankshaft are referenced to the number one piston at TDC on the compression stroke.

2 Positioning the piston(s) at TDC is an essential part of many procedures such as valve seal replacement, timing chain and sprocket replacement and distributor removal.

3 In order to bring any piston to TDC, the crankshaft must be turned using one of the methods outlined below. When looking at the front of the engine, normal crankshaft rotation is clockwise. **Warning:** *Before beginning this procedure, be sure to place the transmission in Neutral and unplug the wire connector at the distributor to disable the ignition system.*

a) *The preferred method is to turn the crankshaft with a large socket and breaker bar attached to the vibration damper bolt threaded into the front of the crankshaft.*

b) *A remote starter switch, which may save some time, can also be used. Attach the switch leads to the S (switch) and B (battery) terminals on the starter motor. Once the piston is close to TDC, use a socket and breaker bar as described in the previous paragraph.*

c) *If an assistant is available to turn the ignition switch to the Start position in short bursts, you can get the piston close to TDC without a remote starter switch. Use a socket and breaker bar as described in paragraph a) to complete the procedure.*

4 Make a mark on the distributor housing directly below the number one spark plug wire terminal on the distributor cap **(see illustration)**. **Note:** *The terminal numbers may be marked on the spark plug wires near the distributor.*

5 Remove the distributor cap as described in Chapter 1.

6 Turn the crankshaft (see paragraph 3 above) until the line on the vibration damper is aligned with the zero mark on the timing indicator **(see illustration)**.

7 The rotor should now be pointing directly at the mark on the distributor housing **(see illustration 3.4)**. If it isn't, the piston may be at TDC on the exhaust stroke. To get the piston to TDC on the compression stroke, turn the crankshaft one complete turn (360-degrees) clockwise. The rotor should now be pointing at the mark.

8 When the rotor is pointing at the number one spark plug wire terminal in the distributor cap (which is indicated by the mark on the housing) and the ignition timing marks are aligned, the number one piston is at TDC on the compression stroke.

9 After the number one piston has been positioned at TDC on the compression stroke, TDC for any of the remaining cylinders can be located by turning the crankshaft 120-degrees at a time and following the firing order (refer to the Specifications).

4 Valve covers - removal and installation

Refer to illustration 4.6

Removal

1 Disconnect the negative cable from the battery.

2 Remove the air cleaner assembly (see Chapter 4).

4.6 Remove the four bolts (arrows) from the valve cover

3 Label and disconnect the wires and hoses which would interfere with removal of the valve covers.

4 Label and detach the spark plug wires and unclip the wire retainers from the studs.

5 Detach any remaining accessories as necessary. If removal of the air conditioning compressor is required, unbolt the unit and carefully set it aside without disconnecting the refrigerant lines. **Warning:** *The air conditioning system is under high pressure. Do not disconnect any refrigerant line or fitting without first having the system discharged by an air conditioning technician.*

Note: *On turbocharged models, remove the turbocharger inlet and outlet exhaust pipes to access the right valve cover* (see Chapter 4A).

6 Remove the valve cover bolts and detach the cover **(see illustration)**. If the cover is stuck, use a soft-face hammer or a block of wood and a hammer to dislodge it. If the cover still won't come loose, pry on it carefully with a putty knife, but don't distort the sealing flange surface. **Note:** *On most models, the left valve cover will have to be angled out from under the AIR pump, but it's not necessary to remove the pump.*

7 Remove all traces of old gasket and sealant with a scraper, then clean the mating surfaces with lacquer thinner or acetone.

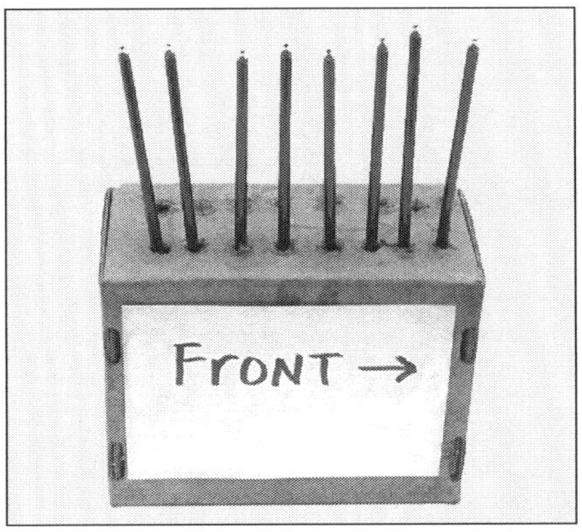

5.4 When removing the pushrods, be sure to mark them and store them separately to ensure installation in their original locations

5.2 Loosen the three rocker arm shaft bolts (arrows) and remove the rocker arms and shaft as an assembly

Installation

8 Apply a thin coating of RTV sealant to the valve cover flange and place gasket on the valve cover.

9 Install the valve cover and tighten the bolts in 1/4-turn increments to the torque listed in this Chapter's Specifications.

10 Reinstall the remaining parts in the reverse order of removal.

11 Run the engine and check for oil leaks.

5 Rocker arms, shafts and pushrods - removal, inspection and installation

Removal

Refer to illustrations 5.2, 5.3 and 5.4

1 Refer to Section 4 and detach the valve cover from the cylinder head.

2 Loosen the rocker arm shaft bolts, a little at a time, to avoid distorting the shaft. Lift off the rocker arms and shafts **(see illustration)**.

3 Remove the plastic rocker arm retainers by pulling them straight out with a pair of pliers **(see illustration)**. With the retainers removed, the rocker arms can be slid off the shaft. Keep them in order so they can be installed in their original positions. **Note:** *If the rocker assembly is being removed for access for another procedure (such as pushrod or cylinder head removal), do not remove the plastic retainers. Normal engine operation hardens the plastic to the point that*

5.3 Remove the rocker arm retainers only if you have to inspect the shaft - the plastic retainers will probably break, so make sure you have new ones on hand

the retainers will break when removed. Don't break them off unless you need to remove the rockers from the shaft.

4 Remove the pushrods and store them separately to make sure they don't get mixed up during installation **(see illustration)**.

Inspection

5 Check each rocker arm for wear, cracks and other damage, especially where the pushrods and valve stems contact the rocker arm faces.

6 Make sure the hole at the pushrod end of each rocker arm is open.

7 Check the pivot areas on the rocker arms and shafts for wear, cracks and galling. If the rocker arms and/or shafts are worn or damaged, replace them with new ones.

8 Inspect the pushrods for cracks and excessive wear at the ends. Roll each pushrod across a piece of plate glass to see if it's bent (if it wobbles, it's bent).

Installation

Refer to illustration 5.11

9 Lubricate the lower end of each pushrod with clean engine oil or moly-base grease and install them in their original locations. Make sure each pushrod seats completely in the lifter.

10 Apply moly-base grease to the ends of the valve stems and the upper ends of the pushrods.

11 Lubricate the rocker arm shaft and slide the rocker arms onto the shaft, install them in

5.11 Reinstall the rockers (numbered with paint before removal) to the shaft in their original sequence

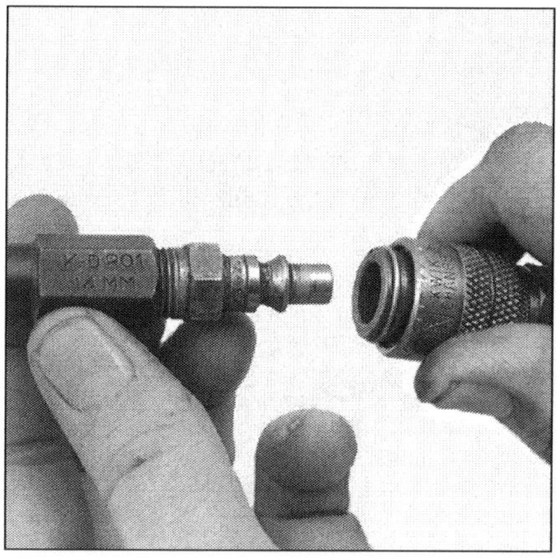

6.4 This is what the air hose adapter that threads into the spark plug hole looks like - they're commonly available in auto parts stores

6.8 Once the spring is depressed, the keepers can be removed with a small magnet or needle-nose pliers (a magnet is preferred to prevent dropping the keepers)

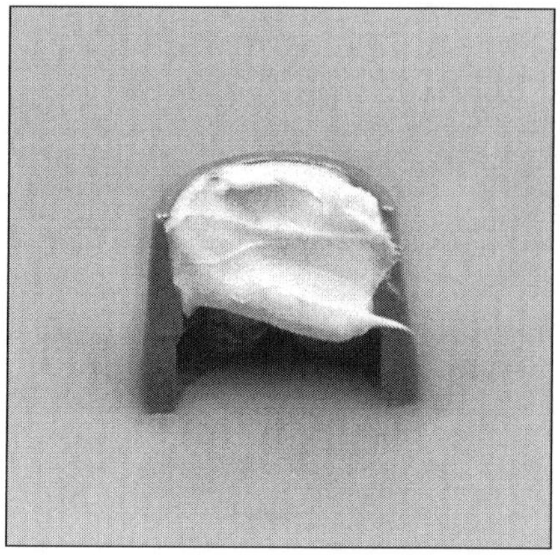

6.17 Apply a small dab of grease to each keeper as shown before installation - it'll hold them in place on the valve stem as the spring is released

their original locations **(see illustration)**. Install the plastic retainers, if removed during disassembly.

12 Install the rocker arm assembly onto the cylinder head. Install the bolts and tighten them in increments to the torque listed in this Chapter's Specifications.

13 Install the valve covers.

6 Valve springs, retainer and seals - replacement

Refer to illustrations 6.4, 6.8 and 6.17

Note: *Broken valve springs and defective valve stem seals can be replaced without removing the cylinder heads. Two special tools and a compressed air source are normally required to perform this operation, so read through this Section carefully and rent or buy the tools before beginning the job. If compressed air isn't available, a length of nylon rope can be used to keep the valves from falling into the cylinder during this procedure.*

1 Refer to Section 4 and remove the valve cover from the affected cylinder head. If all of the valve stem seals are being replaced, remove both valve covers.

2 Remove the spark plug from the cylinder which has the defective component. If all of the valve stem seals are being replaced, all of the spark plugs should be removed.

3 Turn the crankshaft until the piston in the affected cylinder is at top dead center (TDC) on the compression stroke (refer to Section 3 for instructions). If you are replacing all of the valve stem seals, begin with cylinder number one and work on the valves for one cylinder at a time. Move from cylinder to cylinder following the firing order sequence (see this Chapter's Specifications).

4 Thread an adapter into the spark plug hole and connect an air hose from a compressed air source to it **(see illustration)**. Most auto parts stores can supply the air hose adapter. **Note:** *Many cylinder compression gauges utilize a screw-in fitting that may work with your air hose quick-disconnect fitting.*

5 Remove the rocker arm assembly (see Section 5) and the pushrod for the valve with the defective part. If all of the valve stem seals are being replaced, remove all of the pushrods.

6 Apply compressed air to the cylinder.

7 If you don't have access to compressed air, an alternative method can be used. Position the piston at a point just before TDC on the compression stroke, then feed a long piece of nylon rope through the spark plug hole until it fills the combustion chamber. Be sure to leave the end of the rope hanging out of the spark plug hole so it can be removed easily. Use a large breaker bar and socket to rotate the crankshaft in the normal direction of rotation until slight resistance is felt.

8 Stuff shop rags into the cylinder head holes above and below the valves to prevent parts and tools from falling into the engine, then use a valve spring compressor to compress the valve spring. Remove the keepers with small needle-nose pliers or a magnet **(see illustration)**.

9 Remove the spring retainer or rotator, oil shield and valve spring assembly, then remove the umbrella-type guide seal. **Note:** *If air pressure fails to hold the valve in the closed position during this operation, the valve face and/or seat is probably damaged. If so, the cylinder head will have to be removed for additional repair operations.*

10 Wrap a rubber band or tape around the top of the valve stem so the valve won't fall into the combustion chamber, then release the air pressure. **Note:** *If a rope was used instead of air pressure, turn the crankshaft slightly in the direction opposite normal rotation.*

11 Inspect the valve stem for damage. Rotate the valve in the guide and check the end for eccentric movement, which would indicate that the valve is bent.

12 Move the valve up and down in the guide and make sure it doesn't bind. If the valve stem binds, either the valve is bent or the guide is damaged. In either case, the head will have to be removed for repair.

13 Reapply air pressure to the cylinder to retain the valve in the closed position, then remove the tape or rubber band from the valve stem. If a rope was used instead of air pressure, rotate the crankshaft in the normal direction of rotation until slight resistance is felt.

14 Lubricate the valve stem with engine oil and install a new umbrella-type guide seal.

15 Install the valve spring assembly and shield in position over the valve.

16 Install the valve spring retainer or rotator, and compress the valve spring assembly.

17 Position the keepers in the upper groove. Apply a small dab of grease to the inside of each keeper to hold it in place if necessary **(see illustration)**. Remove the pressure from the spring and make sure the keepers are seated.

18 Disconnect the air hose and remove the adapter from the spark plug hole. If a rope was used in place of air pressure, pull it out of the cylinder.

19 Refer to Section 5 and install the pushrods and rocker arm assembly.

20 Install the spark plugs and hook up the wires.

21 Refer to Section 4 and install the valve covers.

22 Start and run the engine, then check for oil leaks and unusual sounds coming from the valve cover area.

7 Intake manifold - removal and installation

Removal

Refer to illustrations 7.4a, 7.4b, 7.5, 7.6, 7.8, 7.12, 7.13 and 7.14

1 Disconnect the negative cable from the battery.

2 Drain the coolant from the radiator (see Chapter 1).

7.4a Remove the two AIR pump and alternator braces (arrows)

7.6 Disconnect the AIR pipe from the rear of the manifold; use a back-up wrench on the fitting

3 Label and remove the wires, hoses, cables and fuel lines from the carburetor (see Chapter 4A).

4 Remove the braces from the intake manifold to both the AIR pump and the alternator **(see illustrations)**. Also remove the bracket that the AIR pump brace is attached to.

5 Remove the engine lifting bracket at the right front of the intake manifold. Remove the heater hose fitting, if necessary **(see illustration)**.

6 At the rear of the manifold, disconnect the AIR system pipe **(see illustration)**. On turbocharged models, refer to Chapter 4A for turbocharger removal.

7 Label and disconnect the spark plug wires from the plugs, then remove the distributor cap and rotor (see Chapter 1).

8 Remove the single Torx-head bolt at the front of the intake manifold **(see illustration)**.

9 Detach the brake booster vacuum pipe at the manifold.

10 Detach the evaporative emission hoses.

11 Disconnect the upper radiator hose, heater hoses and bypass hose.

12 Unbolt the remaining intake manifold bolts and lift it off the engine. If it's stuck, pry carefully against a protrusion on the manifold.

7.4b Remove the AIR pump brace mounting bracket (arrow)

7.8 At the left front of the manifold remove the single Torx-head bolt (arrow)

Do not pry between the gasket surfaces **(see illustration)**.

13 Remove all traces of old gasket material and sealant from the manifold and cylinder head mating surfaces, then clean them with lacquer thinner or acetone **(see illustration)**. Clean the intake manifold bolt holes in the cylinder head with a tap. Compressed air can be used to remove the debris from the holes. **Warning:** *Wear eye protection when using compressed air.* There are several different lengths of intake manifold mounting bolts. Use a marked cardboard sheet with holes in it to store the bolts and studs for proper reassembly.

14 On most engines with considerable mileage, there will be carbon buildup in the EGR passages in the manifold and under the carburetor mounting area **(see illustration)**.

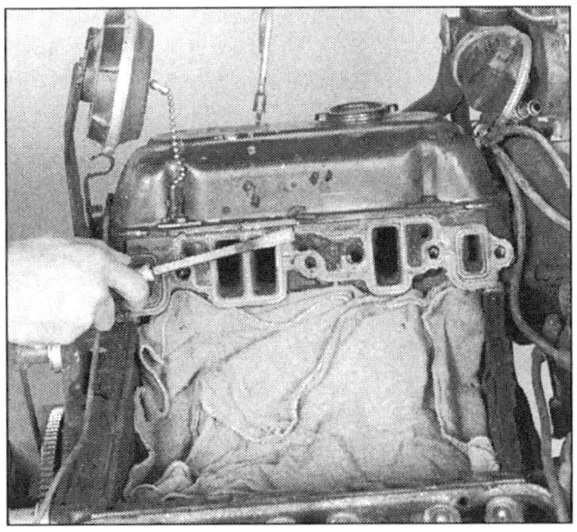

7.13 Cover the lifter valley with rags to catch debris while scraping the old gasket material from the heads

7.5 The rear nut to the front engine-lifting bracket can't be removed unless the heater hose fitting (arrow) is removed first

7.12 Pry the manifold loose at one of the corners; DO NOT pry on the gasket sealing surface

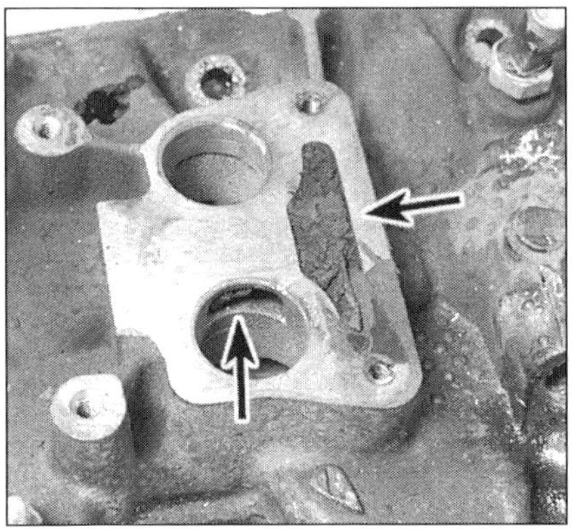

7.14 Carbon deposits in the EGR passages (arrows) should be cleaned out with the intake manifold removed

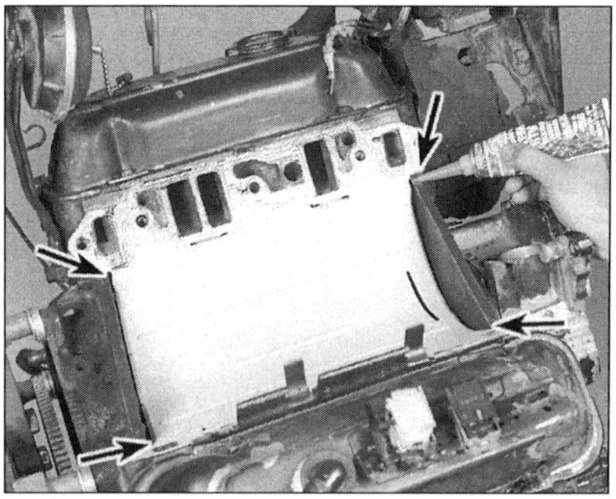

7.16 Apply RTV sealant at the end seal-to-metal gasket junction (arrows)

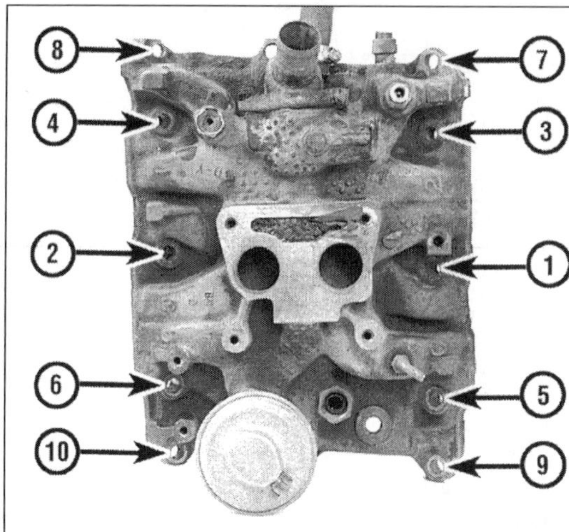

7.18 Intake manifold bolt tightening sequence

Now is the best time to clean these passages, maintaining proper EGR operation. Chip the majority of the material out with a screwdriver, then use carburetor cleaner to dissolve the remaining deposits. Remove the EGR valve and force a stiff wire or coat hanger back and forth through the passages to clear them, then apply more cleaner and blow out the debris with compressed air. **Warning:** *Wear eye protection when using compressed air.*

Installation

Refer to illustrations 7.16 and 7.18

15 Install the new one piece intake manifold gasket onto the engine block. **Note:** *The one-piece gasket is properly in place when its cutouts "snap" under the cylinder head on each side.*

16 Install new seals to each end of the block. Apply a 3/16-inch bead of RTV sealant where the end seals meet the metal gasket **(see illustration)**.

17 Install the intake manifold on the engine and hand tighten the bolts. Install each bolt by size into the designated place. Remember to install the engine lift bracket and front brace bracket under the appropriate bolts and studs

18 Following the sequence shown **(see illustration)**, tighten the manifold bolts, in several steps, to the torque listed in this Chapter's Specifications. Check to make sure the end seals are properly installed.

19 Reinstall the remaining parts in the reverse order of removal.

20 Run the engine, adjust the ignition timing and check for oil and vacuum leaks.

8 Exhaust manifolds - removal and installation

Warning: *Allow the engine to cool completely before performing this procedure.*

Removal

Refer to illustrations 8.6a and 8.6b

8.6a On the right manifold, remove the air conditioning compressor brace (arrows)

8.6b Remove the exhaust manifold bolts and heat shield

1 Detach the cable from the negative battery terminal.

2 Raise the front of the vehicle and support it securely on jackstands. Apply the parking brake and block the rear wheels to keep the vehicle from rolling.

3 Unbolt the exhaust pipes from the manifolds. Use penetrating oil on all exhaust pipe fasteners and allow it to soak in before loosening the fasteners. **Note:** *On many models there are two flange connections on the right manifold, one to the exhaust system and one from the crossover pipe from the other side.*

4 If you are working on the left side, disconnect the EFE pipe and remove the EFE valve (see Chapter 6).

5 Disconnect the spark plug wires from the spark plugs, labeling them as they're disconnected to simplify installation **(see Chapter 1)**.

6 Remove the remaining exhaust manifold mounting bolts **(see illustrations)** and separate the manifold from the engine. **Note:** *On models so equipped, disconnect the wiring connector from the oxygen sensor in the right exhaust manifold. Do not attempt to remove the oxygen sensor from the exhaust manifold unless the sensor or the manifold are to be replaced.*

Installation

7 Installation is the reverse of removal. Be sure to clean the cylinder head and manifold surfaces thoroughly before installing the manifold. Tighten the bolts to the torque listed in this Chapter's Specifications and use anti-seize compound on the threads of all exhaust fasteners.

9 Timing chain, cover and sprockets - inspection, removal and installation

Front cover removal

Refer to illustrations 9.7, 9.8a, 9.8b, 9.10, and 9.11

1 Drain the engine coolant (see Chapter 1).

2 Disconnect the heater hose and lower radiator hose from the water pump. Have a drain pan positioned under the vehicle, as some coolant will spill out.

3 Remove the fuel pump (see Chapter 4).

4 Remove the radiator fan, pulley and drivebelts (see Chapter 3).

5 Remove the oil filter (see Chapter 1).

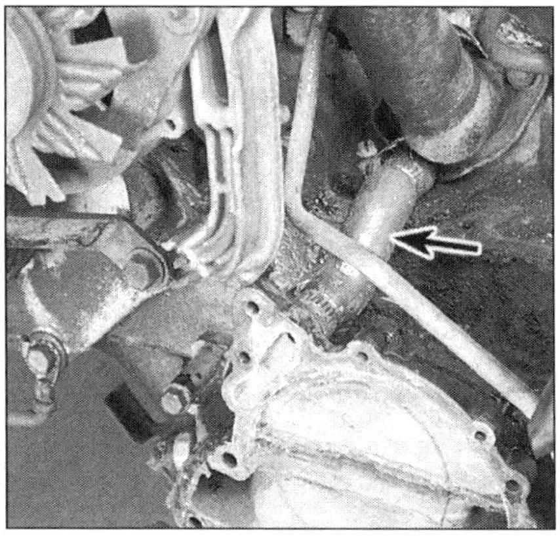

9.7 Loosen the bypass hose clamps so the hose can be disconnected from the front cover - inspect this hose carefully and replace it during this procedure, if necessary

9.8a Remove the front crankshaft pulley

9.8b Use a large breaker bar to loosen and remove the crankshaft damper bolt

9.10 Use a three-bolt puller to draw the vibration damper from the crankshaft

9.11 To remove the front cover, remove the two front oil-pan-to-cover bolts, and the 11 cover-to-block bolts (arrows) - the water pump may remain attached to the front cover

6 Loosen the AIR pump adjusting bolt and position it aside.

7 Loosen the front clamp on the thermostat bypass hose and slide the clamp over the hose **(see illustration)**.

8 Remove the bolts from the crankshaft pulley and detach the pulley. Remove the vibration damper-to-crankshaft bolt **(see illustrations)**. Use a screwdriver or prybar wedged in the starter ring gear on the driveplate to keep the crankshaft from turning

9 Position the engine at TDC for number one cylinder (see Section 3). Remove the distributor (see Chapter 5). Be sure to mark the position of the rotor to the distributor housing and the distributor housing to the front cover to insure proper installation.

10 Attach a puller to the damper and draw it off the crankshaft. A common gear puller should not be used - it may separate the outer portion of the damper from the hub. Use only a puller that bolts to the hub **(see illustration)**.

11 Place a drain pan under the front of the engine. Remove the front cover-to-engine bolts (be prepared for coolant spillage) and the two oil pan-to-front cover bolts, then separate the cover from the engine **(see illustration)**. **Note:** *The water pump may remain on the front cover, if desired, just remove the common mounting bolts.*

Timing chain inspection

Refer to illustration 9.14

12 Before removing the chain and sprockets, visually inspect the teeth on the sprockets for signs of wear and check the chain for looseness. **Note:** *When the front cover is removed, the camshaft thrust button and spring may pop out of the front of the camshaft.*

13 Turn the crankshaft counterclockwise (with the balancer bolt reinserted in the crankshaft snout) just enough to take all the slack from the timing chain on one side of the assembly. On the opposite side, check for play in the chain. If the chain can be moved back-and-forth more than one inch , the chain and sprockets must be replaced.

14 If either sprocket shows any sign of wear they should be replaced with new components. Wear on camshaft sprocket is very common **(see illustration)**. Failure to replace a worn timing chain and sprockets may result in erratic engine performance, loss of power and fuel economy. Also, if the plastic covering on the camshaft sprocket begins to deteriorate, the plastic debris can clog the oil pump pickup in the pan, potentially causing engine failure.

9.14 Worn or missing teeth, as shown here, is common on high-mileage engines with aluminum/nylon constructed camshaft sprockets

15 If any one component (timing chain or either sprocket) requires replacement, the entire set should be replaced.

16 If it's determined the components require replacement, proceed as follows.

Timing chain removal

Refer to illustrations 9.17, 9.18, 9.19 and 9.20

17 Remove the oil slinger from the crank-

9.17 Remove the oil slinger from the crankshaft snout - note the cupped side faces to the front

9.18 Align the timing marks (arrows) on the camshaft and crankshaft sprockets as shown

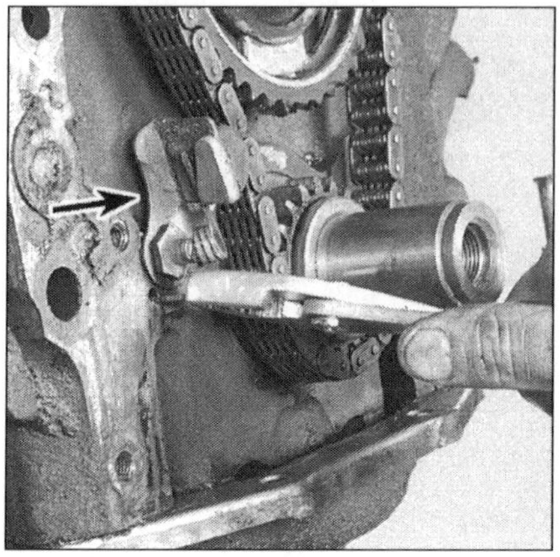

9.19 Pull the spring end out of the block to release the timing chain tensioner, then unbolt it from the block

shaft snout **(see illustration)**.

18 Reinstall the vibration damper mounting bolt and use it to turn the crankshaft clockwise until the marks on the camshaft sprocket and crankshaft sprocket are in exact alignment **(see illustration)**.

19 On 1983 and later models, unbolt and remove the timing chain tensioner assembly **(see illustration)**.

20 Remove the camshaft sprocket mounting bolts **(see illustration)** and detach the camshaft sprocket and timing chain from the front of the engine. You may have to pry behind the sprocket with a screwdriver to dislodge it from the camshaft.

21 If you have to remove the crankshaft sprocket, it can be withdrawn with a gear puller.

Installation

Refer to illustrations 9.26 and 9.29

22 Install the crankshaft sprocket, aligning the keyway with the crankshaft key. A new sprocket may have to be driven onto the crankshaft with a large socket or section of pipe. Be very careful not to crack the crankshaft sprocket when driving it on.

23 Lubricate the thrust (rear) surface of the camshaft sprocket with moly-base grease or engine assembly lube. Install the timing chain over the camshaft sprocket with slack in the chain hanging down.

24 With the timing marks aligned, slip the chain under the crankshaft sprocket and then draw the camshaft sprocket into place with the bolts. Do not hammer or attempt to drive the camshaft sprocket into place, as it could dislodge the Welch plug at the rear of the engine.

25 With the chain and both sprockets in place, check again to make sure the timing marks on the two sprockets are properly aligned. If not, remove the camshaft sprocket and move the chain until the marks align.

26 Lubricate the chain with engine oil and install the camshaft thrust spring and button and the timing chain tensioner **(see illustration)**. Apply a little grease to the fuel pump eccentric portion of the camshaft (just behind the distributor gear). Don't forget to reinstall the oil slinger over the crankshaft snout.

27 Clean all oil, dirt and old gasket material off the sealing surfaces of the cover and engine block. Replace the oil seal as described in Section 10.

28 Remove the oil pump cover and pack the space around the oil pump gears with petroleum jelly or grease (see Section 13). There must be no air space left inside the pump. This is very important in order to insure immediate oil pressure on start-up. Reinstall the oil pump cover using a new gasket.

29 Apply a bead of RTV sealant to the oil pan flange and around the coolant passages. Position a new gasket over the dowel pins **(see illustration)**.

30 Apply sealant to the threads of the bolts surrounding the coolant passages. Place the front cover in position on the engine block and install the mounting bolts. Tighten the bolts to the torque listed in this Chapter's Specifications in a criss-cross pattern (to avoid distorting the cover).

31 Coat the oil seal journal on the damper with moly-base grease.

32 Place the damper in position over the key on the crankshaft. Make sure the damper keyway lines up with the key.

33 Using a damper installation tool, press the damper onto the crankshaft.

34 Remove the installation tool and install the damper bolt. Tighten the bolt to the

9.20 Remove the two camshaft sprocket bolts (arrows) and remove the camshaft sprocket and timing chain together

9.26 Before reinstalling the timing chain cover, insert the spring and button into the front of the camshaft

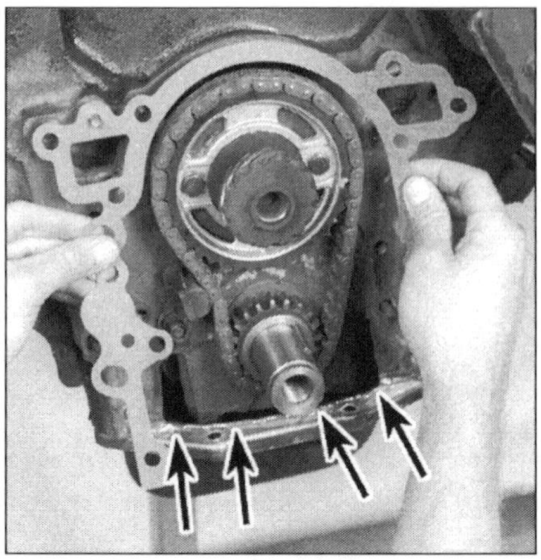

9.29 Apply RTV sealant to the oil pan flange (arrows) and install a new timing chain cover gasket to the block

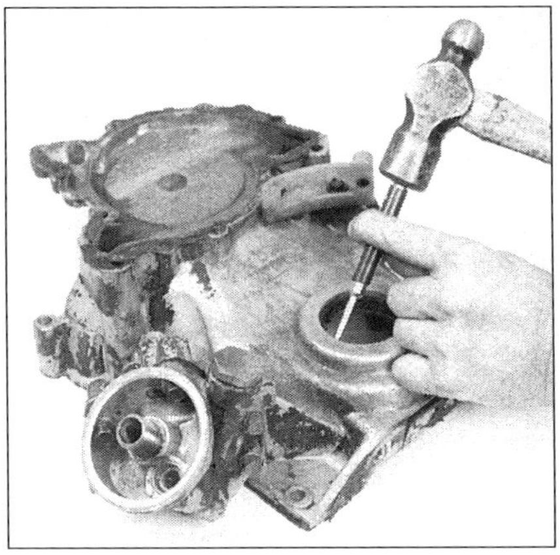

10.1 Drive the oil shedder out of the cover using a punch from the front side

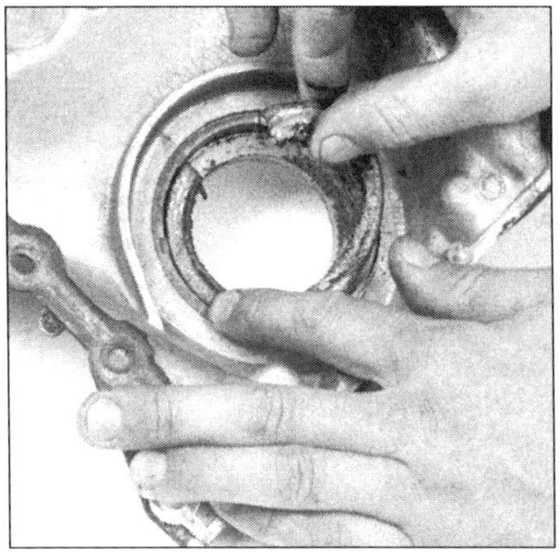

10.3a Clean the groove and install the new seal material with the ends butted together at the top of the cover

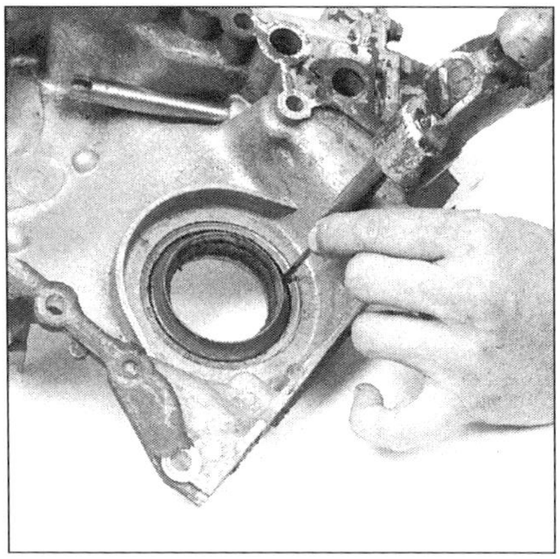

10.3b Install the shedder ring with a large socket and hammer, then stake the ring in place in three places with a small punch

torque listed in this Chapter's Specifications.

35 The remaining installation steps are the reverse of removal. Be sure to refill the cooling system (see Chapter 1). It's also a good idea to change the engine oil, as coolant may have leaked into the crankcase.

10 Crankshaft front oil seal - replacement

Refer to illustrations 10.1, 10.3a, 10.3b and 10.4

1 Remove the front cover from the engine (see Section 9). Using a hammer and punch, drive the oil shedder from the backside of the cover **(see illustration)**.

2 Remove the old seal material from the groove in the front cover and clean the seal cavity thoroughly.

3 Press a new length of seal material into the groove. Position the ends, together, at the top of the groove. Drive the oil shedder into the cover and stake it in three places with a small punch **(see illustrations)**.

4 Use a wooden hammer handle to seat the seal material into the groove **(see illustration)**.

11 Camshaft and lifters - removal, inspection and installation

1 A noisy valve lifter can be isolated when the engine is idling. Hold a mechanic's stethoscope or a length of hose near the location of each valve while listening at the other end.

2 The most likely causes of noisy valve lifters are dirt trapped between the plunger and the lifter body or lack of oil flow, viscosity or pressure. Before condemning the lifters, we recommend checking the oil for fuel contamination, correct level, cleanliness and correct viscosity.

Removal

Refer to illustration 11.11

3 Disconnect the cable from the negative battery terminal.

4 Drain the coolant (see Chapter 1).

5 Remove the radiator (see Chapter 3).

6 If equipped with air conditioning, remove the condenser (see Chapter 3). **Warning:** *The air conditioning system is under high pressure. Do not loosen any fittings or remove any components until after the system has been discharged into an EPA approved container by a dealer service department or automotive air conditioning facility. Always wear eye protection when disconnecting refrigerant fittings.*

7 Remove the valve covers as described in Section 4.

8 Remove the intake manifold as described in Section 7.

9 Remove the rocker arms, shafts and pushrods (see Section 5).

10 There are several ways to extract the lifters from the bores. A special tool designed to grip and remove lifters is manufactured by many tool companies and is widely available, but may not be required in every case. On newer engines without a lot of varnish buildup, the lifters can often be removed with a small magnet or even with your fingers. A machinist's scribe with a bent end can be used to pull the lifters out by positioning the point under the retainer ring in the top of each lifter. **Caution:** *Don't use pliers to remove the lifters unless you intend to replace them with new ones (along with the camshaft). The pliers may damage the precision machined and hardened lifters, rendering them useless.*

11 Before removing the lifters, arrange to store them in a clearly labeled box to ensure they can be reinstalled in their original loca-

10.4 Using a smooth hammer handle, press the seal into the groove completely around the opening

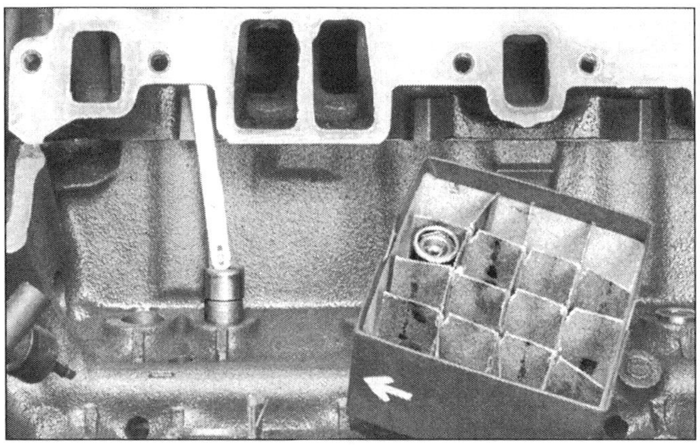

11.11 The lifters on an engine with high-mileage may require a special tool for removal - store the lifters in an organized manner to make sure they're reinstalled in their original locations

11.15a If the bottom of any lifter is worn concave, pitted, scratched or galled, replace the entire set with new lifters and a new camshaft

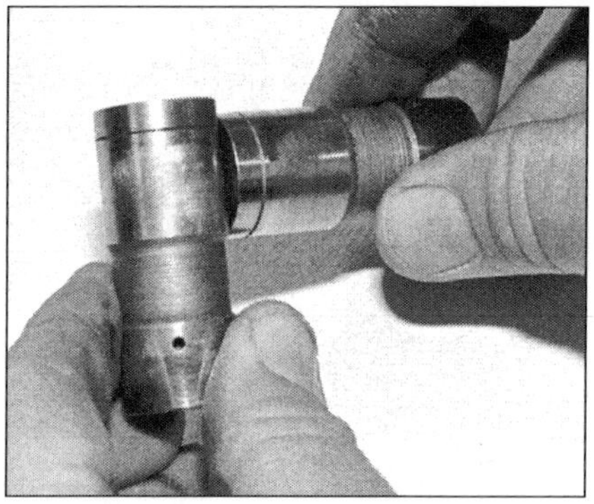

11.15b The foot of each lifter should be slightly convex - the side of another lifter can be used as a straightedge to check it; if it appears concave, it's worn and must not be reused

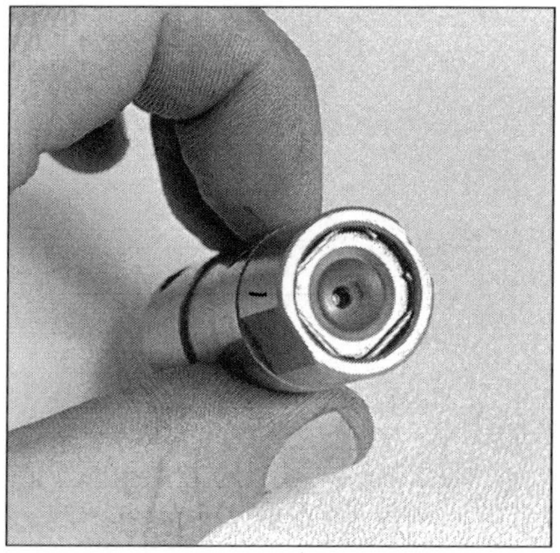

11.15c Check the pushrod seat (arrow) in the top of each lifter for wear

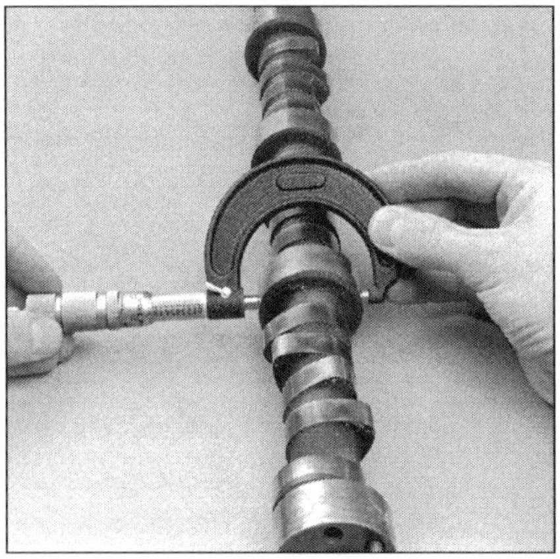

11.17 Using a micrometer, measure the camshaft journals and compare them to Specifications

11.20 Apply moly-based grease or engine assembly lube to the camshaft lobes and bearing journals before installing the camshaft

tions **(see illustration)**.

12 Remove the front cover, timing chain and camshaft sprocket (see Section 9).

13 Carefully draw the camshaft straight out of the engine block. Do this very slowly to avoid damage to the camshaft bearings as the lobes pass over them.

Inspection

Refer to illustrations 11.15a, 11.15b, 11.15c and 11.17

14 Clean the lifters with solvent and dry them thoroughly without mixing them up.

15 Check each lifter wall, pushrod seat and foot for pitting, scuffing, score marks and uneven wear **(see illustration)**. Each lifter foot (the surface that rides on the cam lobe) must be slightly convex, although this can be difficult to determine by eye. If the base of the lifter is concave **(see illustration)**, the lifters and camshaft must be replaced. If the lifter walls are damaged or worn (which isn't very likely), inspect the lifter bores in the engine block as well. If the pushrod seats **(see illustration)** are worn, check the pushrod ends.

16 After the camshaft has been removed from the engine, cleaned with solvent and dried, inspect the bearing journals for uneven wear, pitting and evidence of seizure. If the journals are damaged, the bearing inserts in the block are probably damaged as well. Both the camshaft and bearings will have to be replaced.

17 Measure the bearing journals with a micrometer to determine if they are excessively worn or out-of-round **(see illustration)**.

18 Check the camshaft lobes for heat discoloration, score marks, chipped areas, pitting and uneven wear. Measure the height of all the intake and exhaust lobes. All of the lobe measurements must be within 0.005-inch of the largest measurement (intake and exhaust lobe respectively). If the lifters, lobes and journals check out OK, the camshaft and lifters may be reused.

Installation

Refer to illustration 11.20

19 If new lifters are being installed, a new camshaft must also be installed. If the camshaft is replaced, then install new lifters as well. Never install used lifters unless the original camshaft is used and the lifters can be installed in their original locations!

20 Prior to installing the camshaft, coat each of the lobes and journals with engine assembly lube or moly-base grease **(see illustration)**.

21 Slide the camshaft into the engine block, again taking extra care so you don't damage the bearings.

22 Install the camshaft sprocket and timing chain as described in Section 9.

23 Soak new lifters in oil to remove trapped air, and lube the bottom of the lifters with assembly lube and install them into the engine block.

24 Install the remaining components in the reverse order of removal by referring to the appropriate Chapter or Section.

25 Run the engine and check for oil leaks.

12 Cylinder heads - removal and installation

Warning: *Allow the engine to cool completely before performing this procedure.*

Removal

1 Remove the intake manifold (refer to Section 7). **Note:** *On turbocharged models, refer to Chapter 4A for turbocharger removal.* As soon as the intake manifold is removed, cover the lifter valley with clean shop rags, to prevent dirt loosened during head removal from getting into the lifters.

2 Raise the vehicle and support it securely on jackstands.

3 Refer to Chapter 1 and drain the coolant from the radiator and engine block drain plugs.

Right cylinder head

Refer to illustration 12.6

4 Remove the drivebelts (see Chapter 1).

12.6 Remove the alternator and compressor, then remove these three bolts (arrows) to remove the bracket from the right cylinder head

12.15 Pry carefully on a casting protrusion - don't force a tool between the gasket surfaces

12.17 Carefully remove all traces of old gasket material

5 Remove the alternator (see Chapter 5). If the vehicle is equipped with air conditioning, remove the compressor and set it aside (see Chapter 3). DO NOT disconnect the refrigerant lines.

6 Remove the alternator/compressor mounting bracket **(see illustration)**.

Left cylinder head

7 Remove the oil dipstick.

8 Remove the power steering pump with the mounting bracket and move it to the side, without disconnecting the hoses.

9 Refer to Chapter 6 and remove the AIR pump and its bracket.

Both cylinder heads

Refer to illustration 12.15

10 Disconnect the wires from the spark plugs and remove the spark plug wire clips from the valve cover studs. Remove the valve covers (see Section 4).

11 Remove the exhaust manifolds (see Section 8).

12 Remove the rocker arms, shafts and pushrods (see Section 5).

13 Using a new head gasket, outline the cylinders and bolt pattern on a piece of cardboard. Be sure to indicate the front of the engine for reference. Punch holes at the bolt locations.

14 Loosen the cylinder head bolts in 1/4-turn increments until they can be removed by hand (start at the ends and work toward the center of the head). Store the bolts in the cardboard holder as they're removed - this will ensure that they're reinstalled in their original locations.

15 Lift the head off the engine. If it's stuck, DO NOT pry between the head and block or damage to the mating surfaces will result! To dislodge the head, use a long screwdriver or pry bar to pry under the casting protrusions **(see illustration)**.

Installation

Refer to illustrations 12.17, 12.20 and 12.23

16 If a new cylinder head is being installed, attach the components previously removed from the old head.

17 The mating surfaces of the cylinder head and block must be perfectly clean when the cylinder head is installed. Use a gasket scraper to remove all traces of carbon and old gasket material, then clean the mating surfaces with lacquer thinner or acetone **(see illustration)**. If there's oil on the mating surfaces when the cylinder head is installed, the gasket may not seal correctly and leaks could develop. When working on the block, stuff the cylinders with clean shop rags to keep out debris. Use a vacuum cleaner to remove any debris that falls into the cylinders.

18 Check the block and head mating surfaces for nicks, deep scratches and other damage. If damage is slight, it can be removed with a file; if it's excessive, machining may be the only alternative. Check the cylinder head for warpage with a straightedge and feeler gauges (see Chapter 2C).

19 Use a tap of the correct size to chase the threads in the head bolt holes. Mount each bolt in a vise and run a die down the threads to remove corrosion and restore the threads. Dirt, corrosion, sealant and damaged threads will affect torque readings.

20 Install the gasket over the engine block dowel pins with the mark THIS SIDE UP visible **(see illustration)**.

21 Position the cylinder head over the gasket.

22 Coat the cylinder head bolts with sealant and install them.

23 Tighten the bolts in the recommended sequence **(see illustration)** to the torque

12.20 Install the new gasket over the dowel pins in the block (arrows)

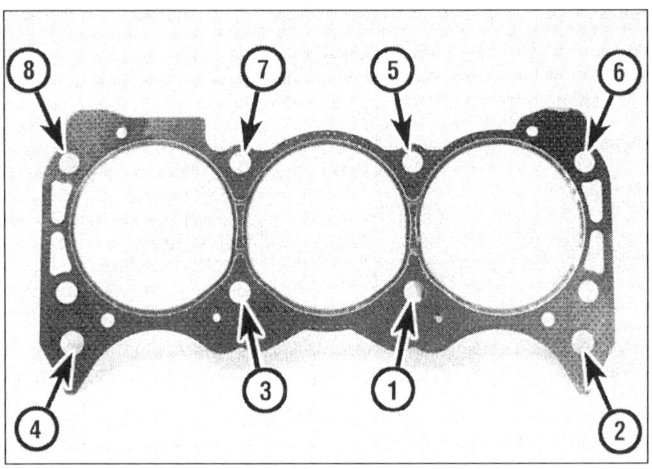

12.23 Cylinder head tightening sequence

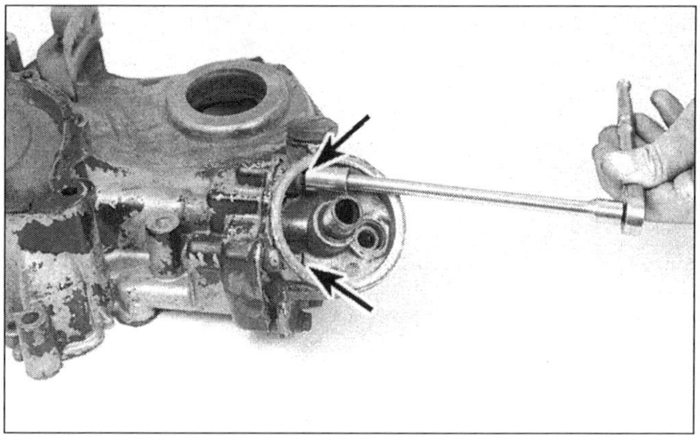

13.2a Remove the bolts holding the oil pump to the front cover - these two bolts (arrows) are exposed only after the oil filter is removed

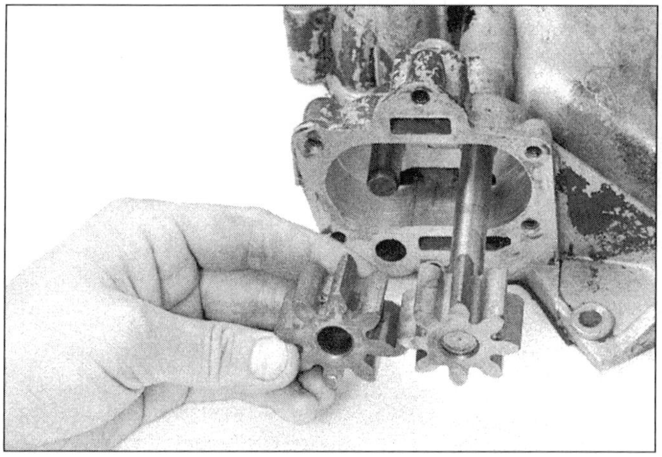

13.2b Pull the oil pump gears out of the housing for inspection

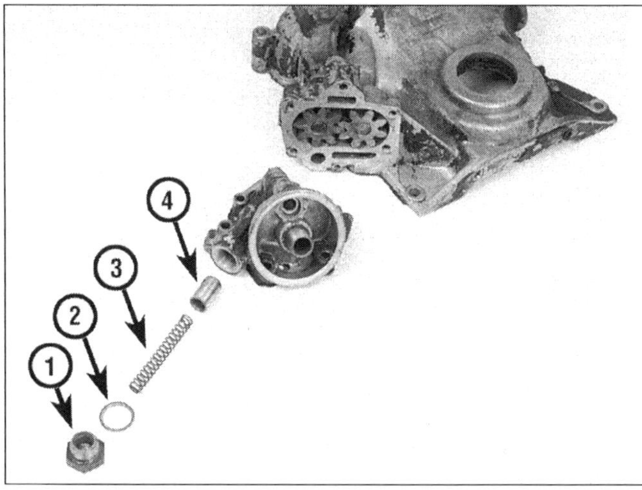

13.4 Oil pump pressure relief components:

1. *Pressure relief cap*
2. *Copper sealing ring*
3. *Oil pressure relief spring*
4. *Oil pressure relief valve*

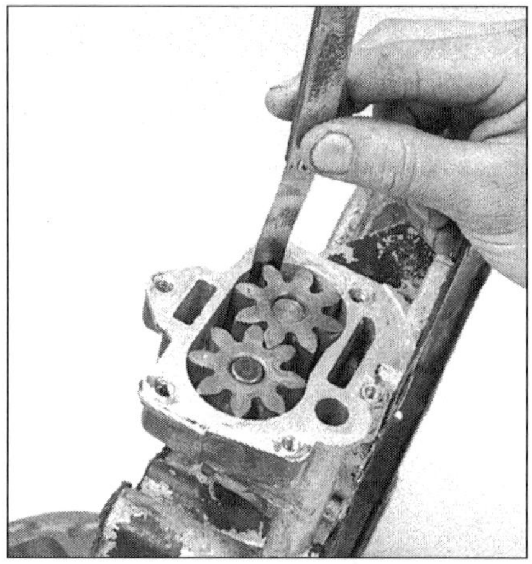

13.9a Check the gear tip clearance in the pump body

listed in this Chapter's specifications. Work up to the final torque in three steps.

24 The remaining installation steps are the reverse of removal.

13 Oil pump - removal, inspection and installation

Removal

Refer to illustrations 13.2a and 13.2b

1 Remove the oil filter (see Chapter 1).

2 Remove the bolts attaching the oil pump cover assembly to the front cover **(see illustration)**. Remove the cover assembly and slide out the oil pump gears **(see illustration)**.

Inspection

Refer to illustrations, 13.4, 13.9a, 13.9b, 13.9c, 13.9d and 13.9e

3 Clean the gears with solvent and inspect them for wear and scoring. If the gears are worn or damaged, replace them as a set.

4 Unscrew the oil pressure relief valve cap, spring and valve **(see illustration)**. Do not remove the oil filter by-pass valve and spring, as they are staked in place.

5 Clean the parts with solvent and inspect the relief valve for wear and scoring. Check to make sure the relief valve spring is not collapsed or worn. Any relief valve spring which is questionable should be replaced with a new one.

6 Check the relief valve clearance in the pump body. The valve should fit snugly in its bore. If excessive side clearance is noted, the valve and/or front cover should be replaced with new components.

7 The filter by-pass valve should be flat and free of nicks, cracks or warping and scratches.

8 Lubricate the pressure relief valve and spring, and install it in the oil pump body. Install the cap and gasket, and tighten the cap securely.

9 Install the gears into the pump body and, using feeler gauges, check the clearance between the tips of the gear teeth and the pump body **(see illustration)**. Now, lay a straightedge across the gears and measure the end clearance between the gears and the gasket surface **(see illustration)**. If either of these two measurements are not within the tolerances listed in this Chapter's Specifications, measure the diameter and length of the gears, and the depth of the pump body, to determine if the gears or the pump body are worn **(see illustrations)**. If the gears are found to be worn, replace them as a set. If the pump body is worn, the front cover must be replaced (see Section 9), and a new set of gears should also be installed.

13.9b Lay a straightedge across the pump body and measure the clearance between the gears and the gasket surface (end clearance)

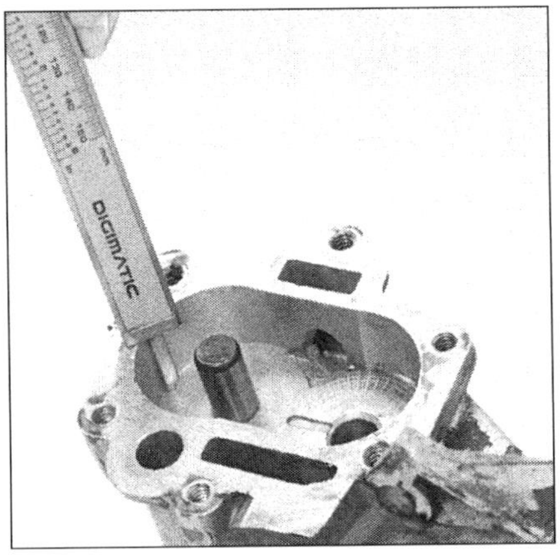

13.9c Measure the depth of the oil pump body cavity

13.9d With a micrometer or precision caliper, measure the gear thickness . . .

13.9e . . . and width, then compare your measurements to the Specifications

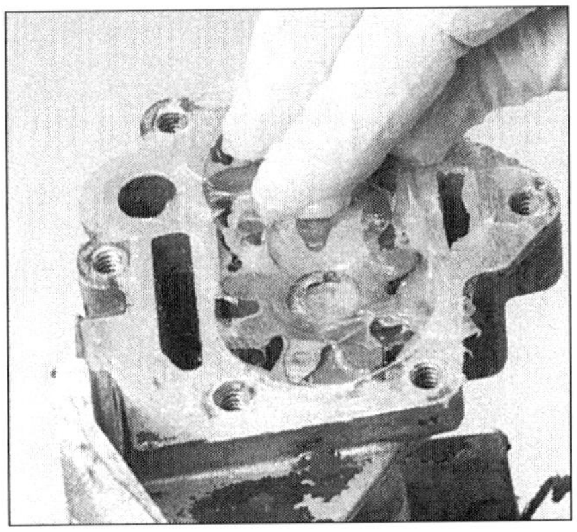

13.11 Pack the oil pump with petroleum jelly to ensure the engine has immediate oil pressure on startup

10 If the condition of the pump is satisfactory at this point, remove the gears and pack the pump body with petroleum jelly. DO NOT use chassis grease or any other lubricant.

Installation

Refer to illustration 13.11

11 Re-install the gears, making sure that petroleum jelly is packed into the gear cavity and between the teeth of the gears **(see illustration)**. If the pump is not packed completely with petroleum jelly, it may not prime when the engine is initially started.

12 Install the pump cover and tighten the bolts to the torque listed in this Chapter's Specifications.

13 Install a new oil filter and add engine oil as necessary. Pay close attention to the oil pressure gauge or warning light during the initial startup and driving period. Shut off the engine and inspect all work if a lack of pressure is indicated.

14.8 Remove the oil pan bolts

14 Oil pan - removal and installation

Note: *The following procedure is based on the assumption the engine is in the vehicle. If it has been removed, simply unbolt the oil pan and detach it from the block.*

Removal

Refer to illustration 14.8

1 Disconnect the negative cable from the battery.

2 Drain the engine oil (see Chapter 1).

3 Raise and safely support the vehicle with heavy-duty jackstands. Refer to Chapter 10 and unbolt the idler arm bracket.

4 Turn the steering wheel fully to the left.

5 Remove the starter motor (see Chapter 5).

6 Refer to Chapter 8, unbolt the final drive unit from the engine and transmission and lower the unit.

7 Remove the flywheel cover (see Chapter 7).

8 Remove the oil pan mounting bolts **(see illustration)**.

9 Carefully separate the pan from the engine block. Don't pry between the block and pan or damage to the sealing surfaces may result and oil leaks could develop. If the pan sticks, use a block of wood and a hammer to break it loose. You may have to turn the crankshaft slightly to maneuver the front of the pan past the crankshaft counterweights.

Installation

Refer to illustration 14.13

10 Scrape off all traces of old gasket material and sealant. Clean the gasket sealing surfaces with lacquer thinner or acetone. Make sure the bolt holes in the block are clean.

11 Check the oil pan flanges for distortion, particularly around the bolt holes and corners. If necessary, place the pan on a block of wood and use a hammer to flatten and restore the gasket surface. If distortion is severe, install a new oil pan.

12 Most 1981 and later V6 engines were equipped, from the factory, with RTV sealant instead of an oil pan gasket. A formed rubber or cork gasket is available for all models and may be preferable to using only RTV sealant.

13 If you're not using a gasket, apply a continuous 3/16-inch diameter bead of RTV sealant on the oil pan flange, to the inside of

14.13 Use some RTV sealant to hold the new gasket in place, then install the pan before the RTV cures

15.1 Give the bolts and a few light taps with a hammer to loosen the rear main cap

15.2b Drive each end of the seal into the groove until it feels tightly packed

the bolt holes. Install the pan while the sealant is still wet. If a gasket is to be used, place it on the oil pan, using a few dabs of RTV sealant to hold it in place **(see illustration)**.

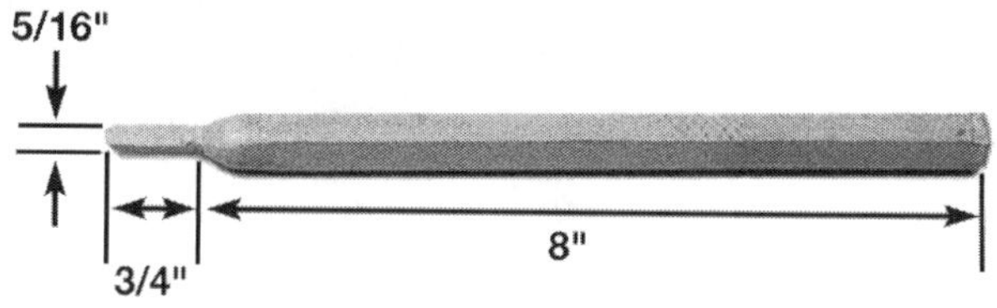

15.2a Grind a piece of 1/2-inch diameter brass or aluminum rod to these dimensions as a rear seal driver

14 Carefully position the pan against the block and install the bolts finger-tight. Tighten the bolts in three steps to the torque listed in this Chapter's specifications. Start at the center of the pan and work out toward the ends in a spiral pattern.

15 The remaining steps are the reverse of removal. **Caution:** *Don't forget to refill the engine with oil before starting it* (see Chapter 1).

16 Start the engine and check carefully for oil leaks at the oil pan.

15 Rear main oil seal - replacement

Refer to illustrations 15.1, 15.2a, 15.2b, 15.3, 15.6a, 15.6b, 15.7a and 15.7b

1 With the oil pan and pickup removed (see Section 14), unbolt the rear main bearing cap. Use the two main cap bolts as levers to rock the cap back and forth to loosen it for removal. **Note:** *It may help to tap the bolts on the side with a hammer to loosen the cap* **(see illustration)**.

2 Insert the special seal packing tool or equivalent **(see illustration)** against the seal. Drive the old seal into its groove until it is packed tight at each end **(see illustration)**.

3 Measure the distance which the seal was driven into the groove, then add 1/16-inch **(see illustration)**. Cut two pieces, the calculated length, from the old seal taken from the bearing cap. Use the bearing cap as a guide when cutting.

4 Place a drop of sealant on each end of these seal pieces and then pack them into the upper groove to fill the gap made previously.

5 Trim the remaining material perfectly flush with the block. Be careful not to harm the bearing surface. Push a thin piece of shim stock between the seal and the crankshaft, to protect the crankshaft, and trim the seal against the shim stock.

6 Install a new rope seal into the main bearing cap groove and push firmly all around using a hammer handle or special tool **(see illustration)**. Make sure the seal is firmly seated, then trim the ends flush with the bearing cap mating surface **(see illustration)**.

7 Apply a *thin* coat of RTV sealant to the bearing cap at the block mating surface **(see illustration)**, install the cap and tighten the bolts finger tight. Soak the new side seals in clean engine oil for at least two minutes. Insert the seals into the grooves on each side of the main bearing cap **(see illustration)**. Make sure the side seals are seated at the bottom of the groove, then tighten the rear main bearing cap to the torque listed in this Chapter's Specifications. The side seals are slightly longer than the bearing cap, DO NOT trim the ends of the seals to fit. Install the oil pan and the remainder of the components. **Note:** *When new seals are installed, they may leak slightly until heat swells the side seals sufficiently. Allow the engine to reach operating temperature before driving.*

15.3 Measure the amount that the seal has been driven up into the groove - here a small screwdriver was used with a sleeve of masking tape (arrow) to serve as a depth indicator

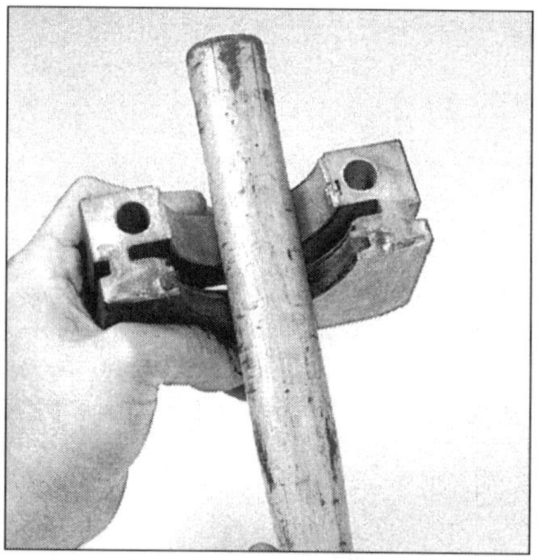

15.6a The new seal material used in the cap can be settled into the groove with a hammer handle or by taping it in with a hammer and large-diameter socket

15.6b Trim the seal with a sharp razor blade flush with the bearing cap

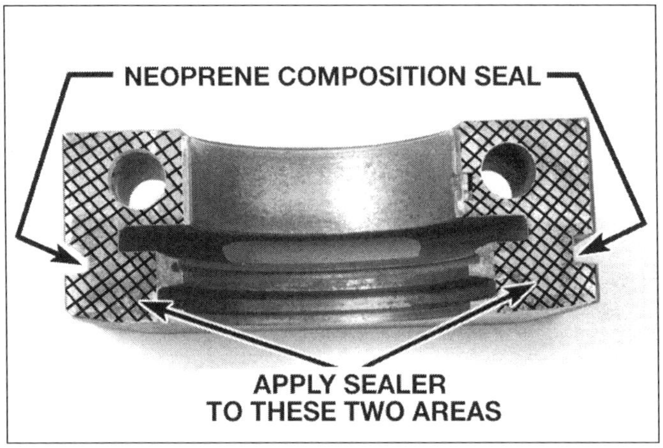

15.7a Before installing the cap, coat the indicated area with a thin film of RTV sealant - do not get RTV on the bearing or seal

15.7b Soak the new side seals in clean engine oil, then install them in the grooves on either side of the rear main bearing cap (arrow) - install the seals after the bearing cap is installed

16 Driveplate - removal and installation

Refer to illustrations 16.2 and 16.3

1 Raise the vehicle and support it securely on jackstands. Support the engine from above with a hoist, then refer to Chapter 7 and remove the transmission.

2 Use a sharp scribe or a marking pen to draw a line from the driveplate to the end of the crankshaft for correct alignment during reinstallation **(see illustration)**.

3 Remove the bolts that secure the driveplate to the crankshaft flange. If difficulty is experienced in removing the bolts due to movement of the crankshaft, use a screwdriver to keep the driveplate from turning **(see illustration)**.

4 Remove the driveplate from the crankshaft flange.

5 Check the starter ring gear for cracked or broken teeth. Lay the driveplate on a flat surface and use a straightedge to check for warpage. Examine the metal between the large holes for evidence of cracks. **Note:** *If your driveplate has clip-on balancing weights (clipped onto the driveplate through one or more of the large holes), make sure they are on firmly.*

6 Clean the mating surfaces of the driveplate and the crankshaft.

7 Position the driveplate against the crankshaft, matching the alignment marks made during removal. Before installing the bolts, apply a thread-locking compound to the threads.

8 Wedge a screwdriver through the driveplate or into the ring gear teeth to keep the crankshaft from turning. Tighten the bolts to the torque listed in this Chapter's Specifications. Working in a criss-cross pattern, tighten the bolts in two or three steps.

9 The remainder of installation is the reverse of the removal procedure.

17 Engine mounts - check and replacement

Check

1 Engine mounts seldom require attention, but broken or deteriorated mounts should be replaced immediately or the added strain placed on the driveline components may cause damage.

2 During the check, the engine must be raised slightly to remove the weight from the mounts. Disconnect the negative battery cable from the battery.

3 Raise the vehicle and support it securely on jackstands, then position the jack under the engine oil pan. Place a wood block between the jack head and the oil pan, then carefully raise the engine just enough to take the weight off the mounts.

4 Check the mounts to see if the rubber is cracked, hardened or separated from the

16.2 To insure proper balance, mark the relationship of the driveplate to the crankshaft

16.3 A large screwdriver wedged in the starter ring rear teeth or one of the holes in the driveplate can be used to keep the driveplate from turning as the mounting bolts are loosened or tightened

metal plates. Sometimes the rubber will split right down the center. Rubber preservative may be applied to the mounts to slow deterioration.

5 Check for relative movement between the mount plates and the engine or frame (use a large screwdriver or pry bar to attempt to move the mounts). If movement is noted, lower the engine and tighten the mount fasteners.

Replacement

6 Remove the fan shroud mounting screws and place the shroud over the fan.

7 Remove the engine mount locknuts, top and bottom. There are two front mounts in a saddle, each attached with a stud top and bottom or a bolt on top and stud below (see Chapter 2B).

8 Raise the front of the engine high enough for the mount studs to clear the frame and the large bracket from the front of the engine. Do not force the engine up too high. If it touches anything before the mounts are free, remove the part for clearance. Place a block of wood between the oil pan and crossmember as a safety precaution.

Note: *On vehicles equipped with self-locking nuts and bolts, replace them with new ones whenever they are disassembled. Prior to assembly, remove hardened residual adhesive from the engine block holes with a proper-size bottoming tap.*

9 Slip the new engine mounts between the bracket and the frame. Make sure that both upper and lower studs go through their respective holes in the chassis and the engine bracket. Lower the engine to its original height and tighten the fasteners securely.

Chapter 2 Part B
V8 engines

Contents

Specifications

Cadillac big V8 engines - 368, 425 and 500 cu. in.

General

Firing order	1-5-6-3-4-2-7-8
Camshaft	
Journal diameter	
500	Not available
368, 425	2.6243 to 2.6250 inches
Lobe lift	Compare the readings for each intake and each exhaust valve. Replace the camshaft if readings vary more than 0.003 inch

Cylinder location and distributor rotation

The blackened terminal shown on the distributor cap indicates the Number One spark plug wire position

Cadillac 368, 425, and 500 cu. in. V8 engines

Torque specifications

	Ft-lbs (unless otherwise indicated)
Intake manifold bolts	30
Exhaust manifold-to-cylinder head bolts	
Long bolt	35
Short bolt	144 in-lbs
Cylinder head bolts	
425, 368	95
500	115
Driveplate-to-crankshaft bolts	75
Oil pan bolts	120 in-lbs
Oil pump cover bolts	180 in-lbs
Crankshaft pulley-to-hub bolts	17
Valve cover bolts	30 in-lbs
Front cover bolts	
5/16-18	120 in-lbs
3/8-16	22
Rocker arm shaft bolts	70
Main bearing cap bolts	90

Cadillac HT4100 V8 engine

General

Firing order	1-8-4-3-6-5-7-2

Camshaft

Journal diameter (all)	Not available
Lobe lift	Compare the readings for each intake and each exhaust valve. Replace the camshaft if readings vary more than 0.005 inch

Torque specifications

	Ft-lbs (unless otherwise indicated)
Intake manifold bolts	
Step 1 (bolts 1 through 4)	180 in-lbs
Step 2 (bolts 5 through 16)	22
Step 3 (all bolts, in sequence)	22
Exhaust manifold-to-cylinder head bolts	20
Camshaft sprocket bolt	35
Crankshaft pulley-to-hub bolts	20
Cylinder head bolts	
Step 1	45
Step 2	90
Driveplate-to-crankshaft bolts	35
Oil pan bolts	120 in-lbs
Valve cover bolts	50 in-lbs
Rocker arm pivot-to-support bolts	20
Rocker arm support-to-head bolt nuts	35
Front cover bolts	180 in-lbs

Cadillac HT 4100 V8 engine

Cylinder location and distributor rotation

The blackened terminal shown on the distributor cap indicates the Number One spark plug wire position

Oldsmobile V8 engines - 307, 350, 403 and 455 cu in

General

Firing order	1-8-4-3-6-5-7-2

Camshaft

Journal diameter	
no. 1	2.0365 to 2.0357 inches
no. 2	2.0165 to 2.0157 inches
no. 3	1.9965 to 1.9957 inches
no. 4	1.9767 to 1.9757 inches
no. 5	1.9565 to 1.9557 inches
Endplay	0.011 to 0.077 inch
Lobe lift	Compare the readings for each intake and each exhaust valve. Replace the camshaft if readings vary more than 0.005 inch

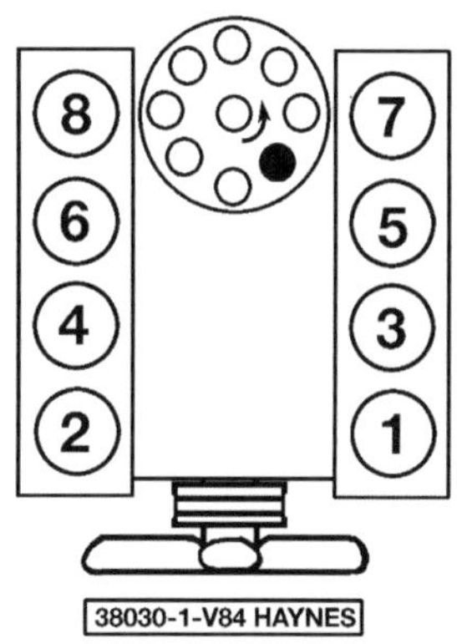

Oldsmobile 455 V8 engine (with points-type ignition)

Torque specifications

	Ft-lbs (unless otherwise indicated)
Intake manifold bolts*	40
Exhaust manifold-to-cylinder head bolts	25
Camshaft sprocket bolt	65
Cylinder head bolts*	
1976 and earlier	85
1977 on	130
Driveplate-to-crankshaft bolts	60
Front cover bolts (see Section 10)	
Lower four (through mounts)	50
Upper bolts (through pump)	22
Vibration damper-to-crankshaft bolt	200 to 310
Oil pan bolts	120 in-lbs
Oil pump cover bolts	96 in-lbs
Crankshaft pulley-to-hub bolts	20
Valve cover bolts	84 in-lbs
Rocker arm pivot bolts	25

** lightly oil threads*

All other Oldsmobile V8 engines

1 General information and engine identification

General information

This Part of Chapter 2 is devoted to in-vehicle repair procedures for the V8 engines. All information concerning engine removal and installation and engine block and cylinder head overhaul can be found in Part C of this Chapter.

Since the repair procedures included in this Part are based on the assumption that the engine is still installed in the vehicle, if they are being used during a complete engine overhaul (with the engine already out of the vehicle and on a stand) many of the steps included here will not apply.

The specifications included in this Part of Chapter 2 apply only to the procedures found here. The specifications necessary for rebuilding the block and cylinder heads are included in Part C.

Engine identification

For most of their history, marques such as Cadillac, Oldsmobile, Buick and other divisions of General Motors had their own distinctive engines. However, since that time, General Motors automobiles have been equipped with various engines, supplied by the nameplate's division or another division. Thus, an Oldsmobile 350 V8 could be original equipment in a Buick, Cadillac or Oldsmobile, and a V6 of Buick origin has been used in both Oldsmobiles and Cadillacs.

On 1972 and newer models, a check of the Vehicle Identification Number (VIN) will help you determine which engine your vehicle has. The VIN is stamped onto a small metal plate that is affixed to the cowl bar, visible through the lower left (driver's side) corner of the windshield (see the introductory pages at the front of this manual). The number gives information concerning the engine, the year of the vehicle, and so on. 1972 through 1980 models use a 13 digit number, the fifth position in the VIN being the character that denotes the type of engine. 1981 and newer models use a 17 digit number, the eighth digit of the VIN reveals which engine is installed. Refer to the accompanying chart to determine which engine you have.

There are some differences between the various makes of engines, but overall, repair and maintenance procedures are nearly identical. Where differences occur, they will be noted. A check of the Specifications chart at the beginning of this Chapter will alert the home mechanic to any differences in the various tolerances. Also check the Vehicle Emission Control Information label, located adjacent to the radiator, for additional engine information. **Note:** *This list does not include the 350 cubic inch diesel engine, an Oldsmobile design available in all of the vehicles covered by this book (in the model years 1979 through 1985). Part A of this Chapter covers the 3.8L and 4.1L V6 engines, which are Buick-designed engines, yet used in Buick, Oldsmobile and Cadillac models.*

V8 ENGINE IDENTIFICATION

VIN CODE	ENGINE TYPE
Cadillac Eldorado	
S (1971 to 1976)	500
S (1977 to 1978)	425
B (1979 only)	350 Olds (MPFI)
8 (1980 only)	350 Olds (MPFI)
9 (1980 only)	368 (TBI)
9 (1981 only)	368 V8-6-4 (TBI)
8 (1982 to 1985)	4.1L (250) Aluminum (HT4100)
Cadillac Seville	
8 (1980 only)	350 Olds (MPFI)
9 (1980 only)	368 (TBI)
9 (1981 only)	368 V8-6-4 (TBI)
8 (1982 to 1985)	4.1L (250) Aluminum (HT4100)
Buick Riviera	
R (1979 and 1980)	350 (Olds)
9 (1981 to 1985)	307 (Olds)
Oldsmobile Toronado	
W (1971 to 1975)	455 (Olds)
S (1976 only)	455 (Olds)
K (1977 and 1978)	403 (Olds)
L (1979)	350 (Olds)
Y (1980)	307 (Olds)
R (1980)	350 (Olds)
Y (1981 to 1985)	307 (Olds)

Cadillac produced two engines that differed from their other conventional V8 engines. In 1981 the 368 V8-6-4, equipped with a Modulated Displacement system, was introduced, but was used for one year only, then dropped. From 1982 through 1985, a 4.1L (250 cu. in.) aluminum engine, commonly referred to as the HT4100, was used.

The 368 Modulated Displacement engine, also known as the V8-6-4, reduces the number of operating cylinders with the use of valve selectors located on the rocker arm assemblies. When energized, these valve selectors deactivate certain cylinders, closing the intake and exhaust valves of those cylinders. As engine load decreases, it will run on six, then four cylinders. When full power is required, the valve selectors are de-energized and all eight cylinders function normally.

The HT4100 engine is constructed of an aluminum block with cast iron cylinder heads. Because the engine is largely aluminum, particular care must be taken to accommodate the characteristics of this metal. Bolts which thread into aluminum must not be over-tightened or the threads may be damaged. The cylinder head tightening procedure must be strictly followed to insure proper sealing of the head gasket. When cleaning the gasket surfaces of the aluminum, use soft wire brushes or dull scrapers. Blow out all debris from the bolt holes to avoid inaccurate torque readings.

2 Repair operations possible with the engine in the vehicle

Many major repair operations can be accomplished without removing the engine from the vehicle.

Clean the engine compartment and the exterior of the engine with some type of degreaser before any work is done. A clean engine will make the job easier and will help keep dirt out of the internal areas of the engine.

Depending on the components involved, it may be a good idea to remove the hood to improve access to the engine as repairs are performed (refer to Chapter 11 if necessary).

If oil or coolant leaks develop, indicating a need for gasket or seal replacement, the repairs can generally be made with the engine in the vehicle. The oil pan gasket (except on 1978 and earlier models), the cylinder head gaskets, intake and exhaust manifold gaskets, timing cover gaskets and the crankshaft oil seals (except for the rear main oil seal on 1978 and earlier models) are accessible with the engine in place.

Exterior engine components, such as the water pump, the starter motor, the alternator, the distributor and the fuel system components, as well as the intake and exhaust manifolds, can be removed for repair with the engine in place.

Since the cylinder heads can be removed without pulling the engine, valve component servicing can also be accomplished with the engine in the vehicle.

Replacement of, repairs to, or inspection of the timing chain and sprockets, camshaft and the oil pump (except on 1978 and earlier Oldsmobile-built engines) are all possible with the engine in place.

In extreme cases, caused by a lack of necessary equipment, repair or replacement of piston rings, pistons, connecting rods and rod bearings is possible with the engine in the vehicle (except on 1978 and earlier models). However, this practice is not recommended because of the cleaning and preparation work that must be performed on the components involved.

3 Top Dead Center (TDC) for number one piston - locating

Refer to illustrations 3.1a and 3.1b

See Chapter 2, Part A, for this procedure. Be sure to use the firing order in the Specifications in this Part of Chapter 2,

3.1a Timing marks on a typical Oldsmobile-built engine

3.1b Timing marks on a typical Cadillac engine

4.4 Move any hoses or wires in the way of removing the valve cover - on most models remove or bend the diverter valve assembly (arrow) out of the way (V8-6-4 shown)

4.6a Valve cover bolt locations (arrows) - HT4100 Cadillac V8

where necessary. Refer to the illustrations here for V8 timing marks **(see illustrations).**

4 Valve covers - removal and installation

Refer to illustrations 4.4, 4.6a, 4.6b, 4.6c and 4.9

1 Disconnect the negative cable from the battery.

2 Remove the air cleaner assembly (see Chapter 4 if necessary).

3 Label and disconnect any emissions or vacuum lines and wires which are routed over the valve cover(s). **Note:** *If you are working on a Cadillac V8-6-4 engine, disconnect the electrical connectors from the modulated displacement valve selectors.*

4 Remove any braces or brackets which block access to the cover(s), noting the way they are mounted to ease reassembly. On some models, the wiring connector to the alternator must be disconnected to clear the right valve cover. On most models, unbolt the AIR diverter valve assembly or bend its bracket slightly to allow removal of the right valve cover **(see illustration).**

5 Detach any remaining accessories as necessary. If removal of the air conditioning compressor is required, unbolt the unit and carefully set it aside without disconnecting the refrigerant lines. **Warning:** *The air conditioning system is under high pressure. Do not disconnect any refrigerant line or fitting without first having the system discharged by an air conditioning technician.*

6 Remove the valve cover bolts **(see illustrations). Note:** *Keep track of the location of nuts/studs used as valve cover fasteners, as well as wiring tabs, hose clamps or other brackets retained by the valve cover fasteners.*

7 Remove the valve cover. **Note:** *On the left cover of some models, the AIR pipe and backpressure transducer* (see Chapter 6) *may have to be bent slightly to clear removal of the valve cover.* **Caution:** *Do not pry on the*

4.6b Valve cover bolt locations (arrows) - Oldsmobile-built V8 (valve cover removed for clarity)

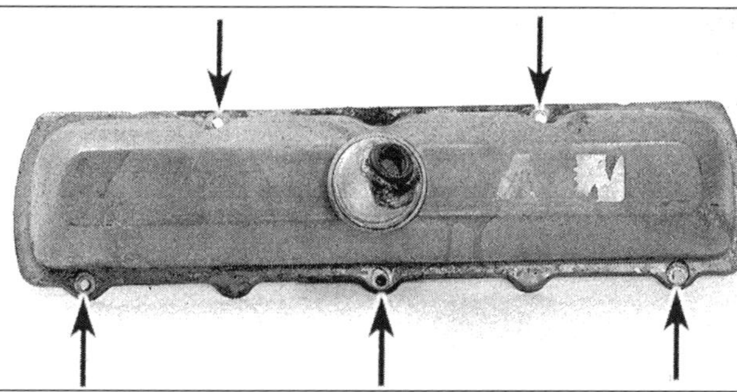

4.6c Valve cover bolt locations (arrows) - big Cadillac V8 (368, 425 and 500)

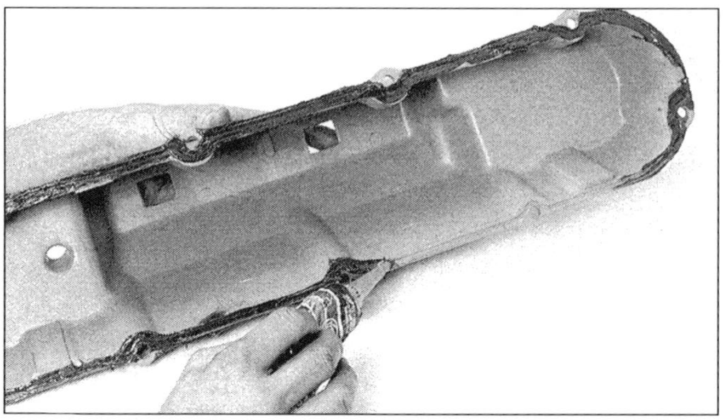

4.9 Install a new valve cover gasket if one was used before, otherwise apply a bead of RTV around the cleaned cover

5.3a Unbolt the rocker arms from the cylinder head - this is an Oldsmobile engine with two rocker arms connected by a common bridge for support

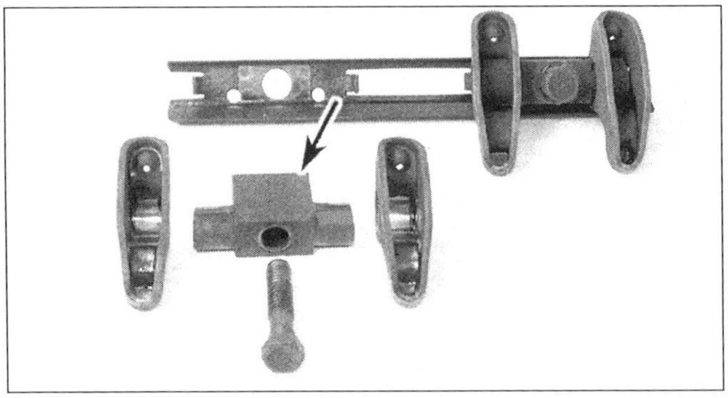

5.3b On 425 and 500 Cadillac V8s, the rocker arms are grouped in pairs on a shaft-like support pedestal (arrow) - two pairs of rockers are assembled with a rocker arm retainer plate beneath them, so each head has two retainer plates

5.3c The HT4100 Cadillac V8 has all of the rocker arms bolted to a support, held to the head studs by five nuts (arrows) and four bolts - remove the nuts/bolts and take the rockers out as an assembly

5.4a Unbolt the valve actuation solenoids (arrows) before removing the rocker arms on V8-6-4 engines

sealing flange. To do so may damage the surface, causing oil leaks. Tap on the sides of the cover with a rubber mallet until it pops loose. The covers on the V8-6-4 engine are plastic; use care in removal.

8 Thoroughly clean the mating surfaces, removing all traces of old gasket material. Use acetone or lacquer thinner and a clean rag to remove any traces of oil.

9 Prepare the cover for installation by applying a continuous bead of RTV sealant **(see illustration)** or a new gasket to the sealing flange. Use the same sealing method the vehicle had, otherwise new bolts of a different length may be required.

10 Install the cover(s) and bolts and tighten them to the torque listed in this Chapter's Specifications. Do not overtighten them, as the covers may be deformed.

11 Reinstall the remaining parts in the reverse order of removal.

12 Run the engine and check for leaks.

5 Rocker arms and pushrods - removal, inspection and installation

Removal

Refer to illustrations 5.3a, 5.3b, 5.3c, 5.4a, 5.4b and 5.5

1 Refer to Section 4 and detach the valve cover(s) from the cylinder head(s).

2 Remove each of the rocker arm bolts or nuts. Place them in order in a cardboard box or rack.

3 Remove each rocker arm assembly, placing each component on the numbered box or rack, or number the components with paint before removal **(see illustrations)**. **Note:** *On HT4100 engines, remove the rocker arm support retaining nuts and bolts (loosen them evenly) and lift the rocker arms and support as a single unit* **(see illustration)**. *The rocker arms can be unbolted and removed from the support for individual replacement if necessary. Be sure to mark each rocker arm pivot Left or Right to insure proper installation.*

4 On the Cadillac V8-6-4, the valve actuation solenoids are on top of the rocker assembly **(see illustrations)**. On the left side of the engine the solenoids are on the two middle cylinders, while solenoids are on the two end cylinders on the right side. Unbolt the solenoids before removing the rockers.

5 Remove the pushrods and store them in order to make sure they don't get mixed up during installation **(see illustration)**.

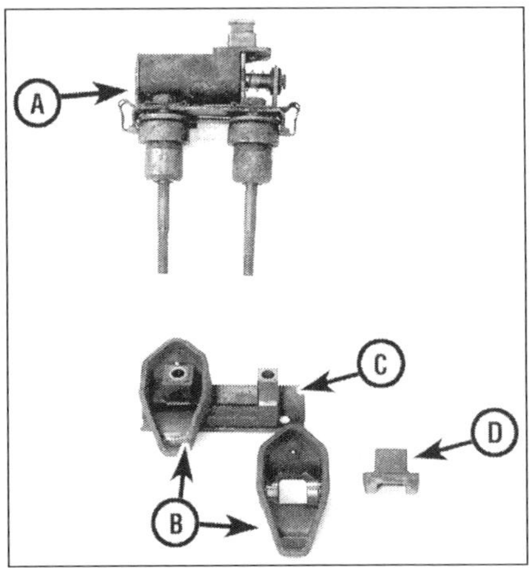

5.4b Keep the valve actuation solenoids (A) together with the rocker arms (B), stands (C) and pivots (D)

5.5 Pull the pushrods out and store them in order so they can be reinstalled in the same locations

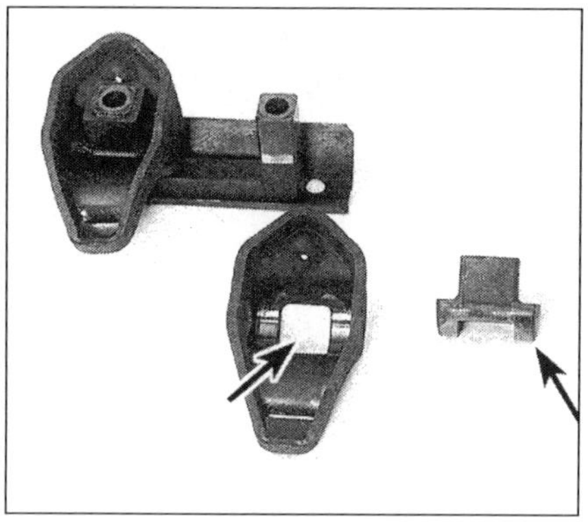

5.8a Inspect the pivots and wear surfaces of the rocker arms (arrows) - 368 Cadillac V8 shown, others similar

Inspection

Refer to illustrations 5.8a, 5.8b and 5.8c

6 Check each rocker arm for wear, cracks and other damage, especially where the pushrods and valve stems contact the rocker arm faces.

6.1a Use a valve spring compressor to compress the spring far enough to remove the keepers with a small magnet - HT4100 V8 shown

6.1b Valve seals can be installed with an appropriate-size deep socket - tap them down just until they seat on the valve guide

5.8b Pay particular attention to the rocker arms closest to the EGR passage (arrows) at the center of the head - these tend to show more rapid wear - 350 Oldsmobile-built V8 shown

7 Make sure the hole at the pushrod end of each rocker arm is open.

8 Check each rocker arm pivot area for wear, cracks and galling. If the rocker arms are worn or damaged, replace them with new ones and use new pivots as well **(see illustrations)**.

9 Inspect the pushrods for cracks and excessive wear at the ends. Roll each pushrod across a piece of plate glass to see if it's bent (if it wobbles, it's bent).

Installation

Refer to illustration 5.12

10 Lubricate the lower end of each pushrod with clean engine oil or moly-base grease and install them in their original locations. Make sure each pushrod seats completely in the lifter.

11 Apply moly-base grease to the ends of the valve stems and the upper ends of the pushrods before positioning the rocker arms over the studs.

12 Set the rocker arms in place, then install the pivots and bolts. Apply moly-base grease to the pivots to prevent damage to the mating surfaces before engine oil pressure builds up **(see illustration)**.

13 The balance of the assembly is the reverse of the disassembly process. Start the engine and check for leaks and valvetrain noise.

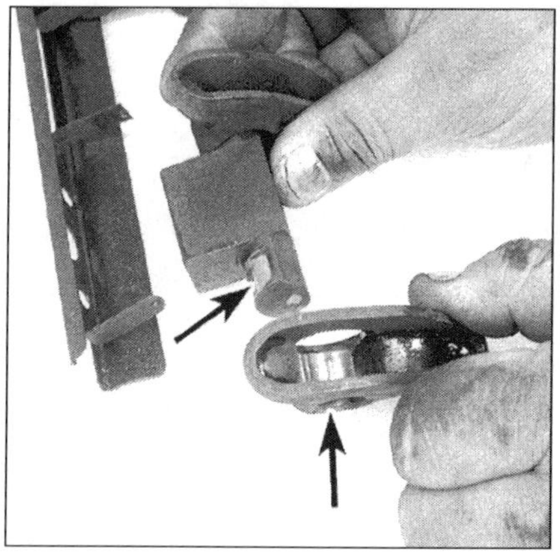

5.8c On 500 and 425 Cadillac V8s, check these areas for wear after cleaning the components

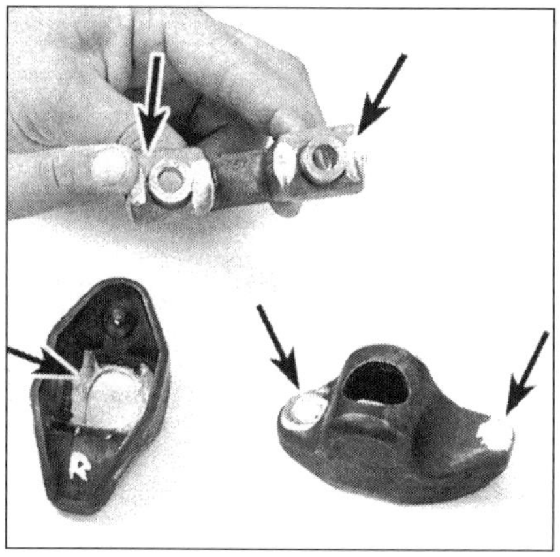

5.12 Apply moly-based lubricant to the wear points (arrows) of the rocker arm components before reassembly

6 Valve spring, retainer and seals - replacement in vehicle

Refer to illustrations 6.1a, 6.1b, 6.1c and 6.1d

Refer to Chapter 2, Part A, for this procedure. Remove the valve covers, rocker arms and pushrods following the appropriate Sections in this Chapter. Refer to the **illustrations in this Section** for variances in V8 seals and valve assemblies.

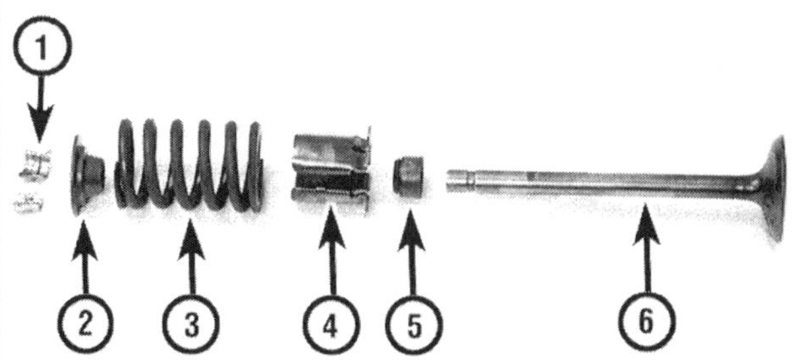

6.1c Relationship of Cadillac HT4100 valve components:

1. *Keepers*
2. *Retainer*
3. *Valve spring*
4. *Valve spring damper*
5. *Intake valve seal*
6. *Intake valve*

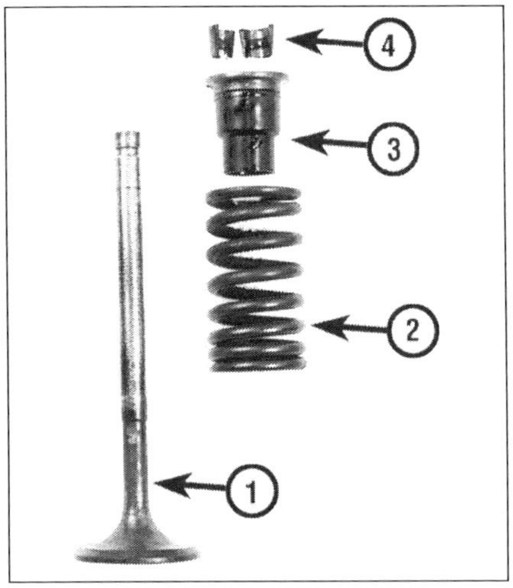

6.1d Relationship of Cadillac 500 and 425 valve components:

1 *Valve*
2 *Valve spring*
3 *Retainer/damper*
4 *Keepers*

7 Intake manifold - removal and installation

Removal

All except HT4100

Refer to illustrations 7.9 and 7.11

1 Disconnect the cable from the negative terminal of the battery.

2 Drain the cooling system (see Chapter 1).

3 Remove the air cleaner assembly.

4 Detach all coolant hoses from the intake manifold.

5 Label and then disconnect any wiring and vacuum, emission and/or fuel lines which attach to the intake manifold. On models with Multi-Port Fuel Injection, detach the injector wires and remove the injectors and fuel rail (see Chapter 4B).

6 Remove the EGR valve, if necessary (see Chapter 6).

7 On engines with the distributor mounted through the manifold, remove the distributor (see Chapter 5). On engines with the distributor in front of the manifold, you may be able to simply remove the distributor cap only, and, by angling the manifold rearward during removal, clear the distributor.

8 Remove the carburetor or throttle body unit (see Chapter 4A).

9 Remove the intake manifold bolts and any brackets, noting their locations, so they may be reinstalled in the same locations **(see illustration)**.

10 Lift off the manifold. If it is difficult to break loose, carefully pry against a casting protrusion. **Caution:** *Do not pry against a sealing surface.* **Note:** *If your engine has a valley cover under the intake manifold, this must be removed to access the valve lifters. Unbolt the cover and lift it out.*

7.9 Remove the engine lifting brackets and throttle linkage mount (arrows), then remove the intake-to-head bolts

7.11 Remove the one-piece, sheetmetal intake manifold gasket and valley cover, then clean the manifold mounting surfaces on the heads

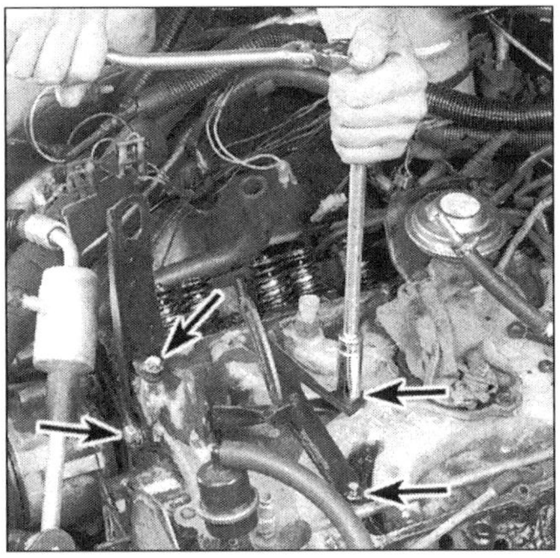

7.15 On the HT4100, unbolt the engine lifting brackets (arrows to bolts) - there is one more bracket at the rear of the engine

7.17 Remove the throttle linkage bracket (arrow) on the left side of the manifold

11 Stuff rags in the exposed ports and passages. Thoroughly clean all sealing surfaces, removing all traces of gasket material **(see illustration)**. Check the exhaust crossover passages in the manifold and the cylinder heads for carbon blockage.

HT4100

Refer to illustrations 7.15, 7.17 and 7.18

12 Follow steps 1 through 8.

13 Refer to Section 4 and remove the valve covers, then refer to Section 5 and remove the rocker arms and rocker arm supports as an assembly.

14 Refer to Chapter 3 for thermostat removal and installation procedures. Unbolt the thermostat housing from the water pump and lift it off as an assembly with the intake manifold.

15 Remove the intake manifold bolts that go through the front and rear engine lifting brackets, then loosen the lower bracket bolts to lean the brackets away from the intake manifold **(see illustration)**.

16 Refer to Chapter 5 and remove the distributor, with the engine set to TDC (see Section 3).

17 Unbolt the air conditioning compressor and move it, without disconnecting the refrigerant lines. Unbolt the throttle linkage bracket at the left rear of the manifold **(see illustration)**.

18 There are four lengths of intake manifold bolts on this engine. Identify and mark each of the 16 intake manifold bolts as to exact

7.18 Pry evenly at the front and rear of the HT4100 intake manifold - there are large dowels locating the manifold (arrow indicates the front dowel)

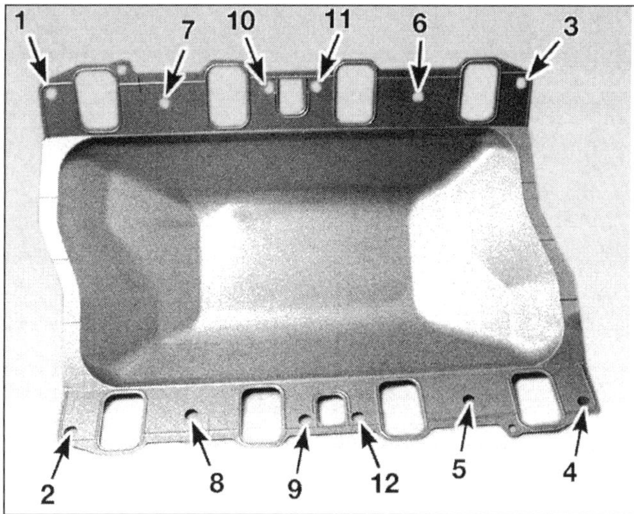

7.23 Intake manifold bolt tightening sequence - Oldsmobile and big Cadillac V8s

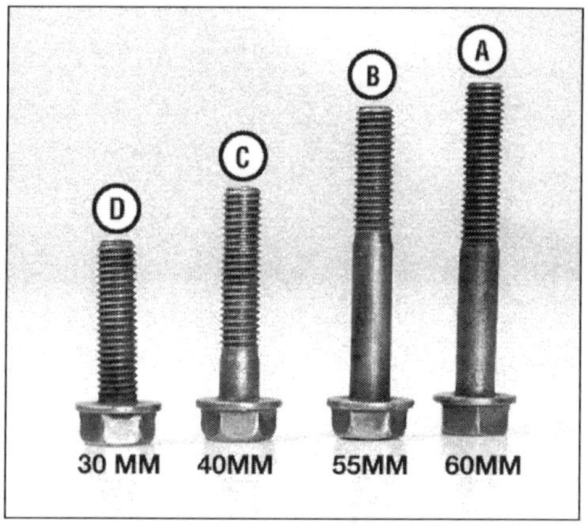

7.29a There are four lengths of intake bolts on the HT4100 engine - keep track of their locations

location upon removal, to aid in later assembly. When all of the bolts are removed, pry up the intake manifold at the ends. **Note:** *The intake manifold fits over a large dowel pin at each end of the block. When prying the manifold off, pry at both ends at the same time to pry the manifold straight up off the dowels* **(see illustration)**.

Installation

All except HT4100

Refer to illustration 7.23

19 Clean the gasket surfaces of the intake manifold with a scraper followed by lacquer thinner or brake system cleaner. If the manifold was equipped with an EGR valve, clean any carbon buildup from the EGR passages with carburetor spray cleaner, using a screwdriver, drill bit or lengths of coat-hanger wire to chip out hard carbon. Make sure the whole passage is clear.

20 Position new gaskets and ridge seals, using RTV sealant in the corners to hold them in place. Use plastic gasket retainers, if provided. Follow the gasket manufacturer's instructions and markings such as "UP", "TOP" or "FRONT".

21 The sheetmetal main gasket should be coated on both sides of the intake port area with Gaskacinch or Coppercoat brush-on sealant. Set it onto the engine, locating it over the dowels in the cylinder heads. The end gaskets should be glued to the block, with the ends tucking into the pockets at the ends of the cylinder heads. Where the end gaskets and the metal gasket meet, apply a small dab of RTV sealant and a thin coat along the top surfaces that face the manifold.

22 Set the manifold into position. Be sure all the bolt holes are lined up and start all the bolts by hand before tightening any of them (lightly oil the threads of the bolts before installation). Remember which bolts the engine lift brackets go under.

23 Tighten the bolts in three stages in the appropriate sequence **(see illustration)** until the torque listed in this Chapter's Specifications is reached. **Note:** *Some engines don't have a specific tightening sequence. If the tightening sequence for your engine isn't shown, tighten the bolts in a similar sequence, in three stages, to the torque listed in this Chapter's Specifications.*

24 Proceed to Step 31.

HT4100

Refer to illustrations 7.29a, 7.29b and 7.30

25 Thoroughly clean the O-ring seating areas of the intake manifold, thermostat housing and water pump, then install new, greased O-rings on the intake manifold end of the thermostat housing and the thermostat housing end of the water pump (see Chapter 3). Push the thermostat housing into the front of the intake manifold.

26 Install the side gaskets with their locating pins registering in the holes in the cylinder heads. **Caution:** *There are LEFT and RIGHT side gaskets for the 1984 and 1985 models. The right-side gasket has a restrictor that controls exhaust crossover flow to the intake manifold, and should be marked "RIGHT BANK". The left-side gasket has a tab that will stick out from the front if installed on the wrong side. If the restrictor gasket is not used on the right side, you could experience driveability problems.*

27 Attach the rubber end seals to the block with gasket cement, then coat the tops with a thin coat of RTV sealant, with a dab of RTV at the corners where they meet the side gaskets.

28 Lower the intake manifold carefully to align it with the dowels at the front and rear of the block. **Caution:** *Make sure the thermostat housing goes over the water pump. With the thermostat cover and thermostat out, you can look through the housing to make sure the O-ring is placed properly.*

29 Install the intake manifold bolts. The HT4100 engine uses three or four different length intake manifold-to-cylinder head bolts **(see illustration)**. To determine which intake manifold-to-cylinder head bolts to use, look for an identifying mark on the intake manifold next to the manifold air temperature sensor, then refer to the chart below **(see illustration)**. **Warning:** *If the incorrect bolts are used, coolant leaks or stripped threads may result.*

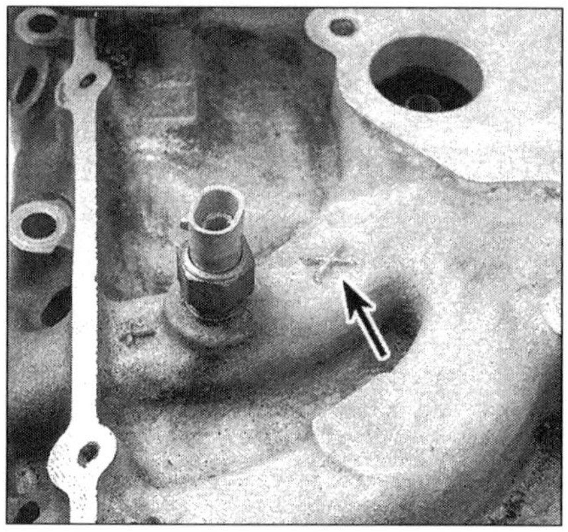

7.29b Look for a mark like this (arrow) to identify which HT4100 intake manifold you have

No mark

This is the 1982 manifold which uses 3 bolt sizes as follows:

40 mm bolt (C) ..... Bolt locations 1, 2, 3, 4, 12, 13 and 16
30 mm bolt (D)...... Bolt locations 5, 6, 7, 8, 9, 10, 11 and 14
60 mm bolt (A)...... Bolt location 15

X mark

This manifold uses four bolt sizes as follows:

55 mm bolt (B)...... Bolt locations 1, 2, 3 4 and 12
30 mm bolt (D)...... Bolt locations 5, 6, 7, and 8
40 mm bolt (C) ..... Bolt locations 9, 10, 11, 14 and 16
60 mm bolt (A)...... Bolt locations 13 and 15

Circle with an X inside

This manifold uses the same bolt locations as the X manifold except for bolt location 12

55 mm bolt (B)...... Bolt location 12

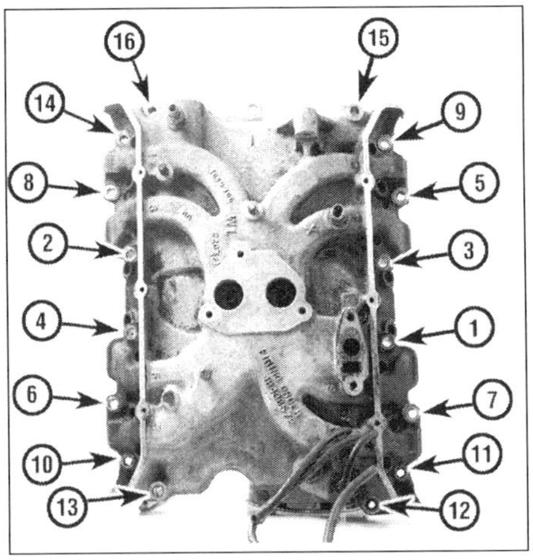

7.30 Intake manifold bolt tightening sequence - HT4100 V8

30 Tighten the bolts in three stages, following the appropriate sequence **(see illustrations)** until the specified torque is reached.

All engines

31 The remainder of installation is the reverse of removal. Be sure to refill the cooling system and change the oil and filter (see Chapter 1), as coolant often gets into the oil during manifold removal.

32 Run the engine and check for fluid and vacuum leaks. Adjust the ignition timing, if the distributor was disturbed (see Chapter 1). Road test the vehicle, checking for proper operation of engine and accessories.

8 Exhaust manifolds - removal and installation

Refer to illustrations 8.7a, 8.7b, 8.8a, 8.8b, 8.9a and 8.9b

Removal

1 Allow the engine to cool completely.

2 Place protective covers on the fenders.

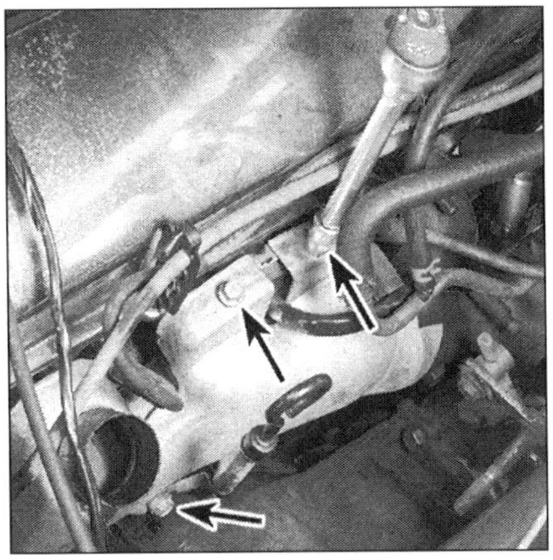

8.7a Remove these three bolts on the HT4100 to remove the heat shield and move the oil dipstick tube

8.7b Two stud nuts (arrows) retain the heat shield on Cadillac 500 and 425 engines

3 Disconnect the negative cable from the battery.

4 Raise the vehicle and support it securely on jackstands.

5 Spray penetrating oil on the threads of fasteners holding the hot air shrouds and the exhaust pipe(s) to the manifold(s) you wish to remove. Go on to the next steps, allowing the penetrating oil to soak in.

6 Remove the air cleaner and hot air duct.

7 Detach the heat shield(s) from the manifold **(see illustrations)**.

8 Label and then remove the spark plug wires (only if they are in the way) and any hoses such as EFE or AIR, as needed **(see illustration)**. On models so equipped (most 1980 and later models), remove the oxygen sensor from the exhaust manifold (see Chapter 6). **Note:** *On some models, a brace for the shift linkage is bolted to the left exhaust manifold and must be removed* **(see illustration)**.

9 Unbolt any engine accessories which block access to the manifold(s) such as the alternator, air conditioning compressor or power steering pump **(see illustrations)**. Refer to the appropriate Chapters (5, 3, 10) for further information. When unbolting the air conditioning compressor, leave the refrigerant lines connected and tie the compressor aside without putting a strain on the fittings. **Warning:** *Do not disconnect any air conditioning line or fitting unless the system pressure has been discharged by a qualified air conditioning technician.*

8.8a On models so equipped, unbolt the AIR injection tube bolts (arrows) from the exhaust manifold - HT4100 shown

8.8b On models with a shift linkage bracket on the left exhaust manifold, remove these 2 nuts (arrows)

8.9a On some Oldsmobile-built V8s, remove this brace from the alternator to the exhaust manifold (arrows indicate nuts)

8.9b On the right side of this HT4100, the diverter valve assembly (upper arrow) is bolted to the same exhaust studs as the AIR tubes (lower arrows)

9.3 Use large breaker bar and a heavy-duty socket on the crankshaft bolt - make sure the engine is securely held at the flywheel while removing this highly-torqued bolt

9.4 Use a bolt-on type puller to remove the damper hub from the crankshaft

9.5 Use a screwdriver or seal removal tool to pull out the front seal, being careful not to nick the crankshaft surface

9.7 Use an appropriate-size socket to drive the new seal squarely into the front cover, to the same depth as the original seal

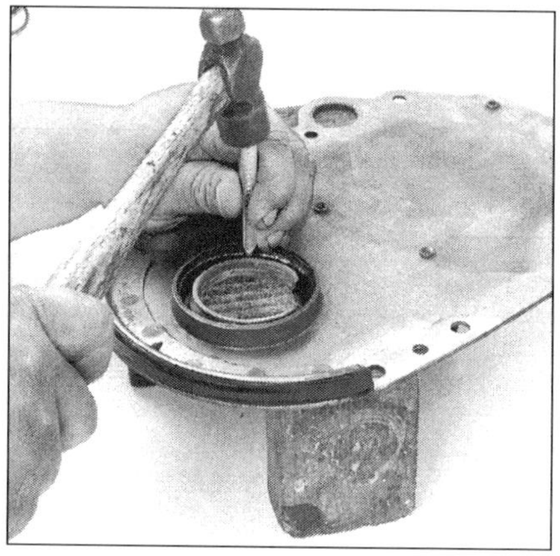

9.8 Support the front cover on wood blocks and drive the seal out from the backside with a hammer and punch - don't distort the seal bore

10 Bend back any lock tabs from the manifold bolt heads and remove the manifold-to-exhaust pipe fasteners. Keep track of the locations of any stud/nut fasteners.

11 Remove the manifold(s) from the engine compartment.

Installation

12 Thoroughly clean and inspect the sealing surfaces, removing all traces of old gasket material. Look for cracks and damaged threads. If the gasket was leaking, take the manifold to an automotive machine shop to inspect/correct for warpage.

13 If replacing the manifold, transfer all parts to the new unit. Using new gaskets (where applicable), install the manifold and start the bolts by hand. **Note:** *On HT4100 engines, be sure to apply a thin layer of graphite dry film lubricant to the exhaust manifold and cylinder head mating surfaces to prevent the exhaust manifold from cracking. On the left side, use graphite on both sides of the inner heat shield, which mounts between the cylinder head and the manifold.*

14 Working from the center outward, tighten the bolts to the torque listed in this Chapter's Specifications. Bend the lock tabs (if equipped) against the bolt heads.

15 Reinstall the remaining components in the reverse order of removal.

16 Run the engine and check for exhaust leaks.

9 Crankshaft front oil seal - replacement

Timing cover in place

Refer to illustrations 9.3, 9.4, 9.5 and 9.7

1 Drain the engine coolant and remove the drivebelts (see Chapter 1).

2 Remove the fan shroud and radiator fan (see Chapter 3).

3 Remove the bolts from the crankshaft pulley (a screwdriver can be used to lock the starter ring gear on the driveplate so the crankshaft won't rotate), then detach the pulley. On Oldsmobile-built engines, remove the vibration damper-to-crankshaft bolt **(see illustration)**. **Warning:** *This bolt is torqued to considerable pressure. It will take lots of leverage and force to remove it unless you have an air-powered impact wrench. Be certain that the engine is securely locked from turning, such as with an assistant wedging a prybar into the driveplate, while you use both hands and a long breaker bar to loosen the bolt. You may even have to use a length of pipe over the breaker bar handle to achieve enough leverage. Make sure you hands are not going to hit anything when the bolt does break loose.*

4 Attach a puller to the damper and draw it off the crankshaft. Be careful not to drop it as it comes free. A common gear puller should not be used - it may separate the outer portion of the damper from the hub. Use only a puller that bolts to the hub **(see illustration)**. **Note 1:** *On some Cadillac engines there is a plug at the front of the crankshaft. Remove it before installing the damper puller.*

Note 2: *On Oldsmobile engines, the threaded hole for the damper bolt is quite large, larger than the front end of most damper removal tools. An adapter or spacer will have to be used to prevent the front of the tool from ruining the threads in the crankshaft.*

5 Carefully pull the seal out of the cover with a seal removal tool **(see illustration)** or pry it out with a large screwdriver. Be careful not to distort the cover or scratch the wall of the seal bore (cover the screwdriver tip with electrical tape to avoid nicking the crankshaft). It's a good idea to apply penetrating oil to the seal-to-cover joint and allow it to soak in before attempting to pull the seal out.

6 Clean the bore to remove any old seal material and corrosion. Position the new seal in the bore with the open end of the seal facing IN. A small amount of oil applied to the outer edge of the new seal will make installation easier.

7 Drive the seal squarely into the bore with a large socket and hammer until it's completely seated **(see illustration)**. Select a socket that's the same outside diameter as the seal (a section of pipe can be used if a socket isn't available). **Caution:** *If the crankshaft has a Woodruff key in place, the socket used must be big enough in diameter to clear the key while driving on the seal.*

9.10 Use a block of wood to squarely drive in the new seal

Timing cover removed

Refer to illustrations 9.8 and 9.10

8 Use a punch or screwdriver and hammer to drive the seal out of the cover from the back side. Support the cover as close to the seal bore as possible **(see illustration)**. Be careful not to distort the cover or scratch the wall of the seal bore. If the engine has accumulated a lot of miles, apply penetrating oil to the seal-to-cover joint on each side and allow it to soak in before attempting to drive the seal out.

9 Clean the bore to remove any old seal material and corrosion. Support the cover on blocks of wood and position the new seal in the bore with the open end of the seal facing IN. A small amount of oil applied to the outer edge of the new seal will make installation easier.

10 Drive the seal into the bore with a wood block and hammer until it's completely seated **(see illustration)**.

Balancer installation

11 On all models, make sure the keyway on the hub is lined up with the key in the crankshaft.

12 On Oldsmobile engines, apply lubricant to the outer seal surface of the balancer, and apply a thin coating of RTV sealant to the crankshaft key and the inner surface of the balancer before drawing on the balancer with an installation tool, available at most auto parts stores. After drawing on the balancer as far as the tool can go, remove the installer and insert the crankshaft bolt and washer and torque to Specifications. **Note:** *Have an assistant hold the driveplate from turning while you apply the torque to the balancer bolt.*

13 On Cadillac engines, use an installer tool only to get the hub far enough onto the crankshaft to be able to install and tighten a balancer-to-crankshaft bolt and washer (not a stock Cadillac part; use a grade-eight bolt). Tighten the bolt to 125 foot pounds, and then remove the bolt and washer. **Note:** *On the HT4100 engine, the balancer hub is a press-fit on the crankshaft. When reinstalling it, use anti-seize lubricant on the crankshaft snout. When the hub has been pulled on far enough, it will bottom out on the crankshaft, then remove the installer and reinstall the crankshaft plug.*

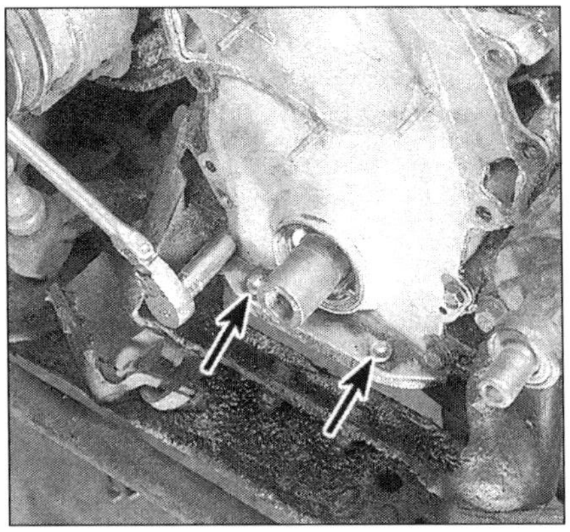

10.8 Remove the front cover bolts and pull off the cover - the front pan bolts must be loosened (arrows indicate the two pan bolts that must be removed on HT4100 engines)

10 Front cover, timing chain and sprockets - removal and installation

Removal

Refer to illustrations 10.8, 10.10, 10.11, 10.12a, 10.12b, 10.13 and 10.14

1 Disconnect the negative cable from the battery.

2 Remove the alternator and brackets as well as the distributor on Cadillac engines (see Chapter 5).

3 Drain the cooling system and disconnect the radiator hoses, heater hose (where applicable) and the small by-pass hose (where applicable). **Note:** *The factory recommends removing the oil pan completely to replace the gaskets when removing the front cover. However, on 1978 and earlier models, oil pan removal requires that the engine be removed from the chassis. The following procedure involves loosening the front bolts of the oil pan and prying the front cover off with the pan still on the engine. To avoid leaks, this requires care in reassembly with gaskets and sealant.*

4 Remove the radiator support, the fan shroud, the fan and pulley and the radiator (see Chapter 3). **Note:** *On some models it is necessary to remove the staples that secure the upper portion of the fan shroud to the lower portion in order to remove the assembly. Most later models have a one-piece fan shroud.*

5 Remove the crankshaft pulley and the vibration damper (see Section 9).

6 Remove the water pump (see Chapter 3). On carbureted models, refer to Chapter 4A and remove the fuel pump. Unbolt and set aside the AIR pump and bracket, and air conditioning compressor and bracket, as applicable, without disconnecting any hoses or lines.

7 On models which have the front engine mount cradle attached with front cover bolts, support the engine from above with a hoist and remove the engine mount bracket at the front cover.

10.10 Remove the camshaft bolt(s) and, if equipped, the fuel pump eccentric (arrow)

8 Remove the nuts and bolts that attach the cover to the engine, then pull the cover free **(see illustration)**. If it's stuck, knock it loose with a hammer and a wood block. Don't pry between the mating surfaces, or oil leaks may result. **Note:** *Loosen the front four oil pan bolts on each side to ease removal and installation of the front cover on Oldsmobile and Cadillac engines, except the HT4100 Cadillac engine which has two bolts joining the front cover to the oil pan.*

9 Using locking pliers, pull the dowel pins (if equipped) out of the engine block. Grind a chamfer on one end of each pin. This will make installation of the cover easier. Thoroughly clean all gasket mating surfaces (do not allow the old gasket material to fall into the oil pan), then wipe them with a cloth soaked in solvent. Clean sealant and gasket material from the exposed front edges of the oil pan.

10 If equipped, remove the fuel pump drive eccentric by unscrewing the bolt from the end of the camshaft **(see illustration)**. Some models with fuel injection still may have a fuel pump eccentric, even though they do not have a mechanical fuel pump.

11 If equipped, slide the oil slinger off of the end of the crankshaft **(see illustration)**.

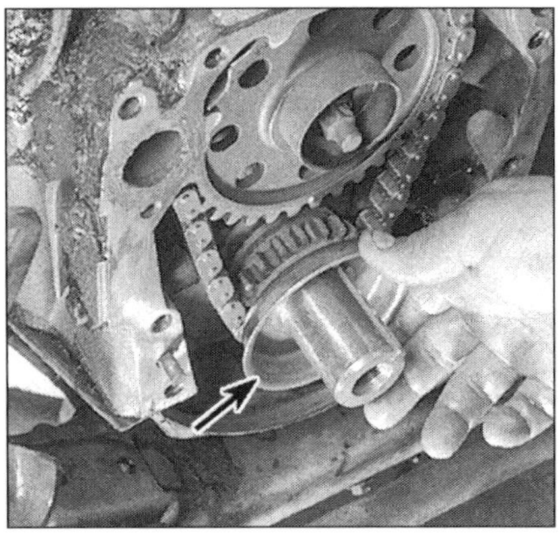

10.11 Slide the oil slinger from the crankshaft, noting which way it was installed

10.12a TDC timing gear marks - big Cadillac engines

10.12b TDC timing gear marks - HT4100 engines

10.13 Remove the camshaft sprocket bolt(s) and take the timing chain and camshaft sprocket out together

10.14 Most crankshaft sprockets will come off with gentle prying with two screwdrivers, but some may require a puller to remove

10.17 If a new timing chain set is installed, the new crankshaft sprocket may have to be tapped on with a large socket and hammer - make sure the keyway is aligned and that the socket doesn't hit the Woodruff key

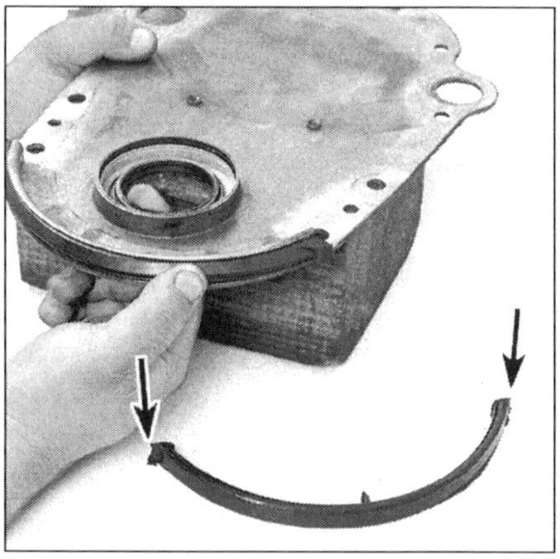

10.23a On all but the HT4100 engines (which are sealed to the pan with RTV), cut off 1/8-inch from each end of the pan seal (arrows) and glue it to the bottom of the front cover

12 Turn the crankshaft until the marks on the camshaft and crankshaft sprockets are perfectly aligned **(see illustrations)**. DO NOT attempt to remove either sprocket or the chain until this is done. Also, do not turn the camshaft or the crankshaft after the sprockets are removed.

13 Remove the bolt(s) or nut that attach(es) the sprocket to the end of the camshaft **(see illustration)**.

14 Generally speaking, the camshaft sprocket and the timing chain can be slipped off the crankshaft sprocket together. If resistance is encountered, it may be necessary to use two screwdrivers to carefully pry the sprocket off of the camshaft. If resistance is encountered on a crankshaft sprocket, a gear puller will be required **(see illustration)**.

15 If the crankshaft and the camshaft are not disturbed while the timing chain and sprockets are out of place, then installation can begin with Step 17. If the engine is completely dismantled, or if the crankshaft or camshaft are disturbed while the timing chain is off, then the engine must be positioned at TDC before the timing chain and sprockets are installed (see Section 3).

Installation

Refer to illustrations 10.17, 10.23a, 10.23b and 10.23c

16 Align the hole in the camshaft sprocket with the dowel pin in the end of the camshaft, then slip the sprocket onto the end of the camshaft. **Note:** *When the camshaft and crankshaft timing marks are aligned, the engine is positioned at TDC compression for cylinder number 6 (Oldsmobile-built engines), cylinder number 4 (Cadillac big V8 engines) and cylinder number 1 (Cadillac HT4100 engine).*

17 Slip the crankshaft sprocket onto the end of the crankshaft (make sure the key and keyway are properly aligned), then turn the crankshaft until the timing mark on the sprocket is pointed straight up (all engines) **(see illustration)**. **Caution:** *On Oldsmobile engines where the keyway slopes up at the engine end of the groove, install the crankshaft gear first without the key in place. Then turn the gear to line up the keyway in the gear and install the key, but only as far in as it was originally installed. With a tight new gear being installed, driving over an in-place key may force the key up at the back of the groove and possibly fracture the gear.*

18 Next, lay the chain over the camshaft sprocket. Slip the other end of the chain under the crankshaft sprocket (keep the timing marks aligned as this is done) and reinstall the camshaft sprocket.

19 Install the fasteners that attach the sprocket to the camshaft, then recheck the alignment of the timing marks.

20 Tighten the camshaft sprocket fastener(s) to the torque listed in this Chapter's Specifications.

21 Be sure to clean the mating surfaces of the front cover and cylinder block, and install a new gasket. **Note:** *Where equipped, be sure to reinstall the oil slinger on the crankshaft before installing the front cover.*

22 Cut off the excess gasket material at the front of the oil pan until it is flush with the engine block.

23 Using a razor knife, trim about 1/8-inch from each end of the new front pan seal and glue it into the groove in the bottom of the front cover with weatherstripping cement

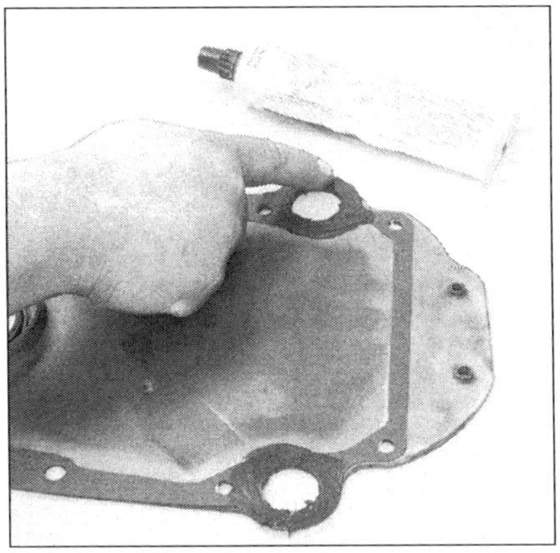

10.23b Glue a new cover gasket to the back of the cover and apply RTV around the water pump passages

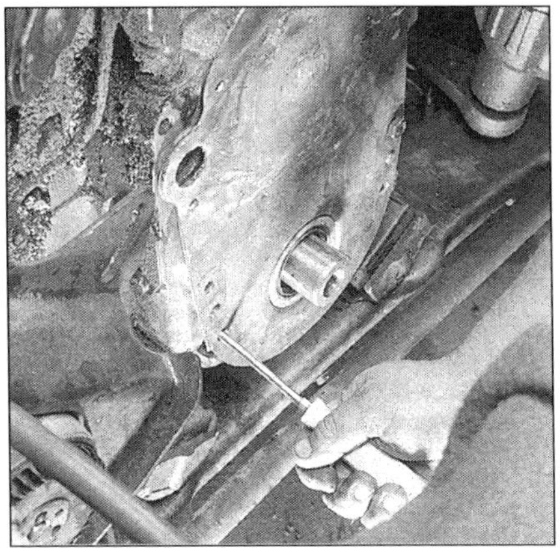

10.23c The cover must be forced down against the pan, compressing the seal, to align the bolt holes - use screwdrivers through two of the lower holes to align the cover holes until two upper bolts can be installed

11.3 Most lifters can be removed with a mechanic's magnet (shown); otherwise use pliers but replace the lifters with new ones

(see illustrations). When this is dry, coat the front of the oil pan, especially where the oil pan meets the block, with RTV sealant and push the front cover back into place, pushing down against the pan and back against the block until the bolt holes line up and the cover bolts can be started. Rotate the cover back and forth and guide the bottom of the cover in using a small screwdriver **(see illustration)**. Feel around the bottom joint between the pan and the cover to make sure the seal hasn't pushed out of place.

24 Apply engine oil to the bolt threads and loosely install two of the bolts to hold the cover in place. Tighten the front oil pan bolts that were loosened for cover removal.

25 Install the dowel pins, chamfered end first, into the engine block.

26 Install the water pump with a new gasket (if removed from cover).

27 Tighten all bolts to the proper torque listed in this Chapter's Specifications and install all components in the reverse order of removal. Apply lubricant to the front hub seal before installing the crankshaft hub (see Section 9).

11 Camshaft and lifters - removal, inspection and installation

Refer to illustrations 11.3 and 11.5

1 Before beginning this procedure, have the air conditioning system discharged so the condenser can be removed. **Warning:** *The air conditioning system is under high pressure. DO NOT loosen any fittings or remove any components until after the system has been discharged. Air conditioning refrigerant should be properly discharged into an EPA-approved container at a dealer service department or an automotive air conditioning facility. Always wear eye protection when disconnecting air conditioning system fittings.* **Note:** *It is possible on some models to unbolt the condenser* (see Chapter 3) *and move it out of the way for camshaft removal (without discharging the refrigerant), but only if it can be done without kinking the refrigerant lines.*

Removal

2 Refer to the appropriate Sections and remove the intake manifold, the rocker arms, the pushrods and the timing chain and camshaft sprocket. The radiator and air conditioning condenser must be removed as well (see Chapter 3).

3 The lifters must be removed before removing the camshaft, and there are several ways to extract the lifters from the bores. A special tool designed to grip and remove lifters is manufactured by many tool companies and is widely available, but it may not be required in every case. On engines without a lot of varnish buildup, the lifters can often be removed with a small magnet or even with your fingers **(see illustration)**. A machinist's scribe with a bent end can be used to pull the lifters out by positioning the point under the retainer ring in the top of each lifter. **Caution:** *Do not use pliers to remove the lifters unless you intend to replace them with new ones (along with the camshaft). The pliers may damage the precision machined and hardened lifters.*

4 Before removing the lifters, arrange to store them in a clearly labeled box to ensure that they are reinstalled in their original locations. Remove the lifters and store them where they will not get dirty. Do not attempt to withdraw the camshaft with the lifters in place.

5 Refer to Sections 3 and 10, set the engine to TDC and remove the timing chain and camshaft sprocket. Thread a long bolt of the proper thread into one of the camshaft sprocket bolt holes to use as a handle when removing the camshaft from the block **(see illustration)**.

6 Carefully pull the camshaft out. Support the cam near the block so the lobes do not nick or gouge the bearings as it is withdrawn.

11.5 Thread a long bolt into the camshaft to aid in withdrawing the camshaft - proceed slowly, being careful not to nick the camshaft bearings in the block with the lobes or journals

Inspection

Camshaft and bearings

7 After the camshaft has been removed from the engine, cleaned with solvent and dried, inspect the bearing journals for uneven wear, pitting and evidence of seizure. If the journals are damaged, the bearing inserts in the block are probably damaged as well. Both the camshaft and bearings will have to be replaced.

8 Measure the bearing journals with a micrometer to determine if they are excessively worn or out-of-round. Camshaft lobe and journal measurement is covered in Part C of this Chapter.

9 Check the camshaft lobes for heat discoloration, score marks, chipped areas, pitting and uneven wear. If the lobes are in good condition and if the lobe lift measurements are as specified, the camshaft can be reused. Check the lobes for wear by measuring all the intake lobe heights with a micrometer. The shortest lobe should be no more than 0.005-inch shorter than the tallest. Make the same checks for the exhaust lobes.

11.15 The back of the engine block has a camshaft plug (arrow) - do not push the camshaft in hard enough to disturb this plug, or an oil leak will result

12.5a On some models (early Cadillac 500 shown) the cruise control canister must be unbolted (arrows) from the rear of the left cylinder head

12.5b On HT4100 engines, remove this vacuum-pump brace from the front of the left cylinder head

Lifters

Caution: *Do not unbolt and remove the lifter carrier assembly on the HT4100 engine. This will destroy the alignment of the lifter bores. Also, don't substitute an incorrect lifter on the HT4100 engine. These special lifters are designed for the valve system on the HT4100 only, and since other types fit the lifter bore, incorrect lifters can easily be installed.*

10 Clean the lifters with solvent and dry them thoroughly without mixing them up.

11 Check each lifter wall, pushrod seat and foot for scuffing, score marks and uneven wear. Each lifter foot (the surface that rides on the cam lobe) must be slightly convex, although this can be difficult to determine by eye (refer to Chapter 2, Part A for lifter inspection procedures). If the base of the lifter is concave, the lifters and camshaft must be replaced. If the lifter walls are damaged or worn (which is not very likely), inspect the lifter bores in the engine block as well. If the pushrod seats are worn, check the pushrod ends.

12 If new lifters are being installed, a new camshaft must also be installed. If a new camshaft is installed, use new lifters as well. Never install used lifters unless the original camshaft is used and the lifters can be installed in their original locations. **Caution:** *On HT4100 engines, do not use a reground or "rebuilt" camshaft. Use only a brand-new factory camshaft to ensure camshaft longevity.* **Note:** *Some engines may be factory-fitted with oversized lifters in some bores. The lifters and the block near their lifter bore is usually marked with an "O", which indicates a .010-inch-oversize lifter is required there.*

Bearing replacement

13 Camshaft bearing replacement requires special tools and expertise that place it outside the scope of the home mechanic. Take the engine block to an automotive machine shop to ensure that the job is done correctly.

Installation

Refer to illustration 11.15

14 Lubricate the camshaft bearing journals and cam lobes with camshaft installation lube.

15 Slide the camshaft into the engine. Support the cam near the block and be careful not to scrape or nick the bearings. **Caution:** *Do not push the camshaft any further into the block than is necessary. The camshaft plug at the rear of the block could be moved enough to create an oil leak* **(see illustration)**.

16 Refer to Section 10 and install the timing chain and sprockets.

17 Lubricate the lifters with clean engine oil and install them in the block. If the original lifters are being reinstalled, be sure to return them to their original locations. If a new camshaft is being installed, be sure to install new lifters as well.

18 The remaining installation steps are the reverse of removal.

19 Before starting and running the engine, change the oil and install a new oil filter (see Chapter 1).

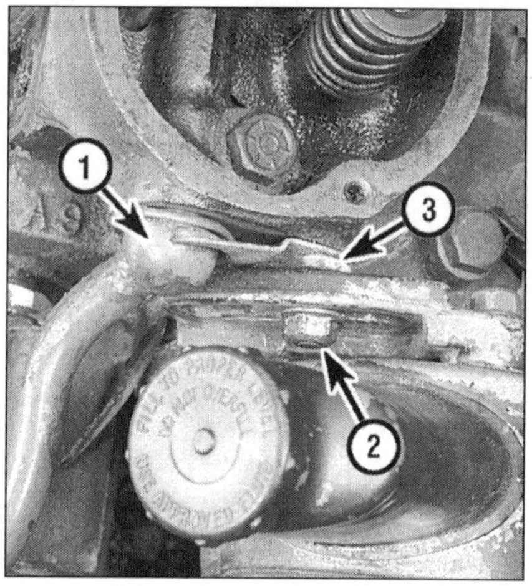

12.5c On some Cadillac V8s, there is an AIR tube (1) connected to the front of each cylinder head - to disconnect them, remove the power steering bracket nut (2), pull the pump away, then remove the stud (3) and the AIR tube clamp

12.5d Where the AIR tubes attach to the head, there are lead seals (arrow) - the seals can be reused if they aren't damaged

12 Cylinder heads - removal and installation

Caution: *The engine must be completely cool when the heads are removed. Failure to allow the engine to cool off could result in head warpage.*

Removal

Refer to illustrations 12.5a, 12.5b, 12.5c, 12.5d, 12.8, 12.9 and 12.11

1 Remove the intake manifold (see Section 7).

2 Remove the valve cover(s) as described in Section 4.

3 Remove the rocker arms and pushrods (see Section 5). On the HT4100 engine, remove the rocker arms and rocker arm supports as an assembly.

4 Remove the exhaust manifolds (see Section 8).

5 Unbolt the engine accessories and brackets as necessary and set them aside **(see illustrations)**. See Chapter 5 for alternator removal. When removing the power steering pump (see Chapter 10), leave the hoses

12.8 Use a deep socket to remove the inner row of head studs on the HT4100 engine

12.9 While the cylinder head is off of an HT4100 engine, a liner-holding tool must be bolted to the engine to keep the liners from moving and losing their O-ring seal

12.11 Scrape the block surface, vacuum up any debris, then clean the surface with lacquer thinner or brake cleaner and a clean rag

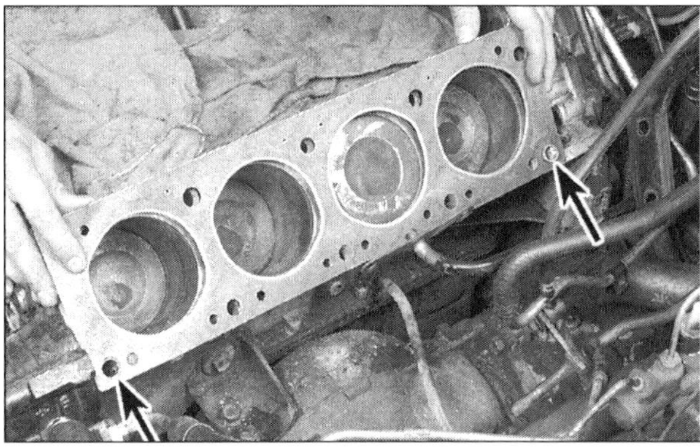

12.14 Install the new head gasket, locating it over the dowels (arrows) on the block

attached and secure the unit in an upright position. The refrigerant lines should remain attached to the air conditioning compressor (see Chapter 3). **Warning:** *The air conditioning system is under high pressure. Do not loosen any hose or fitting until the refrigerant has been discharged by an auto air-conditioning technician.*

6 Recheck to be sure nothing is still connected to the head(s) you intend to remove, including ground wires bolted to the heads, temperature senders or engine lifting brackets.

7 Using a new gasket, outline the cylinders and bolt pattern on a piece of cardboard. Be sure to indicate the front of the engine for reference. Punch holes at the bolt locations.

8 Loosen the head bolts in 1/4-turn increments until they can be removed by hand. Work from bolt to bolt in a pattern that's the reverse of the tightening sequence **(see illustrations 12.17a and 12.17b)**. Store the bolts in the cardboard holder as they are removed; this will insure the bolts are reinstalled in their original holes. **Note 1:** *The top (inner) row of head bolts on the HT4100 engine are studs, which will require a deep socket for removal* **(see illustration)**. **Note 2:** *On V8-6-4 Cadillac engines, the rearmost head bolt on the right cylinder head may not have room for complete withdrawal. Pull the bolt up until its threads are clear of the block (about 7/8-inch up) and apply duct tape to hold the bolt at this height. Remove the head with this bolt in place.*

9 Lift the head(s) off the engine. If excessive resistance is felt, do not pry between the head and block as damage to the mating surfaces may result. To dislodge the head, place a block of wood against the end of it and strike the wood with a hammer, or pry on a casting protrusion. Store the head(s) on their sides to prevent damage to the gasket surface. **Note:** *On HT4100 engines, install a cylinder liner holder, available at most auto parts stores, to the engine block to prevent the liners from shifting in the event the engine is turned over or disturbed* **(see illustration)**. **Caution:** *If the HT4100 engine is turned over while the cylinder heads are removed, the iron cylinder bore liners may lose their sealing at the O-rings in the block, causing water leaks later.*

10 Cylinder head disassembly and inspection procedures are covered in detail in Chapter 2, Part C.

11 Use a gasket scraper to remove all traces of carbon and old gasket material, then clean the mating surfaces with lacquer thinner or acetone or brake system cleaner **(see illustration)**. If there's oil on the mating surfaces when the heads are installed, the gaskets may not seal properly and leaks may develop. When working on the block, cover the lifter valley with shop rags to keep out debris. Use a vacuum cleaner to remove any debris that falls into the cylinders. **Caution:** *The block on HT4100 engines is aluminum - use care not to gouge the surface when cleaning it.*

12 Check the block and head mating surfaces for nicks, deep scratches and other damage. If damage is slight, it can be removed with a file. If the gasket seemed to be leaking, have the head(s) checked for cracks and warpage by an automotive machine shop. Surface damage or warpage can usually be corrected by machining. Cracks normally require replacement.

Installation

Refer to illustrations 12.14, 12.17a and 12.17b

13 Use a tap of the correct size to chase the threads in the head bolt holes. Mount each bolt in a vise and run a die down the threads to remove any corrosion and restore the threads. Dirt, corrosion, sealant and damaged threads will affect torque readings. This kind of fastener and thread cleaning is especially important on the HT4100 aluminum block.

14 If an all-metal gasket is used, apply a thin, even coat of sealant such as K & W Copper Coat to both sides prior to installation. Metal gaskets must be installed with the raised bead UP. Most gaskets have "THIS SIDE UP" stamped into them. Composition gaskets must be installed dry - don't use sealant. Follow the gasket manufacturer's instructions, if available. Position a new gasket over the dowel pins in the block **(see illustration)**.

15 Carefully position the head on the block without denting or disturbing the gasket. **Note:** *If you're working on a Cadillac V8-6-4 engine, remember to have the last bolt of the right head taped in place* (see Step 8) *before installing the head.*

16 Be sure the head bolt holes are clean. Apply a light coating of engine oil to the head bolts, on the threads and under the bolt heads. Head bolts that enter water jacket areas should be coated with a non-hardening sealant such as Permatex Number 2.

17 Install the bolts in their original locations and tighten them finger tight. Follow the recommended sequence **(see illustrations)** and

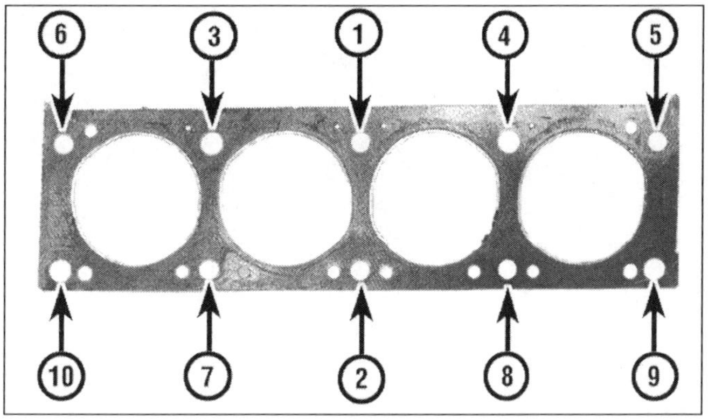

12.17a Cylinder head bolt tightening sequence - HT4100 Cadillac V8

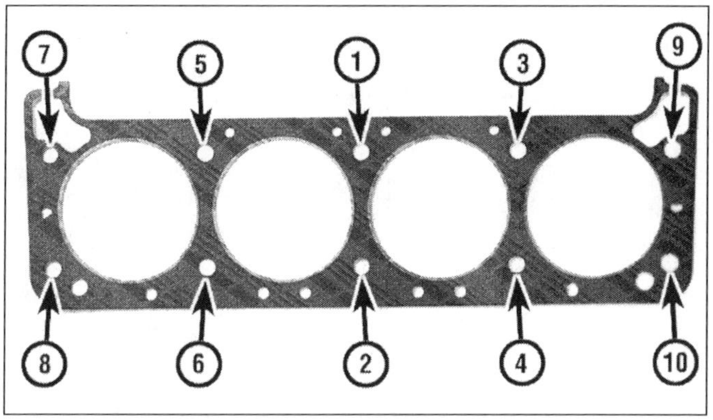

12.17b Cylinder head bolt tightening sequence - big Cadillac and Oldsmobile V8s

tighten the bolts in several steps to the torque listed in this Chapter's Specifications.

18 The remaining installation steps are the reverse of removal.

19 Add coolant, change the oil and filter (see Chapter 1), then start the engine and check carefully for leaks.

13 Oil pump - removal, inspection and installation

Cadillac HT4100 and Oldsmobile-built engines

Removal

Refer to illustration 13.2

1 Remove the oil pan as described in Section 14.

2 Remove the bolts securing the oil pump assembly to the main bearing cap **(see illustration)**. Remove the oil pump with its pickup tube and screen as an assembly from the engine block. Once the pump is removed, the oil pump driveshaft can be withdrawn from the block. **Note 1:** *Do not attempt to remove the washers from the driveshaft. Note that the end with the washers fits into the pump.* **Note 2:** *On some Toronado models, there is a sheetmetal oil deflector that must be removed before unbolting the oil pump from the engine.*

Inspection

3 Because of the critical importance of the oil pump and the risk of engine damage if an overhauled pump doesn't perform like new, we do not recommend overhauling the oil pump on these models. Always replace the pump with a new unit.

Installation

4 To install, slip the driveshaft extension into the oil pump driveshaft, with the washer end closest to the pump. The washer must be in place and should be 1-11/32 inch from the oil pump end of the extension. **Note:** *Pour clean engine oil into the pickup and turn the driveshaft to prime the pump.*

5 Move the pump assembly into position and align the extension with the lower end of the distributor. The distributor drives the oil pump, so it is essential that these two components mate properly. The driveshaft extension fits into the distributor drive gear.

6 Install the bolts and tighten them securely. Make sure the oil pump screen is parallel with the oil pan rails of the block. The screen must be in this position to fit into the oil pan properly.

7 Install the oil pan (see Section 14). Refill the crankcase with oil (see Chapter 1), run the engine and check for leaks.

Cadillac engines, except HT4100

Refer to illustrations 13.10 and 13.13

Removal

8 Except for the HT4100 engine, Cadillac oil pumps are externally mounted to the engine. The oil pan need not be removed.

9 Refer to Chapter 1 and drain the engine oil and remove the oil filter.

10 Remove the screws holding the oil pump to the block, removing th screw by the pressure regulator last **(see illustration)**.

11 Pull the driveshaft out of the pump and scrape the old gasket from the pump body.

Inspection

12 Because of the critical importance of the oil pump and the risk of engine damage if an overhauled pump doesn't perform like new, we do not recommend overhauling the oil pump on these models. Always replace the pump with a new unit.

Installation

Note: *Before installing the oil pump, pack the cavities of the pump with petroleum jelly. This primes the pump and will ensure that oil pressure will build up quickly.*

13.2 HT4100 (shown) and Oldsmobile-built engines have the oil pump bolted to the rear main bearing cap - remove the mounting bolts (arrows indicate the two bolts and a nut on the HT4100, while Oldsmobile pumps have just two bolts)

13.10 Cadillac big V8 pumps are mounted to the front of the block - remove the five bolts (arrows indicate four of them; one more is behind the pump) and pull out the pump and driveshaft - this view is from below the vehicle

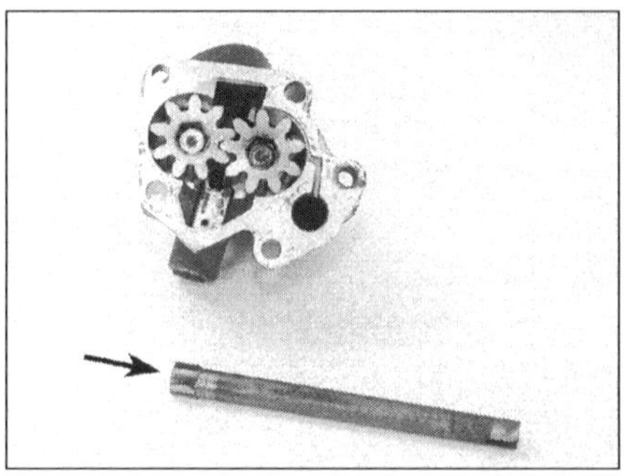

13.13 Lube the gears in the pump, install a new gasket on the pump body and install the hex end (arrow) of the driveshaft into the drive gear in the pump

15.2 Mark the driveplate with reference to the end of the crankshaft before removal - the HT4100 driveplate has only three bolts (arrows) and they are usually Torx-type

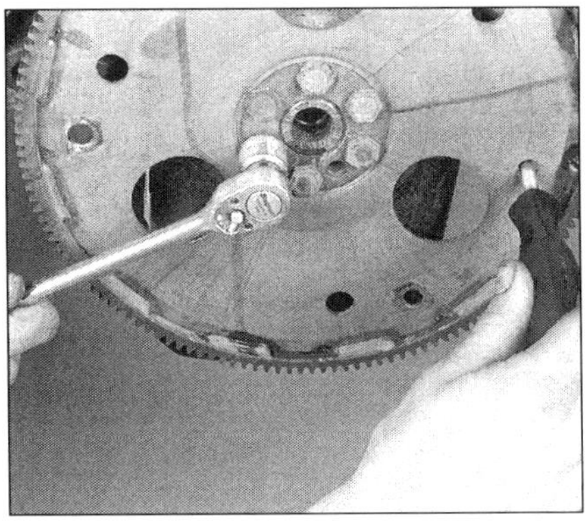

15.3 Hold the driveplate by jamming a large screwdriver through one of the holes and against the block, while removing the driveplate mounting bolts

13 Reinstall the driveshaft in the pump **(see illustration)**. Place a new gasket on the pump and engage the driveshaft with the distributor drive while starting the bolt nearest the regulator portion of the housing. As the bolt is tightened further by hand the pump will mount against the engine and the other bolts can be installed. Tighten the bolts to the torque listed in this Chapter's Specifications.
14 Install a new oil filter and refill the crankcase with new oil (see Chapter 1). Run the engine and check for leaks.

14 Oil pan - removal and installation

Warning: *Do not place any part of your body below the engine when it is supported solely by a jack or hoist.*

Removal

1978 and earlier models

1 Because of the proximity of the transmission to the driver's side pan rail on these engines, removal of the oil pan requires that the engine be removed from the vehicle. Refer to Part C of this Chapter.
2 With the engine supported safely on a stand, remove the oil pan bolts, making note of where any clips, brackets or studs are located.
3 Use a rubber hammer to break the pan-to-block seal.
4 Before installing, thoroughly clean the gasket sealing surfaces on the engine block and on the oil pan. All sealant and gasket material must be removed.

1979 and later models

5 Disconnect the negative battery cable.
6 Refer to Chapter 8 to remove the final drive (differential) unit. **Note:** *Some transmission fluid may leak out when the final drive unit is removed. Have a drain pan in place to catch any fluid.*
7 Refer to Chapter 10 to disconnect the steering center link and move it away from the oil pan.
8 On some models, there may be two sheetmetal braces running from the front crossmember back. Unbolt and remove these for better oil pan access.
9 Drain the engine oil (see Chapter 1).
10 Remove the torque converter shield (see Chapter 7), and the starter motor (see Chapter 5).
11 Use the bolt at the center of the vibration damper to rotate the engine until the timing mark is straight down, at the 6 o'clock position. This will move the forward crankshaft throw upward, providing clearance at the front of the oil pan.
12 On HT4100 models, support the engine from above with a hoist, unbolt the front engine mounts (see Section 17) and raise the engine. Raise the engine slowly until wood blocks can be placed between the engine mounts on the crossmember and the engine block. The blocks should be approximately three inches thick. Check clearances all around the engine as it is raised. Pay particular attention to the distributor and the cooling fan. Lower the engine onto the wood blocks. Make sure it is firmly supported. If a hoist is being used, keep the lifting chains secured to the engine.
13 Remove the oil pan bolts. Note the different sizes and their locations.
14 Remove the oil pan by tilting it down at the rear and then working the front clear of the crossmember. It may be necessary to use a rubber mallet to break the seal - don't pry between the pan and the block!
15 Before installing, thoroughly clean the gasket sealing surfaces on the engine block and on the oil pan. All sealant and gasket material must be removed.

Installation

16 Apply a thin film of sealant to the new side gaskets and fit them to the engine block. All bolt holes should line up properly. If you are working on an HT4100 engine, apply a continuous bead of RTV sealant to the pan, making sure the bead travels around the inside of the bolt holes. Install the pan while the sealant is still wet.
17 Again using sealant, install the front and rear seals to the engine (except on HT4100 engines). Make sure the ends butt with the ends of the side gaskets.
18 Lift the pan into position and install all bolts finger-tight. There is no specific order for tightening the bolts; however, it is a good policy to tighten the end bolts first, and all of the bolts should be started before any are tightened to Specifications.
19 On HT4100 models, remove the wood blocks, lower the engine and reattach the engine mounts (see Section 17).
20 Follow the removal steps in a reverse order. Fill the engine with the correct grade and quantity of oil (see Chapter 1), start the engine and check for leaks.

15 Driveplate - removal and installation

Refer to illustrations 15.2 and 15.3

Removal

1 Refer to Chapter 7 and remove the transmission.
2 Use a scribe or a marking pen to draw a line from the driveplate to the end of the crankshaft for correct alignment during reinstallation **(see illustration)**.
3 Remove the bolts that secure the driveplate to the crankshaft rear flange. If difficulty is experienced in removing the bolts due to movement of the crankshaft, wedge a screwdriver to keep the driveplate from turning **(see illustration)**. **Note:** *There are only three bolts securing the HT4100 driveplate, and they are usually Torx fasteners.*
4 Remove the driveplate from the crankshaft flange, noting the location and installed direction of any spacer rings (if used).
5 Clean any grease or oil from the driveplate. Check for cracked or broken starter ring gear teeth. Lay the driveplate on a flat surface and use a straightedge to check for warpage.
6 Clean the mating surfaces of the driveplate and the crankshaft.

Installation

7 Position the driveplate against the crankshaft, matching the alignment marks made during removal. Before installing the bolts, apply a thread locking compound to the threads.
8 Wedge a screwdriver through the driveplate or into the ring gear teeth to keep the crankshaft from turning. Tighten the bolts to the torque listed in this Chapter's specifications in two or three steps, working in a crisscross pattern.
9 The remainder of installation is the reverse of the removal procedure.

16 Rear main oil seal - replacement

Two-piece neoprene seal (Cadillac engines)

Refer to illustrations 16.5, 16.6, 16.9, 16.10, 16.12 and 16.15

1 Always replace both halves of the rear main oil seal as a unit. While the replacement

16.5 Drive in one end of the upper seal half until the other end protrudes, then pull the seal (arrow) all the way out with a pair of pliers

of this seal is much easier with the engine removed from the car, the job can be done with engine in place (except on 1978 and earlier models, since the engine must be removed for oil pan removal).

2 Remove the oil pan as described in Section 14. On HT4100 engines, also refer to Section 13 to remove the oil pump.

3 Remove the rear main bearing cap from the engine.

16.10 Start the lubricated seal into the groove in the block, using the shoehorn to protect it from the sharp edge of the groove

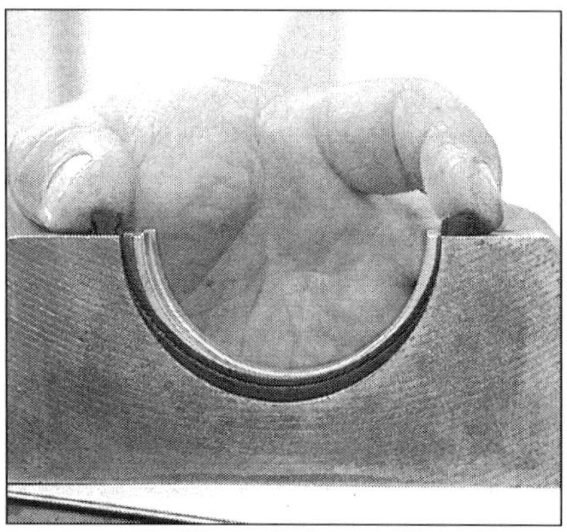

16.12 Seat the bottom half of the seal in the cap by pushing both ends in evenly

16.6 Clean the bearing cap seating surface of any sealant - on HT4100 engines (shown) use a screwdriver to clean out the RTV from the block grooves on either side of the rear main cap

4 Using a screwdriver, pry the lower half of the oil seal from the bearing cap.

5 To remove the upper half of the seal, use a small hammer and a brass pin punch to roll the seal around the crankshaft journal. Tap one end of the seal with the hammer and brass drift (be careful not to strike the crankshaft) until the other end of the seal protrudes enough to pull the seal out with a pair of pliers **(see illustration)**.

6 Clean all seal remnants and foreign material from the bearing cap and block **(see illustration)**. Do not use an abrasive cleaner for this.

7 Inspect components for nicks, scratches or burrs at all sealing surfaces.

8 Coat the seal lips of the new seal with light engine oil. Do not get oil on the seal mating ends. **Caution:** *Do not use any kind of silicone lubricant on the seal lips or oil leakage could develop.*

9 Included in the purchase of the rear main oil seal should be a small plastic installation tool. If not included, make your own by cutting an old feeler gauge blade or shim stock **(see illustration)**.

10 Position the new upper seal half (lubricated) to start into the groove in the block, with the narrow end of the installation tool

16.15 Force RTV into the HT4100 rear main cap grooves (arrows), using a sealant tube fitted with a washer

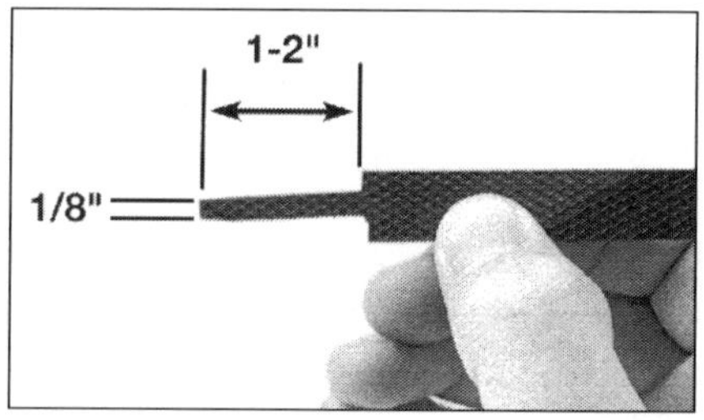

16.9 A "shoehorn" guide for the rear seal can be made from a thin piece of brass shim stock

between the seal and the outward side of the seal groove **(see illustration)**. The lip of the seal should face toward the front of the engine.

11 Roll the seal around the crankshaft, all the time using the tool as a "shoehorn" for protection from the sharp edge of the engine block. When both ends of the seal are flush with the engine block, remove the installation tool, being careful not to withdraw the seal as well.

12 Install the lower half of the oil seal in the bearing cap, pushing it straight in with even pressure at both ends **(see illustration)**. Make sure the seal is firmly seated.

13 Smear a bit of sealant on the bearing cap areas immediately adjacent to the seal ends.

14 Install the bearing cap (with seal) and torque the attaching bolts to about 10 to 12 ft-lbs only. Now tap the end of the crankshaft first rearward (use a block of wood, not a hammer), then forward to line up the thrust surfaces. Retighten the bearing cap bolts to the torque specified in Chapter 2C.

15 On HT4100 engines, inject RTV sealant into the grooves between the rear main cap and the block **(see illustration)**. You'll know when the grooves are full when sealant seeps out at the parting line between the bottom of the block and top of the cap. Watch for it to squirt out either on the crankcase side or at the rear of the block.

Braided fabric seal (Oldsmobile-built engines)

16 Replacing the rope seal on the Oldsmobile V8 engines (in-car) is essentially the same as for the Buick V6, covered in Part A of this Chapter, with the exception that the V8s do not have side seals on either side of their rear main caps like the V6.

17 Engine mounts - check and replacement

Engine mounts seldom require attention, but broken or deteriorated mounts should be replaced immediately or the added strain placed on the driveline components may cause damage. The procedures to check and replace V8 engine mounts are essentially the same as for the V6 engine, as covered in Part A of this Chapter.

Chapter 2 Part C
General engine overhaul procedures

Contents

Specifications

V6 engines (Buick-built)

See Chapter 2, Part A, for additional information

General

Displacement	
3.8L	231 cubic inches
4.1L	252 cubic inches
Oil pressure at 2400 rpm	37 psi
Compression pressure	
Minimum	100 psi
Allowable variation between cylinders	20%
Cylinder head warpage limit	0.003 inch per 6 inches

Valves

Valve stem diameter	
Intake	0.3412 to 0.3401 inch
Exhaust	0.3412 to 0.3405 inch
Valve margin width (limit)	0.025 inch
Valve spring installed height	1.727 inch
Valve stem-to-guide clearance	
Intake	0.0015 to 0.0035 inch
Exhaust	0.0015 to 0.0032 inch

V6 engines (Buick-built) (continued)

Engine block

Cylinder bore diameter	
3.8	3.800 inches
4.1	3.965 inches
Cylinder bore taper/out-of-round	Less than 0.0005 inch

Pistons and rings

Piston-to-bore clearance (measured at top of skirt)	0.0008 to 0.0020 inch
Piston ring end gap	
1979 to 1983	
Compression rings	0.013 to 0.0023 inch
Oil rings	0.015 to 0.035 inch
1984 and 1985	
Compression rings	0.010 to 0.0020 inch
Oil rings	0.015 to 0.055 inch

Crankshaft, connecting rods and bearings

Connecting rod side clearance (total - both rods)	
1979 to 1984	0.006 to 0.023 inch
1985	0.003 to 0.015 inch
Connecting rod bearing oil clearance	0.0005 to 0.0026 inch
Rod and main journal taper/out-of-round limit	0.0015 inch
Crankshaft endplay	0.003 to 0.0011 inch
Main bearing journal diameter	2.4995 inch
Main bearing oil clearance	0.0003 to 0.0018 inch

Torque specifications*

	Ft-lbs
Main bearing cap bolts	100
Connecting rod cap nuts	40

***Note:** *Refer to Part A for additional torque specifications.*

500, 425 and 368 cu in V8 engines (Cadillac-built)

See Chapter 2, Part B, for additional information

General

Oil pressure	35 psi @ 2600 rpm
Compression pressure	
Allowable variation between cylinders	20%
Minimum	100 psi
Cylinder head warpage limit	0.006 inch

Valves

Valve stem diameter	
Intake	0.3415 to 0.3425 inch
Exhaust	
500	0.3415 to 0.3420 inch
425 and 368	0.3413 to 0.3420 inch
Valve seat width in head	1/16 inch
Valve spring free length	2.250 inches
Valve stem-to-guide clearance	
Standard	0.0010 to 0.0027 inch
Limit	0.005 inch

Engine block

Cylinder bore diameter	
500 cu. in.	
Letter A	4.3000 to 4.3002 inches
Letter B	4.3002 to 4.3004 inches
Letter C	4.3004 to 4.3006 inches
Letter D	4.3006 to 4.3008 inches
Letter E	4.3008 to 4.3010 inches
Letter H	4.3010 to 4.3012 inches
Letter J	4.3012 to 4.3014 inches
Letter K	4.3014 to 4.3016 inches
Letter L	4.3016 to 4.3018 inches
Letter M	4.3018 to 4.3020 inches

425 cu. in.	
Letter A	4.0820 to 4.0824 inches
Letter B	4.0824 to 4.0828 inches
Letter C	4.0828 to 4.0832 inches
Letter D	4.0832 to 4.0836 inches
Letter E	4.0836 to 4.0840 inches
368 cu. in.	
Letter A	3.8000 to 3.8004 inches
Letter B	3.8004 to 3.8008 inches
Letter C	3.8008 to 3.8012 inches
Letter D	3.8012 to 3.8016 inches
Letter E	3.8016 to 3.8020 inches
Piston-to-bore clearance (measured at top of skirt)	
500	0.0006 to 0.0010 inch
425 and 368	0.0006 to 0.0014 inch

Pistons and rings

Piston size	
500 cu. in.	
Letter A	4.2992 to 4.2994 inches
Letter B	4.2994 to 4.2996 inches
Letter C	4.2996 to 4.2998 inches
Letter D	4.2998 to 4.3000 inches
Letter E	4.3000 to 4.3002 inches
Letter H	4.3002 to 4.3004 inches
Letter J	4.3004 to 4.3006 inches
Letter K	4.3006 to 4.3008 inches
Letter L	4.3008 to 4.3010 inches
Letter M	4.3010 to 4.3012 inches
425 cu. in.	
Letter A	4.0810 to 4.0814 inches
Letter B	4.0814 to 4.0818 inches
Letter C	4.0818 to 4.0822 inches
Letter D	4.0822 to 4.0826 inches
Letter E	4.0826 to 4.0830 inches
368 cu. in.	
Letter A	3.7990 to 3.7994 inches
Letter B	3.7994 to 3.7998 inches
Letter C	3.7998 to 3.8002 inches
Letter D	3.8002 to 3.8006 inches
Letter E	3.8006 to 3.8010 inches
Piston ring end gap	
Compression rings	
500	0.013 to 0.025 inch
425, 368	0.013 to 0.023 inch
Oil ring, all	0.015 to 0.055 inch
Piston ring side clearance	
Compression rings	0.017 to 0.040 inch
Oil ring	NONE - side sealing

Crankshaft, connecting rods and main bearings

Rod endplay - (total - both rods)	
1971 to 1973	0.008 to 0.016 inch
1974 to 1975	0.011 to 0.021 inch
1976 to 1981	0.008 to 0.020 inch
Crankshaft endplay (all)	0.002 to 0.012 inch
Main bearing journal diameter	3.250 inches
Connecting rod journal diameter	2.500 inches
Main bearing oil clearance	
1971 to 1973	0.0003 to 0.0026 inch
1974 to 1975	0.0001 to 0.0026 inch
1976 to 1981	0.0005 to 0.0026 inch
Connecting rod bearing oil clearance	0.0005 to 0.0028 inch

Torque specifications*	**Ft-lbs**
Connecting rod cap nuts	40
Main bearing cap bolts	90

***Note:** *Refer to Part B for additional torque specifications.*

HT4100 Cadillac V8 engine

See Chapter 2, Part B, for additional information

General

Bore Diameter	3.465 inches
Oil pressure (minimum)	30 psi @ 2600 rpm
Compression pressure	
Allowable variation between cylinders	20%
Minimum	140 psi
Cylinder head warpage limit	0.006 inch

Valves

Valve stem diameter, Intake and exhaust	0.3420 to 0.3413 inch
Valve margin width (minimum)	0.025 inch
Valve spring free length	2.12 inches
Valve spring installed height	1.73 inches
Valve stem-to-guide clearance (new)	0.001 to 0.003 inch
Valve stem-to-guide clearance limit	0.005 inch

Engine block

Cylinder bore diameter	3.465 inches
Piston-to-bore clearance*	0.0010 to 0.0018 inch

***Note:** *Measure pistons at top of skirt, perpendicular to pin*

Pistons and rings

Piston ring end gap	
Compression rings	0.015 to 0.025 inch
Oil rings	0.010 to 0.050 inch
Compression ring side clearance	0.0016 to 0.0037 inch
Oil ring side clearance	None (side sealing)

Crankshaft, connecting rods and main bearings

Connecting rod endplay (side clearance)	0.008 to 0.020 inch
Crankshaft endplay	
New limits	0.001 to 0.007 inch
Worn limits	0.015 inch
Main bearing journal diameter	2.640 inches
Connecting rod journal diameter	1.929 inches
Connecting rod bearing oil clearance	
Production	0.0005 to 0.0028 inch
Wear limit	0.0035 inch
Connecting rod bearing journal out-of-round limit	0.0004 inch
Main bearing oil clearance	
1982 through 1984	0.004 to 0.0027 inch
1985	
No. 1	0.0008 to 0.0031 inch
Nos. 2, 3, 4 and 5	0.0016 to 0.0039 inch

Torque specifications*

	Ft-lbs (unless otherwise specified)
Main bearing cap bolts	85
Connecting rod bolts	22

***Note:** *Refer to Part B for additional torque specifications.*

Oldsmobile V8 engines - 307, 350, 403 and 455 cu. in.

See Chapter 2, Part B, for additional information

General

Oil pressure	30 psi @ 1500 rpm
Compression pressure	
Allowable variation between cylinders	20%
Minimum	100 psi
Cylinder head warpage limit	0.006 inch

Valves

Valve stem diameter	
Intake	0.3425 to 0.3432 inch
Exhaust	0.3420 to 0.3427 inch
Valve margin width (minimum)	0.025 inch

Valve stem-to-guide clearance	
Intake	0.0010 to 0.0027 inch
Exhaust	0.0015 to 0.0032 inch

Engine block

Cylinder bore diameter	
455	4.126 inches
403	4.351 inches
350	4.057 inches
307	3.800 inches
Cylinder bore taper/out-of-round	0.0015 inch maximum
Piston-to-bore clearance	0.00075 to 0.00175 inch

Pistons and rings

Piston ring end gap*	
Compression rings	0.010 to 0.023 inch
Oil ring	0.015 to 0.055 inch
Compression ring side clearance	0.002 to 0.004 inch

***Note:** *Varies by ring manufacturer - use ring maker's specifications, if different.*

Crankshaft, connecting rods and main bearings

Connecting rod endplay (side clearance)	0.006 to 0.020 inch
Crankshaft endplay	0.0035 to 0.0135 inch
Connecting rod journal diameter	
307, 350, 403	2.1248 to 2.1238 inches
455	2.4998 to 2.4988 inches
Main bearing journal diameter	
307, 350, 403	2.4995 to 2.4985 inches
455	3.003 to 2.9993 inches
Main bearing oil clearance	
Nos. 1 through 4	0.0005 to 0.0021 inch
No. 5	
307, 350, 403	0.0015 to 0.0031 inch
455	0.002 to 0.0034 inch
Connecting rod bearing oil clearance (all)	0.0004 to 0.0033 inch

Torque specifications*	Ft-lbs (unless otherwise indicated)
Main bearing cap bolts (nos. 1 through 4)	80
Main bearing cap bolts (rear - no. 5)	120
Connecting rod cap nuts	42

***Note:** *Refer to Part B for additional torque specifications.*

1 General information

Included in this portion of Chapter 2 are the general overhaul procedures for the cylinder heads and internal engine components.

The information ranges from advice concerning preparation for an overhaul and the purchase of replacement parts to detailed, step-by-step procedures covering removal and installation of internal engine components and the inspection of parts.

The following Sections have been written based on the assumption that the engine has been removed from the vehicle. For information concerning in-vehicle engine repair, as well as removal and installation of the external components necessary for the overhaul, see Part A and B of this Chapter and Section 7 of this Part.

The Specifications included in this Part are only those necessary for the inspection and overhaul procedures which follow. Refer to Parts A and B for additional Specifications.

2 Engine overhaul - general information

Refer to illustrations 2.4a, 2.4b, 2.4c and 2.4d

It's not always easy to determine when, or if, an engine should be completely overhauled, as a number of factors must be considered.

High mileage is not necessarily an indication that an overhaul is needed, while low mileage doesn't preclude the need for an overhaul. Frequency of servicing is probably the most important consideration. An engine that's had regular and frequent oil and filter changes, as well as other required maintenance, will most likely give many thousands of miles of reliable service. Conversely, a neglected engine may require an overhaul very early in its life.

Excessive oil consumption is an indication that piston rings, valve seals and/or valve guides are in need of attention. Make sure that oil leaks aren't responsible before deciding that the rings and/or guides are bad. Perform a cylinder compression check to determine the extent of the work required (see Section 3).

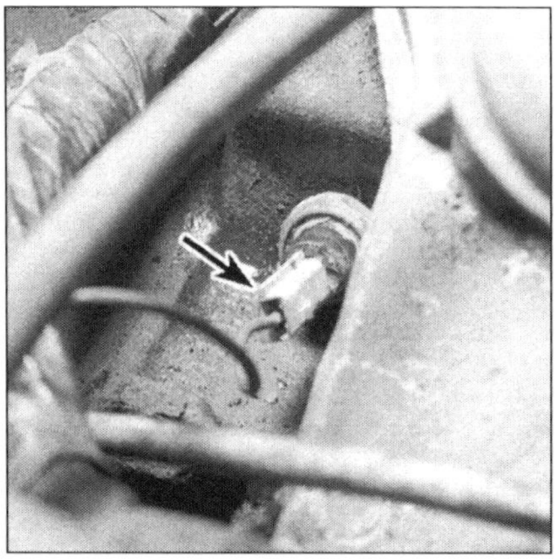

2.4a Oil pressure sending unit location - Cadillac big V8 - at the top of the block, behind the intake manifold

Check the oil pressure with a gauge installed in place of the oil pressure sending unit **(see illustrations)** and compare it to the

2.4b Oil pressure sending unit location - Cadillac HT4100 - above the oil filter at the right rear of the block

2.4c Oil pressure sending unit location - Oldsmobile V8 - top of the block, in front of the intake manifold

2.4d Oil pressure sending unit location - V6 engines - above the right front engine mount

Specifications. If it's extremely low, the bearings and/or oil pump are probably worn out.

Loss of power, rough running, knocking or metallic engine noises, excessive valve train noise and high fuel consumption rates may also point to the need for an overhaul, especially if they're all present at the same time. If a complete tune-up doesn't remedy the situation, major mechanical work is the only solution.

An engine overhaul involves restoring the internal parts to the specifications of a new engine. During an overhaul, the piston rings are replaced and the cylinder walls are reconditioned (rebored and/or honed). If a rebore is done by an automotive machine shop, new oversize pistons will also be installed. The main bearings, connecting rod bearings and camshaft bearings are generally replaced with new ones and, if necessary, the crankshaft may be reground to restore the journals. Generally, the valves are serviced as well, since they're usually in less than-perfect condition at this point. While the engine is being overhauled, other components, such as the distributor, starter and alternator, can be rebuilt as well. The end result should be a like-new engine that will give many trouble-free miles. **Note:** *Critical cooling system components such as the hoses, drivebelts, thermostat and water pump MUST be replaced with new parts when an engine is overhauled.* The radiator should be checked carefully to ensure that it isn't clogged or leaking (see Chapter 3). **Note:** *If you decide to have your short-block or long-block rebuilt by a professional shop, they may not guarantee the engine unless you have the radiator cleaned or rebuilt at a radiator shop.* Also, we don't recommend overhauling the oil pump - always install a new one when an engine is rebuilt.

Before beginning the engine overhaul, read through the entire procedure to familiarize yourself with the scope and requirements of the job. Overhauling an engine isn't difficult, but it is time consuming. Plan on the vehicle being tied up for a minimum of two weeks, especially if parts must be taken to an automotive machine shop for repair or reconditioning. Check on availability of parts and make sure that any necessary special tools and equipment are obtained in advance. Most work can be done with typical hand tools, although a number of precision measuring tools are required for inspecting parts to determine if they must be replaced. Often an automotive machine shop will handle the inspection of parts and offer advice concerning reconditioning and replacement. **Note:** *Always wait until the engine has been completely disassembled and all components, especially the engine block, have been inspected before deciding what service and repair operations must be performed by an automotive machine shop.* Since the block's condition will be the major factor to consider when determining whether to overhaul the original engine or buy a rebuilt one, never purchase parts or have machine work done on other components until the block has been thoroughly inspected. As a general rule, time is the primary cost of an overhaul, so it doesn't pay to install worn or substandard parts.

As a final note, to ensure maximum life and minimum trouble from a rebuilt engine, everything must be assembled with care in a spotlessly clean environment.

3 Cylinder compression check

Refer to illustrations 3.5 and 3.6

1 A compression check will tell you what mechanical condition the upper end (pistons, rings, valves, head gaskets) of your engine is in. Specifically, it can tell you if the compression is down due to leakage caused by worn piston rings, defective valves and seats or a blown head gasket. **Note:** *The engine must be at normal operating temperature and the battery must be fully charged for this check. Also, the choke valve must be all the way open to get an accurate compression reading (if the engine's warm, the choke should be open).*

2 Begin by cleaning the area around the spark plugs before you remove them (compressed air should be used, if available, otherwise a small brush or even a bicycle tire pump will work). The idea is to prevent dirt from getting into the cylinders as the compression check is being done.

3.5 Unplug the HEI connectors (arrows) at the distributor before checking compression

3 Remove all of the spark plugs from the engine (Chapter 1).

4 Block the throttle wide open.

5 On vehicles with "point-type" ignition, detach the coil wire from the center of the distributor cap and ground it on the engine block. Use a jumper wire with alligator clips on each end to ensure a good ground. On vehicles equipped with electronic ignition, the ignition circuit should be disabled by unplugging the primary (low voltage) electrical connectors from the distributor **(see illustration)**. On fuel-injected models, disable the fuel pump by removing the fuel pump fuse.

6 Install the compression gauge in the number one spark plug hole **(see illustration)**.

7 Crank the engine over at least seven compression strokes and watch the gauge. The compression should build up quickly in a healthy engine. Low compression on the first stroke, followed by gradually increasing pres-

3.6 Use a compression gauge with a threaded fitting for the spark plug hole; don't use the type with a conical rubber tip - it relies on hand pressure to create a seal between the gauge and the combustion chamber, and usually gives an inaccurate reading

sure on successive strokes, indicates worn piston rings. A low compression reading on the first stroke, which doesn't build up during successive strokes, indicates leaking valves or a blown head gasket (a cracked head could also be the cause). Deposits on the undersides of the valve heads can also cause low compression. Record the highest gauge reading obtained.

8 Repeat the procedure for the remaining cylinders and compare the results to the Specifications.

9 Add some engine oil (about three squirts from a plunger-type oil can) to each cylinder, through the spark plug hole, and repeat the test.

10 If the compression increases after the oil is added, the piston rings are definitely worn. If the compression doesn't increase significantly, the leakage is occurring at the valves or head gasket. Leakage past the valves may be caused by burned valve seats and/or faces or warped, cracked or bent valves.

11 If two adjacent cylinders have equally low compression, there's a strong possibility that the head gasket between them is blown. The appearance of coolant in the combustion chambers or the crankcase would verify this condition.

12 If one cylinder is 20 percent lower than the others, and the engine has a slightly rough idle, a worn exhaust lobe on the camshaft could be the cause.

13 If the compression is unusually high, the combustion chambers are probably coated with carbon deposits. If that's the case, the cylinder heads should be removed and decarbonized.

14 If compression is way down or varies greatly between cylinders, it would be a good idea to have a leak-down test performed by an automotive repair shop. This test will pinpoint exactly where the leakage is occurring and how severe it is.

4.4 Use a vacuum gauge connected to manifold vacuum (full vacuum available at idle) to test an engine's condition

4 Vacuum gauge diagnostic - checks

Refer to illustration 4.4

A vacuum gauge provides valuable information about what is going on in the engine at a low cost. You can check for worn rings or cylinder walls, leaking head or intake manifold gaskets, incorrect fuel mixtures, restricted exhaust, stuck or burned valves, weak valve springs, improper ignition or valve timing and ignition problems.

Unfortunately, vacuum gauge readings are easy to misinterpret, so they should be used in conjunction with other tests to confirm the diagnosis.

Both the gauge readings and the rate of needle movement are important for accurate interpretation. Most gauges measure vacuum in inches of mercury (in-Hg). As vacuum increases (or atmospheric pressure decreases), the reading will increase. Also, for every 1,000-foot increase in elevation above sea level, the gauge readings will decrease about one inch of mercury.

Connect the vacuum gauge directly to intake manifold vacuum **(see illustration)**. Be sure no hoses are left disconnected during the test or false readings will result.

Before you begin the test, allow the engine to warm up completely. Block the wheels and set the parking brake. With the transmission in Park, start the engine and allow it to run at normal idle speed. **Warning:** *Carefully inspect the fan blades for cracks or damage before starting the engine. Keep your hands and the vacuum tester clear of the fan and do not stand in front of the vehicle or in line with the fan when the engine is running.*

Read the vacuum gauge; an average, healthy engine should normally produce about 17 to 22 inches of vacuum with a fairly steady needle. Refer to the following vacuum gauge readings and what they indicate about the engines condition:

1 A low, steady reading usually indicates a leaking gasket between the intake manifold and throttle body, a leaky vacuum hose, late ignition timing or incorrect camshaft timing. Eliminate all other possible causes, utilizing the tests provided in this Chapter before you remove the timing chain cover to check the timing marks.

2 If the reading is three to eight inches below normal and it fluctuates at that low reading, suspect an intake manifold gasket leak at an intake port.

3 If the needle has regular drops of about two to four inches at a steady rate, the valves are probably leaking. Perform a compression or leak-down test to confirm this.

4 An irregular drop or down-flick of the needle can be caused by a sticking valve or an ignition misfire. Perform a compression or leak-down test and read the spark plugs.

5 A rapid vibration of about four inches-Hg vibration at idle combined with exhaust smoke indicates worn valve guides. Perform a leak-down test to confirm this. If the rapid vibration occurs with an increase in engine speed, check for a leaking intake manifold gasket or head gasket, weak valve springs, burned valves or ignition misfire.

6 A slight fluctuation, say one inch up and down, may mean ignition problems. Check all the usual tune-up items and, if necessary, run the engine on an ignition analyzer.

7 If there is a large fluctuation, perform a compression or leak-down test to look for a weak or dead cylinder or a blown head gasket.

8 If the needle moves slowly through a wide range, check for a clogged PCV system, incorrect idle fuel mixture, throttle body or intake manifold gasket leaks.

9 Check for a slow return after revving the engine by quickly snapping the throttle open until the engine reaches about 2,500 rpm and let it shut. Normally the reading should drop to near zero, rise above normal idle reading (about 5 in-Hg over) and then return to the previous idle reading. If the vacuum returns slowly and doesn't peak when the throttle is snapped shut, the rings may be worn. If there is a long delay, look for a restricted exhaust system (often the muffler or catalytic converter). An easy way to check this is to temporarily disconnect the exhaust ahead of the suspected part and re-test.

5 Engine removal - methods and precautions

If you've decided that an engine must be removed for overhaul or major repair work, several preliminary steps should be taken.

Locating a suitable place to work is extremely important. Adequate work space, along with storage space for the vehicle, will be needed. If a shop or garage isn't available, at the very least a flat, level, clean work surface made of concrete or asphalt is required.

Cleaning the engine compartment and engine before beginning the removal procedure will help keep tools clean and organized.

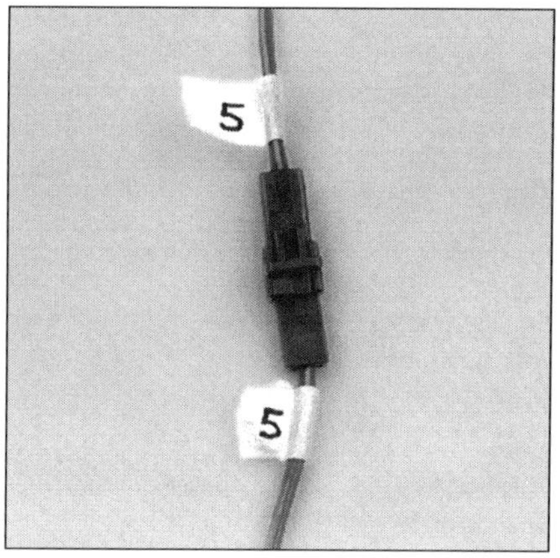

6.5a Label each wire and hose before unplugging the connector

6.5b Make sure any ground wires or straps are disconnected before pulling the engine (HT4100 ground wires shown, on right cylinder head)

6.21 Locate and remove the transmission-to-engine bolts (arrows) - left side shown

An engine hoist or A-frame will also be necessary. Make sure the equipment is rated in excess of the combined weight of the engine and accessories. Safety is of primary importance, considering the potential hazards involved in lifting the engine out of the vehicle.

If the engine is being removed by a novice, a helper should be available. Advice and aid from someone more experienced would also be helpful. There are many instances when one person cannot simultaneously perform all of the operations required when lifting the engine out of the vehicle.

Plan the operation ahead of time. Arrange for or obtain all of the tools and equipment you'll need prior to beginning the job. Some of the equipment necessary to perform engine removal and installation safely and with relative ease are (in addition to an engine hoist) a heavy duty floor jack, complete sets of wrenches and sockets as described in the front of this manual, wooden blocks and plenty of rags and cleaning solvent for mopping up spilled oil, coolant and gasoline. If the hoist must be rented, make sure that you arrange for it in advance and perform all of the operations possible without it beforehand. This will save you money and time.

Plan for the vehicle to be out of use for quite a while. A machine shop will be required to perform some of the work which the do-it-yourselfer can't accomplish without special equipment. These shops often have a busy schedule, so it would be a good idea to consult them before removing the engine in order to accurately estimate the amount of time required to rebuild or repair components that may need work On older engines, the rebuild parts may not be in stock at your local parts store or warehouse, so be prepared for some delay in ordering parts.

Always be extremely careful when removing and installing the engine. Serious injury can result from careless actions. Plan ahead, take your time and a job of this nature, although major, can be accomplished successfully.

6 Engine - removal and installation

Refer to illustrations 6.5a, 6.5b, 6.21 and 6.24

Warning: *Gasoline is extremely flammable, so take extra precautions when you work on any part of the fuel system. Don't smoke or allow open flames or bare light bulbs near the work area, and don't work in a garage where a natural gas-type appliance (such as a water heater or clothes dryer) with a pilot light is present. Since gasoline is carcinogenic, wear latex gloves when there's a possibility of being exposed to fuel, and, if you spill any fuel on your skin, rinse it off immediately with soap and water. Mop up any spills immediately and do not store fuel-soaked rags where they could ignite. The fuel system on fuel-injected models is under constant pressure, so, if any fuel lines are to be disconnected, the fuel pressure in the system must be relieved first* (see Chapter 4 for more information). *When you perform any kind of work on the fuel system, wear safety glasses and have a Class B type fire extinguisher on hand.*

Warning: *The air conditioning system is under high pressure! Have a dealer service department or service station discharge the system before disconnecting any air conditioning system hoses or fittings.*

Removal

1 If the vehicle is fuel-injected, relieve the fuel system pressure (see Chapter 4). Disconnect the negative cable from the battery.

2 Cover the fenders and cowl and remove the hood (see Chapter 11). Special pads are available to protect the fenders, but an old bedspread or blanket will also work.

3 Remove the air cleaner assembly.

4 Drain the cooling system (see Chapter 1).

5 Label the vacuum lines, emissions system hoses, electrical connectors, ground straps and fuel lines, to ensure correct reinstallation, then detach them. Pieces of masking tape with numbers or letters written on them work well **(see illustrations)**. If there's any possibility of confusion, make a sketch of the engine compartment and clearly label the lines, hoses and wires.

6 Label and detach all coolant hoses from the engine.

7 Remove the cooling fan, shroud and radiator (see Chapter 3).

8 Remove the drivebelts (see Chapter 1).

9 Disconnect the fuel lines running from the engine to the chassis (see Chapter 4). Plug or cap all open fittings/lines.

10 Disconnect the accelerator linkage (and TV linkage/speed control cable, if equipped) from the engine (see Chapter 4 and Chapter 7).

11 On power steering equipped vehicles, unbolt the power steering pump (see Chapter 10). Leave the lines/hoses attached and make sure the pump is kept in an upright position in the engine compartment (use wire or rope to restrain it out of the way).

12 On air conditioned vehicles, unbolt the compressor (see Chapter 3) and set it aside. Do not disconnect the hoses.

13 Drain the engine oil (see Chapter 1) and remove the filter.

14 Remove the starter motor (see Chapter 5).

15 Remove the alternator (see Chapter 5).

16 Unbolt the exhaust manifolds from the engine (see Chapter 2A or 2B).

17 Refer to Chapter 7 and remove the torque converter-to-driveplate fasteners.

18 Support the transmission with a jack. Position a wood block between them to prevent damage to the transmission. Special transmission jacks with safety chains are available - use one if possible.

19 Attach an engine sling or a length of chain to the lifting brackets on the engine. If there are no factory lifting brackets, attach the chain to two sturdy, 3/8-inch-diameter or larger bolts, one at either end of the engine.

20 Roll the hoist into position and connect the sling to it. Take up the slack in the sling or chain, but don't lift the engine. You may have to experiment with the location of the hook from the hoist with the lifting sling to get the engine to lift out level or at the angle you

6.24 With the accessories tied out of the way and the engine mount bolts removed, tilt, twist and raise the engine with the hoist until it clears the engine compartment

want. **Warning:** *DO NOT place any part of your body under the engine when it's supported only by a hoist or other lifting device.*
21 Remove the transmission-to-engine block bolts **(see illustration)**.
22 Remove the engine mount-to-frame bolts (see Chapter 2A or 2B).
23 Recheck to be sure nothing is still connecting the engine to the transmission or vehicle. Disconnect anything still remaining.
24 Raise the engine slightly. Carefully work it forward to separate it from the transmission. Be sure the torque converter stays in the transmission (clamp a pair of vise-grips to the housing to keep the converter from sliding out). Slowly raise the engine out of the engine compartment **(see illustration)**. Check carefully to make sure nothing is hanging up.
25 Remove the driveplate and mount the engine on an engine stand.

Installation

26 Check the engine and transmission mounts. If they're worn or damaged, replace them.
27 Raise the transmission slightly to accept the angle of the engine when it is lowered into place.
28 Carefully lower the engine into the engine compartment - make sure the engine mounts line up.
29 Install the transmission-to-engine bolts and tighten them securely. **Caution:** *DO NOT use the bolts to force the transmission and engine together!*
30 Install the driveplate-to-torque converter bolts following the procedure outlined in Chapter 7.
31 Reinstall the remaining components in the reverse order of removal.
32 Add coolant, oil, power steering and transmission fluid as needed.
33 Run the engine and check for leaks and proper operation of all accessories, then install the hood and test drive the vehicle.
34 Have the air conditioning system recharged and leak tested.

7 Engine rebuilding alternatives

The do-it-yourselfer is faced with a number of options when performing an engine overhaul. The decision to replace the engine block, piston/connecting rod assemblies and crankshaft depends on a number of factors, with the number one consideration being the condition of the block. Other considerations are cost, access to machine shop facilities, parts availability, time required to complete the project and the extent of prior mechanical experience on the part of the do-it-yourselfer.

Some of the rebuilding alternatives include:

Individual parts - If the inspection procedures reveal that the engine block and most engine components are in reusable condition, purchasing individual parts may be the most economical alternative. The block, crankshaft and piston/connecting rod assemblies should all be inspected carefully. Even if the block shows little wear, the cylinder bores should be surface-honed.

Short block - A short block consists of an engine block with a crankshaft and piston/connecting rod assemblies already installed. In a rebuilt short-block, all new bearings are incorporated and all clearances will be correct. The existing camshaft, valve train components, cylinder heads and external parts can be bolted to the short block with little or no further machine shop work necessary. In some cases, a rebuilder may include a new camshaft, timing chain and timing gears as part of the rebuilt short-block.

Long block - A long block consists of a short block plus an oil pump, oil pan, cylinder heads, rocker arm covers, camshaft and valve train components, timing sprockets and chain or gears and timing cover. All components are installed with new bearings, seals and gaskets incorporated throughout. The installation of manifolds and external parts is all that's necessary.

Give careful thought to which alternative is best for you and discuss the situation with local automotive machine shops, auto parts dealers and experienced rebuilders before ordering or purchasing replacement parts.

8 Engine overhaul - disassembly sequence

1 It's much easier to disassemble and work on the engine if it's mounted on a portable engine stand. A stand can often be rented quite cheaply from an equipment rental yard. Before the engine is mounted on a stand, the flywheel/driveplate should be removed from the engine.
2 If a stand isn't available, it's possible to disassemble the engine with it blocked up on the floor. Be extra careful not to tip or drop the engine when working without a stand.
3 If you're going to obtain a rebuilt engine, all external components must come off first, to be transferred to the replacement engine, just as they will if you're doing a complete engine overhaul yourself. These include:

Alternator and brackets
Emissions control components
Distributor, spark plug wires and spark plugs
Thermostat and housing cover
Water pump
Carburetor or fuel injection unit
Intake/exhaust manifolds
Oil filter
Engine mounts
Driveplate
Engine rear plate

Note: *When removing the external components from the engine, pay close attention to details that may be helpful or important during installation. Note the installed position of gaskets, seals, spacers, pins, brackets, washers, bolts and other small items.*
4 If you're obtaining a short block, which consists of the engine block, crankshaft, pistons and connecting rods all assembled, then the cylinder heads, oil pan and oil pump will have to be removed as well. See *Engine rebuilding alternatives* for additional information regarding the different possibilities to be considered.
5 If you're planning a complete overhaul, the engine must be disassembled and the internal components removed in the following order:

Rocker arm covers
Intake and exhaust manifolds
Rocker arms and pushrods
Valve lifters
Cylinder heads
Timing cover
Timing chain and sprockets
Camshaft
Oil pan
Oil pump
Piston/connecting rod assemblies
Crankshaft and main bearings

6 Before beginning the disassembly and overhaul procedures, make sure the following items are available. Also, refer to *Engine overhaul - reassembly sequence* for a list of tools and materials needed for engine reassembly.

Common hand tools
Small cardboard boxes or plastic bags for storing parts
Gasket scraper
Ridge reamer
Vibration damper puller
Micrometers

9.2 A small plastic bag, with an appropriate label, can be used to store the valve train components so they can be kept together and reinstalled in their original locations

Telescoping gauges
Dial indicator set
Valve spring compressor
Cylinder surfacing hone
Piston ring groove-cleaning tool
Electric drill motor
Tap and die set
Wire brushes
Oil gallery brushes
Cleaning solvent

9 Cylinder head - disassembly

Refer to illustrations 9.2 and 9.4

Note: *New and rebuilt cylinder heads are commonly available for most engines at dealerships and auto parts stores. Due to the fact that some specialized tools are necessary for the disassembly and inspection procedures, and replacement parts may not be readily available, it may be more practical and economical for the home mechanic to purchase rebuilt replacement heads rather than taking the time to disassemble, inspect and recondition the originals. However, on older engines, existing cores may not be available, in which case your heads will have to be rebuilt.*

1 Cylinder head disassembly involves removal of the intake and exhaust valves and related components. If they're still in place, remove the rocker arm nuts, pivot balls and rocker arms from the cylinder head studs. Label the parts or store them separately so they can be reinstalled in their original locations.

2 Before the valves are removed, arrange to label and store them, along with their related components, so they can be kept separate and reinstalled in the same valve guides they are removed from **(see illustration)**.

3 Compress the springs on the first valve with a spring compressor and remove the keepers **(see Chapter 2A or 2B)**. Carefully release the valve spring compressor and remove the retainer, the spring and the spring seat (if used).

9.4 If the valve won't pull through the guide, deburr the edge of the stem end and the area around the top of the keeper groove with a file or whetstone

4 Pull the valve out of the head, then remove the oil seal from the guide. If the valve binds in the guide (won't pull through), push it back into the head and deburr the area around the keeper groove with a fine file or whetstone **(see illustration)**.

5 Repeat the procedure for the remaining valves. Remember to keep all the parts for each valve together so they can be reinstalled in the same locations.

6 Once the valves and related components have been removed and stored in an organized manner, the heads should be thoroughly cleaned and inspected. If a complete engine overhaul is being done, finish the engine disassembly procedures before beginning the cylinder head cleaning and inspection process.

10 Cylinder head - cleaning and inspection

1 Thorough cleaning of the cylinder heads and related valve train components, followed by a detailed inspection, will enable you to decide how much valve service work must be done during the engine overhaul. **Note:** *If the engine was severely overheated, the cylinder heads may be warped* (see Step 12).

Cleaning

2 Scrape all traces of old gasket material and sealing compound off the head gasket, intake manifold and exhaust manifold sealing surfaces. Be very careful not to gouge the cylinder head. Special gasket removal solvents that soften gaskets and make removal much easier are available at auto parts stores.

3 Remove all built up scale from the coolant passages.

4 Run a stiff wire brush through the various holes to remove deposits that may have formed in them.

5 Run an appropriate size tap into each of the threaded holes to remove corrosion and thread sealant that may be present. If compressed air is available, use it to clear the holes of debris produced by this operation. **Warning:** *Wear eye protection when using compressed air!*

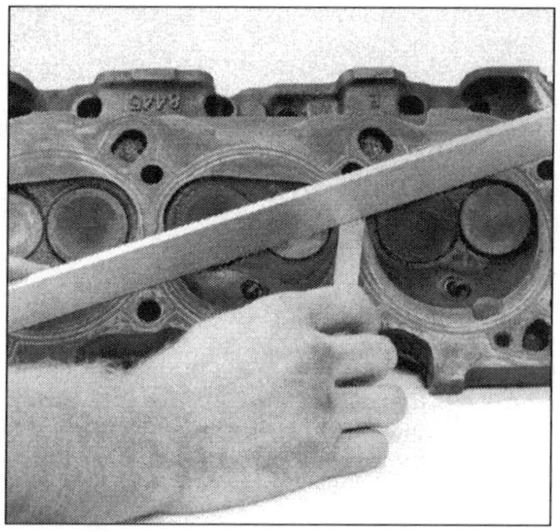

10.12 Check the cylinder head gasket surface for warpage by trying to slip a feeler gauge under the straightedge (see this Chapter's Specifications for the maximum warpage allowed and use a feeler gauge of that thickness)

6 Clean the rocker arm pivot stud threads, when equipped, with a wire brush.

7 Clean the cylinder head with solvent and dry it thoroughly. Compressed air will speed the drying process and ensure that all holes and recessed areas are clean. **Note:** *Decarbonizing chemicals are available and may prove very useful when cleaning cylinder heads and valve train components. They are very caustic and should be used with caution. Be sure to follow the instructions on the container.*

8 Clean the rocker arm components and pushrods with solvent and dry them thoroughly (don't mix them up during the cleaning process). Compressed air will speed the drying process and can be used to clean out the oil passages.

9 Clean all the valve springs, spring seats, keepers and retainers (or rotators) with solvent and dry them thoroughly. Do the components from one valve at a time to avoid mixing up the parts.

10 Scrape off any heavy deposits that may have formed on the valves,
then use a motorized wire brush to remove deposits from the valve heads and stems. Again, make sure the valves don't get mixed up.

Inspection

Note: *Be sure to perform all of the following inspection procedures before concluding that machine shop work is required. Make a list of the items that need attention.*

Cylinder head

Refer to illustrations 10.12 and 10.14

11 Inspect the head very carefully for cracks, evidence of coolant leakage and other damage. If cracks are found, check with an automotive machine shop concerning repair. If repair isn't possible, a new cylinder

10.14 A dial indicator can be used to determine the valve stem-to-guide clearance (move the valve stem as indicated by the arrows)

head should be obtained.

12 Using a straightedge and feeler gauge, check the head gasket mating surface for warpage **(see illustration)**. If the warpage exceeds the specified limit, it can be resurfaced at an automotive machine shop. **Note:** *If the heads are resurfaced, the intake manifold flanges will also require machining.*

13 Examine the valve seats in each of the combustion chambers. If they're pitted, cracked or burned, the head will require valve service that's beyond the scope of the home mechanic.

14 Check the valve stem-to-guide clearance by measuring the lateral movement of the valve stem with a dial indicator attached securely to the head **(see illustration)**. The valve must be in the guide and approximately 1/16-inch off the seat. The total valve stem movement indicated by the gauge needle must be divided by two to obtain the actual clearance. After this is done, if there's still some doubt regarding the condition of the valve guides, they should be checked by an automotive machine shop (the cost should be minimal). If they are beyond recommended clearances, the guides can be replaced at a machine shop.

Valves

Refer to illustrations 10.15 and 10.16

15 Carefully inspect each valve face and stem for uneven wear, deformation, cracks, pits and burned areas **(see illustration)**. Check the valve stem for scuffing and galling and the neck for cracks. Rotate the valve and check for any obvious indication that it's bent. Look for pits and excessive wear on the end of the stem. The presence of any of these conditions indicates the need for valve service by an automotive machine shop.

16 Measure the margin width on each valve **(see illustration)**. Any valve with a margin narrower than specified will have to be replaced with a new one.

Valve components

Refer to illustrations 10.17, 10.18 and 10.19

17 Check each valve spring for wear (on the ends) and pits. Any springs that are shorter than specified have sagged and should not be reused **(see illustration)**. The tension of all springs should be checked with a special fixture before deciding that they're suitable for use in a rebuilt engine (take the springs to an automotive machine shop for this check).

18 Stand each spring on a flat surface and check it for squareness **(see illustration)**. If any of the springs are distorted or sagged, replace all of them with new parts.

19 Check the spring retainers (or rotators) and keepers for obvious wear and cracks. Any questionable parts should be replaced with new ones, as extensive damage will occur if they fail during engine operation. Make sure the rotators If used) operate smoothly with no binding or excessive play **(see illustration)**.

Rocker arm components

20 Check the rocker arm faces (the areas that contact the pushrod ends and valve stems) for pits, wear, galling, score marks and rough spots. Check the rocker arm pivot contact areas and pivot as well. Look for cracks in each rocker arm and nut or bolt. Clean and inspect the pivots and (if equipped) the rocker arm shafts.

21 Inspect the pushrod ends for scuffing and excessive wear. Roll each pushrod on a flat surface, like a piece of plate glass, to determine if it's bent.

22 Check the rocker arm studs in the cylinder heads for damaged threads and secure installation.

23 Any damaged or excessively worn parts

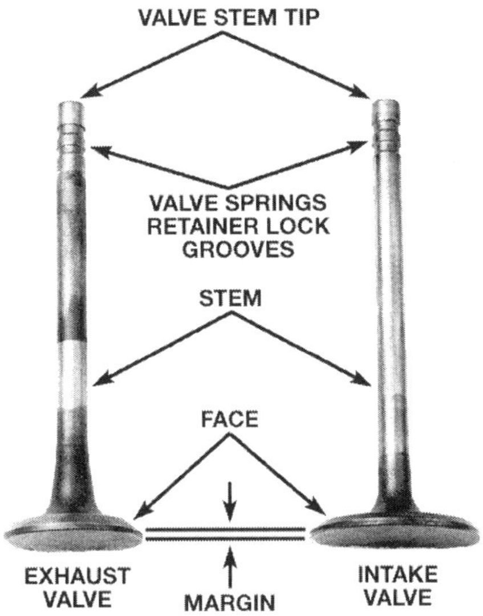

10.15 Using a micrometer or vernier caliper, check for valve wear at the points shown here

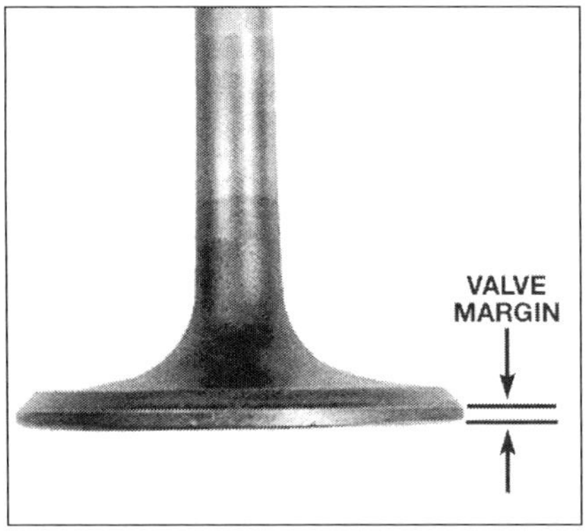

10.16 The margin width on the valve must be as specified (if no margin exists, the valve cannot be reused)

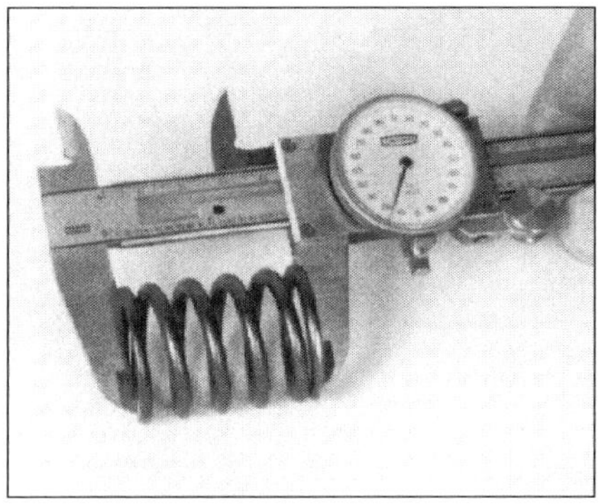

10.17 Measure the free length of each valve spring with a dial or vernier caliper

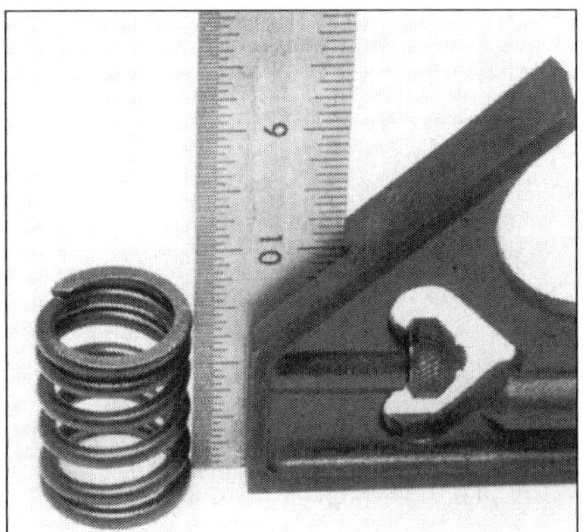

10.18 Check each valve spring for squareness

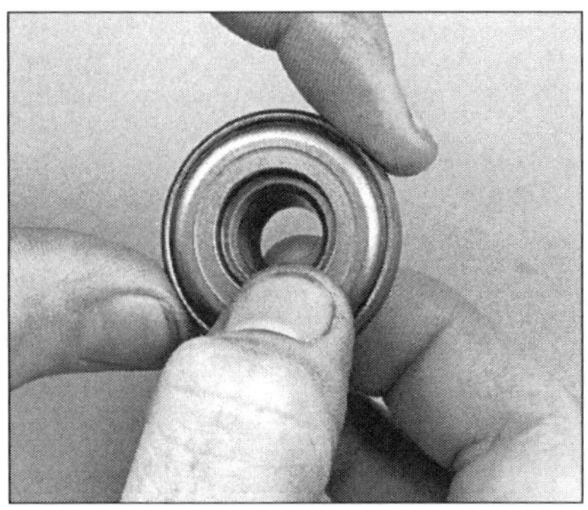

10.19 The exhaust valve rotators can be checked by turning the inner and outer sections in opposite directions - feel for smooth movement and excessive play

must be replaced with new ones.

24 If the inspection process indicates that the valve components are in generally poor condition and worn beyond the limits specified, which is usually the case in an engine that's being overhauled, reassemble the valves in the cylinder head and refer to Section 11 for valve servicing recommendations.

11 Valves - servicing

1 Because of the complex nature of the job and the special tools and equipment needed, servicing of the valves, the valve seats and the valve guides, commonly known as a valve job, should be done by a professional shop.

2 The home mechanic can remove and disassemble the heads, do the initial cleaning and inspection, then reassemble and deliver them to a dealer service department or an automotive machine shop for the actual service work. Doing the inspection will enable you to see what condition the heads and valvetrain components are in and will ensure that you know what work and new parts are required when dealing with an automotive machine shop.

3 The dealer service department, or automotive machine shop, will remove the valves and springs, recondition or replace the valves and valve seats, recondition the valve guides, check and replace the valve springs, spring retainers or rotators and keepers (as necessary), replace the valve seals with new ones, reassemble the valve components and make sure the installed spring height is correct. The cylinder head gasket surfaces will also be resurfaced if they're warped.

4 After the valve job has been performed by a professional, the heads will be in like-new condition. When the heads are returned, be sure to clean them again before installation on the engine to remove any metal particles and abrasive grit that may still be present from the valve service or head resurfacing operations. Use compressed air, if available, to blow out all the oil holes and passages.

Note: *Up until the mid-1970's, most engines were designed to operate on leaded fuels, which are no longer available. Unless the cylinder heads are machined and fitted with hardened valve seats, the new valve job will have a shortened life. Most engines built for unleaded fuel have seats that are "induction-hardened", which is a surface hardening treatment. After two valve jobs (or one sloppy one), much of the hardened area of the factory seat has been machined away, so fitting hardened seats, especially on the exhaust valves, is recommended for any older engine, even if it was originally designed for unleaded gasoline.*

12 Cylinder head - reassembly

Refer to illustration 12.8

1 Regardless of whether or not the heads were sent to an automotive repair shop for valve servicing, make sure they are clean before beginning reassembly.

12.8 Be sure to check the valve spring installed height (the distance from the top of the seat/shims to the top of the shield/bottom of the retainer

2 If the heads were sent out for valve servicing, the valves and related components will already be in place. Begin the reassembly procedure with Step 8.

3 Install new seals on each of the intake valve guides. Using a hammer and a deep socket, gently tap each seal into place until it is completely seated on the guide. Do not twist or cock the seals during installation or they will not seal properly on the valve stems. The umbrella-type seals are installed over the exhaust valves after the valves are in place (Refer to Chapter 2A or 2B for valve seal installation).

Note: *On Oldsmobile engines, the seals are color-coded as follows: intake seals are gray (standard size to .005-inch oversize) or orange (.010 to .013-inch oversize), and ivory-colored for the exhaust seals (standard size to .005-inch oversize) or blue (.010 to .013-inch oversize).*

4 Beginning at one end of the head, lubricate and install the first valve. Apply moly-base grease or clean engine oil to the valve stem.

5 Drop the spring seat or shim(s) over the valve guide and set the valve springs, shield and retainer (or rotator) in place. **Note:** *On Cadillac engines, there is a nylon "oil shedder" shield that goes on after the valve spring is in place, but before the retainer is positioned* **(refer to Chapter 2A or 2B for valve/spring arrangements)**.

6 Compress the springs with a valve spring compressor, position the keepers in the upper groove, then slowly release the compressor and make sure the keepers seat properly. Apply a small dab of grease to each keeper to hold it in place if necessary.

7 Repeat the procedure for the remaining valves. Be sure to return the components to their original locations - do not mix them up!

8 Check the installed valve spring height with a ruler graduated in 1/32-inch increments or a dial caliper. If the heads were sent out for service work, the installed height should be correct (but don't automatically assume that it is). The measurement is taken from the top of each spring seat or shim(s) to the top of the oil shield (or the bottom of the retainer/rotator, the two points are the same) **(see illustration)**. If the height is greater than specified, shims can be added under the springs to correct it. **Caution:** *Do not, under any circumstances, shim the springs to the point where the installed height is less than specified.*

13.1 A ridge reamer is required to remove the ridge from the top of each cylinder - do this before removing the pistons!

9 Apply moly-base grease to the rocker arm faces and the pivots, then install the rocker arms. On V-6 engines, assemble the rocker arms to the shafts, with moly-based lube on the shafts and the rocker arms properly oriented (the rockers are marked "L" for left and "R" for right).

13 Piston/connecting rod assembly - removal

Refer to illustrations 13.1, 13.3 and 13.6

Note: *Prior to removing the piston/connecting rod assemblies, remove the cylinder heads, the oil pan and the oil pump (except externally-mounted pumps) by referring to the appropriate Sections in Chapter 2A or 2B.*

1 Use your fingernail to feel if a ridge has formed at the upper limit of ring travel (about 1/4-inch down from the top of each cylinder). If carbon deposits or cylinder wear have produced ridges, they must be completely removed with a special tool **(see illustration)**. Follow the manufacturer's instructions provided with the tool. Failure to remove the ridges before attempting to remove the piston/connecting rod assemblies may result in piston breakage.

2 After the cylinder ridges have been removed, turn the engine upside-down so the crankshaft is facing up.

3 Before the connecting rods are removed, check the side clearance with feeler gauges. Slide them between the first connecting rod and the crankshaft throw until the play is removed **(see illustration)**. The endplay is equal to the thickness of the feeler

13.3 Check the connecting rod side clearance with a feeler gauge as shown

gauge(s). If the endplay exceeds the service limit, new connecting rods will be required. If new rods (or a new crankshaft) are installed, the endplay may fall under the specified minimum (if it does, the rods will have to be machined to restore it - consult an automotive machine shop for advice if necessary). Repeat the procedure for the remaining connecting rods.

4 Check the connecting rods and caps for identification marks. If they aren't plainly marked, use a small center punch to make the appropriate number of indentations on each rod and cap (1, 2, 3, etc., depending on the engine type and cylinder they're associated with). **Note:** *On HT4100 engines, if the original cylinder liners are to be reused, install a cylinder liner holder, available at most auto parts stores*, see Section 12 in Chapter 2, Part B) *to the engine block to prevent the liners from shifting when the pistons are withdrawn. Also, mark the position of the liners relative to the block with indelible ink to ensure they do not shift.*

5 Loosen each of the connecting rod cap nuts 1/2-turn at a time until they can be removed by hand. Remove the number one connecting rod cap and bearing insert. Don't drop the bearing insert out of the cap.

6 Slip a short length of plastic or rubber hose over each connecting rod cap bolt to protect the crankshaft journal and cylinder wall as the piston is removed **(see illustration)**. **Note:** *The HT4100 engine and V-6 engines use rod bolts that thread into the rod through the cap - there are no separate nuts, and no rubber hoses are required.*

7 Remove the bearing insert and push the connecting rod/piston assembly out through the top of the engine. Use a wooden hammer handle to push on the upper bearing surface in the connecting rod. If resistance is felt, double-check to make sure that all of the ridge was removed from the cylinder.

8 Repeat the procedure for the remaining cylinders.

9 After removal, reassemble the connecting rod caps and bearing inserts in their respective connecting rods and install the cap nuts finger tight. Leaving the old bearing inserts in place until reassembly will help prevent the connecting rod bearing surfaces from being accidentally nicked or gouged.

10 Don't separate the pistons from the connecting rods (see Sec-tion 18 for additional information).

13.6 To prevent damage to the crankshaft journals and cylinder walls, slip sections of rubber or plastic hose over the rod bolts before removing the pistons/rods

14.3 Checking crankshaft endplay with a feeler gauge

14 Crankshaft - removal

Refer to illustrations 14.1, 14.3, 14.4a and 14.4b

Note: *The crankshaft can be removed only after the engine has been removed from the vehicle. It's assumed that the driveplate, vibration damper, timing chain, oil pan, oil pump and piston/connecting rod assemblies have already been removed. If your engine is equipped with a one-piece rear main oil seal, the seal housing must be unbolted and separated from the block before proceeding with crankshaft removal.*

1 Before the crankshaft is removed, check the endplay. Mount a dial indicator with the stem in line with the crankshaft and touching one of the crank throws or the nose of the crankshaft **(see illustration)**.

14.1 Checking the crankshaft endplay with a dial indicator

14.4a All main caps should be marked with numbers or punch marks - this V6 block is marked with numbers and dots (the number of dots indicates which cap it is)

2 Push the crankshaft all the way to the rear and zero the dial indicator. Next, pry the crankshaft to the front as far as possible and check the reading on the dial indicator. The distance that it moves is the endplay. If it's greater than specified, check the crankshaft thrust surfaces for wear. If no wear is evident, new main bearings should correct the endplay.

3 If a dial indicator isn't available, feeler gauges can be used. Gently pry or push the crankshaft all the way to the front of the engine. Slip feeler gauges between the crankshaft and the front face of the thrust main bearing to determine the clearance **(see illustration)**.

4 Check the main bearing caps to see if they're marked to indicate their locations. They should be numbered consecutively from the front of the engine to the rear, usually also marked with a cast-in arrow, which points to the front of the engine **(see illustrations)**. If they aren't, mark them with number stamping dies or a center punch. Loosen the

14.4b Main cap numbering on the HT4100 V8 engine

main bearing cap bolts 1/4-turn at a time each, until they can be removed by hand. Note if any stud bolts are used and make sure they're returned to their original locations when the crankshaft is reinstalled.

5 Gently tap the caps with a soft-face hammer, then separate them from the engine block. If necessary, use the bolts as levers to remove the caps. Try not to drop the bearing inserts if they come out with the caps.

6 Carefully lift the crankshaft out of the engine. It may be a good idea to have an assistant available, since the crankshaft is quite heavy. With the bearing inserts in place in the engine block and main bearing caps, return the caps to their respective locations on the engine block and tighten the bolts finger tight.

15 Engine block - cleaning

Refer to illustrations 15.1, 15.9 and 15.11

1 Remove the core plugs from the engine block. To do this, knock one side of the plugs into the block with a hammer and punch, then grasp them with large pliers and pull them back through the holes **(see illustration)**. **Caution:** *The core plugs (also known as freeze or soft plugs) may be difficult or impossible to retrieve if they're driven into the block coolant passages.*

2 Using a gasket scraper, remove all traces of gasket material from the engine block. Be very careful not to nick or gouge the gasket sealing surfaces.

3 Remove the main bearing caps and separate the bearing inserts from the caps and the engine block. Tag the bearings, indicating which cylinder they were removed from and whether they were in the cap or the block, then set them aside.

4 Remove all of the threaded oil gallery plugs from the block. The plugs are usually very tight - they may have to be drilled out and the holes retapped. Use new plugs when the engine is reassembled.

5 **Caution:** *On HT4100 engines, it is necessary to remove the cylinder liners in order to properly clean the block. Carefully mark the alignment of each liner to the cylinder block if they are to be reused. However, this particular engine is a difficult one for the home mechanic to rebuild, because of the cylinder liners and other rebuilding problems. It is suggested that when rebuilding this engine, have the short-block cleaned and rebuilt at a professional engine shop. They will install new pistons with new, matching liners, carefully fit new O-rings to the bottom of the liners and set the correct liner height in the block.*

15.1 Use a hammer and large punch to knock the core plugs sideways in their bores, then pull them out with pliers

6 If the engine is extremely dirty it should be taken to an automotive machine shop to be steam cleaned or hot tanked.

7 After the block is returned, clean all oil holes and oil galleries one more time. Brushes specifically designed for this purpose are available at most auto parts stores. Flush the passages with warm water until the water runs clear, dry the block thoroughly and wipe all machined surfaces with a light, rust preventive oil. If you have access to compressed air, use it to speed the drying process and to blow out all the oil holes and galleries. **Warning:** *Wear eye protection when using compressed air!*

8 If the block isn't extremely dirty or sludged up, you can do an adequate cleaning job with hot soapy water and a stiff brush. Take plenty of time and do a thorough job. Regardless of the cleaning method used, be sure to clean all oil holes and galleries very thoroughly, dry the block completely and coat all machined surfaces with light oil.

9 The threaded holes in the block must be clean to ensure accurate torque readings during reassembly. Run the proper size tap into each of the holes to remove rust, corrosion, thread sealant or sludge and restore damaged threads **(see illustration)**. If possible, use compressed air to clear the holes of debris produced by this operation. Now is a good time to clean the threads on the head bolts and the main bearing cap bolts as well. **Caution:** *On the HT4100 engine with it's aluminum block, it is important to clean all of the block's threaded holes with taps to remove dirt or corrosion.*

15.9 All bolt holes in the block - particularly the main bearing cap and head bolt holes - should be cleaned and restored with a tap (be sure to remove debris from the holes after this is done)

15.11 A large socket on an extension can be used to drive the new core plugs into the bores

10 Reinstall the main bearing caps and tighten the bolts finger tight.

11 After coating the sealing surfaces of the new core plugs with Permatex no. 2 sealant, install them in the engine block **(see illustration)**. Make sure they're driven in straight and seated properly or leakage could result. Special tools are available for this purpose, but a large socket, with an outside diameter that will just slip into the core plug, a 1/2-inch drive extension and a hammer will work just as well. **Warning:** *On HT4100 engines, tap the plugs into the block slowly and gently to avoid cracking the aluminum block.*

12 Apply non-hardening sealant (such as Permatex no. 2 or Teflon pipe sealant) to the new oil gallery plugs and thread them into the holes in the block. Make sure they're tightened securely.

13 If the engine isn't going to be reassembled right away, cover it with a large plastic trash bag to keep it clean.

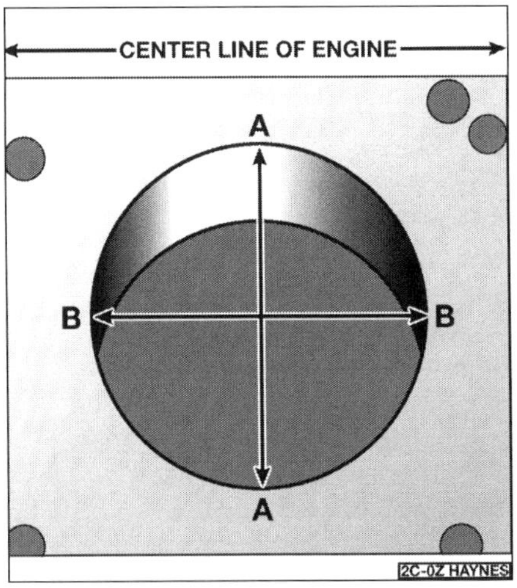

16.4a Measure the diameter of each cylinder at a right angle to the engine centerline (A), and parallel to the engine centerline (B) - out-of-round is the difference between A and B; taper is the difference between A and B at the top of the cylinder and A and B at the bottom of the cylinder

16 Engine block - inspection

Refer to illustrations 16.4a, 16.4b, 16.4c and 16.11

1 Before the block is inspected, it should be cleaned as described in Section 15.

2 Visually check the block for cracks, rust and corrosion. Look for stripped threads in the threaded holes. It's also a good idea to have the block checked for hidden cracks by an automotive machine shop that has the special equipment to do this type of work. If defects are found, have the block repaired, if possible, or replaced.

3 Check the cylinder bores for scuffing and scoring.

4 Check the cylinders for taper and out-of-round conditions as follows **(see illustrations)**:

5 Measure the diameter of each cylinder at the top (just under the ridge area), center and bottom of the cylinder bore, parallel to the crankshaft axis.

6 Next, measure each cylinder's diameter at the same three locations perpendicular to the crankshaft axis.

7 The taper of each cylinder is the difference between the bore diameter at the top of the cylinder and the diameter at the bottom. The out-of-round specification of the cylinder bore is the difference between the parallel and perpendicular readings. Compare your results to this Chapter's Specifications.

8 Repeat the procedure for the remaining pistons and cylinders.

9 If the cylinder walls are badly scuffed or scored, or if they're out-of-round or tapered beyond the limits given in the Specifications, have the engine block rebored and honed at an automotive machine shop. If a rebore is done, oversize pistons and rings will be required.

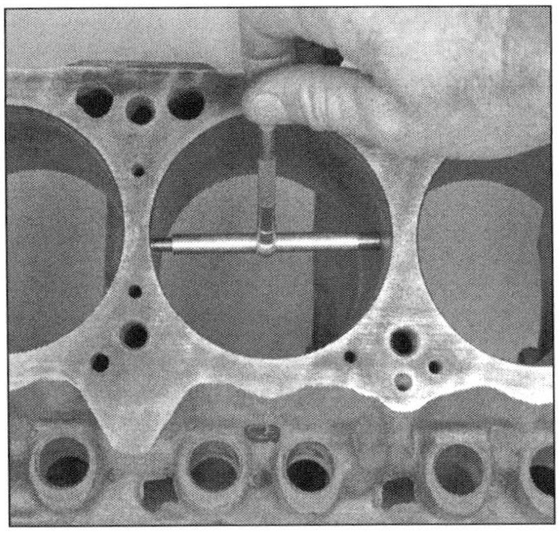

16.4b The ability to "feel" when the telescoping gauge is at the correct point will be developed over time, so work slowly and repeat the check until you're satisfied the bore measurement is accurate

10 If the cylinders are in reasonably good condition and not worn to the outside of the limits, and if the piston-to-cylinder clearances can be maintained properly, then they don't have to be rebored. Honing is all that's necessary (Section 17). **Note:** *It is not recommended to hone the cylinder liners in the HT4100 engine without specialized equipment. It is recommended that the engine be rebuilt by a professional, using new liners with matching new pistons.*

11 The cylinder head surface of the block should be check for warpage using a straightedge and feeler gauge **(see illustration)**. If it is beyond Specifications, the block must be surfaced at a machine shop.

17 Cylinder honing

Refer to illustrations 17.3a and 17.3b

1 Prior to engine reassembly, the cylinder bores must be honed so the new piston rings will seat correctly and provide the best possible combustion chamber seal (except for HT4100 engines, see Step 5 of Section 15). **Note:** *If you don't have the tools or don't want to tackle the honing operation, most automotive machine shops will do it for a reasonable fee.*

2 Before honing the cylinders, install the main bearing caps and tighten the bolts to the specified torque.

3 Two types of cylinder hones are commonly available - the flex hone, or "bottle brush," type and the more traditional surfacing hone with spring-loaded stones. Both will do the job, but for the less experienced mechanic the "bottle brush" hone will probably be easier to use. You'll also need some kerosene or honing oil, rags and an electric drill motor. Proceed as follows:

a) *Mount the hone in the drill motor, compress the stones and slip it into the first cylinder* **(see illustration)**. *Be sure to wear safety goggles or a face shield!*

b) *Lubricate the cylinder with plenty of honing oil, turn on the drill and move the hone up and down in the cylinder at a pace that will produce a fine crosshatch pattern on the cylinder walls. Ideally, the*

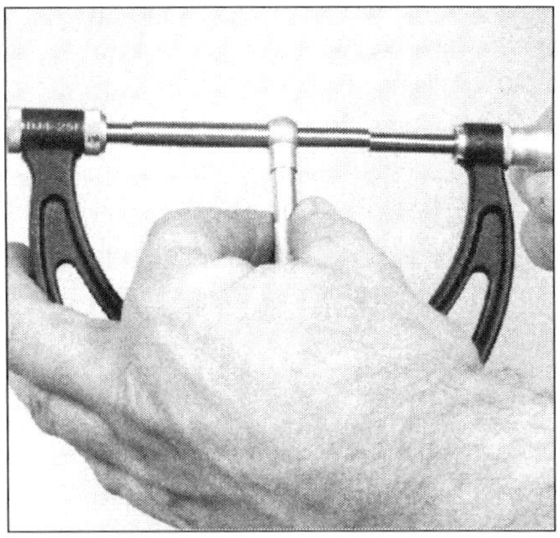

16.4c The gauge is then measured with a micrometer to determine the bore size

16.11 When the top of the block is cleaned, place a straightedge across the deck and try to slip a feeler gauge under it - if the specified gauge fits easily under the straightedge, the block must be surfaced at a machine shop

17.3a A "bottle-brush" hone will produce better results if you've never honed cylinders before

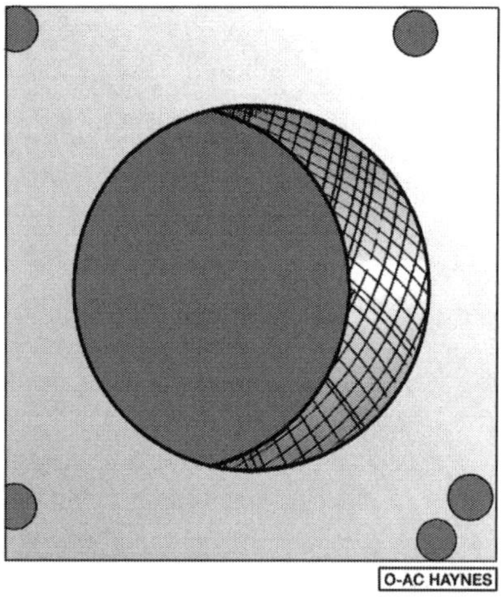

17.3b The cylinder hone should leave a smooth, crosshatch pattern with the lines intersecting at approximately a 45 to 60-degree angle

crosshatch lines should intersect at approximately a 60-degree angle **(see illustration)**. *Be sure to use plenty of lubricant and don't take off any more material than is absolutely necessary to produce the desired finish.* **Note:** *Piston ring manufacturers may specify a smaller crosshatch angle than the traditional 60-degrees - read and follow any instructions included with the new rings.*

c) *Don't withdraw the hone from the cylinder while it's running. Instead, shut off the drill and continue moving the hone up-and down in the cylinder until it comes to a complete stop, then compress the stones and withdraw the hone. If you're using a "bottle brush" type hone, stop the drill motor, then turn the chuck in the normal direction of rotation while withdrawing the hone from the cylinder.*

d) *Wipe the oil out of the cylinder and repeat the procedure for the remaining cylinders.*

4 After the honing job is complete, chamfer the top edges of the cylinder bores with a small file so the rings won't catch when the pistons are installed. Be very careful not to nick the cylinder walls with the end of the file.

5 The entire engine block must be washed again very thoroughly with warm, soapy water to remove all traces of the abrasive grit produced during the honing operation. **Note:** *The bores can be considered clean when a lint-free white cloth - dampened with clean engine oil - used to wipe them out doesn't pick up any more honing residue, which will show up as gray areas on the cloth. Be sure to run a brush through all oil holes and galleries and flush them with running water.*

6 After rinsing, dry the block and apply a coat of light rust preventive oil to all machined surfaces. Wrap the block in a plastic trash bag to keep it clean and set it aside until reassembly.

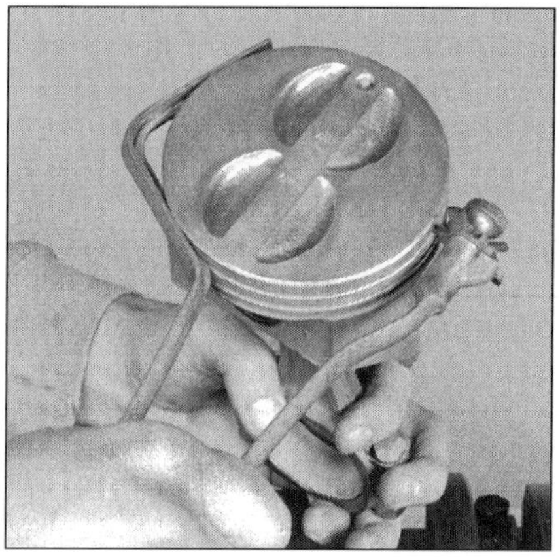

18.4a The piston ring grooves can be cleaned with a special tool, as shown here . . .

18 Piston/connecting rod assembly - inspection

Refer to illustrations 18.4a, 18.4b, 18.10 and 18.11

1 Before the inspection process can be carried out, the piston/connecting rod assemblies must be cleaned and the original piston rings removed from the pistons. **Note:** *Always use new piston rings when the engine is reassembled.*

2 Using a piston ring installation tool, carefully remove the rings from the pistons. Be careful not to nick or gouge the pistons in the process.

3 Scrape all traces of carbon from the top of the piston. A hand-held wire brush or a piece of fine emery cloth can be used once the majority of the deposits have been scraped away. Do not, under any circumstances, use a wire brush mounted in a drill motor to remove deposits from the pistons. The piston material is soft and may be eroded away by the wire brush.

4 Use a piston ring groove cleaning tool to remove carbon deposits from the ring grooves. If a tool isn't available, a piece broken off the old ring will do the job. Be very careful to remove only the carbon deposits - don't remove any metal and do not nick or scratch the sides of the ring grooves **(see illustrations)**.

5 Once the deposits have been removed, clean the piston/rod assemblies with solvent and dry them with compressed air (if available). Make sure the oil return holes in the back sides of the ring grooves are clear.

6 If the pistons and cylinder walls aren't damaged or worn excessively, and if the engine block is not rebored, new pistons won't be necessary. Normal piston wear appears as even vertical wear on the piston thrust surfaces and slight looseness of the top ring in its groove. New piston rings, however, should always be used when an engine is rebuilt.

7 Carefully inspect each piston for cracks around the skirt, at the pin bosses and at the ring lands.

18.4b . . . or a section of broken ring

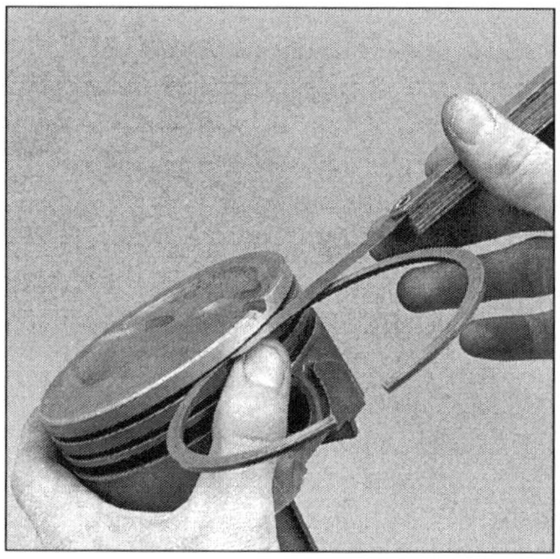

18.10 Check the ring side clearance with a feeler gauge at several points around the groove

8 Look for scoring and scuffing on the thrust faces of the skirt, holes in the piston crown and burned areas at the edge of the crown. If the skirt is scored or scuffed, the engine may have been suffering from overheating and/or abnormal combustion, which caused excessively high operating temperatures. The cooling and lubrication systems should be checked thoroughly. A hole in the piston crown is an indication that abnormal combustion (preignition) was occurring. Burned areas at the edge of the piston crown are usually evidence of spark knock (detonation). If any of the above problems exist, the causes must be corrected or the damage will occur again. The causes may include intake air leaks, incorrect fuel/air mixture, incorrect ignition timing and EGR system malfunctions.

9 Corrosion of the piston, in the form of small pits, indicates that coolant is leaking into the combustion chamber and/or the crankcase. Again, the cause must be corrected or the problem may persist in the rebuilt engine.

10 Measure the piston ring side clearance by laying a new piston ring in each ring groove and slipping a feeler gauge in beside it **(see illustration)**. Check the clearance at

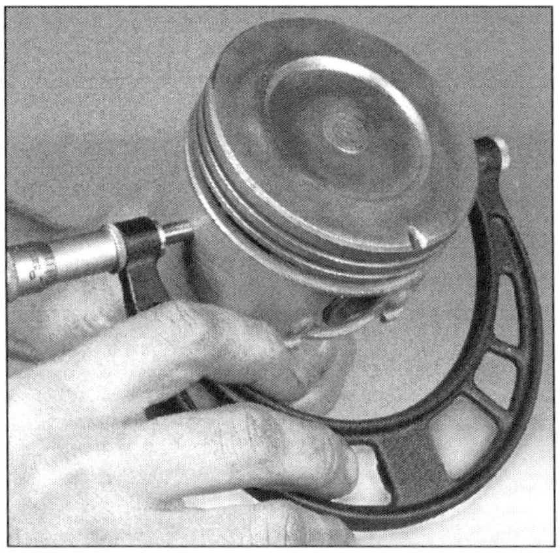

18.11 Measure the piston diameter at a 90-degree angle to the piston pin and in line with it

19.1 The oil holes should be chamfered so sharp edges don't gouge or scratch the new bearings

19.2 Use a wire or stiff plastic bristle brush to clean the oil passages in the crankshaft

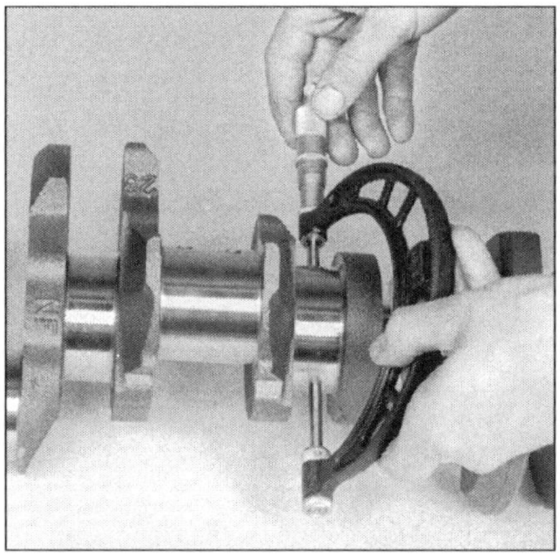

19.5 Measure the diameter of each crankshaft journal at several points to detect taper and out-of-round conditions

19.7 If the seals have worn grooves in the crankshaft journals, or if the seal contact surfaces are nicked or scratched, the new seals will leak

three or four locations around each groove. Be sure to use the correct ring for each groove - they are different. If the side clearance is greater than specified, new pistons will have to be used.

11 Check the piston-to-bore clearance by measuring the bore (see Section 16) and the piston diameter. Make sure the pistons and bores are correctly matched. Measure the piston across the skirt, at a 90-degree angle to and in line with the piston pin **(see illustration)** and 3/16-inch below the cross slot. Subtract the piston diameter from the bore diameter to obtain the clearance. If it's greater than specified, the block will have to be rebored and new pistons and rings installed. **Note:** *On HT4100 engines, if the clearances exceed the specifications, then the cylinder liner must be replaced by an automotive machine shop as the installation requires a special tool to set the cylinder liner height. It is best to purchase new pistons with matched liners.*

12 Check the piston-to-rod clearance by twisting the piston and rod in opposite directions. Any noticeable play indicates excessive wear, which must be corrected. The piston/connecting rod assemblies should be taken to an automotive machine shop to have the pistons and rods resized and new pins installed.

13 If the pistons must be removed from the connecting rods for any reason, they should be taken to an automotive machine shop. While they are there have the connecting rods checked for bend and twist, since automotive machine shops have special equipment for this purpose. **Note:** *Unless new pistons and/or connecting rods must be installed, do not disassemble the pistons and connecting rods.*

14 Check the connecting rods for cracks and other damage. Temporarily remove the rod caps, lift out the old bearing inserts, wipe the rod and cap bearing surfaces clean and inspect them for nicks, gouges and scratches. After checking the rods, replace the old bearings, slip the caps into place and tighten the nuts finger tight. **Note:** *If the engine is being rebuilt because of a connecting rod knock, be sure to install new rods.*

19 Crankshaft - inspection

Refer to illustrations 19.1, 19.2, 19.5 and 19.7

1 Remove all burrs from the crankshaft oil holes with a stone, file or scraper **(see illustration)**.

2 Clean the crankshaft with solvent and dry it with compressed air (if available). **Warning:** *Wear eye protection when using compressed air.* Be sure to clean the oil holes with a stiff brush **(see illustration)** and flush them with solvent.

3 Check the main and connecting rod bearing journals for uneven wear, scoring, pits and cracks.

4 Check the rest of the crankshaft for cracks and other damage. It should be magnafluxed to reveal hidden cracks - an automotive machine shop will handle the procedure.

5 Using a micrometer, measure the diameter of the main and connecting rod journals and compare the results to this Chapter's Specifications **(see illustration)**. By measuring the diameter at a number of points around each journal's circumference, you'll be able to determine whether or not the journal is out-of-round. Take the measurement at each end of the journal, near the crank throws, to determine if the journal is tapered.

6 If the crankshaft journals are damaged, tapered, out-of-round or worn beyond the limits given in the Specifications, have the crankshaft reground by an automotive machine shop. Be sure to use the correct size bearing inserts if the crankshaft is reconditioned.

7 Check the oil seal journals at each end of the crankshaft for wear and damage. If the seal has worn a groove in the journal, or if it's nicked or scratched **(see illustration)**, the new seal may leak when the engine is reassembled. In some cases, an automotive machine shop may be able to repair the journal by pressing on a thin sleeve. If repair isn't feasible, a new or different crankshaft should be installed.

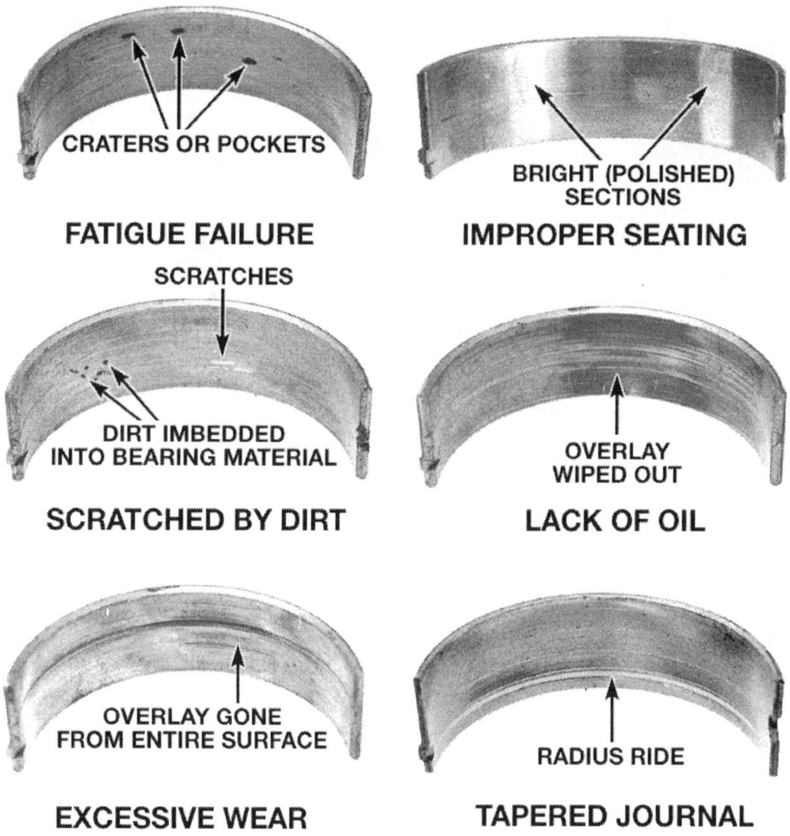

20.1 Typical bearing failures

8 Refer to Section 20 and examine the main and rod bearing inserts.

20 Main and connecting rod bearings - inspection

Refer to illustration 20.1

1 Even though the main and connecting rod bearings should be replaced with new ones during the engine overhaul, the old bearings should be retained for close examination, as they may reveal valuable information about the condition of the engine **(see illustration)**.

2 Bearing failure occurs because of lack of lubrication, the presence of dirt or other foreign particles, overloading the engine and corrosion. Regardless of the cause of bearing failure, it must be corrected before the engine is reassembled to prevent it from happening again.

3 When examining the bearings, remove them from the engine block, the main bearing caps, the connecting rods and the rod caps and lay them out on a clean surface in the same general position as their location in the engine. This will enable you to match any bearing problems with the corresponding crankshaft journal.

4 Dirt and other foreign particles get into the engine in a variety of ways. It may be left in the engine during assembly, or it may pass through filters or the PCV system. It may get into the oil, and from there into the bearings. Metal chips from machining operations and normal engine wear are often present. Abrasives are sometimes left in engine components after reconditioning, especially when parts are not thoroughly cleaned using the proper cleaning methods. Whatever the source, these foreign objects often end up embedded in the soft bearing material and are easily recognized. Large particles will not embed in the bearing and will score or gouge the bearing and journal. The best prevention for this cause of bearing failure is to clean all parts thoroughly and keep everything spotlessly clean during engine assembly. Frequent and regular engine oil and filter changes are also recommended.

5 Lack of lubrication (or lubrication breakdown) has a number of interrelated causes. Excessive heat (which thins the oil), overloading (which squeezes the oil from the bearing face) and oil leakage or throw off (from excessive bearing clearances, worn oil pump or high engine speeds) all contribute to lubrication breakdown. Blocked oil passages, which usually are the result of misaligned oil holes in a bearing shell, will also oil starve a bearing and destroy it. When lack of lubrication is the cause of bearing failure, the bearing material is wiped or extruded from the steel backing of the bearing. Temperatures may increase to the point where the steel backing turns blue from overheating.

6 Driving habits can have a definite effect on bearing life. Driving at low speed in too, high a gear (lugging the engine) puts very high loads on bearings, which tends to squeeze out the oil film. These loads cause the bearings to flex, which produces fine cracks in the bearing face (fatigue failure). Eventually the bearing material will loosen in pieces and tear away from the steel backing. Short-trip driving leads to corrosion of bearings because insufficient engine heat is produced to drive off the condensed water and corrosive gases. These products collect in the engine oil, forming acid and sludge. As the oil is carried to the engine bearings, the acid attacks and corrodes the bearing material.

7 Incorrect bearing installation during engine assembly will lead to bearing failure as well. Tight fitting bearings leave insufficient bearing oil clearance and will result in oil starvation. Dirt or foreign particles trapped behind a bearing insert result in high spots on the bearing which lead to failure.

21 Engine overhaul - reassembly sequence

1 Before beginning engine reassembly, make sure you have all the necessary new parts, gaskets and seals as well as the following items on hand:

Common hand tools
A 1/2-inch drive torque wrench
Piston ring installation tool
Piston ring compressor
Vibration damper installation tool
Short lengths of rubber or plastic hose to fit over connecting rod bolts
Plastigage
Feeler gauges
A fine-tooth file
New engine oil
Engine assembly lube or moly-base grease
Gasket sealant
Thread locking compound

2 In order to save time and avoid problems, engine reassembly must be done in the following general order:

New camshaft bearings (must be installed by an automotive machine shop)
Piston rings
Crankshaft and main bearings
Piston/connecting rod assemblies
Oil pump - except external-mount type
Camshaft and lifters
Oil pan
Timing chain and sprockets
Cylinder heads, pushrods and rocker arms
Timing cover (and oil pump - external-mount type)
Intake and exhaust manifolds
Valve covers
Engine rear plate
Driveplate

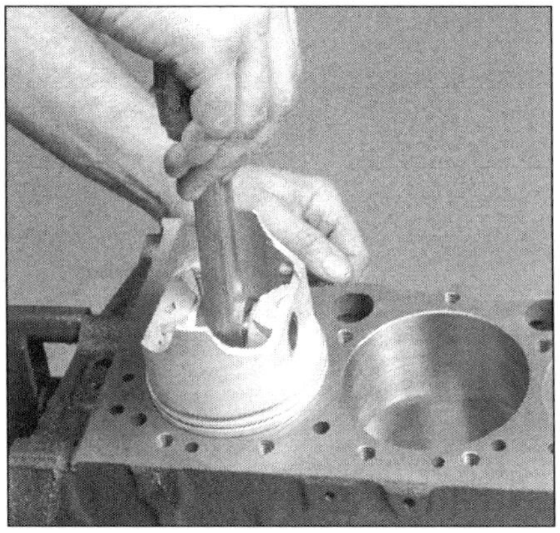

22.3 When checking piston ring end gap, the ring must be square in the cylinder bore (this is done by pushing the ring down with the top of a piston as shown)

22.4 With the ring square in the cylinder, measure the end gap with a feeler gauge

22.5 If the end gap is too small, clamp a file in a vise and file the ring ends (from the outside in only) to enlarge the gap slightly

22 Piston rings - installation

Refer to illustrations 22.3, 22.4, 22.5, 22.9a, 22.9b and 22.12

1 Before installing the new piston rings, the ring end gaps must be checked. It's assumed that the piston ring side clearance has been checked and verified correct (see Section 18).

2 Lay out the piston/connecting rod assemblies and the new ring sets so the ring sets will be matched with the same piston and cylinder during the end gap measurement and engine assembly. **Note:** *The 425, 500 and 368 V8 engines are stamped on the block with an identification number that designates the size of the piston. The letter is located on the cylinder head face of the cylinder block, directly below the cylinder bore.* Refer to the Specifications listed in this Chapter for the correct sizes.

3 Insert the top (number one) ring into the first cylinder and square it up with the cylinder walls by pushing it in with the top of the piston **(see illustration)**. The ring should be near the bottom of the cylinder, at the lower limit of ring travel.

4 To measure the end gap, slip feeler gauges between the ends of the ring until a gauge equal to the gap width is found **(see illustration)**. The feeler gauge should slide between the ring ends with a slight amount of drag. Compare the measurement to the Specifications. If the gap is larger or smaller than specified, double-check to make sure you have the correct rings before proceeding.

5 If the gap is too small, it must be enlarged or the ring ends may come in contact with each other during engine operation, which can cause serious damage to the engine. The end gap can be increased by filing the ring ends very carefully with a fine file. Mount the file in a vise equipped with soft jaws, slip the ring over the file with the ends contacting the file face and slowly move the ring to remove material from the ends. When performing this operation, file only from the outside in **(see illustration)**.

6 Excess end gap isn't critical unless it's greater than 0.040-inch. Again, double-check to make sure you have the correct rings for your engine.

7 Repeat the procedure for each ring that will be installed in the first cylinder and for each ring in the remaining cylinders. Remember to keep rings, pistons and cylinders matched up.

8 Once the ring end gaps have been checked/corrected, the rings can be installed on the pistons.

9 The oil control ring (lowest one on the piston) is usually installed first. It's composed of three separate components. Slip the spacer/expander into the groove **(see illustration)**. If an anti-rotation tang is used, make sure it's inserted into the drilled hole in the ring groove. Next, install the lower side rail. Don't use a piston ring installation tool on the oil ring side rails, as they may be damaged. Instead, place one end of the side rail into the groove between the spacer/expander and the ring land, hold it firmly in place and slide a finger around the piston while pushing the rail into the groove **(see illustration)**. Next, install the upper side rail in the same manner.

10 After the three oil ring components have been installed, check to make sure that both the upper and lower side rails can be turned smoothly in the ring groove.

11 The number two (middle) ring is installed next. It's usually stamped with a mark which must face up, toward the top of the piston. **Note:** *Always follow the instructions printed on the ring package or box - different manufacturers may require different approaches. Do not mix up the top and middle rings, as they have different cross sections.*

12 Use a piston ring installation tool and make sure the identification mark is facing the top of the piston, then slip the ring into

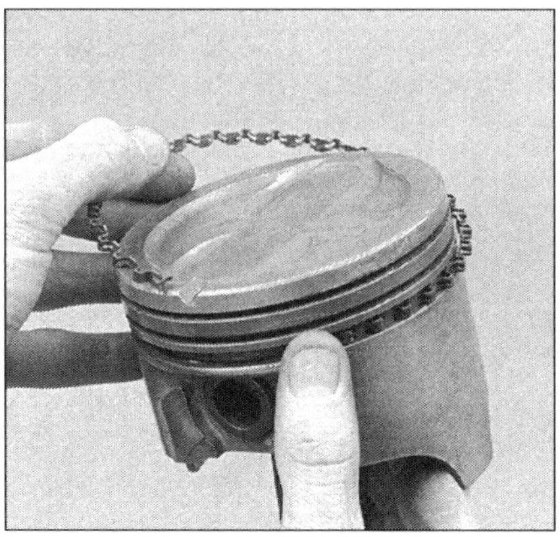

22.9a Install the spacer/expander in the oil control ring groove

22.9b DO NOT use a piston ring installation tool when installing the oil ring side rails

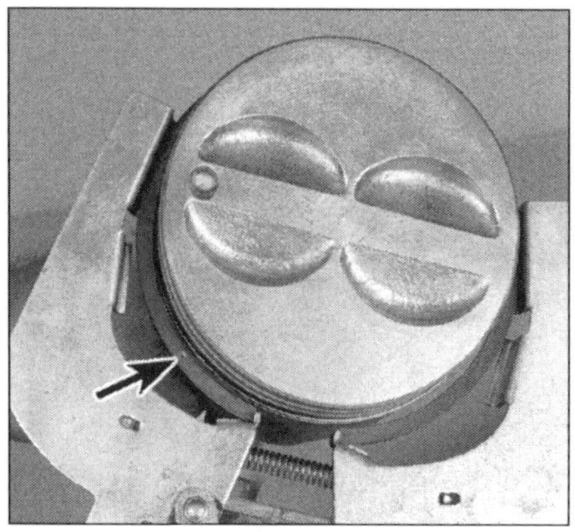

22.12 Install the compression rings with a ring expander - the mark (arrow) must face up

the middle groove on the piston **(see illustration)**. Don't expand the ring any more than necessary to slide it over the piston.

13 Install the number one (top) ring in the same manner. Make sure the mark is facing up. Be careful not to confuse the number one and number two compression rings.

14 Repeat the procedure for the remaining pistons and rings.

23 Rear main oil seal installation

1 In Parts A and B of this Chapter, the procedure is given for replacement of the rear main seal while the engine is in the car, and the crankshaft still in the engine. The procedure is somewhat simpler when the engine is being overhauled, but refer to the illustrations and procedures in those Parts first.

2 On engines with neoprene seals, install the upper half in the groove in the block. Most neoprene seals come with a wax coating to ease installation, don't remove this coating. Seat the seal in the block by pressing the ends flush with the block, pushing evenly on both ends of the seal at the same time. **Caution:** *Do not use any kind of silicone lubricant on the seal lips or oil leakage could develop*.

3 On engines with fabric rear seals (V6's and Oldsmobile V8's), apply some Loctite 414 (or equivalent) to the seal's groove, install one-half of the new seal into the block, and work it into the channel with a large-diameter socket or a wooden hammer handle. Trim the ends with a sharp razor or utility knife, leaving each end sticking up 1/16-inch above the surface of the block. **Note:** *When trimming the seal ends, use a metal backing to cut against, so the seal end is cut clean and square.*

4 With either type of seal, proceed with the crankshaft installation and main bearing selection (see Section 24) after Steps 1 through 3. The following steps should be performed after the Plastigage is removed, the bearings are lubed and the caps are being installed for the last time.

5 Install the lower seal half (neoprene) into the main cap until it is flush with the cap at each end. On fabric seals, install and trim the lower seal to the cap as in Step 3 above. On V6 engines, apply a drop of RTV sealant to the ends of the seals and the rear of the cap **(see Chapter 2A)**.

6 On V6 models, there are two side seals between the cap and the block. Install and tighten the cap bolts to Specifications. Soak the side seals in light engine oil for five minutes, then push them into the grooves between the main cap and the block (see Chapter 2A).

7 On HT 4100 engines, the side seals on the rear main are not separate neoprene seals, but RTV sealant. Clean any old sealant from the cap and block, then install the cap with new main seals in place. Fit a small washer over the tip on your RTV tube, put the tip into the cap-to-block groove and force RTV in **(See Chapter 2B)**. Both grooves

24.11 Lay the Plastigage strips (arrow) on the main bearing journals, parallel to the crankshaft centerline

should be filled completely.

8 On all engines, after the rear cap is tightened to the specified torque, rotate the crankshaft to make sure everything turns properly.

24 Crankshaft - installation and main bearing oil clearance check

Refer to illustrations 24.11 and 24.15

1 Crankshaft installation is the first step in engine reassembly. It's assumed at this point that the engine block and crankshaft have been cleaned, inspected and repaired or reconditioned.

2 Position the engine with the bottom facing up.

3 Remove the main bearing cap bolts and lift out the caps. Lay them out in the proper order to ensure correct installation. **Note:** *On HT4100 engines, each bearing cap has a cast number (1/8, 2/8, 3/8, 4/8 and 5/8) on the bottom starting from the front of the engine* **(see Part B of this Chapter)**. *Do not mismatch them, as they are manufactured specifically for that particular journal.*

4 If they're still in place, remove the original bearing inserts from the block and the main bearing caps. Wipe the bearing surfaces of the block and caps with a clean, lint-free cloth. They must be kept spotlessly clean.

Main bearing oil clearance check

5 Clean the back sides of the new main bearing inserts and lay one in each main bearing saddle in the block. If one of the bearing inserts from each set has a large groove in it, make sure the grooved insert is installed in the block. Lay the other bearing from each set in the corresponding main bearing cap. Make sure the tab on the bearing insert fits into the recess in the block or cap. **Caution:** *The oil holes in the block must line up with the oil holes in the bearing insert.* Do not hammer the bearing into place and

24.15 Measure the width of the crushed Plastigage to determine the main bearing oil clearance (be sure to use the correct scale - standard and metric ones are included)

don't nick or gouge the bearing faces. No lubrication should be used at this time.

6 The flanged thrust bearing must be installed in the proper cap and saddle.

7 Clean the faces of the bearings in the block and the crankshaft main bearing journals with a clean, lint-free cloth.

8 Check or clean the oil holes in the crankshaft, as any dirt here can go only one way - straight through the new bearings.

9 Once you're certain the crankshaft is clean, carefully lay it in position in the main bearings.

10 Before the crankshaft can be permanently installed, the main bearing oil clearance must be checked.

11 Cut several pieces of the appropriate-size Plastigage (they must be slightly shorter than the width of the main bearings) and place one piece on each crankshaft main bearing journal, parallel with the journal axis **(see illustration)**.

12 Clean the faces of the bearings in the caps and install the caps in their respective positions (don't mix them up) with the arrows pointing toward the front of the engine. Don't disturb the Plastigage.

13 Starting with the center main and working out toward the ends, tighten the main bearing cap bolts, in three steps, to the specified torque. Don't rotate the crankshaft at any time during this operation.

14 Remove the bolts and carefully lift off the main bearing caps. Keep them in order. Don't disturb the Plastigage or rotate the crankshaft. If any of the main bearing caps are difficult to remove, tap them gently from side to side with a soft-face hammer to loosen them.

15 Compare the width of the crushed Plastigage on each journal to the scale printed on the Plastigage envelope to obtain the main bearing oil clearance **(see illustration)**. Check the Specifications to make sure it's correct.

16 If the clearance is not as specified, the bearing inserts may be the wrong size (which

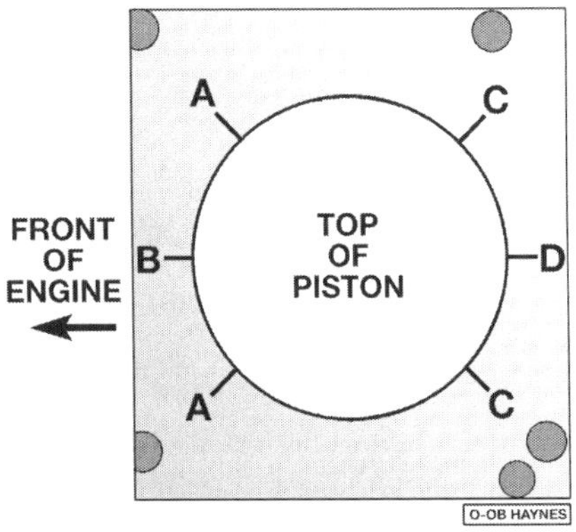

25.5 Ring end gap positions

A Oil ring rail gaps
B Second compression ring gap
C Oil ring spacer gap (position in-between marks)
D Top compression ring gap

means different ones will be required). Before deciding that different inserts are needed, make sure that no dirt or oil was between the bearing inserts and the caps or block when the clearance was measured. If the Plastigage was wider at one end than the other, the journal may be tapered (refer to Section 19).

17 Carefully scrape all traces of the Plastigage material off the main bearing journals and/or the bearing faces. Use your fingernail or the edge of a credit card - don't nick or scratch the bearing faces.

Final crankshaft installation

18 Carefully lift the crankshaft out of the engine.

19 Clean the bearing faces in the block, then apply a thin, uniform layer of moly-base grease or engine assembly lube to each of the bearing surfaces. Be sure to coat the thrust faces as well as the journal face of the thrust bearing.

20 Make sure the crankshaft journals are clean, then lay the crankshaft back in place in the block. The upper half of the rear main seal should be in place in the block (see Section 23).

21 Clean the faces of the bearings in the caps, then apply lubricant to them.

22 Install the caps in their respective positions with the arrows pointing toward the front of the engine. The lower half of the rear main seal should be installed in the cap (see Section 23).

23 Install the bolts.

24 Tighten all except the thrust bearing cap bolts to the specified torque (work from the center out and approach the final torque in three steps).

25 Tighten the thrust bearing cap bolts to 10 to 12 ft-lbs.

26 Tap the ends of the crankshaft forward and backward with a lead or brass hammer to line up the main bearing and crankshaft thrust surfaces.

25.9 The mark or notch on the top of the piston must face forward in the engine

27 Retighten all main bearing cap bolts to the specified torque, starting with the center main and working out toward the ends.

28 Rotate the crankshaft a number of times by hand to check for any obvious binding.

29 The final step is to check the crankshaft endplay with a feeler gauge or a dial indicator as described in Section 14. The endplay should be correct if the crankshaft thrust faces aren't worn or damaged and new bearings have been installed.

25 Piston/connecting rod assembly - installation and rod bearing oil clearance check

Refer to illustrations 25.5, 25.9, 25.11, 25.13 and 25.17

1 Before installing the piston/connecting rod assemblies, the cylinder walls must be perfectly clean, the top edge of each cylinder must be chamfered, and the crankshaft must be in place.

2 Remove the cap from the end of the number one connecting rod (refer to the marks made during removal). Remove the original bearing inserts and wipe the bearing surfaces of the connecting rod and cap with a clean, lint-free cloth. They must be kept spotlessly clean.

Connecting rod bearing oil clearance check

3 Clean the back side of the new upper bearing insert, then lay it in place in the connecting rod. Make sure the tab on the bearing fits into the recess in the rod. Don't hammer the bearing insert into place and be very careful not to nick or gouge the bearing face. Don't lubricate the bearing at this time.

4 Clean the back side of the other bearing insert and install it in the rod cap. Again, make sure the tab on the bearing fits into the recess in the cap, and don't apply any lubricant. It's critically important that the mating surfaces of the bearing and connecting rod are perfectly clean and oil-free when they're assembled.

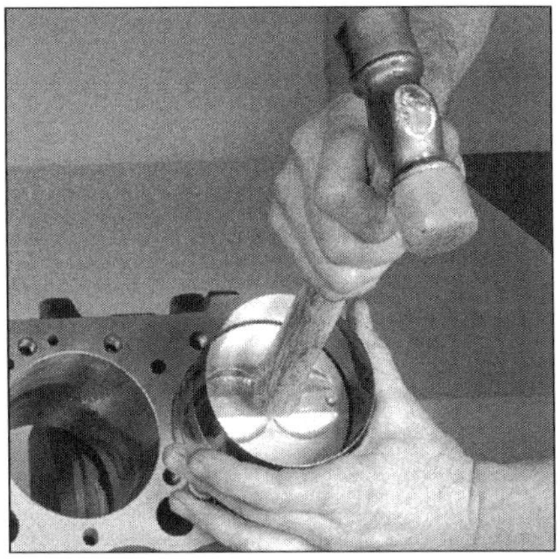

25.11 Drive the piston gently into the cylinder bore with the end of a wooden or plastic hammer handle

5 Stagger the piston rings around the piston as shown in the accompanying illustration **(see illustration)**. This will prevent blowby, loss of compression and excessive oil consumption.

6 Slip a section of plastic or rubber hose over each connecting rod cap bolt.

7 Lubricate the piston and rings with clean engine oil and attach a piston ring compressor to the piston. Leave the skirt protruding about 1/4-inch to guide the piston into the cylinder. The rings must be compressed until they're flush with the piston.

8 Rotate the crankshaft until the number one connecting rod journal is at BDC (bottom dead center) and apply a coat of engine oil to the cylinder walls. **Caution:** *During this procedure on HT4100 engines, the crankshaft must never be turned unless either the cylinder heads are in place or a suitable tool is bolted to the head surface of the block to hold the cylinder liners from moving* **(see Part B of this Chapter)**. *If the engine is turned without the plate tightened in place, the cylinder liners can move enough to break the seal on the O-rings sealing the bottom of the liners to the block, causing coolant leaks later on. It is one of the reasons that we recommend having this engine rebuilt professionally.*

9 With the mark or notch on top of the piston **(see illustration)** facing the front of the engine, gently insert the piston/connecting rod assembly into the number one cylinder bore and rest the bottom edge of the ring compressor on the engine block.

10 Tap the top edge of the ring compressor to make sure it's contacting the block around its entire circumference.

11 Gently tap on the top of the piston with the end of a wooden hammer handle **(see illustration)** while guiding the end of the connecting rod into place on the crankshaft journal. The piston rings may try to pop out of the ring compressor just before entering the cylinder bore, so keep some downward pressure on the ring compressor. Work slowly,

25.13 Lay the Plastigage strips on each rod bearing journal, parallel to the crankshaft centerline

and if any resistance is felt as the piston enters the cylinder, stop immediately. Find out what's hanging up and fix it before proceeding. Do not, for any reason, force the piston into the cylinder - you might break a ring and/or the piston.

12 Once the piston/connecting rod assembly is installed, the connecting rod bearing oil clearance must be checked before the rod cap is permanently bolted in place.

13 Cut a piece of the appropriate-size Plastigage slightly shorter than the width of the connecting rod bearing and lay it in place on the number one connecting rod journal, parallel with the journal axis **(see illustration)**.

14 Clean the connecting rod cap bearing face, remove the protective hoses from the connecting rod bolts and install the rod cap. Make sure the mating mark on the cap is on the same side as the mark on the connecting rod.

15 Install the nuts and tighten them to the torque listed in this Chapter's Specifications, working up to it in three steps. **Note:** *Use a thin-wall socket to avoid erroneous torque readings that can result if the socket is wedged between the rod cap and nut. If the socket tends to wedge itself between the nut and the cap, lift up on it slightly until it no longer contacts the cap. Do not rotate the crankshaft at any time during this operation.*

16 Remove the nuts and detach the rod cap, being very careful not to disturb the Plastigage.

17 Compare the width of the crushed Plastigage to the scale printed on the Plastigage envelope to obtain the oil clearance. Compare it to the Specifications to make sure the clearance is correct **(see illustration)**.

18 If the clearance is not as specified, the bearing inserts may be the wrong size (which means different ones will be required). Before deciding that different inserts are needed, make sure that no dirt or oil was between the bearing inserts and the connecting rod or cap when the clearance was measured. Also, recheck the journal diameter. If the Plasti-

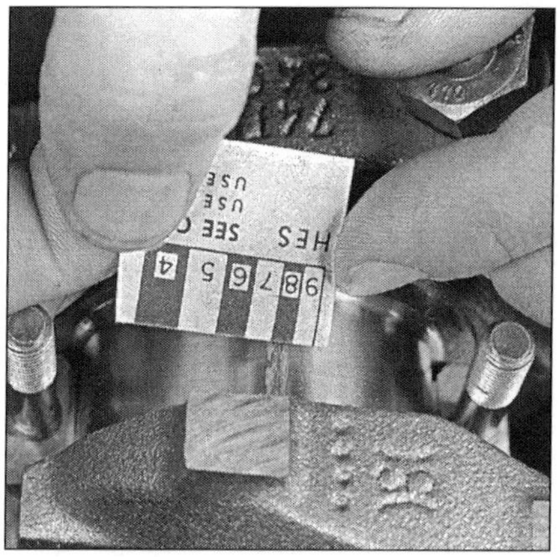

25.17 Measure the width of the crushed Plastigage to determine the rod bearing oil clearance (be sure to use the correct scale - standard and metric ones are included)

gage was wider at one end than the other, the journal may be tapered (refer to Section 19).

Final connecting rod installation

19 Carefully scrape all traces of the Plastigage material off the rod journal and/or bearing face. Be very careful not to scratch the bearing - use your fingernail or the edge of a credit card.

20 Make sure the bearing faces are perfectly clean, then apply a uniform layer of clean moly-base grease or engine assembly lube to both of them. You'll have to push the piston into the cylinder to expose the face of the bearing insert in the connecting rod - be sure to slip the protective hoses over the rod bolts first.

21 Slide the connecting rod back into place on the journal, remove the protective hoses from the rod cap bolts, install the rod cap and tighten the nuts to the specified torque. Again, work up to the torque in three steps.

22 Repeat the entire procedure for the remaining pistons/connecting rods.

23 The important points to remember are:

a) *Keep the back sides of the bearing inserts and the insides of the connecting rods and caps perfectly clean when assembling them.*
b) *Make sure you have the correct piston/rod assembly for each cylinder.*
c) *The notch or mark on the piston must face the front of the engine.*
d) *Lubricate the cylinder walls with clean oil.*
e) *Lubricate the bearing faces when installing the rod caps after the oil clearance has been checked.*

24 After all the piston/connecting rod assemblies have been properly installed, rotate the crankshaft a number of times by hand to check for any obvious binding.

25 As a final step, the connecting rod endplay must be checked. Refer to Section 13 for this procedure.

26 Compare the measured endplay to the Specifications to make sure it's correct. If it was correct before disassembly and the original crankshaft and rods were reinstalled, it should still be right. If new rods or a new crankshaft were installed, the endplay may be inadequate. If so, the rods will have to be removed and taken to an automotive machine shop for resizing.

26 Initial start-up and break-in after overhaul

Warning: *Have a fire extinguisher handy when starting the engine for the first time.*

1 Once the engine has been installed in the vehicle, double-check the engine oil and coolant levels.

2 With the spark plugs out of the engine and the ignition system disabled (see Section 3), crank the engine until oil pressure registers on the gauge or the indicator light goes out.

3 Install the spark plugs, hook up the plug wires and restore the ignition system functions (see Section 3).

4 Start the engine. It may take a few moments for the fuel system to build up pressure, but the engine should start without a great deal of effort. **Note:** *If backfiring occurs through the carburetor or throttle body, recheck the carburetor and ignition timing. If that fails to correct it, check for improper timing chain installation.*

5 As soon as the engine starts, it should be set at a fast idle (to ensure proper oil circulation) and allowed to warm up to normal operating temperature. While the engine is warming up, make a thorough check for oil and coolant leaks.

6 Shut the engine off and recheck the engine oil and coolant levels.

7 Drive the vehicle to an area with minimum traffic, accelerate sharply from 30 to 50 mph, then allow the vehicle to slow to 30 mph with the throttle closed. Repeat the procedure 10 or 12 times. This will load the piston rings and cause them to seat properly against the cylinder walls. Check again for oil and coolant leaks.

8 Drive the vehicle gently for the first 500 miles (no sustained high speeds) and keep a constant check on the oil level. It is not unusual for an engine to use oil during the break-in period.

9 At approximately 500 to 600 miles, change the oil and filter.

10 For the next few hundred miles, drive the vehicle normally. Do not pamper it or abuse it.

11 After 2000 miles, change the oil and filter again and consider the engine broken in.

Chapter 3
Cooling, heating and air conditioning systems

Contents

Specifications

General

Radiator cap pressure rating	15 psi
Thermostat rating	192 to 199-degrees F

Torque specifications

	Ft-lbs (unless otherwise indicated)
Water pump mounting fasteners	
V6 engines (all fasteners)	84 in-lbs
Oldsmobile-built V8 engines **(see illustration 7.12a)**	
Pump to cover screws (A)	156 in-lbs
Pump to block bolts (B)	180 in-lbs
HT4100 Cadillac V8 **(see illustration 7.12c)**	
A	30
B	60 in-lbs
C	84 in-lbs
D	180 in-lbs
500, 425 and 368 Cadillac V8 **(see illustration 7.12b)**	
A	70 in-lbs
B	180 in-lbs
C	22 ft-lbs
Thermostat housing cover bolts	
V-6 engines	156 in-lbs
Oldsmobile-built V8 engines	20
Cadillac V8 engines, 500, 425 and 368	120 in-lbs
Cadillac HT4100 V8	
Upper housing-to-lower housing	20
Lower housing-to-water pump bolt	84 in-lbs
Lower housing-to-water pump stud	30
Coolant temperature sending unit	20
Fan to clutch bolts	20
Water pump pulley nuts	20

1 General information

Engine cooling system

All vehicles covered by this manual employ a pressurized engine cooling system with thermostatically controlled coolant circulation. An impeller-type water pump mounted on the front of the block pumps coolant through the engine. The coolant flows around each cylinder and toward the rear of the engine. Cast-in coolant passages direct coolant around the intake and exhaust ports, near the spark plug areas and in close proximity to the exhaust valve guides.

A wax pellet type thermostat is located in the thermostat housing near the front of the engine. During warm up, the closed thermostat prevents coolant from circulating through the radiator. When the engine reaches normal operating temperature, the thermostat opens and allows hot coolant to travel through the radiator, where it is cooled before returning to the engine.

The cooling system is sealed by a pressure-type radiator cap. This raises the boiling point of the coolant, and the higher boiling point of the coolant increases the cooling efficiency of the radiator. If the system pressure exceeds the cap pressure relief value, the excess pressure in the system forces the spring-loaded valve inside the cap off its seat and allows the coolant to escape through the overflow tube into a coolant reservoir. When the system cools, the excess coolant is automatically drawn from the reservoir back into the radiator.

The coolant reservoir serves as both the point at which fresh coolant is added to the cooling system to maintain the proper fluid level and as a holding tank for overheated coolant.

This type of cooling system is known as a closed design because coolant that escapes past the pressure cap is saved and reused.

Heating system

The heating system consists of a blower fan and heater core located within the heater box, the inlet and outlet hoses connecting the heater core to the engine cooling system and the heater/air conditioning control head on the dashboard. Hot engine coolant is circulated through the heater core. When the heater mode is activated, a flap door opens to expose the heater box to the passenger compartment. A fan switch on the control head activates the blower motor, which forces air through the core, heating the air. The adjustable temperature lever controls how much incoming air is exposed to the heater core, while the fan switch controls how fast the blower pushes the air.

Air conditioning system

The air conditioning system consists of a condenser mounted in front of the radiator, an evaporator mounted adjacent to the heater core, a compressor mounted on the engine, a filter-drier (accumulator) which contains a high-pressure relief valve and the plumbing connecting all of the above.

The blower fan forces the warmer air through the evaporator core (sort of a radiator-in-reverse), transferring the heat from the air to the refrigerant. The liquid refrigerant boils off into low pressure vapor, taking the heat with it when it leaves the evaporator. When the controls are set to NORM mode, outside air is taken in and cooled. When switched to MAX (or HIGH on climate-controlled systems), a vent door closes to recirculate the car's *interior* air instead of outside air. Since the interior air is already somewhat cooled and dehumidified, the MAX setting will provide cooler air conditioning when the outside air is very hot or humid.

2 Antifreeze - general information

Refer to illustration 2.7

Warning: *Do not allow antifreeze to come in contact with your skin or painted surfaces of the vehicle. Rinse off spills immediately with plenty of water. Antifreeze is highly toxic if ingested. Never leave antifreeze lying around in an open container or in puddles on the floor; children and pets are attracted by it's sweet smell and may drink it. Check with local authorities about disposing of used antifreeze. Many communities have collection centers which will see that antifreeze is disposed of safely. Never dump used antifreeze on the ground or pour it into drains.*

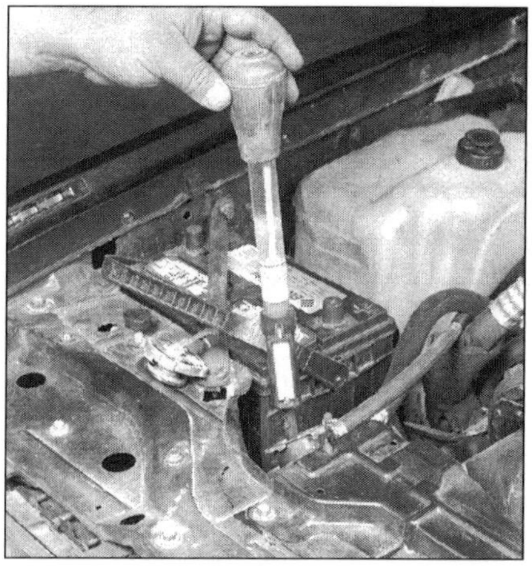

2.7 An inexpensive hydrometer can be used to test the condition of your coolant

Note: *Non-toxic antifreeze is now manufactured and available at local auto parts stores, but even these types should be disposed of properly.*

Caution: *The HT4100 engine requires a special antifreeze supplement to seal against internal and external leakage. Whenever you refill the radiator, add this special sealant to the radiator. This solution is available at dealer parts departments. Also, make sure the antifreeze meets specifications for aluminum-block engines.*

The cooling system should be filled with a water/ethylene glycol based antifreeze solution, which will prevent freezing down to at least -20 degrees F, or lower if local climate requires it. It also provides protection against corrosion and increases the coolant boiling point.

The cooling system should be drained, flushed and refilled at least every other year (see Chapter 1). The use of antifreeze solutions for periods of longer than two years is likely to cause damage and encourage the formation of rust and scale in the system. If your tap water is "hard", use distilled water with the antifreeze.

Before adding antifreeze to the system, check all hose connections, because antifreeze tends to leak through very minute openings. Engines do not normally consume coolant. Therefore, if the level goes down find the cause and correct it.

The exact mixture of antifreeze-to-water which you should use depends on the relative weather conditions. The mixture should contain at least 50-percent antifreeze, but should never contain more than 70-percent antifreeze. Consult the mixture ratio chart on the antifreeze container before adding coolant.

Hydrometers are available at most auto parts stores to test the ratio of antifreeze to water **(see illustration)**.

3 Thermostat - check and replacement

Warning: *Wait until the engine is completely cool before beginning this procedure.*

Caution: *Do not drive the vehicle without a thermostat. The computer (when equipped) may stay in an open loop and emissions and fuel economy will suffer, and the heater may not operate properly.*

Check

1 Before assuming the thermostat is to blame for a cooling system problem, check the coolant level (see Chapter 1), drivebelt tension (see Chapter 1) and temperature indicator light operation.

2 If the engine takes a long time to warm up, the thermostat is probably stuck open. Replace the thermostat.

3 If the engine runs hot, use your hand to check the temperature of the upper radiator hose. If the hose is not hot, but the engine is, the thermostat is probably stuck in the closed position, preventing the coolant inside the engine from escaping to the radiator. Replace the thermostat.

4 If the upper radiator hose is hot, it means that the coolant is flowing and the thermostat is open. Consult the *Troubleshooting* section at the front of this manual for further diagnosis.

Replacement

Refer to illustrations 3.8a, 3.8b, 3.9 and 3.12

5 Disconnect the negative battery cable.

6 Drain the cooling system (see Chapter 1).

7 Remove the upper radiator hose from the thermostat housing on the intake manifold. If equipped, remove the smaller bypass hose from the thermostat housing. **Note:** *Since this hose is difficult to replace without removing the thermostat housing, now is a good time to install a new piece of bypass hose between the water pump and the thermostat housing.*

8 Remove the bolts or nuts from the thermostat housing and detach the housing **(see illustrations)**. Be prepared for some coolant to spill as the gasket seal is broken. On some models, a throttle return spring bracket may be mounted under the left bolt/nut.

9 Remove the thermostat, noting the way it was installed **(see illustration)**.

10 Remove all traces of gasket material from the sealing surfaces. On HT4100 engines, be very careful not to damage the delicate aluminum surface.

11 Install the thermostat, making sure the

3.8a Remove these two bolts (arrows) to remove the thermostat housing from the intake manifold - Oldsmobile-manufactured engine shown, most Cadillac V8's similar

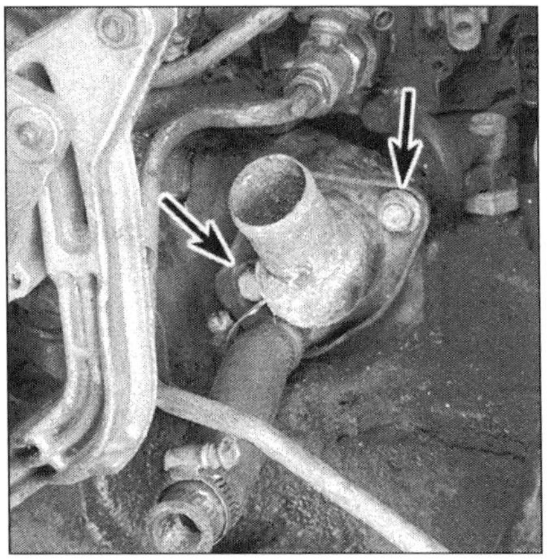

3.8b On V6 engines, the thermostat housing is "buried" below and behind the distributor (here removed for clarity) - note the bypass hose (arrows indicate housing bolts)

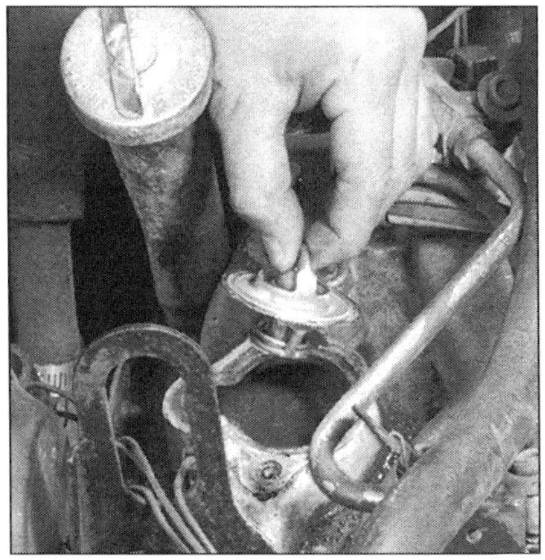

3.9 Note the direction of the thermostat - the spring end goes toward the engine

3.12 Here the new thermostat is in place and the cover is fitted with a new gasket and RTV sealant - the new bypass hose has also been installed

4.9 Remove the bolts holding the fan shroud to the radiator support

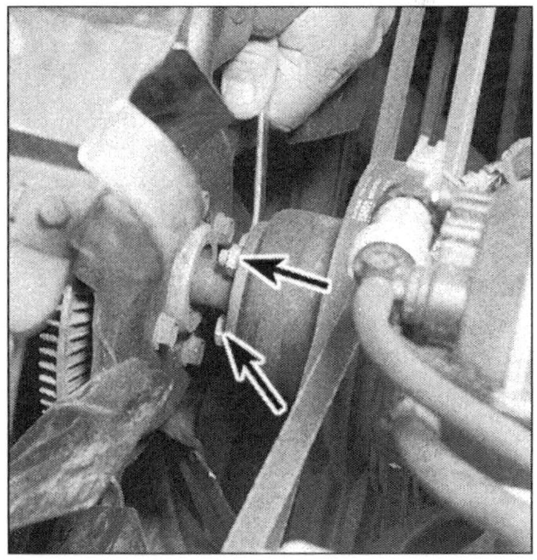

4.10 Remove the nuts/bolts holding the fan assembly to the water pump/pulley (arrows indicate two of the four)

spring end is directed into the engine, then apply gasket sealant to both sides of a new gasket and position it on the engine. **Note:** *Some mechanics prefer to glue the gasket to the thermostat cover, using RTV sealant on only the engine side of the gasket.*

12 Install the thermostat housing and bolts **(see illustration)**. Tighten the bolts to the torque listed in this Chapter's Specifications, reattach the radiator hose and tighten the clamp on the bypass hose (if equipped). **Note:** *The clamps on the bypass hose should already be in place when the thermostat housing is installed.*

13 Refill the cooling system (see Chapter 1).

4 Engine cooling fan and clutch - check and replacement

Check

1 Most vehicles covered by this manual are equipped with thermostatically controlled fan clutches. Some models may have solid-hub type fans.

2 Begin the clutch check with a lukewarm engine (start it when cold and let it run for two minutes only).

3 Remove the key from the ignition switch for safety purposes.

4 Turn the fan blades and note the resistance. There should be moderate resistance, depending on temperature. If the fan spins freely by hand, the clutch should be replaced.

5 Drive the vehicle until the engine is warmed up. Shut it off and remove the key.

6 Turn the fan blades by hand and again note the resistance. There should be a noticeable increase in resistance.

7 If the fan clutch fails this check or is locked up, replacement is indicated. If excessive fluid is leaking from the hub or lateral play over 1/4-inch is noted, replace the fan clutch. **Note:** *Excessive noise from the fan assembly at all times when the engine is above high idle indicates the clutch may be locked up.*

8 If any fan blades are bent, don't straighten them! The metal will be weakened and blades could fly off during engine operation. Replace the fan with a new one.

Replacement

Refer to illustrations 4.9, 4.10, 4.11 and 4.12

9 Most models have a one-piece fan shroud with bolts holding it to the radiator support. Remove the bolts and pull the fan shroud back over the fan and the front of the engine **(see illustration)**. **Note:** *Some models have a two-piece shroud, with staples attaching the upper half to the lower. Pry these staples out or cut them with diagonal pliers.*

10 Remove the fasteners holding the fan assembly to the water pump hub **(see illustration)**. If the assembly is held to the water pump with bolts, replace the first two bolts removed with studs for alignment, then remove the rest, without loosening the belts. Other models have studs already; just remove the nuts.

11 Detach the fan and clutch assembly

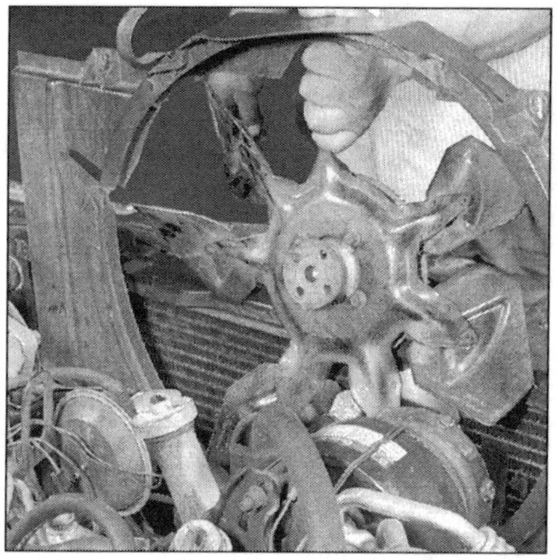

4.11 Remove the fan, fan clutch and shroud at the same time

4.12 Remove the four bolts holding the fan to the clutch

5.4a Disconnect the two transmission cooling lines (arrows) from the radiator

(see illustration). **Caution:** *When the fan and clutch are removed from the engine, always store the clutch with the radiator side down to prevent silicone fluid inside from leaking out or into the bearing.*

12 Unbolt the fan from the clutch **(see illustration)**.

13 Installation is the reverse of removal. If the upper shroud was fastened to the lower with staples, align the two shrouds and drill several holes on each side, fitting them either with sheetmetal screws or plastic wire-ties.

14 Tighten all fasteners securely.

5.4b On some models, a heater hose (arrow) may be attached directly to the top of the radiator

5 Radiator and coolant tank - removal and installation

Radiator

Refer to illustrations 5.4a, 5.4b, 5.5, 5.6 and 5.9

Warning: *The engine must be completely cool before beginning this procedure!*

1 Disconnect the negative battery cable.

2 Drain the radiator, referring to Chapter 1.

3 Refer to Section 4 and remove the fan and fan shroud.

4 Disconnect the radiator upper and lower hoses and the automatic transmission cooling lines **(see illustration)**. Have a pan ready to catch drips of transmission fluid that may come out. On HT4100 engines, also disconnect the engine oil cooler lines at the right side of the radiator. **Note:** *One some models there may be a heater hose that attaches directly to the top of the radiator, rather than to the intake manifold* **(see illustration)**.

5 Remove the upper metal panel at the top of the radiator **(see illustration)**.

6 Lift the radiator straight up and out of the engine compartment **(see illustration)**. Be careful not to scratch the paint on the front nosepiece (if equipped). If coolant drips on any body paint, immediately wash it off with clear water as the antifreeze solution can damage the finish.

7 With the radiator removed, it can be inspected for leaks or damage. Green stains (on copper radiators, or white stains (on aluminum radiators) indicate leakage. If in need of repairs, have a professional radiator shop or dealer perform the work, as special equipment and techniques are required.

8 Bugs and dirt can be cleaned from the radiator by using compressed air and a soft brush. Do not bend the cooling fins as this is done.

9 Inspect the rubber mounting pads which the radiator sits on and replace as necessary. Most models will have two rubber-lined insulators at the top and two at the bottom, in the radiator cradle **(see illustration)**.

10 Lift the radiator into position, making sure it is seated in the mounting pads.

11 Install the upper insulators, radiator cover, shroud, hoses and lines in the reverse order of removal.

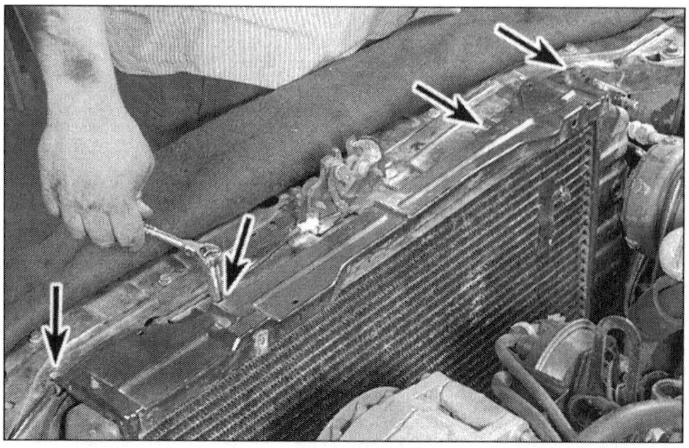

5.5 Remove the screws (arrows) and take off the sheetmetal panel above the radiator

5.6 Lift the radiator straight up and out

5.9 The radiator is supported top and bottom with rubber insulators - make sure they are all in place when reinstalling the radiator

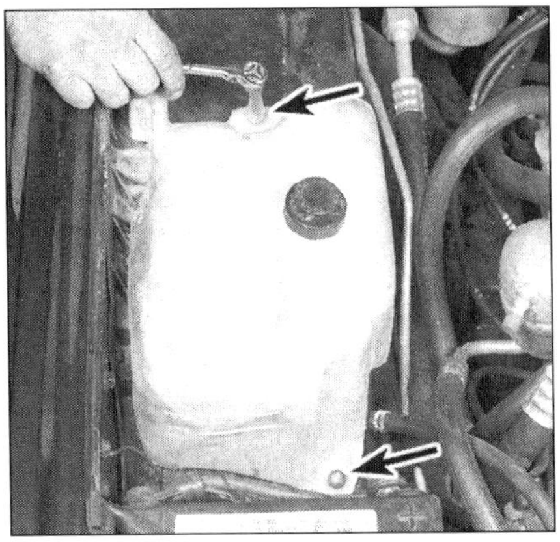

5.15 Remove the nuts or screws (arrows) holding the coolant reservoir to the fender panel

6.2 The water pump weep hole (arrow, pump removed for clarity) may be easier to see on the car with a flashlight and small mirror

12 Connect the negative battery cable and fill the radiator as described in Chapter 1.
13 Start the engine and check for leaks. Allow the engine to reach normal operating temperature (upper radiator hose hot) and add coolant until the level reaches the bottom of the filler neck.
14 Install cap with arrows aligned with the overflow tube.

Coolant tank

Refer to illustration 5.15

15 To remove the coolant tank, disconnect the overflow hose at the radiator. Remove the screws or nuts holding the tank to the inner fender panel **(see illustration)**.
16 When lifting the tank out of the vehicle, keep the overflow hose(s) up to prevent drips. **Caution:** *Anti-freeze can damage painted surfaces. Clean up any spills right away.*
17 To better see the coolant level in the tank, clean the inside of the tank of any rust deposits or scale with hot, soapy water. Use a wad of cloth taped to the end of a bent coat hanger to scrub hard-to-reach areas inside the tank, then rinse with clear water.

6 Water pump - check

Refer to illustration 6.2

1 Water pump failure can cause overheating of and serious damage to the engine. There are a couple of ways to check the operation of the water pump while it's installed on the engine. If either of the following quick checks indicates water pump failure, it should be replaced immediately.
2 A seal protects the water pump impeller shaft bearing from contamination by engine coolant. If the seal fails, weep holes in the top and bottom of the water pump snout **(see illustration)** will leak coolant. If the weep hole is leaking, shaft bearing failure will follow. Replace the water pump immediately. **Note:** *A small amount of black discoloration is normal around the weep hole, but the presence of brown residue or dripping water indicates replacement is required.*
3 Besides contamination by coolant after a seal failure, the water pump impeller shaft bearing can also be prematurely worn out by an improperly-tensioned drivebelt. When the bearing wears out, it emits a high-pitched squealing sound. If noise is coming from the water pump during engine operation, the shaft bearing has failed. Replace the water pump immediately.
4 To identify excessive bearing wear before the bearing actually fails, grasp the water pump pulley and try to force it up and down or from side to side. If the pulley can be moved either horizontally or vertically, the bearing is nearing the end of its service life. Replace the water pump.
5 Its possible for a water pump to be bad, even if it doesn't howl or leak water. If the engine's coolant has been worn out for too long, the fins on the back of the impeller can corrode away until the pump is no longer effective. The only way to check this is to remove the pump for examination.

7 Water pump - removal and installation

Refer to illustrations 7.5, 7.6, 7.7, 7.9a, 7.9b, 7.11, 7.12a, 7.12b and 7.12c

Note: *It is not economical or practical to overhaul a water pump. If failure occurs, a new or rebuilt unit should be purchased to replace the faulty water pump.*
1 Disconnect the negative battery cable.
2 Refer to Chapter 1 to drain the radiator.
3 Refer to Section 4 and remove the fan and clutch (or spacer if equipped) along with the fan shroud. **Caution:** *When the fan and clutch are removed from the engine, always store the clutch with the radiator side down to prevent silicone fluid inside from leaking out or into the bearing.*
4 It is now necessary to loosen and remove all drivebelts from the water pump pulley. The number of belts will depend upon model, year, and equipment. Loosen the adjusting and pivot bolts of each affected component (air pump, alternator, air conditioning compressor, power steering pump) and push the component toward the engine to loosen the belt enough to be removed from the water pump pulley (see Chapter 1).
5 Disconnect and remove all mounting brackets which are attached to the water pump. These may include the alternator, air conditioning compressor or power steering brackets **(see illustration)**. On some models, the component itself, such as the compressor, may have to be removed first to allow the bracket to be removed. On HT4100 models, the power steering pulley may have to be removed with a puller to access one of the mounting bracket bolts.

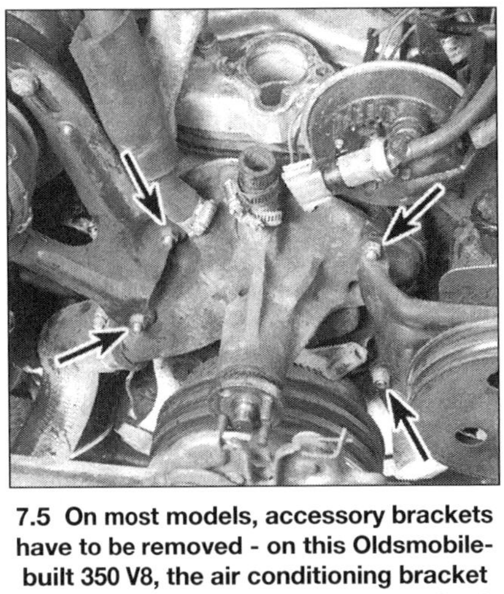

7.5 On most models, accessory brackets have to be removed - on this Oldsmobile-built 350 V8, the air conditioning bracket and power steering bracket are retained by nuts (arrows) on water pump studs

7.6 Radiator and bypass hoses (arrows) connected to the water pump (V6 engine shown)

7.7 Remove the bolts and tap the pump loose - this engine has four stud/bolts (arrows); remember their locations

7.9a On the HT4100, clean the bottom cavity of the thermostat housing, lubricate the O-ring (being held in this photo) and install it on the water pump, then push the thermostat housing down onto the pump

7.9b Clean the adapter (arrow), fit it with a new, lubricated O-ring at each end, and push it into the back of the thermostat housing (HT4100 engine)

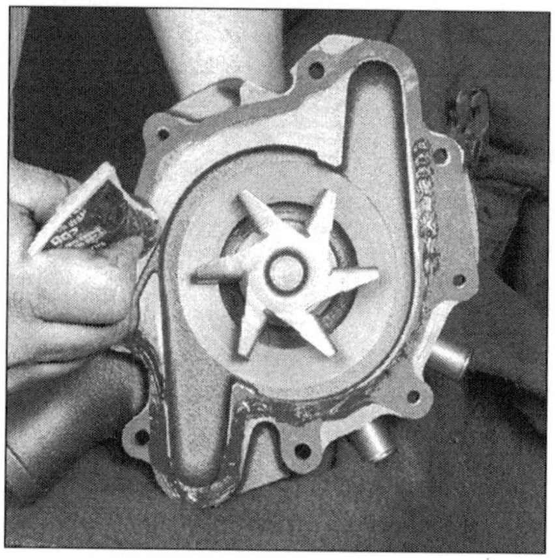

7.11 Coat the pump with a thin film of RTV sealant, install the gasket, then put a thin coat of RTV sealant on the engine side of the gasket and install the pump

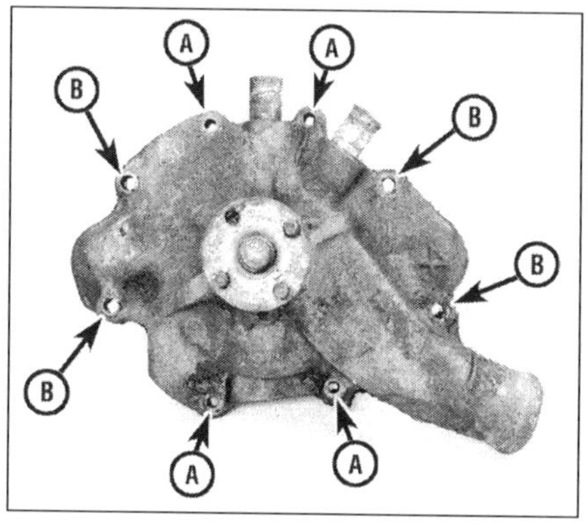

7.12a Water pump bolt locations on Oldsmobile engines - see the Specifications for the torque values

A 156 in-lbs B 180 in-lbs

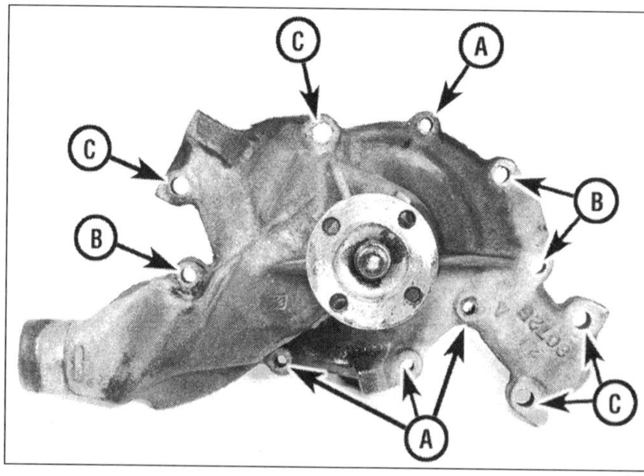

7.12b Water pump bolt locations on big Cadillac V8 engines - see the Specifications for the torque values

6 Disconnect the lower radiator hose and, if attached to the pump, the heater and/or bypass hoses **(see illustration)**. **Note:** *On the HT4100 engine, the thermostat housing fits into tight O-rings on both the water pump and the intake manifold. It should remain with the water pump and be pulled out away from the intake manifold when replacing the water pump.*

7 Remove the remaining bolts which secure the water pump to the front cover of the engine. The bolts are different sizes, so be sure to note their locations and which ones are studs **(see illustration)**. Pull the water pump away from the engine. If the pump is stuck to the engine, tap it gently with a soft-face hammer.

8 If installing a new or rebuilt water pump, transfer all fittings and studs to the new water pump.

9 On the HT4100 engine, pull the thermostat housing from the pump and clean its O-ring surfaces thoroughly. Then lubricate the small-diameter O-ring with white grease and install the housing on the new water pump **(see illustration)**. Then clean the adapter and fit it with new, greased O-rings and press it into the backside of the thermostat housing **(see illustration)**.

10 Clean the gasket surfaces of the front cover completely using a gasket scraper or putty knife, then follow with lacquer thinner.

11 Use a thin coat of gasket sealant on the new gasket and install the new water pump **(see illustration)**. Place the pump into position on the front cover and secure it loosely with the bolts. On HT4100 engines, push the pump straight toward the engine, aligning the O-ringed adapter into the intake manifold as you go.

12 Tighten all water pump bolts to the torque listed in this Chapter's Specifications **(see illustrations)**. Use sealant on those

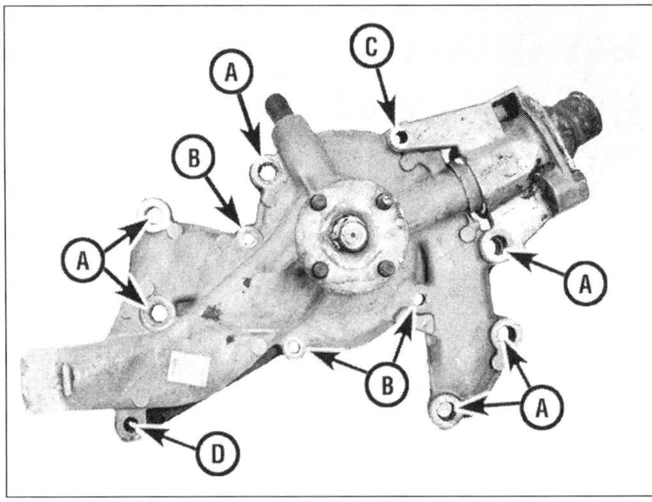

7.12c Water pump bolt locations on HT4100 Cadillac V8 engines - see the Specifications for the torque values

8.1a Coolant temperature sending unit location - V6 engines - at the front of the intake manifold, hidden by the distributor (distributor removed here for clarity)

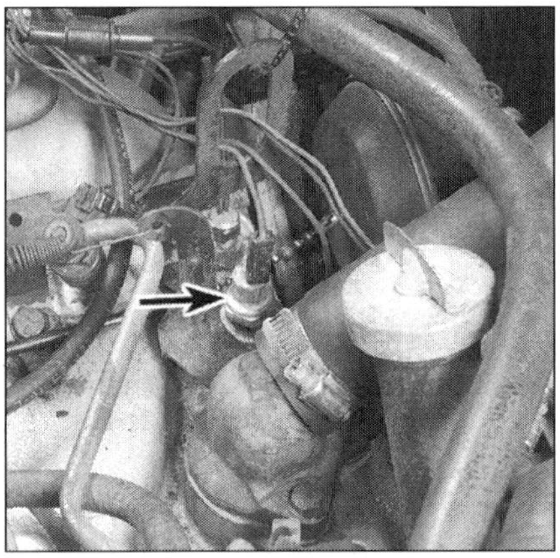

8.1b Coolant temperature sending unit location - Oldsmobile-manufactured V8 engines - just left of the thermostat housing

8.1c Coolant temperature sending unit location - Cadillac big V8 engines - at the front (under the compressor, compressor removed here for clarity)

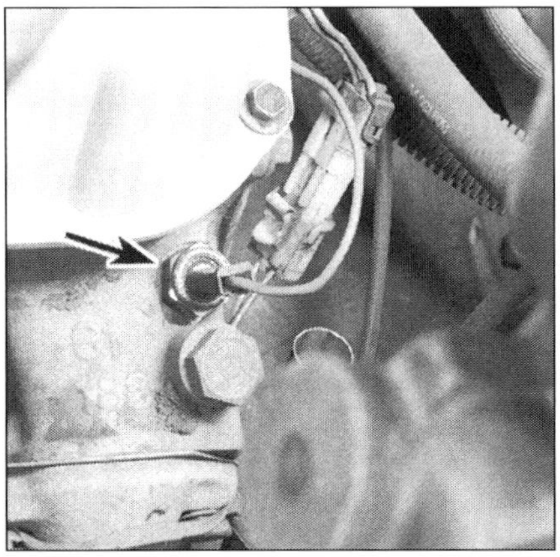

8.1d Location of "engine metal temperature" sending unit - Cadillac engines

8.1e Location of "engine metal temperature" sending unit - Oldsmobile-manufactured engines

bolts immediately next to the water passages in the block, and on Olds;mobile-manufactured engines, use oil on the four bolts that thread into the plate behind the pump.

13 Install the engine components in the reverse order of removal, tightening the fasteners securely.

14 Adjust all drivebelts to the proper tension (see Chapter 1).

15 Connect the negative battery cable and fill the radiator with a mixture of ethylene glycol antifreeze and water in a 50/50 mixture. Start the engine and allow it to idle until the upper radiator hose gets hot. Check for leaks. With the engine hot, fill it with more coolant mixture until the level is at the bottom of the filler neck. Install the radiator cap and check coolant level periodically over the next few miles of driving. Top off the coolant recovery tank to the indicated level.

8 Coolant temperature sending unit - check and replacement

Refer to illustrations 8.1a, 8.1b, 8.1c, 8.1d and 8.1e

Check

1 If the COOLANT TEMPERATURE light doesn't come on when the ignition switch is turned to START, check the bulb. If the light stays on even with the engine cold, unplug the wire at the sending unit **(see illustrations)**. If the light goes off, replace the sending unit. If the light stays on, the wire is grounded somewhere in the harness. **Note:** *Some models are equipped with an additional STOP ENGINE TEMPERATURE light. This is activated when the engine metal temperature sensor located on the cylinder head is heated to an excessive temperature* **(see illustration)**. *Check the STOP ENGINE TEMPERATURE light by opening the driver's door while the ignition is in LOCK or OFF position. The light should glow and the buzzer should sound. The light should not glow when the ignition is in the START mode.*

Replacement

2 Allow the engine to cool completely.

3 Unplug the wire connected to the sending unit.

4 Unscrew the sending unit and quickly install the new unit to prevent loss of coolant. **Note:** *The "engine metal temperature" sender is not connected to a water passage and should be installed with NO sealant!*

5 Connect the wire and check indicator operation.

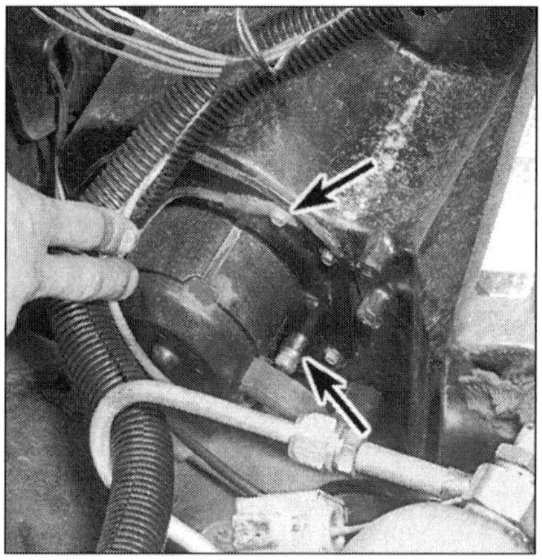

9.2 Blower motor location - typical - lower arrow shows location of power connector, upper arrow indicates ground wire

9.3 Apply fused battery power to the power connector, and a good ground to the motor - the motor should operate

9.6 Blower motor resistor (arrow) location in the engine compartment - typical

9 Blower motor circuit - check and component replacement

Refer to illustrations 9.2, 9.3, 9.6 and 9.7

1 Disconnect the negative battery cable.

2 The blower unit is located in the right-rear corner of the engine compartment **(see illustration)**. If the blower doesn't work, check the fuse and all connections in the circuit for looseness and corrosion. Make sure the battery is fully charged.

3 If the blower motor does not operate, disconnect the electrical connectors, and apply a ground wire and fused battery power to the motor side of the connectors **(see illustration)**. If the motor doesn't operate, replace it. If the motor does operate, the problem is somewhere in the circuit.

4 To begin checking the circuit, turn the ignition key On (engine not running) and check for battery voltage at the power connector on the motor when the blower speed switch is on HIGH. If battery voltage is not present, there is a problem in the ignition feed circuit.

5 If the motor is good, but doesn't operate at any speed, the heater/air conditioning control switch is probably faulty. Remove the heater/air conditioner control assembly (see Section 11) and check for continuity through the switch in each position.

6 If the blower motor operates at High speed, but not at one or more of the lower speeds, check the blower motor resistor, located on the left side of the blower/evaporator housing in the engine compartment **(see illustration)**. **Note:** *On some Oldsmobile models, the resistor is mounted on the housing, but below the blower motor.*

7 Disconnect the electrical connector from the blower motor resistor. Remove the screws and withdraw the resistor from the housing. **Note:** *Some models with climate control systems have a more elaborate blower resistor called a power module* **(see illustration)**. *It offers many more variable blower speeds and is also part of the air conditioning compressor cycling circuit.*

8 Using a continuity tester on the blower motor resistor - there should be continuity between all terminals. If not, replace the resistor.

10 Blower motor - removal and installation

Refer to illustrations 10.2 and 10.3

1 Disconnect the battery negative cable.

2 If the blower motor must be replaced, disconnect the wiring connector to the blower, pull off the drain hose, then remove the mounting screws and pull the blower assembly out of the housing **(see illustration)**. **Note:** *There are some 1970's Toronado models where access to the blower motor is very restricted when working from the engine compartment. For these models, it is easier to take out the plastic inner splash shield from the right-front fender for access to the blower from below.*

3 The fan can be removed and used again on the new blower motor by removing the clip or nut holding the fan on the motor shaft **(see illustration)**.

4 Installation is the reverse of removal. Check for proper operation.

9.7 The power module is larger than a conventional resistor and can be identified by the two large heat sinks

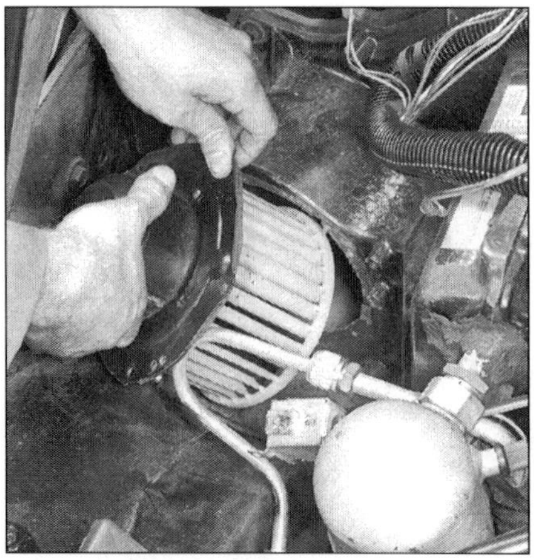

10.2 Remove the screws and pull the blower motor and fan from the blower/evaporator housing - typical

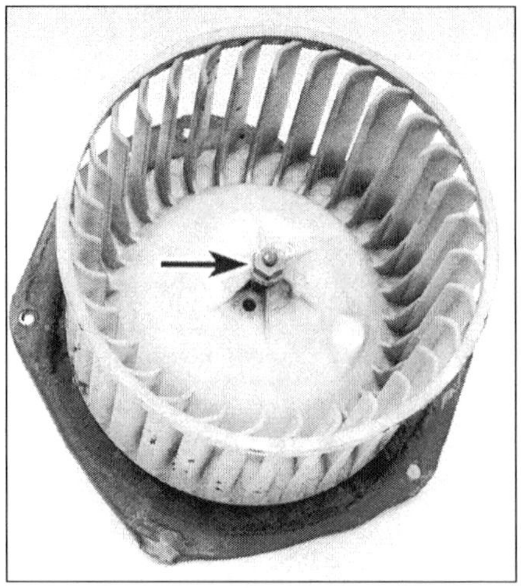

10.3 The fan is retained to the blower motor with a clip or a nut (arrow)

11.4 Remove these screws (arrows) to remove the control panel from the dashboard

11 Heater and air conditioning control assembly - check, removal and installation

Refer to illustrations 11.4 and 11.5

1 Many different systems have been used in Cadillac, Oldsmobile and Buick vehicles during the years covered by this manual. Automatic Temperature Control and Electronic Climate Control incorporate many different types of computer and automatic devices to regulate the temperature within the vehicle. In some, the various functions are controlled by cables; in others the actuation is electrical or by vacuum controls. Many systems have a combination of two or three of these methods of actuation. The following steps cover the basics of the most typical systems.

2 Disconnect the battery cable from the negative battery terminal.

3 Remove the trim bezel that surrounds the heater/air conditioning control assembly (see Chapter 11).

4 Remove the control assembly retaining screws **(see illustration)**.

5 Pull the heater/air conditioning control assembly from the instrument panel enough to see the cable, vacuum or electrical connections at the back of the control unit, and disconnect the blend-air control cable, electrical connectors and vacuum lines from the control assembly **(see illustration)**. **Caution:** *Be careful when removing vacuum lines to avoid cracking the plastic connectors and causing a vacuum leak (possibly internal within the control assembly).*

6 To install the control assembly, reverse the removal procedure. **Caution:** *When reconnecting vacuum lines to the control assembly, do not use any lubricant to make them slip on easier, as it can affect vacuum operation. If necessary, use a very small amount of plain water to make reconnection easier.*

11.5 Pull the control assembly out of the dash far enough to disconnect the connectors at the rear (arrows)

Control assembly vacuum check

Refer to illustrations 11.8 and 11.10

7 Put the controls through all of their modes with the vehicle running. If necessary, have someone else operate the controls while you look under the dashboard to observe the action of the various vacuum motors controlling airflow and temperature modes. If there is any position of the controls that gives air from the heater ducts *and* the air conditioning ducts, this indicates a vacuum leak.

8 Vacuum is supplied to the heater/air conditioning control assembly by tubing attached to the intake manifold. A check valve is used in the line. Inspect the supply line, from the intake manifold to the control assembly, for damage or leaks. **Note:** *On models with automatic climate control, the check valve is in the programmer unit that operates the air mix door* **(see illustration)**. The programmer is the black box mounted to the right side of the heater/air conditioning housing under the dashboard. To inspect it, remove the mounting screws and snap loose the rod connecting it to the blend-air door.

9 Pull the heater/air conditioning control panel away from the instrument panel and disconnect the vacuum harness from the control assembly. On climate-control models, the control panel will have electrical connectors, not vacuum lines. The vacuum lines run from the programmer to each of the mode actuators. Apply 8 inches of vacuum to each of the ports on the harness connector and observe the functions of that vacuum circuit.

10 If any of the circuits don't hold vacuum, follow the lines to their destination **(see illustration)**, isolate the source of the leak and repair it.

11 If there is vacuum in the line to the actuator when that function is selected, and there is no leak detected, check for binding of the door the actuator operates. If the door operates freely, independent of the actuator, then the actuator needs replacing.

11.8 On models with climate control, the programmer (arrow) controls the air mix door - check the electrical and vacuum connections to it

11.10 Trace the vacuum lines to their destination and check for vacuum at the hose end when vacuum is applied at the control assembly - check the actuators (arrows) to see if they operate - left arrow here indicates the mode door actuator, the right arrow is the defroster door actuator (assembly removed from below the dash for clarity)

12 Heater core - removal and installation

Refer to illustrations 12.4, 12.7, 12.10, 12.11a, 12.11b, 12.11c, 12.11d, 12.12, 12.13a and 12.13b

1 The heater core is contained within the heater/air conditioning assembly. The assembly is divided by the firewall, with the blower motor and evaporator located in a housing on the engine side, and the heater core in a housing inside the car, under the dashboard. Generally, if only the heater core is being removed, there is no need to evacuate the refrigerant from the air conditioning system or to remove the engine-side housing. **Note:** *There are a number of variations in removal details for the years and models of vehicle covered by this book. The following procedure is a general one that should apply to most models.*

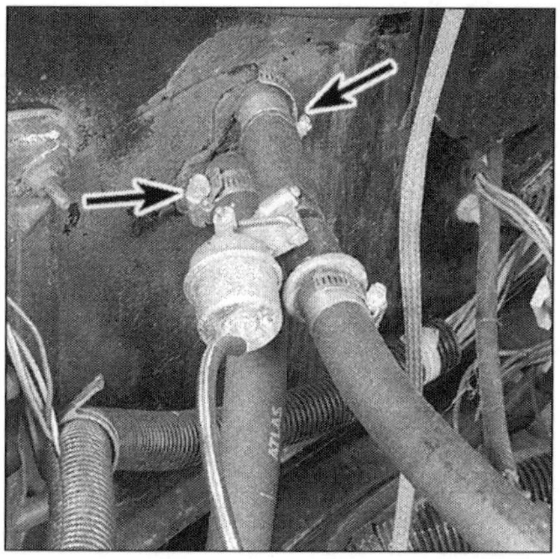

12.4 Disconnect the two heater hoses (arrows) at the firewall - the vacuum canister on the hose is the heater water valve actuator

12.7 With the glove box liner removed there is access to the blend-air door rod (right arrow) - on climate-control models also disconnect the aspirator hose (left arrow)

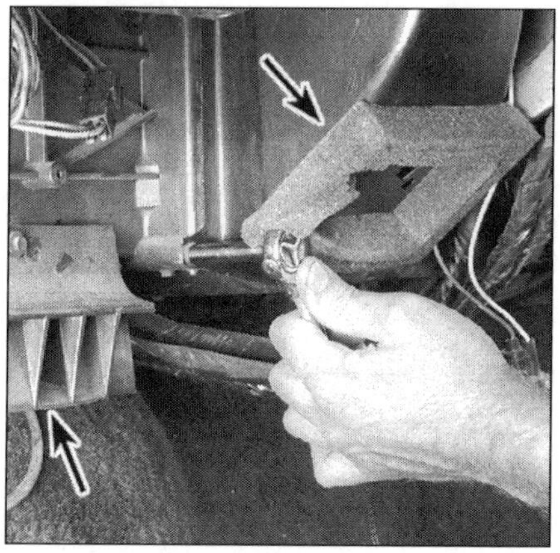

12.10 Remove the screws retaining these two ducts (arrows) to the rear of the heater/air conditioning assembly

2 Disconnect the negative battery cable.

3 Drain the cooling system (see Chapter 1).

4 Disconnect the heater hoses at the firewall **(see illustration)**.

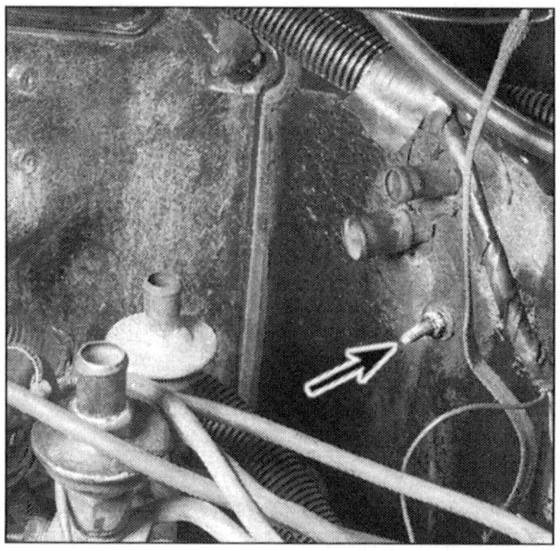

12.11a Most heater units have three or four studs holding them to the firewall - one (arrow) is below and to the left of where the heater hoses attach at the firewall (engine-compartment side)

5 Remove the top and bottom portions of the instrument panel (see Chapter 12). **Note:** *It may not be necessary on all models to remove the top (padded section) of the instrument panel. The panel must be removed only if the defroster ducting is to be unbolted.*

6 Disconnect and tag any electrical connectors or vacuum control lines that are attached to the heater/air conditioning assembly under the dash. **Note:** *There may be some wiring or vacuum lines from the heater/air conditioning assembly that are bundled to the speedometer cable or other dashboard wiring with plastic wire-ties. Cut these wire-ties.*

7 Refer to Chapter 12 and remove the glove box liner for access to the portion of the heater/air conditioning assembly behind it. Disconnect the rod to the blend-air door by squeezing the plastic connector and pulling it out of the arm **(see illustration)**. On climate-control models, this rod is connected to the programmer. unscrew the programmer from the heater/air conditioning assembly **(see illustration 11.8)**.

8 Disconnect the control assembly on the dash and set it aside (see Section 11).

9 On some models, the defroster ducting will have to be unbolted to allow enough maneuvering room to pull out the heater core assembly from below. Try the following steps first to see if the procedure can be completed without removing the dash pad to get at the defroster screws. If not, remove the screws holding the duct to the cowl and heater case. The defroster ducting will probably not come out of the vehicle, but will now be loose enough to allow removal of the heater/air conditioning assembly.

10 Remove the screws retaining the central dash duct and the driver-side floor duct **(see illustration)**.

11 Remove the nuts that retain the heater/air conditioning assembly to the firewall **(see illustrations)**. **Note:** *Some of the fasteners are screws that hold the assembly to the firewall from inside the car, while studs on the assembly have nuts located on the engine side of the firewall.* **Caution:** *Some of the engine-side studs/nuts may be coated with paint or undercoating. Remove this from the threads before taking the nuts off, or the studs may break or be forced out of the heater case.*

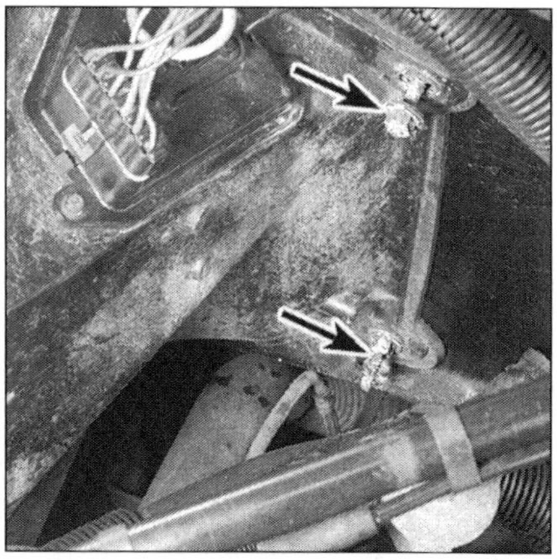

12.11b Remove the nuts (arrows) from the two studs at the left end of the evaporator case on the engine-compartment side

12.11c Refer to Section 9 and remove the blower resistor - on some models there is a stud/nut (arrow) hidden inside

12.11d There may also be one or two screws (arrow) to remove from the interior side

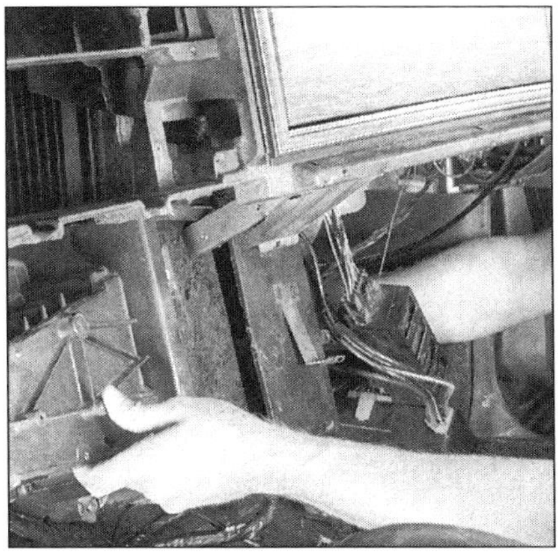

12.12 Pull the heater/air conditioning assembly down and out from the dash area

12 Carefully lower the heater/air conditioning assembly from under the dash **(see illustration)**. **Caution:** *Have some rags or old towels on the floor to protect the carpet from any coolant that may spill.*

13 Remove the screws that secure the heater core to the housing, and remove the core **(see illustrations)**.

14 Installation is the reverse of removal. **Note:** *Make sure to transfer any weatherstripping/sealing material from the old core to the new one.*

12.13a Separate the front and rear halves of the assembly case

12.13b Remove this one screw (arrow) and clamp to allow removal of the heater core from the front half of the case

13 Air conditioning and heating system - check and maintenance

Refer to illustration 13.1

Warning: *The air conditioning system is under high pressure. DO NOT loosen any fittings or remove any components until after the system has been discharged. Air conditioning refrigerant should be properly discharged into an EPA-approved recovery container at a dealer service department or an automotive air conditioning facility. Always wear eye protection when disconnecting air conditioning system fittings.*

1 The following maintenance steps should be performed on a regular basis to ensure that the air conditioner continues to operate at peak efficiency:

a) *Check the tension of the air conditioning compressor drivebelt and adjust it if necessary* (refer to Chapter l).

b) *Visually inspect the condition of the hoses, looking for any cracks, hardening and other deterioration.* **Note:** *Don't remove any hoses until the system has been discharged.*

c) *Make sure the fins of the condenser aren't covered with foreign material, such as leaves or bugs. A soft brush and compressed air can be used to remove them.* **Warning:** *Always wear eye protection when using compressed air!*

d) *Be sure the evaporator drain is open by slipping a wire into the evaporator housing drain occasionally* **(see illustration)**.

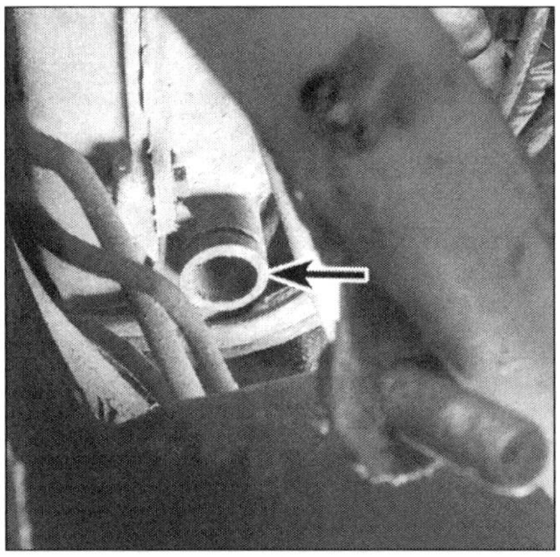

13.1 Occasionally check the drain (arrow) from the evaporator housing - it is difficult to see even from underneath, but is at the bottom of the housing and close to the firewall

2 The air conditioning compressor should be run about 10 minutes at least once every month. This is especially important to remember during the winter months because long-term non-use can cause hardening of the seals.

3 Leaks in the air conditioning system are best spotted when the system is brought up to operating temperature and pressure, by running the engine with the air conditioning ON for five minutes. Shut the engine off and inspect the air conditioning hoses and connections. Traces of oil usually indicate refrigerant leaks.

4 Because of the complexity of the air conditioning system and the special equipment required to effectively work on it, accurate troubleshooting of the system should be left to a professional technician.

5 The most common cause of poor cooling is simply a low system refrigerant charge. If a noticeable drop in cool air output occurs, the following quick check will help you determine if the refrigerant level is low. For more complete information on the air conditioning system, refer to the *Haynes Automotive Heating and Air Conditioning Manual*.

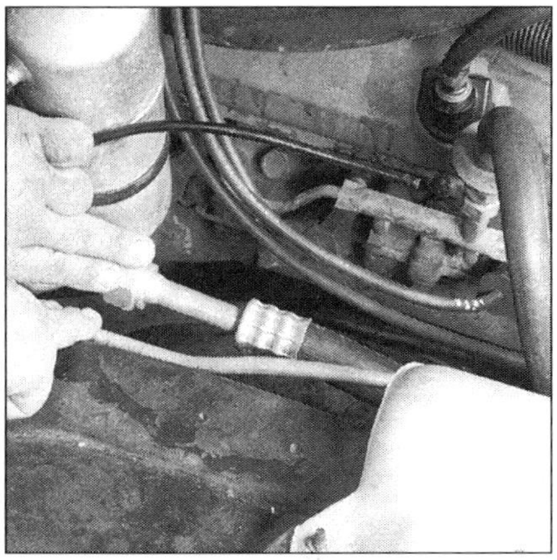

13.8 Feel the evaporator inlet and outlet pipes with the engine running and the air conditioning on

Checking the refrigerant charge

Refer to illustration 13.8

6 Warm the engine up to normal operating temperature.

7 Place the air conditioning temperature selector at the coldest setting and put the blower at the highest setting. Open the doors (to make sure the air conditioning system doesn't cycle off as soon as it cools the passenger compartment).

Accumulator systems

8 With the compressor engaged - the clutch will make an audible click and the center of the clutch will rotate. After the system reaches operating temperature, feel the two pipes (the evaporator inlet pipe and the surface of the accumulator) connected to the evaporator at the firewall **(see illustration)**.

9 If the system is operating properly, the two surfaces will both be about the same temperature and both colder than the outside air by the same amount. Insert a thermometer in the center air distribution duct while operating the air conditioning system - the temperature of the output air should be 35 to 40-

14.1a Most early models have a receiver/drier mounted up front near the radiator - the sight glass on a receiver/drier is on top (arrow)

14.1b The sight glass on some models is visible through a hole in the radiator support

14.3 Use two wrenches when disconnecting refrigerant lines - this is the later-model system with an accumulator, mounted just in front of the evaporator

degrees F below the ambient air temperature (down to approximately 40-degrees F). If the air isn't as cold as it used to be, the system probably needs a charge. Further inspection or testing of the system is beyond the scope of the home mechanic and should be left to a professional.

10 If the accumulator inlet pipe has frost accumulation or feels cooler than the accumulator surface, the refrigerant charge is low. Add refrigerant.

Receiver-drier systems (with sight glass)

11 Most of the earlier (non-accumulator) systems use a thermal limiter circuit to protect the compressor (on top of the evaporator housing). When the thermal limiter fuse burns out, the compressor clutch won't engage. Simply plug in a new one. Later models, with an accumulator, do not use a thermal limiter fuse.

12 If bubbles (with the engine running and air conditioning ON) appear in the sight glass (normally located near the top of the receiver-drier) **(see illustrations 14.1a and 14.1b)**, this is an indication of either a small refrigerant leak or air in the refrigerant. If air is in the refrigerant, the receiver-dryer or accumulator is probably contaminated with moisture and should be replaced.

13 If the sight glass takes on a mist-like appearance or shows many bubbles, this indicates a large refrigerant leak. In such a case, do not operate the compressor at all until the fault has been corrected.

14 Frosting of the high pressure liquid line (which runs between the condenser, receiver-drier and expansion valve) indicates that either the drier or the high pressure line is restricted. The line will have to be cleared or the receiver-drier replaced.

All systems

15 The combination of bubbles in the sight glass, a very hot suction line and, possibly, overheating of the engine is an indication that either the condenser is not operating properly or the refrigerant is overcharged. Check the tension of the drivebelt and adjust it, if necessary (see Chapter 1). Check for foreign matter covering the fins of the condenser and clean them, if necessary. Also check for proper operation of the cooling system. If no fault can be found in these checks, the condenser may have to be replaced.

16 Because of federal restrictions on the sale of R-12 refrigerant, it isn't practical anymore for refrigerant to be added by the home mechanic. When the system needs recharging, take the vehicle to a dealer service department or professional air conditioning shop for evacuation, leak-testing and recharging.

Heating system

17 If the carpet under the heater core is damp or smells of coolant, or if coolant vapors are coming through the vents, the heater core is leaking. Refer to Section 12 for the replacement procedure.

18 The air coming out of the heater vents isn't hot, the problem could stem from any of the following causes:

a) *The thermostat is stuck open, preventing the engine coolant from warming up enough to carry heat to the heater core. Replace the thermostat* (see Section 3).
b) *The heater water valve is blocked or malfunctioning. Replace the water valve.*
c) *A heater hose is blocked, preventing the flow of coolant through the heater core. Feel both hoses at the firewall. They should be hot, and when the heater is operating and the blower is on, the inlet hose should be hotter than the outlet hose. If one of the hoses is cool, there is an obstruction in either the hoses or the heater core. Detach the heater hoses and attach a garden hose to the inlet fitting of the core and backflush the core.*
d) *If flushing the hoses and core fails to remove the obstruction, replace the hoses and core.*

14 Air conditioning accumulator/receiver- drier - removal and installation

Refer to illustrations 14.1a, 14.1b and 14.3

Warning: *The air conditioning system is under high pressure. DO NOT loosen any fittings or remove any components until after the system has been discharged. Air conditioning refrigerant should be properly discharged into an EPA-approved recovery container at a dealer service department or an automotive air conditioning facility. Always wear eye protection when disconnecting air conditioning system fittings.*

1 The receiver-drier, which acts as a reservoir and filter for the refrigerant, is the canister-shaped object mounted ahead of the condenser or adjacent to it **(see illustrations)**.

2 Later models use an accumulator system. The accumulator is also a canister-shaped object, but it's mounted next to the evaporator case.

3 Disconnect the two lines from the accumulator or receiver-drier. Cap the open fittings immediately to prevent moisture from entering the system **(see illustration)**.

4 Remove the accumulator or receiver-drier from its bracket.

5 Installation is the reverse of removal.

6 Have the system evacuated, charged and leak tested. If a new accumulator or receiver-drier was installed, add refrigerant oil according to the component manufacturer's instructions.

15 Air conditioning compressor - removal and installation

Refer to illustrations 15.3, 15.5, 15.6a and 15.6b

Warning: *The air conditioning system is under high pressure. DO NOT loosen any fit-*

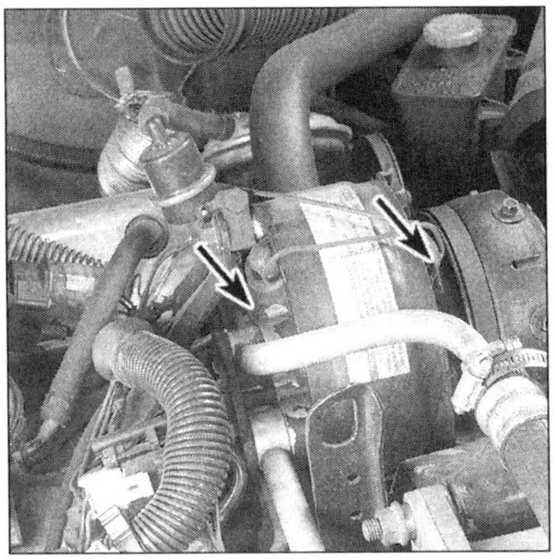

15.3 Disconnect the electrical connectors (arrows) from the compressor

15.5 Remove the bolt holding the refrigerant lines to the rear of the compressor - typical

15.6a Remove these bolts (arrows) to remove the compressor on older systems

tings or remove any components until after the system has been discharged. Air conditioning refrigerant should be properly discharged into an EPA-approved recovery container at a dealer service department or an automotive air conditioning facility. Always wear eye protection when disconnecting air conditioning system fittings.

1 Have the air conditioning system discharged by a dealer or air conditioning shop.

2 Disconnect the negative battery cable.

3 Disconnect the compressor wiring harness **(see illustration)**.

4 Remove the drivebelt (see Chapter 1).

5 Disconnect the refrigerant lines from the rear of the compressor. Plug the open fittings to prevent entry of dirt and moisture **(see illustration)**.

6 Unbolt the compressor from the mounting brackets and lift it out of the vehicle **(see illustrations)**. Plug the open lines to prevent entry of dirt or moisture.

7 If a new compressor is being installed, follow the directions furnished with the compressor regarding the draining of excess oil prior to installation.

8 Installation is the reverse of removal. Replace any O-rings with new ones specifically made for the purpose and lubricate them with refrigerant oil.

9 Have the system evacuated, recharged and leak tested by the shop that discharged it.

16 Air conditioning condenser - removal and installation

Refer to illustrations 16.4 and 16.6

Warning: *The air conditioning system is under high pressure. DO NOT loosen any fittings or remove any components until after the system has been discharged. Air conditioning refrigerant should be properly discharged into an EPA-approved recovery container at a dealer service department or an automotive air conditioning facility. Always wear eye protection when disconnecting air conditioning system fittings.*

15.6b Most later-model rotary compressors have a bracket front and rear - remove the through-bolts and pull the compressor out

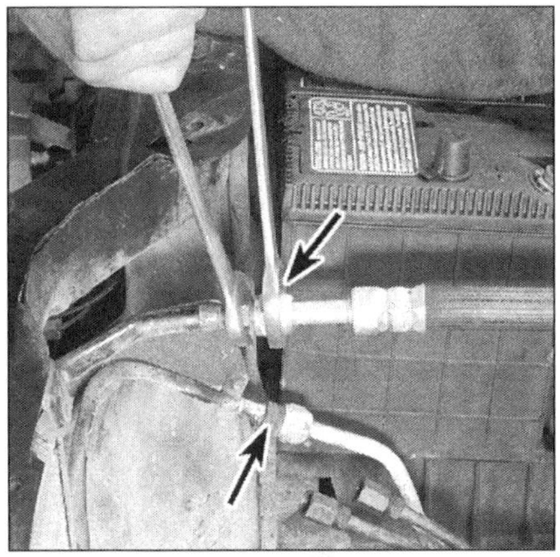

16.4 Remove these two lines (arrows) from the condenser - typical model - always use two wrenches

1 Have the air conditioning system discharged by a dealer service department or air conditioning shop.

2 Disconnect the negative cable from battery.

3 Drain the cooling system (see Chapter 1).

4 Disconnect the refrigerant lines from the condenser **(see illustration)**.

5 Remove the radiator (see Section 5). **Note:** *One some models it may be possible to remove only the radiator support, leave the radiator in place, and unbolt and remove the condenser from in front of the radiator.*

6 Remove the mounting bolts from the condenser brackets **(see illustration)**.

7 Lift the condenser out of the vehicle and plug the lines to prevent dirt and moisture from entering.

16.6 Unbolt the condenser mounting bolts and pull up the condenser - don't loose the rubber isolators at the bottom - some models may have bolts at the bottom as well

17.4 Locations of the six screws and two nuts (two right arrows) retaining the left half of the evaporator housing

17.6 Remove the screws holding the housing halves together and remove the evaporator core (arrow)

8 If the same condenser will be reinstalled, store it with the line fittings on top to prevent oil from draining out.

9 If a new condenser is being installed, pour one ounce of refrigerant oil into the new condenser prior to installation.

10 Reinstall the components in the reverse order of removal. Be sure the rubber pads are in place under the condenser. Also, be sure to use new O-rings on the refrigerant lines and lubricate them with a small amount of refrigerant oil.

11 Have the system evacuated, recharged and leak tested by the shop that discharged it.

17 Air conditioning evaporator and expansion valve - removal and installation

Refer to illustrations 17.4 and 17.6

Warning: *The air conditioning system is under high pressure. DO NOT loosen any fittings or remove any components until after the system has been discharged. Air conditioning refrigerant should be properly discharged into an EPA-approved recovery container at a dealer service department or an automotive air conditioning facility. Always wear eye protection when disconnecting air conditioning system fittings.*

1 Have the air conditioning system discharged by a dealer service department or air conditioning shop.

2 Disconnect the negative cable from battery.

3 Refer to Section 14 and disconnect the inlet and outlet refrigerant lines from the evaporator. On models with an accumulator, it is the accumulator you are disconnecting, while on receiver-drier systems it is the lines going forward.

4 Disconnect any electrical connectors on the evaporator housing, including the blower motor resistor, blower motor, and on later-model vehicles with climate control, the power module and ambient temperature switch **(see illustration)**. **Note:** *On some models, there may also be a vacuum connection on the evaporator housing.*

5 Remove the nuts on the studs holding the housing to the firewall **(see illustration 12.11b)**. The bottom ones may be more accessible from under the vehicle.

6 Remove any clips or screws securing the two halves of the housing together, split them apart and remove the evaporator core from inside **(see illustration)**.

7 Installation is the reverse of the removal process. Make sure that any sealing materials are reused and if you install a new unit that you add new refrigerant oil in the amount specified by the manufacturer or rebuilder.

8 Have the system evacuated, leak-tested and recharged at a dealer or air conditioning shop.

Chapter 4 Part A
Fuel and exhaust systems - carbureted engines

Contents

Specifications

Fuel system pressure

All carbureted models	2 to 10 psi

Torque specifications

	Ft-lbs
Carburetor mounting bolts	
Dualjet carburetor	
Front	10
Rear	15
Quadrajet carburetor	
Front	11
Rear	15

1 General information

Warning: *Gasoline is extremely flammable, so take extra precautions when you work on any part of the fuel system. Don't smoke or allow open flames or bare light bulbs near the work area, and don't work in a garage where a natural gas-type appliance (such as a water heater or a clothes dryer) with a pilot light is present. Since gasoline is carcinogenic, wear latex gloves when there's a possibility of being exposed to fuel, and, if you spill any fuel on your skin, rinse it off immediately with soap and water. Mop up any spills immediately and do not store fuel-soaked rags where they could ignite. When you perform any kind of work on the fuel system, wear safety glasses and have a Class B type fire extinguisher on hand.*

Fuel system

The fuel system on carbureted models consists of a fuel tank mounted under the rear of the vehicle, a mechanically operated fuel pump and a carburetor. The carburetor is either a two or four-barrel type (Dualjet or Quadrajet). A combination of metal and rubber fuel hoses is used to connect these components.

There are two types of choke systems on the carburetors: the electric choke and the hot air choke. The electric choke is controlled by battery voltage while the hot air choke element is controlled by hot air during warm-up passing over the heating element in the choke housing. On the electric choke systems, at temperatures above 60-degrees F, the temperature sensing switch closes and current is supplied to the ceramic heater. As the heater warms, it causes the spring to pull the choke plate open within 1 to 1-1/2 minutes. On hot air chokes, warm air is directed through a tube over the thermostatic coil, expanding the coil and moving the choke rod and choke valve into the open position. **Note:** *Early model choke systems incorporate a heating element that is mounted inside the intake manifold and covered by a sheet-metal housing. An actuator rod positions the choke as the heating element expands from the heated air circulating through the element.*

The carburetor is either a two or four-barrel type (Dualjet or Quadrajet), depending on engine displacement and year of production. Later models are equipped with electronic feedback carburetors. These carburetors are linked with a variety of sensors and output actuators to help control the amount of emissions.

Here is a list of the various carburetors used on these models:

Two-barrel carburetors (Dualjet)
- 2MC, M2ME
- E2ME feedback carburetor

Four-barrel carburetors (Quadrajet)
- M4MC, M4ME
- E4ME, E4MC, E4MA (high altitude) feedback carburetors

The fuel system is interrelated with the emissions control systems on all models produced for sale in the United States. Components of the emissions control systems are described in Chapter 6.

2.1 Install a T-fitting between the carburetor and the inlet fuel line and attach a fuel pressure gauge onto the T section

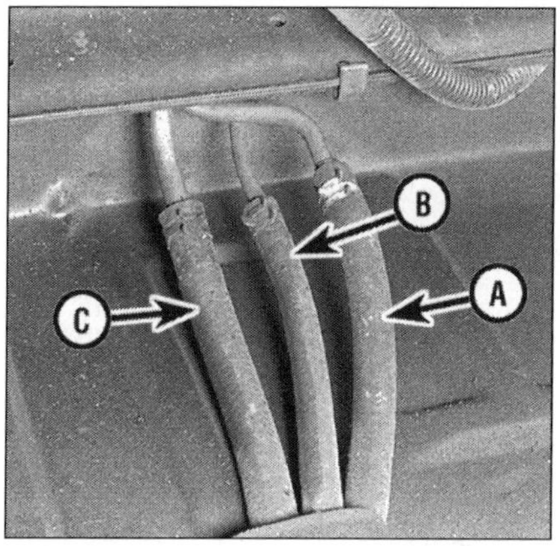

3.10a Typical fuel return (A), vapor (B) and feed lines (C) (carbureted engines)

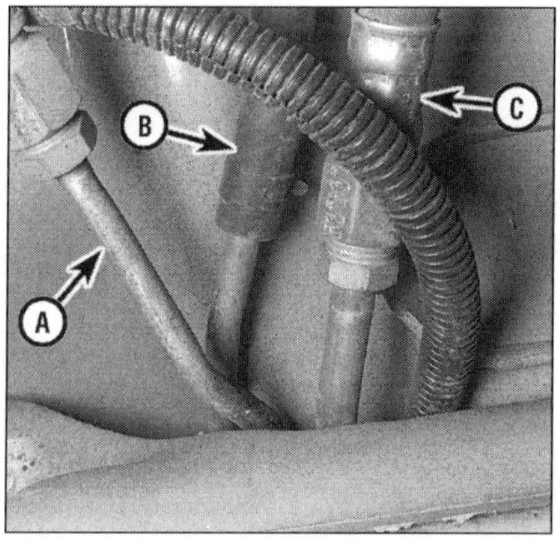

3.10b Typical fuel return (A), vapor (B) and feed lines (C) (fuel-injected engines)

Exhaust system

The exhaust system includes two exhaust manifolds, an exhaust oxygen sensor, a catalytic converter (1975 and later models), a resonator (some models), an exhaust pipe, and a muffler.

The catalytic converter is an emission control device added to the exhaust system to reduce pollutants. A single or dual-bed converter is used in combination with a three-way (reduction) catalyst. Refer to Chapter 6 for more information regarding the catalytic converter.

2 Fuel pump/fuel pressure check

Refer to illustration 2.1

Warning: *Gasoline is extremely flammable, so take extra precautions when you work on any part of the fuel system. See* **Warning** *in Section 1.*

Note: *It is a good idea to check the fuel pump and lines for any obvious damage or fuel leakage. Also check all hoses from the tank to the pump, particularly the suction hoses at the fuel tank and pump which, if they have are cracked, may not allow fuel to the fuel pump. It is also possible for the fuel pump diaphragm to rupture internally and leak fuel into the crankcase. If you have excess fuel consumption or fuel smell, and you can't find any external leaks, check the condition of the engine oil for any signs of fuel mixing with the engine oil; the oil level will usually be abnormally high and the oil will be thinned out and have a fuel smell.*

1 Disconnect the fuel line from the carburetor and install a T-fitting. Connect a fuel pressure gauge to the T-fitting with a section of fuel hose **(see illustration)**.

2 Start the engine and allow it to idle. The pressure on the gauge should be 2 to 10 psi. It should remain constant and return to zero slowly when the engine is shut off. **Note:** *If the engine will not start, crank the engine until you get a reading on the gauge.*

3 An instant pressure drop indicates a faulty outlet valve and the fuel pump must be replaced.

4 If the pressure is too high, check the air vent to see if it is plugged before replacing the pump.

5 If the pressure is too low, be sure the fuel hoses and lines are in good shape and not plugged, then replace the pump.

3 Fuel lines and fittings - repair and replacement

Warning: *Gasoline is extremely flammable, so take extra precautions when you work on any part of the fuel system. See* **Warning** *in Section 1.*

1 Always relieve the fuel pressure before servicing fuel lines or fittings if the system is equipped with an electric fuel pump (Section 2 in Chapter 4B).

2 The fuel lines extend from the fuel tank to the engine compartment. The lines are secured to the underbody with clip and screw assemblies. Both fuel feed lines must be occasionally inspected for leaks, kinks and dents.

3 If evidence of dirt is found in the system or fuel filter during disassembly, the line should be disconnected and blown out. Check the fuel strainer on the fuel gauge sending unit (see Section 5) for damage and deterioration.

Steel tubing

4 If replacement of a fuel line or emission line is called for, use welded steel tubing, available at most auto parts stores.

5 Don't use copper or aluminum tubing to replace steel tubing. These materials cannot withstand normal vehicle vibration.

6 Because fuel lines used on fuel injected vehicles are under high pressure, they require special consideration.

7 Most fuel lines have threaded fittings with O-rings. Any time the fittings are loosened to service or replace components:

- a) *Use a back-up wrench while loosening and tightening the fittings.*
- b) *Check all O-rings for cuts, cracks and deterioration. Replace any that appear worn or damaged.*
- c) *If the lines are replaced, always use original equipment parts, or parts that meet the manufacturer's standards specified in this Section.*

Rubber hose

8 When rubber hose is used to replace a metal line, use reinforced, fuel resistant hose with the word "Fluoroelastomer" imprinted on it. Hose(s) not clearly marked like this could fail prematurely and could fail to meet Federal emission standards. Hose inside diameter must match line outside diameter.

9 Don't use rubber hose within four inches of any part of the exhaust system or within ten inches of the catalytic converter. Metal lines and rubber hoses must never be allowed to chafe against the frame. A minimum of 1/4-inch clearance must be maintained around a line or hose to prevent contact with the frame.

Removal and installation

Refer to illustrations 3.10a, 3.10b, 3.16 and 3.17

Note: *The following procedure and accompanying illustrations are typical for vehicles covered by this manual.*

10 Relieve the fuel pressure (fuel-injected models) and disconnect the fuel feed, return or vapor line at the fuel tank **(see illustrations)**.

11 Detach the bracket from the rear crossmember.

12 Detach the bracket from the rear end of the left frame member, just in front of the left rear wheel.

13 Detach the three brackets from the left frame member.

14 Detach the bracket from the left front end of the left frame member, just behind the left front wheel.

15 Detach the bracket from the lower left rear corner of the engine compartment.

16 Detach the hose clamps (carbureted) or the threaded fitting(s) (fuel injected) that

3.16 Typical fuel feed and return line threaded fittings, which are used on fuel-injected models

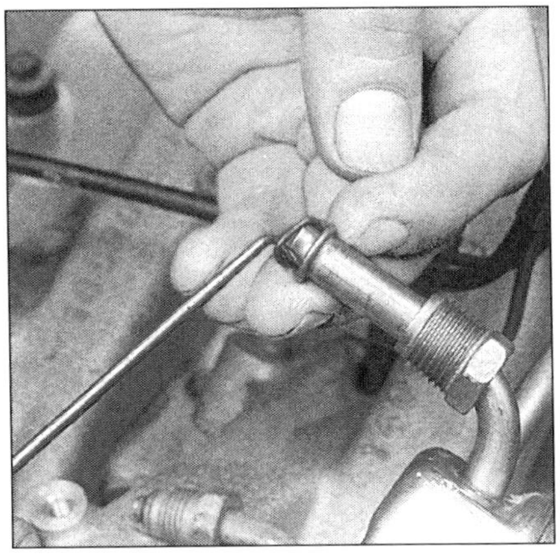

3.17 Always replace the fuel line O-rings

4.1 The fuel pump on some models is on the left side of the timing chain housing; on others it's on the right side of the engine block

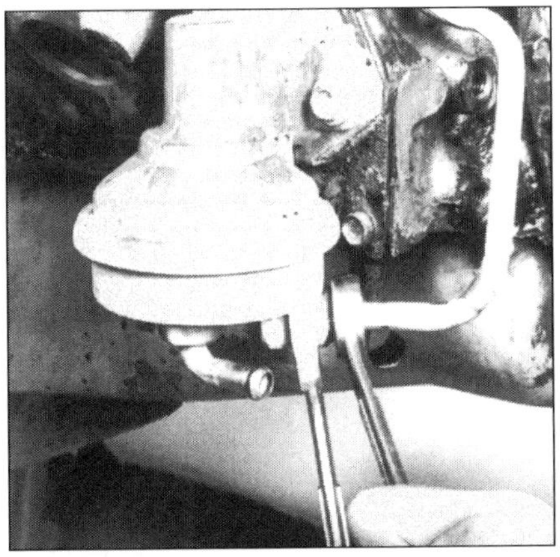

4.3 When detaching the fuel lines from a mechanical pump, use two wrenches so you don't bend or kink the metal fuel lines or the pipes protruding from the pump

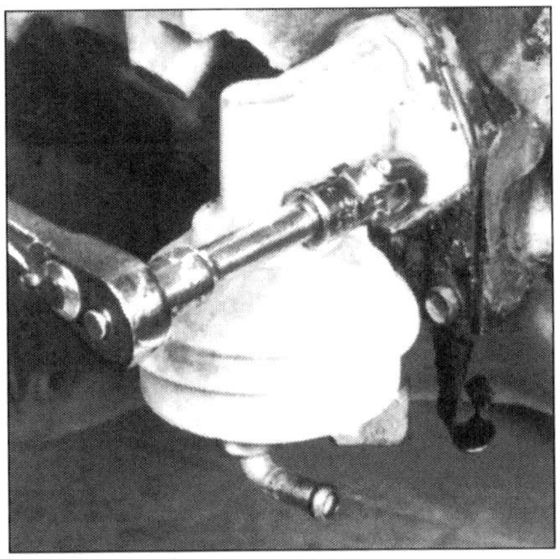

4.4a To remove a mechanical pump from the engine, remove the two mounting bolts . . .

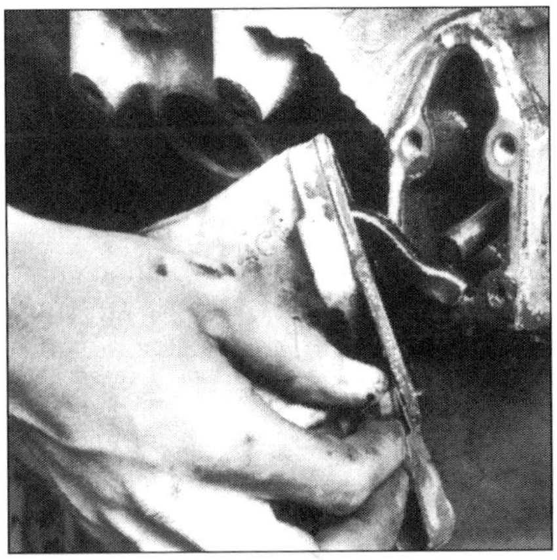

4.4b . . . then separate the pump and gasket from the block (be sure to remove all old gasket material from the pump and block mating surfaces)

attach the metal lines to the engine compartment fuel hoses **(see illustration)**.

17 Installation is the reverse of removal. Be sure to use new O-rings at the threaded fittings **(see illustration)**.

Repair

18 In repairable areas, cut a piece of fuel hose four inches longer than the portion of the line removed. If more than a six inch length of line is removed, use a combination of steel line and hose so hose lengths won't be more than ten inches. Always follow the same routing as the original line.

19 Cut the ends of the line with a tube cutter. Using the first step of a double flaring tool, form a bead on the end of both line sections. If the line is too corroded to withstand bead operation without damage, the line should be replaced.

20 Use a screw type hose clamp. Slide the clamp onto the line and push the hose on. Tighten the clamps on each side of the repair.

21 Secure the lines properly to the frame to prevent chafing.

4 Fuel pump - removal and installation

Refer to illustrations 4.1, 4.3. 4.4a and 4.4b

Warning: *Gasoline is extremely flammable, so take extra precautions when you work on any part of the fuel system. See* **Warning** *in Section 1.*

Note: *It is a good idea to check the fuel pump and lines for any obvious damage or fuel leakage. Also check all hoses from the tank to the pump, particularly the suction hoses at the fuel tank and pump which, if they have are cracked, may not allow fuel to the fuel pump. It is also possible for the fuel pump diaphragm to rupture internally and leak fuel into the crankcase. If you have excess fuel consumption or fuel smell, and you can't find any external leaks, check the condition of the engine oil for any signs of fuel mixing with the engine oil; the oil level will usually be abnormally high and the oil will be thinned out and have a fuel smell.*

1 On some models, the fuel pump is bolted to the engine block near the water pump; on others it's mounted on the timing chain housing **(see illustration)**.

2 Place clean rags or newspaper under the fuel pump to catch any gasoline spilled during removal.

3 Carefully unscrew the fuel line fittings and detach the lines from the pump **(see illustration)**. A flare-nut wrench should be used to prevent damage to the fittings.

4 Unbolt and remove the fuel pump **(see illustrations)**. Using a gasket scraper or putty knife, carefully remove all traces of old gasket material from the engine block and fuel pump (if the same one will be reinstalled).

5 Before installation, coat both sides of the new gasket with RTV sealant, hold the fuel pump in place and install the bolts. If the fuel pump is difficult to set in place to install the bolts, rotate the engine crankshaft to reposition the drive eccentric. Rotate it about 1/4-turn at first. If this doesn't make the pump easier to install, rotate the crankshaft another 1/4-turn.

6 Attach the lines to the pump and tighten

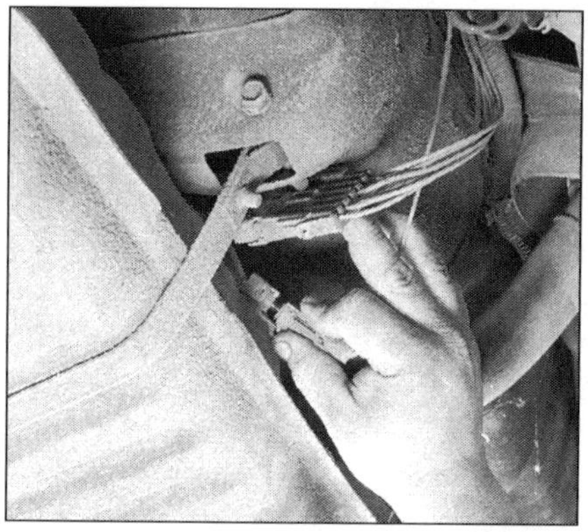

5.5 Disconnect the fuel pump electrical connector on fuel tanks equipped with an in-tank fuel pump

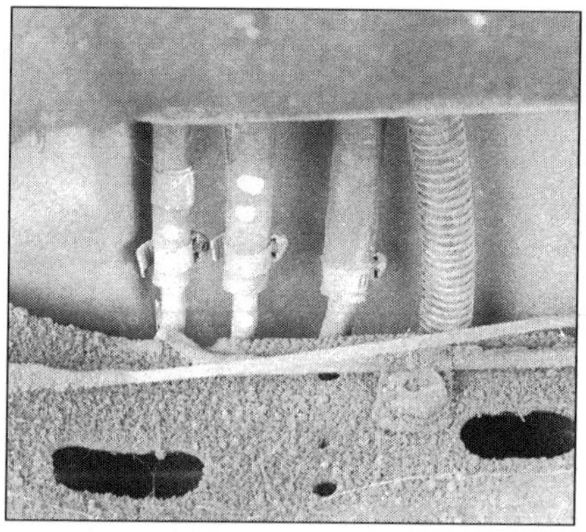

5.6 Mark the fuel lines with paint to avoid any reassembly problems

5.8 Disconnect the fuel tank straps (arrows)

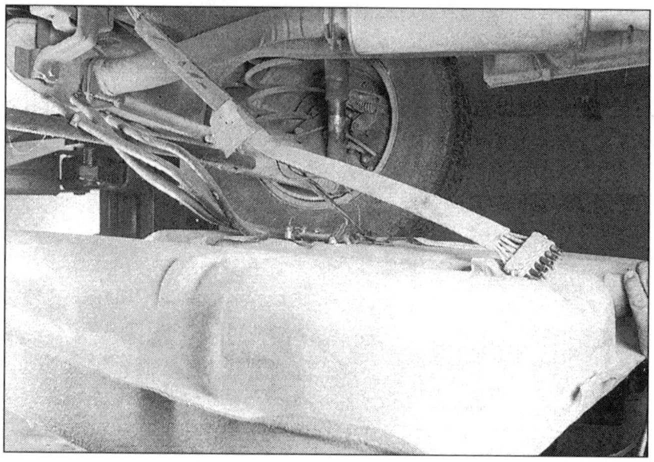

5.9 Lower the fuel tank carefully and disconnect any hoses or electrical connectors

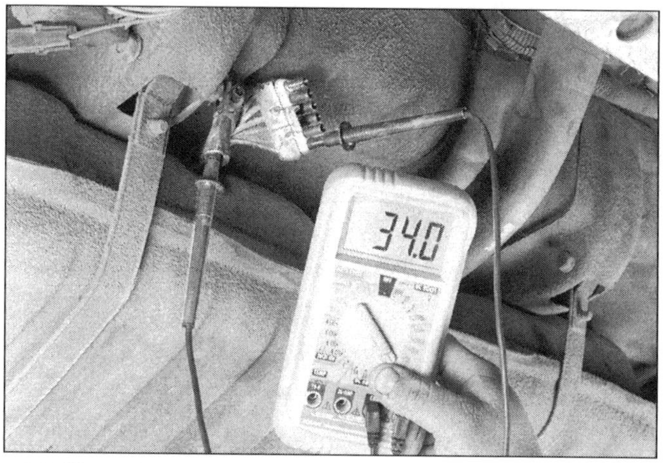

7.2 Check the resistance of the fuel level sending unit with the fuel tank in place. This fuel tank is low on fuel as indicated by the low resistance reading

the fittings securely (use a flare-nut wrench, if available, to prevent damage to the fittings).

7 Run the engine and check for fuel and oil leaks.

5 Fuel tank - removal and installation

Refer to illustrations 5.5, 5.6, 5.8 and 5.9

Warning: *Gasoline is extremely flammable, so take extra precautions when you work on any part of the fuel system. See* **Warning** *in Section 1.*

1 If the tank is full or nearly full, drive the vehicle to use up the gas.

2 Remove the tank cap to relieve the fuel pressure.

3 Detach the cable from the negative terminal of the battery.

4 Raise the vehicle and place it securely on jackstands.

5 Locate the electrical connector for the electric fuel pump and fuel gauge sending unit in front of the tank, and unplug it **(see illustration)**. If the vehicle doesn't have a connector, see Step 9 below.

6 Disconnect the fuel feed and return lines, the vapor line and the filler neck and vent tubes **(see illustration)**.

7 Support the fuel tank with a floor jack.

8 Disconnect both fuel tank retaining straps **(see illustration)**.

9 Lower the tank enough to disconnect the wires and ground strap from the fuel pump/fuel gauge sending unit, if you haven't already done so **(see illustration)**.

10 Remove the tank from the vehicle.

11 Installation is the reverse of removal.

6 Fuel tank cleaning and repair - general information

1 All repairs to the fuel tank or filler neck should be done by an experienced professional - the job is potentially dangerous! Even after cleaning and flushing of the fuel system, explosive fumes can remain and ignite during repair of the tank.

2 If the fuel tank is removed from the vehicle, it shouldn't be stored in an area where sparks or open flames could ignite the fumes coming out of it. Be especially careful inside a garage where a natural gas-type appliance is located, because the pilot light could cause an explosion.

7 Fuel level sending unit - check and replacement

Warning: *Gasoline is extremely flammable, so take extra precautions when you work on any part of the fuel system. See* **Warning** *in Section 1.*

Check

Refer to illustrations 7.2, 7.5a and 7.5b

1 Raise the vehicle and secure it on jackstands.

2 Position the probes of an ohmmeter onto the fuel level sending unit electrical connector terminals **(see illustration)** and check for resistance. **Note:** *There will be many variations for all the years and models. Refer to the wiring diagrams at the end of Chapter 12 for additional information concerning the fuel level sending unit wire colors.*

3 First, check the resistance of the sending unit with the fuel tank completely full. The resistance of the sending unit should be about 110 ohms.

4 Wait until the tank is nearly empty and check the resistance of the unit again. The resistance should be approximately 23 ohms.

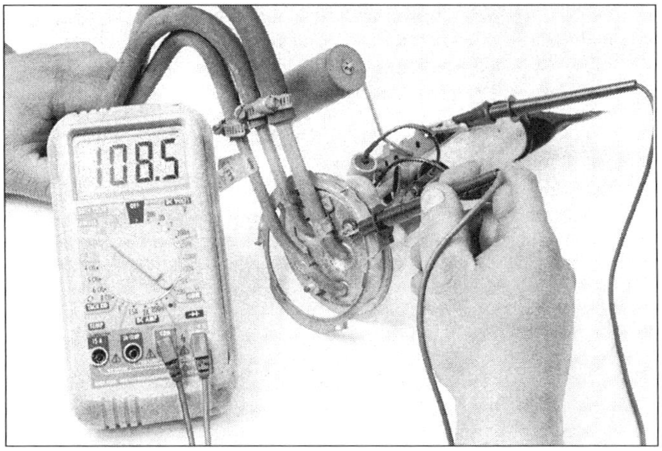

7.5a Check the resistance of the fuel level sending unit on the bench with the float completely raised (full tank) and . . .

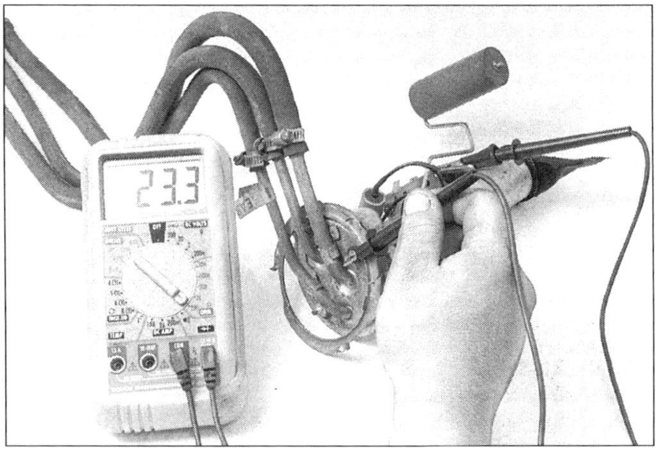

7.5b . . . with the float lowered (empty tank) there should be a clear change in resistance values

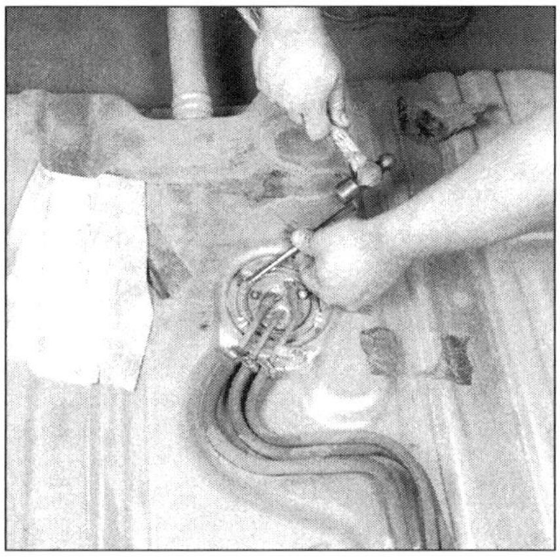

7.9 Use a brass punch to tap the lock ring counterclockwise until the tabs align with the recess areas of the fuel tank

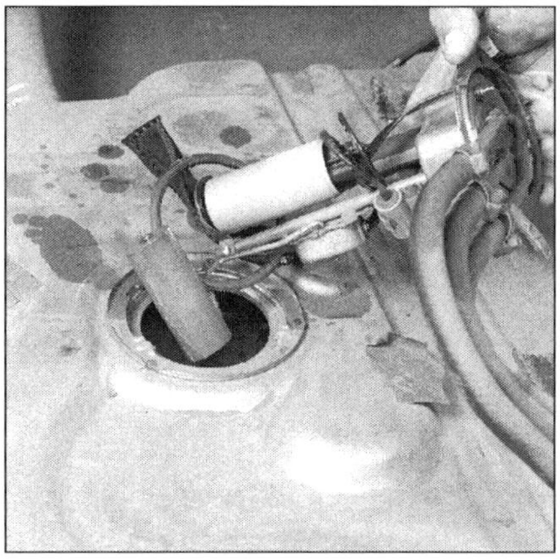

7.10 Remove the fuel sending unit from the tank. Be careful not to damage the float

8.3 Lift the air cleaner assembly from the engine compartment

5 If the readings are incorrect or there is very little change in resistance as the float travels from full to empty, replace the fuel level sending unit assembly. **Note:** *Another check for the fuel level sending unit is to remove it from the tank* (see Step 6) *and check the resistance while moving the float from full (arm at highest point of travel) to empty (arm at lowest point of travel* **(see illustrations)**.

Replacement

Refer to illustrations 7.9 and 7.10

6 Relieve the fuel system pressure (see Section 2).

7 Disconnect the cable from the negative battery terminal.

8 Remove the fuel tank (see Section 5).

9 The fuel pump/sending unit assembly is located inside the fuel tank. It is held in place by a cam that locks into the designated tabs in the fuel tank. Using a brass punch, carefully tap the locking cam until the tabs align with the recesses **(see illustration)**.

10 Lift the fuel pump/sending unit assembly from the fuel tank **(see illustration)**. **Caution:** *The fuel level float and sending unit are delicate. Do not bump them against the tank during removal or the accuracy of the sending unit may be affected.*

11 Inspect the condition of the rubber gasket around the opening of the tank. If it is dried, cracked or deteriorated, replace it.

12 Remove the bolts from the fuel level sending unit and separate it from the assembly.

13 Installation is the reverse of removal.

8 Air cleaner assembly - removal and installation

Refer to illustration 8.3

1 Remove the air filter from the air cleaner housing (see Chapter 1).

2 Disconnect any vacuum hoses or electrical connectors that would interfere with air cleaner removal and mark them with pieces of numbered tape for reassembly purposes.

3 Lift the air cleaner housing from the engine compartment **(see illustration)**.

4 Installation is the reverse of removal.

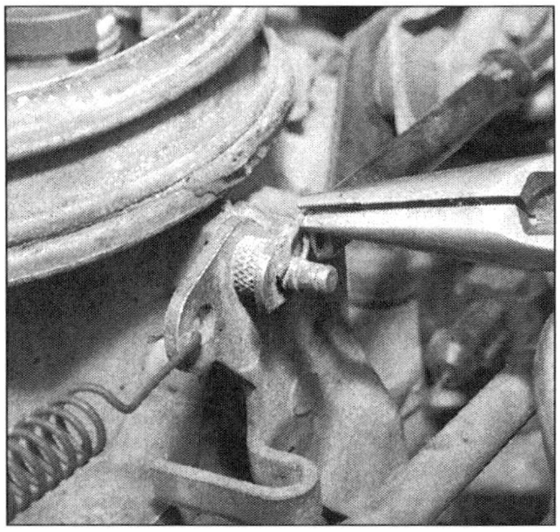

9.1 Remove the clip that retains the accelerator cable to the throttle shaft

9 Accelerator cable - removal, installation and adjustment

Refer to illustrations 9.1, 9.2 and 9.4

Removal

1 Remove the accelerator cable from the throttle linkage by prying the cable end off the shaft using a small screwdriver. Some models

use a clip to retain the accelerator cable onto the throttle shaft **(see illustration)**.

2 Remove the accelerator cable from the bracket assembly **(see illustration)**.

3 Detach the screws and the clips retaining the lower instrument trim panel on the driver's side and remove the trim piece (see Chapter 11).

4 Working inside the vehicle, up under the driver's side of the dash, pull the cable end out and then up from the accelerator pedal slot **(see illustration)**.

5 To disconnect the cable at the firewall, remove the cable rubber grommet by pushing it into the engine compartment using a blunt screwdriver.

Installation

6 Installation is the reverse of removal. **Note:** *To prevent possible interference, flexible components (hoses, wires, etc.) must not be routed within two inches of moving parts, unless routing is controlled.*

7 Operate the accelerator pedal and check for any binding condition by completely opening and closing the throttle.

8 If necessary, at the engine compartment side of the firewall, apply sealant around the accelerator cable to prevent water from entering the passenger compartment.

Adjustment

9 There is no specific adjustment on these types of accelerator cables but it will be necessary to adjust the kickdown cable for the automatic transmission (see Chapter 7).

10 Carburetor diagnosis and overhaul - general information

Warning: *Gasoline is extremely flammable, so take extra precautions when you work on any part of the fuel system. See* **Warning** *in Section 1.*

Diagnosis

1 A thorough road test and check of carburetor adjustments should be done before any major carburetor service work. Specifications for some adjustments are listed on the *Vehicle Emissions Control Information* (VECI) label found in the engine compartment.

2 Carburetor problems usually show up as flooding, hard starting, stalling, severe backfiring and poor acceleration. A carburetor that's leaking fuel and/or covered with wet looking deposits definitely needs attention.

3 Some performance complaints directed at the carburetor are actually a result of loose, out-of-adjustment or malfunctioning engine or electrical components. Others develop when vacuum hoses leak, are disconnected or are incorrectly routed. The proper approach to analyzing carburetor problems should include the following items:

a) *Inspect all vacuum hoses and actuators for leaks and correct installation* (see Chapter 6).

9.2 Squeeze the tabs and push the cable assembly through the mounting bracket

b) *Tighten the intake manifold and carburetor mounting nuts/bolts evenly and securely.*

c) *Perform a cylinder compression test* (see Chapter 2).

d) *Clean or replace the spark plugs as necessary* (see Chapter 1).

e) *Check the spark plug wires* (see Chapter 1).

f) *Inspect the ignition primary wires.*

g) *Check the ignition timing (follow the instructions printed on the Vehicle Emissions Control Information label).*

h) *Check the fuel pump pressure/volume* (see Section 2).

I) *Check the heat control valve in the air cleaner for proper operation* (see Chapter 1).

j) *Check/replace the air filter element* (see Chapter 1).

k) *Check the PCV system* (see Chapters 1 and 6).

l) *Check/replace the fuel filter* (see Chapter 1). *Also, the strainer in the tank could be restricted.*

m) *Check for a plugged exhaust system.*

n) *Check EGR valve operation* (see Chapter 6).

o) *Check the choke - it should be completely open at normal engine operating temperature* (see Chapter 1).

p) *Check for fuel leaks and kinked or dented fuel lines* (see Chapters 1 and 4).

q) *Check accelerator pump operation with the engine off (remove the air cleaner cover and operate the throttle as you look into the carburetor throat - you should see a stream of gasoline enter the carburetor).*

r) *Check for incorrect fuel or bad gasoline.*

s) *Check the valve clearances (if applicable) and camshaft lobe lift* (see Chapters 1 and 2).

t) *Have a dealer service department or repair shop check the electronic engine and carburetor controls (if equipped).*

4 Diagnosing carburetor problems may require that the engine be started and run with the air cleaner off. While running the engine without the air cleaner, backfires are possible. This situation is likely to occur if the carburetor is malfunctioning, but just the removal of the air cleaner can lean the fuel/air mixture enough to produce an engine backfire. **Warning:** *Don't position any part of your body, especially your face, directly over the carburetor during inspection and servicing procedures. Wear eye protection!*

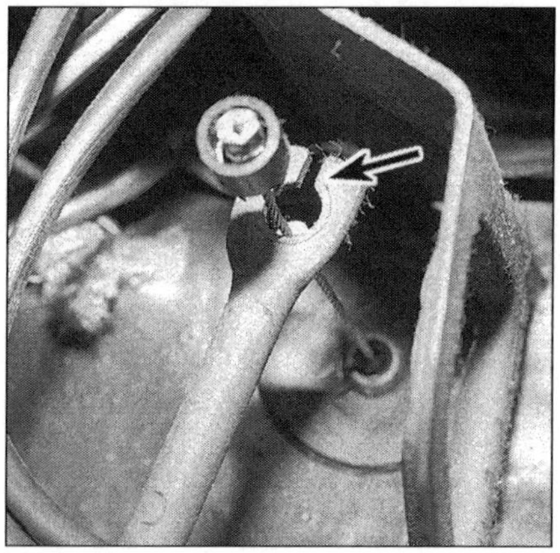

9.4 Pull the accelerator cable out and pass it through the slot (arrow) located on the top of the pedal arm

Overhaul

Refer to illustration 10.5a, 10.5b and 10.5c

5 Once it's determined that the carburetor **(see illustrations)** needs an overhaul, several options are available. If you're going to attempt to overhaul the carburetor yourself, first obtain a good quality carburetor rebuild kit (which will include all necessary gaskets, internal parts, instructions and a parts list). You'll also need some special solvent and a means of blowing out the internal passages of the carburetor with air.

6 An alternative is to obtain a new or rebuilt carburetor. They're readily available from dealers and auto parts stores. Make absolutely sure the exchange carburetor is identical to the original. A tag is usually attached to the top of the carburetor or a number is stamped on the float bowl. It'll help determine the exact type of carburetor you have. When obtaining a rebuilt carburetor or a rebuild kit, make sure the kit or carburetor matches your application exactly. Seemingly insignificant differences can make a large difference in engine performance.

7 If you choose to overhaul your own carburetor, allow enough time to disassemble it carefully, soak the necessary parts in the cleaning solvent (usually for at least one-half day or according to the instructions listed on the carburetor cleaner) and reassemble it, which will usually take much longer than disassembly. When disassembling the carburetor, match each part with the illustration in the carburetor kit and lay the parts out in order on a clean work surface. Overhauls by inexperienced mechanics can result in an engine which runs poorly or not at all. To avoid this, use care and patience when disassembling the carburetor so you can reassem-

10.5a Exploded view of a typical 2M series Dualjet carburetor

1 *Screw (2) - front vacuum break*
2 *Front vacuum break assembly*
3 *Hose - front vacuum break*
4 *Hose - rear vacuum break*
5 *Screw (2) - rear vacuum break*
6 *Rear vacuum break assembly*
7 *Pin - pump lever*
8 *Lever - pump*
9 *Rod - pump*
10 *Screw - choke lever*
11 *Lever - choke shaft*
12 *Screw (2) - bowl cover (tapered head)*
13 *Screw and lockwasher (5) - bowl cover*
14 *Bowl cover assembly*
15 *Gasket - bowl cover*
16 *Pump assembly*
17 *Spring - pump*
18 *Baffle - pump well*
19 *Insert - aneroid cavity*
20 *Power piston assembly*
21 *Spring - metering rod*
22 *Metering rod (2)*
23 *Spring - power piston*
24 *Insert - float bowl*
25 *Float and lever assembly*
26 *Hinge pin - float*
27 *Rotary valve and gasket*
28 *Plug - pump disc*
30 *Jet (2) - main metering*
31 *Screw (3) - choke cover retainer*
32 *Retainer (3) - choke cover*
33 *Choke cover assembly*
34 *Gasket - choke cover (non-electric models)*
35 *Screw and lockwasher - choke housing*
36 *Choke housing assembly*
37 *Tube - vacuum passage*
38 *Link - rear vacuum break*
39 *Screw - choke coil lever*
40 *Lever - choke coil*
41 *Shaft assembly - intermediate choke*
42 *Cam - fast idle*
43 *Seal - choke housing shaft hole*
44 *Seal - intermediate choke shaft*
45 *Rod - choke*
46 *Lever - intermediate choke*
47 *Screw and lockwasher (4) - throttle body*
48 *Throttle body assembly*
49 *Cap (2) - idle limiter*
50 *Needle - idle adjusting*
51 *Spring - idle adjusting needle*
52 *Gasket - throttle body*
53 *Filter nut - fuel inlet*
54 *Gasket - filter nut*
55 *Filter - fuel*
56 *Spring - filter*
57 *Float bowl assembly*

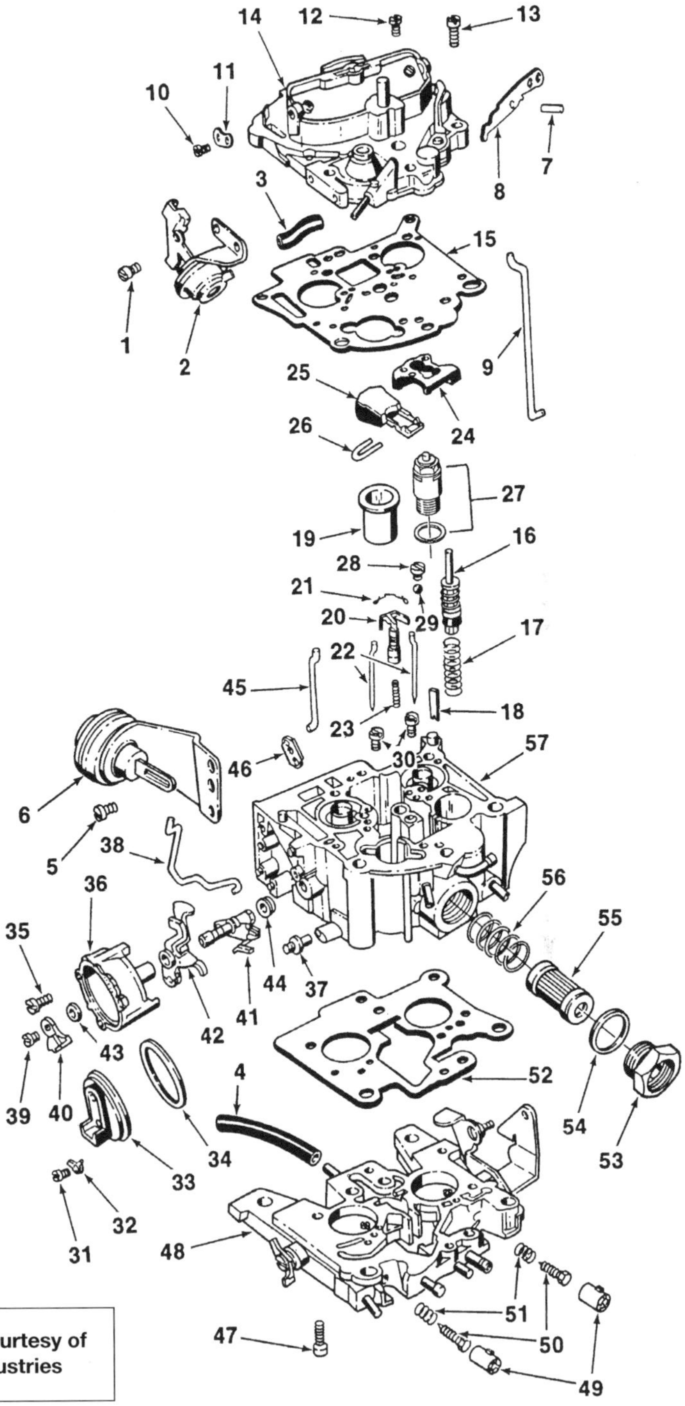

Illustration courtesy of Tomco Industries

ble it correctly.

8 Because carburetor designs are constantly modified by the manufacturer in order to meet increasingly stringent emissions regulations, we cannot include overhaul procedures for all carburetors covered by this manual. You'll receive a detailed, well illustrated set of instructions with any carburetor overhaul kit; they'll apply in a more specific manner to the carburetor on your vehicle.

11 Choke heater - testing

Hot air choke heater

Refer to illustrations 11.1, 11.2a, 11.2b and 11.2c

Note: *Early model choke systems incorporate an externally mounted heating element that is mounted inside the intake manifold and covered by a metal housing. An actuator rod positions the choke as the heating element expands from the heated air circulating through the element. Later model choke systems incorporate an integral choke assembly attached to the carburetor body. A hot air inlet pipe feeds warm air from the manifold to the heating element inside the choke housing.*

1 With the engine cold, start the engine and allow it to warm up to operating temper-

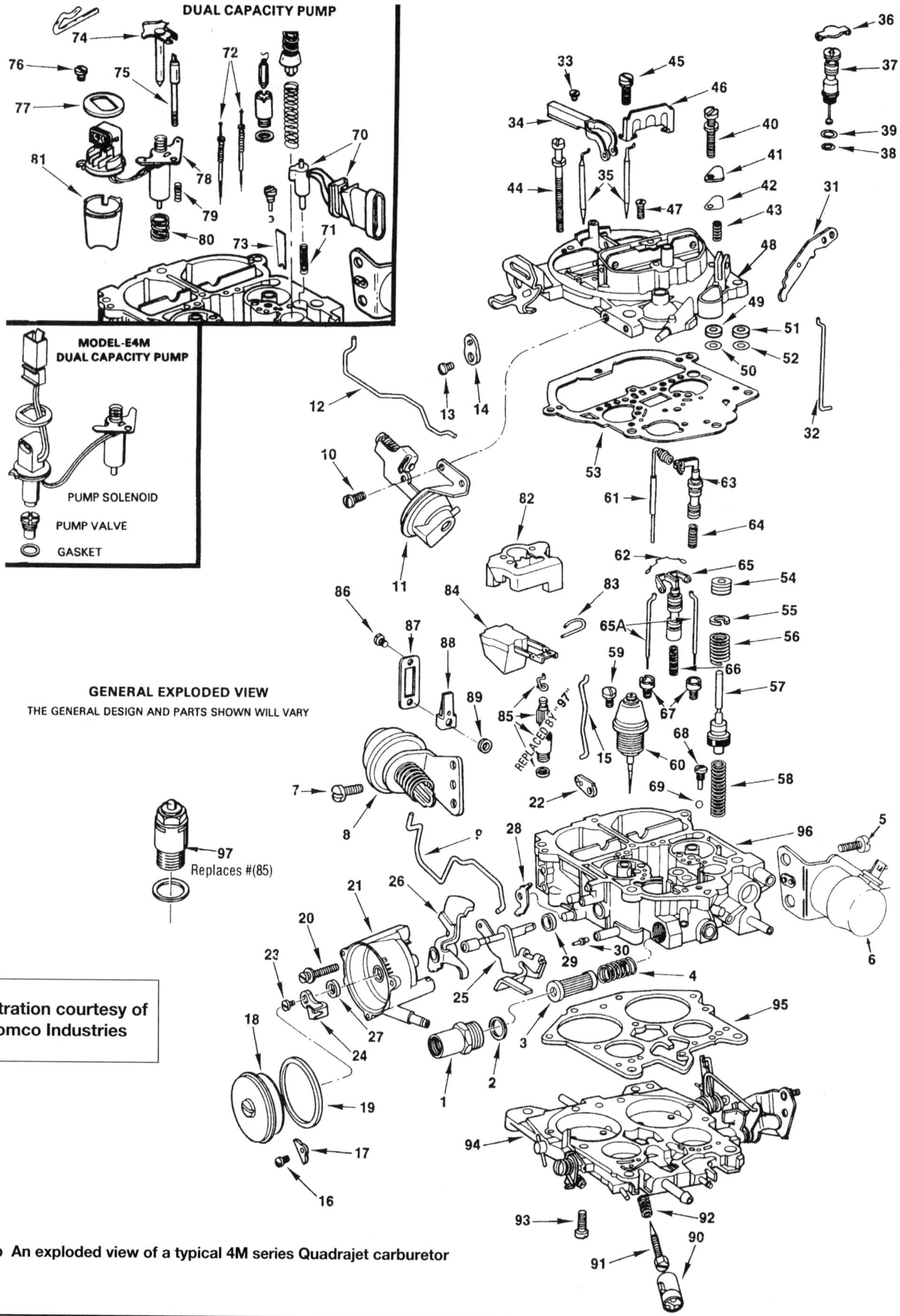

Illustration courtesy of Tomco Industries

10.5b An exploded view of a typical 4M series Quadrajet carburetor

10.5c Parts list for a typical 2M series Quadrajet carburetor

1 *Fuel filter nut*
2 *Fuel filter nut gasket*
3 *Fuel filter*
4 *Fuel filter spring*
5 *Solenoid screw*
6 *Idle speed solenoid*
7 *Rear vacuum break screw*
8 *Rear vacuum break assembly*
9 *Rear vacuum break rod*
10 *Front vacuum break screw*
11 *Front vacuum break assembly*
12 *Front vacuum break rod*
13 *Choke lever screw*
14 *Choke lever*
15 *Choke rod*
16 *Choke cover retainer rivet*
17 *Choke cover retainer*
18 *Choke cover assembly*
19 *Choke cover gasket*
20 *Choke housing screw*
21 *Choke housing assembly*
22 *Intermediate choke lever*
23 *Choke coil lever screw*
24 *Choke coil lever*
25 *Intermediate choke shaft*
26 *Fast idle cam*
27 *Choke housing seal*
28 *Secondary lockout cam*
29 *Intermediate choke shaft seal*
30 *Vacuum passage tube*
31 *Pump lever*
32 *Pump rod*
33 *Secondary metering rod holder screw*
34 *Secondary metering rod holder*
35 *Secondary metering rods*
36 *Air bleed valve cover*
37 *Idle air bleed valve*
38 *Lower bleed valve O-ring*
39 *Upper bleed valve O-ring*
40 *Vent cover screw*
41 *Vent cover*
42 *Vent cover gasket*
43 *Vent valve spring*
44 *Airhorn screw - long*
45 *Airhorn screw - short*
46 *Air baffle*
47 *Airhorn screw - special*
48 *Airhorn assembly*
49 *Pump stem seal*
50 *Pump stem seal retainer*
51 *T.P.S. plunger seal*
52 *T.P.S. plunger seal retainer*
53 *Airhorn gasket*
54 *Pump stem spacer*
55 *Pump spring retainer*
56 *Pump spring*
57 *Pump stem assembly*
58 *Pump return spring*
59 *Aneroid assembly screw*
60 *Aneroid assembly*
61 *Auxiliary metering rod*
62 *Metering rod spring*
63 *Auxiliary power piston*
64 *Auxiliary power piston spring*
65 *Power piston assembly*
65A *Main metering rods*
66 *Power piston assembly spring*
67 *Main jets*
68 *Pump discharge ball screw*
69 *Pump discharge ball*
70 *Throttle position sensor assembly*
71 *T.P.S. spring*
72 *Main metering rod and spring*
73 *Pump well baffle*
74 *Solenoid plunger*
75 *Solenoid lean mixture adjustment screw*
76 *ECM connector screw*
77 *ECM connector gasket*
78 *ECM connector and solenoid assembly*
79 *Lean mixture screw*
80 *Solenoid spring*
81 *Well insert*
82 *Fuel bowl insert*
83 *Float hinge pin*
84 *Float and lever assembly*
85 *Needle and seat assembly*
86 *Hot idle compensator cover screw*
87 *Hot idle compensator cover*
88 *Hot idle compensator assembly*
89 *Hot idle compensator gasket*
90 *Idle limiter cap (2)*
91 *Idle needle (2)*
92 *Idle needle spring (2)*
93 *Throttle body screw*
94 *Throttle body*
95 *Throttle body gasket*
96 *Main body*
97 *Rotary inlet valve*

11.1 Press the actuator rod to make sure there is tension on the choke lever when the engine is cold (early model hot air choke system shown)

11.2a On early models, remove the bolts (arrows) from the choke assembly and . . .

11.2b . . . remove the choke assembly from the intake manifold

ature. Visually inspect the choke as it opens during warm-up **(see illustration).** It may be necessary to step on the accelerator pedal to allow the fast idle cam to reposition itself in relation to the fast idle screw. Also, use your finger to touch the hot air inlet pipe and thermostatic coil to make sure it is warm. **Caution:** *To avoid burns, do not touch the hot choke parts for extended lengths of time.*

2 If the choke housing or hot air inlet pipe remains cool, check for loss of vacuum, possible restricted heat inlet pipe or restriction in the manifold choke heat stove. On later style chokes, a vacuum bleed inside the carburetor draws the hot air through the housing, so a disruption in vacuum will cause the choke not to open. If the choke parts are hot, it will be necessary to remove the choke assembly to check the heater element **(see illustrations)**. The heater element must expand (uncoil) when the temperatures go up. If the choke element remains coiled (closed) or uncoiled (open) and does not change with temperature changes, replace it with a new part.

Electric choke heater

Refer to illustration 11.3

Caution: *If there is any loss of electrical current to the choke heater, operation of any type, including idling, should be avoided. Loss of power to the choke will cause the choke to remain partly closed during engine operation. A very rich air/fuel mixture will be created and result in abnormally high exhaust system temperatures, which may cause damage to the catalytic converter or other underbody parts of the vehicle.*

3 With the engine cold, connect a jumper

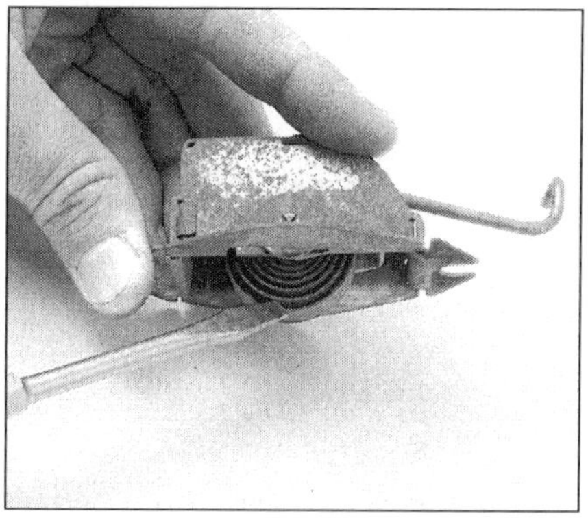

11.2c On all models, check the choke coil for damage and corrosion, as well as loss of spring tension

wire from the choke heater terminal to the positive battery terminal **(see illustration).** The choke heater housing should start becoming hot and the choke plate in the carburetor should slowly open after some time. Be sure it opens completely in about five minutes or replacement is necessary. **Note 1:** *As the heater is heating the choke coil, occasionally tap the accelerator to allow the choke to open.* **Note 2:** *The electric assist choke system consists of a thermostatic spring and cover (choke assembly), temperature sensing switch and a ceramic (positive temperature coefficient) heater. At temperatures below 60-degrees, the switch is open and no current is supplied to the ceramic heater located within the thermostatic spring. At temperatures above 60-degrees F, the temperature sensing switch closes and current is supplied to the ceramic heater. As the heater warms, it causes the spring to pull the choke plate open within 1 to 1-1/2 minutes.*

4 If the choke heater tests okay, but the choke valve does not open in normal operation, check for voltage to the choke heater when the engine is cold and the ignition switch is in the ON position.

5 If no voltage is present in Step 4, repair the open in the power circuit to the choke heater (be sure to check the fuse first!).

12 Carburetor - adjustments

Mixture control solenoid plunger adjustment (feedback models only)

Refer to illustrations 12.1 and 12.4

Note: *A feedback carburetor can be identified by the electrical connector for the mixture control solenoid, shown in illustration 12.4, toward the lower left corner of the illustration. Only feedback carburetors have such an electrical connector.*

Measuring plunger travel

Note: *If you're reassembling the carburetor after overhaul, just set the air horn in place when measuring the plunger travel (there's no need to install the gasket or screws, and you may need to remove the air horn again to adjust the travel).*

11.3 Later models have a choke housing on the right side of the carburetor (it has a black plastic cover) - electric chokes have an electrical connector like this one (A) with a wire hooked up to it. Hot air heaters have a small metal tube hooked up to a fitting on the housing (B)

12.4 . . . press lightly on the gauge until it bottoms the plunger and measure again. The difference between the two measurements is the travel

1 Insert a special carburetor float gauge tool (available from auto parts stores and tool manufacturers) into the vertical "D"-shaped vent hole in the air horn casting next to the idle air bleed valve cover **(see illustration)**. It may be necessary to file material off the side of the gauge to make clearance for the tool to enter without binding.

2 First, press down on the gauge and make sure the gauge moves up and down freely without any binding.

3 With the gauge resting against the plunger (no pressure applied), sight across the air horn and record the mark on the gauge that lines up with the top of the air horn casting (upper edge).

4 Lightly press DOWN on gauge until the plunger bottoms. Record this measurement **(see illustration)**.

5 Now, subtract the first measurement

12.1 To measure plunger travel, first measure the plunger height with no pressure applied to the gauging tool, then . . .

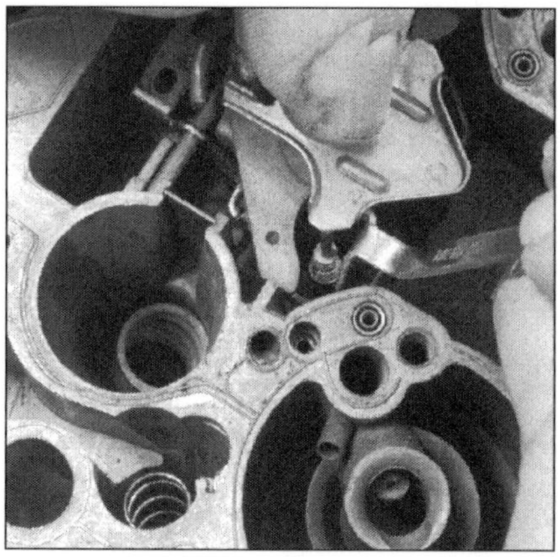

12.8a To adjust the lean-stop, place the gauging tool (being held at right) on the metering jet and under the solenoid plunger, as shown, then depress the plunger and turn the adjusting screw until the plunger bottoms against the lean stop and touches the top of the gauging tool simultaneously

from the second measurement and record the difference. This reading is the total plunger travel.

6 If the difference in travel is between 3/32 and 5/32-inch, no adjustment is necessary. If the difference is less than 3/32-inch (not enough travel) or greater than 5/32-inch (too much travel), adjust the plunger travel, as follows.

Adjusting plunger travel

Note 1: *This adjustment usually is not required after overhaul if you kept the adjustment at its original setting. It is only necessary if the travel is not correct or the duty cycle (percent "on time") is incorrect as determined by the* System performance test (see Section 15).

Note 2: *The air horn must be removed from the carburetor during this procedure; however, the procedure can be performed with the carburetor on or off the vehicle.*

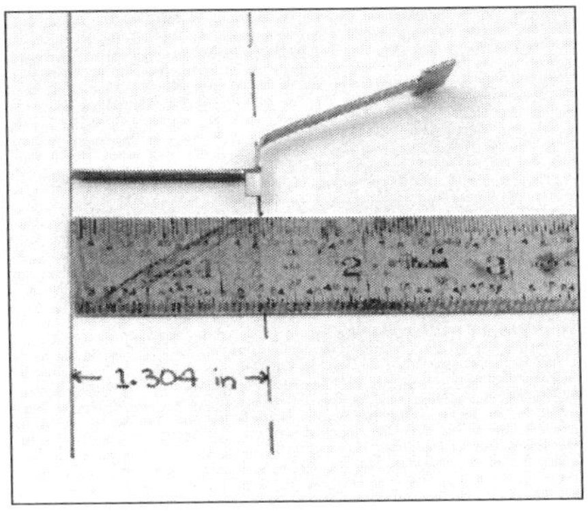

12.8b The gauging tool, shown here, allows you to precisely set the lean-stop at 1.304 inches

Note 3: *These carburetors are equipped with either a* **four-point** *mixture control solenoid adjustment system (earlier feedback systems) or a* **two-point** *mixture control solenoid adjustment system (mainly on 1985 and 1986 models). The four-point system is equipped with separate lean-stop and rich-stop adjustments that correctly adjust the travel of the solenoid plunger from rich to lean. The* **two-point** *system uses an integral rich limit stop bracket that essentially limits the travel of the plunger going up (rich) as well as the plunger going down (lean). Therefore, only one adjustment is required.*

All feedback models

Refer to illustrations 12.8a and 12.8b

7 Remove the air horn from the carburetor. Also remove the solenoid plunger and the plastic float-bowl insert, then reinstall the plunger (removing the insert will allow access to the float-bowl area). **Note:** *On two-point systems, it will be necessary to remove the solenoid adjusting screw and rich-stop before the solenoid plunger and insert can be removed. Prior to removing the screw, turn it clockwise until the plunger bottoms, counting the number of turns. After the insert is removed, reassemble the plunger and stop, setting the adjusting screw the same number of turns from the lightly-bottomed position.*

8 Now install a special gauging tool (available from auto parts stores and automotive tool suppliers) onto the base of the metering jet and directly under the solenoid plunger. This tool is made specifically to measure the solenoid plunger travel **(see illustrations)**, which should be 1.304 inches (approximately 1-5/16 inches).

9 Apply very slight pressure to the solenoid plunger with the tip of your finger to bottom it. Slowly turn the lean-stop screw with the special adjustment tool until it (the solenoid plunger) just touches the gauging tool when it's bottomed against the lean stop. This is the factory-specified distance for the lean-stop adjustment.

10 If you have a four-point system, proceed to Step 11. If you have a two-point system, the adjustment is complete. Turn the adjusting screw clockwise to the lightly-bottomed position, counting the number of turns, then unscrew and remove the screw, rich stop and plunger. Install the insert and reassemble the parts, turning the adjusting screw in the same number of turns. Install the air horn and proceed to Step 16.

12.13a On four-point systems, if the travel is not correct after setting the lean-stop, unscrew . . .

Models with four-point adjustment systems only

Refer to illustrations 12.13a, 12.13b and 12.15

11 Reinstall the air horn, along with a new gasket, onto the carburetor main body, but attach it temporarily with two screws only.

12 Recheck the solenoid plunger travel as described earlier in this procedure. If the travel is correct, completely assemble the air horn and proceed to Step 16 to finish the job.

13 If the plunger travel is still not correct, remove the air horn, invert it and remove the rich-stop screw **(see illustrations)**.

14 With the rich-stop screw removed, drive the plug out of the air horn using a punch and a hammer. Reinstall the rich-stop screw.

15 Reinstall the carburetor air horn. Insert the special float gauge into the "D"-shaped vent hole (see *Measuring plunger travel* earlier in this procedure) and, using the special carburetor tool, turn the rich-stop screw **(see illustration)** until the total solenoid plunger travel is 1/8-inch.

12.15 Using a special tool to adjust the rich-stop screw on four-point systems

12.13b . . . and remove the rich-stop screw from the carburetor air horn

All feedback models

16 With the plunger travel correctly set and the air horn reinstalled, install the replacement plugs into the carburetor body. Be sure to install the hollow end down.

Adjustments for all carburetors

17 Several on-vehicle adjustments are necessary to fine-tune engine performance. Make these adjustments after overhaul or anytime engine performance is poor and you suspect carburetor problems.

Float level check and adjustment

Refer to illustration 12.19

Note: *This procedure is normally not necessary after overhaul if the float level was carefully set during reassembly.*

18 These carburetors are equipped with a slotted access hole to insert a special float level tool for quick-checking the float level adjustment. These tools are available from auto parts stores and tool manufacturers. This procedure will allow the home mechanic to find out if the float level is incorrect and the cause of any driveability problems such as hard starting, flooding or a rich-running condition.

19 First, with the engine running at idle and the choke wide open, carefully insert the gauge into the vent slot (next to the air

12.19 Using a gauge, the "wet" float level can be checked on the vehicle, without removing the air horn

12.22 The idle mixture screws (arrows) are located in the front lower section on the Quadrajet carburetor - a special flexible adjusting tool (in use here) is necessary to access the screws on many engines

cleaner mounting stud) in the air horn and allow it to rest against the float inside the carburetor (do not press down on the gauge) **(see illustration)**.

20 Sight across the top of the air horn and observe the mark on the gauge directly at eye level as it lines up with the top of the casting at the vent slot. The setting should be within 1/16-inch of the specified float level setting. Refer to your carburetor specification sheet (included with overhaul kits) for the correct float setting.

21 If the setting varies more than 1/16-inch, remove the air horn and adjust the float level (instructions are included in overhaul kits).

Idle mixture adjustment

Refer to illustrations 12.22

Note: *On some later models with D-shaped mixture screw heads, a special screwdriver, available at most auto parts stores, will be necessary to make this adjustment.*

22 With the engine idling at the proper speed, turn each idle mixture screw clockwise **(see illustration)** until the idle speed drops a noticeable amount. Now slowly turn the mixture screw counterclockwise until the maximum rpm is achieved, but no further. Work from one mixture screw to the other, making sure both screws are about the same number of turns out from the lightly-bottomed position; this assures there's a mixture balance. After the idle mixture adjustment is correct, check the idle speed again to make sure it's still correct.

Fast idle speed adjustment

Refer to illustration 12.23

23 With the engine warmed up, hook up a tachometer according to the meter manufacturer's instructions, then position the fast idle speed adjusting screw on the second highest step of the fast-idle cam. The speed with the engine warm should be approximately 1700 rpm. If the speed is significantly more or less than 1700 rpm, turn the fast idle speed screw **(see illustration)** until the speed is correct.

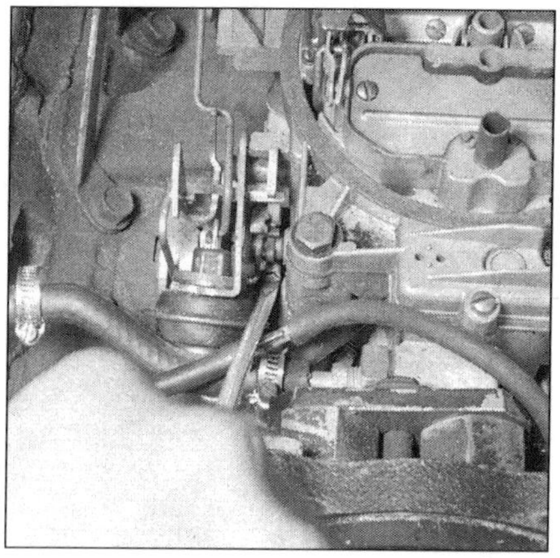

12.23 The fast-idle adjusting screw is located on the right side of the carburetor - it rests against the fast-idle cam when the choke is on

Feedback carburetor adjustments

24 Depending upon the engine size and year of the vehicle, feedback carburetor systems require several on-vehicle adjustments to fine-tune engine performance.

Idle speed control (ISC) system

Refer to illustrations 12.29, 12.31, 12.33a and 12.33b

25 If the carburetor has just been overhauled, the ISC solenoid has just been replaced with a new one or the vehicle is having a fluctuating idle problem, it is necessary to check the ISC system adjustments.

26 First, place the transmission in Neutral, set the parking brake and block the drive wheels. Connect a tachometer according to the manufacturer's instructions.

27 With the A/C off (if equipped), start the engine and warm it up to normal operating temperature (closed loop).

28 Turn the ignition OFF and unplug the connector from the ISC motor.

29 Fully retract the ISC plunger by applying 12 volts to terminal C (run a fused jumper wire from the battery's positive terminal) of the ISC motor connector and grounding terminal D **(see illustration)**. **Note 1:** *Do not allow the battery voltage (12V) to contact terminal C any longer than necessary to retract the ISC plunger. Prolonged contact will cause damage to the motor. Also, it is very important to never connect a voltage source across terminals A and B, as it may damage the internal throttle contact switch.* **Note 2:** *If the ISC solenoid does not respond when battery voltage is applied to the C and D terminals, it is faulty and should be replaced.*

30 Start the engine and allow it to return to normal operation (closed loop). Have an assistant place his foot firmly on the brake and place the transmission in DRIVE.

31 With the plunger completely retracted (from Step 5), turn the idle stop screw **(see illustration)** to attain the minimum idle speed. The minimum base idle speed is usually about 450 rpm in DRIVE. Consult your

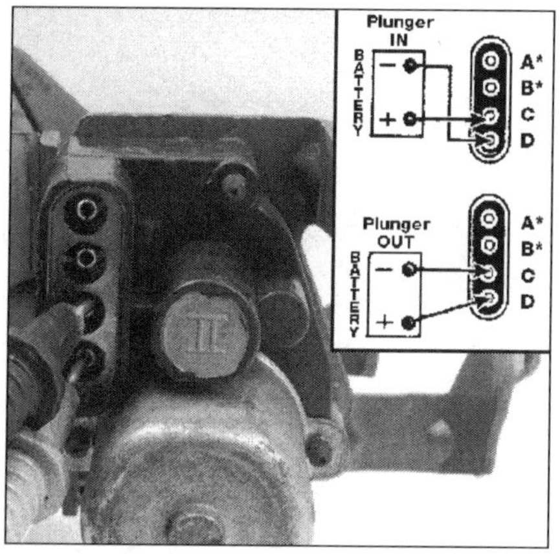

12.29 Using jumper wires, apply battery voltage to terminals C and D to extend or retract the ISC solenoid plunger

12.31 Location of the idle-stop screw (arrow) on feedback carburetors (on non-feedback carburetors, this is the curb-idle speed screw)

VECI label under the hood of the engine compartment to verify the idle specifications.

32 Now, with the transmission In DRIVE and an assistant holding his foot firmly on the brake pedal, fully extend the plunger by applying battery positive voltage (12V) to terminal D of the ISC connector and grounding terminal C **(see illustration 12.29)**. **Note:** *Do not allow the battery voltage (12V) to contact terminal D any longer than necessary to retract the ISC plunger. Prolonged contact will cause damage to the motor. Also, it is very important to never connect a voltage source across terminals A and B as it may damage the internal throttle contact switch.*

33 With the ISC plunger fully extended, check the idle speed, which should be approximately 900 rpm in DRIVE. If necessary, adjust the plunger length **(see illustrations)**. Consult your VECI label under the hood of the engine compartment to verify the idle specifications. **Note:** *When the ISC plunger is in the fully extended position, the plunger must also be in contact with the throttle lever (on carburetor) to prevent possible internal damage to the ISC solenoid.*

34 If the ISC motor was removed and the

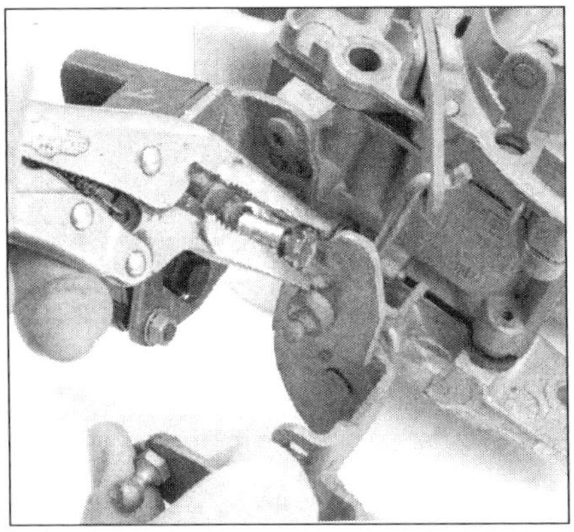

12.33a Adjust the ISC plunger by turning the plunger end with pliers (carburetor removed from engine for clarity), but . . .

12.41 The special gauging tool shown is necessary to check the idle air bleed valve adjustment. Use a large screwdriver, as shown here, to adjust the valve

plunger length changed, double-check the maximum allowable speed (see Step 33). If necessary, readjust the plunger until the correct speed is obtained.

35 Reconnect the harness connector to the ISC motor.

Idle air bleed valve (E2ME and E4ME) (feedback carburetors)

Refer to illustrations 12.38 and 12.41

36 To gain access to the idle air bleed valve, it is necessary to first remove the idle air bleed valve cover. Often, if the carburetor has been overhauled before, the cover has already been removed. If it has not been removed before, the air bleed is probably still at its factory setting and should not be tampered with unless it's known to be incorrect.

37 With the engine off, cover all the bowl vents, air inlets and air intakes with masking tape to prevent any metal chips from falling into the carburetor.

38 Carefully align a Number 35 drill bit (0.110 inches) on one end of the steel rivet heads and drill only enough to remove the rivet head from the carburetor. Use a drift and hammer to remove the remaining rivet from the assembly **(see illustration)**.

39 Lift off the cover and remove any pieces

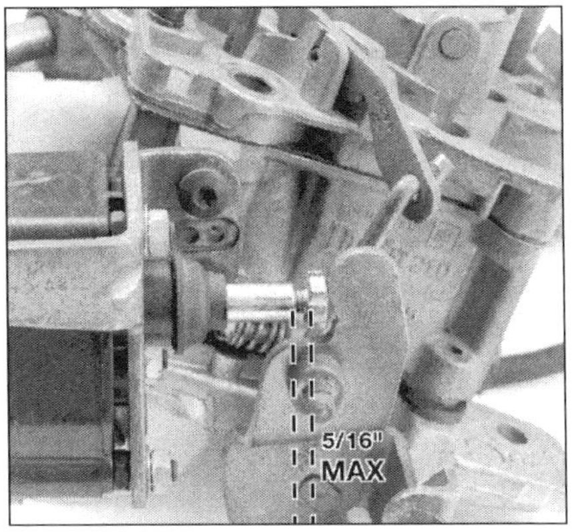

12.33b . . . do not unscrew the plunger end more than 5/16-inch from its all-the-way-in setting

12.50 DO NOT adjust the ILC plunger to a point where the screw is extending more than 1-inch

of metal, rivets or debris from the carburetor body. Discard the idle air bleed valve cover.

40 Using compressed air (if available) blow out any remaining pieces of metal from the carburetor area. **Warning:** *Be sure to wear safety goggles whenever using compressed air.*

41 Install a special gauging tool (available from auto parts stores and automotive tool suppliers) into the "D"-shaped vent hole **(see illustration)**. The upper end of the tool should be positioned over the open cavity next to the idle air bleed valve.

42 While holding the gauging tool down lightly, engage the solenoid plunger against the solenoid stop. Adjust the idle air bleed valve so that the gauging tool will pivot over and just contact the top of the valve.

43 Remove the gauging tool. Next, it will be necessary to check the duty cycle (on-time) of the mixture control solenoid to verify that the air bleed is adjusted properly or if the idle mixture must be adjusted (see Section 15).

44 Disconnect the canister purge hose and plug the end (canister side). Start the engine and allow it to reach normal operating temperature (closed loop). Follow the procedure for checking the M/C solenoid duty cycle in Section 15. If the dwell average is not within 25 to 35 degrees, then it will be necessary to

12.38 Be sure to protect the carburetor when drilling out the air-bleed rivets (otherwise, metal chips could fall into the carburetor!)

adjust the idle mixture (refer to the procedure in this Chapter).

Idle load compensator (ILC) (some later engines)

Refer to illustrations 12.50 and 12.52

45 The idle load compensator (ILC) is used instead of an ISC solenoid on some later engines to control curb idle speed. The ILC uses manifold vacuum to sense changes in engine load and compensates by changing the idle speed. The idle load compensator is adjusted at the factory. It is not necessary to make any adjustments unless the curb idle speed is out of adjustment or the ILC solenoid was faulty and had to be replaced. Before adjusting the ILC, make sure the vacuum lines to the anti-diesel solenoid, vacuum regulator, ILC solenoid and all the components that require vacuum are in order and not leaking. Check the vacuum schematic on the VECI label under the hood for the correct vacuum routing.

46 Connect a tachometer according to the manufacturer's instructions. Remove the air cleaner and plug the hose to the thermal vacuum valve (TVV). Disconnect and plug the vacuum hose to the EGR valve. Disconnect and plug the vacuum hose to the canister purge port. Disconnect and plug the vacuum hose to the ILC.

47 Back out the idle-stop screw on the carburetor three turns **(see illustration 12.31)**.

48 Turn the A/C system OFF (if equipped). Place the transmission in PARK (automatic) or NEUTRAL (manual), apply the emergency brake and place a block under each of the drive wheels.

49 Start the engine and allow it to reach normal operating temperature. On automatic transmission models, have an assistant place his foot firmly on the brake pedal and place the transmission in DRIVE. The ILC plunger should be fully extended with no vacuum applied. Using back-up wrenches, adjust the ILC plunger to obtain 750 rpm, plus or minus 50 rpm.

50 Next, measure the distance from the jam nut to the tip of the plunger **(see illustra-**

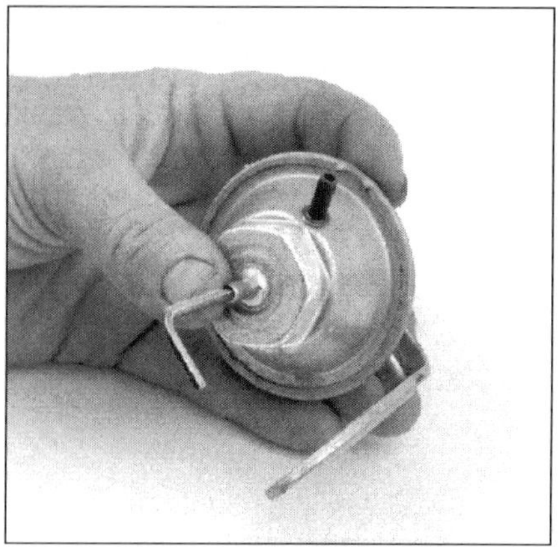

12.52 Use a 3/32-inch Allen wrench to adjust the ILC solenoid (removed from vehicle for clarity)

12.58 To adjust the TPS, drill out and remove the access plug (carburetor shown removed from vehicle for clarity) . . .

12.62 . . . then use a small screwdriver to turn the adjusting screw until the voltmeter readings are correct

tion). It should not exceed 1-inch. If the plunger measures more than 1-inch, check for other carburetor problems.

51 Remove the plug from the vacuum hose and reconnect it to the ILC and observe the idle speed. Idle speed should be 450 rpm (vehicle in NEUTRAL (manual) or DRIVE with the brake applied). If the idle speed is correct, proceed to Step 9).

52 If the idle speed is not correct, it will be necessary to adjust the ILC diaphragm. Stop the engine and remove the ILC. Remove the center cap from the center outlet tube. Using a 3/32-inch Allen wrench, insert it through the open center tube to engage the idle speed adjusting screw inside **(see illustration)**. If the idle speed was low, turn the adjusting screw counterclockwise ONE turn to increase the idle speed approximately 75 rpm. Conversely, turn the screw clockwise ONE turn to lower the idle speed about 75 rpm. **Note:** *Turn the adjusting screw TWO full turns to raise or lower the idle speed approximately 150 rpm and consequently use the same ratio to calculate the necessary rpm change desired for the situation.*

53 Re-install the ILC onto the carburetor and attach the springs and other related parts. Recheck the idle speed. Make sure the engine is completely warmed up (closed loop). If it is not correct, repeat the ILC adjustment procedure.

54 The last adjustment must be performed on the engine after the TPS value has been reset by the ECM. This can be accomplished by turning off the ignition for 10 seconds or more. Using a hand-held vacuum pump, apply vacuum to the ILC vacuum tube inlet to fully retract the plunger.

55 Adjust the idle stop screw on the carburetor to obtain 450 rpm with the vehicle in NEUTRAL (manual) or DRIVE with the brake applied.

56 Place the vehicle in PARK and stop the engine. Remove the plug from the ILC vacuum hose and install the hose onto the ILC. Reconnect all the vacuum hoses, install the air cleaner and gaskets.

Throttle position sensor (TPS)

Refer to illustrations 12.58 and 12.62

57 The throttle position sensor is equipped with an adjustment screw that is covered over with a factory-installed plug. Do not remove the plug unless it has been determined with careful testing that the TPS is out of adjustment. Refer to Section 15 in this Chapter for complete diagnostic procedures for checking the TPS. This is a critical adjustment that must be performed correctly.

58 Using a 0.076-inch (5/64-inch) drill bit, carefully drill a hole in the aluminum plug covering the TPS adjustment screw **(see illustration)**. Drill only enough metal to start a self-tapping screw.

59 Start a number 8 X 1/2-inch long self-tapping screw into the drilled hole in the plug, turning the screw just enough to ensure good thread engagement in the hole.

60 Place a wide blade section of screwdriver between the screw head and the air horn casting. Carefully pry against the screw head to remove the plug. It is also possible to use a slide hammer.

61 Install jumper wires by backprobing the electrical connector onto the correct terminals of the TPS electrical connector, then connect a digital voltmeter between the wires connected to the B (center) and C (bottom) terminals of the TPS connector on the carburetor.

62 With the engine off and ignition on and the throttle closed, turn the screw until the voltage reading is approximately 0.48 volts **(see illustration)**.

63 Make sure the voltage is correct. Then install a new plug into the air horn. Drive the plug into place until it is flush with the raised boss on the casting.

13 Carburetor - removal and installation

Warning: *Gasoline is extremely flammable, so take extra precautions when you work on any part of the fuel system. See* **Warning** *in Section 1.*

Removal

Refer to illustration 13.9

1 Remove the fuel tank cap to relieve the tank pressure.

2 Remove the air cleaner from the carburetor. Be sure to label all vacuum hoses attached to the air cleaner housing.

3 Disconnect the accelerator cable from the throttle lever (see Section 9).

4 Disconnect the TV cable from the throttle lever (see Chapter 7).

5 If equipped, disconnect the cruise control actuating lever or chain from the throttle lever.

6 Clearly label all vacuum hoses and fittings, then disconnect the hoses.

7 Disconnect the fuel line from the carburetor using a flare-nut wrench. Also use a back-up wrench to hold the large (usually 1-inch) fitting nut on the carburetor; this will prevent twisting the fuel line when the large nut loosens, as it usually does.

8 Label the wires and terminals, then unplug all electrical connectors.

9 Remove the mounting bolts **(see illustration)** and detach the carburetor from the intake manifold. Remove the carburetor mounting gasket. Stuff a shop rag into the intake manifold openings to prevent debris from falling into the manifold.

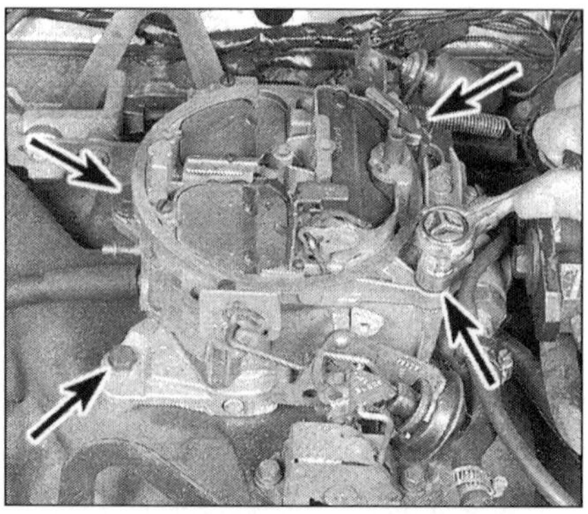

13.9 Remove the four carburetor bolts (arrows) (Quadrajet shown, Dualjet similar)

Installation

10 Use a gasket scraper to remove all traces of gasket material and sealant from the intake manifold (and the carburetor, if it's being reinstalled), then remove the shop rag from the manifold openings. Clean the mating surfaces with lacquer thinner or acetone.
11 Place a new gasket on the intake manifold.
12 Position the carburetor on the gasket and install the mounting bolts.
13 To prevent carburetor distortion or damage, tighten the fasteners, in a criss-cross pattern, 1/4-turn at a time, to the torque listed in this Chapter's Specifications.
14 The remaining installation steps are the reverse of removal.
15 Check and, if necessary, adjust the idle speed (see Chapter 1).
16 Refer to Chapter 7 to adjust the TV cable (1979 and later models only).
17 Start the engine and check carefully for fuel leaks.

14 Electronic feedback carburetor systems - general information

1 The electronic feedback carburetor system relies on an electronic signal, which is generated by an exhaust gas oxygen sensor, to control a variety of devices and keep emissions within limits. The system works in conjunction with a three-way catalyst to control the levels of carbon monoxide, hydrocarbons and oxides of nitrogen. The feedback carburetor system also works in conjunction with the computer. The two systems share certain sensors and output actuators; therefore, diagnosing this system will require a thorough check of all the feedback carburetor components.
2 The system operates in two modes: open loop and closed loop. When the engine is cold, the air/fuel mixture is controlled by the computer in accordance with a program designed in at the time of production. The air/fuel mixture during this time will be richer to allow for proper engine warm-up. When the engine is at operating temperature, the system operates in closed loop and the air/fuel mixture is varied depending on the information supplied by the exhaust gas oxygen sensor.
3 Here is a list of the various sensors and output actuators involved with these feedback carburetor systems:

Coolant temperature sensor (ECT)
Exhaust Gas Oxygen sensor (O2)
High energy Electronic Ignition (HEI) (see Chapter 5)
Early Fuel Evaporation (EFE) system (see Chapter 6)
Mixture Control Solenoid
Electronic Control Module (ECM)
Throttle Position Sensor (TPS)
Vehicle Speed Sensor (VSS)
Barometric Pressure Sensor (BARO) or Barometric Manifold Absolute Pressure (MAP) sensor

15.3 Use a jumper wire (arrow) to connect the tachometer lead to the TACH terminal on the distributor (HEI systems only)

Idle Speed Control (ISC) switch
Park/Neutral switch (see Chapter 7)

Refer to Section 15 for the diagnostic checks for the feedback carburetor system components.

15 Electronic feedback carburetor information sensors and output actuators - check and replacement

Note: *Feedback carburetor systems are equipped with a self diagnosis system that allows the home mechanic to view trouble codes for helping diagnose fuel and emission system problems. Refer to Chapter 6 for the complete procedure for extracting trouble codes from the C3 system.*

Here are some simple checks for testing the main components (actuators and sensors) of the feedback carburetor system:

Idle Speed Control (ISC) motor

General description

1 The ISC motor is a more advanced version of a throttle positioner. The motor is under direct control of the computer, which has the desired idle speed programmed into its memory. The computer compares the actual idle speed from the engine (taken from the distributor or crankshaft position sensor ignition impulses) to the desired rpm reference in memory. When the two do not match, the ISC plunger is moved in or out. This automatically adjusts the throttle to hold the idle speed, regardless of engine loads.
2 Many ISC motors have a throttle contact switch at the end of the plunger. The position of the switch determines whether or not the ISC should control idle speed. When the throttle lever is resting against the ISC plunger, the switch contacts are closed, at which time the computer moves the ISC motor to the programmed idle speed. When the throttle lever is not contacting the ISC plunger, the switch contacts are open and

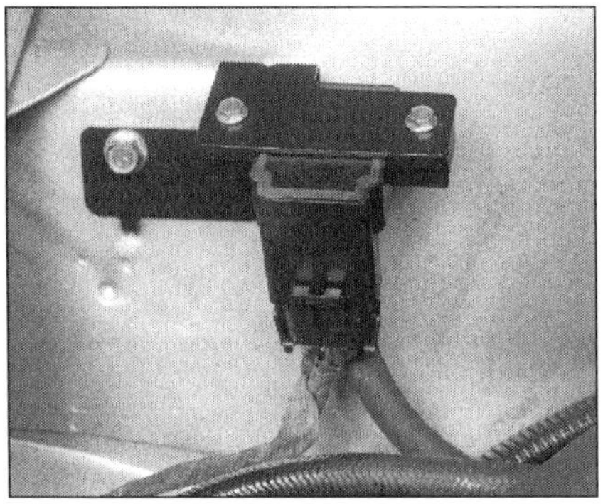

15.6 A typical MAP sensor - they're sometimes mounted on the firewall, like this one, or on the side of the air cleaner housing

the ECM stops sending the idle speed commands and the driver controls engine speed.

Check

Refer to illustration 15.3

3 With the engine warmed to normal operating temperature, remove the air cleaner assembly and any other components that obscure your view of the ISC motor. Hook up a tachometer **(see illustration)** in accordance with the manufacturer's instructions and check the VECI label under the hood to determine what the correct idle rpm should be.
4 Have an assistant start the engine. Check that the engine rpm is correct. Have your assistant turn on the air conditioning (if equipped), headlights and any other electrical accessories. If the vehicle is equipped with power steering, have your assistant turn the steering wheel from side-to-side. Note the reading on the tachometer. The engine speed should remain stable at the correct idle speed. If the vehicle is equipped with an automatic transmission, block the wheels and have your assistant set the parking brake, place his/her foot firmly on the brake pedal and place the transmission in Drive. Again the engine rpm should remain stable at the correct speed. **Warning:** *Do not stand in front of the vehicle during this test.*
5 If the ISC motor is not functioning as it should, first check the condition of the wiring and electrical connector(s). Make sure the connector is securely attached and there is no corrosion at the terminals. For further diagnosis of this system, refer to factory service manual for your particular vehicle or take the vehicle to a dealer service department or other qualified shop.

MAP (Manifold Absolute Pressure) sensor

General description

Refer to illustration 15.6

6 The MAP sensor (sometimes referred to as the pressure differential sensor) reports engine load to the computer which uses the information to adjust spark advance and fuel enrichment **(see illustration)**. The MAP sensor measures intake manifold pressure and

vacuum on the absolute scale (from zero instead of from sea-level atmospheric pressure (14.7 psi) as most gauges and sensors do). The MAP sensor reads vacuum and pressure through a hose connected to the intake manifold. A pressure-sensitive ceramic or silicon element and electronic circuit in the sensor generates a voltage signal that changes in direct proportion to pressure.

7 Under low-load, high-vacuum conditions, the computer leans the fuel/air mixture and advances the spark timing for better fuel economy. Under high-load, low-vacuum conditions, the computer richens the fuel/air mixture and retards timing to prevent detonation. The MAP sensor serves as the electronic equivalent of both a vacuum advance on a distributor and a power valve in the carburetor.

Check

8 Anything that hinders accurate sensor input can upset both the fuel mixture and ignition timing. This includes the MAP sensor itself as well as shorts or opens in the sensor wiring circuit and/or vacuum leaks in the intake manifold or vacuum hose. Some of the most typical driveability symptoms associated with problems in the MAP sensor circuit include:

1) *Detonation and misfire due to increased spark advance and a lean fuel mixture.*
2) *Loss of power and/or fuel economy and sometimes even black smoke due to retarded ignition timing and a very rich fuel mixture.*
3) *Poor fuel economy*
4) *Hard starts and/or stalling.*

Note: *A vacuum leak in the hose to the MAP sensor causes the MAP sensor to indicate a higher than normal pressure (less vacuum) in the manifold, which makes the computer think the engine is under much more load than it really is. As a result, the ignition timing is retarded and the fuel mixture is richened.*

9 When a MAP sensor trouble code is detected, be sure to first check for vacuum leaks in the hoses or electrical connectors or wiring damage in the MAP sensor circuit. Kinks in the line, blockage or splits can occur and deter the sensor's ability to respond accurately to the changes in the manifold pressure. check for anything that is obvious and easily repaired before actually replacing the sensor itself.

10 A MAP sensor will typically produce a voltage signal that will drop with decreasing manifold pressure (rising vacuum). Test specifications will vary according to the manufacturer and engine type. A typical MAP sensor will read 4.6 to 4.8 volts with 0 in-Hg vacuum applied. Raise it to 5 in-Hg vacuum and the reading should drop to about 3.75 volts. Raise it up again to 20 in-Hg and the reading should drop to about 1.1 volts.

Barometric pressure (BARO) sensor

General description

11 The BARO sensor detects ambient pressure changes that occur as the result of changes in the weather and/or the altitude of the vehicle. It then sends an electronic signal to the ECM that is used to adjust the air fuel ratio and spark timing.

15.21a Check the TPS signal voltage and observe that, as the throttle opens, the signal voltage INCREASES

Check

12 A problem with the BARO sensor will usually set a Code 32. To check the sensor, begin by checking the voltage from terminal A to terminal B at the sensor electrical connector. Compare your voltage reading with the chart below.

Altitude (in feet)	Voltage range
Below 1000	3.8 to 5.5
1000 to 2000	3.6 to 5.3
2000 to 3000	3.5 to 5.1
3000 to 4000	3.3 to 5.0
4000 to 5000	3.2 to 4.8
5000 to 6000	3.0 to 4.6
6000 to 7000	2.9 to 4.5
7000 to 8000	2.8 to 4.3
8000 to 9000	2.6 to 4.2
9000 to 10000	2.5 to 4.0

13 Connect a hand-held vacuum pump to the port of the sensor (you may have to remove a small filter to do this), apply 10 in-Hg to the sensor and check the voltage again.

14 If the change is more than 2.3 volts, replace the sensor.

15 If the voltage change is less than 1.2 volts, check for a short between sensor terminals B and C. If there's no short, replace the sensor.

16 If the voltage change is between 1.2 to 2.3 volts, the problem lies in the wire to ECM terminal no. 1, a bad connection at the ECM or a defective ECM.

Throttle Position Sensor (TPS)

General description

17 The TPS is either mounted externally on the throttle body or inside of the carburetor. The TPS output voltage varies according to the angle of the throttle. Its job is to inform the computer about the rate of throttle opening and relative throttle position. A separate Wide Open Throttle (WOT) switch may be used to signal the computer when the throttle is wide open. The TPS consists of a variable resistor that changes resistance as the throttle changes its opening. By signaling the computer when the throttle opens, the computer can richen the fuel mixture to retain the proper air/fuel ratio. The initial setting of the TPS is very important because the voltage signal the computer receives tells the computer the exact position of the throttle at idle.

15.21b First check the TPS resistance with the throttle closed and . . .

Check

Refer to illustration 15.21a, 15.21b and 15.21c

18 Throttle Position Sensors typically have their own types of driveability symptoms that can be distinguished from other information sensors. The most common symptom of a faulty or misadjusted sensor is hesitation or stumble during acceleration. The same symptom of a bad accelerator pump in a non-feedback, carbureted engine.

19 There are basically two voltage checks you can perform to test the Throttle Position Sensor. **Note:** *It is best to have the correct wiring diagram for the vehicle when performing the following checks.*

20 The first test is for the presence of voltage at the TPS supply wire with the ignition key ON. The sensor cannot deliver the correct signal without the proper supply voltage. You can determine the function of each individual wire (ground, supply, signal wire) by probing each one with a voltmeter and checking the different voltages. The voltage that remains constant when the throttle is opened and closed will be the supply voltage. If there's no voltage at any of the wires, there's probably an open or short in the wiring harness to the sensor.

21 The second check is for the proper voltage change that occurs as the throttle opens and closes. As the throttle goes from closed-to-wide open, the voltage at the signal wire should typically increase smoothly from 1 volt to 5 volts **(see illustration)**. To check the resistance of the sensor, unplug the electrical connector and hook up an ohmmeter to the supply and signal terminals. With the ignition key OFF, slowly move the throttle through the

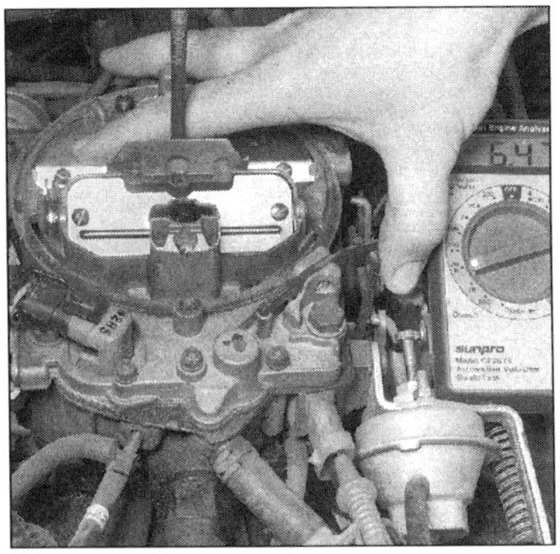

15.21c . . . then with the throttle open. Resistance should INCREASE

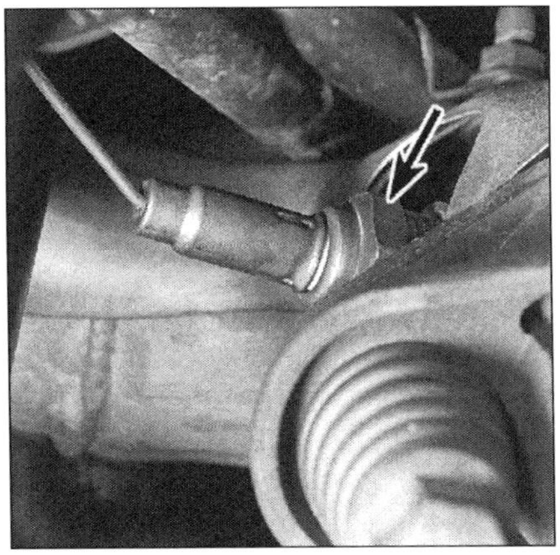

15.23 A typical oxygen sensor (arrow) mounted in the exhaust manifold

15.30 Check for a millivolt signal on the oxygen sensor electrical connector (usually located near the firewall)

complete range **(see illustrations)**. Observe carefully for any unusual changes in the resistance (the change should be smooth) as it increases from low to high.

22 Also, be sure to check for trouble codes. Be sure you have checked all the obvious items before replacing the TPS.

Oxygen sensor

General description

Refer to illustration 15.23

23 The oxygen sensor is located in the exhaust manifold (or in the exhaust pipe near the exhaust manifold) and produces a voltage signal proportional to the content of oxygen in the exhaust **(see illustration)**. A higher oxygen content across the sensor tip will vary the oxygen differential, thereby lowering the sensor's output voltage. On the other hand, lower oxygen content will raise the output voltage. Typically the voltage ranges from 0.10 volts (lean) to 0.90 volts (rich). The computer uses the sensor's input voltage to adjust the air/fuel mixture, leaning it out when the sensor detects a rich condition or enriching it when it detects a lean condition. When the sensor reaches operating temperature (600-degrees F), it will produce a variable voltage signal based on the difference between the amount of oxygen in the exhaust (internal) and the amount of oxygen in the air directly surrounding the sensor (external). The ideal stoichiometric fuel/air ratio (14.7:1) will produce about 0.45 volts.

24 There are basically two types of oxygen sensors on the market. The most popular type uses a zirconia element in its tip. The latest type of oxygen sensor uses a titania element. Instead of producing its own voltage, the titania element resistance will alter a voltage signal that is supplied by the computer itself. Although the titania element works differently than the zirconia element, the results are basically identical. The biggest difference is that the titania element responds faster and allows the computer to maintain more uniform control over a wide range of exhaust temperatures.

25 Contamination can directly affect engine performance and life span of the oxygen sensor. There are basically three types of contamination; carbon, lead and silicon. Carbon buildup due to a rich-running condition will cause inaccurate readings and increase the problem's symptoms. Diagnose the fuel injection system or carburetor feedback controls for correct fuel adjustments. Once the system is repaired, run the engine at high rpm without a load (parked in the driveway) to remove the carbon deposits. Avoid leaded gasoline as it causes contamination of the oxygen sensor. Also, avoid using old-style silicone gasket sealant (RTV) that releases volatile compounds into the crankcase which eventually wind up on the sensor tip. Always check to make sure the RTV sealant you are using is compatible with modern emission systems.

26 Before an oxygen sensor can function properly it must reach a minimum operating temperature of 600-degrees F. The warm-up period prior to this is called "open loop." In this mode, the computer detects a low coolant temperature (cold start) and wide open throttle (warm-up) condition. Until the engine reaches operating temperature, the computer ignores the oxygen sensor signals. During this time span, the emission controls are not precise! Once the engine is warm, the system is said to be in "closed loop" (using the oxygen sensor's input). Some manufacturers have designed an electric heating element to help the sensor reach operating temperature sooner. A typical heated sensor will consist of a ground wire, a sensor output wire (to the computer) and a third wire that supplies battery voltage to the resistance heater inside the oxygen sensor. Be careful when testing the oxygen sensor circuit! Clearly identify the function of each wire or you might confuse the data and draw the wrong conclusions.

Check

27 Sometimes an apparent oxygen sensor problem is not the sensor's fault. An air leak in the exhaust manifold or a fouled spark plug or other problem in the ignition system causes the oxygen sensor to give a false lean-running condition. The sensor reacts only to the content of oxygen in the exhaust, and it has no way of knowing where the extra oxygen came from.

28 When checking the oxygen sensor it is important to remember that a good sensor produces a fluctuating signal that responds quickly to the changes in the exhaust oxygen content. To check the sensor you will need a 10 mega-ohm digital voltmeter. Never use an ohmmeter to check the oxygen sensor and never jump or ground the terminals. This can damage the sensor.

29 Connect the meter to the oxygen sensor circuit. select the mV (millivolt) scale. If the engine is equipped with a later style (heated) oxygen sensor, be sure you are connected to the signal wire and not one of the heater or ground wires. Start the engine and let it idle. Typically, the meter will respond with a fluctuating millivolt reading when connected properly. Also, be sure the engine is in closed loop (warmed-up to operating temperature).

30 Watch very carefully as the voltage fluctuates. The display will flash values ranging from 100 mV to 900 mV (0.1 to 0.9 volt). The numbers will flash very quickly, so be observant. Record the high and low values over a period of one minute. With the engine operating properly, the oxygen sensor should average approximately 500 mV (0.5 volt) **(see illustration)**.

31 To further test the oxygen sensor, remove a vacuum line and observe the readings as the engine stumbles from the excessively LEAN mixture. The voltage should LOWER to an approximate value of 200 mV (0.2 volt). Install the vacuum line. Now, obtain some propane gas mixture (bottled) and connect it to a vacuum port on the intake manifold. Start the engine and open the propane valve (open the propane valve only partially and do so a little at a time to prevent over-enriching the mixture). This will create a RICH mixture. Watch carefully as the readings INCREASE. **Warning:** *Propane gas is highly flammable. Be sure there are no leaks in your connections or an explosion could result.* If the oxygen sensor responds correctly to the makeshift lean and rich conditions, the sensor is working properly.

15.40 Connect the dwellmeter to the electrical connector (arrow) near the carburetor and observe the engine rpm on one meter (right side) and the dwell on the other meter (left side)

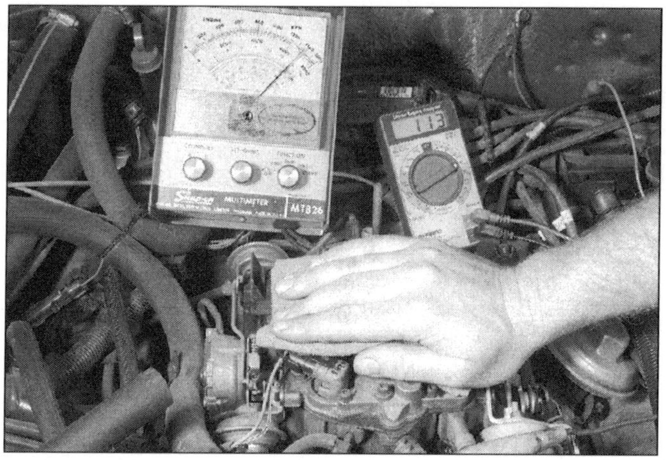

15.44a Place a rag over the carburetor air horn and watch the dwell go LEAN to compensate for a rich running condition

Mixture control (M/C) solenoid

General description

Refer to illustrations 15.40, 15.44a and 15.44b

32 The mixture control (M/C) solenoid is a device that controls fuel flow from the bowl to the main well and at the same time controls the idle circuit air bleed.

33 The mixture control (M/C) solenoid is located in the float bowl where the power piston used to be. It is equipped with a spring loaded plunger that moves up and down like a power piston but more rapidly. Certain areas on the plunger head contact the metering rods and an idle air bleed valve. Plunger movement controls both the metering rods and the idle air bleed valve simultaneously.

34 When the mixture control solenoid is energized it moves down causing the metering rods to move into the jets and restrict the flow of fuel into the main well. The idle air bleed plunger opens the air bleed and allows air into the idle circuit. Both these movements reduce fuel flow and thereby LEANS out the system.

35 When the plunger is de-energized, the M/C solenoid moves up, causing the metering rods to move out of the jets and allow more fuel to the main well, less idle air and increased fuel flow. Here the solenoid is in the RICH position.

36 The mixture control solenoid varies the air/fuel ratio based on the electrical input from the ECM. When the solenoid is ON, the fuel is restricted and the air is admitted. This gives a lean air/fuel ratio (approximately 18:1). When the solenoid is OFF, fuel is admitted and the air/fuel ratio is approximately 13:1. During closed loop operation, the ECM controls the M/C solenoid to approximately 14.7:1 by controlling the ON and OFF time of the solenoid.

37 As the solenoid "on time" changes, the up time and down time of the metering rods also changes. When a lean mixture is desired, the M/C solenoid will restrict fuel flow through the metering jet 90-percent of the time, or, in other words, a lean mixture will be provided to the engine.

38 This lean command will read as 54-degrees on the dwell meter (54-degrees is 90-percent of 60-degrees), and means the M/C solenoid has restricted fuel flow 90-percent of the time. A rich mixture is provided when the M/C solenoid restricts it only 10-percent of the time and allows a rich mixture to flow to the engine. A rich command will have a dwellmeter reading of 6-degrees (10-percent of 60-degrees); the M/C solenoid has restricted fuel flow 10-percent of the time. On some engines dwellmeter readings can vary between 5-degrees and 55-degrees, rather than between 6-degrees and 54-degrees. The ideal mixture would be shown on the dwellmeter with the needle varying or swinging back and forth, anywhere between 10-degrees and 50-degrees. "Varying" means the needle continually moves up and down the scale. The amount it moves does not matter, only the fact that it does move. The dwell is being varied by the signal sent to the ECM by the oxygen sensor in the exhaust manifold.

39 The following checks assume the engine has been tuned and the ignition system is in order.

40 The dwellmeter is used to diagnose the M/C solenoid system. This is done by connecting a dwellmeter to the pigtail connector in the M/C solenoid wiring harness **(see illustration)**.

41 In the older style contact-points ignition systems, the dwellmeter reads the period of time that the points were closed (or "dwelled" together). That period of time was when voltage flowed to the ignition coil. In the feedback carburetor system, the dwellmeter is used to read the time that the ECM closes the M/C solenoid circuit to ground, allowing voltage to operate the M/C solenoid. Dwell, as used in feedback system performance diagnosis, is the time that the M/C solenoid circuit is closed (energized). The dwellmeter will translate this time into degrees. The "6-cylinder" (0-degrees to 60-degrees) scale on the dwellmeter is used for this reading. The ability of the dwellmeter to make this kind of conversion makes it an ideal tool to check the amount of time the ECM internal switch is closed, thus energizing the M/C solenoid. The only difference is that the degree scale on the meter is more like percent of solenoid "on time" rather than "degrees of dwell".

42 First set the dwellmeter on the 6-cylinder position, then connect it to the M/C solenoid dwell lead to measure the output of the ECM. Do not allow the terminal to touch ground, including hoses. You must use the 6-cylinder position when diagnosing all engines, whether the engine you're working on is a 4, 6, or 8 cylinder engine. **Note:** *Some older dwellmeters may not work properly on the feedback carburetor systems. Don't use any dwellmeter which causes a change in engine operation when it is connected to the solenoid lead.*

The 6-cylinder scale on the dwellmeter provides evenly divided points, for example:

15-degrees = 1/4 scale
30-degrees = midscale
45-degrees = 3/4 scale

Connect the positive clip lead of the dwellmeter to the M/C solenoid pigtail connector. Attach the other dwellmeter clip lead to ground. Do not allow the clip leads to contact other conductive cables or hoses which could interfere with accurate readings.

43 After connecting the dwellmeter to a warm, operating engine the dwell at idle and part throttle will read between 5-degrees and 55-degrees and will be varying. That is, the needle will move continuously up and down the scale. What matters is that the needle does move, not how much it moves. Typical needle movement will occur between the 30 and 35-degree range in a normal operating feedback system. Needle movement indicates that the engine is in "closed-loop," and that the dwell is being varied by signals from the ECM. However, if the engine is cold, has just been restarted, or the throttle is wide open, the dwell will be fixed and the needle will be steady. Those are signs that the

15.44b Disconnect a vacuum line and observe the dwell "on time" indicate rich (low reading) to compensate for the lean running condition

15.48a Install a clamp onto the purge hose from the charcoal canister to prevent entrance of vapors into the carburetor

engine is in "open-loop."

44 Diagnostic checks to find a condition without a trouble code are usually made on a warm engine (in "closed-loop") easily checked by making sure the upper radiator hose is hot. There are three ways of distinguishing "open" from "closed-loop" operation.

1. *A variation in dwell will occur only in "closed-loop."*
2. *Test for closed loop operation by restricting airflow to the carburetor to choke the engine* **(see illustration). Warning:** *Use a thick rag (not your bare hand) and keep your face away from the carburetor. If the dwellmeter moves up scale, that indicates "closed-loop."*
3. *If you create a large vacuum leak and the dwell drops down, that also indicates "closed-loop"* **(see illustration)**.

45 Basically, "closed loop" indicates that the ECM is using information from the exhaust oxygen sensor to influence operation of the Mixture Control (M/C) solenoid. The ECM still considers other information such as engine temperature, RPM, barometric and manifold pressure and throttle position along with the exhaust oxygen sensor information.

46 During "open-loop" all information except the exhaust oxygen sensor input is considered by the ECM to control the M/C solenoid. Accurate readings from the oxygen sensor are not attained until the sensor is completely hot (600-degrees F).

Note: *The exhaust oxygen sensor may cool below its operational temperature during prolonged idling. This will cause an open loop condition, and make the diagnostic information not usable during diagnosis. Engine RPM must be increased to warm the exhaust oxygen sensor, and again re-establish "closed loop". Diagnosis should begin over at the first step after "closed-loop" is resumed.*

Coolant temperature sensor

47 On V6 engines, the sensor is located on the right front of the intake manifold, near the thermostat housing. On V8 engines, it's located at the extreme left front corner of the intake manifold. Refer to Chapter 6, Section 6 for the coolant temperature sensor diagnostic procedure.

System performance test

Refer to illustration 15.48a and 15.48b

48 First, start the engine and then ground the diagnostic terminal (terminals A and B) using a small jumper wire (see Chapter 6, Section 4). This will allow the feedback system to run on the preset default values, thereby not allowing the computer to make any running adjustments. **Caution:** *It is important NOT to crank the engine while the diagnostic connector is grounded.* Disconnect the purge hose from the charcoal canister and plug it (or simply clamp it shut) **(see illustration)**. Disconnect the bowl vent hose at the carburetor and plug the hose on the canister side. These two steps will not allow any recirculated crankcase vapors to enter the carburetor during testing. Connect a tachometer according to the manufacturers' instructions. Disconnect the M/C solenoid and ground the M/C solenoid dwell lead **(see illustration)**. Run the engine at 3,000 rpm and while holding the throttle steady, reconnect the M/C solenoid and observe the rpm. If the engine is equipped with an electric cooling fan, the rpm may lower when it turns on. Remove the dwell lead before returning to idle.

49 The test results will be either:

a) *the engine will drop below 300 rpm*
b) *the engine will NOT drop below 300 rpm and may increase rpm*

50 If the engine does not drop below 300 rpm, check the wiring on the M/C solenoid for any damaged connectors and if they are OK, check the carburetor on-vehicle adjustments in Section 12.

51 If the engine drops below 300 rpm, connect a dwellmeter to the M/C solenoid dwell

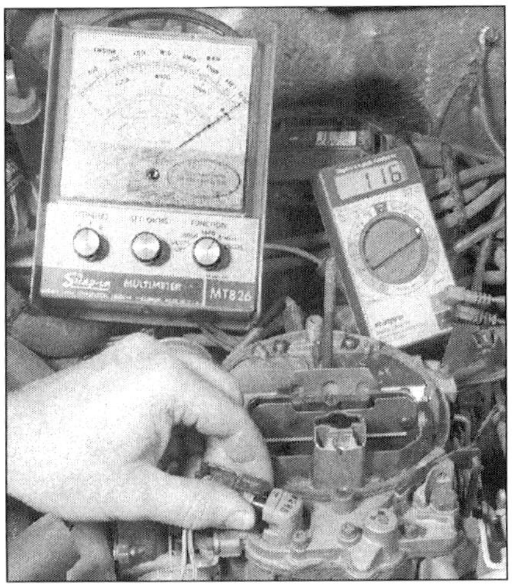

15.48b With the dwellmeter and tachometer properly installed, disconnect the M/C solenoid connector and observe the gauge. Rpm should drop below 300 from normal

lead **(see illustration 15.40)**. Be sure to read the information on "closed loop" operation and dwellmeters in the preceding Sections. Set the carburetor on the high step of the fast idle cam and run the engine for one minute or until the dwell starts to vary (whichever happens first). Return the engine to idle and observe the dwell. In most cases the dwell should vary between 10 and 50-degrees but there are several types of problems that may occur. **Note:** *The following tests must be performed with the diagnostic connector still grounded (terminals A and B) unless otherwise indicated.*

Fixed dwell under 10-degrees

52 This condition indicates that the feedback system is responding RICH to offset a very lean condition in the engine. One way to separate the problem is to choke the carburetor with the engine at part throttle. This will either increase or decrease the dwell.

53 If the dwell increases, check for a vacuum leak in the hoses, gaskets, AIR system etc. Also, check for an exhaust leak near the oxygen sensor, any hoses that are misrouted and an EGR valve that is not operating or that is leaking.

54 If the dwell does not increase, check the oxygen sensor, the wiring harness from the ECM to the oxygen sensor, TPS, TPS voltage and/or the ECM. If necessary, have the system diagnosed by a dealer service department or other repair shop.

Fixed dwell between 10 and 50-degrees

55 This condition indicates that the feedback system is stuck in one mode (open loop) because of a faulty coolant temperature sensor, oxygen sensor or TPS. Start the diagnosis by running the engine at part throttle for one minute. Then with the engine idling, observe the dwell, remove the connector from the coolant sensor and jump the terminals on the connector. This will ground the signal and indicate to the ECM that the sensors are functioning (grounded). The dwell reading should not be fixed with the sensor grounded. Check each sensor for the correct resistance and voltage signal from its respective electrical connector.

Fixed dwell over 50-degrees

56 This condition indicates that the feedback system is responding LEAN to offset a very rich condition in the engine. Start the diagnosis by running the engine at fast idle for about two minutes and then let it return to idle. This procedure makes sure that the feedback system is in closed-loop (warmed-up). Next, disconnect the large vacuum hose to the PCV valve and cause a major vacuum leak. Do not allow the engine to stall. The dwell should drop by approximately 20-degrees. If it does, check the carburetor on-vehicle adjustments in Section 12. Also, check the evaporative canister for fuel overload or leaks in the purge control system that would cause an over-rich condition in the carburetor.

57 If the dwell does not drop, check the oxygen sensor, oxygen sensor signal voltage and their respective wiring circuits for any problems.

16 Turbocharger - general information

The turbocharger increases power by using an exhaust gas-driven turbine to pressurize the fuel/air mixture before it enters the combustion chambers. The amount of boost (intake manifold pressure) is controlled by the wastegate (exhaust bypass valve). The wastegate is operated by a spring-loaded actuator assembly which controls the maximum boost level by allowing some of the exhaust gas to bypass the turbine. The wastegate is controlled by the computer.

Only the Buick Riviera models covered in this manual are equipped with the turbocharger option on the 3.8L V6 engine from 1979 through 1985. The 1985 Riviera is equipped with Sequential Electronic Fuel Injection along with the Distributorless Ignition System (DIS). These particular engines are not covered in this manual. The 1979 through 1984 Riviera turbocharged V6 engines are equipped with the Rochester Quadrajet carburetor. These Rivieras were the first front wheel drive turbocharged vehicles produced in the United States. This turbocharger set-up is rated at 200 horsepower.

17 Turbocharger - check

General checks

1 While it is a relatively simple device, the turbocharger is also a precision component which can be severely damaged by an interrupted oil or coolant supply or loose or damaged ducts.

2 Due to the special techniques and equipment required, checking and diagnosis of suspected problems dealing with the turbocharger should be left to a dealer service department. The home mechanic can, however, check the connections and linkages for security, damage and other obvious problems. Also, the home mechanic can check components that govern the turbocharger such as the wastegate solenoid, bypass valve and wastegate actuator. Refer to the checks later in this Section.

3 Because each turbocharger has its own distinctive sound, a change in the noise level can be a sign of potential problems.

4 A high-pitched or whistling sound is a symptom of an inlet air or exhaust gas leak.

5 If an unusual sound comes from the vicinity of the turbine, the turbocharger can be removed and the turbine wheel inspected. **Caution:** *All checks must be made with the engine off and cool to the touch and the turbocharger stopped or personal injury could result. Operating the engine without all the turbocharger ducts and filters installed is also dangerous and can result in damage to the turbine wheel blades.*

6 With the engine turned off, reach inside the housing and turn the turbine wheel to make sure it spins freely. If it doesn't, it's possible the cooling oil has sludged or coked from overheating. Push in on the turbine wheel and check for binding. The turbine should rotate freely with no binding or rubbing on the housing. If it does the turbine bearing is worn out.

7 Check the exhaust manifold for cracks and loose connections.

8 Because the turbine wheel rotates at speeds up to 140,000 rpm, severe damage can result from the interruption of coolant or contamination of the oil supply to the turbine bearings. Check for leaks in the coolant and oil inlet lines and obstructions in the oil drain-back line, as this can cause severe oil loss through the turbocharger seals. Burned oil on the turbine housing is a sign of this. **Caution:** *Whenever a major engine bearing such as a main, connecting rod or camshaft bearing is replaced, the turbocharger should be flushed with clean oil.*

Wastegate boost pressure test procedure

9 The wastegate turbocharger provides additional low speed boost without over-boost at high speeds. This increases low speed torque and better driveability. It is important that the wastegate assembly is working properly.

10 Remove the wastegate actuator hose and install a hand-held vacuum pump onto the actuator assembly.

11 Apply approximately 3 in.Hg. vacuum to the actuator. The actuator rod should move slightly and hold its position.

12 If the test results are incorrect, replace the wastegate actuator.

13 If the test results are correct but the turbocharger boost seems insufficient, have a dealer service department perform a road test to check boost pressure while the vehicle attains wide open acceleration.

18 Turbocharger - replacement and wastegate adjustment

Caution: *The turbocharger is a high-speed component, balanced and assembled to very fine tolerances. Do not disassemble it or try to repair it. Turbochargers should only be overhauled or repaired by authorized turbocharger repair shops or damage could result to the turbocharger and/or the engine.*

Removal

1 Disconnect the negative battery cable.

2 Disconnect the exhaust outlet pipe from the turbocharger. Be sure to use penetrating spray to lubricate the threads before attempting to remove them from the turbocharger.

3 Raise the vehicle and support it securely on jackstands.

4 Disconnect the exhaust outlet pipe from the catalytic converter and separate the outlet pipe from the engine compartment.

5 Disconnect the turbocharger inlet pipe from the turbocharger housing and exhaust manifold and separate the pipe from the assembly.

6 Disconnect the oil supply line located in the center of the turbocharger and by the oil pressure switch on the engine block and separate the oil supply line from the engine. Be ready with a rag to catch any oil from the lines as they are disconnected.

7 Remove the clip that attaches the wastegate actuator rod and separate the rod from the actuator.

8 Remove the six bolts, three lockplates and three clamps holding the turbocharger to the exhaust manifold and remove the tur-

19.1 Be sure to spray penetrating lubricant onto the exhaust flange nuts before removing them from the exhaust flange

19.4 Exhaust system hangers are usually secured to the pipes by U-type bolts

bocharger, being careful not to damage the wastegate actuator rod, line or bracket). **Note:** *The wastegate actuator is precisely adjusted, be careful when laying the complete turbocharger unit on the bench, so as not to disturb wastegate actuator alignment.*

Installation

9 Use a tap to clean the threads in the turbocharger mounting portion of the intake manifold and coat the bolts with anti-seize compound. Bolt the turbocharger onto the intake manifold, using a new gasket.

10 Reinstall the oil drain line fitting and line with a new gasket.

11 Prime the center bearing of the turbocharger with oil by squirting a few ounces of clean engine oil into the oil supply hole on top, while turning the compressor wheel, then install the supply line. **Warning:** *The turbine or compressor wheels have very sharp blades; do not turn the blades with your fingers. Use a plastic pen.*

12 The remainder of installation is the reverse of removal.

Wastegate adjustment

13 The turbocharger wastegate controls over-boosting and is precisely adjusted at the factory. It need not be readjusted unless it is damaged or the components have been replaced.

14 Install a dial indicator to check the movement of the actuator rod at the turbocharger. Pull the hose from the actuator and apply 15 psi pressure to the actuator. This will seat the components.

15 Release the air pressure and zero the dial indicator. Apply 3 in.Hg. of vacuum to the actuator (with a hand pump/gauge or regulated shop air) while watching the dial indicator. The rod should move a total of 0.015 inches.

16 If adjustment is necessary, have the turbocharger serviced at a dealer service department.

19 Exhaust system servicing - general information

Refer to illustrations 19.1 and 19.4

Warning: *Inspection and repair of exhaust system components should be done only after it has cooled completely. Also, when working under the vehicle, make sure it's securely supported on jackstands.*

1 The exhaust system consists of the exhaust manifolds, the catalytic converter, the muffler, the resonator (not all models), the tailpipe and all connecting pipes, brackets, hangers and clamps **(see illustration)**. The exhaust system is attached to the body with mounting brackets and rubber hangers. If any of the parts are improperly installed, excessive noise and vibration will be transmitted to the body.

2 Conduct regular inspections of the exhaust system to keep it safe and quiet. Look for any damaged or bent parts, open seams, holes, loose connections, excessive corrosion or other defects which could allow exhaust fumes to enter the vehicle. Deteriorated exhaust system components should not be repaired; they should be replaced with new parts.

3 If the exhaust system components are extremely corroded or rusted together, welding equipment will probably be required to remove them. The convenient way to accomplish this is to have a muffler repair shop remove the corroded sections with a cutting torch. If, however, you want to save money by doing it yourself (and you don't have a welding outfit with a cutting torch), simply cut off the old components with a hacksaw. If you have compressed air, special pneumatic cutting chisels can also be used. If you do decide to tackle the job at home, be sure to wear safety goggles to protect your eyes from metal chips and work gloves to protect your hands.

4 Here are some simple guidelines to follow when repairing the exhaust system:

a) *Work from the back to the front when removing exhaust system components.*
b) *Apply penetrating oil to the exhaust system component fasteners to make them easier to remove.*
c) *Use new gaskets, hangers and clamps* **(see illustration)** *when installing exhaust system components.*
d) *Apply anti-seize compound to the threads of all exhaust system fasteners during reassembly.*
e) *Be sure to allow sufficient clearance between newly installed parts and all points on the underbody to avoid overheating the floor pan and possibly damaging the interior carpet and insulation. Pay particularly close attention to the catalytic converter and heat shield.*

Notes

Chapter 4 Part B
Fuel and exhaust systems - fuel-injected engines

Contents

Specifications

Fuel injection system pressure

MPFI systems	
With vacuum to regulator	29 to 35 psi (@ 15 in. Hg.)
Without vacuum to regulator	36 to 42 psi
TBI systems	9 to 12 psi
Hold pressure	No more than a 5 psi drop in two minutes

Injector resistance

TBI injectors	1.0 ohm
MPFI injectors	2.5 ohms

Torque specifications

	Ft-lbs (unless otherwise indicated)
Throttle body mounting bolts	
TBI systems	15
MPFI systems	17
Fuel inlet nut (TBI)	28
Fuel outlet nut (TBI)	22
Fuel meter cover screws (TBI)	22 in-lbs
Fuel meter body screws (TBI)	35
Fuel rail mounting bolts (MPFI)	60 in-lbs

1 General information

Warning: *Gasoline is extremely flammable, so take extra precautions when you work on any part of the fuel system. Don't smoke or allow open flames or bare light bulbs near the work area, and don't work in a garage where a natural gas-type appliance (such as a water heater or a clothes dryer) with a pilot light is present. Since gasoline is carcinogenic, wear latex gloves when there's a possibility of being exposed to fuel, and, if you spill any fuel on your skin, rinse it off immediately with soap and water. Mop up any spills immediately and do not store fuel-soaked rags where they could ignite. The fuel system on fuel-injected models is under constant pressure, so, if any fuel lines are to be disconnected, the fuel pressure in the system must be relieved first. When you perform any kind of work on the fuel system, wear safety glasses and have a Class B type fire extinguisher on hand.*

Fuel system

The fuel system on fuel-injected models consists of a fuel tank, an electric fuel pump located either next to the fuel tank or in the fuel tank (some models have both), a fuel pump relay, an air cleaner assembly and either one of two fuel injection systems: Throttle Body Injection (TBI) or Multi Port Fuel Injection (MPFI). The TBI system is easily identified by the large throttle body with two injectors mounted side by side, while the MPFI system uses injectors mounted on the intake manifold, positioned to shoot fuel into the intake port of each cylinder.

Throttle Body Injection (TBI) systems

Note: *General Motors designates this system as the Digital Fuel Injection (DFI) system. Throttle Body Injection or TBI is the more common term used to describe DFI.*

These systems utilize two injectors, centrally mounted in a carburetor-like throttle body. The injectors are electric solenoid valves, and fuel is delivered to the injectors at a constant pressure level. To maintain the fuel pressure at a constant level, excess fuel is returned to the fuel tank.

A signal from the Electronic Control Module (ECM) opens the solenoids, allowing fuel to spray through each injector into the throttle body. The amount of time the injector is held open by the ECM determines the fuel/air mixture ratio.

General Motors calls this system Digital Fuel Injection (DFI) but for the purpose of using common terminology amongst U.S auto makers, the term Throttle Body Injection system will be used.

Multi Port Fuel Injection (MPFI) system

This system utilizes eight solenoid-activated injectors to control the fuel/air ratio. Instead of two injectors mounted in a centrally located throttle body, one injector is installed above each intake port. The throttle body serves only to control the amount of air passing into the system.

MPFI systems were installed on 1976 through 1980 Cadillac Eldorados and 1980 Sevilles.

Fuel pump and lines

Fuel is circulated from the fuel tank to the fuel injection system and back to the fuel tank through a pair of metal lines running along the underside of the vehicle. An electric fuel pump is located either next to the fuel tank or inside the fuel tank. A vapor return system routes all vapors back to the fuel tank through a separate return line.

The fuel pump will operate as long as the engine is cranking or running and the ECM is receiving ignition reference pulses from the electronic ignition system. If there are no reference pulses, the fuel pump will shut off after two or three seconds while cranking. **Note:** *TBI systems are equipped with one fuel pump located in the fuel tank. MPFI systems are equipped with two fuel pumps. The external pump, located next to the fuel tank, acts as the main pump while the in-tank pump serves as a priming pump.*

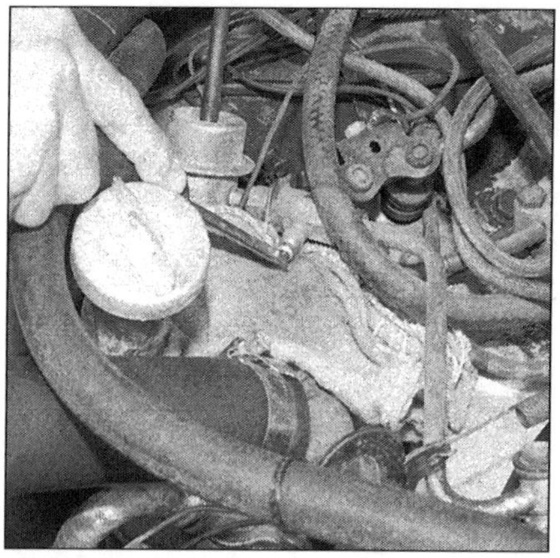

2.4 Place shop towels under the Schrader valve and, using a small screwdriver, bleed the fuel into the towels (it's a good idea to cover the valve with a rag before depressing the valve core)

Exhaust system

The exhaust system includes two exhaust manifolds, an exhaust oxygen sensor, a catalytic converter (1975 and later models), a resonator (some models), an exhaust pipe, and a muffler.

The catalytic converter is an emission control device added to the exhaust system to reduce pollutants. A single or dual-bed converter is used in combination with a three-way (reduction) catalyst. Refer to Chapter 6 for more information regarding the catalytic converter.

2 Fuel pressure relief procedure

Refer to illustration 2.4

Warning: *Gasoline is extremely flammable, so take extra precautions when you work on any part of the fuel system. See the* **Warning** *in Section 1.*

Note: *After the fuel pressure has been relieved, it's a good idea to wrap a shop towel around any fuel connection you're disconnecting to absorb the residual fuel that may leak out.*

1 Disconnect the negative battery cable.

2 Before servicing any fuel system component, you must relieve the fuel pressure to minimize the risk of fire or personal injury.

3 Remove the cap from the gas tank - this will relieve any pressure built up in the tank.

4 Use one of the following methods to relieve the fuel pressure:

a) *Attach a fuel pressure gauge to the Schrader valve on the fuel rail. Place the gauge bleeder hose in an approved fuel container. Open the valve on the gauge to relieve the pressure.*

b) *Locate the Schrader valve at the rear of the engine on TBI systems or near the front of the engine on MPFI systems* **(see illustration)**. *Remove the cap from the valve, place several shop towels around the valve and, using the tip of a small screwdriver, depress the core of the Schrader valve until the fuel pressure is relieved.*

5 Dispose of the gasoline-soaked towels in a covered, fire-safe container.

6 After the fuel system has been serviced, reconnect the negative battery cable.

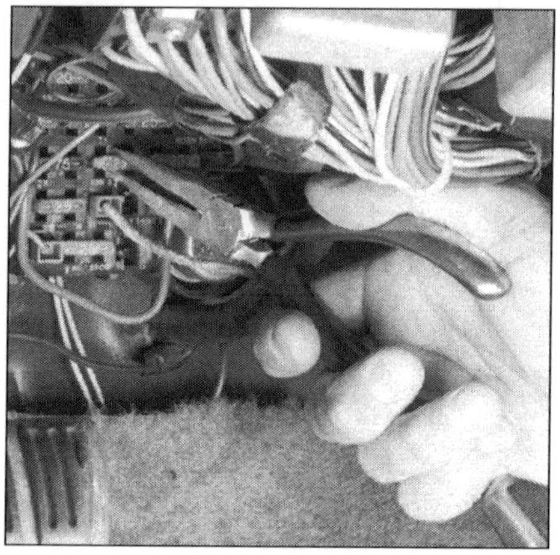

3.2 Location of the EFI fuse on an MPFI-equipped Cadillac Eldorado

3 Fuel pump/fuel pressure check

Warning: *Gasoline is extremely flammable, so take extra precautions when you work on any part of the fuel system. See the* **Warning** *in Section 1.*

Note 1: *To perform the fuel pressure test, you will need to obtain a fuel pressure gauge and adapter set (fuel line fittings).*

Note 2: *After the fuel pressure has been relieved. it's a good idea to lay a shop towel over any fuel connection to be disassembled, to absorb the residual fuel that may leak out when servicing the fuel system.*

Preliminary inspection

Refer to illustrations 3.2, 3.3a, 3.3b, 3.4a and 3.4b

1 Should the fuel system fail to deliver the proper amount of fuel, or any fuel at all, inspect it as follows. Remove the fuel filler cap. Have an assistant turn the ignition key to the On position (engine not running) while you listen at the fuel filler opening. You should hear a whirring sound that lasts for a couple of seconds.

2 If you don't hear anything, check the fuel pump fuse **(see illustration)** (see Chapter 12). If the fuse is blown, replace it and see if it blows again. If it does, trace the fuel pump circuit for a short. If it isn't blown, check for battery voltage to the fuel pump. If no power is present, the problem could be in

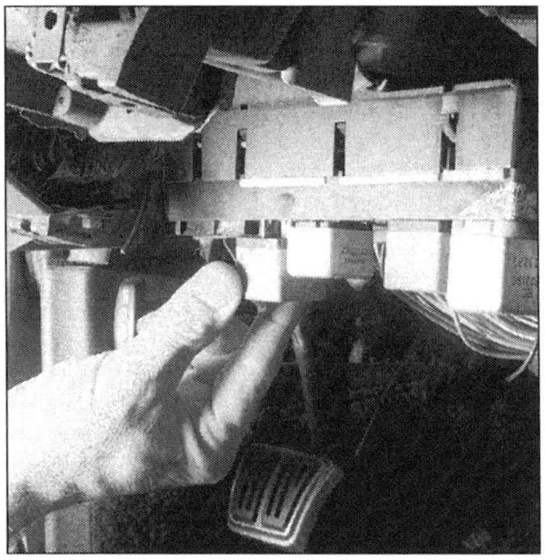

3.3a Locate the fuel pump relay under the dash near the steering column

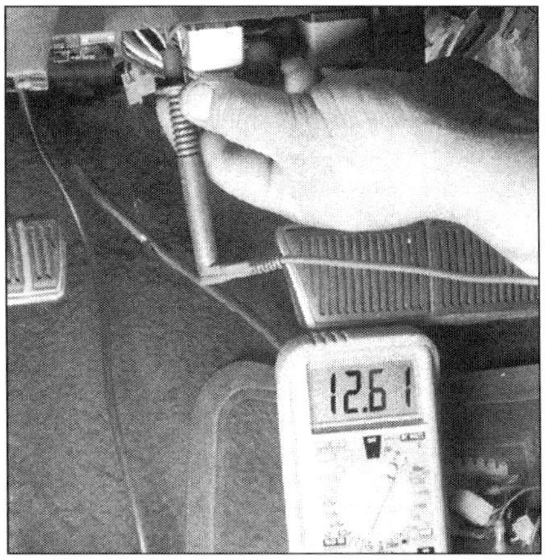

3.3b Check for power to the fuel pump relay with the ignition key ON and the engine cranking (TBI system shown)

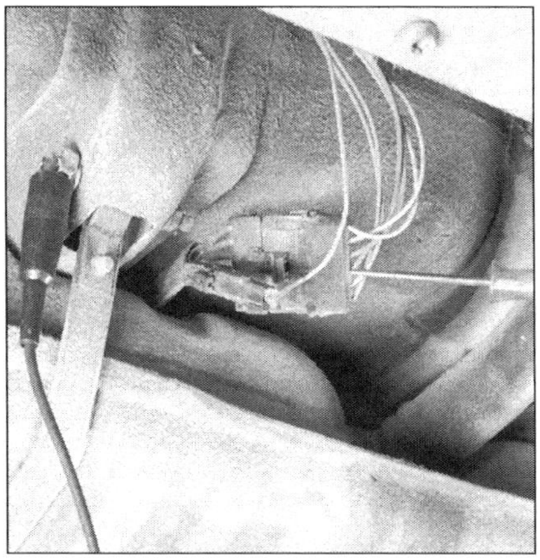

3.4a Use a test light or a voltmeter to check for voltage to the fuel pump (in-tank fuel pump shown)

the fuel pump circuit from the relay panel to the fuel pump or the relay itself.

3 Check for battery voltage to the fuel pump relay connector **(see illustrations)**. If there is battery voltage present, have the relay tested at a dealer service department or other qualified automotive repair shop. **Note:** *The MPFI system on 1976 through 1980 models does not incorporate a fuel pump relay to control the fuel pump circuit. Instead, the computer functions as the switching mechanism for the voltage to the fuel pump.*

4 If voltage is present, disconnect the fuel pump electrical connector next to the fuel tank **(see illustrations)** and check for battery voltage. You will need an assistant to turn the ignition key. If there is no voltage present, check the fuse(s) and the wiring circuit for the fuel pump relay (see Chapter 12). **Note 1:** *Watch carefully for the voltage signal because it lasts approximately two seconds before it is switched off.* **Note 2:** *Refer to the Wiring diagrams at the end of Chapter 12 if you're unable to determine the color of the fuel pump wires*

Operating pressure check

Refer to illustrations 3.7a, 3.7b and 3.9

5 Detach the cable from the negative battery terminal.

6 Relieve the fuel system pressure (see Section 2).

7 Remove the cap from the fuel pressure test port and attach a fuel pressure gauge **(see illustrations)**. If you don't have the correct adapter for the test port, remove the Schrader valve and connect the gauge hose to the fitting. Tighten the hose clamp securely.

8 Attach the cable to the negative battery terminal.

9 Start the engine. With the engine idling, measure the fuel pressure. It should be as listed in this Chapter's Specifications. On MPFI systems, detach the vacuum hose from the fuel pressure regulator - the fuel pressure reading should immediately increase. If the pressure doesn't rise when the hose is disconnected, check for vacuum at the disconnected hose. If vacuum is present, the fuel

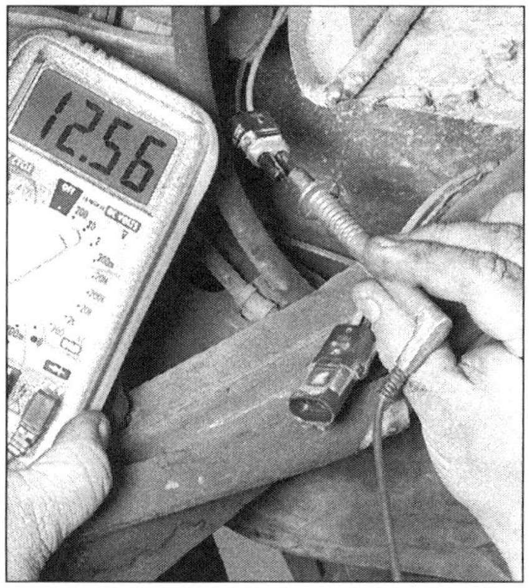

3.4b Use a test light or a voltmeter to check for voltage to the fuel pump (external fuel pump shown)

pressure regulator is faulty. Next, connect a hand-held vacuum pump to the pressure reg-

3.7a Connect the fuel pressure gauge to the Schrader valve (test port) located on the fuel feed line near the back of the engine on TBI fuel systems

3.7b On MPFI fuel systems, install the fuel pressure gauge to the test port located on the fuel rail near the front of the engine

3.9 Apply vacuum to the fuel pressure regulator and see if the fuel pressure decreases

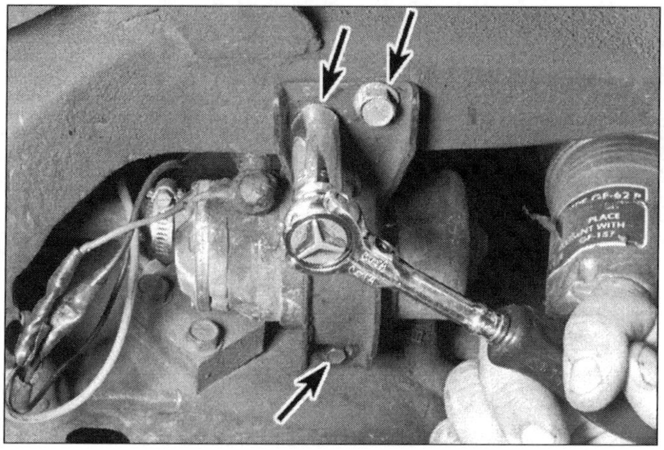

4.2 Remove the bolts (arrows) from the fuel pump bracket (external fuel pump shown)

ulator and apply vacuum **(see illustration).** Fuel pressure should decrease as vacuum increases. Reconnect the vacuum hose. **Note:** *On TBI systems it will not be possible to check unregulated fuel pressure. Throttle body injected models are equipped with an internal fuel pressure regulator. Raise the engine rpm and see if the fuel pressure increases. If there is no response from the fuel pressure regulator, have the TBI system checked at a dealer service department.*

10 If the fuel pressure is too high, check for a pinched or clogged fuel return hose or pipe. If the fuel return line is not obstructed, replace the fuel pressure regulator (see Section 7 for TBI or Section 8 for MPFI).

11 If the pressure is lower than specified, inspect the fuel filter - make sure it's not clogged. Look for a pinched or clogged fuel hose between the fuel tank and the fuel injection assembly. If the fuel feed line is OK, pinch the fuel return hose with a pair of pliers. If the pressure rises, replace the fuel pressure regulator. If the pressure is still low, either the fuel pump is not putting out enough pressure or is leaking, or a fuel injector (or injectors) may be leaking.

12 Turn the ignition switch to Off, wait five minutes and recheck the pressure on the gauge. Compare the reading with the hold pressure listed in this Chapter's Specifications. If the hold pressure is less than specified:

a) *The fuel lines may be leaking.*
b) *The fuel pressure regulator may be allowing the fuel pressure to bleed through to the return line.*
c) *A fuel injector (or injectors) may be leaking.*
d) *The fuel pump may be defective.*

4 Fuel pump - removal and installation

Warning: *Gasoline is extremely flammable, so take extra precautions when you work on any part of the fuel system. See the* **Warning** *in Section 1.*

Note: *TBI systems are equipped with one fuel pump located in the fuel tank. MPFI systems are equipped with two fuel pumps. The external pump, located next to the fuel tank, acts as the main pump while the in-tank pump serves as a priming pump.*

Chassis-mounted electric pump (MPFI systems)

Refer to illustration 4.2

1 Detach the cable from the negative battery terminal. Relieve the fuel system pressure.

2 Unbolt the brackets and detach the electrical connectors and fuel lines from the pump for removal **(see illustration)**. Plug the fuel lines to prevent leakage.

3 Installation is the reverse of removal.

Electric in-tank pump

4 Relieve the fuel system pressure (see Section 2).

5 Disconnect the cable from the negative battery terminal.

6 Remove the fuel tank (see Chapter 4A).

7 The fuel pump/sending unit assembly is located inside the fuel tank. It is held in place by a cam that locks into corresponding tabs in the fuel tank. Using a brass punch, carefully tap the locking cam counterclockwise until the tabs align with the recesses.

8 Lift the fuel pump/sending unit assembly from the fuel tank. **Caution:** *The fuel level float and sending unit are delicate. Do not bump them against the tank during removal or the accuracy of the sending unit may be affected.*

9 Inspect the condition of the rubber gasket around the opening of the tank. If it is dried, cracked or deteriorated, replace it.

10 Remove the strainer from the lower end of the fuel pump. If it is dirty, clean it with a suitable solvent and blow it out with compressed air. If it is too dirty to be cleaned, replace it.

11 Disconnect the electrical connector from the fuel pump.

12 Separate the fuel pump from the assembly.

13 Installation is the reverse of removal. Reassemble the fuel pump to the sending unit bracket assembly and insert the assembly into the fuel tank.

14 Install the fuel tank (see Chapter 4A).

5 Fuel injection system - general information

General Information

The fuel system on fuel-injected models consists of a fuel tank, an electric fuel pump located next to the fuel tank and/or in the fuel tank, a fuel pump relay, an air cleaner assembly and either one of two fuel injection systems: Throttle Body Injection (TBI) or Multi Port Fuel Injection (MPFI). The TBI system is easily identified by the large throttle body with two injectors mounted side by side, while the MPFI uses injectors mounted in a fuel rail, positioned to shoot fuel into the intake ports of each cylinder.

Throttle Body Injection (TBI) system

Note: *General Motors refers to this system as the Digital Fuel Injection (DFI) system. Throttle Body Injection or TBI is the more common term used to describe DFI.*

The main component of the TBI system is the Throttle Body Injection (TBI) unit, which is mounted on the intake manifold just like a carburetor. The TBI unit is made up of two major assemblies: the throttle body and the fuel metering assembly.

The throttle body contains two throttle plates, controlled by the accelerator pedal, similar to a carburetor. Attached to the exterior of the body are the Throttle Position Sensor (TPS), which sends throttle position information to the ECM, and the Idle Air Control (IAC) assembly, which is used by the ECM to maintain a constant idle speed during normal

6.11a Place the tip of the stethoscope onto the fuel injector body and listen for clicking sounds as the solenoid opens and closes (TBI model shown)

6.11b Check all eight injectors for proper operation (MPFI system shown)

engine operation.

The fuel metering assembly contains the fuel pressure regulator and the two fuel injectors. The regulator dampens the pulsations of the fuel pump and maintains a steady pressure at the injectors. The fuel injectors are controlled by the ECM through an electrically operated solenoid. The amount of fuel injected into the intake manifold is varied by the length of time the injector plunger is held open.

Multi Port Fuel Injection (MPFI) system

Multi port Fuel Injection (MPFI) consists of an air intake manifold, the throttle body, the injectors, the fuel rail assembly, two electric fuel pumps and associated plumbing. **Note:** *The MPFI system does not incorporate a fuel pump relay to govern the fuel pump circuit. Instead, the computer functions as the source and switching mechanism for the voltage to the fuel pump*

Air is drawn through the air cleaner and throttle body. A Manifold Absolute Pressure (MAP) sensor, located under the dash inside of the computer, compensates for temperature and pressure variations.

While the engine is running, the fuel constantly circulates through the fuel rail, which removes vapors and keeps the fuel cool while maintaining sufficient pressure to the injectors under all running conditions.

As with TBI, the operation of the MPFI injection system is controlled by the ECM so that it works in conjunction with the rest of the vehicle functions to provide optimum driveability and emissions control.

Because the MPFI system meters fuel and air precisely, it is important to the proper operation of the vehicle that the fuel and air filters be changed at the specified intervals.

6 Fuel injection system - check

Warning: *Gasoline is extremely flammable, so take extra precautions when you work on any part of the fuel system. See the* **Warning** *in Section 1.*

6.12a Checking the resistance on a TBI injector

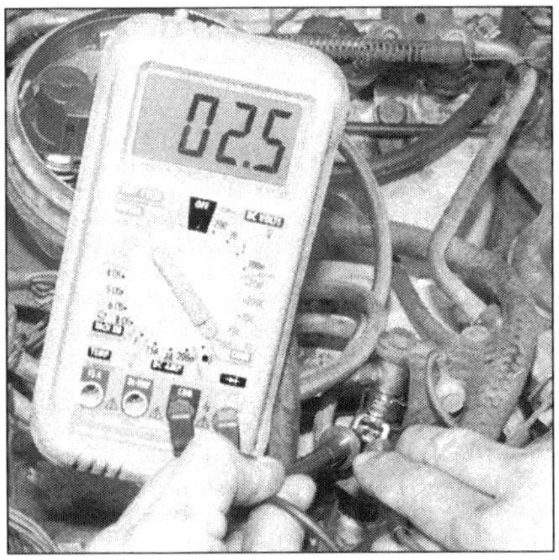

6.12b Checking the resistance on an MPFI injector

Note: *The following procedure is based on the assumption that the fuel pump is working and the fuel pressure is adequate* (see Section 3).

Preliminary checks

1 Check all electrical connectors that are related to the system. Loose electrical connectors and poor grounds can cause many problems that resemble more serious malfunctions.

2 Check to see that the battery is fully charged, as the control unit and sensors depend on an accurate supply voltage in order to properly meter the fuel.

3 Check the air filter element - a dirty or partially blocked filter will severely impede performance and economy (see Chapter 1).

4 If a blown fuse is found, replace it and see if it blows again. If it does, search for a grounded wire in the harness to the fuel pump.

System checks

Refer to illustrations 6.11a, 6.11b, 6.12a, 6.12b, 6.13a and 6.13b

5 Check the ground wire connections on the intake manifold for tightness. Check all electrical connectors that are related to the system. Loose connectors and poor grounds can cause many problems that resemble more serious malfunctions.

6 Check to see that the battery is fully charged, as the control unit and sensors depend on an accurate supply voltage in order to properly meter the fuel.

7 Check the air filter element - a dirty or partially blocked filter will severely impede performance and economy (see Chapter 1).

8 If a blown fuse is found, replace it and see if it blows again. If it does, search for a grounded wire in the harness to the fuel pump.

9 Check the condition of all vacuum hoses connected to the intake manifold.

10 Remove the air intake duct from the throttle body and check for dirt, carbon or other residue build-up. If it's dirty, clean it with carburetor cleaner and a toothbrush.

11 With the engine running, place an automotive stethoscope against each injector, one at a time, and listen for a clicking sound, indicating operation **(see illustrations)**. If you don't have a stethoscope, place the tip of a screwdriver against the injector and listen through the handle. **Note:** *On models with TBI, you can actually look at the injector spray pattern to see if the injector is working properly.*

12 Unplug the injector electrical connector(s) and check the resistance of each injec-

6.13a Disconnect the harness connector from the injector and install an injector test light or "noid" light (TBI system shown)

6.13b Checking for the injector signal on an MPFI system

7.6 Carefully peel away the old fuel meter outlet passage gasket and fuel meter cover gasket with a razor blade

7.7 Never remove the four pressure regulator screws (arrows) from the fuel meter cover

7.14 To remove either injector electrical connector, depress the two tabs on the front and rear of each connector and lift straight up

7.16 To remove an injector, slip the tip of a flat-bladed screwdriver under the lip of the lug on top of the injector and, using another screwdriver as a fulcrum, carefully pry the injector up and out

tor **(see illustrations)**. Compare the values to the Specifications listed in this Chapter.

13 Install an injector test light ("noid" light) into each injector electrical connector, one at a time **(see illustrations)**. Crank the engine over. Confirm that the light flashes evenly on each connector. This will test for voltage to the injectors.

14 The remainder of the system checks can be found in the following Sections.

7 Throttle Body Injection (TBI) unit - removal, overhaul and installation

Warning: *Gasoline is extremely flammable, so take extra precautions when you work on any part of the fuel system. See the* **Warning** *in Section 1.*

Note: *Because of its relative simplicity, the throttle body assembly does not need to be removed from the intake manifold or disassembled for component replacement. However, for the sake of clarity, the following procedures are shown with the TBI assembly removed from the vehicle.*

1 Relieve system fuel pressure (see Section 2).

2 Detach the cable from the negative terminal of the battery.

3 Remove the air cleaner housing assembly, adapter and gaskets.

Fuel meter cover/fuel pressure regulator assembly

Refer to illustrations 7.6 and 7.7

Note: *The fuel pressure regulator is housed in the fuel meter cover. Whether you are replacing the meter cover or the regulator itself, the entire assembly must be replaced. The regulator must not be removed from the cover.*

4 Unplug the electrical connectors to the fuel injectors.

5 Remove the long and short fuel meter cover screws and remove the fuel meter cover.

6 Remove the fuel meter outlet passage gasket, cover gasket and pressure regulator seal. Carefully remove any old gasket material that is stuck with a razor blade **(see illustration)**. **Caution:** *Do not attempt to re-use either of these gaskets.*

7 Inspect the cover for dirt, foreign material and casting warpage. If it is dirty, clean it with a clean shop rag soaked in solvent. Do not immerse the fuel meter cover in cleaning solvent - it could damage the pressure regulator diaphragm and gasket. **Warning:** *Do not remove the four screws* **(see illustration)** *securing the pressure regulator to the fuel meter cover. The regulator contains a large spring under compression which, if accidentally released, could cause injury. Disassembly might also result in a fuel leak between the diaphragm and the regulator housing. The new fuel meter cover assembly will include a new pressure regulator.*

8 Install the new pressure regulator seal, fuel meter outlet passage gasket and cover gasket.

9 Install the fuel meter cover using Loctite 262 or equivalent on the screws. **Note:** *The short screws go next to the injectors.*

10 Attach the electrical connectors to both injectors.

11 Attach the cable to the negative terminal of the battery.

12 With the engine off and the ignition on, check for leaks around the gasket and fuel line couplings.

13 Install the air cleaner, adapter and gaskets.

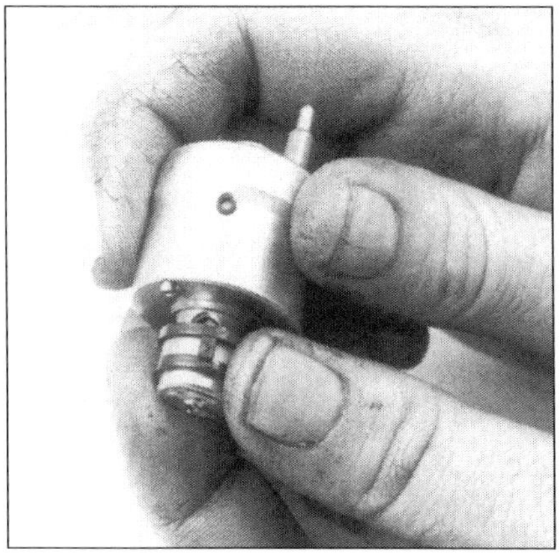

7.21 Slide the new filter onto the nozzle of the injector

7.22 Lubricate the lower O-ring with transmission fluid then place it on the shoulder in the bottom of the injector cavity

7.23 Place the steel back-up washer on the shoulder near the top of the injector cavity

Fuel injector(s)

Refer to illustrations 7.14, 7.16, 7.21, 7.22, 7.23, 7.24 and 7.25

Note: *When replacing a fuel injector, be sure to use one having the identical part number. Injectors from other models are calibrated with different flow rates but can be interchanged with other TBI units. Check with a dealer parts department for correct identification.*

14 To unplug the electrical connectors from the fuel injectors, squeeze the plastic tabs and pull straight up **(see illustration).**

15 Remove the fuel meter cover/pressure regulator assembly. **Note:** *Do not remove the fuel meter cover assembly gasket - leave it in place to protect the casting from damage during injector removal.*

16 Use two screwdrivers **(see illustration)** to pry out the injector(s).

17 Remove the upper (larger) and lower (smaller) O-rings and filter from the injector(s).

18 Remove the steel backup washer from the top of each injector cavity.

19 Inspect the fuel injector filters for evidence of dirt and contamination. If present, check for the presence of dirt in the fuel lines and fuel tank.

20 Be sure to replace the fuel injector with an identical part. Injectors from other models can fit in the TBI assembly but are calibrated for different flow rates.

21 Slide the new filter into place on the nozzle of the injector **(see illustration)**.

22 Lubricate the new lower (smaller) O-ring with automatic transmission fluid and place it on the small shoulder at the bottom of the fuel injector cavity in the fuel meter body **(see illustration)**.

23 Install the steel back-up washer in the injector cavity **(see illustration)**.

24 Lubricate the new upper (larger) O-ring with automatic transmission fluid and install it on top of the steel back-up washer **(see illustration)**. **Note:** *The back-up washer and the large O-ring must be installed before the injector. If they aren't, improper seating of the large O-ring could cause fuel leakage.*

7.24 Lubricate the upper O-ring with transmission fluid then install it on top of the steel washer

7.25 Make sure that the lug is aligned with the groove in the bottom of the fuel injector cavity

25 To install an injector, align the raised lug on the injector base with the notch in the fuel meter body cavity **(see illustration)**. Push down on the injector until it is fully seated in the fuel meter body. **Note:** *The electrical terminals should be parallel with the throttle shaft.*

26 Install the fuel meter cover assembly and gasket.

27 Attach the cable to the negative terminal of the battery.

28 With the engine off and the ignition on, check for fuel leaks.

29 Attach the electrical connectors to the fuel injectors.

30 Install the air cleaner housing assembly, adapter and gaskets.

Throttle Position Sensor (TPS)

31 Remove the two TPS attaching screws and retainers and remove the TPS from the throttle body.

32 If you intend to re-use the same TPS, do not attempt to clean it by soaking it in any liquid cleaner or solvent. The TPS is a delicate electrical component and can be damaged by solvents.

33 Install the TPS on the throttle body while lining up the TPS lever with the TPS drive lever.

34 Install the two TPS attaching screws and retainers. Adjust the TPS (refer to Chapter 6).

35 Install the air cleaner housing assembly, adapter and gaskets.

36 Attach the cable to the negative terminal of the battery.

Idle Speed Control (ISC) motor

37 Unplug the electrical connector from the ISC motor.

38 Remove the ISC mounting bolts and remove the ISC motor from the TBI unit. Installation is the reverse of removal.

Fuel meter body assembly

Refer to illustrations 7.43 and 7.45

39 Unplug the electrical connectors from the fuel injectors.

40 Remove the fuel meter cover/pressure regulator assembly, fuel meter cover gasket, fuel meter outlet gasket and pressure regulator seal.

41 Remove the fuel injectors.

7.43 Remove the fuel inlet and outlet nuts from the fuel meter body

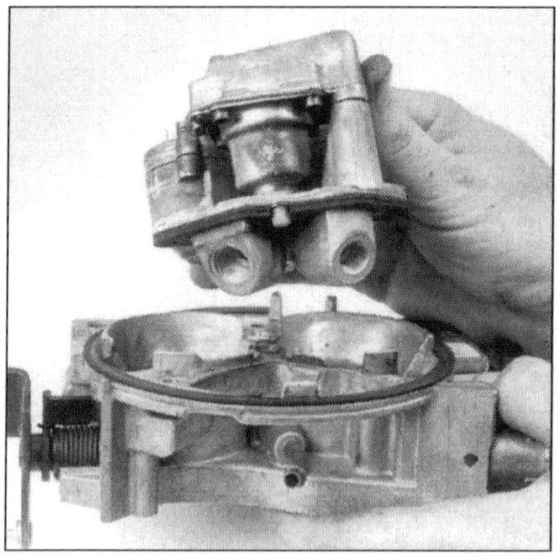

7.45 Once the fuel inlet and outlet nuts are off and the screws are removed, pull the fuel meter body straight up to separate it from the throttle body

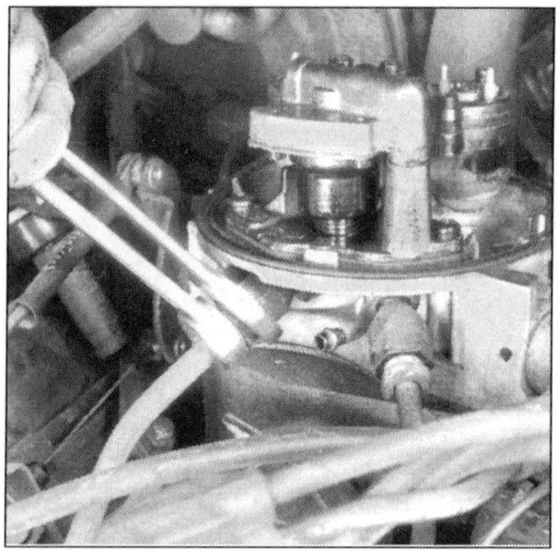

7.58 When disconnecting the fuel feed and return lines from the fuel inlet and outlet nuts, be sure to use a back-up wrench to prevent damage to the lines

42 Unscrew the fuel inlet and return line threaded fittings, detach the lines and remove the O-rings.

43 Remove the fuel inlet and outlet nuts and gaskets from the fuel meter body assembly **(see illustration)**. Note the locations of the nuts to ensure proper reassembly. The inlet nut has a larger passage than the outlet nut.

44 Remove the gasket from the inner end of each fuel nut.

45 Remove the fuel meter body-to-throttle body attaching screws and remove the fuel meter body from the throttle body **(see illustration)**.

46 Install the new throttle body-to-fuel meter body gasket. Match the cut-out portions in the gasket with the openings in the throttle body.

47 Install the fuel meter body on the throttle body. Coat the fuel meter body-to-throttle body attaching screws with thread locking compound before installing them.

48 Install the fuel inlet and outlet nuts, with new gaskets, in the fuel meter body and tighten the nuts to the torque listed in this Chapter's Specifications. Install the fuel inlet and return line threaded fittings with new O-rings. Use a back-up wrench to prevent the nuts from turning.

49 Install the fuel injectors.

50 Install the fuel meter cover/pressure regulator assembly.

51 Attach the cable to the negative terminal of the battery.

52 Attach the electrical connectors to the fuel injectors.

53 With the engine off and the ignition on, check for leaks around the fuel meter body, the gasket and around the fuel line nuts and threaded fittings.

54 Install the air cleaner housing assembly, adapters and gaskets.

Throttle body assembly

Refer to illustrations 7.58 and 7.59

55 Unplug all electrical connectors - the ISC motor, TPS and fuel injectors. Detach the grommet with the wires from the throttle body.

56 Detach the throttle linkage, return spring(s), transmission control cable (automatics) and, if equipped, cruise control.

57 Clearly label, then detach, all vacuum hoses.

58 Using a back-up wrench, detach the inlet and outlet fuel line nuts **(see illustration)**. Remove the fuel line O-rings from the nuts and discard them.

59 Remove the TBI mounting bolts **(see illustration)** and lift the TBI unit from the intake manifold. Remove and discard the TBI manifold gasket.

60 Place the TBI unit on a holding fixture (Kent-Moore J-9789-118 or BT-3553 or equivalent). **Note:** *If you don't have a holding fixture, and decide to place the TBI directly on a work bench surface, be extremely careful when servicing it. The throttle valve can be easily damaged.*

61 Remove the fuel meter body-to-throttle body attaching screws and separate the fuel meter body from the throttle body.

62 Remove the throttle body-to-fuel meter body gasket and discard it.

63 Remove the TPS.

64 Invert the throttle body on a flat surface for greater stability and remove the ISC motor.

65 Clean the throttle body assembly in a cold immersion cleaner. Clean the metal parts thoroughly and blow dry with compressed air. Be sure that all fuel and air passages are free of dirt or burrs. **Caution:** *Do not place the TPS, ISC motor, pressure regulator diaphragm, fuel injectors or other components containing rubber in the solvent or cleaning bath. If the throttle body requires cleaning, soaking time in the cleaner should be kept to a minimum. Some models have throttle shaft dust seals that could lose their effectiveness by extended soaking.*

66 Inspect the mating surfaces for damage that could affect gasket sealing. Inspect the throttle lever and valve for dirt, binds, nicks and other damage.

7.59 Remove the throttle body mounting bolts (arrows)

67 Invert the throttle body on a flat surface for stability and install the ISC motor and the TPS.

68 Install a new throttle body-to-fuel meter body gasket and place the fuel meter body assembly on the throttle body assembly. Coat the fuel meter body-to-throttle body attaching screws with thread locking compound and tighten them securely.

69 Using a new TBI-to-manifold gasket, install the TBI unit and tighten the mounting bolts to the torque listed in this Chapter's Specifications.

70 Install new O-rings on the fuel line nuts. Install the fuel line and outlet nuts by hand to prevent stripping the threads. Using a back-up wrench, tighten the fittings securely.

71 Attach the vacuum hoses, throttle linkage, return spring(s), transmission control cable (automatics) and, if equipped, cruise control cable. Attach the grommet, with wire harness, to the throttle body.

72 Plug in all electrical connectors, making sure that the connectors are fully seated and latched.

73 Check to see if the accelerator pedal is free by depressing the pedal to the floor and

7.82 Turn the ISC plunger until the correct idle speed is obtained

8.2 Spray carburetor cleaner onto the throttle shaft and throttle valve inside the throttle body housing

8.9 Check for battery voltage to the Fast Idle Valve while the engine is running during cold start-up

releasing it with the engine off.

74 Connect the negative battery cable, and, with the engine off and the ignition on, check for leaks around the fuel line nuts.

75 Check the TPS output and adjust if necessary (see Chapter 6).

ISC motor adjustment

Refer to illustration 7.82

76 Warm the engine to normal operating temperature.

77 Connect a tachometer in accordance with the tool manufacturer's instructions.

78 Open the Set Timing connector (refer to Chapter 1 timing specifications and procedure).

79 Disconnect the electrical connector from the TPS.

80 Turn the ignition key Off for 10 seconds and observe the position of the ISC plunger. It should be fully extended.

81 When the ISC plunger is fully extended, disconnect the ISC electrical connector. Using a jumper wire, connect terminals A and B on the ISC electrical connector. Terminals A and B are the top two slots on the connector.

82 Reconnect the TPS and start the engine. The engine should idle at 1,500 rpm +/- 100 rpm. If the engine speed is incorrect, turn the plunger until the idle speed is correct **(see illustration)**.

83 Reconnect the ISC motor and repeat the test. The engine should maintain the correct idle speed. Be sure the TPS is correctly adjusted if the idle speed fluctuates (refer to Chapter 6).

84 Disconnect all the testing instruments and reconnect the Set Timing connector. Turn the engine Off and observe the plunger move to its fully extended position.

85 The adjustment procedure may set a diagnostic code in the C3 system. If the CHECK ENGINE light comes on, refer to Chapter 6, Section 4, and erase them from the ECM memory.

86 Install the air cleaner housing assembly, adapter and gaskets.

8 Multi Port Fuel Injection (MPFI) system - component check and replacement

Warning: *Gasoline is extremely flammable, so take extra precautions when you work on any part of the fuel system. See the* **Warning** *in Section 1.*

Throttle body

Check

Refer to illustration 8.2

1 Remove the air cleaner assembly (see Chapter 4A).

2 Have an assistant depress the throttle pedal while you watch the throttle valve. Check that the throttle valve moves smoothly when the throttle is moved from closed (idle position) to fully open (wide open throttle). **Note:** *Spray carburetor cleaner into the throttle body, especially around the shaft area* **(see illustration)** *to free-up any binding caused by the accumulation of carbon deposits or sludge buildup.*

3 Wiggle the throttle lever while watching the throttle shaft inside the bore. If it appears worn (loose), replace the throttle body unit.

Removal

4 Disconnect the electrical connectors and vacuum lines from the throttle body. Label them to insure correct installation.

5 Remove the nuts from the base of the throttle body.

6 Lift the throttle body from the intake manifold.

7 Installation is the reverse of removal.

Fast Idle Valve

Check

Refer to illustrations 8.9 and 8.10

8 The Fast Idle Valve is made of a plastic body, an electric heating element, a spring, a plunger and a thermal sensitive element. The valve is installed in the top section of the throttle body and it is connected to the fuel pump circuit directly through the ECM. At cold starting temperatures, the fast idle valve opens, allowing extra air to bypass the throttle thereby raising the rpm. The heater, which is supplied with voltage through the fuel pump circuit, warms the thermal element which expands, forcing the spring and plunger toward the orifice. This action closes the air off to the throttle, decreasing rpm. The Fast Idle Valve will be inoperative after the heating element reaches 140-degrees F. The valve closes as a function of ambient temperature. If the air temperature is warm (68-degrees F) the total operating time will be about 90 seconds. If the air temperature is very cold (about 20-degrees F), the total amount of time will be about 5 minutes.

9 To check the Fast Idle Valve, make sure the engine is completely cold and start the engine. Using a voltmeter, check for voltage to the fast idle valve. There should be approximately 12 volts available **(see illustration)**.

10 Remove the Fast Idle Valve (see Steps 11 through 14). Check for corrosion within the plunger and thermal-sensitive element **(see illustration)**. If there are large amounts of deposits and foreign material, replace the valve with a new part.

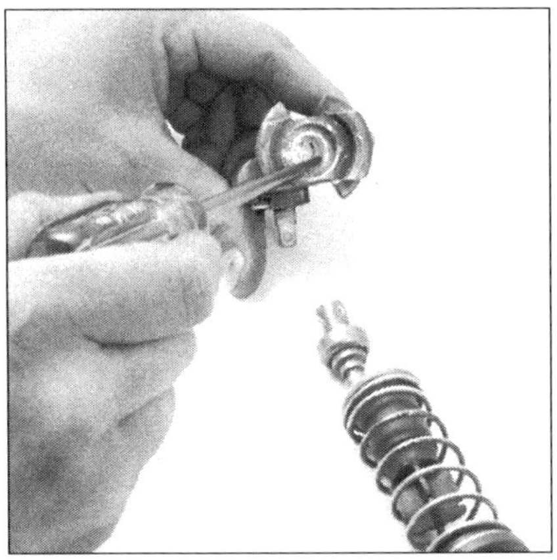

8.10 Examine the Fast Idle Valve for deposits

8.13 Push down and turn the Fast Idle Valve counterclockwise to release it from the cut-out portion of the throttle body

Removal

Refer to illustration 8.13

11 Unplug the electrical connector from the Fast Idle Valve.

12 Remove the air cleaner housing stud from the throttle body.

13 Push down and twist the Fast Idle Valve counterclockwise until the locking tab located on the top section of the valve releases from the throttle body recess **(see illustration)**.

14 Lift the fast idle valve from the throttle bore. **Caution:** *The fast idle valve itself is an electrical component and must not be soaked in any liquid cleaner, as damage may result.*

Installation

15 Installation is reverse of removal. Make sure the locking tab is secure within the throttle body as the fast idle valve is under spring tension.

Throttle Position Sensor (TPS)

Check

16 Check for stored trouble codes in the ECM (see Chapter 6).

17 To check the operation and replacement of the TPS, refer to the *Information sensors* Section in Chapter 6.

Fuel rail and injectors

Refer to illustrations 8.21 and 8.23

Warning: *Before any work is performed on the fuel lines, fuel rail or injectors, the fuel system pressure must be relieved* (see Section 2).

18 Detach the cable from the negative terminal of the battery.

19 Remove the fuel pressure regulator (see Steps 32 through 37).

20 Label and unplug the injector electrical connectors.

21 Remove the fuel inlet line from the fuel rail **(see illustration)**.

22 Detach the fuel return hose from the fuel pressure regulator.

23 Remove the fuel rail bracket retaining bolts **(see illustration)**.

24 Carefully remove the fuel rail bracket leaving the fuel injectors inside the fuel rail assembly. Some of the injectors may stick to the intake manifold instead. Remove them from the intake manifold and install them into the fuel rail assembly to keep all the injectors in order. Be sure to label each injector for ease of assembly.

25 To remove the fuel injectors, carefully pull them out of the fuel rail.

26 Remove the injector O-ring seals. There are two seals for each injector. One is used to seal the fuel rail and the other to seal the intake manifold.

27 Install the new O-ring seals on the injectors and lubricate them with a light film of engine oil.

28 Install the injectors into the fuel rail assembly.

29 Secure the injectors with the fuel rail bracket.

30 Installation is the reverse of the removal procedure. Check carefully for leaks before placing the vehicle into normal service.

Fuel pressure regulator

Check

31 Refer to Section 3 for the fuel pressure checking procedure.

Replacement

32 Disconnect the cable from the negative terminal of the battery.

33 Relieve the fuel system pressure (see Section 2).

34 Disconnect the vacuum hose from the fuel pressure regulator.

35 Remove the fuel return pipe clamp from the fuel pressure regulator.

36 Use a back-up wrench on the fuel pressure regulator, unscrew the flare nut from the return line fitting and remove the fuel pressure regulator from the fuel rail.

37 Reassembly is the reverse of disassembly. Be sure to replace the seal, otherwise a dangerous fuel leak may develop. When installing the seal, lubricate it with a light film of engine oil.

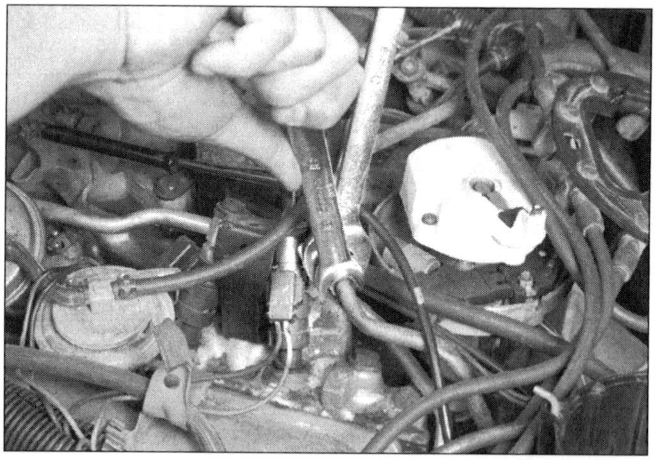

8.21 Use two wrenches to detach the fuel lines from the fuel rail (if available, use a flare-nut wrench on the fuel line fitting to prevent rounding off the corner of the fitting)

8.23 Remove the mounting bolts (arrows) from the fuel rail brackets and lift the assembly from the intake manifold

Chapter 5
Engine electrical systems

Contents

Specifications

Ignition system

Ignition coil resistance	
Breaker-points system	
Primary resistance	1.7 to 2.0 ohms
Secondary resistance	3,000 to 20,000 ohms
HEI system	
Primary resistance	0.4 to 0.5 ohms
Secondary resistance	6,000 to 30,000 ohms
Pick-up coil resistance	500 to 1,500 ohms

1 General information

The engine electrical systems include all ignition, charging and starting components. Because of their engine-related functions, these components are discussed separately from chassis electrical devices such as the lights, the instruments, etc. (which are included in Chapter 12).

Always observe the following precautions when working on the electrical systems:

a) Be extremely careful when servicing engine electrical components. They are easily damaged if checked, connected or handled improperly.

b) The alternator is driven by an engine drivebelt which could cause serious injury if your hands, hair or clothes become entangled in it with the engine running.

c) Both the alternator and the starter are connected directly to the battery and could arc or even cause a fire if mishandled, overloaded or shorted out.

d) Never leave the ignition switch on for long periods of time with the engine off.

e) Don't disconnect the battery cables while the engine is running.

f) Maintain correct polarity when connecting a battery cable from another source, such as a vehicle, during jump starting.

g) Always disconnect the negative cable first and hook it up last or the battery may be shorted by the tool being used to loosen the cable clamps.

It's also a good idea to review the safety-related information regarding the engine electrical systems located in the Safety First section near the front of this manual before beginning any operation included in this Chapter.

2 Battery - removal and installation

Refer to illustration 2.2

1 **Caution:** *Always disconnect the negative cable first and hook it up last or the battery may be shorted by the tool being used to loosen the cable clamps. Disconnect both cables from the battery terminals.*

2 Remove the battery hold-down clamp **(see illustration)**.

3 Lift out the battery. Use the proper lifting technique - the battery is heavy.

4 While the battery is out, inspect the battery carrier (tray) for corrosion (See Chapter 1).

2.2 Remove the bolts (arrow) that retain the brace above the battery

5 If you are replacing the battery, make sure that you get an identical battery, with the same dimensions, amperage rating, "cold cranking" rating, etc.

6 Installation is the reverse of removal.

3 Battery - emergency jump starting

Refer to the Booster battery (jump) starting procedure at the front of this manual.

4 Battery cables - check and replacement

1 Periodically inspect the entire length of each battery cable for damage, cracked or burned insulation and corrosion. Poor battery cable connections can cause starting problems and decreased engine performance.

2 Check the cable-to-terminal connections at the ends of the cables for cracks, loose wire strands and corrosion. The presence of white, fluffy deposits under the insulation at the cable terminal connection is a sign that the cable is corroded and should be replaced. Check the terminals for distortion, missing mounting bolts and corrosion.

3 When removing the cables, always disconnect the negative cable first and hook it up last or the battery may be shorted by the tool used to loosen the cable clamps. Even if only the positive cable is being replaced, be sure to disconnect the negative cable from the battery first (see Chapter 1 for further information regarding battery cable removal).

4 Disconnect the old cables from the battery, then trace each of them to their opposite ends and detach them from the starter solenoid and ground. Note the routing of each cable to insure correct installation.

5 If you are replacing either or both of the old cables, take them with you when buying new cables. It is vitally important that you replace the cables with identical parts. Cables have characteristics that make them easy to identify: positive cables are usually red, larger in cross-section and have a larger diameter battery post clamp; ground cables are usually black, smaller in cross-section and have a slightly smaller diameter clamp for the negative post.

6 Clean the threads of the solenoid or ground connection with a wire brush to remove rust and corrosion. Apply a light coat of battery terminal corrosion inhibitor, or petroleum jelly, to the threads to prevent future corrosion.

7 Attach the cable to the solenoid or ground connection and tighten the mounting nut/bolt securely.

8 Before connecting a new cable to the battery, make sure that it reaches the battery post without having to be stretched.

9 Connect the positive cable first, followed by the negative cable.

5 Ignition system - general information

1 In order for the engine to run correctly, it is necessary for an electrical spark to ignite the fuel/air mixture in the combustion chamber at exactly the right moment in relation to engine speed and load. The ignition coil converts low tension voltage from the battery into high tension voltage, powerful enough to jump the spark plug gap in the cylinder, providing that the system is in good condition and that all adjustments are correct.

2 The ignition system equipped on pre-1975 cars as standard equipment is a conventional distributor with mechanical breaker points. On 1975 and later models, a breakerless High Energy Ignition (HEI) system is used.

Breaker-points ignition system

3 The ignition system is divided into the primary (low tension) circuit and the secondary (high tension) circuit.

4 The primary circuit consists of the battery lead to the starter motor, the lead to the ignition switch, the calibrated resistance wire from the ignition switch to the coil primary winding and the lead from the coil low tension windings to the breaker points and condenser in the distributor.

5 The secondary circuit consists of the coil secondary winding, the high tension lead from the coil to the distributor cap, the distributor cap, rotor and the spark plug leads and spark plugs.

6 The system functions in the following manner. Low voltage in the coil is converted into high voltage by the opening and closing of the breaker points in the distributor. This high voltage is carried via the brush in the center of the distributor cap to the rotor arm on the distributor shaft. Every time the end of the rotor passes one of the spark plug wire terminals on the cap, the spark jumps the gap from the rotor arm to the terminal and is carried by the spark plug wire to the spark plug, where it jumps the spark plug gap to ground.

7 Ignition advance is controlled by both mechanical and vacuum operated systems. The mechanical governor mechanism consists of two weights which, due to centrifugal force, move out from the distributor shaft as the engine speed rises. As they move outwards, they rotate the cam relative to the distributor shaft, advancing spark timing. The weights are held in position by two light springs. It is the tension of these springs which determines correct spark advancement.

8 The vacuum control system consists of a diaphragm, one side of which is connected via a vacuum line to the carburetor, the other side to the contact breaker plate. Vacuum in the intake manifold and carburetor varies with engine speed and throttle opening. As the vacuum changes, it moves the diaphragm, which rotates the contact breaker plate slightly in relation to the rotor, thus advancing or retarding the spark. Control is fine-tuned by a spring in the vacuum assembly.

HEI ignition system

1975 through 1980

9 The Delco-Remy High Energy Ignition (HEI) system is a pulse triggered, transistor controlled, inductive discharge system.

10 A magnetic pick-up inside the distributor contains a permanent magnet, pole-piece and pick-up coil. A toothed wheel, rotating inside the pole piece, induces a voltage in the pick-up coil. When the teeth on the wheel and pole piece line up, a signal passes to the electronic module to open the coil primary circuit. The primary circuit current collapses and a high voltage is induced in the coil secondary winding. This high voltage is directed to the spark plugs by the distributor rotor in a manner similar to a conventional system. A capacitor suppresses radio interference.

11 The HEI system features a longer spark duration than a conventional breaker point ignition system, and the dwell period increases automatically with engine speed. These characteristics are desirable for lean firing and EGR-diluted mixtures.

12 The ignition coil and the electronic module are both housed in the distributor cap. Other than the distributor cap and rotor, the distributor does not require routine servicing.

13 Spark timing is advanced by mechanical and vacuum devices similar to those used on conventional breaker point distributors (described above). The TCS system is eliminated.

14 An Electronic Spark Selection (ESS) system was used on Cadillac models beginning in 1980. The ESS system is able to advance or retard the spark under certain operating conditions, improving fuel economy and reducing exhaust emissions. The main component of the system is the decoder module, mounted on the firewall. The decoder which is located on the firewall, is connected to the distributor through a five-wire plug. These ignition systems contain a specialized 5 pin HEI ESS module, a timer core, pole piece, pick-up coil, capacitor and speed sensor.

15 The ESS system works like a normal HEI ignition system with the exception of the spark advance. The pick-up coil senses the rotation of the timer core, located on the distributor shaft. An induced alternating current is fed to the ESS controller which informs the computer of the ignition advance. When this signal is received by the HEI module, the module cuts current flow through the primary windings of the ignition coil. This creates additional buildup of current which causes a surge of voltage through the secondary windings of the ignition coil. The ESS decoder uses three modes of ignition characteristics to control the engine. Cranking and cold engine operation (retarded timing) and high speed cruising (advanced timing). Coolant temperature is sensed indirectly through the EGR control solenoid.

1981 and later

16 Since 1981, HEI systems have been equipped with Electronic Spark Timing (EST). All spark timing changes are carried out by the Electronic Control Module (ECM), which monitors data from various engine sensors, computes the desired spark timing and sig-

6.1 The ignition system should be checked with a spark tester - if the ignition system produces a spark that will jump the tester gap, it's functioning properly

6.6a Checking for battery voltage on the positive terminal of the ignition coil (points-type ignition)

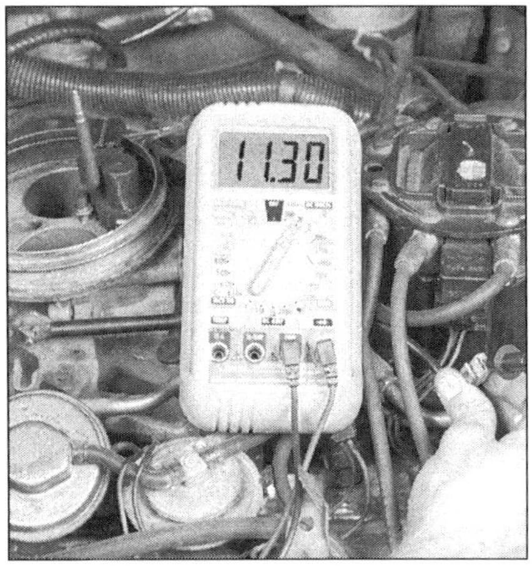

6.6b Checking for battery voltage on the BAT terminal on the ignition coil (HEI ignition)

nals the distributor to alter spark timing accordingly. Vacuum and mechanical advance is eliminated. The electronic module which is located in the distributor has three terminals instead of four terminals for the early, non-computerized HEI systems from 1975 through 1980. The three and four terminal modules cannot be interchanged. The computer is located near the glovebox inside the passenger compartment. These models are divided into Federal and California designed ignition systems for emissions. Vacuum from the engine is routed to the ECM and into an atmospheric pressure sensor or MAP sensor.

17 Distributors for some of the engines from 1982 are equipped with a Hall Effect switch and shutter blades. The Hall Effect switch acts as a second pick-up coil and timer core for sending signals to the ECM. While the engine is cranking, the primary pick-up coil sends cylinder firing information to the ECM but after the engine starts and enters into cruise mode, the Hall Effect switch takes over this function. The distributor module is connected to the EST system using a four wire connector. The ECM meanwhile reads data from several information sensors throughout the engine. These information sensors are discussed in Chapter 6.

18 Some models in 1982 and 1983 utilize a spark retard system to control excess engine detonation. An Electronic Spark Control (ESC) system utilizes a knock sensor, and the ECM, to allow maximum spark advance without spark knock. The ESC system improves driveability and fuel economy.

6 Ignition system - check

Refer to illustrations 6.1, 6.6a and 6.6b

Warning: *Because of the very high secondary voltage generated by the ignition system - particularly the High Energy Ignition (HEI) system - extreme care should be taken whenever this check is performed.*

1 If the engine will not start even though it turns over, check for spark at the spark plug by installing a calibrated ignition system tester to one of the spark plug wires **(see illustration)**. **Note:** *The tool is available at most auto parts stores. Be sure to get the correct tool for your particular ignition system (breaker-points or HEI).*

2 Connect the clip on the tester to a ground such as a metal bracket or valve cover bolt, crank the engine and watch the end of the tester for bright blue, well defined sparks.

3 If sparks occur, sufficient voltage is reaching the plugs to fire the engine. However the plugs themselves may be fouled, so remove and check them as described in Chapter 1 or replace them with new ones.

4 If no sparks occur, detach the coil secondary wire from the distributor cap, connect the tester to the coil wire and repeat the test (breaker-points systems only).

5 If sparks now occur, the distributor cap, rotor or spark plug wires may be defective. Remove the distributor cap and check the cap, rotor and spark plug wires as described in Chapter 1. Replace defective parts as necessary. If moisture is present in the distributor cap, use WD-40 or something similar to dry out the cap and rotor, then reinstall the cap and repeat the spark test at the spark plug wire.

6 If no sparks occur at the coil wire, check the primary wire connections at the coil to make sure they are clean and tight. Check for voltage to the ignition coil **(see illustrations)**. Battery voltage should be available to the ignition coil with the ignition switch ON. **Note:** *If the reading is 7 volts or less, repair the primary circuit from the ignition switch to the ignition coil.*

7 The coil-to-cap wire may be bad (breaker-points systems only), check the resistance with an ohmmeter and compare it to the Specifications. Make any necessary repairs and repeat the test.

8 If there's still no spark, check the ignition module (HEI system) (see Section 11), the ignition coil (see Section 8) or other internal components that may be defective.

9 If there is still no spark (see Step 1), check the ignition points (refer to Chapter 1). If the points appear to be in good condition (no pits or burned spots on the point surface) and the primary wires are hooked up correctly, adjust the points as described in Chapter 1.

10 If there is still no spark at the plugs, check for a ground or open circuit in the distributor/points circuit. There may be a damaged points terminal causing the ignition voltage to become shorted or diminished.

7 Distributor - removal and installation

Removal

Refer to illustrations 7.5a, 7.5b, 7.6a and 7.6b

1 After disconnecting the negative battery terminal cable, disconnect the primary lead from the coil (or distributor cap on HEI models).

2 Disconnect all electrical leads from the distributor. To find the connectors, trace the wires from the distributor.

3 Look for a raised "1" on the distributor cap. This marks the location for the number one cylinder spark plug wire terminal. If the cap does not have a mark for the number one spark plug, locate the number one spark plug and trace the wire back to its corresponding terminal on the cap.

4 Remove the distributor cap (see Chapter 1) and turn the engine over until the rotor is pointing toward the number one spark plug terminal (see locating TDC procedure in Chapter 2).

5 Make a mark on the edge of the distributor base directly below the rotor tip and in

7.5a After rotating the engine until the rotor is pointing at the terminal for the number one spark plug, mark the edge of the distributor base directly beneath the rotor

line with it **(see illustration)**. Also, mark the distributor base and the engine block to ensure that the distributor is installed correctly **(see illustration)**.

6 Remove the distributor hold-down bolt and clamp **(see illustrations)**, then pull the distributor straight up to remove it. **Caution:** *DO NOT turn the engine while the distributor is removed, or the alignment marks will be useless.*

Installation

Note: *If the crankshaft has been moved while the distributor is out, locate Top Dead Center (TDC) for the number one piston* (see Chapter 2) *and position the distributor and rotor accordingly.*

7 Insert the distributor into the engine in exactly the same relationship to the block that it was in when removed.

8 To mesh the helical gears on the camshaft and the distributor, it may be necessary to turn the rotor slightly. If the distributor doesn't seat completely, the hex shaped recess in the lower end of the distributor shaft is not mating properly with the oil pump shaft. Recheck the alignment marks between

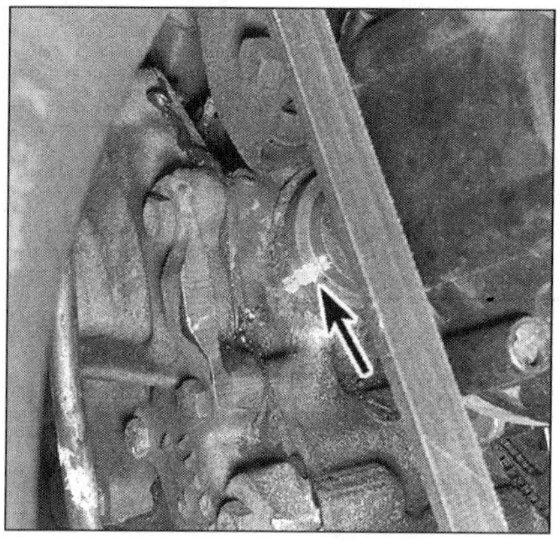

7.5b Mark the base of the distributor and the engine block to insure proper installation

the distributor base and the block to verify that the distributor is in the same position it was in before removal. Also check the rotor to see if it's aligned with the mark you made on the edge of the distributor base.

9 Place the hold-down clamp in position and loosely install the bolt.

10 Install the distributor cap.

11 Plug in the module electrical connector (where applicable).

12 Reattach the spark plug wires to the plugs (if removed).

13 Connect the cable to the negative terminal of the battery.

14 Check the ignition timing (see Chapter 1) and tighten the distributor hold-down bolt securely.

8 Ignition coil - check and replacement

Check

1 If the engine is hard to start, misses at high speed or cuts out during acceleration, the coil may be faulty. First, make sure the battery and the distributor are in good condition, the points (if equipped) are properly

7.6a Some distributor hold-down bolts can be removed with a combination wrench . . .

adjusted and the plugs and plug wires are in good shape. If the problem persists, perform the following test:

Breaker-points ignition system

Refer to illustrations 8.3a and 8.3b

2 Before performing any of the following coil electrical checks, make sure that the coil is clean, free of any carbon tracks and that all connections are tight and free of corrosion. Also make sure that both battery terminals are clean and that the cables are securely attached (especially the ground strap at the negative terminal).

3 Detach the coil high tension cable from the distributor cap. Hold the end of the cable about 3/16-inch away from some grounded part of the engine, turn the ignition on and operate the starter. A bright blue spark should jump the gap.

a) *If the spark is weak, yellowish or red, spark voltage is insufficient. If the points, condenser and battery are in good condition, the coil is probably weak. Check the coil primary and secondary resistance (see illustrations). Refer to the Specifications listed in the beginning of the Chapter. If the coil windings are damaged the resistance will be exces-*

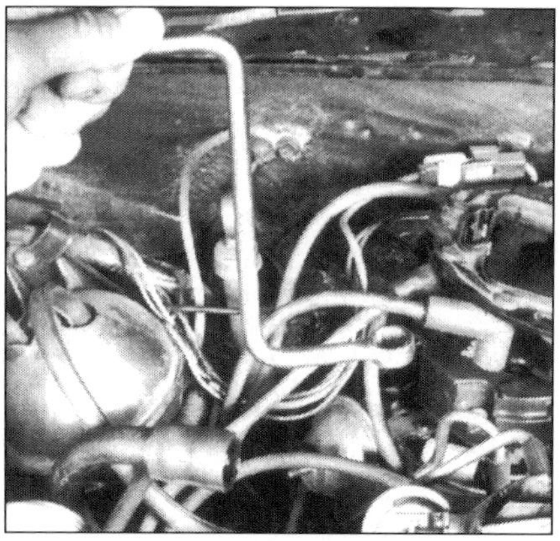

7.6b . . . others may require a special distributor wrench

8.3a Measure the primary resistance between the ignition coil positive (+) and negative (-) terminals (points-type ignition)

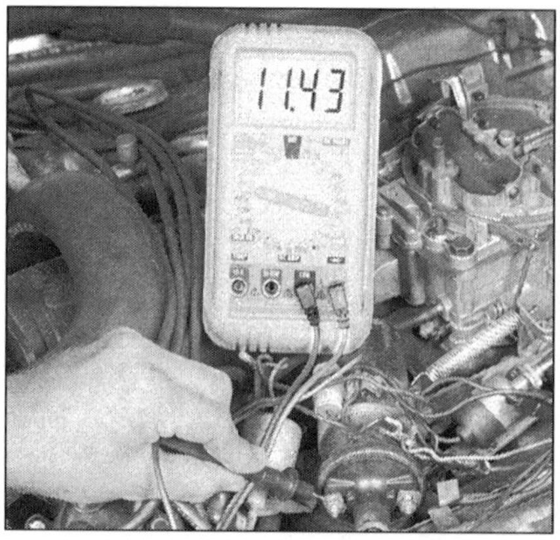

8.3b Measure the secondary resistance between the positive (+) terminal and the ignition coil tower (points-type ignition)

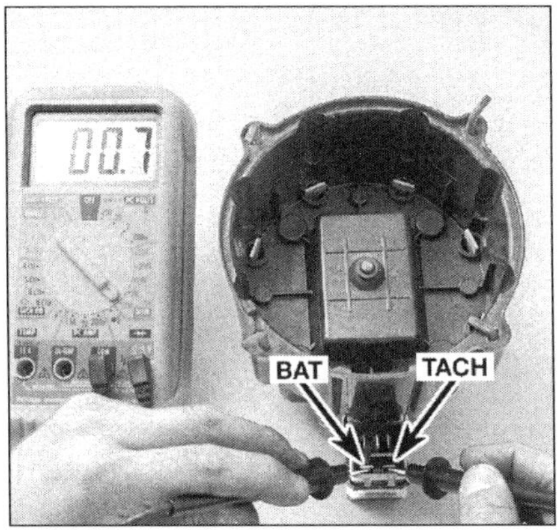

8.6 Measure the primary resistance across the BAT and TACH terminals (HEI ignition)

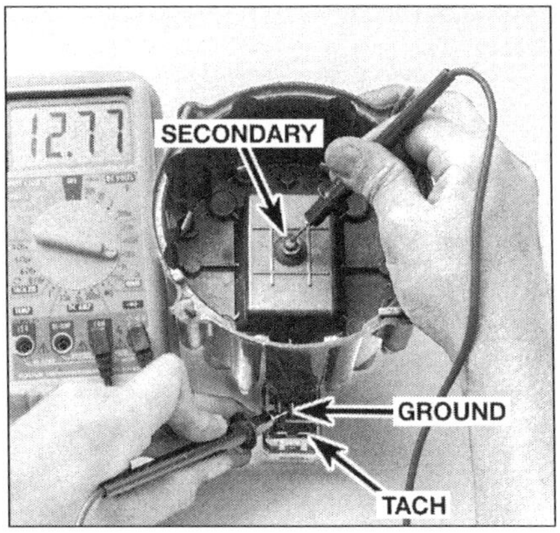

8.7 Measure the secondary resistance across the SECONDARY and GROUND terminals (HEI ignition)

8.10 To remove a conventional coil, simply detach the high tension cable and the primary leads and remove the mounting bracket bolts

sively high. Replace the coil.

b) *If there is no spark at all, try to locate the trouble before replacing the coil. Remove the distributor cap. Turn the engine until the points are open, or separate the points with a small piece of cardboard. Turn on the ignition switch. Using a 12-volt bulb with two test leads, attach one lead to ground somewhere on the engine and the other lead to first one of the coil's primary terminals and then the other:*
   1) *If the bulb lights when touched to the primary terminal that leads to the distributor, the coil is getting current and the primary windings are okay.*
   2) *If the bulb lights when touched to the other primary terminal but not when attached to the one leading to the distributor, the primary windings are faulty and the coil is no good.*
   3) *If the light does not go on when connected to either primary connection, the coil is not the problem. Check the ignition switch and starter solenoid.*
   4) *If the bulb lights when touched to both primary terminals (the coil is receiving current at both primary terminals), remove the high-tension cable from the center distributor cap tower and try shorting across the open distributor points with the tip of a clean (no oil) screwdriver.*
      (a) *If a spark jumps from the coil's high tension secondary wire to a grounded point on the engine as the screwdriver is removed, the points are either contaminated by oil, dirt or water, or they're burned.*
      (b) *If the screwdriver fails to produce a spark at the high tension wire, disconnect the primary wire that passes between the coil and the distributor and attach a test wire to the coil in its place. Ground the other end of the wire against the engine block, then pull it away (the test wire is simulating the points: grounding the wire is just like closing the points; pulling it away creates the same effect - producing a spark from the coil's high tension wire - as opening the points).*
         (1) *If a spark jumps from the high-tension cable when the test wire is removed from the ground, the coil is okay. Either the points are grounded or the condenser is shorted.*
         (2) *If a spark does not jump during this test, the secondary windings of the coil are faulty. Replace the coil.*

4 Sometimes, a coil checks out perfectly but the engine is still hard to start and misses at higher speeds. The problem may be inadequate spark voltage caused by reversed coil polarity. If you have recently tuned up the engine or performed any service work involving the coil, it's possible that the primary leads to the coil were accidentally reversed. To check for reversed polarity, remove one of the spark plug leads and hold it about 1/4-inch from the spark plug terminal or any ground point. Then insert the point of a pencil between the ignition lead and the plug while the engine is running (if the plug connector terminals are deeply recessed in a boot or insulating shield, straighten all but one bend in a paper clip and insert the looped end into the plug connector).

a) *If the spark flares on the ground or spark plug side of the pencil, the polarity is correct.*
b) *If the spark flares between the ignition lead and the pencil, however, the polarity is wrong and the primary wires should be switched at the coil.*

HEI ignition system

Refer to illustrations 8.6 and 8.7

5 Remove the distributor cap.

6 Attach the leads of an ohmmeter across the two primary coil terminals as shown **(see illustration)**. The indicated resistance should be less than one ohm.

7 Using the high scale, attach one lead of the ohmmeter to the SECONDARY terminal in the middle of the distributor and the other lead to the GROUND terminal **(see illustration)**. Also attach the ohmmeter leads across the SECONDARY and TACH terminals. If both readings indicate infinite resistance, replace the coil.

Replacement

Breaker-points ignition system

Refer to Illustration 8.10

8 Detach the cable from the negative terminal of the battery.

9 Disconnect the high tension cable from the coil.

10 Detach the primary electrical connectors from the coil. If there is any doubt as to where they go, be sure to mark them before removal to ensure that they are re-installed correctly. Unscrew the mounting bolts then remove the coil **(see illustration)**.

11 Installation is the reverse of removal

HEI ignition system

Refer to Illustrations 8.14, 8.16 and 8.17

12 Detach the cable from the negative terminal of the battery.

13 Disconnect the electrical connectors from the distributor cap.

14 Remove the coil cover screws and the cover **(see illustration)**.

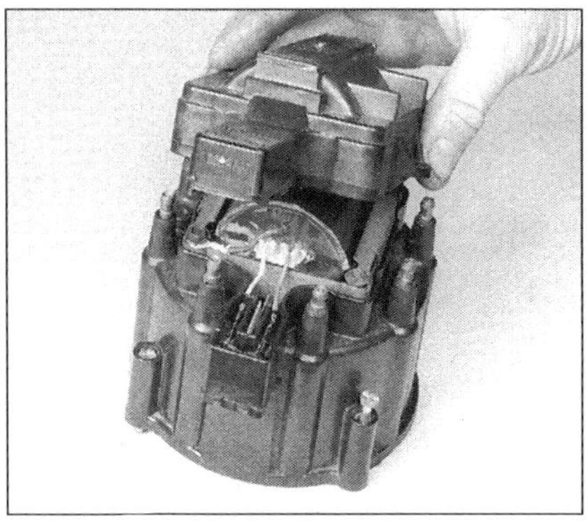

8.14 To access the HEI ignition coil, remove the coil cover screws and the cover

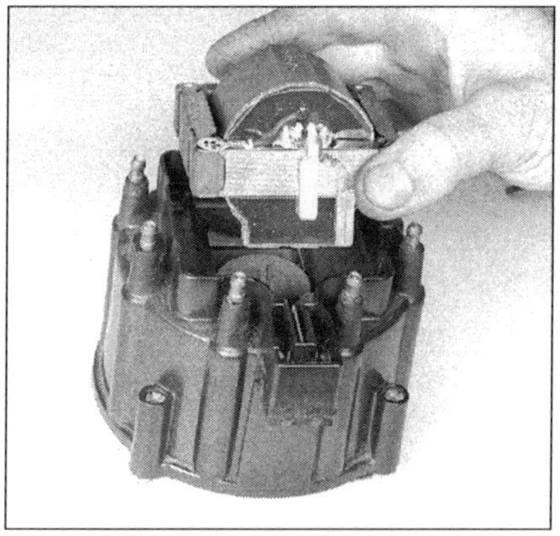

8.16 To separate the coil from the distributor cap, clearly mark the wires, detach the coil ground wire and push the terminals from the underside of the cap

15 Remove the screws securing the coil to the cap.

16 Note the position of each wire, marking them if necessary. Remove the coil ground wire, then push the terminals from the underside of the cap. Remove the coil from the distributor cap **(see illustration)**.

17 Installation is the reverse of the removal procedure. Be sure that the center electrode is in good condition **(see illustration)** and that the leads are connected to their original positions.

8.17 Before installing a new coil, make sure that the center electrode is in good condition

9 Vacuum advance - check and replacement

Check

Refer to illustration 9.45

1 Refer to Chapter 1, Ignition timing check and adjustment, and hook up a timing light as described there.

2 Start the engine and set the speed at approximately 2,500 rpm.

3 Observe the timing marks at the front of the engine and remove the vacuum hose from the vacuum advance control unit on the distributor. When the hose is removed, the timing mark on the crankshaft pulley should appear to move closer to the stationary mark on the timing tab. When the hose is reconnected, the mark should move away again.

4 If reconnecting the vacuum hose produces an abrupt increase in advance, or none at all, the vacuum advance control unit is probably defective. **Note:** *Another method to check the vacuum advance assembly is to connect a vacuum pump to the vacuum advance* **(see illustration)** *and observe the distributor plate for the proper movement.*

9.4 Apply vacuum to the vacuum advance unit and observe movement of the distributor plate

Replacement

Refer to illustration 9.5

5 Remove the distributor cap and rotor **(see illustration)**.

6 Remove the two screws that retain the vacuum advance mechanism to the distributor housing.

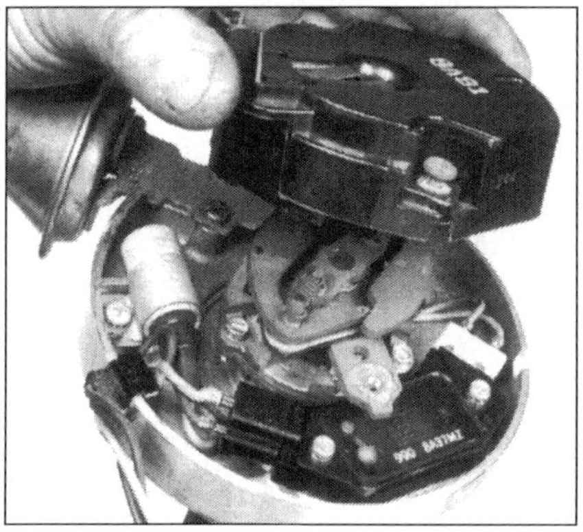

9.5 To detach the rotor, remove the two screws on top that attach it to the centrifugal advance mechanism

7 Unhook the advance arm from the distributor plate by pushing down on it with a narrow punch, then remove the unit from the distributor.

8 Installation is the reverse of the removal procedure.

10 Centrifugal advance - check and replacement

Check

Refer to illustration 10.4

1 Refer to Chapter 1, Ignition timing check and adjustment, and hook up a timing light as described there.

2 With the engine running at idle speed and the light properly connected, disconnect and plug the vacuum hose from the vacuum advance control unit on the distributor.

3 Observe the timing marks on the front of the engine and slowly increase engine speed. The timing mark on the crankshaft pulley should appear to move smoothly in a direction away from the stationary mark on the timing tab. Then when the engine is slowed down, the mark should return to its original position.

4 If the above conditions are not met, the advance mechanism inside the distributor should be checked for broken governor springs and sticking weights **(see illustration)**.

10.4 An example of a worn centrifugal advance weight - note the elongated hole

Replacement

Refer to illustration 10.7

5 Remove the distributor cap.

6 Remove the two screws that retain the rotor **(see illustration 9.5)**.

7 Remove the centrifugal weight springs and carefully lift the weights off the distributor shaft **(see illustration)**.

8 Installation is the reverse of removal.

10.7 Remove the centrifugal weight springs (arrows)

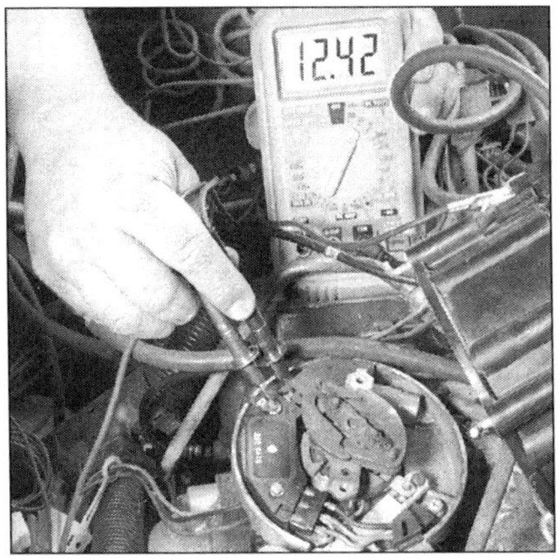

11.2 Check for battery voltage to the ignition module with the ignition key ON (engine not running)

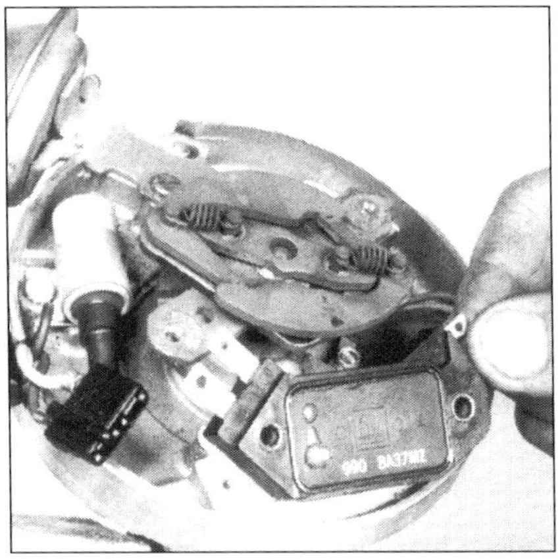

11.10 To remove the ignition module, remove the two mounting screws, unplug the connectors and lift the module out

11 Ignition module - check and replacement

Check

Refer to illustration 11.2

1 Remove the cap from the distributor (see Chapter 1).

2 With the ignition coil leads connected to the distributor, check for battery voltage to the ignition module. **Note:** *The ignition wiring to the distributor cap is short and will not allow much movement. Use a jumper wire from the BAT terminal on the distributor cap to the pink wire.*

3 If battery voltage exists, check the pick-up coil (see Section 12).

4 If the module is receiving power and the pick-up coil, ignition coil and secondary circuit are good, most likely the ignition module is defective. Have the module checked at a dealer service department.

Replacement

Refer to illustration 11.10

Note: *It's not necessary to remove the distributor from the engine to replace the ignition module.*

5 Disconnect the cable from the negative terminal of the battery.

6 Remove the air cleaner to provide room to work around the distributor.

7 Remove the distributor cap and wires as an assembly and position them out of the way (see Chapter 1).

8 Remove the rotor.

9 Carefully detach the electrical connectors from the module terminals.

10 Remove the screws and lift out the module **(see illustration)**.

11 Installation is the reverse of removal. Be sure to apply the silicone dielectric grease supplied with the new module to the distributor base - DO NOT use any other type of grease! If the grease isn't used, the module will overheat and destroy itself.

12 Pick-up coil - check and replacement

Check

Refer to illustrations 12.3 and 12.4

1 Disconnect the cable from the negative battery terminal.

2 Unplug the electrical connectors, disengage the latches and remove the distributor cap and rotor.

3 To test the pick-up coil, remove the pick-up coil leads from the module. Connect the negative ohmmeter probe to the distributor body and the positive probe to the pick-up coil electrical connector **(see illustration)**. Resistance should be infinite. If continuity is indicated, there is a short to ground in the pick-up coil. Replace the pick-up coil.

4 Next, measure the pick-up coil resistance across the two pick-up coil terminals. It should be 500 to 1,500 ohms **(see illustration)**. If the resistance is incorrect, replace the pick-up coil.

5 Flex the pick-up coil leads and pull on the connectors (with the ohmmeter connected to the pick-up coil leads). Any change in resistance would indicate a broken wire in the pick-up coil, replace the pick-up coil.

Replacement

Refer to illustrations 12.8 and 12.9

6 Remove the distributor (see Section 7).

7 Place the distributor in a vise, using blocks of wood to protect it.

8 Mark the relative positions of the gear and shaft. Drive the roll pin out **(see illustration)**. Remove the gear and pull the shaft from the distributor housing.

9 Remove the aluminum shield (if equipped) for access to the pick-up coil. Carefully pry the retaining clip from the distributor shaft and remove the pick-up coil and pole piece assembly **(see illustration)**.

10 Reassembly is the reverse of the disassembly procedure. After reassembly, spin the distributor shaft to make sure there is no contact between the pick-up coil and the pick-up teeth. Loosen and retighten the teeth to eliminate the contact, if necessary.

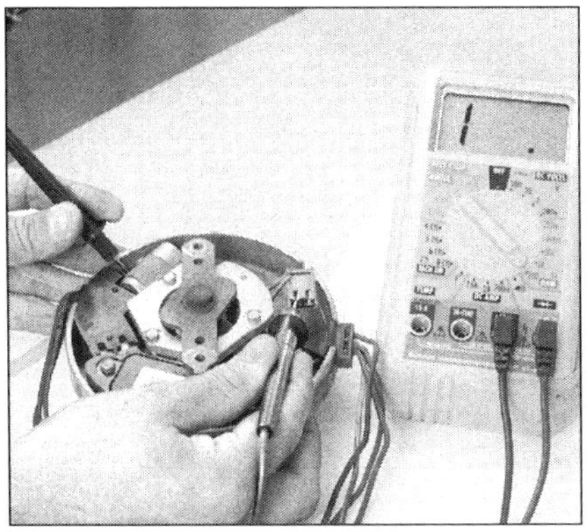

12.3 Connect the ohmmeter to the pick-up coil terminal and the distributor body. If continuity is indicated, there is a short from the pick-up coil wiring to the distributor body

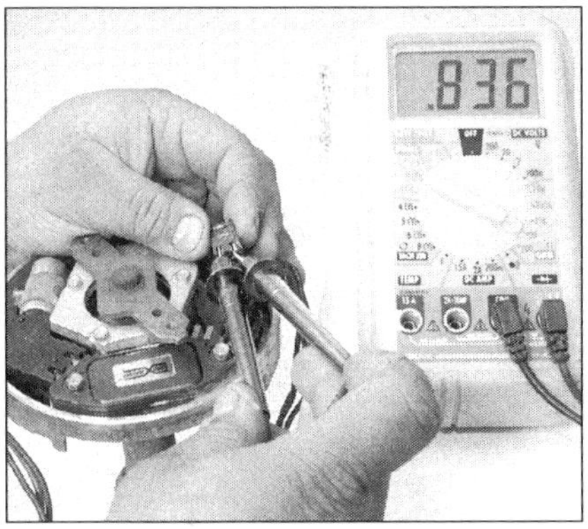

12.4 Measure the resistance of the pick-up coil. It should be between 500 and 1,500 ohms

13 Charging system - general information and precautions

The charging system includes the alternator, either an internal or an external voltage regulator, a charge indicator, the battery, a fusible link and the wiring between all the components. The charging system supplies electrical power for the ignition system, the lights, the radio, etc. The alternator is driven by a drivebelt at the front (right end) of the engine.

These models are equipped with Delco-Remy Delcotron alternators. Several different types with different amperage ratings are used. Early units, up to and including 1972, use an external voltage regulator. Later units are equipped with an internal voltage regulator and are referred to as the SI integral regulator charging system. This refers to the arrangement of the diode trio in relation to the rectifier bridge.

The purpose of the voltage regulator is to limit the alternator's voltage to a preset value. This prevents power surges, circuit overloads, etc., during peak voltage output.

14 Charging system - check

1 If a malfunction occurs in the charging circuit, don't automatically assume that the alternator is causing the problem. First check the following items:

- a) *Check the drivebelt tension and its condition. Replace it if worn or deteriorated.*
- b) *Make sure the alternator mounting and adjustment bolts are tight.*
- c) *Inspect the alternator wiring harness and the connectors at the alternator and voltage regulator. They must be in good condition and tight.*
- d) *Check the fusible link (if equipped) located between the starter solenoid and the alternator. If it's burned, determine the cause, repair the circuit and replace the link (the vehicle won't start and/or the accessories won't work if the fusible link blows).*
- e) *Start the engine and check the alternator for abnormal noises (a shrieking or squealing sound indicates a bad bushing - do not confuse this noise with a squealing drivebelt).*
- f) *Check the specific gravity of the battery electrolyte. If it's low, charge the battery (doesn't apply to maintenance free batteries).*
- g) *Make sure the battery is fully charged (one bad cell in a battery can cause overcharging by the alternator).*

2 Using a voltmeter, check the battery voltage with the engine off. It should be approximately 12 volts.

3 Start the engine and check the battery voltage again. It should now be approximately 14 to 15 volts.

4 Turn on the headlights. The voltage should drop, and then come back up, if the charging system is working properly.

5 If the voltage reading is less or more than the specified charging voltage, replace the voltage regulator (refer to Section 17).

6 If the battery is discharging due to a current drain with the ignition Off, check for a draw as follows:

12.8 To remove the distributor shaft, drive the roll pin out of the shaft with a hammer and punch, remove the gear, shim and tanged washer from the shaft, inspect the shaft for any burrs that might prevent its removal, then pull it out (be careful not to lose the washer at the upper end of the shaft)

- a) *Disconnect the battery cables (negative first, then positive). Inspect the battery posts and the cable clamps for corrosion. Clean them thoroughly if necessary* (see Chapter 1).
- b) *Reconnect the positive cable to its terminal on the battery. Remove the fuse for the clock, if the vehicle is so equipped. With the key off and the doors closed, insert a test light between the negative battery post and the disconnected negative cable clamp.*
  - 1) *If the test light does not come on, reattach the clamp and proceed to the next Step.*
  - 2) *If the test light glows brightly, there is a short in the electrical system of the vehicle. The short must be repaired before the charging system can be checked.* **Note:** *The test light will glow dimly on later models, due to the "keep alive memory" of the ECM, radio, clock etc.*
  - 3) *Disconnect the alternator wiring harness.*

12.9 The pick-up coil and pole piece assembly can be removed after carefully prying out the C-clip

- a) *If the light goes out, the alternator is bad.*
- b) *If the light stays on, pull each fuse until the light goes out (this will tell you which circuit is shorted).*

15 Alternator - removal and installation

Refer to illustrations 15.2a, 15.2b and 15.3

1 Disconnect the cable from the negative terminal of the battery.

2 Loosen the alternator adjustment and pivot bolts and detach the drivebelt **(see illustrations)**.

3 Disconnect the electrical connectors from the alternator **(see illustration)**.

4 Remove the adjustment and pivot bolts and separate the alternator from the engine.

5 If you are replacing the alternator, take the old alternator with you when purchasing a replacement unit. Make sure the new/rebuilt unit is identical to the old alternator. Look at the terminals - they should be the same in number, size and location as the terminals on the old alternator. Finally, look at the identification markings - they will be stamped in the housing or printed on a tag or plaque affixed

15.2a To remove the drivebelt, loosen the alternator pivot bolt . . .

15.2b . . . then loosen the adjustment bolt and slip off the belt - finally, remove the pivot and adjustment bolts and remove the alternator

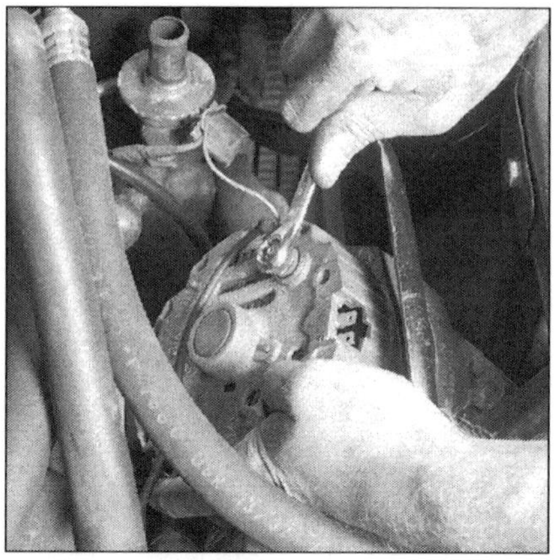

15.3 Tilt the alternator slightly and remove the connectors from the back

16.2 Paint an alignment mark on the alternator body between each end frame

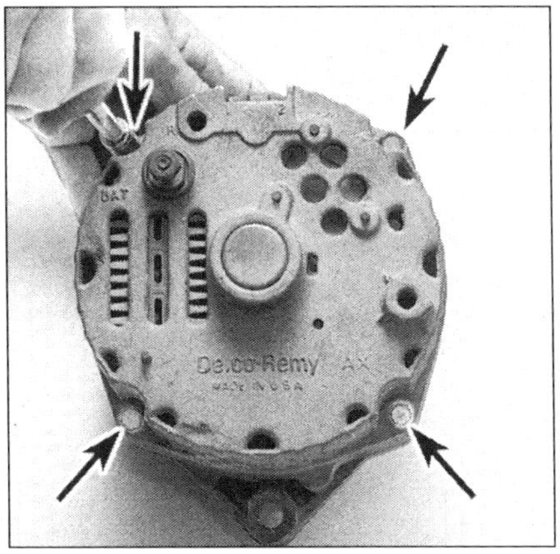

16.3 Remove the bolts (arrows) securing the rear end frame to the drive end frame

16.4 Separate the two halves

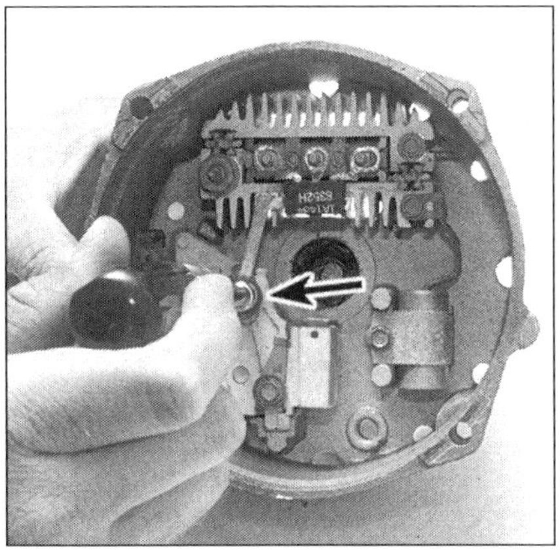

16.5 Remove the screw (arrow) retaining the diode trio to the regulator/brush assembly

16.6 Remove the three nuts (arrows) from the rectifier bridge

16.7 Lift the diode trio from the alternator

to the housing. Make sure these numbers are the same on both alternators.

6 Many new/rebuilt alternators do not have a pulley installed, so you may have to switch the pulley from the old unit to the new/rebuilt one. When buying an alternator, find out the shop's policy regarding pulleys - some shops will perform this service free of charge.

7 Installation is the reverse of removal.

8 After the alternator is installed, adjust the drivebelt tension (see Chapter 1).

9 Check the charging voltage to verify proper operation of the alternator (see Section 14).

16 Alternator components - check and replacement

Refer to illustrations 16.2, 16.3, 16.4, 16.5, 16.6, 16.7, 16.8, 16.9, 16.10, 16.13, 16.14a, 16.14b, 16.14c, 16.14d, 16.14e, 16.15a, 16.15b, 16.16a, 16.6b, 16.17a, 16.17b and 16.17c

1 Remove the alternator (see Section 15) and place it on a clean workbench.

2 Paint an alignment mark on each side of the end frame to insure correct reassembly **(see illustration)**.

3 Remove the four bolts that secure the two end frames together **(see illustration)**.

4 Separate the two halves. The rotor will remain in one half while the stator will remain in the other half **(see illustration)**.

5 Remove the screw retaining the diode trio to the brush assembly **(see illustration)**

6 Remove the three nuts from the rectifier bridge **(see illustration)**.

7 Lift the diode trio from the alternator assembly **(see illustration)**.

8 Remove the stator from the end frame **(see illustration)**.

9 Remove the brush assembly and voltage regulator **(see illustration)**.

10 Remove the nut and washer from the output stud. Remove the screws retaining the rectifier bridge to the rear end frame and lift

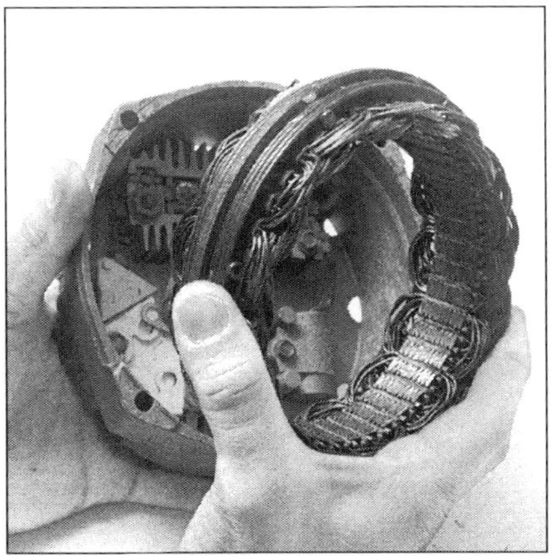

16.8 Separate the stator from the end frame

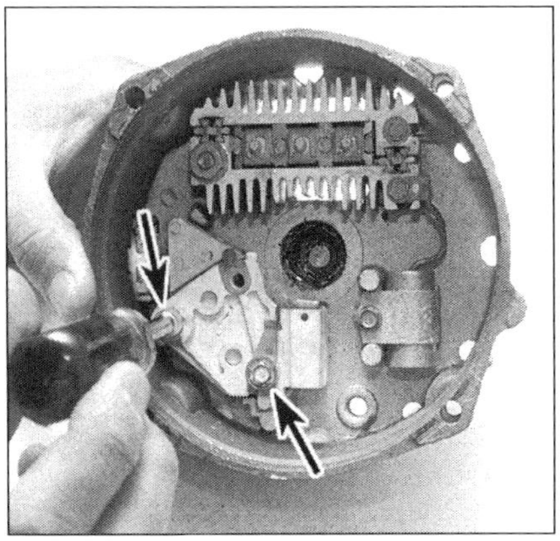

16.9 Remove the two remaining screws (arrows) and remove the brush assembly and voltage regulator

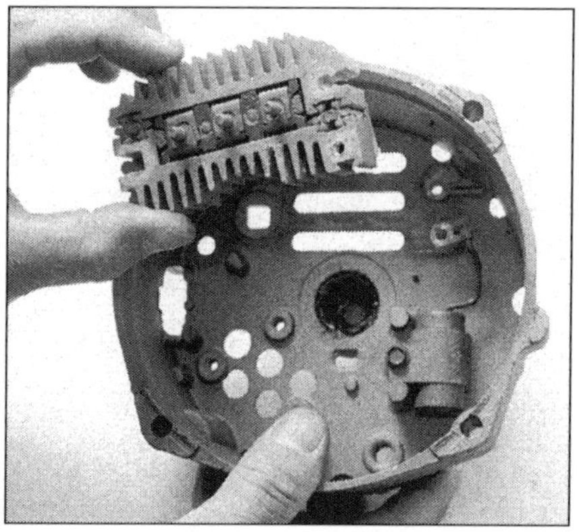

16.10 Remove the rectifier assembly from the end frame

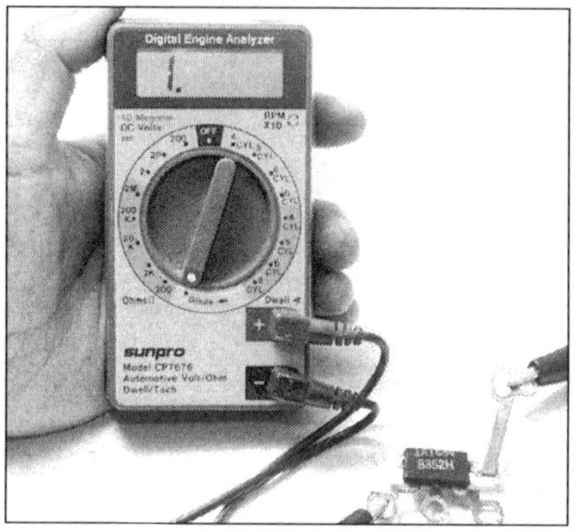

16.14b Reverse the probes to check the continuity in the other direction. The diode should allow continuity in one direction only

the assembly out **(see illustration)**.

11 Remove the nut and washer and separate the front pulley and fan from the drive end frame.

12 Remove the rotor from the drive end frame.

13 Remove the condenser mounting bolt and condenser **(see illustration)**.

14 Test the diodes as follows:

a) *Test the diode trio by installing the negative probe of the multimeter onto the leg and the positive probe onto each terminal of the diode trio. Using the diode testing function on the multimeter, continuity should exist in one position only* **(see illustrations)**. *Reverse the polarity of the test by changing the position of the probes. Continuity should NOT exist. This checks the unidirectional capability of the operating diode. Next, repeat this test for each of the other two diodes (total six checks). Each diode should have the exact same characteristics. It will be necessary to use a multimeter that includes a diode check function. This function allows slight current application to the diode to assist in opening the voltage gate.*

b) *To test the rectifier assembly, follow the exact same procedure as detailed above. Be sure to use a multimeter with a diode check function. Use a screwdriver to lift the tabs off the contact surface to separate the negative and positive diode rectifiers. Make sure the tabs do not touch the posts, the heat sinks or each other. Install the multimeter probes on the tabs and the cooling fins on one side of the rectifier, then the other, to obtain results* **(see illustrations)**. *If the test results are incorrect for any one of the diodes, replace the complete unit.*

15 Test the rotor as follows:

a) *Check for an open between the two slip rings* **(see illustration).** *There should be 1 to 5 ohms resistance between the slip rings.*

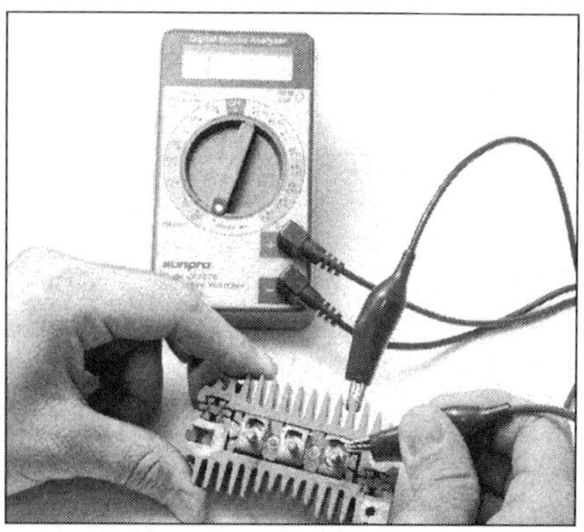

16.14d Reverse the probes to check the continuity in the other direction. Continuity should NOT exist. The rectifier bridge diodes should allow continuity in one direction only

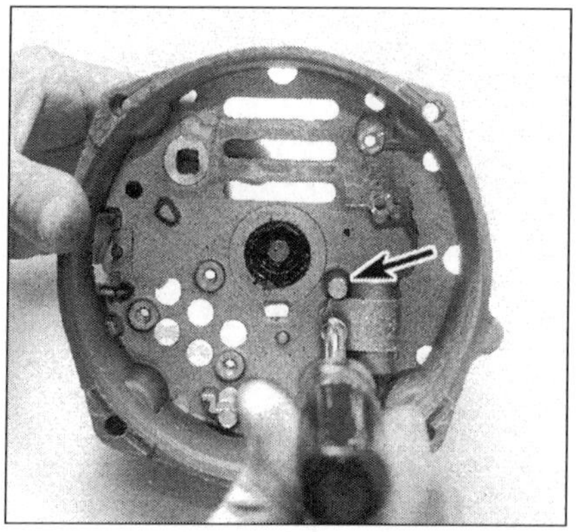

16.13 Remove the condenser mounting bolt

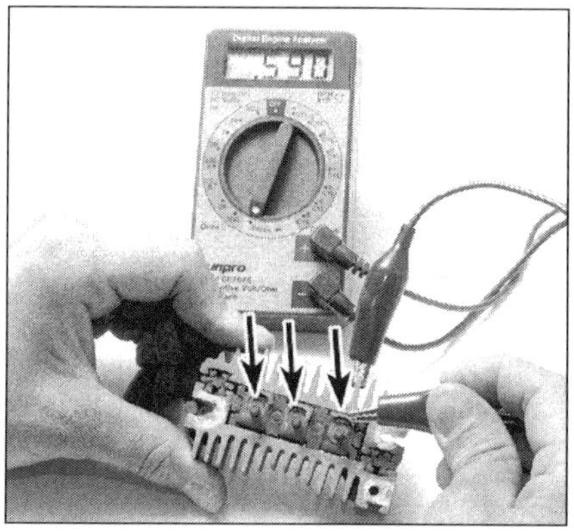

16.14c To test the three diodes (arrows) on the top side of the rectifier bridge, install the positive probe onto the cooling fin and touch the negative probe to each metal tab. Continuity should exist through each diode

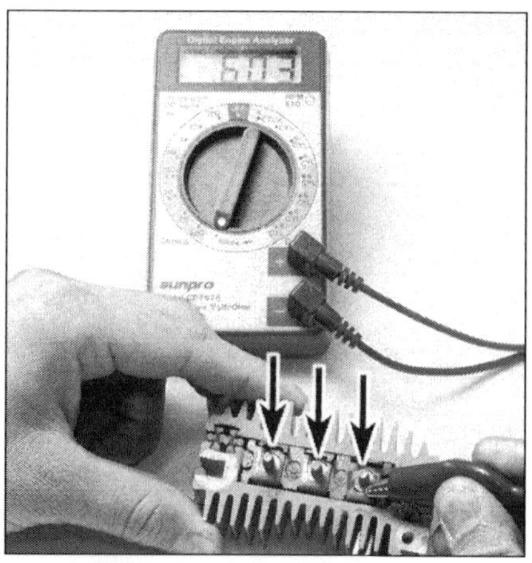

16.14e Test the three diodes (arrows) on the bottom row in the same manner

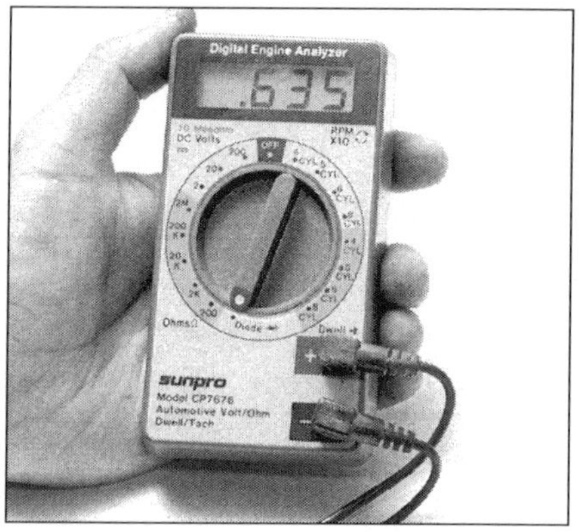

16.14a To test the diode trio, install the negative probe on the extension leg and the positive probe onto each diode (in turn). Continuity should exist through each diode

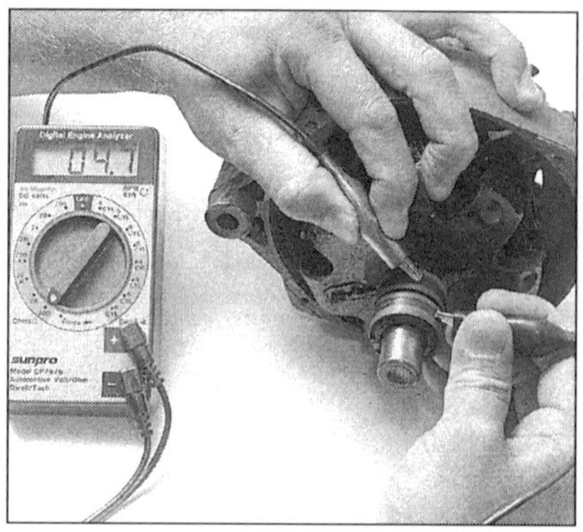

16.15a To test the rotor, check for an open between the two slip rings. There should be 1 to 5 ohms resistance

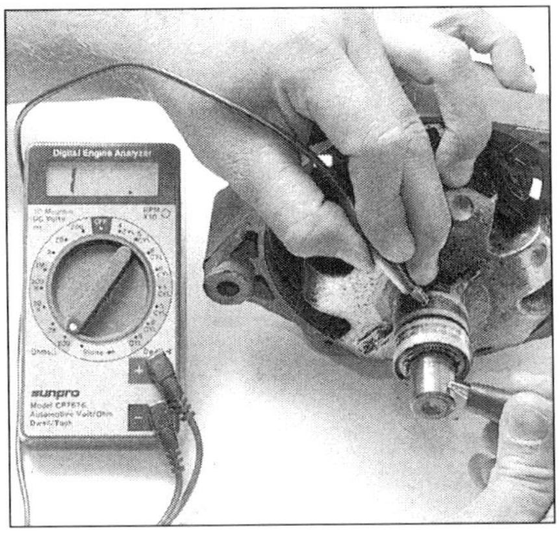

16.15b Also, check the rotor slips rings and the rotor for possible grounds. Continuity should NOT exist between the slip ring and the shaft or frame

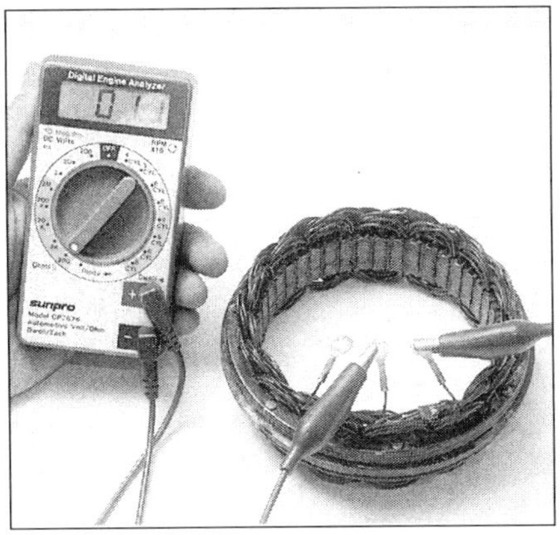

16.16a To test the stator, check for opens between each end terminal of the stator windings. Continuity should exist between all the terminals

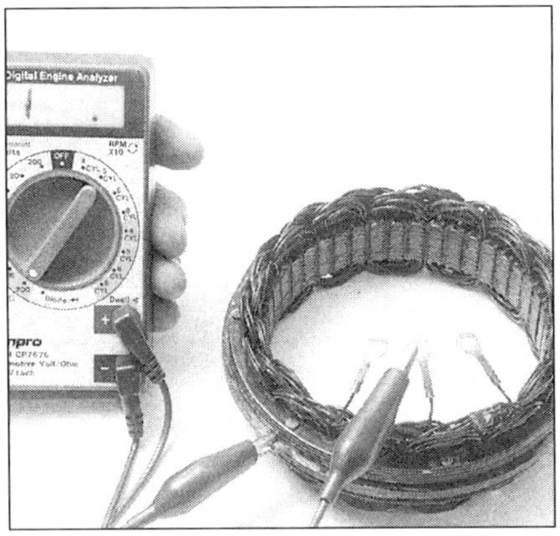

16.16b Also, check for a grounded stator winding to the end frame. Continuity should NOT exist between any terminal and the frame

16.17a Apply a small amount of grease to the bearing surface

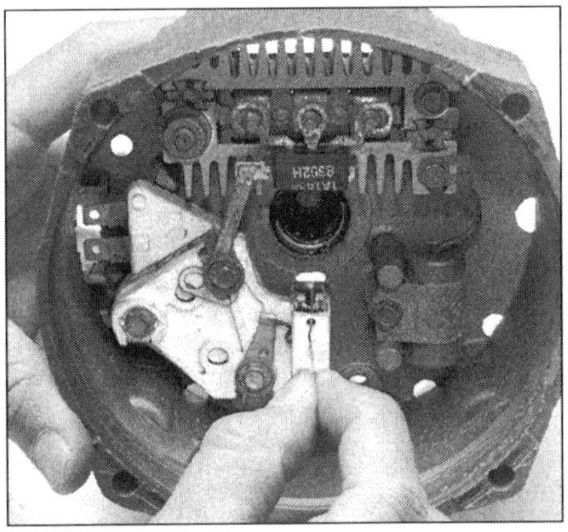

16.17b Press the two brushes into the holder and slide a paper clip through the eyelet to keep the brushes in the holder assembly

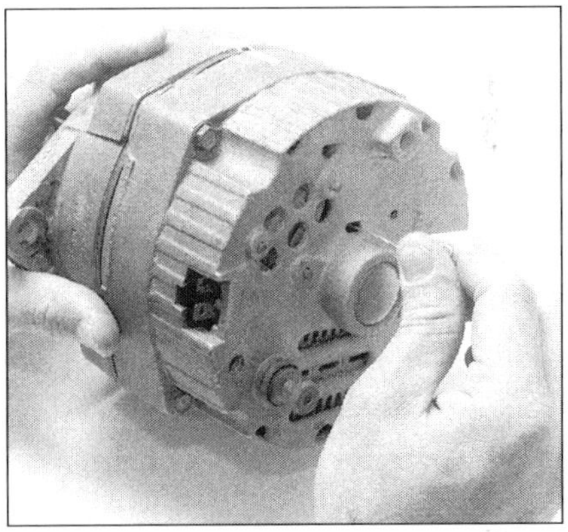

16.17c After the alternator is completely assembled remove the wire or paper clip to release the brushes

b) *Check for grounds between each slip ring and the rotor* **(see illustration)**. *There should be no continuity (infinite resistance) between the rotor and either slip ring. If the rotor fails either test, or if the slip rings are excessively worn, the rotor is defective.*

16 Test the stator as follows:

a) *Check for opens between each end terminal of the stator windings* **(see illustration)**. *If either reading is high (infinite resistance), the stator is defective.*

b) *Check for a grounded stator winding between each stator terminal and the frame* **(see illustration)**. *If there's continuity between any stator winding and the frame, the stator is defective.*

17 Reassembly is a reversal of disassembly. Observe the following points:

a) *Take great care to position the insulating washers and sleeves correctly on the rectifier bridge and brush assembly screws.*

b) *Place a small amount of grease onto the bearing surface before installing the alternator halves together* **(see illustration)**.

c) *Press the brushes into the holder and insert a stiff wire (such as a straightened-out paper clip) through the small hole in the back of the alternator to hold the brushes in a retracted position* **(see illustration)**. *This will prevent them from catching on the slip rings as the alternator halves are assembled.*

d) *Clean the brush contact surfaces on the slip rings before installing the end-frame*

e) *Make sure that the marks on the rear end frame and drive end frame (which were made before dismantling) are in alignment.*

f) *Tighten the pulley nut securely.*

g) *Remove the wire or paper clip from the end-frame to permit the brushes to release onto the slip rings* **(see illustration)**.

17 Voltage regulator (external type)-check and replacement

1 A discharged battery will normally be due to a fault in the voltage regulator, but before testing the unit, perform the following:

a) *Check the drivebelt tension.*

b) *Test the condition of the battery.*

c) *Check the charging circuit for loose connections and broken wires.*

d) *Make sure that lights or other electrical accessories have not been switched on inadvertently.*

e) *Check the generator indicator lamp for normal illumination with the ignition switched on and off, and with the engine idling and stationary.*

2 Disconnect the battery ground cable. Disconnect the harness connector from the regulator.

3 Under no circumstances should the voltage regulator or field relay contacts be cleaned since any abrasive materials will destroy the contact material.

4 Voltage regulator point (0.014-inch) and air-gap (0.067-inch) adjustments can be checked with a feeler gauge of the specified thickness. Check the voltage regulator point opening of the upper contacts with the lower contacts just touching. Adjustments are made by carefully bending the upper contact arm. Check the voltage regulator air gap with the lower contacts touching and adjust it, if necessary, by turning the nylon nut.

5 The field relay point opening may be adjusted by bending the armature stop. The air gap is checked with the points just touching and is adjusted by bending the flat contact support spring. **Note:** *The field relay will*

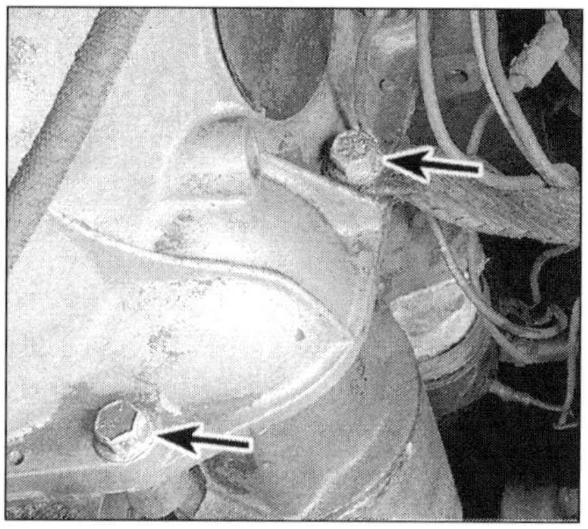

20.4a Starter mounting bolt locations (arrows) for the HT4100 engine

normally operate satisfactorily even if the air-gap is outside the specified limits, and should not be adjusted when the system is functioning satisfactorily.

6 If the regulator must be replaced, simply remove the mounting screws.

7 Installation is the reverse of the removal procedure. Ensure that the rubber gasket is in place on the regulator base.

18 Starting system - general information and precautions

The sole function of the starting system is to turn over the engine quickly enough to allow it to start.

The starting system consists of the battery, the starter motor, the starter solenoid and the wires connecting them. The solenoid is mounted directly on the starter motor or is a separate component located in the engine compartment.

The solenoid/starter motor assembly is installed on the lower part of the engine, next to the transmission bellhousing.

When the ignition key is turned to the Start position, the starter solenoid is actuated through the starter control circuit. The starter solenoid then connects the battery to the starter. The battery supplies the electrical energy to the starter motor, which does the actual work of cranking the engine.

The starter motor can only be operated when the transmission selector lever is in Park or Neutral.

Always observe the following precautions when working on the starting system:

a) *Excessive cranking of the starter motor can overheat it and cause serious damage. Never operate the starter motor for more than 15 seconds at a time without pausing to allow it to cool for at least two minutes.*
b) *The starter is connected directly to the battery and could arc or cause a fire if mishandled, overloaded or shorted out.*
c) *Always detach the cable from the negative terminal of the battery before working on the starting system.*

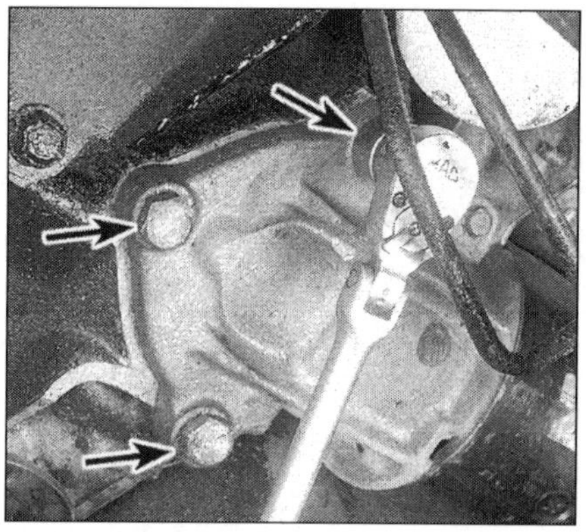

20.4b Typical starter motor mounting bolt locations (arrows) for models with Oldsmobile engine - other models have two vertical mounting bolts

19 Starter motor - testing in vehicle

Note: *Before diagnosing starter problems, make sure the battery is fully charged.*

1 If the starter motor does not turn at all when the ignition switch is operated, make sure the shift lever is in Neutral or Park.

2 Make sure that the battery is charged and that all cables, both at the battery and starter solenoid terminals, are clean and secure.

3 If the starter motor spins but the engine is not cranking, the overrunning clutch in the starter motor is slipping and the starter motor must be replaced.

4 If, when the switch is actuated, the starter motor does not operate at all but the solenoid clicks, then the problem lies with either the battery, the main solenoid contacts or the starter motor itself, or the engine is seized.

5 If the solenoid plunger cannot be heard when the switch is actuated, the battery is bad, the fusible link is burned (the circuit is open) or the solenoid itself is defective.

6 To check the solenoid, connect a jumper lead between the battery (positive terminal) and the ignition switch terminal (the small terminal) on the solenoid. If the starter motor now operates, the solenoid is OK and the problem is in the ignition switch, neutral start switch or in the wiring.

7 If the starter motor still does not operate, remove the starter/solenoid assembly for disassembly, testing and repair.

8 If the starter motor cranks the engine at an abnormally slow speed, first make sure that the battery is charged and that all terminal connections are tight. If the engine is partially seized, or has the wrong viscosity oil in it, it will crank slowly.

9 Run the engine until normal operating temperature is reached, then disconnect the coil wire from the distributor cap and ground it on the engine.

10 Connect a voltmeter positive lead to the battery positive post and then connect the negative lead to the negative post.

11 Crank the engine and take the voltmeter readings as soon as a steady figure is indicated. Do not allow the starter motor to turn for more than 15 seconds at a time. A reading of nine volts or more, with the starter motor turning at normal cranking speed, is normal. If the reading is nine volts or more but the cranking speed is slow, the motor is faulty. If the reading is less than nine volts and the cranking speed is slow, the solenoid contacts are probably burned, the starter motor is bad, the battery is discharged or there is a bad connection.

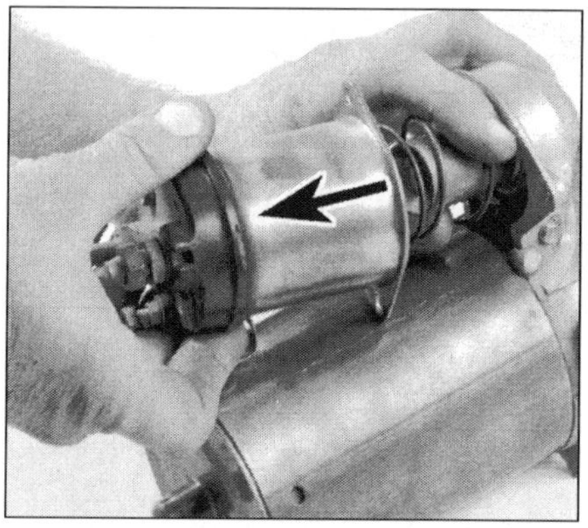

21.3 To disengage the solenoid from the starter, turn it in a clockwise direction

20 Starter motor - removal and installation

Refer to illustrations 20.4a and 20.4b

1 Detach the cable from the negative terminal of the battery.

2 Raise the vehicle and support it securely on jackstands.

3 Clearly label, then disconnect the wires from the terminals on the starter motor and solenoid.

4 Remove the starter motor mounting bolts **(see illustrations)**. Remove the starter.

5 Installation is the reverse of removal.

21 Starter motor solenoid - removal and installation

Refer to illustration 21.3

1 Remove the starter unit (see Section 20).

2 Disconnect the connector strap from the starter motor terminal. Remove the two screws which secure the solenoid housing to the end-frame assembly.

3 Twist the solenoid in a clockwise direction to disengage the flange key and then withdraw the solenoid **(see illustration)**.

4 Install the solenoid to the starter motor by first checking that the return spring is in position on the plunger and then insert the solenoid body into the drive housing and turn the body counterclockwise to engage the flange key.

5 Install the two solenoid securing screws and connect the starter motor connector strap.

Chapter 6
Emissions and engine control systems

Contents

1 General information

Refer to illustrations 1.1a, 1.1b, 1.1c, 1.5a and 1.5b

To prevent pollution of the atmosphere from incompletely burned or evaporating gases, and to maintain good driveability and fuel economy, a number of emission control systems, such as the following, are used on your vehicle **(see illustrations)**:

Positive Crankcase Ventilation (PCV) system
Air Injection Reactor (AIR) system
Inlet Air Temperature Control system
Evaporation Control System (ECS)/ Evaporative Emissions Control System (EECS)
Exhaust Gas Recirculation (EGR) system
Catalytic converter
Computer Controlled Catalytic Converter (C4) system
Computer Command Control (C3) system
Electronic Spark Timing (EST)
Electronic Spark Control (ESC)
Electronic Spark Selection (ESS)
V8-6-4 Modulated Displacement System (1981 Cadillac Eldorado and Seville)

The Sections in this Chapter include general descriptions, checking procedures within the scope of the home mechanic and component replacement procedures (when possible) for each of the systems listed above.

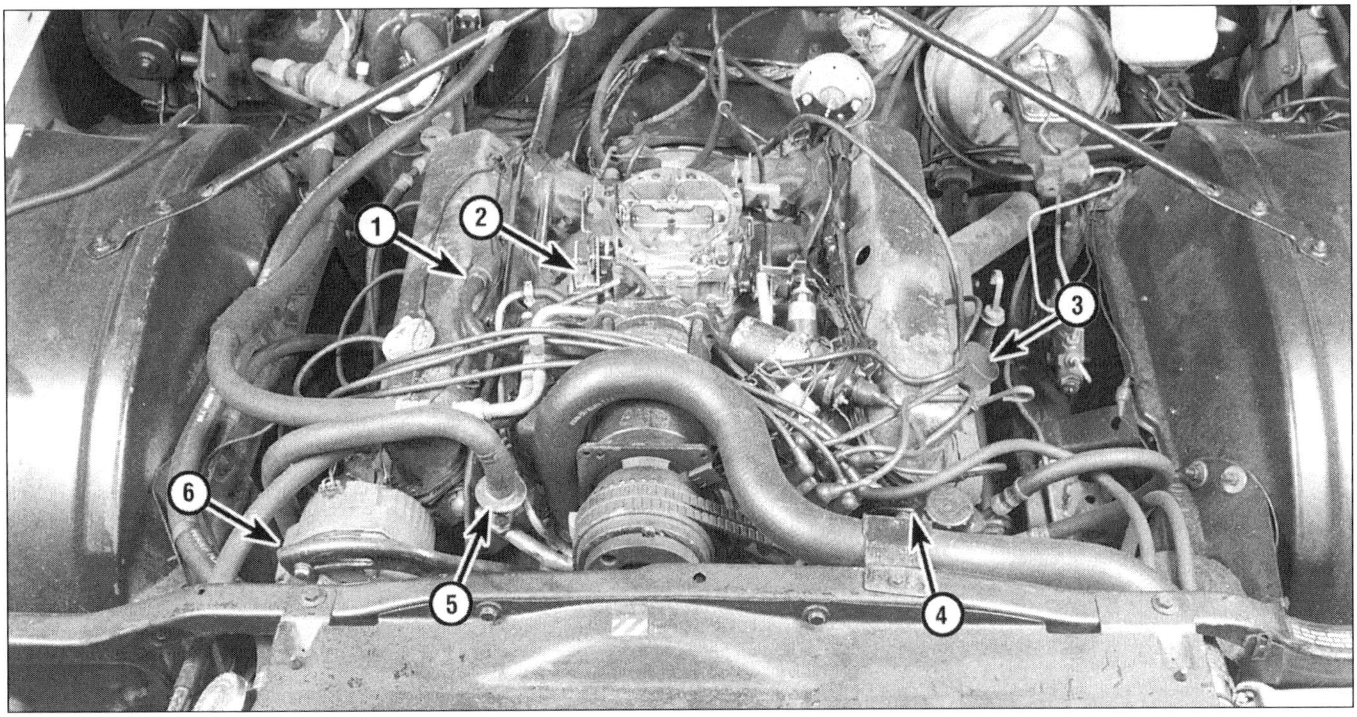

1.1a Emission and engine control system component locations (typical carbureted model)

1 *PCV valve*
2 *Hot air choke (mounted in intake manifold)*
3 *Heated air Intake duct*
4 *Air injection tube (attached to front of cylinder head)*
5 *Air injection check valve*
6 *Diverter valve and air pump (under alternator)*

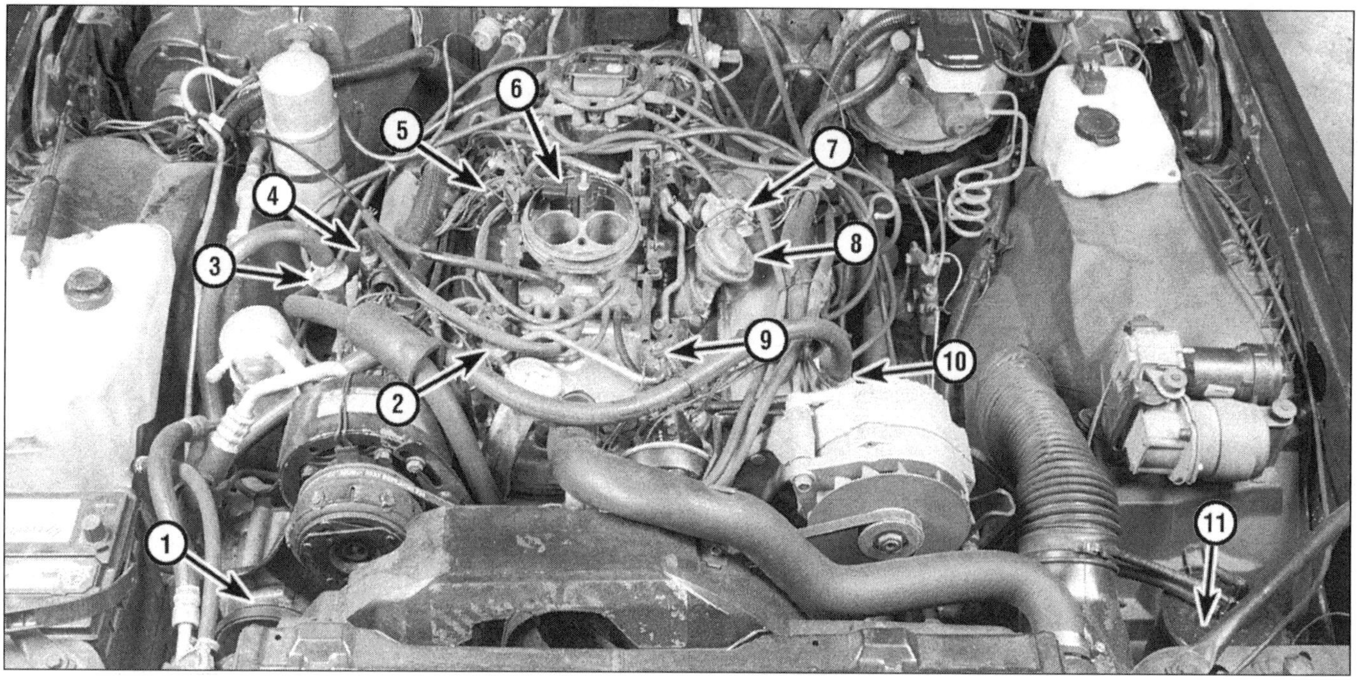

1.1b Emission and engine control system component locations (typical MPFI model)

1 *Air pump*
2 *Fuel pressure regulator*
3 *Air injection check valve*
4 *PCV valve*
5 *EGR control solenoid*
6 *Fast idle control valve*
7 *EGR backpressure transducer*
8 *EGR valve*
9 *Fuel injector*
10 *Air injection check valve*
11 *ECS system charcoal canister*

Before assuming that an emissions control system is malfunctioning, check the fuel and ignition systems carefully. The diagnosis of some emission control devices requires specialized tools, equipment and training. If checking and servicing become too difficult or if a procedure is beyond your ability, consult a dealer service department. This doesn't mean, however, that emission control systems are particularly difficult to maintain and repair. You can quickly and easily perform many checks and do most of the regular maintenance at home with common tune-up and hand tools. **Note:** *Because of a Federally mandated extended warranty which covers the emission control system components, check with your dealer about warranty coverage before working on any emissions-related*

1.1c Emission and engine control system component locations (typical TBI model)

1 *Air injection system pump (located under alternator)*
2 *Air control solenoid*
3 *Air switching valve*
4 *Divert solenoid*
5 *EGR valve*
6 *Fuel injectors*
7 *Heated air intake duct*
8 *ECS system charcoal canister*

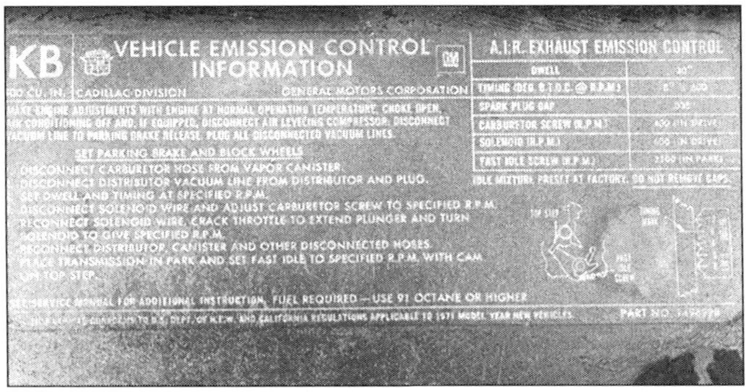

1.5a The Vehicle Emission Control Information (VECI) label is located in the engine compartment on the radiator support and contains information on the emission devices and emissions-related adjustments

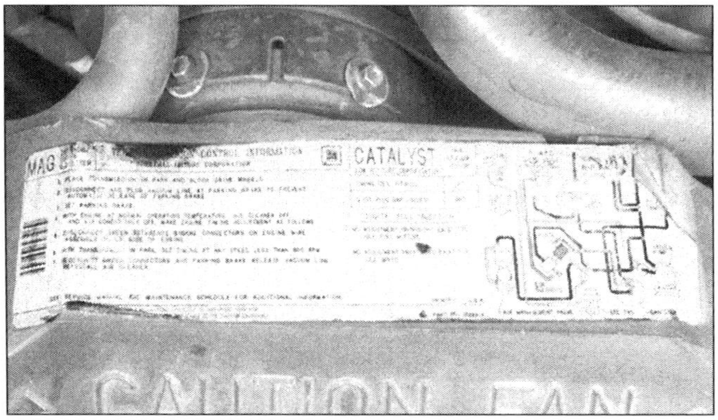

1.5b Many later VECI labels, such as this one, also include a vacuum hose routing diagram

systems. Once the warranty has expired, you may wish to perform some of the component checks and/or replacement procedures in this Chapter to save money.

Pay close attention to any special precautions outlined in this Chapter. It should be noted that the illustrations of the various systems may not exactly match the system installed on your vehicle because of changes made by the manufacturer during production or from year to year. Remember - the most frequent cause of emissions problems is simply a loose or broken vacuum hose or wire, so always check the hose and wiring connections first.

The VECI label is located in the engine compartment **(see illustrations)**. This label contains important emissions specifications and adjustment information, and a vacuum hose routing and emission component location schematic. When servicing the engine or emissions systems, the VECI label in your particular vehicle should always be checked for up-to-date information.

2 Air Injection Reactor (AIR) system

General description

Refer to illustrations 2.3 and 2.4

1 The Air Injection Reactor (AIR) system reduces hydrocarbons in the exhaust by pumping additional oxygen into the exhaust port of the cylinder head, exhaust manifold, or the catalytic converter. The oxygen-rich air helps combust the unburned hydrocarbons before they are expelled as exhaust.

2 The AIR system operates at all engine speeds, but it bypasses air for a short time during deceleration and at high speeds, because air added to the over-rich fuel/air mixture present in the exhaust during these conditions can cause backfiring or popping through the exhaust.

2.3 Layout of the AIR system on an MPFI engine

A Check valves
B Air pump
C Air diverter valve
D Manifold and injection tubes

3 The AIR system consists of an engine-driven injection pump at the front of the engine, air diverter valve attached to the pump housing **(see illustration)**, the manifold and injection tubes running into each port at the exhaust manifolds, and a check valve for each hose between the pump and the injection tubes on either side of the engine.

4 Later versions of the AIR system **(see illustration)** are under ECM control:

a) *When the engine is cold, the ECM energizes an AIR control solenoid. This allows air to flow to an AIR switching valve. The AIR switching valve is energized to direct air to the exhaust ports.*
b) *On a warm engine, or in "closed loop" mode, the ECM de-energizes the AIR switching valve, directing air between the beds of the catalytic converter. This provides extra oxygen for the oxidizing catalyst to decrease HC and CO levels, while keeping oxygen levels low in the first bed of the converter. This enables the reducing catalyst to effectively decrease the levels of oxides of nitrogen (NOx).*
c) *If the AIR control valve detects a rapid increase in manifold vacuum (deceleration) certain operating modes (wide open throttle, for example), or the ECM*

2.4 Layout of the AIR system on a typical TBI model

A Divert solenoid
B Air switching valve
C Air control solenoid
D Air pump (underneath alternator)

2.6a Remove the bolts that retain the front pulley to the air pump

2.6b Remove the pulley and then the plastic air filter element from the pump

2.7a Loosen the clamp and remove the hose from the check valve

self-diagnostic system detects a problem in the C3 or C4 system, air is diverted (divert mode) to the air cleaner or directly to the atmosphere.

d) The divert mode prevents backfiring through the exhaust system. Throttle closure at deceleration creates a fuel-air mixture which is temporarily too rich to burn completely. This mixture, when it reaches the exhaust, becomes burnable when combined with injected air. The next spark would ignite this mixture, causing an exhaust backfire, but momentary diverting of injected air prevents it.

e) The air flow and control hoses transmit pressurized air to the catalytic converter or to the exhaust ports via internal passages in the intake manifold, or through external firing.

f) The check valve prevents backflow of exhaust gas into the AIR distribution system. The valve prevents backflow when the air pump bypasses at high speeds and loads, or when the air pump malfunctions.

Checking

Refer to illustrations 2.6a, 2.6b, 2.7a, 2.7b and 2.10

Note: *The following checks generally apply to all AIR systems. However, where ECM controlled systems differ in design from older types, diagnosis is beyond the scope of the home mechanic.*

5 Properly installed and adjusted air injection systems are fairly reliable and seldom cause problems. However, a malfunctioning system can cause engine surge, backfiring and over-heated spark plugs or catalytic converters. The air pump is the most critical component of this system and the belt at the front of the engine which drives the pump should be your first check. If the belt is cracked or frayed, replace it with a new one. Check the tension of the drive belt by pressing it with your finger. There should be about 1/2-inch of play in the belt when pushed halfway between the pulleys. If the belt is too loose, adjust it (see Chapter 1).

6 Check the condition of the air pump filter. Remove the bolts that secure the pulley to the air pump **(see illustration)**. Remove the plastic filter element and inspect it for excessive dirt and clogged passages. Replace it with a new filter if necessary **(see illustration)**.

7 To check for proper air delivery from the pump, follow the hoses from the pump to where they meet the injection tube/manifold assembly on each side of the engine. Loosen the clamps and disconnect the hoses **(see illustration)**. Start the engine and, with your fingers or a piece of paper, verify that air is flowing out of these hoses **(see illustration)**. Accelerate the engine and observe the air flow, which should increase in relation to engine speed. If this is the case, the pump is working satisfactorily. If air flow was not present, or did not increase, check for crimps in the hoses, proper drivebelt tension and for a leaking diverter valve, which can be heard with the pump operating.

2.7b Start the engine and use your thumb to verify that air is being pumped through the hoses. Accelerate the engine - airflow should increase with engine speed. If it does, the pump is working. If there is no airflow from the pump, check for crimps in the hoses, a loose drivebelt or a leaky diverter valve

2.10 The best method to check for vacuum to the diverter valve is to use a vacuum gauge

8 To check the diverter valve, sometimes called the "gulp" valve or anti-backfire valve, make sure all hoses are connected and start the engine. Locate the muffler on the valve, which is a canister unit with holes in it.

9 Being careful not to touch any of the moving engine components, place your hand near the muffler outlet holes and check that no air is escaping with the engine at idle speed. Now have an assistant depress the accelerator pedal to accelerate the engine and then quickly let off the pedal. A momentary blast of air should be felt discharging through the diverter valve muffler.

10 If no air discharge was felt, disconnect the smaller vacuum hose at the diverter valve. Place your finger over the end of the hose and again have your assistant depress the accelerator and let it off. As the engine is decelerating, a vacuum should be felt **(see illustration)**. If vacuum was felt, replace the diverter valve with a new one. If no vacuum was felt, the vacuum hose or engine vacuum source is plugged, requiring a thorough

2.36 To remove the injector tubes, detach the delivery hoses at the check valves, loosen the threaded connectors on the exhaust manifold at each exhaust port (use a flare-nut wrench), slide the connectors up on the injection tubes so the threads are out of the exhaust manifold and pull the injection tube/air manifold assembly from the engine exhaust manifold. On some models the injector tubes will slide out of the exhaust manifold with the assembly

cleaning to eliminate the problem.

11 Two check valves are located on the air manifold assembly. Their function is to prevent exhaust gases from flowing back into the air pump. To find out if they are functioning properly, disconnect the two air supply hoses where they attach to the check valves. Start the engine and, being careful not to touch any moving engine components, place your hand or a piece of paper over the outlet of the check valve (be careful - if exhaust gas leaks out, it will be hot). No exhaust should flow out of the check valve. The valve can be further checked by turning off the engine, allowing it to cool, and orally blowing through the check valve (toward the air manifold). Then attempt to blow through it in the other direction. If the valve is allowing you to blow through it backwards, it is faulty and should be replaced.

12 Another check for this system is for leaks in the hose connection and/or hoses themselves. Leaks can often be detected by sound or feel with the pump in operation. If a leak is suspected, use a soapy water solution to verify this. Pour or sponge the solution of detergent and water on the hoses and connections. With the pump running, bubbles will form if a leak exists. The air delivery hoses are of a special design to withstand engine temperatures, so if they are replaced make sure the new hoses are of the proper standards.

Component replacement

Air pump

13 As mentioned earlier, some air pumps share a common drivebelt with the alternator while others use their own belt. The particular

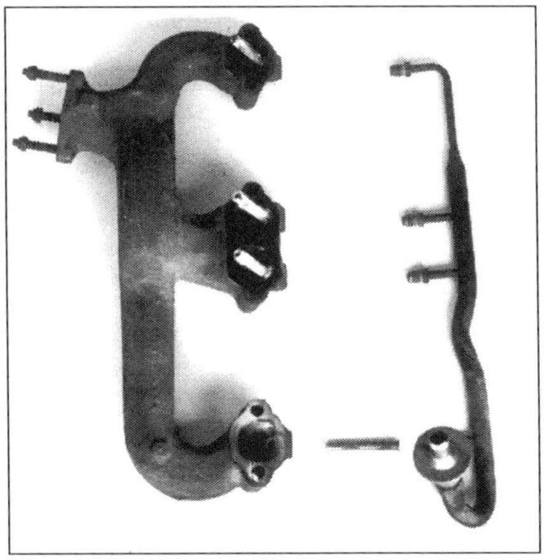

2.38 Internal extension tubes must be pressed out, after the exhaust manifold is removed from the engine

layout on the vehicle being serviced will affect the removal and installation procedure somewhat.

14 Disconnect the air delivery hoses at the air pump. Note the position of each hose for assembly.

15 Disconnect the vacuum source hose at the diverter valve.

16 Compress the drivebelt to keep the air pump pulley from turning, and remove the bolts and washers securing the pulley to the pump.

17 To get some slack in the belt, loosen the alternator adjusting bolt and the pivot bolt. Push the alternator inward until the belt and air pump pulley can be removed from the pump.

18 Remove the bolts which secure the air pump to its brackets and then lift the pump and diverter valve assembly from the engine compartment. On some models it may be necessary to first remove the pulley.

19 If the diverter valve is to be installed onto the new air pump, remove the bolts securing it to the pump and separate the two components.

20 Check the pump for evidence that exhaust gas has entered it, indicating a failure of one or both check valves.

21 Install the diverter valve to the new air pump using a new gasket. Tighten the attaching bolts securely.

22 Install the air pump to its engine mounting brackets with the attaching bolts loose. The exception to this is on models where the mounting bolts are inaccessible with the pulley installed. In this case, the pump mounting bolts should be tightened securely at this point.

23 Install the pump pulley with the bolts, only hand tight at this time.

24 Place the drive belt into position on the air pump pulley and adjust the belt by gently prying on the alternator until about 1/2-inch of play is felt in the belt when pushed with your fingers half-way between the pulleys. Tighten the alternator bolts, keeping the belt tension at this point.

25 Keep the pump pulley from turning by compressing the drive belt and tighten the pulley bolts securely.

26 Connect the hoses to the air pump and diverter valve. Make sure the connections are tight.

27 Tighten the mounting bolts for the pump securely.

28 Check the operation of the air pump as outlined previously.

Diverter valve

29 Disconnect the vacuum signal line and air delivery hoses at the diverter valve. Note the position of each for assembly.

30 Remove the bolts which secure the valve to the air pump and remove the diverter valve from the engine compartment.

31 When purchasing a new diverter or bypass valve, keep in mind that, although many of the valves are similar in appearance, each is designed to meet particular requirements of various engines. Therefore, be sure to install the correct valve.

32 Install the new diverter valve to the air pump or pump extension with a new gasket. Tighten the securing bolts.

33 Connect the air delivery and vacuum source hoses and check the operation of the valve as outlined previously.

Air manifold and/or injection tubes

Refer to illustrations 2.36 and 2.38

34 Due to the high temperatures at this area, the connections at the exhaust manifold may be difficult to loosen. Commercial penetrating oil applied to the thread of the injection tubes may help in the removal procedure.

35 Disconnect the air delivery hoses at the manifold check valves.

36 Loosen the threaded connectors on the exhaust manifold at each exhaust port **(see illustration)**. Slide the connectors upwards on the injection tubes so the threads are out of the exhaust manifold. On models with an AIR manifold running between the cylinder heads, remove the accessories on the front of the engine that are in the way, then remove the clamp bolt and clamp from the front of each cylinder head.

37 Pull the injection tube/air manifold assembly from the engine exhaust manifold (or cylinder heads) and out of the engine compartment. Depending on the model year, injection tube extensions leading inside the engine may come out with the assembly.

38 On models where the extension tubes remain inside the exhaust manifold, they must be pressed out after the exhaust manifold is removed from the engine **(see illustration)**. On models with the head-to-head type of AIR manifold, remove the seals from the holes in the cylinder heads and install new ones.

39 If the exhaust manifold was removed from the engine to clean or replace the extensions, reinstall the manifold with extensions to the engine, using a new gasket. Tighten the bolts to the torque listed in the Chapter 2

2.44 Use backup wrenches to remove the check valve from the threaded fittings. Be sure not to bend or twist the manifold while loosening the check valve

Specifications Section.

40 Thread each of the injection tube connectors loosely into the exhaust manifold, using an anti-seize compound on the threads. After each of the connectors is sufficiently started, tighten each securely.

41 Connect the air supply hoses to the check valves.

42 Start the engine and check for leaks as previously described.

Check valve

Refer to illustration 2.44

43 Disconnect the air supply hose at the check valve.

44 Using two wrenches on the flats provided, remove the check valve from the air manifold assembly **(see illustration)**. Be careful not to bend or twist the delicate manifold or injection tubes as this is done.

45 Installation is a reversal of the removal procedure.

3 Inlet air temperature control system

General description

1 Various versions of this system go by different names, but their purpose is always the same - to improve engine efficiency and reduce hydrocarbon emissions during the initial warm-up period of the vehicle.

2 Two basic methods are used to achieve this goal:

a) *Forced air pre-heat system: Some form of exhaust valve is incorporated inside the exhaust pipe to recirculate warm exhaust gases which are then used to pre-heat the carburetor and choke.*

b) *Warm air from the exhaust manifold is routed into the air cleaner, then through the carburetor.*

3 This system has its greatest effect on engine performance and emissions output during the first few miles of driving (depending on the outside temperature). Once the engine reaches its normal operating temperature, the flapper valves in the exhaust pipe and air cleaner open, allowing for normal engine operation.

3.10 Locate the actuator and rod assembly (arrow) on the heat valve

4 Because of this cold-engine-only function, it is important to periodically check this system to prevent poor cold engine performance and overheating of the fuel mixture once the engine has reached operating temperatures. If either the exhaust heat valve or air cleaner valve sticks in the 'no heat' position, the engine will run poorly, stall and waste gas until it has warmed up on its own. A valve sticking in the 'heat' position causes the engine to run as if it is out of tune, because of the constant flow of hot air to the carburetor.

5 The main component of the initial system is a heat valve inside the exhaust pipe on the right side of the engine (called a heat riser on early models). In 1975, General Motors introduced a new inlet air temperature control system known as the Early Fuel Evaporation (EFE) system. It also has a valve in the exhaust pipe, but uses manifold vacuum to actuate the valve. Instead of a spring and weight, an actuator and Thermal Vacuum Switch TVS control the heat valve. A Thermostatic Air Cleaner (TAC or THERMAC) consisting of a temperature sensor, vacuum diaphragm and heat stove completes the system. Initial checking procedures can be found in Chapter 1.

Checking

Forced air pre-heat system

6 The conventional heat riser, installed on cars built through 1974, should be checked often for free operation (see Chapter 1, Section 25 for the check procedure). Because of the high exhaust temperatures and its location, which is open to the elements, corrosion frequently keeps the valve from operating freely, or even freezes it in position.

7 To check the heat riser operation, locate it on the exhaust manifold (it can be identified by an external weight and spring), and with the engine cold, try moving the counterweight. The valve should move freely with no binding. Now have an assistant start the engine (still cold) while the counterweight is observed. The valve should move to the closed position and then slowly open as the engine warms.

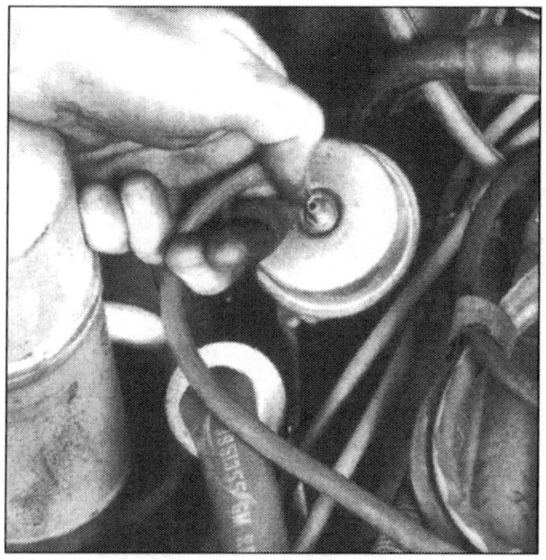

3.11 If the actuator rod is not working properly, you can check the EFE system by disconnecting the vacuum hose at the actuator and placing your thumb over the end - with the engine cold and at idle, you should feel suction indicating proper vacuum - if you do, replace the actuator

8 A stuck or binding heat riser valve can usually be loosened by soaking the valve shaft with solvent as the counterweight is moved back and forth. Light taps with a hammer may be necessary to free a tightly stuck valve. If this proves unsuccessful, the heat riser must be replaced with a new one after disconnecting it from the exhaust pipe.

Early Fuel Evaporation (EFE) System

Refer to illustrations 3.10 and 3.11

9 In 1975, General Motors introduced a replacement for the heat riser known as the Early Fuel Evaporation (EFE) system. The EFE system performs the same function as the heat riser but uses manifold vacuum to open and close the heat valve. Some vehicles are equipped with an electrical type EFE, which uses a heater grid located underneath the primary base of the carburetor.

10 To check the EFE system, locate the actuator and rod assembly **(see illustration)** which is located on a bracket attached to the right exhaust manifold. Have an assistant start the engine (it must be cold). Observe the movement of the actuator rod which leads to the heat valve inside the exhaust pipe. It should immediately operate the valve to the closed position. If it does, the system is operating correctly.

11 If the actuator rod doesn't move, disconnect the vacuum hose at the actuator and place your thumb over the open end **(see illustration)**. With the engine cold and at idle, you should feel a suction, indicating proper

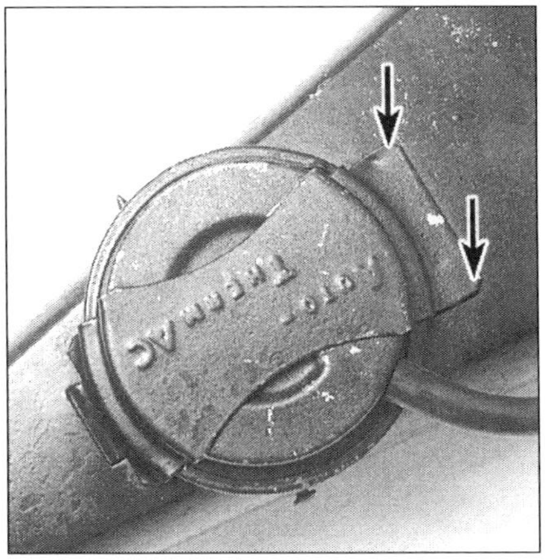

3.35 To remove the vacuum motor, label and detach the hoses, then drill out the spot welds (arrows), slide out the retaining strap, lift up the motor and tilt it to one side to unhook the linkage at the control damper assembly

vacuum. If there is vacuum at this point, replace the actuator with a new one.

12 If there is no vacuum in the line, this is an indication that either the hose is crimped or plugged, or the thermal vacuum switch threaded into the water outlet is not functioning properly. Replace the hose or switch as necessary.

13 To make sure the Early Fuel Evaporation System is disengaging once the engine has warmed, continue to observe the actuating rod as the engine reaches normal operating temperature (approximately 180-degrees depending on engine size). The rod should again move, indicating the valve is in the open position.

14 If, after the engine has warmed, the valve does not open, disconnect the vacuum hose at the actuator and check for vacuum with your thumb. If there is no vacuum, replace the actuator. If there is vacuum, replace the TVS switch on the water outlet housing.

Thermostatic Air Cleaner (TAC/THERMAC)

15 THERMAC components can be quickly and easily checked for proper operation, (see Chapter 1 for routine checking procedures and illustrations).

16 With the engine off, observe the damper door inside the air cleaner snorkel. If this is difficult because of the direction in which the snorkel is pointing, use a small mirror. The valve should be open (all air flows through the snorkel and none through the exhaust manifold hot-air duct at the underside of the air cleaner housing).

17 Have an assistant start the engine while you observe the flapper door inside the snorkel. With the engine cold and at idle, the damper door should close off all air from the snorkel, allowing heated air from the exhaust manifold to enter the air cleaner intake. As the engine warms to operating temperature, the damper door should move, allowing outside air through the snorkel to be included in the mixture. Eventually, the door should recede to the point where most of the incoming air is through the snorkel and not the exhaust manifold passage.

3.44 Remove the metal tabs that locate the sensor onto the air cleaner

18 If the damper door does not close off the snorkel to outside air when the cold engine is first started, disconnect the vacuum hose at the snorkel vacuum motor, place your thumb over the hose end and check for vacuum. If there is vacuum to the motor, verify that the damper door and link are not frozen or binding within the air cleaner snorkel. Replace the vacuum motor if the hose routing is correct and the damper door moves freely.

19 If there is no vacuum to the motor in the above test, check the hoses for cracks, crimps or disconnections. If the hoses are clear and in good condition, replace the temperature sensor inside the air cleaner housing.

Component replacement

Actuator and rod assembly

20 Disconnect the vacuum hose from the actuator.

21 Remove the two nuts which attach the actuator to the bracket.

22 Disconnect the rod from the heat valve and remove the actuator and rod from the engine compartment.

23 Installation is the reverse of removal.

Exhaust heat valve

24 Remove the crossover exhaust pipe.

25 Disconnect the actuating rod from the heat valve.

26 Remove the valve from inside the exhaust pipe.

27 Installation is the reverse of removal.

Thermal vacuum switch (TVS)

28 Drain the engine coolant until the fluid level is below the engine water outlet (thermostat) housing. (On some V6 models, the TVS is located on the intake manifold).

29 Disconnect the hoses from the TVS switch. Note their positions for reassembly.

30 Using a suitable wrench, remove the TVS switch.

31 Apply a soft setting sealant uniformly to the threads of the new TVS switch. Make sure that none of the sealant gets on the sensor end of the switch.

32 Install the switch and tighten it securely.

33 Connect the vacuum hoses to the switch in their original positions and add coolant as necessary.

Air cleaner vacuum motor

Refer to illustration 3.35

34 Remove the air cleaner assembly from the engine and disconnect the vacuum hose from the motor.

35 Drill out the two spot welds **(see illustration)** which secure the vacuum motor retaining strap to the snorkel tube.

36 Remove the motor attaching strap.

37 Lift up the motor, cocking it to one side to unhook the motor linkage at the control damper assembly.

38 To install, drill a 7/64-inch hole in the snorkel tube at the center of the retaining strap.

39 Insert the vacuum motor linkage into the control damper assembly.

40 Using sheetmetal screws, attach the motor and retaining strap to the snorkel. Make sure the sheet metal screws do not interfere with the operation of the damper door.

41 Connect the vacuum hose to the motor and install the air cleaner assembly.

Air cleaner temperature sensor

Refer to illustration 3.44

42 Remove the air cleaner from the engine and disconnect the vacuum hoses at the sensor.

43 Carefully note the position of the sensor. The new sensor must be installed in exactly the same position.

44 Pry up the tabs on the sensor retaining clip and remove the sensor and clip from the air cleaner **(see illustration)**.

45 Install the new sensor with a new gasket in the same position as the old one.

46 Press the retaining clip on the sensor, taking care not to damage the control mechanism in the center of the sensor.

47 Connect the vacuum hoses and install the air cleaner on the engine.

4 Computer Controlled Catalytic Converter (C4)/ Computer Command Control (C3) systems (1980 and later models) - description and code access

General description

1 The C4 system first became available on 1980 models. In 1981, the C4 system was replaced by the Computer Command Control (C3) System. Both systems control exhaust

emissions while retaining driveability by maintaining a continuous interaction between all of the emissions systems on your vehicle. A malfunction in the system is signaled by a CHECK ENGINE or SERVICE SOON light on the dash. On the C4 system, the CHECK ENGINE or SERVICE SOON light will remain on as long as the engine is running. With the diagnostic system activated, this same lamp will flash the trouble code related to the cause of the malfunction. On the C3 system, the CHECK ENGINE or SERVICE SOON light will remain on until the problem is identified and repaired and the code is erased from memory. In other words, the C3 system stores trouble codes in its memory, but the C4 system doesn't. **Note 1:** *C4 systems are capable of self diagnostics but because they are equipped with short term memory, the codes must be accessed immediately and with the engine running before they are lost.* **Note 2:** *Some models are equipped with the Automatic Climate Control system that allows the home mechanic to access trouble codes using the buttons and display screen.*

2 The C4/C3 System requires special tools for maintenance and repair, so most service work on it should be left to your dealer or a qualified technician. Although it seems complex, the system is easily understood in terms of its various components and their functions.

Electronic control module (ECM)

3 The electronic control module (ECM) is essentially a small on-board computer (located under the dash on most vehicles) which monitors numerous engine functions and controls many engine-related systems. The ECM contains a Programmable Read Only Memory (PROM) calibration unit which tailors each ECM's performance to conform to the vehicle. The PROM is programmed with the vehicle's particular design, weight, axle ratio, etc., and cannot be used in another ECM in a car which differs in any way.

4 The ECM receives continuous data from the various information sensors, processes it in accordance with PROM instructions, then sends electronic signals to system components, modifying their performance (see next Section).

Oxygen (O_2) sensor

5 The oxygen sensor is mounted in the exhaust pipe, upstream of the catalytic converter. It monitors the exhaust stream and sends information to the ECM on how much oxygen is present. The oxygen level is determined by how rich or lean the fuel mixture is.

Mixture Control (M/C) solenoid (feedback carburetor systems only)

6 The M/C solenoid controls the fuel flow through the carburetor idle and main metering circuits. The solenoid cycles ten times per second, constantly adjusting the fuel/air mixture. The ECM energizes the solenoid to keep emissions within limits based on information it receives from the oxygen sensor.

Coolant temperature sensor

7 This sensor monitors coolant temperature and sends this information to the ECM. The ECM alters the air/fuel ratio accordingly for conditions such as cold starting. The ECM also performs various switching functions on the EGR, EFE and AIR management systems, depending on engine temperature. This feedback from the coolant sensor can also activate the hot temperature light.

Pressure sensors

8 The ECM uses information from the Barometric Pressure Sensor (BARO) and Manifold Absolute Pressure (MAP) sensor to adjust engine performance. The BARO sensor senses ambient pressure changes that occur as a result of changes in the weather and the altitude of the vehicle. It then sends an electronic signal to the ECM that is used to adjust the air-fuel ratio and spark timing.

9 The MAP sensor measures changes in manifold pressure and provides this information to the ECM. The pressure changes reflect the need for adjustments in air-fuel mixture, spark timing (EST), etc., that are needed to maintain good vehicle performance under various driving conditions.

10 The MAP sensor and BARO sensor on TBI systems is located near the glovebox, tucked in the corner under the dash. The MAP and BARO sensor on the MPFI system is an integral part of the ECM. Vacuum is routed from the throttle body, through the dash and directly to the ECM.

Manifold Air Temperature (MAT) sensor

11 The MAT sensor, mounted on the intake manifold ahead of the throttle body, measures the temperature of the incoming air/fuel mixture and sends this information to the ECM. When it senses a low temperature, its resistance is high. When it senses a high temperature, its resistance is low.

Throttle position sensor (TPS)

12 Mounted on the carburetor body, the TPS is actuated by the throttle plate and sends a variable voltage signal to the ECM: when the throttle plate is closed, the voltage signal is low, but as the throttle plate is opened, the voltage increases. The ECM uses this voltage signal to recognize throttle position.

Idle speed control (ISC) motor

13 The idle speed control motor maintains a low idle speed without stalling under changing conditions. The ECM controls the idle speed control motor on the carburetor to adjust the idle.

Electronic spark timing (EST)

14 The High Energy Ignition (HEI) distributor used with the C4/C3 system does not use centrifugal or vacuum advance. Spark timing is controlled electronically by the ECM, except under certain conditions, such as cranking the engine.

Transmission Converter Clutch/Torque Converter Clutch (TCC)

15 The ECM controls an electric solenoid mounted in the automatic transmission. When the vehicle reaches a specified speed, the ECM energizes the solenoid and allows the torque converter to mechanically couple the engine to the transmission. When operating conditions indicate the transmission should operate as a normal, fluid-coupled transmission (deceleration, passing, etc.), the solenoid is de-energized. The transmission also returns to normal (fluid-coupled) automatic operation when the brake pedal is depressed.

Air Injection Reactor (AIR)

16 When the engine is cold, the ECM energizes an air switching valve which allows air to flow to the exhaust ports to lower carbon monoxide (CO) and hydrocarbon (HC) levels in the exhaust.

Exhaust gas recirculation (EGR)

17 The ECM controls ported vacuum to the EGR with a solenoid valve. When the engine is cold, the solenoid is energized to block vacuum to the EGR valve until the engine is warm.

Evaporative emission system (ECS/EECS)

18 When the engine is cold or idling, the ECM solenoid blocks vacuum to the valve at the top of the charcoal canister. When the engine is warm and at a specified rpm, the ECM de-energizes the valve, releasing the collected vapors into the intake manifold.

Early fuel evaporation (EFE)

19 The ECM controls a valve which shuts off the system until the engine is warm.

C4/C3 system trouble codes

20 The C4/C3 system is analogous to the central nervous system in the human body. The sensors (nerve endings) constantly relay information to the ECM (brain), which processes the data and, if necessary, sends out a command to change the operating parameters of the engine (body). Here's a specific example of how one portion of this system operates: An oxygen sensor, located in the exhaust manifold, constantly monitors the oxygen content of the exhaust gas. If the percentage of oxygen in the exhaust gas is incorrect, an electrical signal is sent to the ECM. The ECM takes this information, processes it and then sends a command to the fuel injection system, telling it to change the air/fuel mixture. This happens in a fraction of a second and it goes on continuously when the engine is running. The end result is an air/fuel mixture ratio which is constantly maintained at a predetermined ratio, regardless of driving conditions.

21 One might think that a system which uses an on-board computer and electrical

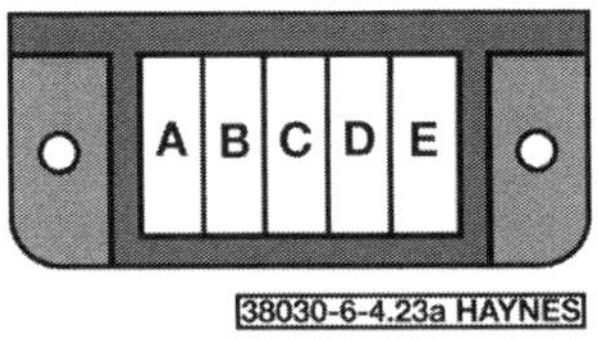

4.23a On 1981 and 1982 carbureted models, connect a jumper wire between terminals D and E on the diagnostic connector to read trouble codes

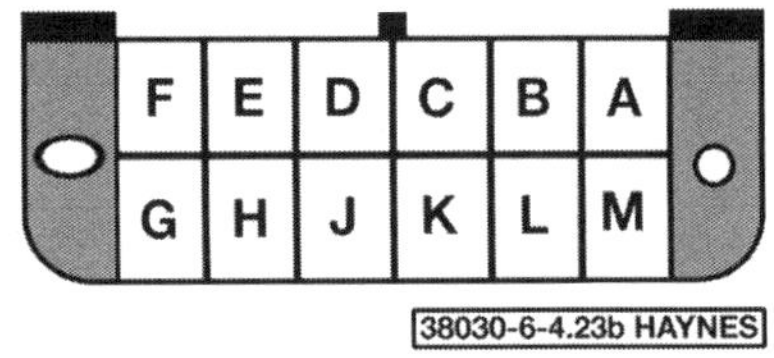

4.23b On 1983 and later carbureted models, connect a jumper wire between terminals A and B of the diagnostic connector to read trouble codes

4.26 On models with TBI fuel injection, press the OFF and WARMER buttons on the climate control system simultaneously to begin the diagnostic sequence. The trouble codes will appear on the digital display

sensors would be difficult to diagnose. This is not necessarily the case. The C4/C3 system has a built-in diagnostic feature which indicates a problem by flashing a CHECK ENGINE or SERVICE SOON light on the instrument panel. When this light comes on during normal vehicle operation, a fault in one of the information sensor circuits or the ECM itself has been detected. More importantly, the source of the malfunction is stored in the ECM's memory. **Note 1:** *Later models are equipped with the "SERVICE NOW" dash light which indicates a Hard Code or an immediate failure in the system.*

Accessing trouble codes

Refer to illustrations 4.23a, 4.23b and 4.26

22 Various trouble code access procedures are used on these models, depending on the fuel system used. When the ECM sets a trouble code, the light will come on and a trouble code will be stored in memory. If the problem is intermittent, the light will go out after ten seconds, when the fault goes away. On 1983 and later models, the trouble code will stay in the ECM memory until the battery voltage to the ECM is interrupted.

307 (5.0L) and 350 (5.7L) Oldsmobile-built V8's and all V6's

Note: *1980 Cadillac 5.7L engines with Multi-Port Fuel Injection (MPFI) do not store trouble codes.*

23 These engines all use feedback carburetors. To access the trouble codes on these models, you must ground a diagnostic terminal to put the ECM in diagnostic mode. **Note:** *The computer on 1980 through 1982 models does not possess long-term memory. Once the CHECK ENGINE or SERVICE SOON light appears on the dash, it will be necessary to access the trouble codes without turning the engine off or the trouble codes will erase.*

On ***1980 models****, locate a green connector in the wiring harness coming directly out of the ECM (the ECM is located under the dash, on the passenger's side, behind the glove box). With the engine running, connect the single terminal in this connector to a good chassis ground.*

1981 and 1982 models *use a 5-pin Assembly Line Diagnostic Link (ALDL), located under the dash, just below the instrument panel. Attach one end of a short jumper wire to terminal D and the other end to terminal E while the engine is running* **(see illustration).**

1983 and later models *use a 12-pin ALDL located under the dash on the driver's side kick* panel **(see illustration)**. *Connect a jumper wire between terminals A and B to enter the diagnostic mode. Install the jumper wire with the ignition OFF and once the jumper wire is installed, turn the ignition key to ON (engine not running).*

24 When the diagnostic mode has been entered, the ECM will display a Code 12 by flashing the CHECK ENGINE, SERVICE ENGINE SOON or SERVICE NOW light. A Code 12 is simply one flash, followed by a brief pause, then two flashes in quick succession. This code will be flashed three times. If no other codes are stored, Code 12 will continue to flash until the diagnostic terminal ground is removed.

25 After flashing Code 12 three times, the ECM will display any stored trouble codes. Each code will be flashed three times, then Code 12 will be flashed again, indicating that the display of any stored trouble codes has been completed.

HT4100 and 368 (6.0 liter) Cadillac-manufactured V8 engines

26 These models are equipped with Cadillac's throttle-body fuel injection system, referred to as Digital Fuel Injection. This system can be accessed using the Automatic Climate Control panel. Turn the ignition key ON (engine not running). Simultaneously press the OFF and WARMER buttons on the Automatic Climate Control panel **(see illustration)**. Wait until two quotation marks are visible on the display screen. Shortly thereafter "-1.8.8"" will be displayed. Code -1.8.8 indicates the beginning of the diagnostic trouble codes. Also, the purpose of code -1.8.8 is to verify that the numbers will be displayed in their entirety. If code 38 or 31 appear, the display lights are not functioning properly, leading to code misinterpretation. Trouble codes will be displayed numerically from the lowest denominations to the highest. The code numbers will not flash but instead they will cycle again and repeat themselves for review. After the codes have been repeated three complete times, code .7.0 will appear. This indicates the start of the switch tests. **Note:** *On the third pass only, hard trouble codes will be displayed. These codes indicate an immediate trouble area that keeps the "SERVICE" light on continuously. If no codes are displayed during the third pass, the "SERVICE" light should be off.*

27 Once code .7.0 is displayed, the system is ready to access hard trouble codes. Here the operator can access several different levels of information. These are the choices.

A........ Switch tests
B........ Engine data display
C .... Output cycling tests
D .... Fixed spark mode
E........ Exit diagnostics or Clear codes

28 The following procedure describes the method to enter the Switch Test mode.

1) *First step on the brake pedal and observe code .7.1. If the code does not change, the brake circuit to the ECM is not operating properly.*
2) *Next, step on the brake pedal again and observe the code .7.2. This checks the cruise control brake circuit operation.*
3) *Next, step on the accelerator pedal and observe code .7.3. Slowly press the pedal from the idle position to wide open throttle and then slowly release the pedal back down to the idle position. Do not step on the pedal and let it snap back to idle or the necessary information will not be recorded by the ECM.*
4) *Next, shift the transmission lever into drive and then neutral and observe code .7.4. This switch test checks the transmission select signal to the ECM.*
5) *Next, shift the transmission lever into reverse and then into park and observe code .7.5. This switch test checks the operation of the reverse switch.* **Note:** On vehicles not equipped with the cruise control option, the following three codes will be handled differently. *Allow the code to be displayed and wait ten seconds. The next code will be displayed and wait ten seconds again until the computer goes through this empty*

code display until the operator is ready for code .7.8.

6) *Next, switch the cruise control instrument panel switch to ON and back to OFF and observe code .7.6.*
7) *Next, turn the cruise control instrument panel switch ON, depress and release the "set/coast" button and observe code .7.7.*
8) *Next, turn the cruise control instrument panel switch ON, depress and release the "resume/acceleration" switch and observe code .7.8.*
9) *Next, depress and release the "instant/average button" on the Fuel Data panel and observe code .7.9.*
10) *Next, press and release the "reset" button on the Fuel Data panel and observe code .8.0.*
11) *Next, press and release the "outside temperature" button twice and observe the clutch engage and disengage. It may be necessary to start the engine and operate the A/C system in AUTO mode selected on the ECC panel.* **Note:** *Press the "Defogger" button on 1981 models to access this switch test.*
12) *Now, after all switch test codes have been checked, the computer will have checked all the circuits and functions for operation. The tests that did not pass will display themselves one by one starting with the lowest number first. After all the switch test trouble codes have been displayed, the panel will display .0.0 and then .7.0 which is the starting point for the switch test mode. The remaining test modes,* ***Engine data display, Output cycling tests*** *etc, can be accessed from this setting. Because of the complexity of the information and the diagnostic procedures involved with the remaining test modes, have the vehicle diagnosed by a dealer service department.*

Canceling trouble codes

29 On ALDL systems, remove the fuse marked ECM or ECM/BAT for ten seconds or more to clear the codes from the ECM memory. Refer to Chapter 12 for additional information on fuse and relay locations.

30 On Automatic Climate Control systems, press the OFF and HI buttons simultaneously. Hold in this position until .0.0 appears. After a short period, .7.0 will be displayed. Turn the ignition OFF for at least 10 seconds before entering the diagnostic mode again.

Trouble codes

The following is a list of the typical trouble codes which may be encountered while diagnosing these systems. Also included are simplified troubleshooting procedures. If the problem persists after these checks have been made, more detailed service procedures will have to be done by a dealer service department.

Trouble code	Circuit or system	Probable cause
Code 12	Distributor-to-ECM	This is the normal code when the engine isn't running. It is not stored in memory. If additional codes are stored in the ECM, they will appear after this code has flashed three times. If the code appears while the engine is running, no reference pulses from the distributor are reaching the ECM. Check the HEI module and wiring between the associated wiring.
Code 13	Oxygen sensor	The engine must run up to five minutes at part throttle under road load before this code will set. Check for a sticking or misadjusted throttle position sensor. Check the oxygen sensor wires and connectors. Replace the oxygen sensor if necessary (see Section 6).
Code 14	Coolant sensor	This code indicates a shorted coolant sensor circuit. The engine must run up to two minutes before this code will set. If the engine is experiencing overheating problems, the problem must be rectified before continuing. Check all wiring and connectors associated with the coolant temperature sensor. Replace the sensor if necessary.
Code 13 and 14 at same time	Coolant sensor	See Code 43.
Code 15	Coolant sensor circuit	The temperature sensor circuit is open. The engine must run for five minutes under 800 rpm to set this code. See Code 14 probable cause, then check the wiring connections at the ECM.
Code 16	Alternator voltage out of range	See Chapter 5 for alternator checks. Could also be an ECM malfunction.
Code 17	Crank signal circuit	Crank signal circuit shorted. Check 3-amp crank fuse if it's blown, the ECM is probably faulty. If it's not blown, check the wire between the fuse and the orange connector at the ECM for a short to ground.
Code 18	Crank signal circuit	Crank signal circuit open. Check the fuse - if it's blown, repair the short circuit condition in the wire between the ignition switch and the fuse or between the fuse and the ECM. If it's not blown, check the same wires for an open circuit condition. If the circuit is OK, the ECM is probably malfunctioning.
Code 19	Fuel pump circuit	Fuel pump circuit shorted. Check oil pressure switch fuel pump relay and associated wiring harnesses. Check electrical connectors at ECM. May be a faulty ECM.
Code 20	Fuel pump circuit	Check fuel pump fuse, oil pressure switch, fuel pump relay and associated wiring. ECM may be malfunctioning.
Code 21	WOT switch	The Wide Open Throttle (WOT) switch is shorted or the closed throttle switch (if equipped) is open. On some year models, Code 21 may refer to the TPS switch (see below) or to both WOT and TPS switches.
Code 21	TPS switch	Check for a sticking or misadjusted Throttle Position Sensor (TPS) plunger. The engine must run for at least 10 seconds at 800 rpm, or at the specified curb idle, to set the code. Check all wiring and connectors between the TPS and the ECM. Adjust or replace the TPS.

Trouble code	Circuit or system	Probable cause
Code 22	TPS switch	The engine must run 20 seconds at the specified curb idle to set this code. Check the Throttle Position Sensor (TPS) adjustment. Check the ECM connector. Replace the TPS.
Code 23 (Carbureted models)	Mixture control solenoid	Check for an open or grounded mixture control circuit solenoid circuit from the feedback carburetor to the ECM.
Code 23 (TBI models)	EST/bypass circuit problem	Check for an open 'set timing' connector. Check electrical connectors at the distributor and the ECM. Check all associated wiring. Could be defective HEI module or ECM.
Code 24	VSS	A fault in the Vehicle Speed Sensor (VSS) circuit should appear only when the vehicle is in motion and the engine has run at least five minutes. Disregard this code if it is set when the drivewheels are turning. Check the connectors at the ECM. Check the TPS adjustment.
Code 25 (V8-6-4 only)	Modulated displacement failure	Take the vehicle to a dealer service department or other repair shop for diagnosis.
Code 25 (HT4100 only)	EST circuit problem	See TBI code 23.
Code 26	Throttle switch circuit	Throttle switch circuit shorted. Check wiring to TPS. Check wiring and connectors to ECM and firewall connector Could be faulty TPS or ECM.
Code 27	Throttle switch circuit	Throttle switch circuit open. See Code 26.
Code 28	Open fourth gear circuit	Check electrical connectors at transmission. Check wiring between TCC connector and ECM. Could be faulty fourth gear pressure switch or malfunctioning ECM. Take the vehicle to a dealer service department or other repair shop for further diagnosis and possible repair.
Code 28	Idle speed control	Shorted idle speed control (ISC) system. Possible problems include a shorted ISC motor, defective wiring or electrical connectors to the ISC motor or a defective ECM. Go to a dealer service department or other repair shop for further diagnosis and possible repair.
Code 29	ISC motor defective	ISC switch not controlling the idle speed. Have the ISC motor diagnosed by a dealer service department.
Code 29	Shorted fourth gear circuit	Check electrical connectors at transmission. Check wiring between TCC connector and ECM. Could be faulty fourth gear pressure switch or malfunctioning ECM. Take the vehicle to a dealer service department or other repair shop for further diagnosis and possible repair.
Code 30	ISC circuit problem	Check TPS adjustment. Check ISC motor - motor may be burned out or gears may be stripped. Check the wiring between the ISC motor and the ECM. ECM may be defective.
Code 31 (TBI models)	MAP sensor circuit	MAP sensor circuit shorted. Check wiring between the sensor and the ECM. May be faulty MAP sensor or ECM.
Code 32 (carbureted models)	BARO sensor circuit	Baro sensor voltage to ECM indicated low. Check BARO sensor and circuit.
Code 32 (TBI models)	MAP sensor circuit	MAP sensor circuit open. See TBI code 31.
Code 33 (TBI models)	MAP/BARO sensor correlation	Check the wiring between the MAP and BARO sensors and the ECM. Check the hose between the MAP sensor and the manifold. The sensor(s) could be defective or the ECM may be faulty.
Code 34	Vacuum sensor or MAP sensor	This code will set when the signal voltage from the Manifold Absolute Pressure (MAP) sensor circuit signal is too high. The engine must idle for up to five minutes to set this code. The ECM will substitute a fixed MAP value and use the TPS to control fuel delivery. Replace the MAP sensor.
Code 35 (TBI models)	BARO sensor circuit	BARO sensor circuit shorted. Check wiring between BARO sensor and ECM. Could be faulty BARO sensor or defective ECM.
Code 36	BARO sensor circuit	BARO sensor circuit open. See TBI code 35.
Code 37	MAT sensor circuit	MAT sensor circuit shorted. Check wiring between sensor and ECM. Could be faulty MAT sensor or ECM. Remove sensor from intake manifold - if it appears burned, replace it.
Code 38	MAT sensor circuit	MAT sensor circuit open. See above.
Code 39	TCC engagement problem	Check the electrical connectors at the transmission. Check the wiring between the transmission electrical connectors and the ECM. Take the vehicle to a dealer service department or other repair shop.

Trouble code	Circuit or system	Probable cause
Code 41	EST circuit	No distributor reference pulses to the ECM at specified engine vacuum (about 8 inches Hg). This code will store in memory. Also, see below.
Code 42	EST circuit	Electronic Spark Timing bypass circuit or EST circuit is grounded or open. A malfunctioning HEI module can cause this code.
Code 43	ESC unit	The Electronic Spark Control (ESC) retard signal has been on for too long or the voltage is too low.
Code 44	Oxygen sensor	The exhaust is lean. Indicated by the oxygen sensor after the engine has run in closed loop, part throttle at road load up to five minutes. Check the ECM wiring connectors. Check for vacuum leakage at the base gasket, vacuum hoses or the intake manifold gasket. Replace the oxygen sensor.
Code 45	Oxygen sensor	The exhaust is rich. Indicated by the oxygen sensor after the vehicle has run in closed loop, part throttle at road load up to five minutes. Check the evaporative charcoal canister and its components for the presence of fuel. Replace the oxygen sensor. **Note:** *A Code 33 or 34 may also cause a Code 45 - so check them first.*
Code 44 and 45 at same time	Oxygen sensor	Indicates a faulty oxygen sensor circuit.
Code 51	PROM unit	Faulty Programmed Read Only Memory (PROM) or improper PROM installation. Make sure that the PROM or MEM-CAL is properly in the ECM. Replace the PROM or MEM-CAL.
Code 52	ECM unit	Battery power to ECM has been lost. Code should clear when power is restored.
Code 53 (V6 models)	ECM unit	Faulty ECM.
Code 53 (1983 and later HT4100)	Distributor signal interrupt	See code 12.
Code 52 and 53	ECM unit	If the Check Engine light is off, there is an intermittent ECM problem. If the Check Engine light is on, at same time the ECM is faulty. Replace it.
Code 54 (Carbureted models)	Mixture control solenoid	High voltage from M/C solenoid indicated. Check for a shorted solenoid and/or a damaged ECM.
Code 55	ECM or oxygen sensor	Make sure that the ECM ground connectors are tight. If they are, either the ECM or the oxygen sensor is faulty. Replace the ECM and/or the oxygen sensor.
Code 60	Transmission not in DRIVE (cruise control circuit)	Clear the code, drive the vehicle and see if it sets again. If it does, take the vehicle to a dealer service department or other repair shop for further diagnosis.
Code 63	Car and set speed tolerance exceeded (cruise control circuit)	See probable cause for code 60.
Code 64	Car acceleration exceeds normal limits	See probable cause for code 60.
Code 65	Coolant temperature exceeds limit (cruise control circuit)	See probable cause for code 60.
Code 66	Engine rpm exceeds maximum limit (cruise control circuit)	See probable cause for code 60.
Code 67	Short in the RESUME selection	See probable cause for code 60.
Code .7.0	System ready	System ready for further testing.
Code .7.1	Brake light circuit	ECM not receiving brake light signals from the brake light circuit. Check bulbs and brake light circuit for possible broken filaments or damaged harness wires.
Code .7.2	Throttle switch circuit	Check for a binding throttle linkage or stuck ISC plunger. Replace ISC motor. Check wiring from ISC motor to ECM. Could be defective ECM.
Code .7.3	Drive switch circuit	ECM not receiving the signal indicating the transmission is in DRIVE. Check 20 amp body fuse in fuse panel for a blown filament. Check the circuit for the Automatic Door Lock switch.
Code .7.4	Back-up light switch circuit	ECM not receiving the signal that indicates the transmission is in reverse. Check back-up light switch and circuit.
Code .7.5	Cruise ON/OFF circuit test	ECM not receiving the signal that indicates the cruise control system is activated. Check circuit.

Trouble code	Circuit or system	Probable cause
Code .7.6	"Set-Coast" circuit test	ECM not receiving the signal that indicates the Set-Coast button is activated. Check circuit.
Code .7.7	"Resume-Acceleration" circuit test	ECM not receiving the signal that indicates the Resume-Acceleration selection is activated. Check the circuit.
Code .7.8	MPG "Average" circuit defective	Average button on the MPG display is defective Check circuit for shorts or damaged wring.
Code .7.9	MPG "Reset" circuit	Reset button on the MPG display is defective. Check circuit for shorts or damaged wiring.
Code .8.0	A/C clutch circuit test	A/C clutch circuit from the ECM defective or shorted. Check the circuit for shorts or damaged wiring.
Code -1.8.8	Initial stage detection	Code 1.8.8 indicates the start of the trouble code display.
Code .9.0	Engine data display	Code .9.0 indicates the start of the engine data.
Code .9.5	Output cycling or cylinder select	System ready for output cycling or cylinder select.
Code .9.6	Output cycling	System ready for output cycling.
Code .9.7	Cylinder select	System ready for system select.
Code .0.0	All diagnostics complete	Self diagnosis system completes message.

Note: *Where replacement of one of the above systems, units or devices is recommended, it should be recognized that replacement will not always solve the problem. For this reason, you may want to seek professional advice before purchasing any replacement parts.*

5.5a Remove the mounting screws (arrows) and remove the ECM (MPFI system ECM shown)

5.5b Mounting screw locations (arrows) on a typical TBI fuel-injection system ECM

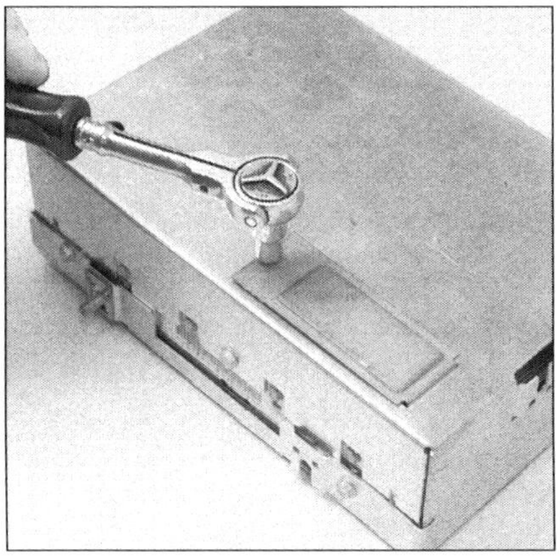

5.10 Remove the PROM cover bolt, then lift the cover off the ECM

5 Electronic Control Module (ECM) and Programmable Read Only Memory (PROM) - removal and installation

ECM

Refer to illustrations 5.5a and 5.5b

1 The Electronic Control Module (ECM) is located under the dash, on the right side, behind the glove box.

2 To remove it, disconnect the negative battery cable from the battery.

3 Remove the screws from the under-dash panel on the right side. Remove the panel (see Chapter 11).

4 Remove the right side kick panel.

5 Remove the retaining bolts **(see illustrations)** and carefully slide the ECM down far enough to disconnect the electrical connectors.

6 Disconnect all the electrical connectors from the ECM. **Caution:** *To prevent electrostatic discharge damage to the ECM, never touch the connector pins or components on the ECM circuit board.*

PROM

7 To allow one model of ECM to be used for many different vehicles, a device called a PROM (Programmable Read Only Memory) is used. To access the PROM, remove the cover. The PROM **(see illustrations 5.5a and 5.5b)** is located inside the ECM and contains information on the vehicle's weight, engine, transmission, axle ratio, etc. One ECM part number can be used by many GM vehicles but the PROM is very specific and must be used only in the vehicle for which it was designed.

8 For this reason, it is essential to check the latest parts book and Service Bulletin information for the correct part number when replacing a PROM. An ECM purchased at the dealer is purchased without a PROM. The PROM from the old ECM must be carefully removed and installed in the new ECM.

PROM replacement

Refer to illustrations 5.10, 5.11, 5.14, 5.16 and 5.18

9 Turn the ECM so that the bottom cover is facing up and place it on a clean work surface.

10 Remove the PROM access cover **(see illustration)**.

11 Using a PROM removal tool (usually supplied with new PROMs), grasp the PROM carrier at the narrow ends. Gently rock the carrier from end to end while carefully pulling up.

12 The PROM carrier and PROM should lift out of the PROM socket easily.

13 Note the reference end of the PROM carrier before setting it aside, so you will be

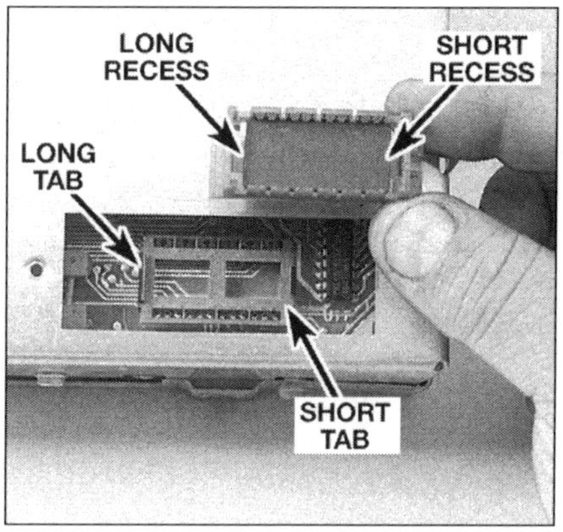

5.13 Make sure the locating tabs on the ECM coincide with the recess grooves in the PROM

able to install the new prom with the same orientation **(see illustration)**.

14 If you are replacing the ECM, remove the new ECM from its container and check the service number to make sure that it is the same as the number on the old ECM **(see illustration)**.

15 If you are replacing the PROM, remove the new PROM from its container and check the service number to make sure that it is the same as the number of the old PROM.

16 Position the PROM/PROM carrier assembly squarely over the PROM socket with the small notched end of the carrier aligned with the small notch in the socket at the pin on one end. Press on the PROM carrier until it seats firmly in the socket **(see illustration)**.

17 If the PROM is new, make sure that the notch in the PROM is matched to the small notch in the carrier. **Caution:** *If the PROM is installed backwards and the ignition switch is turned on, the PROM will be destroyed.*

18 Using the tool, install the new PROM carrier in the PROM socket of the ECM **(see illustration)**. The small notch of the carrier should be aligned with the small notch in the socket. Press on the PROM carrier until it is firmly seated in the socket. **Caution:** *Do not press on the PROM - press only on the carrier.*

19 Attach the access cover to the ECM and tighten the two screws.

20 Install the ECM in the support bracket, plug in the electrical connectors to the ECM and install the hush panel.

21 Start the engine.

22 Enter the diagnostic mode (see Section 4). If no trouble codes occur, the PROM is correctly installed.

23 If Trouble Code 51 occurs, or if the CHECK ENGINE/SERVICE ENGINE SOON light comes on and remains constantly lit, the PROM is not fully seated, is installed backwards, has bent pins or is defective.

24 If the PROM is not fully seated, pressing firmly on both ends of the carrier should correct the problem.

25 If the pins have been bent, remove the PROM, straighten the pins and reinstall the PROM. If the bent pins break or crack when you attempt to straighten them, discard the

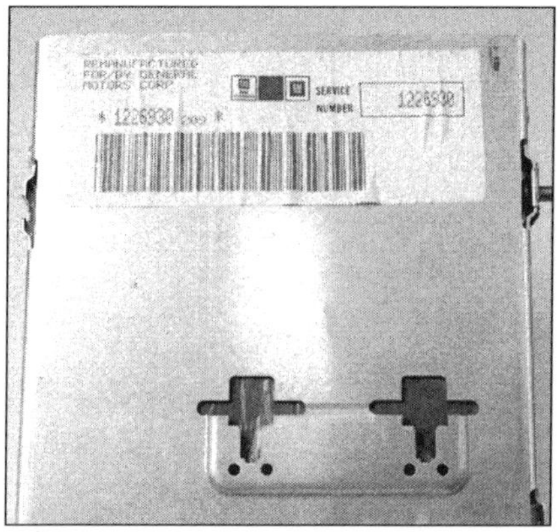

5.14 The ECM service number is printed on a label attached to the ECM

PROM and replace it with a new one.

26 If careful inspection indicates that the PROM is fully seated, has not been installed backwards and has no bent pins, but the CHECK ENGINE/SERVICE ENGINE SOON light remains lit, the PROM is probably faulty and should be replaced.

6 Information sensors - check and replacement

Note: *The following information pertains to fuel-injected models and some 1980 and later carbureted models. For more information on carbureted models see Chapter 4A.*

Engine Coolant Temperature (ECT) sensor

General description

1 The coolant temperature sensor is a thermistor (a resistor which varies the value of its resistance in accordance with temperature changes). The change in the resistance value will directly affect the voltage signal from the coolant thermosensor. As the sensor temperature DECREASES, the resistance will INCREASE. As the sensor temperature INCREASES, the resistance will DECREASE. A failure in the coolant sensor circuit should set either a Code 14 or a Code 15. These codes indicate a failure in the coolant temperature circuit, so the appropriate solution to the problem will be either repair of a wire or replacement of the sensor. The sensor can also be checked with an ohmmeter, by measuring its resistance when cold, then warming up the engine and taking another measurement.

Checking

Refer to illustrations 6.2 and 6.5

2 To check the sensor, check its resistance while it is completely cold (50 to 80-degrees F = 5,700 to 2,200 ohms) **(see illustration)**. Next, start the engine and warm it up until it reaches operating temperature. The resistance should be lower (170 to 200 degrees F = 200 to 300 ohms). To check the

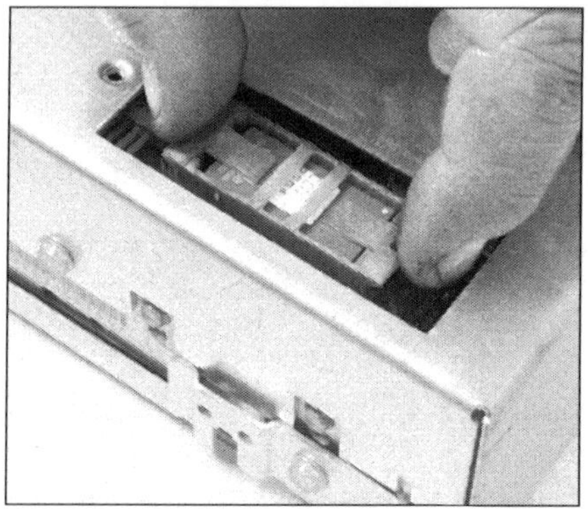

5.16 To install the PROM, press only on the ends until the retaining clips snap into the ends of the PROM - make sure the notches in the PROM are aligned with the small notches in the socket

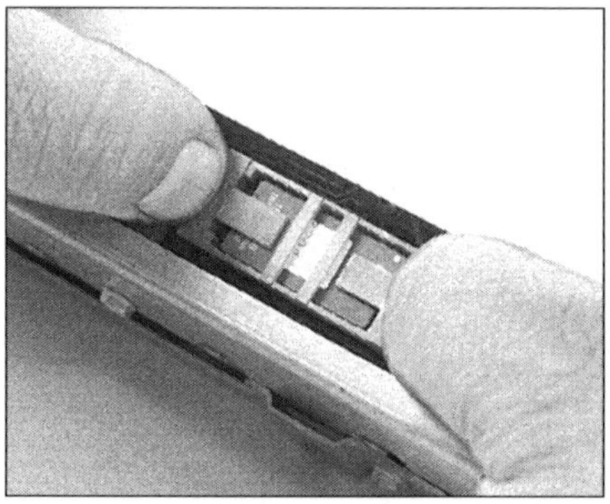

5.18 Press each side of the PROM in evenly

sensor resistance, disconnect the harness connector from the ECT sensor and measure across the two terminals on the sensor harness. **Note 1:** *The coolant temperature sensor on the MPFI system will have a much narrower range of resistance. Cold resistance values will range from 900 to 1,000 ohms and warm temperatures will range from 20 to 400 ohms.* **Note 2:** *In the event the coolant temperature sensor is difficult to position the ohmmeter probes, it will be necessary to*

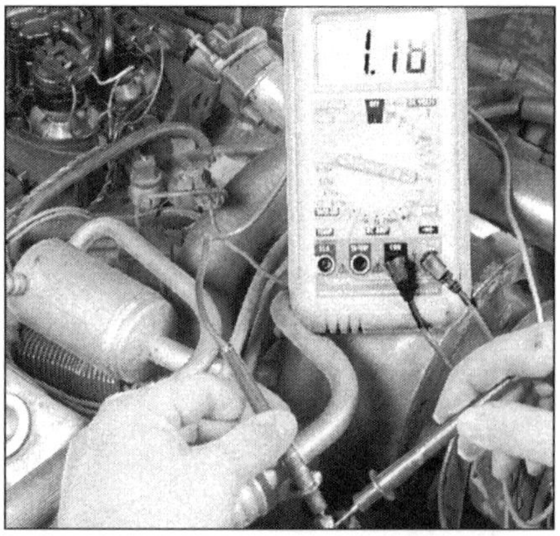

6.2 Install one probe inside the center core and the other probe on the outside (ground) terminal of the coolant temperature sensor

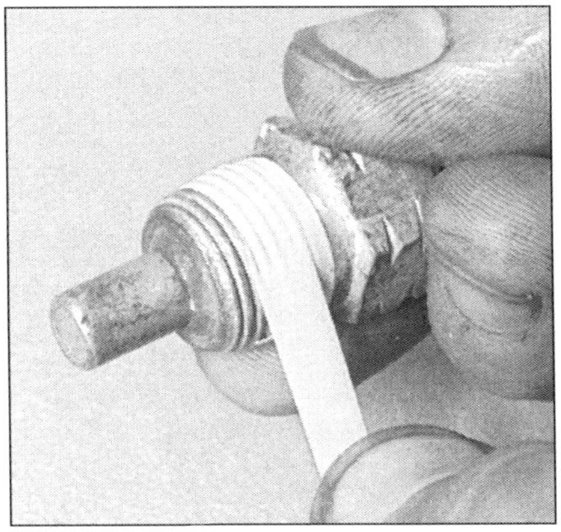

6.5 To prevent coolant leakage, be sure to wrap the temperature sensor threads with Teflon tape before installation

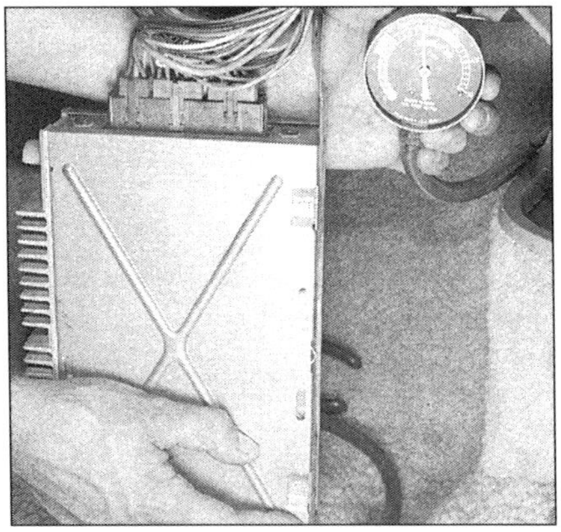

6.7 On MPFI models, be sure the MAP sensor in the computer is receiving the proper vacuum signal

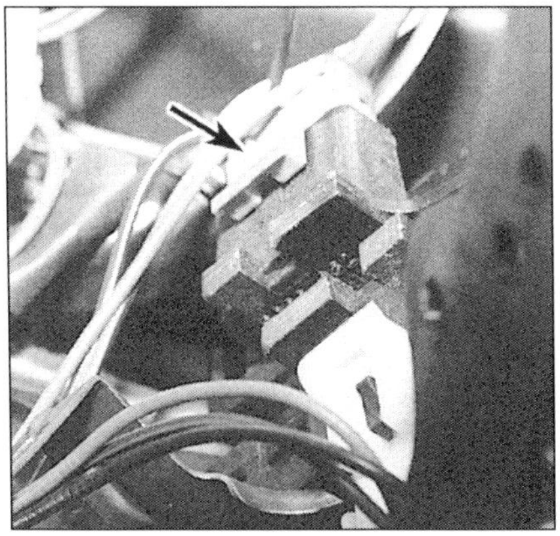

6.9 On TBI models, the MAP and BARO sensors are located under the dash (arrows)

remove the sensor and perform the tests in a pan of heated water to simulate the conditions. **Note 3:** *The ECT sensor on TBI systems is located on the right side of the engine, under the alternator and tucked in the front cover. The ECT sensor on the MPFI system is located on the left side of the engine near the thermostat housing.*

3 On TBI systems, check the reference voltage from the ECM (computer) to the ECT with the ignition key ON (engine not running). It should be approximately 5.0 volts. Install the positive probe of the ohmmeter onto the yellow (+) wire and the negative probe onto the black (-) wire. Refer to the wiring diagrams at the end of Chapter 12 for the correct wire colors. **Note:** *Do not attempt to check the reference voltage on the MPFI system. The computer and the wiring harness differ greatly from the TBI system.*

Replacement

Warning: *Wait until the engine is completely cool before beginning this procedure.*

4 To remove the sensor, release the locking tab, unplug the electrical connector, then carefully unscrew the sensor. **Caution:** *Handle the coolant sensor with care. Damage to this sensor will affect the operation of the entire fuel injection system.*

5 Before installing the new sensor, wrap the threads with Teflon sealing tape to prevent leakage and thread corrosion **(see illustration)**.

6 Installation is the reverse of removal.

Manifold Absolute Pressure (MAP) sensor and Barometric (BARO) Pressure Sensor

General description

Refer to illustration 6.7

7 The Manifold Absolute Pressure (MAP) sensor monitors the intake manifold pressure changes resulting from changes in engine load and speed and converts the information into a voltage output. The BARO sensor monitors the ambient pressure changes from altitude and weather conditions and converts the information into a voltage output signal. The ECM uses the MAP sensor to control fuel delivery and ignition timing. A failure in the MAP sensor circuit should set a Code 33 or 34. The MAP sensor and BARO sensor on the TBI systems is located near the glovebox tucked in the corner under the dash. The MAP and BARO sensor on the MPFI system is an integral part of the ECM. Vacuum is routed from the throttle body, through the dash and directly to the ECM **(see illustration)**.

8 The MAP sensor SIGNAL voltage to the ECM varies from below 2 volts at idle (high vacuum) to above 4 volts with the ignition key ON (engine not running) or wide open throttle (WOT) (low vacuum). These values correspond with the altitude and pressure changes the vehicle experiences while driving.

Check

Refer to illustrations 6.9

9 Check the REFERENCE voltage from the computer to the MAP sensor. Use pins or paper clips to backprobe the MAP or BARO sensor electrical connector.

TBI systems

MAP sensor .... gray wire (+) and pink/black wire (-)
BARO sensor .... gray wire (+) and black/white wire (-)
Feedback carburetors .... gray wire (+) and black wire (-)

The voltage should be approximately 5.0 volts. **Note 1:** *The MAP sensor on the MPFI system is an integral part of the ECM. Have the sensor diagnosed by a dealer service department.* **Note 2:** *The MAP and BARO sensor are difficult to reach on TBI systems. Remove the glovebox and lower instrument panel to gain access* **(see illustration)**.

10 Check the SIGNAL voltage. Connect the leads of the voltmeter to:

TBI systems

MAP sensor .... dark blue/gray wire (+) and pink/black wire (-)
BARO sensor .... gray/black wire (+) and black/white wire (-)
Feedback carburetors .... light green wire (+) and black wire (-)

With the ignition ON (engine not running) the voltage reading should be about 4.5 to 5 volts. Remove the vacuum line from the sensor and install a hand held vacuum pump. Apply vacuum and observe the voltage decrease as vacuum increases. With approximately 15 in-Hg vacuum applied, MAP sensor SIGNAL voltage should produce approximately 1.5 to 2.0 volts.

Replacement

11 To replace the sensor, detach the vacuum hose, unplug the electrical connector and remove the mounting screws. Installation is the reverse of removal.

Air temperature sensor

General description

12 The air temperature sensor or Manifold Air Temperature (MAT) sensor is located on the intake manifold. This sensor acts as a thermistor (a resistor which changes the value of its resistance as the temperature changes). When the intake air is cold, the sensor resistance is high, therefore the ECM will read a high signal voltage. If the intake air is warm, the resistance is low giving the ECM a low voltage reading. The sensor values range from 2,700 ohms at 70-degrees F to 240 ohms at 190-degrees F. The ECM supplies approximately 5.0 volts (REFERENCE voltage) to the sensor. A failure in the sensor circuit should set either a Code 23 or Code 25. **Note :** *The air temperature sensor on the MPFI system will have a much narrower range of resistance than the TBI system sensor. Cold resistance values will range from 900 to 1,000 ohms and warm temperatures will range from 20 to 400 ohms.*

Check

Refer to illustration 6.13a, 6.13b and 6.14

13 Measure the resistance across the sensor terminals **(see illustrations)** by measuring their resistance when cold, then warming the sensor up (a hair dryer can be used for this) and taking another measurement. The resistance of the sensor should be HIGH when the temperature is low. Next, start the

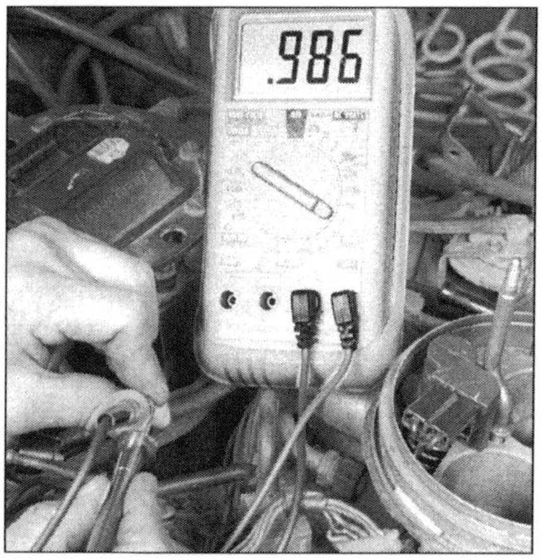

6.13a Measure the air temperature sensor resistance on MPFI systems

6.13b Checking the air temperature sensor resistance (TBI systems)

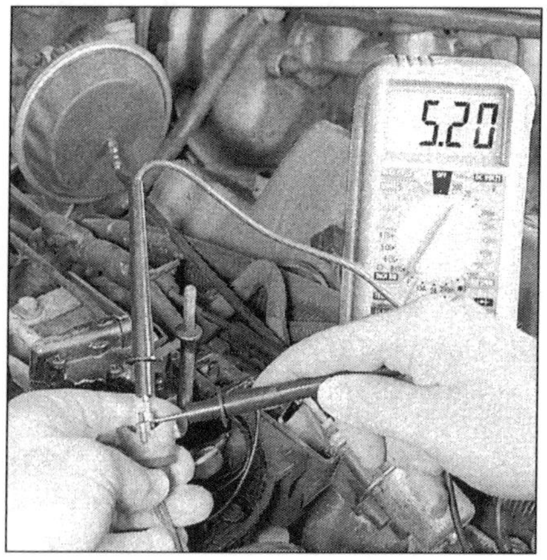

6.14 On TBI systems, install the positive (+) probe of the ohmmeter into the center of the terminal and the negative probe onto the outside of the terminal

engine and let it idle. Wait awhile and let the engine reach operating temperature. Turn the ignition key OFF, disconnect the MAT sensor and check the resistance across the terminals. The resistance should be LOW when the air temperature is high. If the sensor does not exhibit this change in resistance, replace the sensor with a new part.

14 On TBI systems, measure the REFERENCE voltage. Disconnect the MAT electrical sensor and, with the ignition key ON (engine not running), probe the terminals on the connector, checking for voltage **(see illustration)**. The VOM should read approximately 5.0 volts at one of the terminals - if not, the circuit to the sensor is open or grounded. **Note:** *Do not attempt to check the reference voltage on the MPFI system. The computer and the wiring harness differ greatly from the TBI system.*

Replacement

15 To remove the air temperature sensor, disconnect the electrical connector and unscrew the sensor from the intake manifold.

16 Installation is the reverse of removal.

Oxygen sensor

General description

17 The oxygen sensor, which is located in the exhaust manifold, monitors the oxygen content of the exhaust gas stream. The oxygen content in the exhaust reacts with the oxygen sensor to produce a voltage output which varies from 0.1-volt (high oxygen, lean mixture) to 0.9-volts (low oxygen, rich mixture). The ECM constantly monitors this variable voltage output to determine the ratio of oxygen to fuel in the mixture. The ECM alters the air/fuel mixture ratio by controlling the pulse width (open time) of the fuel injectors. A mixture ratio of 14.7 parts air to 1 part fuel is the ideal mixture ratio for minimizing exhaust emissions, thus allowing the catalytic converter to operate at maximum efficiency. It is this ratio of 14.7 to 1 which the ECM and the oxygen sensor attempt to maintain at all times. These models are equipped with a single wire O2 sensor (no heater).

18 The oxygen sensor produces no voltage when it is below its normal operating temperature of about 600-degrees F. During this initial period before warm-up, the ECM operates in OPEN LOOP mode.

19 If the engine reaches normal operating temperature and/or has been running for two or more minutes, and if the computer detects a malfunction, the ECM will set a code 13, 44 or 45.

20 When there is a problem with the oxygen sensor or its circuit, the ECM operates in the open loop mode - that is, it controls fuel delivery in accordance with a programmed default value instead of feedback information from the oxygen sensor.

21 The proper operation of the oxygen sensor depends on four conditions:

a) ***Electrical*** - *The low voltages generated by the sensor depend upon good, clean connections which should be checked whenever a malfunction of the sensor is suspected or indicated.*
b) ***Outside air supply*** - *The sensor is designed to allow air circulation to the internal portion of the sensor. Whenever the sensor is removed and installed or replaced, make sure the air passages are not restricted.*
c) ***Proper operating temperature*** - *The ECM will not react to the sensor signal until the sensor reaches approximately 600 degrees-F. This factor must be taken into consideration when evaluating the performance of the sensor.*
d) ***Unleaded fuel*** - *The use of unleaded fuel is essential for proper operation of the sensor. Make sure the fuel you are using is of this type.*

22 In addition to observing the above conditions, special care must be taken whenever the sensor is serviced.

a) *The oxygen sensor has a permanently attached pigtail and electrical connector which should not be removed from the sensor. Damage or removal of the pigtail or electrical connector can adversely affect operation of the sensor.*
b) *Grease, dirt and other contaminants should be kept away from the electrical connector and the louvered end of the sensor.*
c) *Do not use cleaning solvents of any kind on the oxygen sensor.*
d) *Do not drop or roughly handle the sensor.*
e) *The silicone boot must be installed in the correct position to prevent the boot from being melted and to allow the sensor to operate properly.*

Checking

Refer to illustration 6.23

23 Check the O_2 sensor millivolt signal. Locate the oxygen sensor electrical connector and carefully backprobe it using a long pin. Install the positive probe of a voltmeter onto the signal wire (purple) and the negative probe to ground. **Note:** *Consult the wiring diagrams at the end of Chapter 12 for additional information on the oxygen sensor electrical connector wire color designations.* Monitor the SIGNAL voltage (millivolts) as the engine goes from cold to warm **(see illustration)**.

6.23 The oxygen sensor (arrow) is located in the exhaust manifold

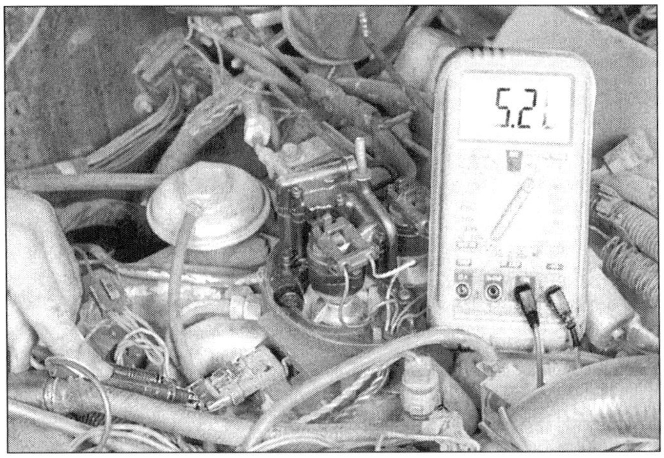

6.36 Checking the TPS REFERENCE voltage (TBI models)

6.37a Checking the TPS SIGNAL voltage on (TBI models)

24 The oxygen sensor will produce a steady voltage signal of approximately 0.1 to 0.2 volts with the engine cold (open loop). After a period of approximately two minutes, the engine will reach operating temperature and the oxygen sensor will start to fluctuate between 0.1 to 0.9 volts (closed loop). If the oxygen sensor fails to reach the closed loop mode or there is a very long period of time until it does switch into closed loop mode, replace the oxygen sensor with a new part.
25 If the oxygen sensor fails any of these tests, replace it with a new part.

Replacement

Note: *Because it is installed in the exhaust manifold or pipe, which contracts when cool, the oxygen sensor may be very difficult to loosen when the engine is cold. Rather than risk damage to the sensor (assuming you are planning to reuse it in another manifold or pipe), start and run the engine for a minute or two, then shut it off. Be careful not to burn yourself during the following procedure.*
26 Disconnect the cable from the negative terminal of the battery.
27 Raise the vehicle and place it securely on jackstands.
28 Carefully disconnect the electrical connector from the sensor.
29 Carefully unscrew the sensor from the exhaust manifold.
30 Anti-seize compound must be used on the threads of the sensor to facilitate future removal. The threads of new sensors will already be coated with this compound, but if an old sensor is removed and reinstalled, recoat the threads.
31 Install the sensor and tighten it securely.
32 Reconnect the electrical connector of the pigtail lead to the main engine wiring harness.
33 Lower the vehicle, take it on a test drive and check to see that no trouble codes set.

Throttle Position Sensor (TPS)

Note: *For information on the TPS used on 1980 and later carbureted models (feedback systems), see Chapter 4, Part A.*

TBI systems

General description

34 The Throttle Position Sensor (TPS) is located on the end of the throttle shaft on the throttle body. By monitoring the output voltage from the TPS, the ECM can determine fuel delivery based on throttle valve angle (driver demand). A broken or loose TPS can cause intermittent bursts of fuel from the injector and an unstable idle because the ECM thinks the throttle is moving.
35 A problem in any of the TPS circuits will set a Code 21 or 22. Once a trouble code is set, the ECM will use an artificial default value for the TPS and some vehicle performance will return.

Checking

Refer to illustrations 6.36, 6.37a and 6.37b

36 Locate the Throttle Position Sensor (TPS) on the throttle body. Using a voltmeter, check the REFERENCE voltage from the ECM. Install the positive probe (+) onto the gray (reference wire) and negative probe (-) onto the black (ground wire) **(see illustration)**. The voltage should read approximately 5.0 volts.
37 Next, check the TPS SIGNAL voltage. With the throttle fully closed, install the positive probe (+) of the voltmeter onto the dark blue wire and the negative probe (-) onto the black wire **(see illustration)**. Gradually open the throttle valve and observe the TPS sensor voltage. Observe a smooth change in the voltage values as the sensor travels from idle to full throttle. The voltage should increase from approximately 0.5 volts at closed throttle to approximately 4.5 volts at wide-open throttle **(see illustration)**. If the readings are incorrect, replace the TPS sensor.

Replacement

Refer to illustration 4.44

38 Disconnect the electrical connector from the TPS.
39 Remove the Torx drive screws from the TPS and remove the TPS from the throttle body.
40 Install the TPS onto the throttle body with the throttle in the closed position. Make sure the arm on the TPS is above the actuating lever on the throttle body. Install the screws, but leave them loose until the TPS is adjusted.

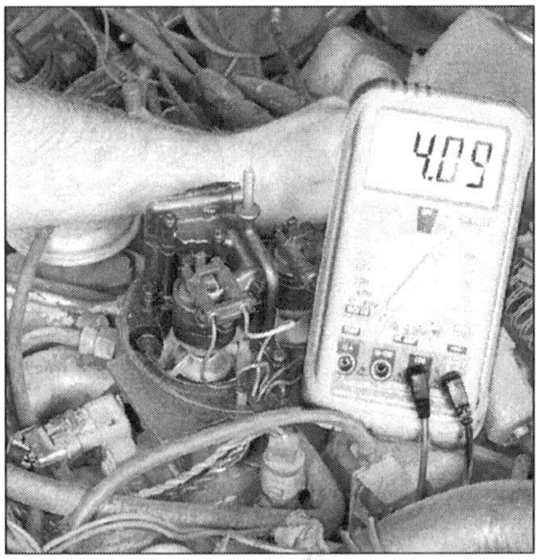

6.37b Now slowly rotate the throttle lever and observe that SIGNAL voltage increases

Adjustment

41 Connect the electrical connector to the TPS and connect a voltmeter to the dark blue and black wire terminals as described in Step 37. Turn the ignition On and rotate the TPS until the voltmeter reads 0.5 volts. Tighten the TPS mounting screws.

MPFI systems

General description

42 The Throttle Position Sensor (TPS) is located on the end of the throttle shaft on the throttle body. This type of TPS acts as a switching device for the computer. As the sensor arm varies with increased throttle action, the TPS signals the computer the position by means of a series of stepped switch positions. As a result, the computer varies the air/fuel mixture according to the driving conditions (accelerator position).

Checking

43 Turn the ignition key ON (engine not run-

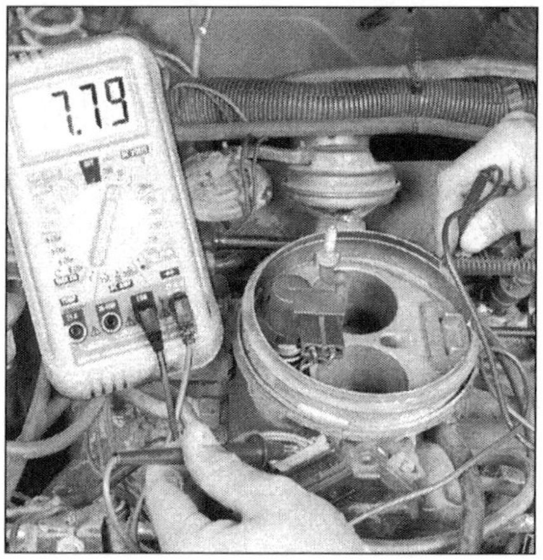

6.44 Check for voltage to the TPS with the ignition key ON (engine not running)

6.48 TPS adjustment on the MPFI system

6.49 Location of the TPS adjustment screws (arrows) on the MPFI system

ning) and listen very carefully at the TPS. Slowly increase throttle position using your hand and listen for clicks on the TPS. As the accelerator cable is throttled, definite clicks will indicate that the TPS is selecting the new position of the accelerator.

44 Check for battery voltage to the TPS. With the ignition key ON (engine not running), check for voltage on the green wire. Battery voltage (approximately 12-volts) should exist **(see illustration)**. If there is no sign of battery voltage to the TPS, check the wiring harness to the ECM.

Adjustment

Refer to illustrations 6.48 and 6.49

45 Loosen the two screws that retain the TPS to the throttle body slightly so the TPS can rotate. Do not loosen the screws excessively or the TPS will slip after it is adjusted and before the screws are tightened.

46 With the throttle valves in the idle position, rotate the TPS counterclockwise until the end stop makes contact.

47 Rotate the throttle lever until the first click is heard (ignition key must be on). Tighten the screws temporarily.

48 Install a 0.020 inch feeler gauge between the throttle lever and idle stop screw **(see illustration)**. The gauge must not fit (tight fit is acceptable) or the clearance must be adjusted.

49 If the clearance is over 0.020 inches, loosen the screws **(see illustration)** and turn the TPS slightly clockwise and recheck the clearance.

50 If switch cannot be adjusted, replace the switch with a new part.

Neutral Start switch

51 The Neutral Start switch, located on the automatic transmission on early models and on the steering column on later models, indicates to the ECM when the transmission is in Park or Neutral. This information is used for Transmission Converter Clutch (TCC), Exhaust Gas Recirculation (EGR) and Idle Speed Control (ISC) motor operation. **Caution:** *The vehicle should not be driven with the Neutral Start switch disconnected because idle quality will be adversely affected.*

52 For more information regarding the Neutral Start switch, which is part of the Neutral start and back-up light switch assembly, see Chapter 7.

Vehicle Speed Sensor (VSS)

General description

53 There are two types of vehicle speed sensors on the MPFI and TBI systems. The MPFI system uses a twin magnet type housed within a special box on the distributor. Two magnets attached to two rotors in the distributor interact with two reed switches on the housing to detect vehicle speed. TBI systems detect engine speed from the seven terminals in the HEI module in the distributor. The ECM controls spark advance in accordance with the speed of the engine.

Check

54 To check the VSS, it will be necessary to have a dealer service department or qualified repair shop diagnose problems with the VSS or its circuitry.

Crankshaft sensor (1977 403 cu.in. Toronado)

General description

55 The 1977 Oldsmobile Toronado ignition system incorporates an HEI system without vacuum advance. Timing is advanced and retarded using information from the sensors (coolant temperature sensor, crankshaft sensor) and controller (Electronic Control Module) or computer. The crankshaft sensor is located at the front of the engine, on the left side of the block near the exhaust manifold, under the alternator. The computer will advance the timing using the module and HEI ignition system but it will vary the amount if the vehicle is either a California model or a 49 States model. The computer detects engine speed and crankshaft position which in turn allows it to calculate precise timing for the fuel injection and the ignition system.

Check

56 To check the crankshaft sensor, with the ignition key ON (engine not running) check for battery voltage to the crankshaft harness on the red wire. Reach down and unscrew the cable connector from the crankshaft sensor and probe the red wire. Battery voltage should be present. If not, check the 10 amp EST fuse in the fuse panel (see Chapter 12). Also, consult the wiring diagrams at the end of Chapter 12 for additional information on the crankshaft circuit and the ignition circuit.

57 Also, check the voltage signal from the computer to the sensor on the light blue and purple wire. There should be 8 to 10 volts available. If all the checks are correct, replace the crankshaft sensor.

Adjustment

58 Use a special wire feeler gauge to check the clearance between the sensor and the pulse generator disc on the crankshaft. There should be 0.045 to 0.055 inch clearance.

Replacement

59 Disconnect the negative terminal from the battery.

60 Disconnect the electrical connector from the crankshaft sensor.

61 Mark the position of the crankshaft sensor with a pencil or paint to insure correct reinstallation and adjustment. Remove bolts from the crankshaft sensor and lift the sensor from the timing cover.

62 Installation is the reverse of removal. Tighten the bolts to the torque listed in this Chapter's Specifications.

7 V8-6-4 Modulated Displacement System (1981 Cadillac Eldorado and Seville) - general information and check

General information

1 Cadillac introduced the V8-6-4 system on 1981 Eldorado models equipped with the

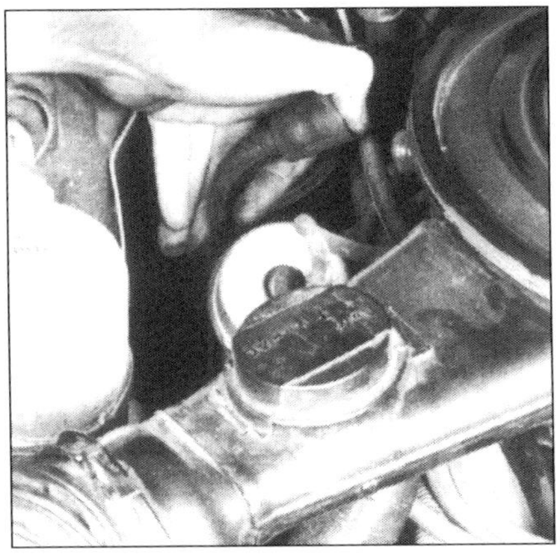

8.6 To check for proper vacuum, remove the top plate of the air cleaner housing, locate the small PCV filter on the inside of the air cleaner housing, detach the hose leading to this filter and, with the engine idling, place your thumb lightly over the end of the hose and leave it there for about 30 seconds - you should feel a slight suction

368 cu. in. engine. Cadillac designed this system to decrease the inefficiency from throttle control problems when the engine is running at slow speeds. The engineers designed a system that temporarily cancels the use of up to four cylinders that are not needed during low power conditions and employs them once again during high-power demand conditions. As a result there are fewer cylinders experiencing throttle loss and the fuel requirement is lessened.

2 At low power conditions, valve selectors deactivate both intake and exhaust valves on two or four cylinders. When full power is required, normal valve operation is restored. In each of the deactivated cylinders, the piston continues to travel, but the intake and exhaust valves are closed, therefore not allowing fuel/air mixture into the combustion chamber.

3 This system consists of special valve selectors, information sensors and linkage. The information is shared by the Throttle Body Injection (TBI) system. Refer to Chapter 4B for additional information on the fuel injection system and components. Valve selectors are installed onto cylinders 1, 4, 6 and 7. In the six cylinder mode, cylinders 1 and 4 are deactivated. In the four cylinder mode, cylinders 1, 4, 6 and 7 are deactivated.

4 The valve selectors control the point of pivot of the rocker arm assembly. During active operation, the rocker arms pivot near the center of the fulcrum point of the rocker arm. As the cam reaches the highest point of the lobe travel, the valve opens and allows the fuel/air mixture to enter. When the valve selector is activated, the rocker arm pivot location changes away from the valve thereby not allowing the particular valve to open.

5 Because the V8-6-4 engines suffer from decreased vacuum levels during the 6 and 4 cylinder modes, they are equipped with a belt driven vacuum pump that is installed onto the power steering pump.

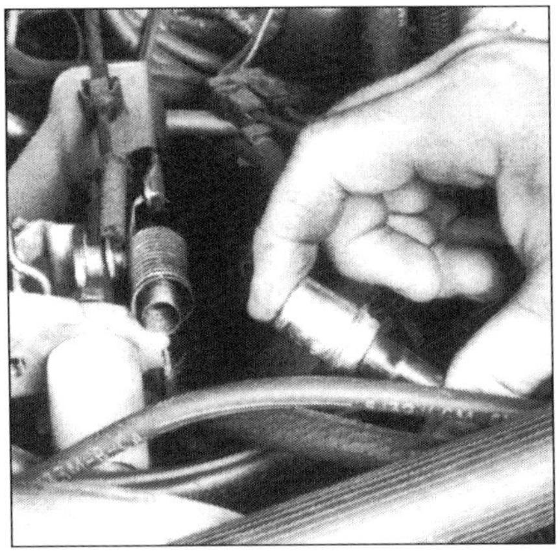

8.9 To check for a clogged PCV valve, remove the valve from the rocker arm cover and, with the engine running, place your finger over the end of the valve and feel for suction - it should be fairly strong

Check

6 Check for code 25 using the self diagnosis and trouble code system described in Section 4. If there are no trouble codes stored, check the entire system.

7 Disconnect the harness connector between the ECM and the modulated displacement solenoids and check for battery voltage on the orange wire. Approximately 12 volts should be present.

8 If no voltage is present, have the ECM checked by a dealer service department. Also, check the circuit to the computer from the harness connector.

9 If voltage is present, check the modulated displacement solenoids located under each valve cover. First, make sure the 20 amp body fuse is intact and battery voltage is present. Next, install a test light onto the positive terminal of the battery and with the solenoids disconnected, probe each solenoid. If the test light illuminates, the solenoid is grounded and must be replaced.

10 If all the MD solenoids check out, start the engine and with the solenoids disconnected, jumper each solenoid (one-by-one) and listen for changes in the engine speed. If the solenoids activate properly, the engine will change idle quality dramatically.

11 If all the tests are correct and the engine continues to experience driveability problems, check the coolant temperature sensor and the information sensors involved with the fuel system (see Section 6).

8 Positive Crankcase Ventilation (PCV) system

General description

1 The positive crankcase ventilation, or PCV as it is more commonly called, reduces hydrocarbon emissions by circulating fresh air through the crankcase to pick up blow-by gases, which are then re-routed through the carburetor or intake manifold to be reburned by the engine.

2 The main components of this simple system are vacuum hoses and a PCV valve which regulates the flow of gases according to engine speed and manifold vacuum.

Checking

Refer to illustrations 8.6 and 8.9

3 The PCV system can be checked for proper operation quickly and easily. This system should be checked regularly, as carbon and sludge deposited by the blow-by gases will eventually clog the PCV valve and/or system hoses. When the flow of the PCV system is reduced or stopped, common symptoms are rough idling or a reduced engine speed at idle.

4 To check for proper vacuum in the system, remove the top plate of the air cleaner and locate the small PCV filter on the inside of the air cleaner housing.

5 Disconnect the hose leading to this filter. Be careful not to break the molded fitting on the filter.

6 With the engine idling, place your thumb lightly over the end of the hose **(see illustration)**. Leave it there for about 30 seconds. You should feel a slight pull, or vacuum. The suction may be heard as your thumb is released. This will indicate that air is being drawn all the way through the system. If a vacuum is felt, the system is functioning properly. Check that the filter inside the air cleaner housing is not clogged or dirty. If in doubt, replace the filter with a new one, which is an inexpensive safeguard.

7 If there is very little vacuum, or none at all, at the end of the hose, the system is clogged and must be inspected further.

8 Shut off the engine and locate the PCV valve. Carefully pull it from its rubber grommet. Shake it and listen for a clicking sound. If the valve does not click freely, replace the valve with a new one.

9 Now start the engine and run it at idle speed with the PCV valve removed. Place your finger over the end of the valve and feel for suction **(see illustration)**. This should be relatively strong vacuum which will be felt immediately.

10 If little or no vacuum is felt at the PCV valve, turn off the engine and disconnect the vacuum hose from the other end of the valve. Run the engine at idle speed and check for vacuum at the end of the hose just disconnected. No vacuum at this point indicates that the vacuum hose or inlet fitting at the engine is plugged. If it is the hose which is blocked, replace it with a new one or remove it from the engine and blow it out sufficiently with compressed air. A clogged passage at the carburetor or manifold requires that the component be removed and thoroughly cleaned of carbon build-up. A strong vacuum felt going into the PCV valve, but little or no

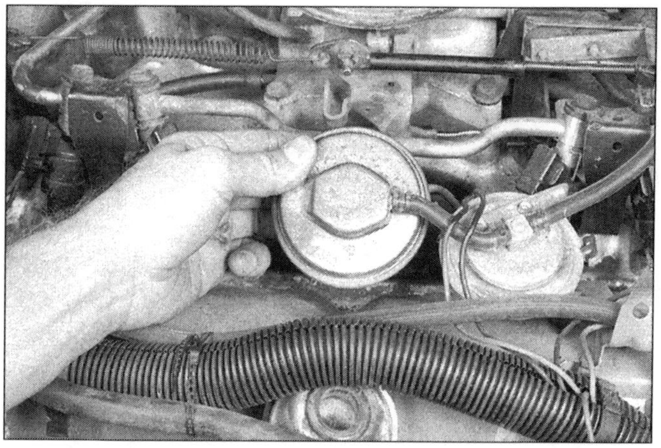

9.7 Using the tip of your finger, press the EGR valve diaphragm up to make sure it moves smoothly without binding

9.8 Use a hand-held vacuum pump to apply vacuum to the EGR valve

vacuum coming out of the valve, indicates a failure of the PCV valve, requiring replacement with a new one.

11 When purchasing a new PCV valve make sure it is the proper one. Each PCV valve is metered for specific engine sizes and model years. An incorrect PCV valve may pull too much or too little vacuum, possibly causing damage to the engine.

12 Information on removing and installing the PCV valve can be found in Chapter 1.

9 Exhaust Gas Recirculation (EGR) system

General description

1 The EGR system is used to reduce oxides of nitrogen (NOx) from the exhaust. Formation of these pollutants takes place at very high temperatures; consequently, it occurs during the peak temperature period of the combustion process. To reduce peak temperatures, and thus the formation of NOx, a small amount of exhaust gas is taken from the exhaust system and recirculated in the combustion cycle.

2 To tap this exhaust supply without an extensive array of pipes and connections in the exhaust system, additional exhaust passages are cast into the intricate runner system of the intake. Because of this arrangement, most of the EGR routing components are hidden from view under the manifold.

3 Two basic types of EGR valves are used - Vacuum Modulated EGR and Exhaust Back Pressure EGR. When Vacuum Modulated EGR is used, the amount of exhaust gas admitted to the intake manifold depends on a vacuum signal (ported vacuum) which is controlled by throttle position. When the throttle is closed (idle or deceleration), there is no vacuum signal to the EGR valve because the vacuum port is above the closed throttle valve. As the throttle valve is opened, a ported vacuum signal is supplied to the EGR valve, admitting exhaust gas to the intake manifold. The Exhaust Backpressure Modulated EGR uses a transducer located inside the EGR valve to control the operating vacuum signal. The vacuum signal is generated in the same manner as for the Vacuum Modulated EGR system. The integral transducer uses exhaust gas pressure to control an air bleed within the valve to modify the vacuum signal from the carburetor. Two types of backpressure EGR valves are used; positive backpressure and negative backpressure. The latest versions of the EGR valve are ECM-controlled. EGR flow is regulated by an ECM-controlled solenoid in the vacuum line. The ECM uses data from various combinations of sensors - such as the coolant temperature sensor, throttle position sensor, MAP sensor and distributor signal - to regulate the solenoid.

4 The EGR system does not recirculate gases when the engine is idling or decelerating. The system is also regulated by the thermal vacuum switch, which does not allow the system to operate until the engine has reached normal operating temperature.

5 Common engine problems associated with the EGR system are: rough idling or stalling when at idle, rough engine performance upon light throttle application and stalling on deceleration.

Checking

Refer to illustrations 9.7, 9.8, 9.13 and 9.18

6 Locate the EGR valve. The location varies from year to year, but on most models it is located on the intake manifold, adjacent to the right side of the carburetor. Initial checking, with illustrations, can be found in Chapter 1.

7 Place your finger under the EGR valve and push upwards on the diaphragm plate **(see illustration)**. The diaphragm should move freely from the open to the closed position. If it doesn't, replace the EGR valve.

8 Now start the engine and run it at idle speed. With your finger, manually depress the EGR diaphragm. If the valve or adjacent accessories are hot, wear gloves to prevent burning your fingers. The engine should lose speed, stumble or even stall. If the engine does not change speed, the EGR passages should be checked for blockage. This will require that the intake manifold be removed (see Chapter 2). If the valve passes this test, apply approximately 15 in-Hg vacuum with a hand vacuum pump **(see illustration)**; the engine should again stumble. If not, replace the valve. Any further checking of the positive backpressure type EGR valve will require special tools, so a questionable valve is best replaced with a new one at this point. Negative backpressure type EGR valves can be further tested as follows:

9.13 Check for a vacuum signal from the EGR control solenoid

9 Allow the engine to reach its normal operating temperature. Have an assistant depress the accelerator slightly and hold the engine at a constant speed above idle.

10 Detach the vacuum signal line at the EGR valve and verify that the diaphragm plate moves downward and engine speed increases.

11 Reattach the vacuum line to the valve. The diaphragm plate should move upward with a decrease in engine speed.

12 If the diaphragm doesn't move, make sure the engine is at its normal operating temperature. Repeat the test if in doubt.

13 To verify that vacuum is reaching the EGR valve, detach the vacuum hose at the valve and, with the engine running and the

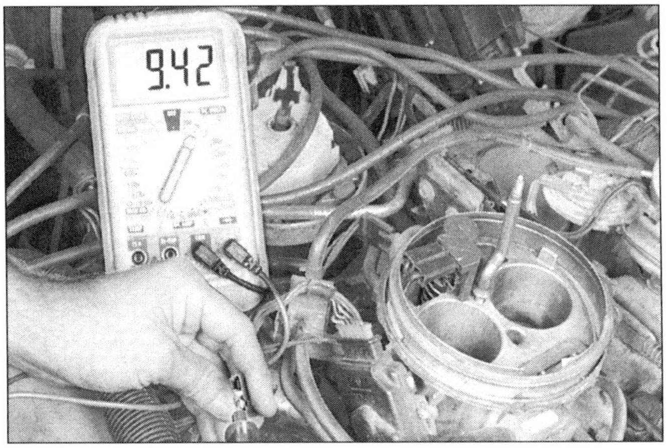

9.18 Check for battery voltage to the EGR control solenoid

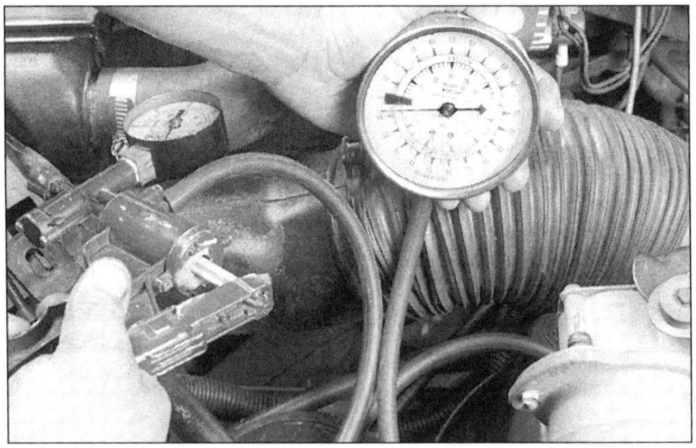

10.8 Use a hand pump to pressurize the charcoal canister. Observe the pressure gauge and make sure the canister does not leak

throttle slightly opened, verify that there's vacuum at the end of the hose **(see illustration)**. If there is vacuum, replace the EGR valve with a new one. If there is no vacuum signal, follow the vacuum hose to its source, inspecting for disconnections, cracks, breaks or blockage in the lines.

14 On all but a few early models, the EGR system uses some kind of vacuum valve to regulate the amount of exhaust gas admitted to the intake air-fuel mixture. Some of the more common valves are the Vacuum Controlled Valve (VCV), which regulates the EGR in accordance with engine intake vacuum; the Thermal Vacuum Switch (TVS) which regulates EGR valve operation in relation to engine temperature; and the electronically operated, ECM-controlled solenoid, which also acts in accordance with engine coolant temperature. Early models without this type of regulation have the vacuum hose routed directly to the carburetor.

15 This vacuum switch opens as the coolant temperature increases, allowing vacuum to reach the EGR valve. The exact temperature varies from year to year, but is indicative of the normal operating temperature of the particular engine.

16 To test a vacuum-actuated switch, check the vacuum signal with a vacuum gauge (if the switch on your vehicle is a solenoid under ECM control, diagnosis should be left to a dealer).

17 Disconnect the vacuum hose at the EGR valve, connect the vacuum gauge to the disconnected end of the hose and start the engine, then have an assistant depress the accelerator slightly and note this reading. As the accelerator is depressed, the vacuum reading should increase.

18 If the gauge does not respond to the throttle opening, disconnect the hose which leads from the carburetor to the vacuum switch **(see illustration)**. Repeat the test with the vacuum gauge attached to the vacuum hose end of the switch. If the vacuum gauge responds to accelerator opening, the vacuum switch is defective and should be replaced with a new one.

Component replacement

EGR valve

19 If the gauge still does not respond to an increase in throttle opening, check for a plugged hose or a problem with the carburetor/throttle body.

20 Disconnect the vacuum hose at the EGR valve.

21 Remove the nuts or bolts which secure the valve to the intake manifold.

22 Lift the EGR valve from the engine.

23 Clean the mounting surfaces of the EGR valve. Remove all traces of gasket material.

24 Place the new EGR valve, with a new gasket, on the intake manifold. Install the spacer, if used. Tighten the attaching bolts or nuts.

25 Connect the vacuum signal hose.

Thermal vacuum switch

26 Drain the engine coolant until the coolant level is beneath the switch.

27 Disconnect the vacuum hose at the EGR valve, connect the vacuum gauge to the disconnected end of the hose and start the engine, noting their positions for reassembly.

28 Using a suitable wrench, remove the switch.

29 When installing the switch, apply thread sealer to the threads, being careful not to allow the sealant to touch the bottom of the sensor.

30 Install the switch and tighten it securely.

10 Evaporation Control System (ECS)/Evaporative Emission Control System (EECS)

General description

Refer to illustration 10.8

1 The Evaporation Control System is one of the most trouble-free systems in the emissions network. Its function is to reduce hydrocarbon emissions. Basically, this is a closed fuel system which reroutes wasted fuel back to the gas tank and stores fuel vapors instead of venting them to the atmosphere.

2 Because it has few moving parts, the ECS/EECS system requires no periodic maintenance other than replacement of the filter in the bottom the charcoal canister at the recommended intervals.

3 The strong smell of fuel vapors is a tip-off that the system is not operating properly. So is engine starvation induced by lack of fuel during acceleration.

4 A pressure/vacuum gasoline filler cap must be used on vehicles equipped with ECS/EECS. A standard cap can render the system ineffective and possibly even collapse the fuel tank. The ECS/EECS system consists of a special gas tank with fill limiters and vent connections, a charcoal canister with an integral purge valve and a filter which stores vapor from the fuel tank to be burned by the carburetor, a carburetor bowl vent valve and the system of hoses connecting these components.

5 Earlier versions of the purge valve are regulated by coolant temperature: at coolant temperatures below the switching point, canister purge is controlled by an internal orifice in the switch. At coolant temperatures above the switching point, the switch opens, allowing canister purge to be controlled by manifold vacuum from the carburetor port. Later versions of the EECS are equipped with a canister purge valve under ECM control.

6 With the engine cold and at room temperature, disconnect the fuel tank line at the charcoal canister (on all models, the canister is located inside the engine compartment). Each of the hose connections should be labeled. Make sure you label them yourself if they're not already marked, to prevent improper assembly.

7 As this hose is disconnected, check for the presence of liquid fuel in the line. Fuel in this vapor hose is an indication that the vent controls or pressure-vacuum relief valve in the gas cap are not functioning properly.

8 Hook up a pressure device on the end of the fuel vapor connector on the charcoal canister. Apply 15 psi pressure to the line and check for excessive loss of pressure **(see illustration)**.

9 Check for a fuel vapor smell in the engine compartment and around the gas tank.

10 Remove the fuel filler cap and check for pressure in the gas tank.

11 If there is a large loss of pressure or a fuel odor, inspect all lines for leaks or deterioration.

12 With the fuel filler cap removed, apply pressure again and check for obstructions in the vent line.

13 To check the purge valve built into the canister, start the engine, allow it to reach normal operating temperatures, and disconnect the vacuum signal line running from the engine to the canister. With your thumb over the end of the hose, raise the engine speed to about 1500 rpm and check for vacuum. If there is no vacuum signal, check the EGR operation as described in this Chapter. The vacuum signal for the canister and the EGR valve originate from the same source.

14 The purge line to the charcoal canister functions with the PCV vacuum source, so if there is no vacuum when this hose is disconnected from the canister, check the PCV valve vacuum.

15 Checking an ECM-controlled purge valve is beyond the scope of the home mechanic.

Charcoal canister and filter - replacement

16 Chapter 1 contains all information concerning the servicing of the Evaporation Control System, in particular the replacement of the canister filter.

11 Electronic Spark Timing (EST) system

General description

Note: *Always consult the VECI label for the exact timing procedure for your vehicle.*

1 To provide improved engine performance, fuel economy and control of exhaust emissions, the Electronic Control Module (ECM) controls distributor spark advance (ignition timing) with the Electronic Spark Timing (EST) system.

2 The EST systems consists of the distributor, ECM or controller, coolant temperature sensor, ignition system (secondary wires, cap, rotor, plugs, module, pick-up coil, coil) and wiring harness. There are several variations on the EST system depending upon year and geographical location (California, Federal, High Altitude etc).

3 On 1978 and 1979 Toronados, the EST system consists of a three-terminal module instead of the usual four-terminal connector. The controller (ECM) is located near the glovebox inside the vehicle passenger compartment. The controller is connected to the harness by a 4-wire or 6-wire harness connector. A white vacuum hose is connected from the intake manifold to the controller (ECM) to monitor manifold vacuum to the atmospheric pressure sensor.

4 On some 1980 through 1985 Oldsmobile and Buick models, the EST system consists of a seven-terminal module (internal coils) instead of the usual four-terminal connector. Some models are also equipped with a Hall Effect switch inside the distributor along with the pick-up coil. This unit acts a second pick-up coil and timer core when the engine is in RUN mode. The pick-up coil acts as signal generator when the engine is cranking.

Checking

5 The ECM will set spark timing at a specified value when the diagnostic "Test" terminal in the ALDL connector is grounded. To check for EST operation, the timing should be checked at 2,000 rpm with the terminal ungrounded. Then ground the test terminal. If the timing changes at 2000 rpm, the EST is operating. A fault in the EST system will usually set Trouble Code 42. Refer to Chapter 1 for the complete timing procedure.

12 Electronic Spark Control (ESC) system

General description

1 Irregular octane levels in modern gasoline can cause detonation in an engine. Detonation is sometimes referred to as "spark knock."

2 The Electronic Spark Control (ESC) system, used on some 1980 models, is designed to retard spark timing up to 20 degrees to reduce spark knock in the engine. This allows the engine to use maximum spark advance to improve driveability and fuel economy.

3 There are three basic components to the ESC system; a distributor, a detonation sensor and a computer (ECM). The ESC knock sensor sends a voltage signal of 8 to 10-volts to the ECM when no spark knock is occurring and the ECM provides normal advance. When the knock sensor detects abnormal vibration (spark knock), the ESC module (5-pin) turns off the circuit to the ECM and the voltage at the ECM drops to zero volts. The ECM then retards the EST distributor until spark knock is eliminated.

4 Failure of the ESC knock sensor signal or loss of ground at the ESC module will cause the signal to the ECM to remain high. This condition will result in the ECM controlling the EST as if no spark knock is occurring. Therefore, no retard will occur and spark knock may become severe under heavy engine load conditions. At this point, the ECM will set a Code 43.

5 Loss of the ESC signal to the ECM will cause the ECM to constantly retard EST. This will result in sluggish performance and cause the ECM to set a Code 43.

Checking

6 First check the operation of the detonation or knock sensor. Check the coolant level (see Chapter 1), check the timing (see Chapter 1) and reconnect the vacuum advance hose to the distributor.

7 Connect a tachometer according to the manufacturer's specifications, start the engine and set the fast idle cam onto the high lobe to attain at least 1,800 rpm. Use a hammer or steel rod and tap on the intake manifold in the area around the knock sensor. Observe the idle speed drop approximately 200 rpm and the timing retard significantly. Timing and engine rpm should return to normal after approximately 20 seconds after the test is stopped.

8 Check the knock sensor. First check to make sure the electrical connector is not damaged. Also, check the resistance of the detonation sensor. Install the positive probe (+) of the ohmmeter to the center terminal and the negative probe (-) to ground (intake manifold) and observe the meter should read 175 to 375 ohms. If the sensor is not within this range, replace it with a new part. If the sensor checks out, diagnose the harness for any shorts or damaged wiring to the knock sensor (see Chapter 12 wiring diagrams).

9 Check the ignition system. Perform the necessary ignition system checks to verify that the module, coil and pick-up coil are operating properly (see Chapter 5).

Component replacement

ESC sensor

10 Detach the cable from the negative terminal of the battery.

11 Disconnect the wiring harness connector from the ESC sensor.

12 Remove the ESC sensor from the block.

13 Installation is the reverse of the removal procedure.

ESC module

14 Detach the cable from the negative terminal of the battery.

15 Remove the engine cover.

16 Locate the module at the rear of the engine compartment.

17 Detach the wiring harness electrical connector from the module.

18 Remove the module mounting bolts and remove the module.

19 Installation is the reverse of removal.

13 Electronic Spark Selection (ESS) system

General Information

1 The Electronic Spark Selection (ESS) system is featured on 1979 Cadillac Eldorado models. This system is able to advance or retard the ignition spark curve to alter the performance characteristics depending on the driving conditions.

2 The system must reach 1,200 rpm to attain the maximum advance on the timing.

3 Spark retard is also controlled on California models when start-up engine tempera-

tures are below 130 degrees F (California vehicles only). With the timing retarded, this allows the exhaust temperature to increase with the late combustion, the catalytic converter reaches warm-up temperature faster, resulting in higher exhaust gas temperatures. Only California vehicles are equipped with spark retard at cold operating temperatures while all others have normal spark advance.

4 The ESS system includes the electronic decoder, the HEI ignition system, the ignition module and the distributor. The pick-up coil signal is sent to the decoder to provide engine speed and ignition timing characteristics. The ESS distributor has a five pin electrical connector rather than the usual four pin electrical connector. The electronic decoder signal either delays or delivers the primary current to the ignition coil.

5 Other sensors input information into the decoder to control the ignition spark advance or retard (California only). The coolant temperature sensor, the EGR control solenoid, the fuel economy switch and the ignition switch help control signals to the engine decoder. The engine coolant temperature is monitored directly at the EGR control solenoid. Also, this solenoid is controlled by the computer to change the exhaust gas recirculation capabilities.

Checking

6 By-pass the decoder and check the ignition timing. Disconnect the four-wire connector between the decoder and the distributor and jumper the green wire (number 2) to the black wire (number 4). Check the ignition timing (see Chapter 1) using a timing light and check that the timing is six degrees advanced with the ESS system disconnected.

7 Check for battery voltage to the decoder with the ignition key ON (engine not running). Battery voltage should exist on pink wire (num-ber 3).

8 Disconnect the 3-pin EGR control solenoid connector and observe the ignition timing. The timing should retard by six degrees. If the timing does not retard, check for an open circuit in the brown wire. If the circuit to the decoder is complete, replace the decoder. **Note:** *Do not disconnect the 2-pin connector from the solenoid harness.*

9 Disconnect the vacuum hose at the fuel economy switch. Timing should retard (see Chapter 1). If the timing does not retard, check the fuel economy switch and the circuit for open circuit.

10 Reconnect the decoder harness connector and any vacuum lines that were removed.

14 Catalytic converter

General description

1 The catalytic converter is an emission control device added to the exhaust system to reduce hydrocarbon and carbon monoxide pollutants. This converter contains beads which are coated with a catalytic substance containing platinum and palladium.

2 It is imperative that only unleaded gasoline be used in a vehicle equipped with a catalytic converter. Unleaded fuel reduces combustion chamber deposits, corrosion and prevents lead contamination of the catalyst.

3 Periodic maintenance of the catalytic converter is not required; however, if the car is raised for other service it is advisable to inspect the overall condition of the catalytic converter and related exhaust components.

4 If the catalytic converter has been ruled by an official inspection station to be ineffective, the converter can be replaced with a new one, or the coated beads drained and replaced. Physical damage and the use of leaded fuels are the main causes of a malfunctioning catalytic converter.

5 It should be noted that the catalytic converter can reach very high temperatures in operation. Because of this, any work performed to the converter or in the general area where it is located should be done only after the system has sufficiently cooled. Also, caution should be exercised when lifting the vehicle with a hoist, as the converter can be damaged if the lifting pads are not properly positioned.

6 There are no functional tests which the home mechanic can make to determine if the catalytic converter is performing its task.

Component replacement

Catalytic converter

7 Raise the car and support it firmly with jackstands. The converter and exhaust system should be cool before proceeding.

8 Disconnect the converter at the front and rear. On most models a flange is used with four bolts and nuts to secure the converter to its mating exhaust pipes. If the fasteners are frozen in place due to high temperatures and corrosion, apply a penetrating oil liberally and allow it to soak in. As a last resort, the fasteners will have to be carefully cut off with a hacksaw.

9 Gently separate the inlet and outlet converter flanges from the exhaust pipes and remove the converter from under the vehicle.

10 Installation is a reversal of the removal process; however, always use new nuts and bolts.

Catalyst

11 Two types of catalytic converters are used on the vehicles covered in this manual. The monolith converter has coated rods which cannot be serviced. If failure occurs, the entire converter must be replaced with a new one. The catalyst in bead type converters can be changed by draining and filling the beads through a plug at the bottom of the converter.

12 With specialized equipment, the beads can be replaced with the converter still positioned under the car. This is definitely a job for a dealer who has the equipment and training necessary to perform this operation.

13 Bead replacement is more easily done with the converter removed from the car (see above).

14 With the converter on a workbench, remove the pressed fill plug. This is done by driving a small chisel between the converter shell and the fill plug lip. Deform the lip until pliers can be used to remove the plug. Be careful not to damage the converter shell surface where the plug seals.

15 Once the plug is removed, drain the beads into a container for disposal. Shake the converter vigorously to remove all beads.

16 To fill the catalytic converter with new beads, raise the front of the converter to approximately 45-degrees and pour the beads through the fill hole. Tapping lightly on the converter seam with a hammer as the beads are poured in will help to settle them. Continue tapping and pouring until the converter is full.

17 A special service fill plug will be required to replace the stock one which was removed. This consists of a bridge, bolt and fill plug and is installed as follows:

a) *Install the bolt into the bridge and put the bridge into the converter opening. Move it back and forth to loosen the beads across the opening (bolt centered).*
b) *Remove the bolt from the bridge and put the washer and fill plug, dished side out, over the bolt.*
c) *While holding the fill plug and washer against the bolt head, thread the bolt four or five turns into the bridge.*
d) *After fill plug has seated against the converter housing, tighten the bolt to 28 ft-lbs.*

18 Install the converter, start the engine and check for leaks.

Notes

Chapter 7
Automatic transmission

Contents

Specifications

Torque specifications

	Ft-lbs (unless otherwise noted)
Differential-to-transmission bolts	See Chapter 8
Transmission-to-engine bolts	
425	30
325/325-4L	35
Torque converter-to-driveplate bolts	
425	40
325/325-4L	41
Vacuum modulator retaining bolt	18

1 General information

All vehicles covered in this manual come equipped with an automatic transmission: the three-speed Turbo Hydra-Matic (THM) 425 is used on 1970 through 1978 Cadillac Eldorados and 1970 through 1978 Oldsmobile Toronados; 1979 through 1981 Eldorados, Toronados and Buick Rivieras are equipped with the three-speed THM 325; all 1982 through 1985 models use a 325-4L, which has an extra gearset for an overdrive 4th gear and a lock-up torque converter.

Due to the complexity of the automatic transmissions covered in this manual and the need for specialized equipment to perform most service operations, this Chapter contains only general diagnosis, routine maintenance, adjustment and removal and installation procedures.

If the transmission requires major repair work, it should be left to a dealer service department or an automotive or transmission repair shop. You can, however, remove and install the transmission yourself and save the expense, even if the repair work is done by a transmission shop.

2 Diagnosis - general

Note: *Automatic transmission malfunctions may be caused by five general conditions: poor engine performance, improper adjustments, hydraulic malfunctions, mechanical malfunctions or malfunctions in the computer or its signal network (models equipped with computer-controlled lock-up torque converter). Diagnosis of these problems should always begin with a check of the easily repaired items: fluid level and condition* (see Chapter 1), *shift linkage adjustment and throttle linkage adjustment. Next, perform a road test to determine if the problem has been corrected or if more diagnosis is necessary. If the problem persists after the preliminary tests and corrections are completed, additional diagnosis should be done by a dealer service department or transmission repair shop.* Refer to the Troubleshooting Section *at the front of this manual for information on symptoms of transmission problems.*

Preliminary checks

1 Drive the vehicle to warm the transmission to normal operating temperature.

2 Check the fluid level as described in Chapter 1:

a) *If the fluid level is unusually low, add enough fluid to bring the level within the designated area of the dipstick, then check for external leaks* (see below).
b) *If the fluid level is abnormally high, drain off the excess, then check the drained fluid for contamination by coolant. The presence of engine coolant in the automatic transmission fluid indicates that a failure has occurred in the internal radiator walls that separate the coolant from the transmission fluid* (see Chapter 3).
c) *If the fluid is foaming, drain it and refill the transmission, then check for coolant in the fluid or a high fluid level.*

3 Check the engine idle speed. **Note:** *If the engine is malfunctioning, do not proceed with the preliminary checks until it has been repaired and runs normally.*

4 Check the throttle valve cable for freedom of movement. Adjust it if necessary (see Section 6). **Note:** *The throttle cable may function properly when the engine is shut off and cold, but it may malfunction once the engine is hot. Check it cold and at normal engine*

3.2a To find the relay lever, locate the shift lever on the steering column (A) on the firewall, just below the power brake booster, and follow the upper shift rod (B) down to the relay lever

operating temperature.

5 Inspect the shift linkage (see Section 3). Make sure it's properly adjusted and that the linkage operates smoothly.

Fluid leak diagnosis

6 Most fluid leaks are easy to locate visually. Repair usually consists of replacing a seal or gasket. If a leak is difficult to find, the following procedure may help.

7 Identify the fluid. Make sure it's transmission fluid and not engine oil or brake fluid (automatic transmission fluid is a deep red color).

8 Try to pinpoint the source of the leak. Drive the vehicle several miles, then park it over a large sheet of cardboard. After a minute or two, you should be able to locate the leak by determining the source of the fluid dripping onto the cardboard.

9 Make a careful visual inspection of the suspected component and the area immediately around it. Pay particular attention to gasket mating surfaces. A mirror is often helpful for finding leaks in areas that are hard to see.

10 If the leak still cannot be found, clean the suspected area thoroughly with a degreaser or solvent, then dry it.

11 Drive the vehicle for several miles at normal operating temperature and varying speeds. After driving the vehicle, visually inspect the suspected component again.

12 Once the leak has been located, the cause must be determined before it can be properly repaired. If a gasket is replaced but the sealing flange is bent, the new gasket will not stop the leak. The bent flange must be straightened.

13 Before attempting to repair a leak, check to make sure the following conditions are corrected or they may cause another leak. **Note:** *Some of the following conditions cannot be fixed without highly specialized tools and expertise. Such problems must be referred to a transmission repair shop or a dealer service department.*

3.2b Loosen the adjuster nut or bolt at the relay lever to free up the upper shift rod, then put the steering column shift lever in the Neutral position

Gasket leaks

14 Check the pan periodically. Make sure the bolts are tight, no bolts are missing, the gasket is in good condition and the pan is flat (dents in the pan may indicate damage to the valve body inside).

15 If the pan gasket is leaking, the fluid level or the fluid pressure may be too high, the vent may be plugged, the pan bolts may be too tight, the pan sealing flange may be warped, the sealing surface of the transmission housing may be damaged, the gasket may be damaged or the transmission casting may be cracked or porous. If sealant instead of gasket material has been used to form a seal between the pan and the transmission housing, it may be the wrong sealant.

Seal leaks

16 If a transmission seal is leaking, the fluid level or pressure may be too high, the vent may be plugged, the seal bore may be damaged, the seal itself may be damaged or improperly installed, the surface of the shaft protruding through the seal may be damaged or a loose bearing may be causing excessive shaft movement.

17 Make sure the dipstick tube seal is in good condition and the tube is properly seated. Periodically check the area around the speedometer gear or sensor for leakage. If transmission fluid is evident, check the O-ring for damage.

Case leaks

18 If the case itself appears to be leaking, the casting is porous and will have to be repaired or replaced.

19 Make sure the oil cooler hose fittings are tight and in good condition.

Fluid comes out vent pipe or fill tube

20 If this condition occurs, the transmission is overfilled, there is coolant in the fluid, the case is porous, the dipstick is incorrect, the vent is plugged, the transmission is overheated or the drain back holes are plugged.

3.5a To put the transmission shift lever into the Park position, rotate it all the way forward (counterclockwise)

3 Shift linkage - check and adjustment

Check

1 Checking the shift linkage isn't something you need to do very often. However, it's a good idea to check the linkage anytime the engine and/or transmission is replaced, the vehicle is involved in an accident or the vehicle has "slop" in the linkage. As the shift lever on the steering column moves from Park to Reverse to Neutral to Drive to Low, it moves a shift lever on the transmission up and down via a pair of rods: an upper rod between the steering column shift lever and the relay lever (both levers are on the firewall) and a lower rod between the relay lever and the shift lever on the transmission. The shift lever on the transmission has six "detent" positions, one for each gear. As you move the shift lever on the transmission to each gear position, you'll hear an audible "click. The position of the shift lever on the transmission must correspond to the position of the shift lever on the steering column. For example, if the shift lever on the steering column indicates Park, the shift lever on the transmission must be in Park; if the shift lever on the column indicates Reverse, the shift lever on the transmission must also indicate Reverse; and so on. If the engine starts in any other gear than Park or Neutral, or if the pointer for the shift lever indicates a gear position other than the gear the shift lever is actually in, either the shift linkage or the shift indicator pointer is out of adjustment.

Adjustment

Refer to illustrations 3.2a, 3.2b, 3.5a and 3.5b

2 Set the parking brake securely and block the wheels, then locate the adjuster nut or bolt for the upper rod at the relay lever **(see illustrations)** and loosen it.

3 Put the steering column shift lever in the Neutral position.

4 Raise the front of the vehicle and place it securely on jackstands.

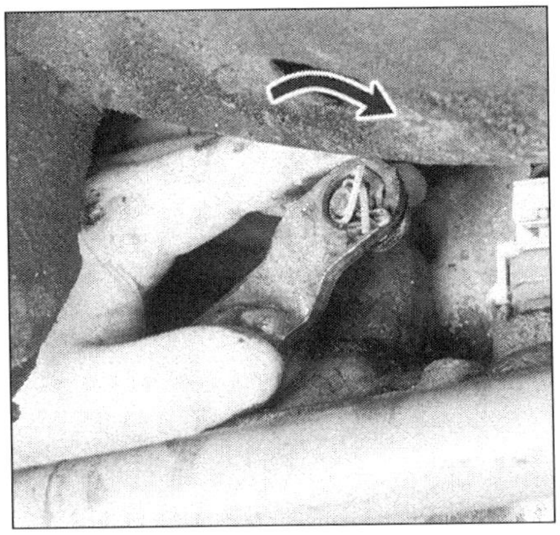

3.5b To put the transmission shift lever into the Neutral position, click the lever back two positions (two clicks) to the third (Neutral) detent position

5 Working underneath the vehicle, click the transmission shift lever forward (counterclockwise) until it reaches the highest detent position **(see illustration)**. The transmission is now in Park. Then push down on the relay rod or the shift lever two detent positions (two clicks) to the third detent position **(see illustration)**. The transmission is now in Neutral.

6 With an assistant holding the steering column shift lever in the Neutral position, tighten the adjuster nut or bolt for the upper rod. If you don't have an assistant to hold the shift lever in Neutral, hang a small weight from the shift lever to hold it in place while you tighten the adjuster nut or bolt.

7 To check your work, verify that the shift lever operates smoothly, that the engine starts only in Park or Neutral, and that the pointer for the column shift lever points at the gear position on the indicator panel corresponding to the gear in which the transmission is actually in. If the pointer doesn't point to the gear that the transmission is in, adjust the pointer as follows:

Adjusting the shift indicator

Refer to illustrations 3.8a, 3.8b, 3.10a, 3.10b, 3.10c and 3.10d

8 The shift indicator needle is linked to a guide clip on the "shift bowl" (the ring encircling the steering column which is rotated as the shift lever is moved from one gear to another). As the shift bowl is rotated, it moves the indicator needle to the corresponding indicated gear on the gear position indicator panel just below the instrument cluster. All shift indicator devices work the same way. However, there are some slight design differences in the units used in various models **(see illustrations)**. Early (1971 and 1972, and some 1973) models use a link rod to connect the clip to the indicator needle; all other models use a wire cable between the clip and the indicator needle. Also, early link-type units and some later cable-type units use a set screw threaded through the clip; other units have no screw. But, basically, there are just two types. The shift indicator pointer on the instrument cluster must point to the gear which the transmission is actually in. If the pointer for the shift lever indicates a gear position other than the gear the transmission is in, the indicator must be adjusted. The adjustment procedure is similar for all models.

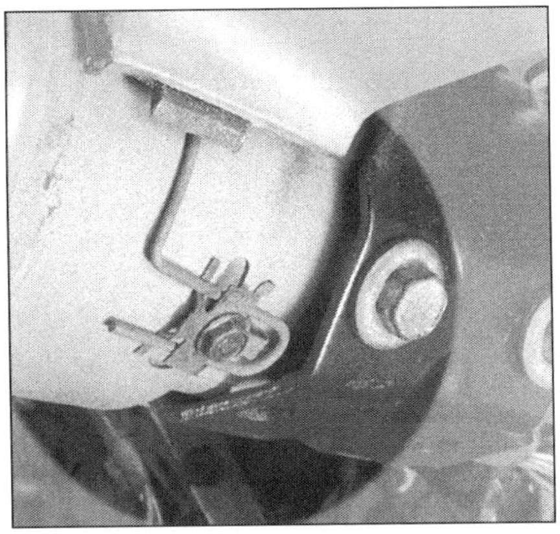

3.8a A typical link-type shift indicator mechanism

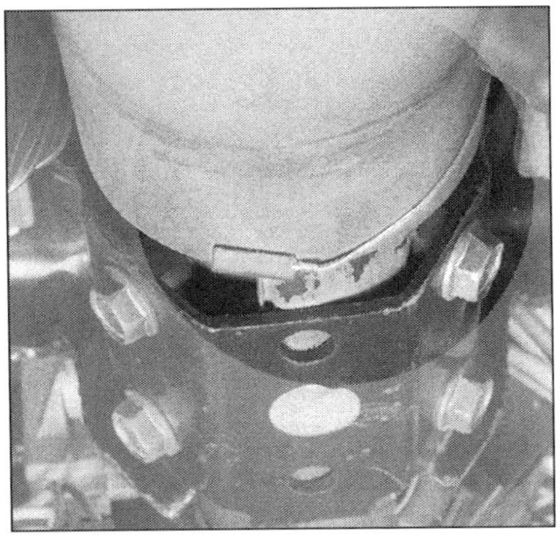

3.8b A typical cable-type shift indicator mechanism

3.10a To adjust the shift indicator needle on 1971, 1972 and some 1973 models, loosen the guide clip set screw, put the shift lever in the Neutral position (or as close to "N" on the gear position indicator panel as it will go) . . .

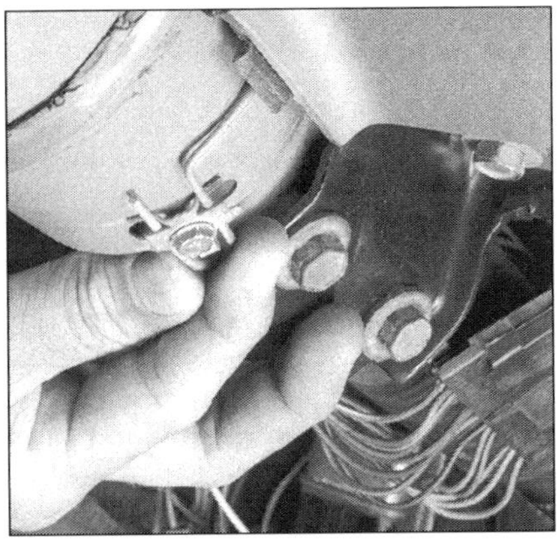

3.10b . . . slide the guide clip until the shift indicator needle is pointing at the middle of the "N", hold the clip in this position and tighten the set screw

3.10c To adjust the shift indicator needle on some 1973 and all later models, pry the guide clip from the shift bowl, put the shift lever in the Neutral position (or as close to "N" as it will go) . . .

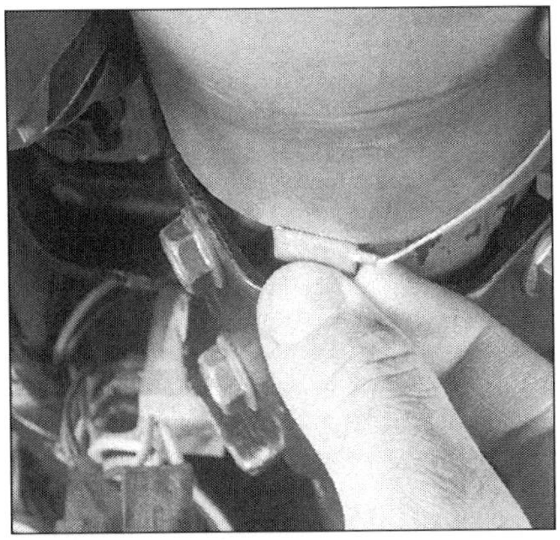

3.10d . . . move the clip until the pointer is pointing at the middle of the "N" on the shift indicator panel, make sure the wire between the guide clip and the indicator is taut, and push the clip back onto the shift bowl

9 Remove the steering column cover and/or dashboard lower trim panel, as necessary (see Chapter 11).

10 Put the shift lever in the Neutral position, remove the guide clip set screw, if equipped, pry the clip off the shift bowl **(see illustrations)**, move it until the indicator needle is

4.3 Typical carburetor-mounted detent switch (arrow) (accelerator pedal-mounted switches look and work essentially the same way)

4.5 To test a detent switch, hook up a test light or voltmeter to the detent switch and ground terminals: turn on the ignition, but don't start the engine. The test light should be off. Now open the throttle linkage to its wide-open position or depress the accelerator pedal all the way to the floor. The light should come on. If it doesn't come on, the switch needs to be either adjusted or replaced (carburetor-mounted switch shown, but an accelerator pedal-mounted switch is tested the same way)

4.6 To adjust a carburetor-mounted detent switch, loosen the mounting screws (the other screw, obscured by the switch in the foreground, is right next to the screw with the wrench on it), insert a #42 (0.094-inch) wire gage or drill bit into the calibrating hole, adjust the position of the switch so the lever just touches the accelerator relay rod or throttle lever, hold the switch in this position, tighten the mounting screws and remove the wire gage or drill bit

pointing at the "N" on the shift indicator panel, then push the clip back onto the shift bowl. If the clip has a set screw, make sure the screw is snug (don't overtighten it or you'll strip the threads). Make sure the link or wire between the guide clip and the indicator needle is taut.

4 Downshift (detent) switch (THM 425) - check, adjustment and replacement

1 The detent switch initiates full-throttle downshifts. When the accelerator pedal is depressed to its wide-open position, the detent switch closes the circuit to the detent solenoid on the transmission case, inside the sump, next to the upper valve body casting. This detent solenoid controls a detent valve inside the valve body. The detent valve is controlled by the opposing forces of line pressure on one end and spring pressure on the other. When the detent solenoid is energized by the detent switch, it opens a small needle valve inside an exhaust passage, allowing line pressure to the detent valve to bleed off. Spring force moves the detent valve to its open position, causing a 3-2 or 2-1 downshift. At any accelerator pedal position other than wide-open throttle, the detent switch opens the circuit to the detent solenoid, the solenoid is de-energized, the exhaust passage is closed and line pressure overcomes spring pressure, moving the detent valve to its closed position. The detent switch is located either at the throttle linkage or at the accelerator pedal.

Check

Refer to illustrations 4.3 and 4.5

Note: *Make sure the carburetor is properly adjusted before beginning this procedure.*

2 If the detent switch is located at the carburetor throttle linkage, remove the air cleaner assembly (see Chapter 4).

3 Locate the detent switch **(see illustration)**.

4 Raise the vehicle and place it securely on jackstands.

5 Hook up a 12-volt test light between the detent switch terminal and ground **(see illustration)**. Turn on the ignition, but don't start the engine. The test light should be off. Now open the throttle linkage to its wide-open position or depress the accelerator pedal all the way to the floor. The light should come on. If it doesn't come on, the switch needs to be either adjusted or replaced.

Adjustment

Switch at carburetor throttle linkage

Refer to illustration 4.6

6 The carburetor-mounted switch is adjusted by altering its position in relation to the throttle lever. Loosen the mounting screws and insert a #42 (0.094-inch) wire gage into the calibrating hole **(see illustration)** located below the lower electrical terminal (the shank of a properly sized drill bit will work if a gage is not available). Adjust the position of the switch so the lever just touches the accelerator relay rod or the throttle lever or arm. Hold the switch in this position, tighten the mounting screws and remove the wire gage or drill bit. The switch should now make contact above 60 degrees of throttle opening.

Switch at accelerator pedal

7 The accelerator pedal-mounted switch (Buicks and Oldsmobiles) is self-adjusting. To set it, push in the switch plunger (toward the firewall) as far as it will go. Then depress the accelerator pedal all the way to the floor. The switch should adjust itself automatically. If it doesn't, replace it.

Replacement

8 Disconnect the electrical leads from the switch, remove the two bolts (carburetor-mounted type) or single bolt (accelerator pedal type) attaching the switch to its bracket and remove the switch.

9 Installation is the reverse of removal. Be sure to adjust the switch as described above.

5 Vacuum modulator (THM 425) - check and replacement

Check

Refer to illustration 5.1

1 The vacuum modulator **(see illustration)** controls throttle pressure in the valve body by regulating line pressure in relation to intake manifold vacuum, which is an indication of engine torque. It consists of a flexible rubber diaphragm inside a metal housing, a spring, a pushrod and a spool valve that opens or closes a passageway inside the valve body. The half of the housing near the transmission is vented to atmospheric pressure. The other half is connected to intake manifold vacuum. This vacuum chamber also contains a spring that pushes against the diaphragm, which uses a pushrod to move a valve spool into or out of its bore in relation to intake manifold vacuum. At idle, intake vacuum is high, which pulls the diaphragm out, against spring pressure, moving the spool valve out of its bore, closing off line pressure to the valve body. As the throttle valve in the

5.1 The vacuum modulator is located on the right underside of the transmission; to remove the modulator, detach the vacuum line (upper arrow), remove the retainer bolt (lower arrow) and retainer, note which direction the vacuum pipe faces, and pull out the modulator

carburetor or throttle body starts to open, intake vacuum begins to drop. At a certain point, the decreasing vacuum pulling the diaphragm is overcome by the spring pushing against it, and the spool valve begins to move into its bore. At wide open throttle (zero vacuum), the spool valve is pushed all the way into its bore, allowing full line pressure to the valve body. In actual operation, the spool valve moves in and out in response to incremental changes in vacuum, regulating line pressure to the valve body in accordance with engine torque.

2 Raise the vehicle and place it securely on jackstands.

3 There are two quick and easy ways to check the modulator: first, disconnect the vacuum line at the modulator and note whether any ATF drips out of the line or the modulator vacuum housing. If it does, the diaphragm is torn. If no ATF comes out, hook up a hand vacuum pump to the modulator, apply vacuum and note whether the vacuum chamber holds a vacuum. If it doesn't, the diaphragm is torn. If the modulator fails either of these two tests, replace it. (A third test - applying vacuum to the vacuum chamber and noting whether the pushrod and spool valve move toward the modulator - requires removal of the modulator.)

Replacement

4 Detach the vacuum line from the modulator, remove the vacuum modulator retaining bolt and retainer **(see illustration 5.1)**.

5 Note the direction in which the vacuum line pipe faces, then remove the modulator from the transmission. DO NOT remove the modulator bushing unless it's damaged.

6 If you're planning to reinstall the same modulator valve, remove the old O-ring from the modulator and discard it.

7 Installation is the reverse of removal. Be sure to use a new O-ring, make sure the vacuum line pipe is facing the same direction as

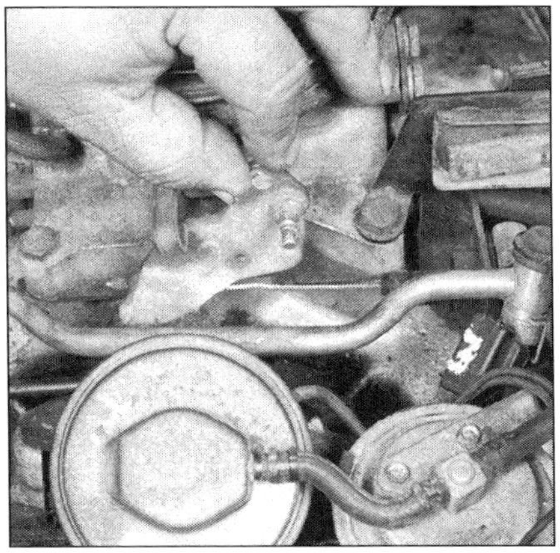

6.3 To check the TV cable, open the throttle lever wide open and let go - the cable should slide easily in both directions through the cable housing and return to its original state

before, install the retainer and tighten the modulator retaining bolt to the torque listed in this Chapter's Specifications.

6 Throttle valve (TV) cable (THM 325/325-4L) - check, adjustment and replacement

Check

Refer to illustration 6.3

Note: *The following check does not verify correct TV cable adjustment. If you suspect an improperly adjusted cable, go through the adjustment procedure below.*

1 The THM 325 and 325-4L use a TV cable instead of the vacuum modulator and downshift switch used by the THM 425. The TV cable, which connects the throttle plate in the carburetor or throttle body to a TV plunger in the valve body, controls detent downshifts, line pressure, part-throttle downshifts, shift feel and shift points. A sticking or misadjusted TV cable can cause delayed shifts or full-throttle shifts.

2 Check the TV cable with the shift lever in Neutral and the engine idling. Set the parking brake firmly and block the wheels to prevent any vehicle movement. As an added precaution, have an assistant in the driver's seat applying the brake pedal.

3 Rotate the throttle lever and pull the cable forward **(see illustration)**. It should easily slide through the cable housing with no binding or jerky operation. Release the cable. It should return to its original location with the cable stop against the cable terminal.

4 If the TV cable does not operate as described, the cause is a defective or misadjusted cable or damaged components at either end of the cable.

Adjustment

Refer to illustrations 6.5a and 6.5b

Note: *The engine should NOT be running*

6.5a On most models, the adjuster mechanism is located next to the carburetor or throttle body (arrow), but, on some models, it may be located near the accelerator pedal, in the passenger compartment

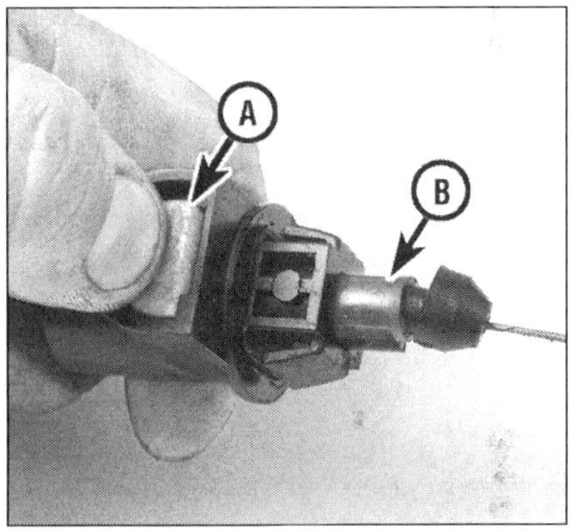

6.5b Details of a typical adjuster mechanism (removed from vehicle for clarity)

A *Re-adjust tab*
B *Slider*

during this adjustment.

5 Push down on the adjuster mechanism re-adjust tab, then push the cable housing/slider into the adjuster mechanism as far as it will go **(see illustrations)**.

6 Release the re-adjust tab.

7 Turn the throttle lever to the wide open throttle (WOT) position, which will automatically adjust the cable. Release the throttle lever. **Note:** *Don't use excessive force at the throttle lever to adjust the TV cable. If great effort is required to adjust the cable, disconnect the cable at the transmission end and check for free operation. If it's still difficult, replace the cable. If it's now free, suspect a bent TV link in the transmission or a problem with a throttle lever.*

8 After adjustment check for proper operation.

Replacement

Refer to illustrations 6.10a, 6.10b, 6.11, 6.13, 6.14 and 6.15

9 Remove the air cleaner (see Chapter 4).

6.10a Squeeze the locking tangs together . . .

6.10b . . . and pull the slider and TV cable assembly through the bracket, away from the throttle lever

6.11 Detach the TV cable from the pin on the throttle lever and remove the cable

6.13 Remove the TV cable hold-down bolt from the transmission

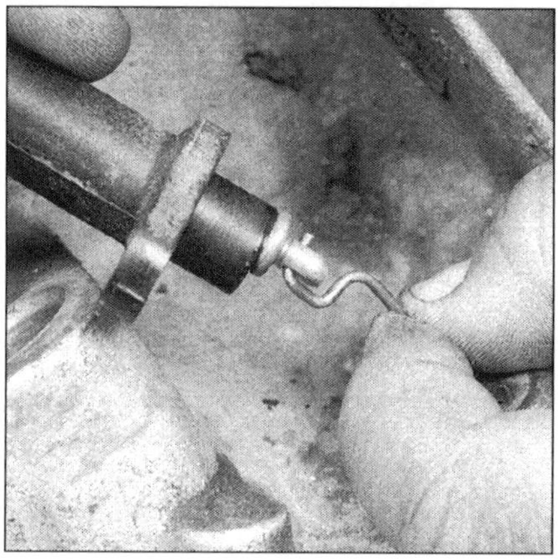

6.14 Pull up on the TV cable and disengage it from the link

6.15 Pull out the old seal and install a new one

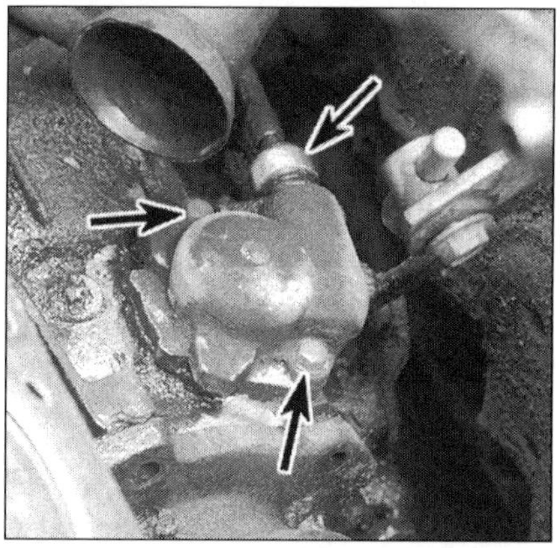

7.2 To remove the governor assembly from a 1979 or later model, unscrew the threaded retaining ring for the speedometer cable (upper arrow) and detach the speedometer cable, then remove the two governor housing retaining bolts (arrows)

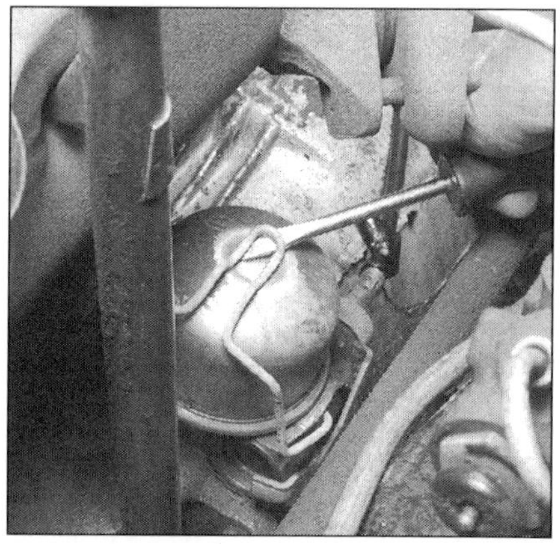

7.3 To remove the governor from a 1971 through 1978 model, pry off the retaining clip, remove the cover and lift out the governor assembly

10 Squeeze the locking tabs and shove the slider through the bracket, away from the throttle lever **(see illustrations)**.

11 Detach the TV cable from the throttle lever **(see illustration)** and pull the cable assembly from the cable bracket.

12 Raise the vehicle and place it securely on jackstands.

13 Remove the cable housing hold-down bolt **(see illustration)**.

14 Pull up on the cable and disengage it from the link **(see illustration)**.

15 Pull out the old seal and install a new one **(see illustration)**.

16 Installation is the reverse of removal. Be sure to route the new cable the same way as the old one. When you're done, adjust the cable (see Steps 5 through 8).

7 Governor - inspection and replacement

Refer to illustrations 7.2, 7.3, 7.7a, 7.7b, 7.8a and 7.8b

1 The governor valve controls governor pressure, which opposes throttle pressure to control upshifts and downshifts in accordance with the vehicle's road speed. The governor valve is driven by the transmission output shaft, so its rotational speed - and governor pressure - rises and falls with vehicle speed. Governor pressure provides a road speed signal to the hydraulic system that produces automatic upshifts as road speed increases, and downshifts as speed decreases.

2 On 1979 and later models, unscrew the threaded retainer ring for the speedometer cable and detach the cable from the speedometer driven gear **(see illustration)**.

3 On 1971 through 1978 models, remove

7.7a Inspect the teeth on the speedometer and governor drive gears for wear and damage, and make sure that the speedometer drive gear bearing turns freely; if either drive gear is damaged or worn, or if the bearing makes a grating sound when turned, replace the governor

7.8b Dig out the old O-ring from its groove around the speedometer driven gear shaft with an awl (it's too deeply embedded to use anything softer), but be careful! And apply a little fresh oil to the new seal when installing it

the governor retaining clip **(see illustration)**; on 1979 and later models, remove the governor retaining bolts **(see illustration 7.2)**.

4 Remove the governor valve assembly.

5 Wipe out the governor valve bore in the transmission with a clean shop rag and inspect it for rust and scoring.

6 Wash the governor valve thoroughly in clean solvent and blow it dry with compressed air.

7 If the governor is from a 1971 through 1978 model, the only thing you can inspect is the drive gear at the lower end of the shaft; the governor assembly (balls, springs, weighted arms) is enclosed in a metal housing that can't be removed. If the governor is from a 1979 or later model **(see illustrations)**, carefully inspect the following parts. Is the speedometer drive gear bearing noisy or sticking? Is the speedometer or governor drive gear damaged? Are the teeth worn or broken? Are the check-ball springs broken,

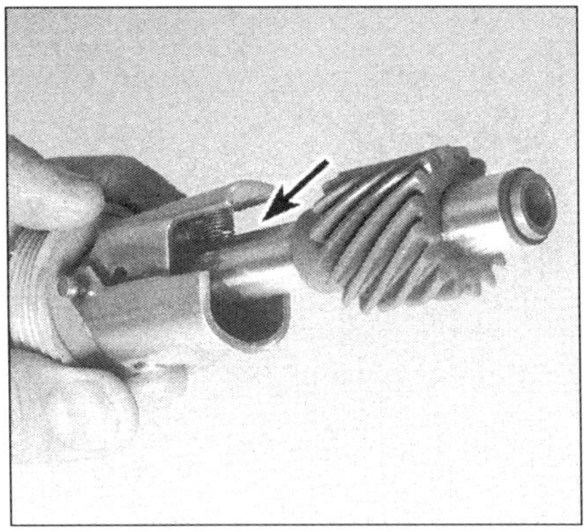

7.7b Inspect the check-ball spring (arrow) and check ball for each weighted arm; the springs should not be loose or distorted and the balls must move freely in and out of the passages they control in the sleeve; again, if there's any obvious damage or wear, replace the governor

8.1a A typical neutral start/back-up light switch (arrow) used on 1971 through 1978 models (electrical connector unplugged for clarity)

distorted or loose? Are the check balls scored, galled or sticking? Do the weighted arms bind or stick? If the governor assembly is damaged or worn in any way, replace it.

8 Installation is the reverse or removal. Be sure to apply a liberal coat of fresh ATF to the governor shaft, O-ring and drive gear. Be sure to use new O-rings on the governor housing and speedometer driven gear shaft **(see illustrations)**.

8 Neutral start and back-up light switch - check, replacement and adjustment

Note: *Later models do not use an electrical neutral start switch. A mechanical block in the steering column prevents the engine from cranking in positions other than Park or Neutral. However, these models use a back-up light switch that's physically similar in appearance to the earlier neutral start/backup light*

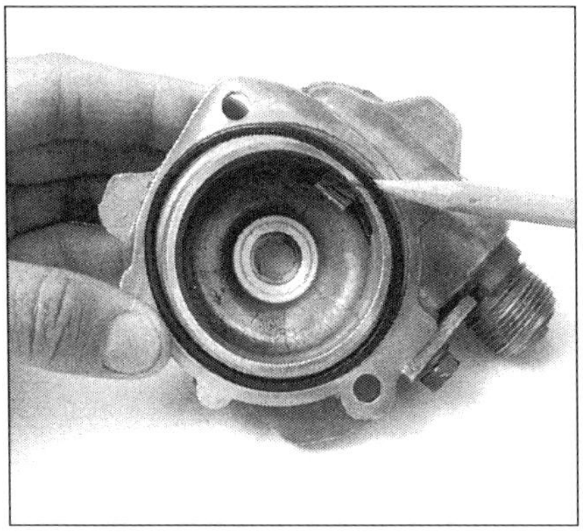

7.8a Remove the old governor housing O-ring with a pencil to protect the O-ring groove from gouging; be sure to lubricate the new O-ring with a little clean engine oil before installing it

8.1b A typical back-up light switch (arrow) used on 1979 and later models (no neutral start switch; that function is handled by a mechanical system in the column)

switch and is adjusted basically the same way. Diagnosis and disassembly of the mechanical type neutral start system is not recommended.

Check

Refer to illustrations 8.1a, 8.1b and 8.5

1 The Neutral start and back-up light switch **(see illustrations)** is located on top of the steering column, near the firewall. When the switch is operating properly, the engine should start only when the shift lever is in Park or Neutral, and the back-up lights should come on when the shift lever is in Reverse. If the engine starts in any other gear, or the back-up lights don't come on, either the shift linkage is out of adjustment or the switch needs to be adjusted or replaced.

2 Make sure the shift linkage is properly adjuster (see Section 3).

3 Verify that there's voltage available at the switch with the ignition key turned to On.

4 Verify that the switch has continuity when it's in Park, Neutral or Reverse (1971 through 1978 models) or when it's in Reverse (1979 and later models) as follows.

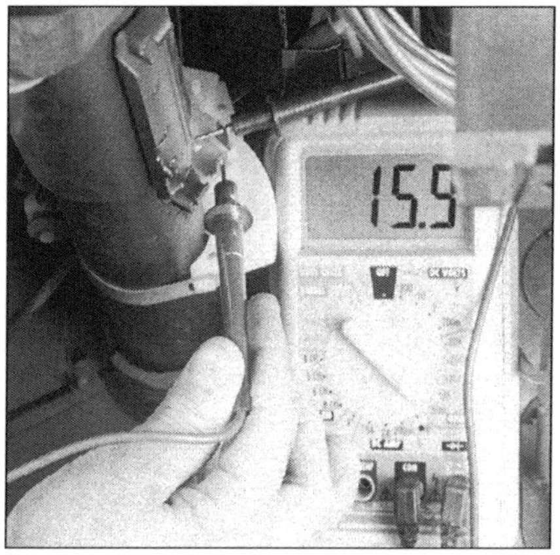

8.5 To check a neutral start/back-up light switch, unplug the electrical connector and check continuity of the appropriate terminals with the shift lever in Park and Neutral, then check continuity of the appropriate terminals with the shift lever in Reverse (shown, on a later back-up-lights-only type switch)

8.9 To remove a neutral start/back-up light switch, remove the small retaining screw on the left side of the column, remove the band that clamps the switch to the column, then lift the switch straight up

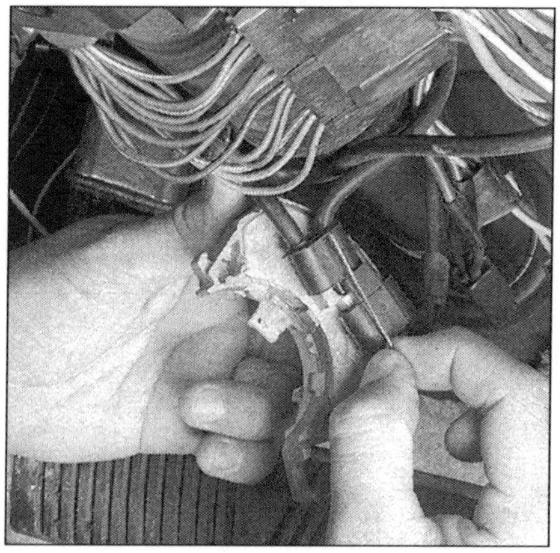

8.10 On 1971 through 1978 models, remove this wire retainer and detach the vacuum block assembly from the back of the neutral start/back-up light switch

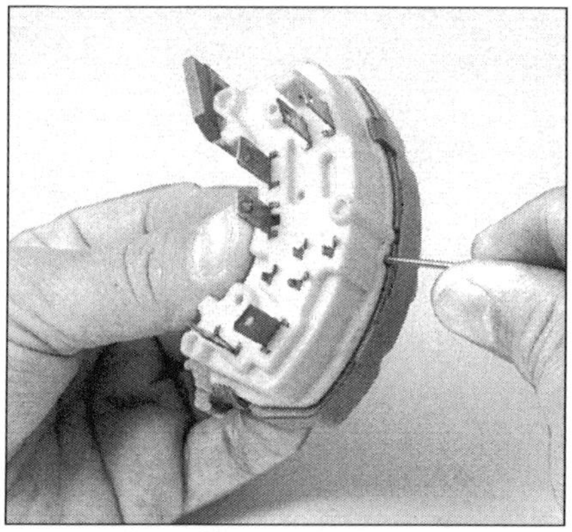

8.11a On 1971 through 1978 models, slide the carrier tang to the neutral position, insert a 0.090-inch diameter gage pin through the hole in the switch cover, then slide the carrier tang back-and-forth a tiny bit until the pin drops through the alignment hole in the inner plastic slide; leave this pin in place until the switch has been installed, but be sure to remove it before shifting out of Neutral

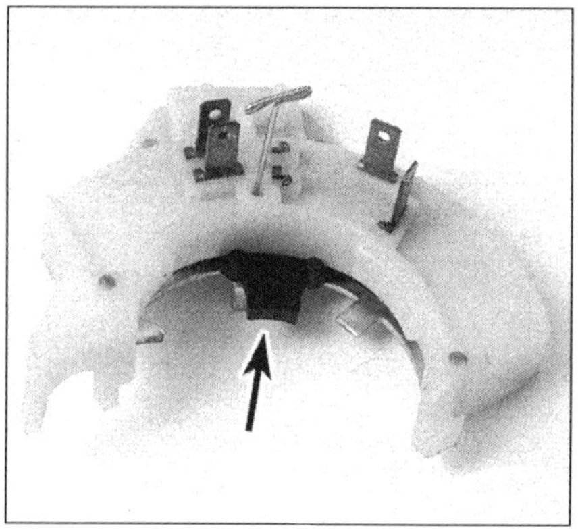

8.11b On 1979 and later models, slide the carrier tang (arrow) to the neutral position and insert a 0.040-inch diameter gage pin through the hole in the switch housing as shown, then jiggle the carrier back-and-forth a little until the pin drops through the alignment hole in the carrier tang; leave this pin in place until the switch has been installed, but be sure to remove it before shifting out of Neutral

5 Unplug the electrical connector and, using an ohmmeter **(see illustration)**, verify that there's continuity when the switch is in Park or Neutral (neutral start terminals) and Reverse (back-up light terminals). There are many terminal arrangements on various switches, so how do you know which terminals to check? You don't! But it's easy to figure out. There are no more than six terminals: two are for the neutral start switch, two are for the back-up lights and two are for the seatbelt warning buzzer, if equipped. Early switches have only four terminals (neutral start and back-up lights, but no seatbelt buzzer); 1979 and later switches also have four terminals (back-up lights and seatbelt buzzer, but no neutral start). So try each pair of terminals in Neutral, Park and Reverse, and you'll figure it out. The neutral start switch should have continuity only when the switch carrier tang (the sliding contact that moves as the shift lever is rotated) is in the Neutral or Park position. The back-up light switch should have continuity only when the switch carrier tang is in the Reverse position. **Note:** *If testing the switch on the steering column proves difficult or inconclusive, remove it and check it on the bench instead.*

6 If the switch doesn't operate as described, try adjusting it (see below) and retest.

7 If the switch doesn't operate as described after adjustment, replace it (see below).

Replacement and adjustment

Refer to illustrations 8.9, 8.10, 8.11a, 8.11b and 8.12

8 Unplug the electrical connector(s). If there is more than one connector, make sure you label or mark the connectors and terminals.

9 Remove the switch retaining screw **(see illustration)** and clamp.

10 If there are parking brake release vacuum lines attached to the back of the switch, remove the wire retainer and detach the vacuum line assembly **(see illustration)**.

11 If you're installing the old switch, adjust it by sliding the carrier tang to the Neutral position and inserting a 0.080-inch diameter gage pin (1971 through 1978 models) or a 0.040-inch diameter pin (1979 and later models) through the hole in the switch housing and the alignment hole in the sliding plastic carrier (older models) or the carrier tang (newer models). If you don't have a gage pin, use a drill bit or a needle **(see illustrations)**. Jiggle the tang back and forth a little to verify that the gage pin has gone all the way through the housing and the tang. Do not remove the pin until the switch is installed. (A new switch will have a shear pin already installed; when you shift out of Neutral, it will shear off.)

12 Use an ohmmeter to verify that the switch has continuity with the carrier tang in neutral **(see illustration)**.

13 Installation is the reverse of removal. Make sure the column shift lever is in the Neutral position and the carrier tang on the switch is locked into the neutral position by the gage pin (or shear pin on a new switch). Do not pull out the gage pin until the switch retaining clamp is in place and the retaining screw has been tightened. Make sure the electrical connectors are plugged into the correct terminals.

14 Verify that the car starts in Neutral, then remove the gage pin. If you installed a new switch, simply move the shift lever all the way to the right (Low), then move it all the way to the left (Park) to shear off the pin.

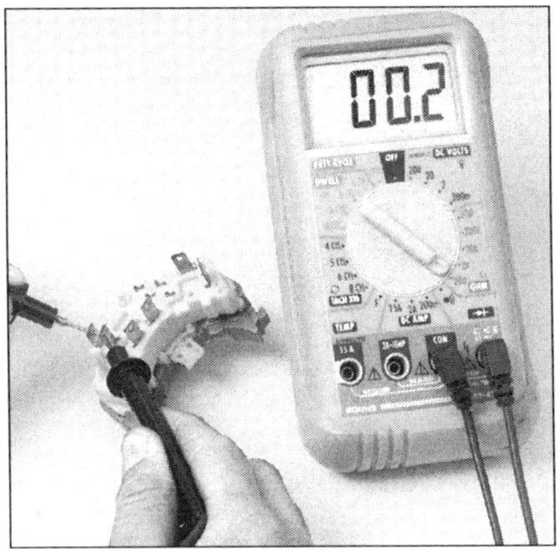

8.12 Using an ohmmeter, verify that the switch has continuity with the carrier tang in the neutral position

9 Transmission mounts - check and replacement

Refer to illustration 9.2

1 Raise the vehicle and place it securely on jackstands.

2 Inspect the rubber insulator on the transmission mounts for deterioration, cracking and separation of the rubber from the metal brackets. Try to pry the mount back and forth and up and down. There should be very little movement of the mount plates relative to the rubber insulators. Replace the mount(s) if there is.

3 To replace a transmission mount, support the transmission with a floor jack, remove the nuts and bolts, raise the transmission slightly with a jack and remove the rubber insulator.

4 Installation is the reverse of removal.

10 Transmission - removal and installation

Removal

Refer to illustrations 10.1a, 10.1b, 10.3, 10.4, 10.6a, 10.6b, 10.8a, 10.8b, 10.9, 10.13a, 10.13b, 10.13c, 10.13d, 10.14, 10.16, 10.19, 10.21a, 10.21b, 10.21c, 10.21d, 10.21e, 10.21f, 10.21g, 10.22 and 10.23

1 On 1971 through 1978 models, disconnect the oil cooler lines from the transmission. Be sure to plug the lines. Disconnect the cooler line bracket from the front left upper corner of the differential **(see illustrations)**.

2 Remove the upper differential-to-transmission bolts and the differential-to-engine support bracket bolts (see Chapter 8). (The rest of differential-to-transmission bolts and the right output shaft bearing support bolts can be removed after the vehicle is raised.)

3 Remove the upper transmission-to-engine bolts **(see illustration)**. (The rest of the bolts can be removed after the vehicle is raised.)

4 Disconnect the speedometer cable **(see illustration)** and remove the governor (see Section 7). Cover or plug the hole to prevent dirt from entering the transmission.

5 Raise the vehicle and support it securely on jackstands.

6 Remove the crossmember, if equipped, from behind the transmission **(see illustra-**

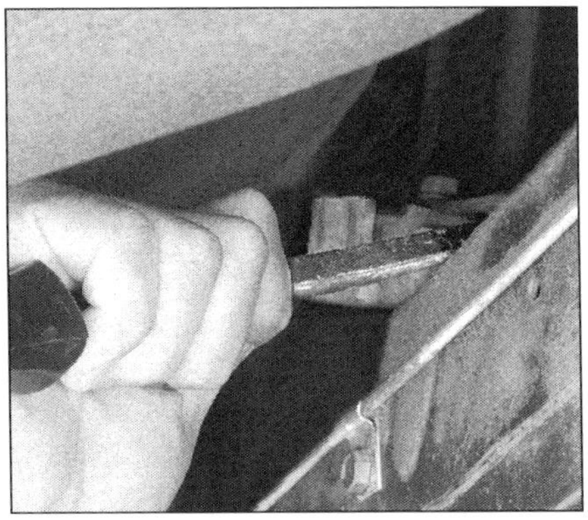

9.2 To check either transmission mount, insert a large screwdriver or prybar into the space between the transmission mount bracket and the crossmember and try to lever the transmission back and forth and up and down - the mount should allow little flex; if it does flex a lot, make sure the mount nuts and bolts are tight and carefully inspect it for cracks, tears and general deterioration; if tightening the mount fasteners fails to tighten it up, or if you find any sign of damage or deterioration, replace the mount

10.1b On 1971 through 1978 models, remove this bolt (arrow) to detach the cooler line bracket from the differential

10.4 Unscrew the threaded fitting (arrow) for the speedometer cable and disconnect the cable from the transmission

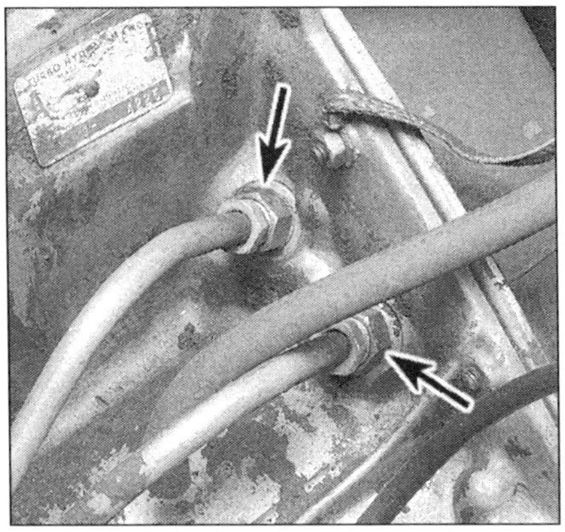

10.1a The oil cooler line fittings (arrows) are located at the upper left corner of the transmission on 1971 through 1978 models; plug the lines to keep out dirt and moisture

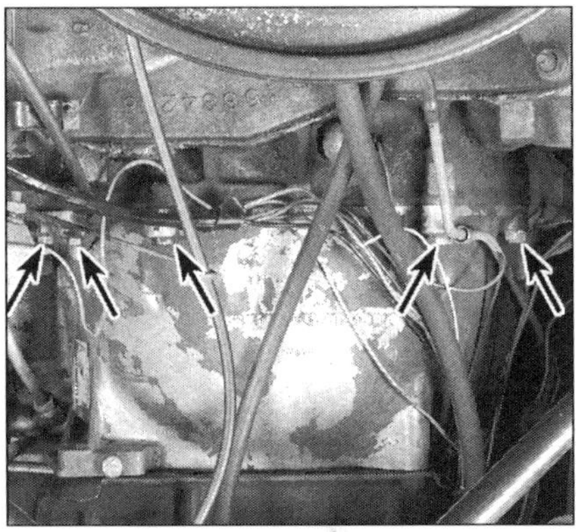

10.3 Upper transmission-to-engine bolts (arrows) (THM 425 shown, THM 325/325-4L similar)

10.6a On 1979 and later models, remove the bolt and nuts (arrows) from both ends of the crossmember behind the transmission (right end of crossmember shown, left end similar) . . .

10.6b . . . then remove the crossmember

10.8a To detach the lower shift rod from the shift lever at the transmission, remove the cotter pin . . .

10.8b . . . disengage the pin from the lever and set the rod aside where it won't be damaged during transmission removal

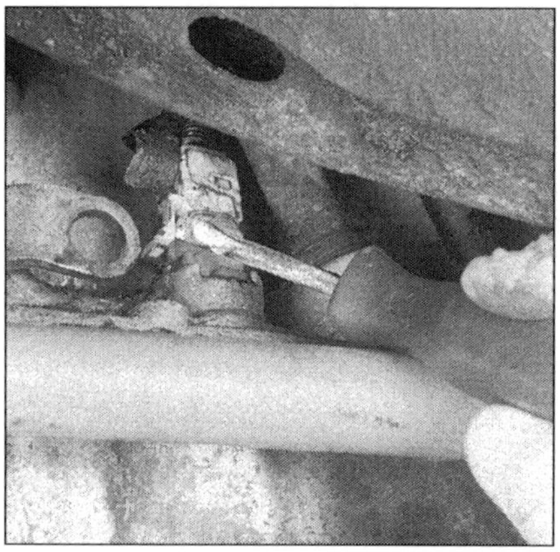

10.9 On 1982 and later models, unplug the electrical connector for the TCC

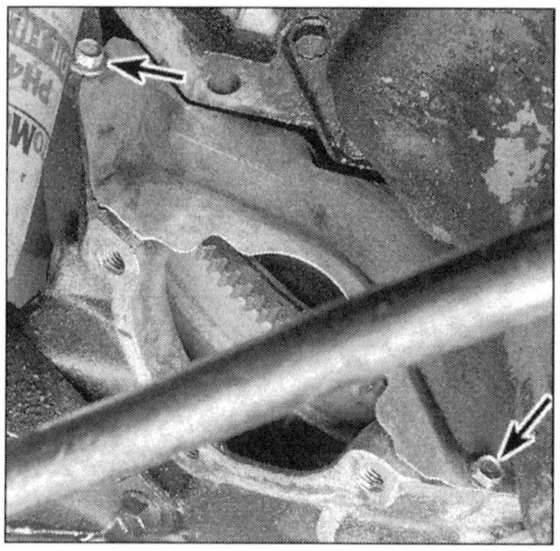

10.13a Upper left and lower torque converter access cover bolts (arrows) on a typical 1979 or later model

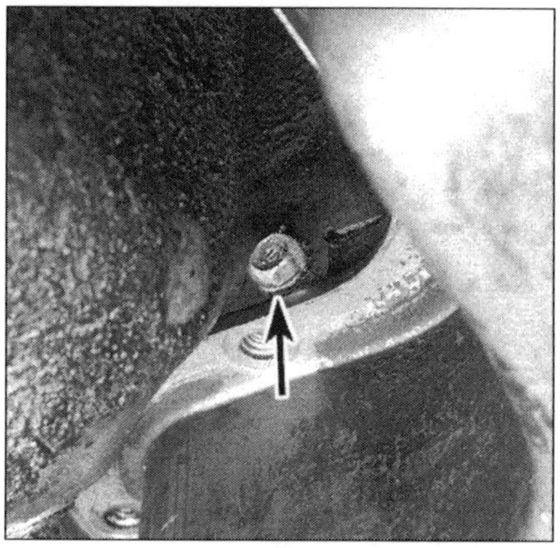

10.13b Lower right torque converter access cover bolt (arrow) on typical 1979 or later model

tions). Also remove any exhaust components which will interfere with transmission removal (see Chapter 4).

7 Drain the transmission fluid (see Chapter 1).

8 Disconnect the shift linkage rod from the shift lever on the transmission **(see illustrations)**.

9 Clearly label, then unplug, the electrical connector for the downshift switch solenoid (1971 through 1978 models) or torque converter clutch (1982 and later models) **(see illustration)**. Label and unplug any other electrical connectors. Set the wiring harnesses safely aside so that they won't be damaged during removal of the transmission.

10 On 1971 through 1978 models, detach the vacuum line from the modulator (see Section 5). Detach any other vacuum lines which might be damaged during transmission removal.

11 On 1979 and later models, disconnect the TV cable from the transmission (see Section 6).

12 Remove the starter motor (see Chapter 5).

13 Remove the torque converter cover bolts and remove the cover **(see illustrations)**.

14 Mark the relationship of the flywheel to the torque converter with white paint so they can be reinstalled in the same position **(see illustration)**.

15 Remove the torque converter-to-flywheel bolts. Turn the crankshaft bolt for access to each bolt.

16 On 1979 and later models, disconnect the threaded fittings for the oil cooler lines **(see illustration)**. Fluid will leak out, so have plugs available for the fittings on the transmission. Connect the two disconnected lines

10.13c Two lower bolts (arrows) on a typical 1971 through 1978 model (upper left bolt, not visible in this photo, is located above the starter hole (same location as upper left bolt on later models, as shown in illustration 10.13a)

10.13d When you remove (and install) the torque converter access cover, be aware that the upper right corner is notched to fit over a stud

10.14 Mark the relationship of the flywheel to the torque converter with white paint so they can be reinstalled in the same position, then remove each torque converter-to-flywheel bolt (arrow) by turning the crankshaft

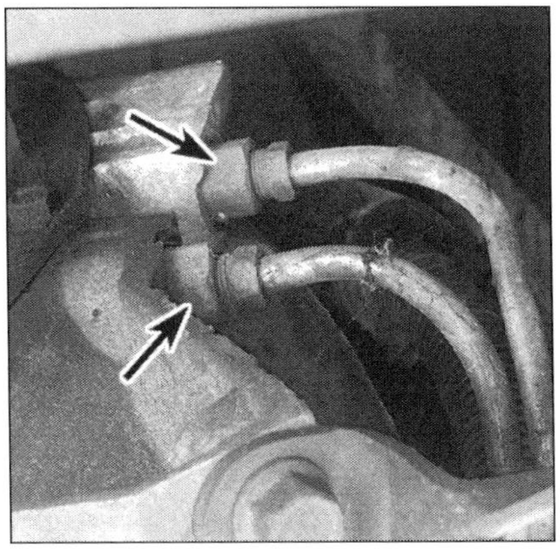

10.16 The oil cooler line fittings (arrows) are located at the lower right corner of the transmission on 1979 and later models; be sure to plug the lines to keep out dirt and moisture

10.19 Place a jack, preferably a transmission jack, or a jack with a transmission-type adapter, under the transmission

10.21a On 1971 through 1978 models, remove the left transmission mount bracket nut (arrow) and remove the mount and bracket (bracket bolts not visible)

10.21b On 1971 through 1978 models, remove the right transmission mount bracket nut (arrow) . . .

10.21c . . . remove the bracket bolts (arrows) and remove the right bracket

with a short section of 3/8-inch fuel line to prevent leakage from the lines.

17 Remove the differential (see Chapter 8).

18 Support the engine from above with an engine hoist or with a chain looped over a length of 4X4 wood laid across the fenders. (We don't recommend using a floor jack to support the engine from below; it won't leave enough room to maneuver the floor jack for the transmission.)

19 Support the transmission with a floor jack - preferably a jack made for this purpose **(see illustration)**. Safety chains will help steady the transmission on the jack.

20 Remove the lower transmission-to-engine bolt(s).

21 Remove the rear mount nuts and bolts **(see illustrations)**.

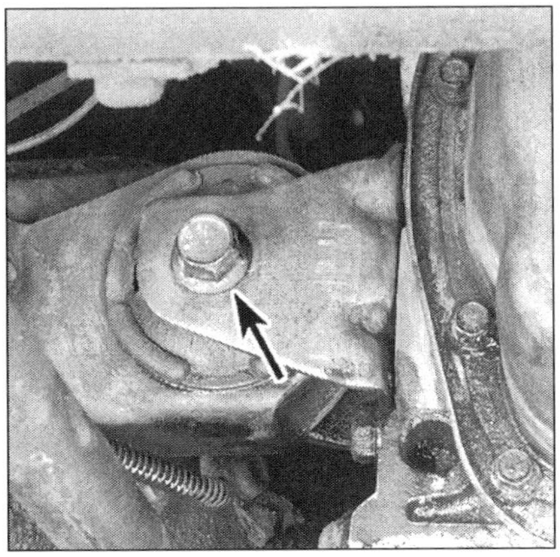

10.21d On 1979 and later models, remove the left transmission mount through-bolt (arrow) . . .

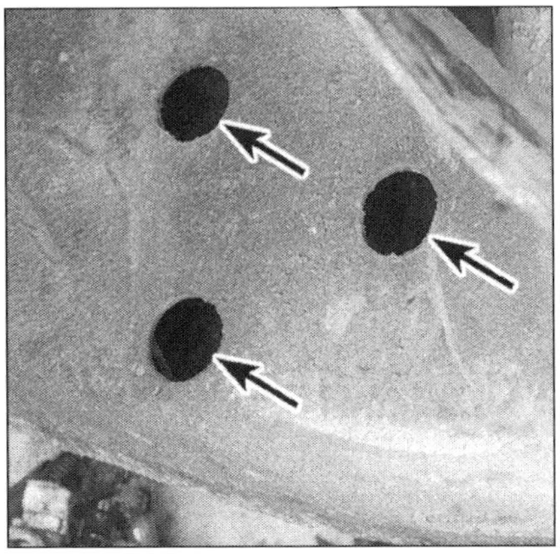

10.21e . . . remove the three bolts from the holes (arrows) in the left frame member . . .

10.21f . . . and pry out the left mount with a large screwdriver or prybar (you can leave the left mount bracket attached to the transmission)

10.21g On 1978 and later models, remove the right transmission mount bracket bolts (arrows) from the transmission and remove the bracket and mount (other bolts not visible)

22 Before removing the transmission assembly, make sure the torque converter is detached from the flywheel **(see illustration)**.
23 Secure the torque converter to the transmission so that it will not fall out during removal. Slide the transmission to the rear and lower it slightly, then check for any wire harness brackets on the top of the transmission **(see illustration)**.
24 Lower the transmission and wheel it out from under the vehicle.

10.22 Make sure the torque converter is completely disconnected from the flywheel before removing the transmission, and make sure the torque converter doesn't fall out while the transmission is being lowered

Installation

25 Make sure prior to installation that the torque converter hub is securely engaged in the pump.
26 With the transmission secured to the jack, raise the transmission into position, making sure to keep it level so the torque converter does not slide forward. Connect the transmission cooler lines.
27 Turn the torque converter to line up the torque converter and flywheel bolt holes. The white paint mark on the torque converter and the stud made during Step 15 must line up.

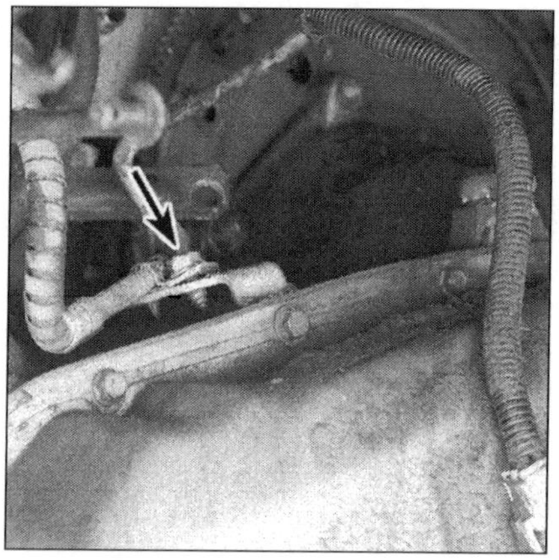

10.23 Lower the transmission just enough to check the top for any vacuum line or wiring harness clamps, such as this harness clamp (arrow) on a 1983 model

28 Move the transmission carefully forward until the dowel pins are engaged and the torque converter is engaged.
29 Installation is the reverse of removal. Be sure to tighten all transmission-to-engine and differential-to-transmission bolts to the torque listed in this Chapter's Specifications.
30 Remove all stands and lower the vehicle.
31 Fill the transmission with the specified fluid (see Chapter 1), run the vehicle and check for fluid leaks.

Chapter 8
Driveaxles and differential

Contents

Specifications

Torque specifications

	Ft-lbs
Differential-to-transmission bolts	30
Driveaxle/hub nut	
Buick	175
Cadillac	
1971 through 1978	110
1979 on	175
Oldsmobile	
1971 through 1973	150
1974	140
1975 through 1978	200
1979 on	175
Driveaxle-to-output shaft bolts	
Buick	60
Cadillac	
1971 through 1978	65
1979 on	60
Oldsmobile	
1971 through 1974	65
1975 through 1978	75
1979 on	60
Output shaft retaining bolt (1971 through 1978 models)	40

1 General information and inspection

Warning: *The procedures in this Chapter involve working under the vehicle, so make sure it's securely supported on sturdy jackstands.*

Power from the engine passes to the front wheels through the transmission, the differential and a pair of equal-length driveaxles. The differential is bolted to the front of the transmission and to the left side of the engine block. A pair of flanged output shafts are splined into the differential side gears. Because the differential is offset to the left, a longer right output shaft makes up the difference. The outer end of the right output shaft is supported by a bracket bolted to the right side of the block.

The inner CV joints are bolted to the flanged outer ends of the output shafts. The outer CV joints are splined into the hub and bearing assembly at each steering knuckle. An axle nut secures the outer CV joint to the hub and bearing assembly.

Each driveaxle assembly consists of three parts: A "tripod" type inner CV joint, a ''ball-and-cage" type outer CV joint and an axleshaft which connects the two. Outer CV joint housings have a splined stub axle which engages with the front hub and is retained by a large nut. Inner CV joint housings are bolted directly to the output shaft flanges. The right driveaxle assembly has a torsional damper on the middle of the axleshaft.

As the driveaxles move through their range of travel, ball bearings inside the CV joint housings allow them to operate at various lengths and angles. These bearings must be lubricated with special grease and protected by rubber boots. It's a good idea to inspect the boots for tears. Torn boots allow dirt and moisture to enter the CV joints; if not fixed, a simple tear accelerates bearing wear and causes premature failure.

Inspection

Periodically, inspect the boots for leaks, damage and deterioration (see Chapter 1). Replace damaged CV joint boots immediately or the CV joints may be damaged. You must remove the driveaxle (see Section 2) to replace the boots. Some auto parts stores carry a convenient alternative: ''Split-type" replacement boots can be installed without removing the driveaxle from the vehicle. This design is handy for emergency repairs when you're traveling, but it's not a substitute for one-piece boots. When a boot is torn, you must remove the driveaxle and disassemble, clean and inspect the CV joint to make sure no moisture and dirt have already caused damage.

The most common symptoms of worn or damaged CV joints, besides lubricant leaks, are: a clicking noise in turns, a clunk when accelerating from a coasting condition or vibration at highway speeds. To check for wear in the CV joints and driveaxle shafts,

2.3a If the hub turns as you unscrew the driveaxle/hub nut, use a large screwdriver or prybar to immobilize the hub

2.3b Remove the large washer behind the driveaxle/hub nut

2.4 Remove the six bolts (arrows) that attach the inner CV joint to the output shaft flange

grasp each axle (one at a time) and rotate it in both directions while holding the CV joint housings. Watch for movement, indicating worn splines or sloppy CV joints. Also, check the driveaxle shafts for cracks and distortion.

2 Driveaxles - removal and installation

Removal

Refer to illustrations 2.3a, 2.3b, 2.4 and 2.6

1 Apply the parking brake and block the rear wheels. Remove the wheel cover and the three lug nuts securing the mount for the wheel cover lock bolt, if equipped. Remove the driveaxle/hub nut cotter pin and nut lock. **Note:** *If the vehicle is equipped with wheels that won't allow the socket for the hub nut to pass through, the wheel will have to be removed and the hub immobilized as shown in illustration 2.3a.*

2 Loosen the remaining wheel lug nuts, raise the front of the vehicle and support it securely on jackstands. Remove the lug nuts and the front wheel.

3 Remove the brake caliper and support it with a piece of wire, then remove the brake disc (see Chapter 9). **Caution:** *Don't let the caliper hang by the brake hose.* Remove the hub nut and washer **(see illustrations)**.

4 Remove the inner CV joint-to-output shaft bolts **(see illustration)**.

5 Support the lower control arm with a floor jack, then disconnect the steering knuckle from the upper balljoint (see Chapter 10). **Warning:** *The jack must remain in this position throughout the remainder of the procedure.* Separate the tie-rod end from the steering knuckle and disconnect the lower end of the shock absorber from the lower control arm (see Chapter 10).

6 Remove the driveaxle assembly **(see illustration)**.

7 While the driveaxle is removed, inspect the differential oil seal and, if it's leaking, replace it (see Section 4). If you removed the right driveaxle assembly, inspect the right output shaft bearing by rotating the shaft and listening to the bearing. If it sounds dry or noisy, remove the right output shaft (see Section 4) and take it to an automotive machine shop to have the old bearing pressed off and a new unit pressed on.

2.6 Swing out the upper end of the steering knuckle as far as it will go and pull out the driveaxle

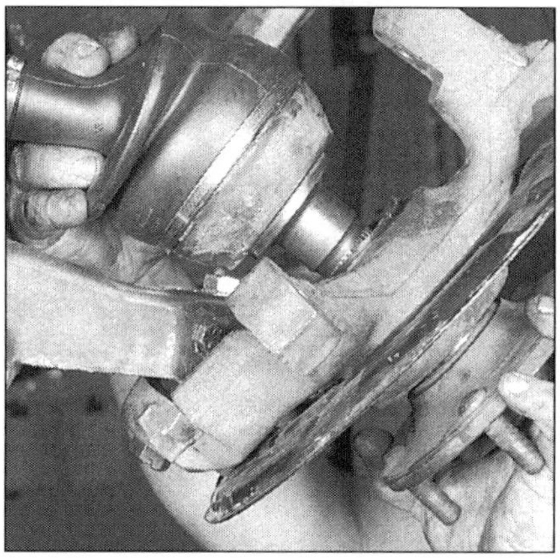

2.9 Lubricate the driveaxle splines and guide them carefully through the hub - make sure you don't damage the lip of the wheel bearing seal

Installation

Refer to illustration 2.9

8 Place the driveaxle in position and install the bolts that attach the inner CV joint to the output shaft flange.

9 Apply a small amount of multi-purpose grease to the splines at the outer end of the driveaxle. Guide the splined end into the hub **(see illustration)**. Secure the outer end of the driveaxle with the washer and hub nut. Just hand tighten the nut - don't try to tighten it yet.

10 Reattach the lower end of the shock absorber to the lower control arm (see Chapter 10).

11 Reattach the steering knuckle to the upper balljoint, then connect the tie-rod end to the steering arm (see Chapter 10). Install the brake caliper (see Chapter 9).

12 Tighten the inner CV joint-to-output shaft flange bolts to the torque listed in this Chapter's Specifications.

13 Install the wheel and lug nuts. Lower the vehicle. **Note:** *If the vehicle is equipped with wheels that won't allow the socket for the hub nut to pass through, immobilize the hub as shown in illustration 2.3a, tighten the nut to the torque listed in this Chapter's Specifications, then install the wheel.*

14 Tighten the driveaxle/hub nut to the torque listed in this Chapter's Specifications, then install the nut lock and a new cotter pin. Turn the nut a little tighter, if necessary, to install a new cotter pin; don't back off the nut to install the cotter pin. Tighten the wheel lug nuts to the torque listed in the Chapter 1 Specifications. Install the wheel cover.

15 Have the front end alignment checked.

3 Driveaxle boot replacement and CV joint inspection

1 Loosen the wheel lug nuts, then raise the vehicle and support it securely on jackstands.

2 Remove the driveaxle (see Section 2).

3.3a Cut off the old hose clamps with a pair of diagonal cutters (you can also chisel the clamps off, but it's easier with cutters)

3.3b The big retainer on 1979 and later model boots is pressed onto the CV joint housing; knock it off with a hammer and punch

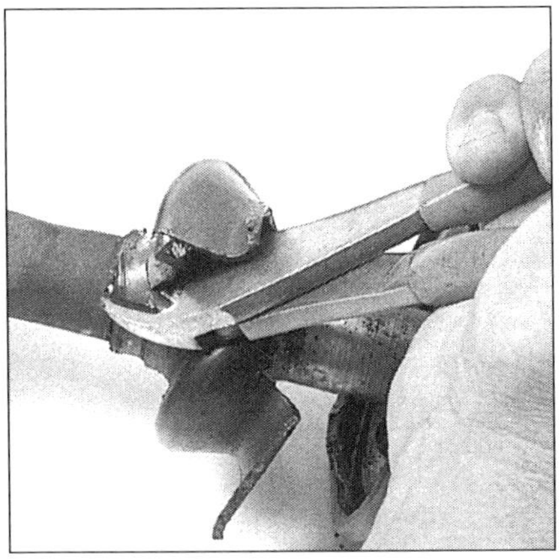

3.3c Cut off the pieces of the old boot

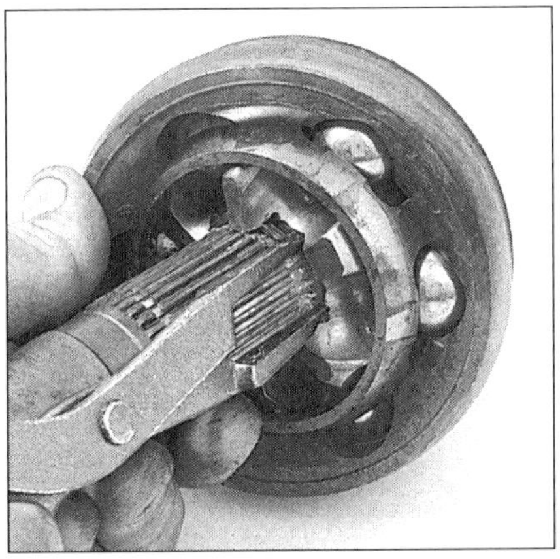

3.3d To release the axleshaft from the inner bearing race, expand the snap ring with a pair of large snap-ring pliers . . .

3.3e . . . then pull the axleshaft straight out of the inner race; if it's stuck, carefully tap on the hub areas of the inner race with a brass punch

3.3f Press down on the inner race far enough to allow a ball bearing to be removed; if it's difficult to tilt, gently tap the cage and inner race with a brass punch and hammer

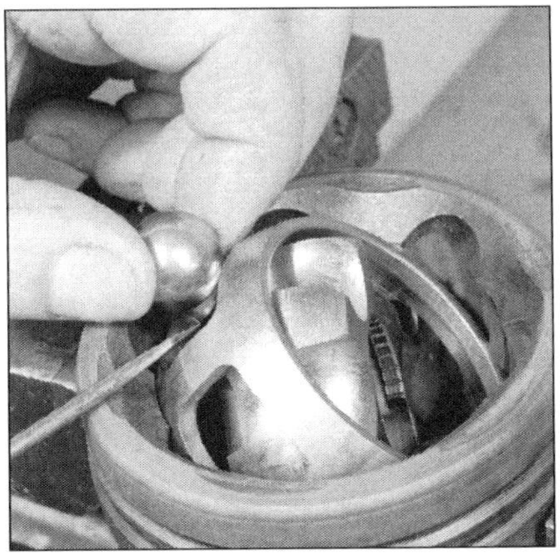

3.3g Pry the balls out of the cage, one at a time, with a blunt screwdriver or wooden tool

3.3h Tilt the inner race and cage 90-degrees, then align the windows in the cage (A) with the lands of the housing (B) and rotate the inner race up and out of the outer race

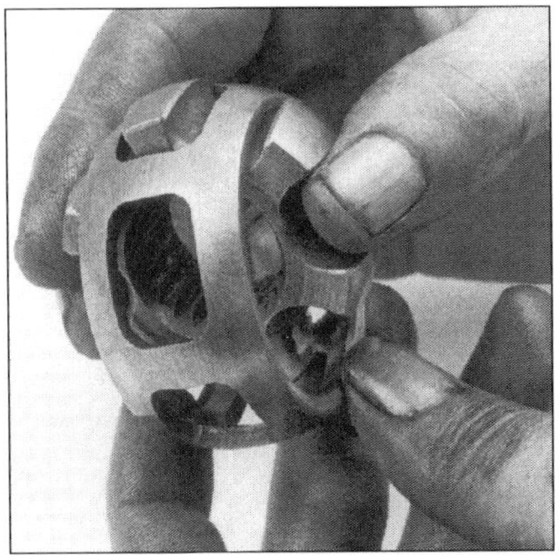

3.3i Align the inner race lands with the cage window and rotate the inner race out of the cage

Outer CV joint

Refer to illustrations 3.3a through 3.3bb

Note: *For some of the following steps, putting the driveaxle in a bench vise makes disassembly and reassembly easier. If you use a vise, be sure to use wood blocks to protect it from the vise jaws.*

3 Refer to the accompanying illustrations to remove, clean, inspect and lubricate the outer CV joint and install a new boot **(see illustrations)**.

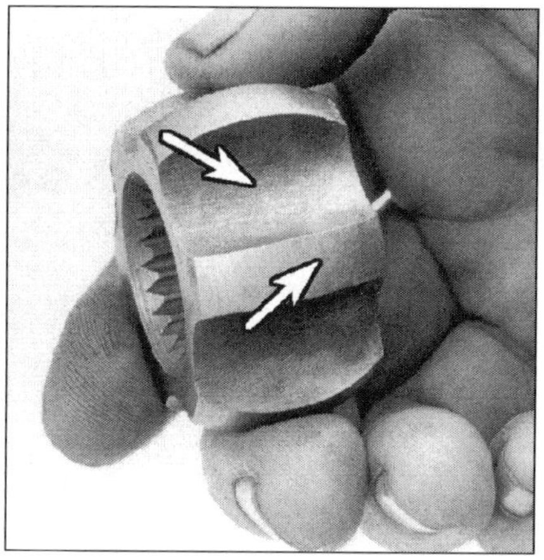

3.3j After cleaning the components with solvent, check the inner race lands and grooves for pitting and score marks

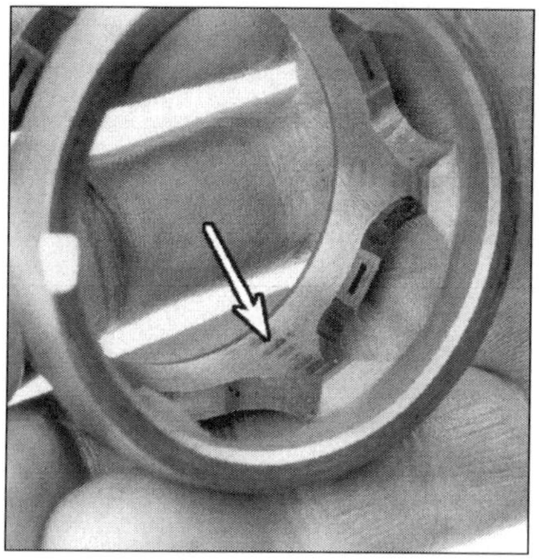

3.3k Check the cage for cracks, pitting and score marks - shiny spots are normal and don't affect operation

3.3l With the race and cage tilted at 90-degrees, lower the assembly into the housing

3.3m Rotate the assembly by gently tapping with a hammer and brass punch, then . . .

3.3n . . . press the balls into the cage windows, repeating until all of the balls are installed

3.3o Use needle-nose pliers to lower the snap-ring into the groove . . .

3.3p . . . then seat it into the groove with snap-ring pliers (note that the two ends of the snap-ring must be located in their special recess)

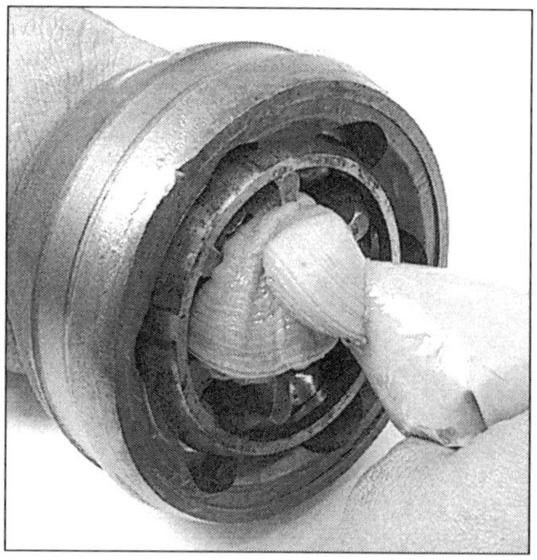

3.3q Pack the assembled CV joint assembly with new CV joint grease by filling the splined hole in the inner race . . .

3.3r . . . then insert a wooden dowel (with a slightly smaller diameter than the axleshaft) into the splined hole and push down to force the grease into the surrounding joint; repeat this procedure until the bearing is completely packed

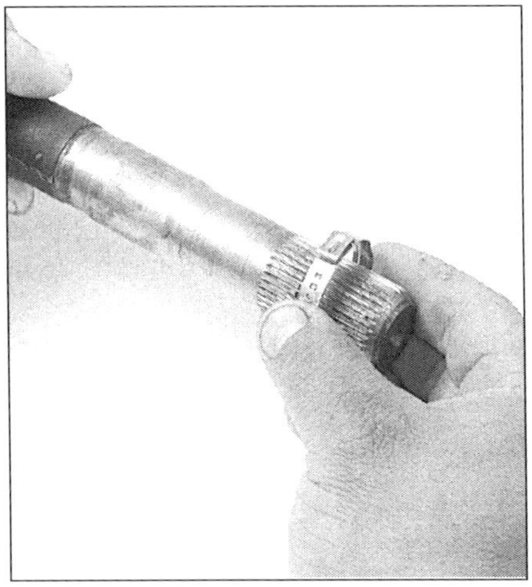

3.3s Slip a new small-end boot clamp over the axleshaft

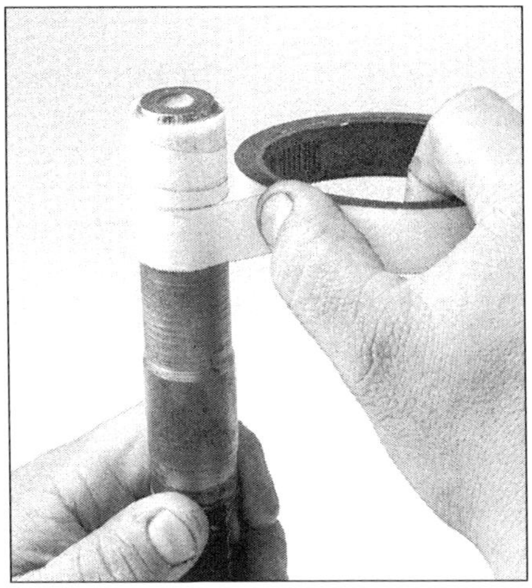

3.3t Tape the splines of the axleshaft to protect the new boot

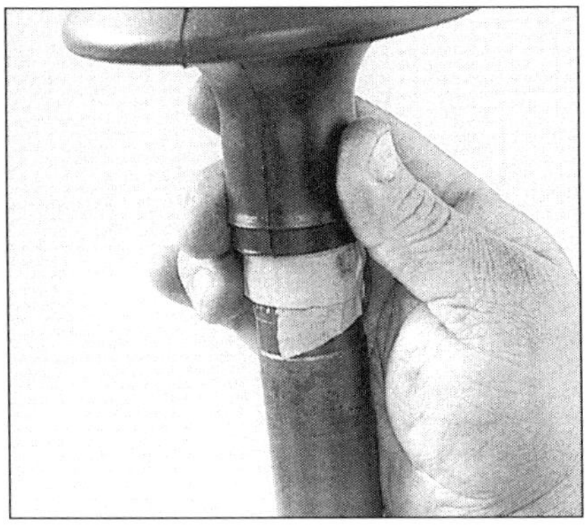

3.3u Carefully slip the new boot over the taped end of the axleshaft; use a little grease if necessary - some boots are a very tight fit and can be torn if forced to slide over the often rough surface of an old axleshaft

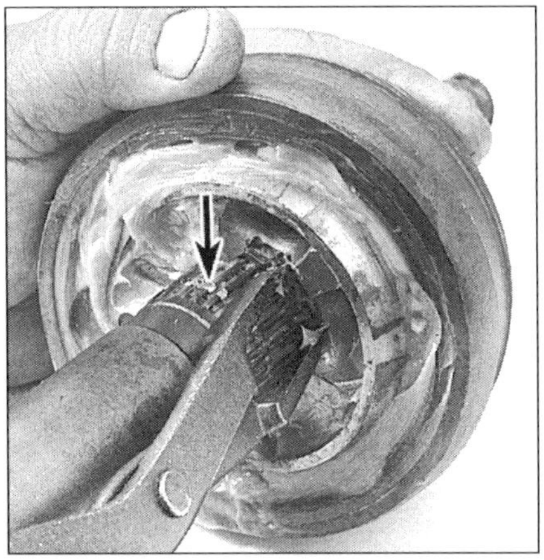

3.3v Once the new boot is on, remove the tape and insert the axleshaft into the outer CV joint assembly; make sure the splines are inserted far enough to allow the snap-ring to engage the groove (arrow) near the end of the splines (to verify that the axleshaft is properly engaged, try to pull the axleshaft out of the CV joint)

3.3w Pack the new boot with the rest of the CV joint grease

3.3x Secure the large boot clamp on 1978 and earlier models with a pair of boot clamp pliers like these (available at most auto parts stores) - this is one type of clamp you're likely to encounter

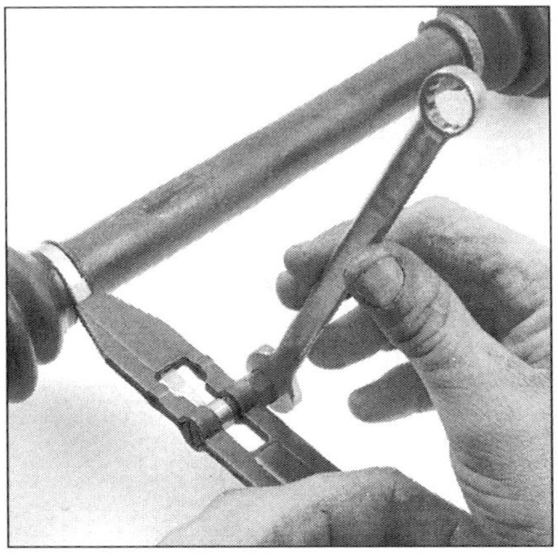

3.3y Another variation of boot clamp is the "band" type, which requires a special tightening tool. Install the band with its end pointing in the direction of axle rotation and tighten it securely . . .

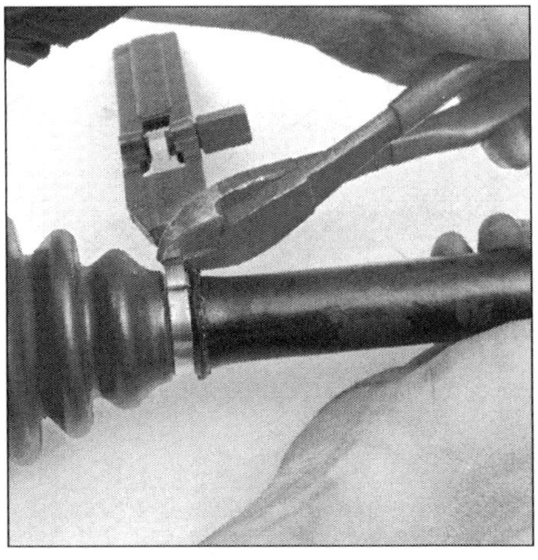

3.3z . . . then bend the end of the clamp back and cut off the excess (see illustration 3.3bb for the proper positioning of the small end of the boot)

3.3aa To install a new boot retainer on 1979 and later models, place the driveaxle assembly in a bench vise as shown, with the new retainer resting on the jaws (don't clamp it!), then carefully tap the outer CV joint housing into the retainer as shown. Every couple of taps, rotate the entire assembly to ensure that the retainer doesn't become cocked

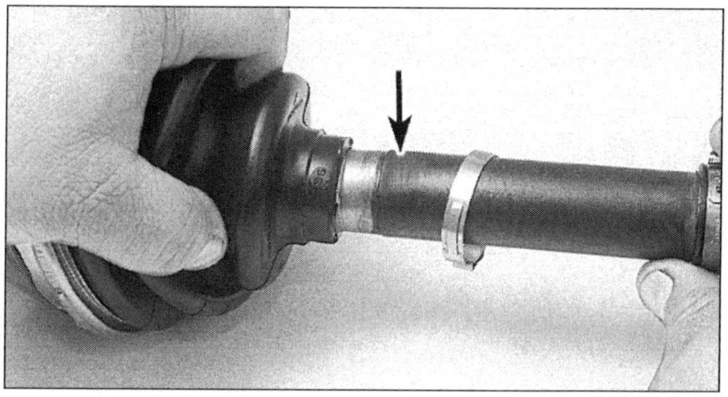

3.3bb Position the small end of the boot at the step (arrow) before installing the new clamp (see illustration 3.3x, y and z)

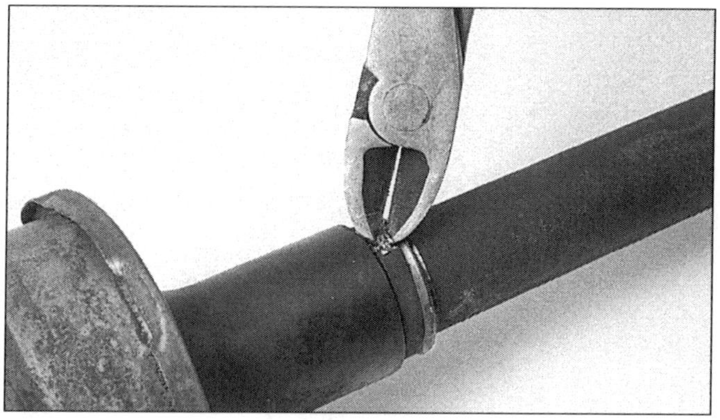

3.4a Cut off the old boot clamp

3.4b On 1971 through 1978 models, pry the boot retainer loose from the inner CV joint housing . . .

3.4c . . . then tap off the retainer with a hammer and punch or chisel . . .

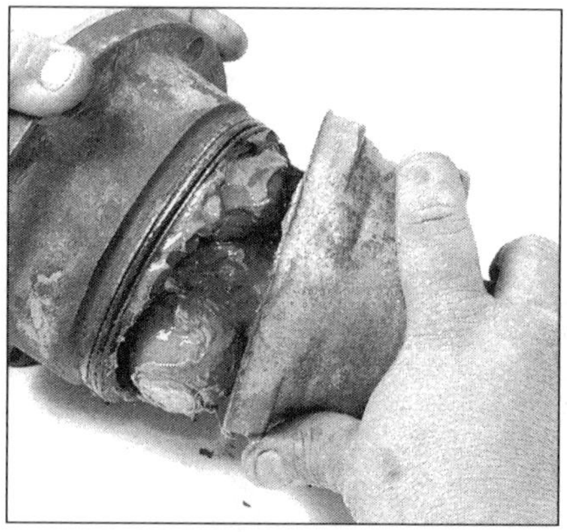

3.4d . . . and separate the retainer from the housing

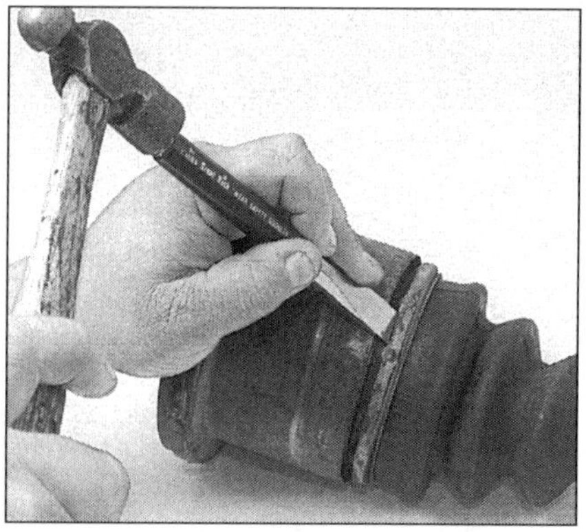

3.4e On 1979 and later models, simply knock the boot retainer off with a hammer and punch or chisel

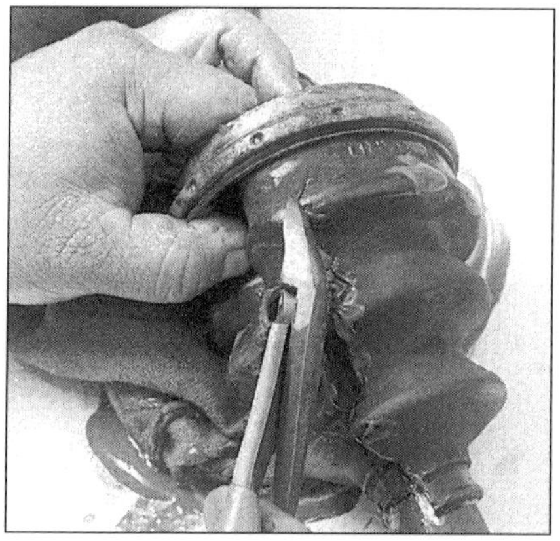

3.4f cut the old boot off

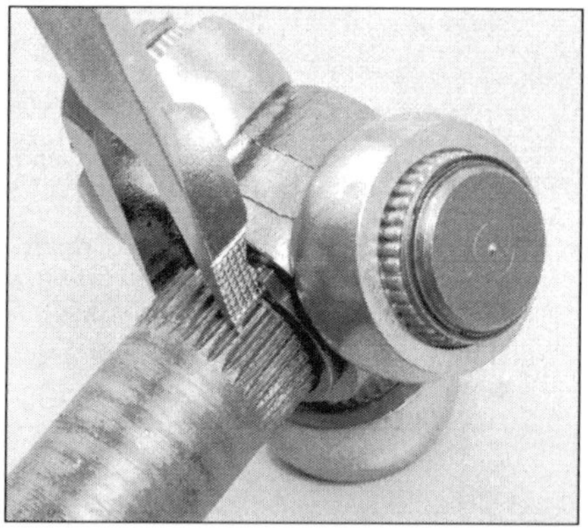

3.4g Spread the spider assembly stop-ring apart and slide it towards the center of the shaft

3.4h Slide the spider assembly back to expose the front retaining ring and remove it

Inner CV joint

Refer to illustrations 3.4a through 3.4z

4 Refer to the accompanying illustrations to remove, clean, inspect and lubricate the inner CV joint and install a new boot **(see illustrations)**.

All driveaxles

5 Install the driveaxle assembly (see Section 2).

6 Install the wheels, remove the jackstands and lower the vehicle. Tighten the wheel lug nuts to the torque listed in the Chapter 1 Specifications.

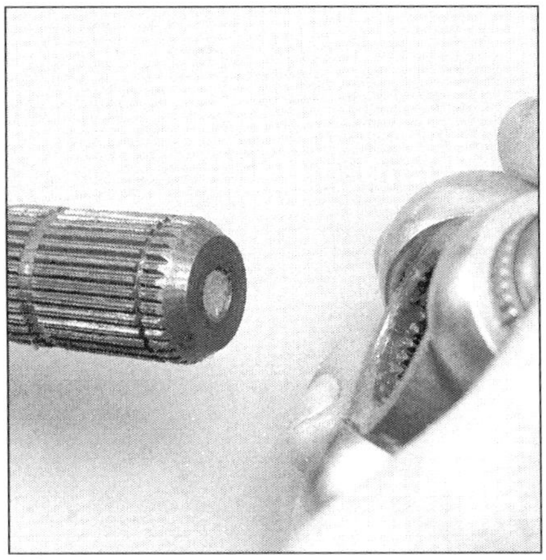

3.4i Slide the spider off the driveaxle, holding the bearings in place; it's a good idea to use tape or a cloth wrapped around the spider bearing assembly to retain them

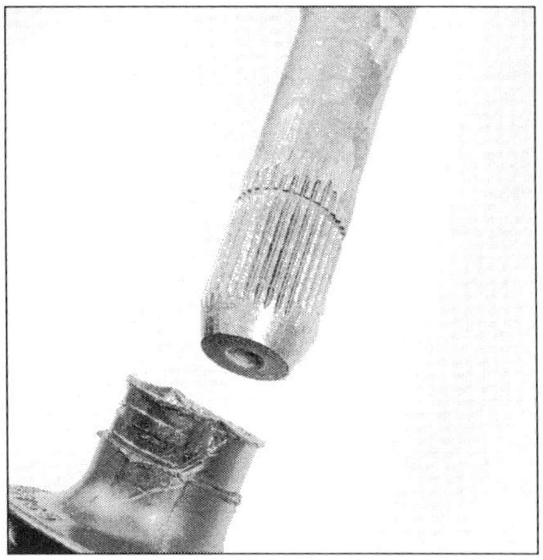

3.4j Slide the stop ring and any remnants of the boot off the axle

3.4k Clean all the old grease out of the CV joint housing and spider assembly, then remove each bearing, one at a time

3.4l Carefully disassemble each section of the spider assembly, clean the needle bearings with solvent and inspect the rollers, spider cross, bearings . . .

3.4m . . . and inner CV joint housing for scoring, pitting and other evidence of abnormal wear; if you find any sign of damage, replace the inner CV joint assembly

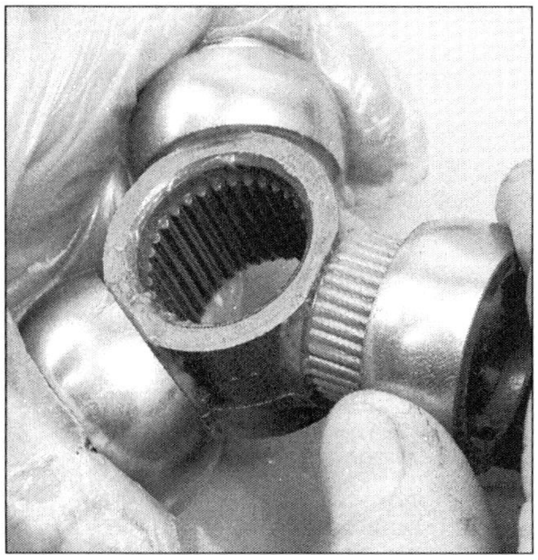

3.4n Apply a coat of CV joint grease to the inner bearing surfaces to hold the needle bearings in place and slide the bearing over them

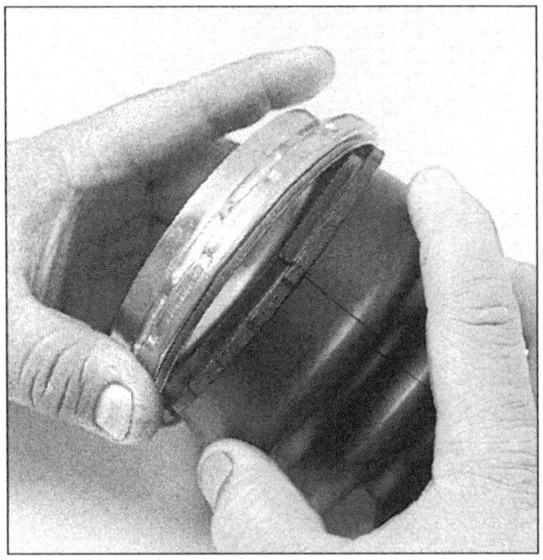

3.4o On 1979 and later models, slip the new boot into the new retainer

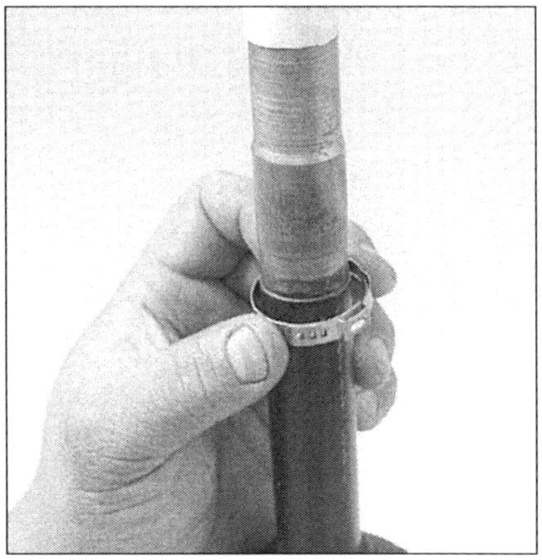

3.4p Wrap the driveaxle splines with tape to avoid damaging the boot, then slide the new boot clamp . . .

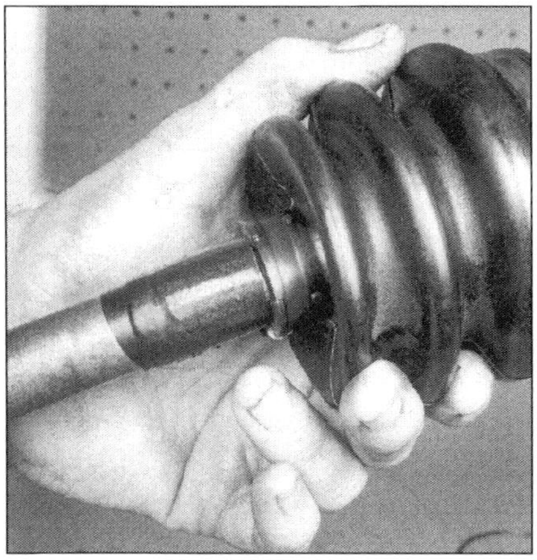

3.4q . . . and boot onto the axleshaft

3.4r Slide the spider stop-ring onto the axleshaft, past the groove in which it seats

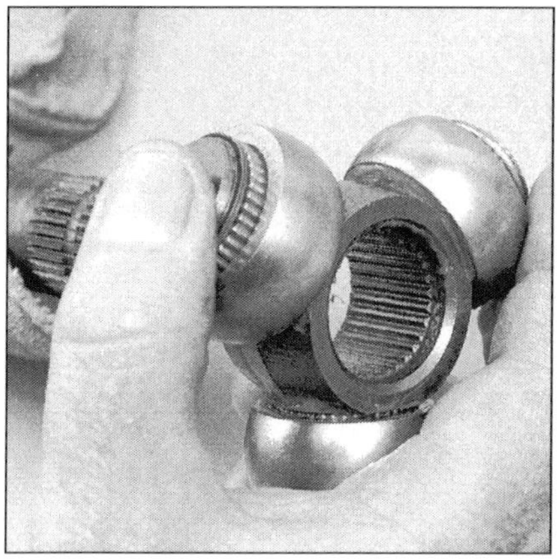

3.4s Install the spider bearing with the recess in the counterbore facing the end of the driveaxle

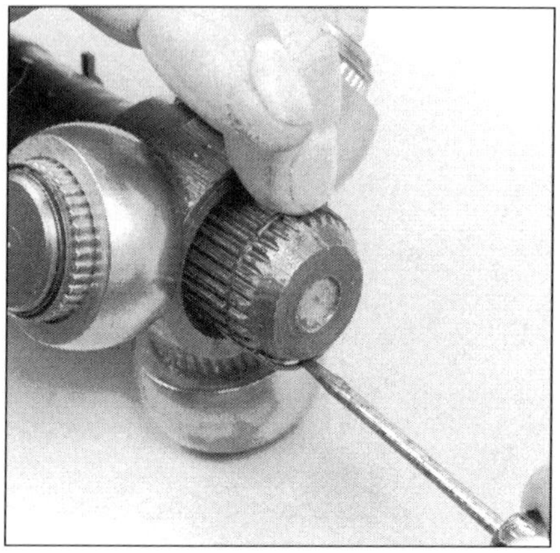

3.4t Use a screwdriver to install the outer snap-ring, then slide the spider assembly against it and install the stop-ring in its groove

3.4u Squirt some new CV joint grease into the bottom of the joint housing, insert the bearing assembly into the housing and squirt some more grease into the bearing recesses

3.4v On 1971 through 1978 models, slide the boot and retainer down onto the housing . . .

3.4w . . . tap it onto the housing until it's fully seated . . .

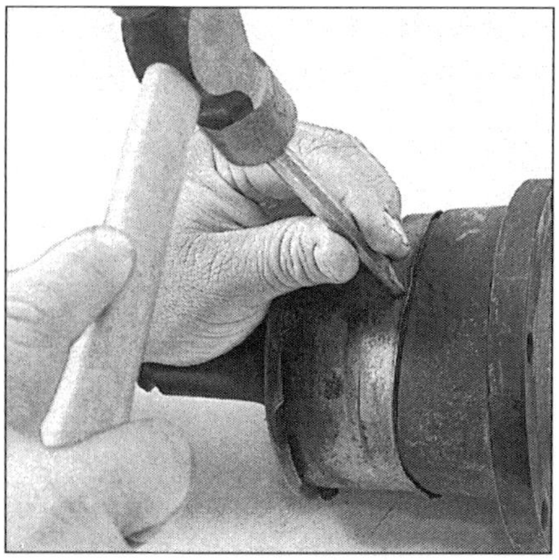

3.4x . . . and peen down the retainer as shown

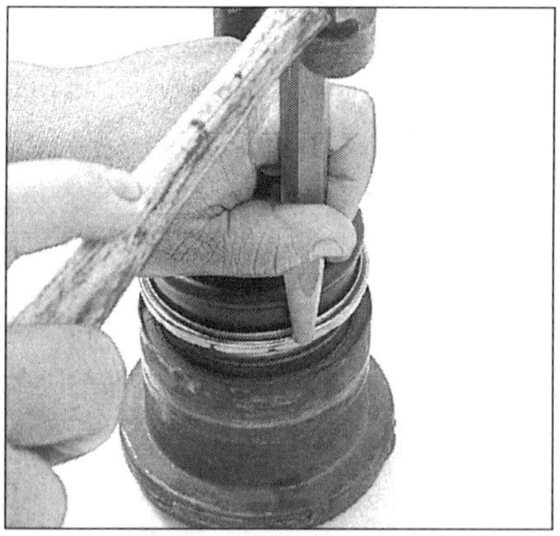

3.4y On 1979 and later models, seat the new boot retainer on the housing and carefully tap the retainer onto the housing until it's fully seated

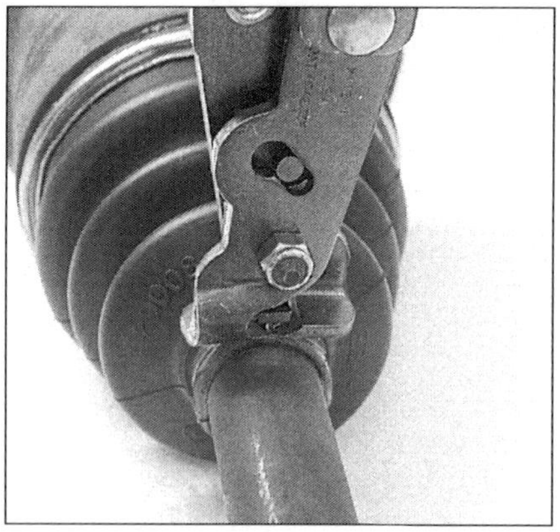

3.4z Use a pair of boot clamp pliers to crimp the new boot clamp (see illustrations 3.3x through 3.3z) if you have "band" type clamps

7 Tighten the driveaxle/hub nut to the torque listed in this Chapter's Specifications, then install the nut lock and a new cotter pin (see Section 2).

8 Have the front end alignment checked.

4 Differential oil seals - replacement

Refer to illustrations 4.4, 4.5a, 4.5b, 4.6, 4.8, 4.9, 4.10 and 4.11

1 Apply the parking brake and block the rear wheels. Remove the wheel cover and the three lug nuts securing the mount for the wheel cover lock bolt, if equipped. Remove the driveaxle/hub nut cotter pin and nut lock. **Note:** *If the vehicle is equipped with wheels that won't allow the socket for the hub nut to pass through, the wheel will have to be*

4.4 Before attempting to pull out the left output shaft on 1971 through 1978 models, remove this retaining bolt (arrow)

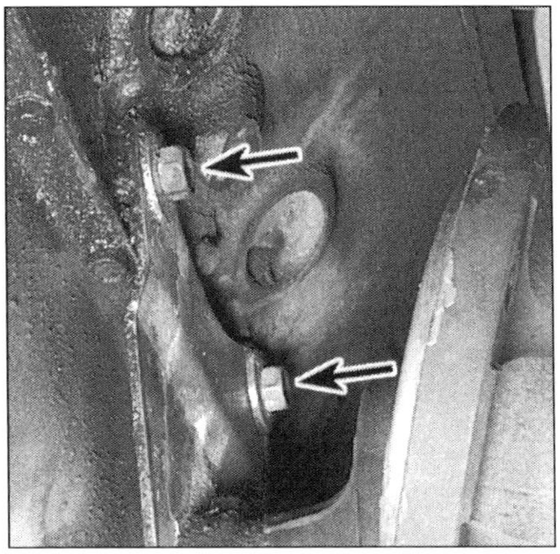

4.5a To detach the support bracket for the right output shaft, remove these bolts (arrows)

4.5b To remove the small support bracket, remove these two bolts (arrows)

4.6 Remove the output shaft from the differential side gear (left shaft shown)

4.8 Use a seal removal tool to remove the old differential seal (left side shown)

4.9 To install a new differential side gear seal, tap it into place with a large socket with an outside diameter slightly smaller than the outside diameter of the seal (right side shown)

removed and the hub immobilized as shown in illustration 2.3a. Raise the vehicle and place it securely on jackstands.

2 Remove the driveaxle (see Section 2).

3 Drain the differential lubricant (see Chapter 1).

4 If you're replacing the left seal on a 1971 through 1978 model, remove the retaining bolt from the output shaft flange **(see illustration)**.

5 If you're replacing the right seal, unbolt the support bracket **(see illustrations)**.

6 If you're replacing the left seal on a 1971 through 1978 model, simply pull out the output shaft **(see illustration)**; if you're working on a 1979 or later model, give the output shaft flange a few sharp taps with a brass drift and hammer to pop loose the internal snap-ring. Inspect this snap-ring; if it's loose, replace it.

7 If you're replacing the right seal, simply pull the right output shaft straight out (the bearing and support bracket will come with it - they're pressed onto the shaft).

8 Use a seal removal tool to remove the seal **(see illustration)**.

9 Using a big socket with an outside diameter slightly smaller than the outside diameter of the seal, tap the new seal into place until it's fully seated **(see illustration)**.

4.10 To check the right output shaft support bearing, grasp the support bracket firmly and turn the output shaft flange back and forth - the bearings should be smooth and quiet; if they're not, have them replaced

10 If you removed the right output shaft, inspect the bearing for wear **(see illustration)**. If the support bearing is worn, take the output shaft and support bearing assembly to an automotive machine shop and have the bearing replaced (the bearing is pressed onto the output shaft, so you can't remove or install it at home without a hydraulic press).

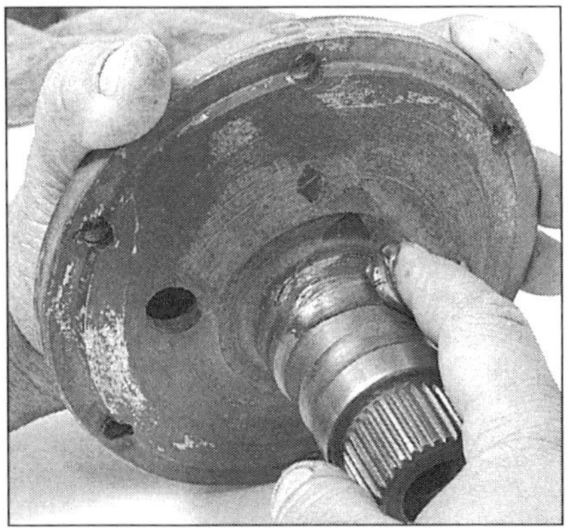

4.11 Be sure to coat the seal friction surface and the splines of the output shaft with grease

11 Coat the inner lip of the new seal, and the splines and seal friction surface of the output shaft with multi-purpose grease **(see**

5.1 Remove these bolts (arrows) and remove the differential-to-engine block bracket (exhaust manifold removed for clarity)

illustration), then carefully insert the shaft through the seal and into the side gear. Make sure you don't tear the new seal.

12 If you're installing the left output shaft on a 1971 through 1978 model, install the shaft retaining bolt and tighten it to the torque listed in this Chapter's Specifications. If you're installing the left output shaft on a 1979 or later model, make sure you feel the retaining ring snap into place.

13 If you're installing the right output shaft, install the support bolts and the bolts for the small reinforcement bracket and tighten them securely.

14 Install the driveaxle assembly (see Section 2).

15 Fill the differential with the recommended type of lubricant (see Chapter 1).

16 Remove the jackstands and lower the vehicle.

17 Have the front-end alignment checked.

5 Differential - removal and installation

Refer to illustrations 5.1, 5.2, 5.8a, 5.8b, 5.9a and 5.9b

1 Disconnect the cable from the negative terminal of the battery. Working from above, remove the differential-to-engine block bracket **(see illustration)**.

2 Remove the upper differential-to-transmission bolts **(see illustration)**. If you're working on a 1978 or earlier model, unbolt the transmission fluid filler tube bracket from the exhaust manifold, then remove the filler tube (1978 and earlier models). Also remove the bracket that secures the transmission cooler lines.

3 Loosen the wheel lug nuts, raise the front of the vehicle and place it securely on jackstands. Remove the front wheels. Turn the steering wheel all the way to the left.

4 Drain the differential lubricant.

5 Unbolt the inner CV joints from the output shaft flanges (see Section 2). Support the driveaxles out of the way with pieces of wire.

6 Remove the output shafts (see Section 4).

7 Place a floor jack underneath the differential assembly. It is recommended that the jack be equipped with a transmission support fixture, as the differential unit is very heavy. On 1978 and earlier models, remove the left tie strut from between the frame and the crossmember.

8 Remove the side and lower differential-to-transmission bolts **(see illustrations)**.

9 Using a large screwdriver or prybar, pry the differential assembly toward the front of the vehicle to disengage the splines from the transmission **(see illustrations)**.

10 Slowly lower the jack and remove the differential. It would be a good idea to have someone help you guide the differential down.

11 Installation is the reverse of removal. Be sure to tighten the differential-to-transmission bolts to the torque listed in this Chapter's Specifications. Refill the differential with the proper lubricant (see Chapter 1).

5.2 Upper differential-to-transmission bolts (arrows)

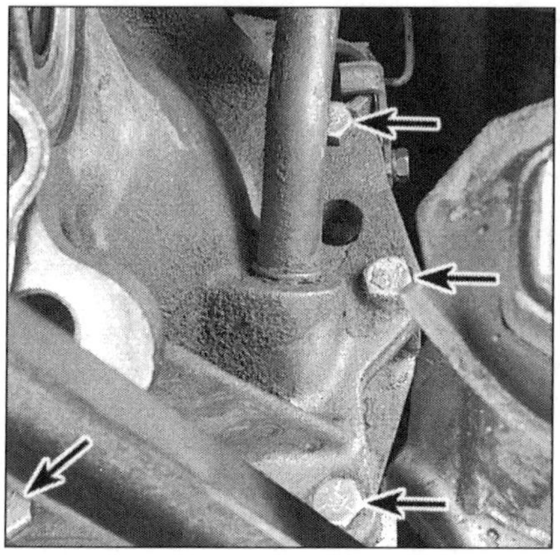

5.8a Left and lower differential-to-transmission bolts (arrows)

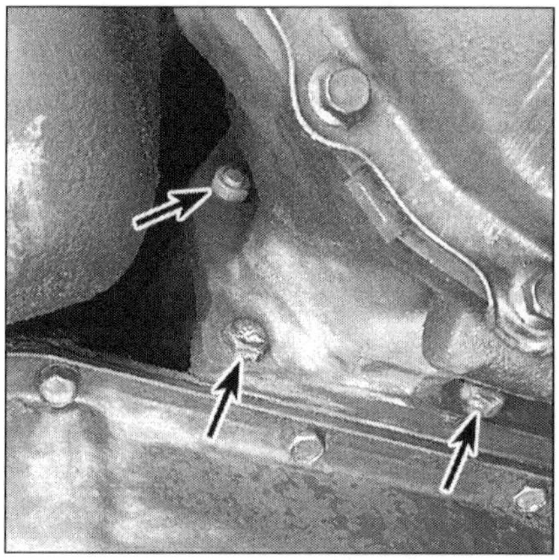

5.8b Right and lower differential-to-transmission bolts (arrows)

5.9a Use a large prybar or screwdriver to lever the differential far enough forward . . .

5.9b . . . to disengage the pinion shaft from the splined output shaft on the front of the transmission

Chapter 9 Brakes

Contents

Specifications

Brake fluid type	See Chapter 1
Disc brakes	
Minimum brake pad thickness	See Chapter 1
Disc minimum thickness	Refer to the dimension cast into the disc
Disc runout limit	No more than 0.004 inch
Drum brakes	
Minimum brake lining thickness	See Chapter 1
Drum maximum diameter	Refer to the dimension cast into the drum
Drum out-of-round	0.006 inch maximum
Drum taper	0.003 inch maximum
Torque specifications	**Ft-lbs**
Master cylinder mounting nuts	20 to 25
Power booster mounting nuts	20 to 25
Caliper mounting bolts	35 to 40
Wheel cylinder mounting bolts	15 to 17
Brake hose fitting-to-caliper bolt	30
Wheel lug nuts	See Chapter 1

2.5 Before removing the caliper, use a large C-clamp to depress the piston back into the caliper; otherwise, you may not be able to fit the caliper and new pads over the disc

2.6a The brake pads may contain asbestos dust, which is carcinogenic, so ALWAYS wash down the disc and caliper assembly with brake cleaner before beginning work; do NOT use compressed air!

2.6b To detach the caliper from the steering knuckle, remove these bolts (arrows) (do NOT unscrew the brake hose fitting unless you're planning to overhaul the caliper)

2.6c To remove the caliper from the disc, lift it straight off

2.6d Remove the outer brake pad . . .

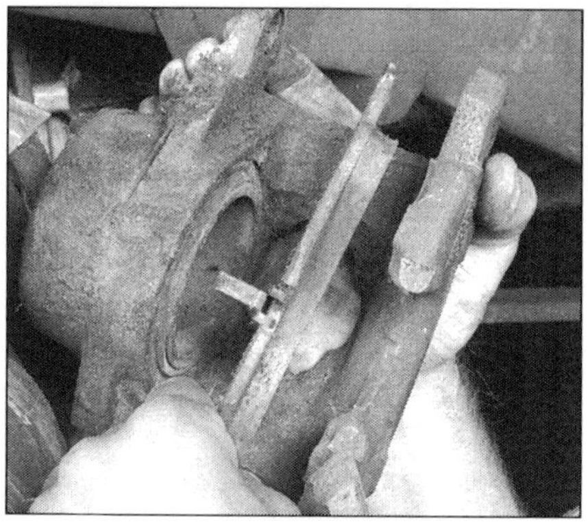

2.6e . . . and the inner pad

1 General information

The vehicles covered by this manual are equipped with hydraulically operated front and rear brake systems. The front brakes are disc type and the rear brakes are drum or disc type. Both the front and rear brakes are self adjusting; the disc brakes automatically compensate for pad wear, and the drum brakes incorporate an adjustment mechanism which is activated as the brakes are applied when the vehicle is driven in Reverse.

Hydraulic system

The hydraulic system consists of two separate circuits. The master cylinder has separate reservoirs for the two circuits and in the event of a leak or failure in one hydraulic circuit, the other circuit will remain operative. A visual warning of circuit failure or air in the system is given by a warning light activated by displacement of the piston in the pressure differential switch portion of the combination valve from its normal "in balance" position.

Combination valve

A combination valve, located in the engine compartment, consists of three sections providing the following functions. The metering section limits pressure to the front brakes until a predetermined front input pressure is reached and until the rear brakes are activated. There is no restriction at inlet pressures below three psi, allowing pressure equalization during non-braking periods. The proportioning section proportions outlet pressure to the rear brakes after a predetermined rear input pressure has been reached, preventing early rear wheel lock-up under heavy brake loads. The valve is also designed to assure full pressure to one brake system should the other system fail. The pressure differential warning switch incorporated into the combination valve is designed to continuously compare the front and rear brake pressure from the master cylinder and energize the dash warning light in the event of either a front or rear brake system failure. The design of the switch and valve are such that the switch will stay in the "warning" position once a failure has occurred. The only way to turn the light off is to repair the cause of the failure and apply a brake pedal force of 450 psi.

Power brake booster

The power brake booster, utilizing engine manifold vacuum and atmospheric pressure to provide assistance to the hydraulically operated brakes, is mounted on the firewall in the engine compartment.

Parking brake

The parking brake operates the rear brakes only, through cable actuation. It's activated by a pedal mounted on the left side kick panel.

Service

After completing any operation involving disassembly of any part of the brake system, always test drive the vehicle to check for proper braking performance before resuming normal driving. When testing the brakes, perform the tests on a clean, dry, flat surface. Conditions other than these can lead to inaccurate test results.

Test the brakes at various speeds with both light and heavy pedal pressure. The vehicle should stop evenly without pulling to one side or the other. Avoid locking the brakes, because this slides the tires and diminishes braking efficiency and control of the vehicle.

Tires, vehicle load and front-end alignment are factors which also affect braking performance.

2 Disc brake pads - replacement

Warning: *The dust created by the brake system may contain asbestos, which is harmful to your health. Never blow it out with compressed air and don't inhale any of it. An approved filtering mask should be worn when*

2.6f Anytime you're not actually holding the caliper, hang it from the suspension with a piece of wire or a coat hanger; do NOT allow the caliper to hang by the brake hose

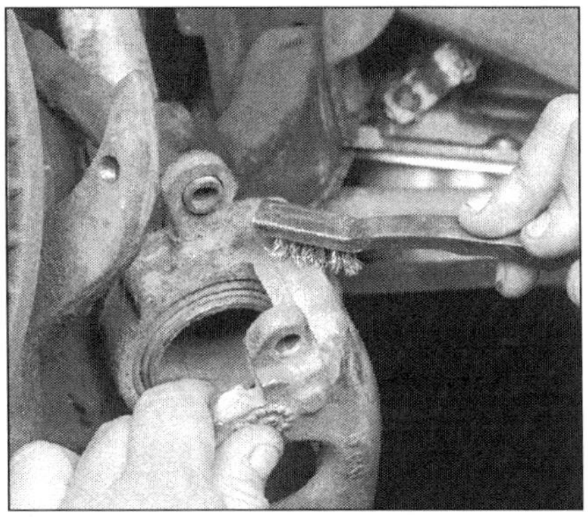

2.6g Scrub off the sliding surfaces on the caliper and the steering knuckle with a wire brush; make sure you remove all old grease, rust and dirt

2.6h Apply a thin coat of brake grease to the sliding surfaces on the steering knuckle and the caliper

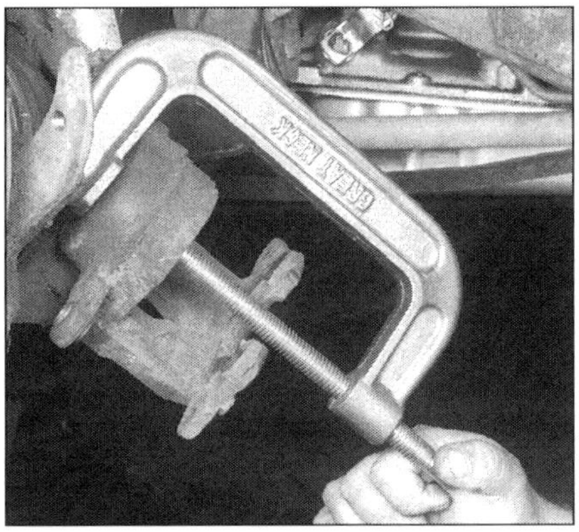

2.6i If the piston has moved out of the caliper bore, depress it again with a C-clamp

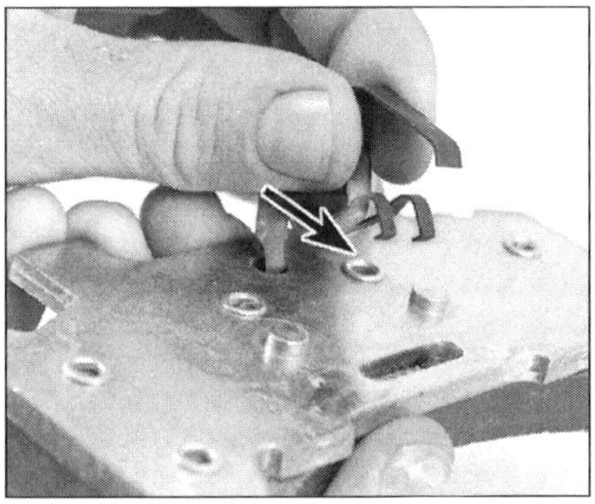

2.6j Transfer the retaining spring from the old inner pad to the new one - hook the end of the spring in the hole at the top of the pad, then insert the two prongs of the spring into the slot on the backing plate

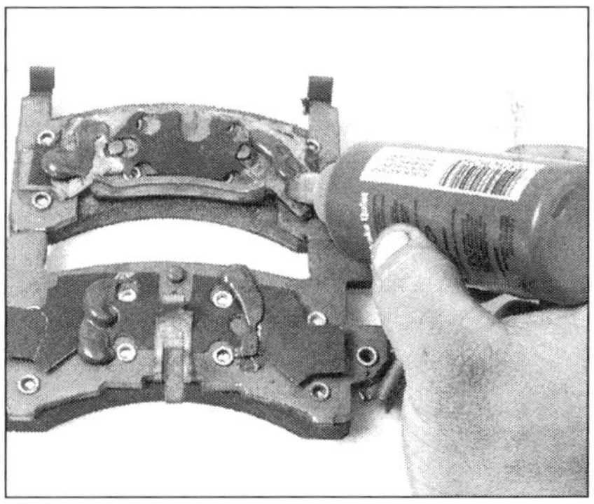

2.6k Apply a coat of anti-squeal compound to the backing plates of the new brake pads - let the compound dry for a few minutes before installing the pads

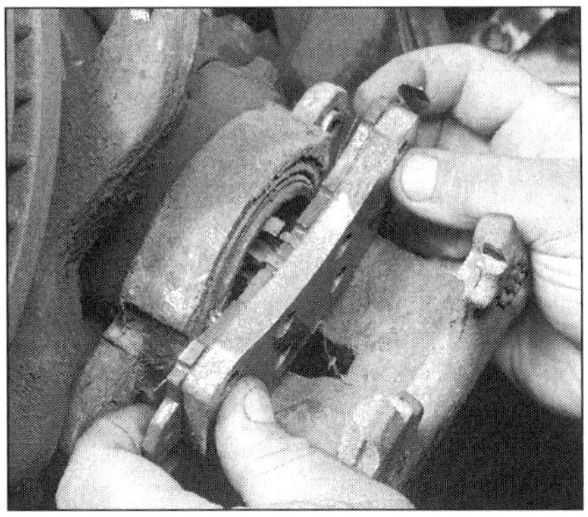

2.6l Install the new inner pad; make sure the spring clip is fully seated into the piston recess

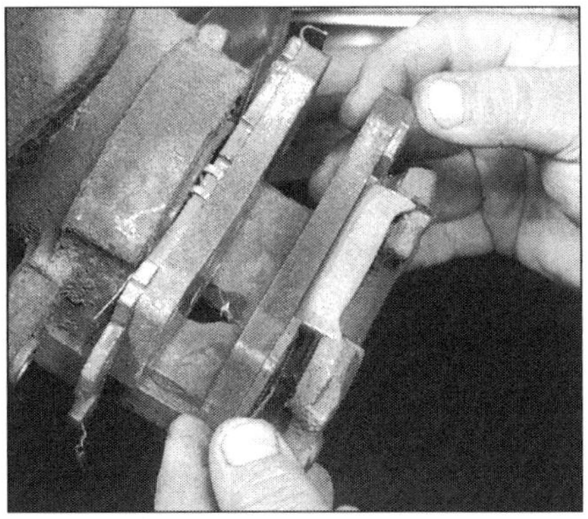

2.6m Install the new outer pad as shown

2.6n Install the caliper and new pads over the disc, install the caliper retaining bolts and tighten them to the torque listed in this Chapter's Specifications

working on the brakes. Do not, under any circumstances, use petroleum-based solvents to clean brake parts. Use brake system cleaner only! Finally, always replace both front or both rear disc brake pads at the same time - never replace the pads on only one wheel.

1 Remove the cover from the brake fluid reservoir.

2 Loosen the wheel lug nuts, raise the vehicle and support it securely on jackstands.

3 Remove the wheels. Work on one brake assembly at a time, using the assembled brake for reference if necessary.

4 Inspect the brake disc carefully as outlined in Section 4. If machining is necessary, follow the information in that Section to remove the disc, at which time the pads can be removed from the calipers as well.

Front brake

Refer to illustrations 2.5 and 2.6a through 2.6o

5 Push the piston back into the bore to provide room for the new brake pads. A C-clamp can be used to accomplish this **(see illustration)**. As the piston is depressed to the bottom of the caliper bore, the fluid in the master cylinder will rise. Make sure it doesn't overflow. If necessary, siphon off some of the fluid.

6 Follow the accompanying illustrations, beginning with **illustration 2.6a**, for the pad replacement procedure. Be sure to stay in order and read the caption under each illustration.

2.6o After refilling the master cylinder and pumping the brake pedal to seat the pads, use adjustable pliers to bend the upper ears of the outer pad until the ears are flush with the caliper housing, with no clearance

2.7a Disconnect the brake line from the rear caliper with a flare-nut wrench and cap the open line

2.7b Pull the parking brake cable to the rear and disengage it from the parking brake lever

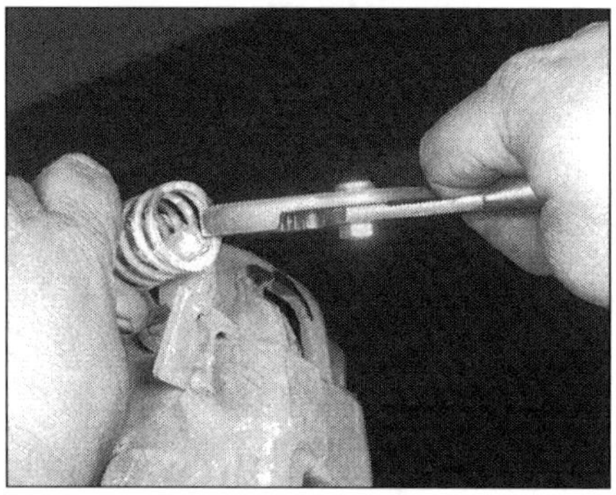

2.7c Remove the parking brake lever return spring

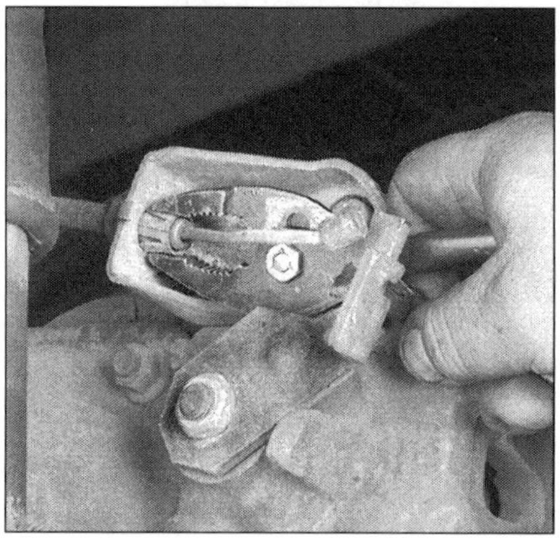

2.7d Squeeze the tangs on the parking brake cable ferrule and slide the cable out of the bracket

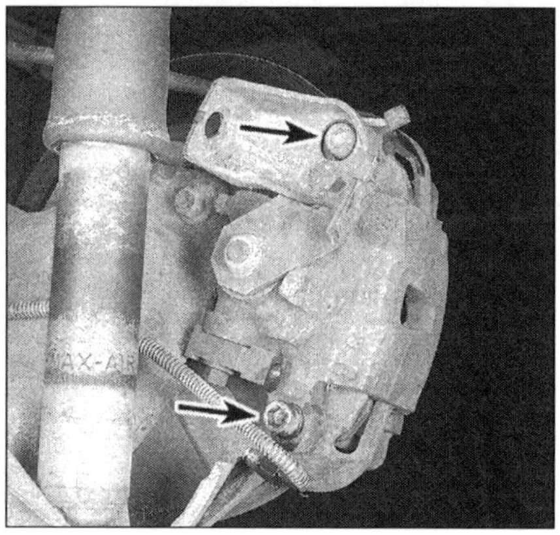

2.7e Remove the rear caliper bolts (arrows)

2.7f Remove the rear caliper assembly

2.7g Remove the outer brake pad

2.7h Remove the inner brake pad. To make room for the new pads, remove the parking brake lever, seal and washer, then depress the piston to the bottom of its bore (see illustrations 3.21h, i, j and v). Reinstall the parking brake lever, seal and washer (see illustrations 3.21w through z)

7 When reinstalling the caliper, be sure to tighten the mounting bolts to the torque listed in this Chapter's Specifications. After the job has been completed and before driving the vehicle, firmly depress the brake pedal a few times to bring the pads into contact with the disc.

Rear brake

Refer to illustrations 2.7a through 2.7q

Caution: *Operation of the rear disc brake adjuster mechanism is critical on these models. If any problems with rear brake adjustment are encountered, you may have to overhaul the caliper (see Section 3).*

8 Follow the accompanying illustrations, beginning with **illustration 2.7a**, for the pad replacement procedure. Be sure to stay in order and read the caption under each illustration.

9 When reinstalling the caliper, be sure to tighten the mounting bolts to the torque listed in this Chapter's Specifications. Bleed the brakes as described in Section 10. After the job has been completed and before driving the vehicle, firmly depress the brake pedal a few times to bring the pads into contact with the disc. **Note:** *This may require heavy pedal pressure, as the friction of the parking brake actuator screw must be overcome as the piston moves out towards the pads.*

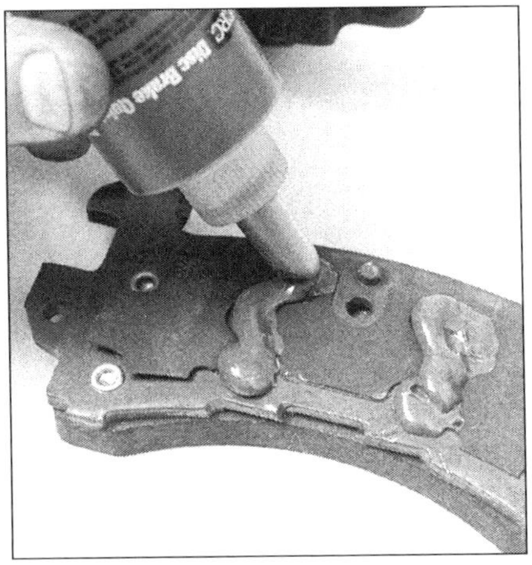

2.7i Apply anti-squeal compound to the brake pad backing plates - let the compound dry for a few minutes before installing the pads

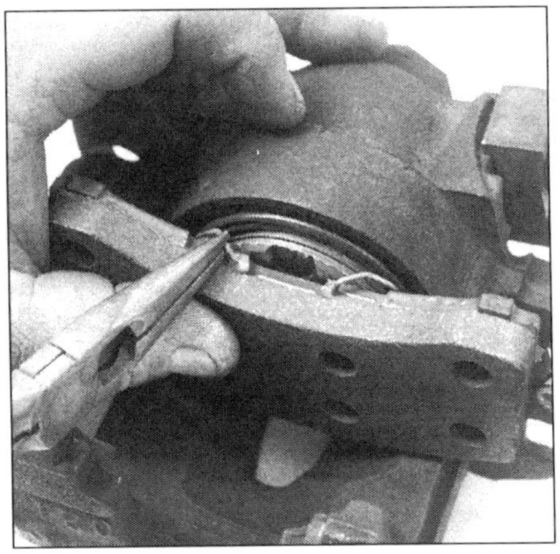

2.7j Place the inner pad against the piston, making sure the post on the pad backing plate engages with the D-shaped cutout on the piston (if it doesn't, turn the piston with the tips of a pair of needle-nose pliers) - lift the ends of the dampening spring onto the pad backing plate, as shown here

2.7k Install the new outer pad

2.7l Install the caliper assembly over the rear disc

2.7m Install the caliper retaining bolts and tighten them to the torque listed in this Chapter's Specifications

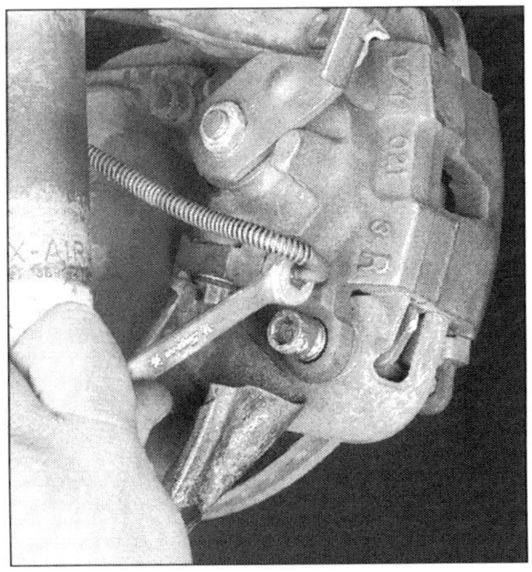

2.7n Connect the brake line fitting and tighten it to the torque listed in this Chapter's Specifications

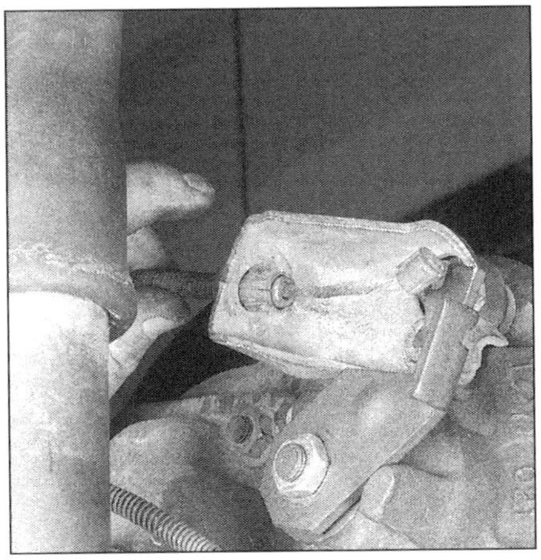

2.7o Insert the parking brake cable through the cable bracket; pull the cable through until the cable ferrule tangs lock against the bracket

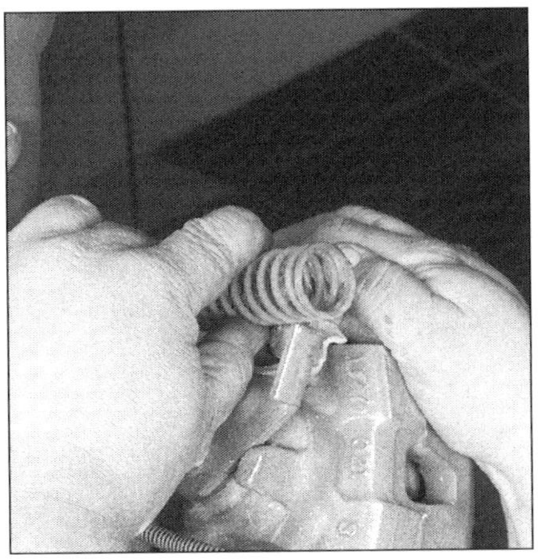

2.7p Install the parking brake lever return spring

2.7q Pull firmly on the cable and engage it with the parking brake lever. Finally, bleed the brakes, have an assistant depress the brake pedal firmly, then bend the ears of the outer pad against the caliper (see illustration 2.6o)

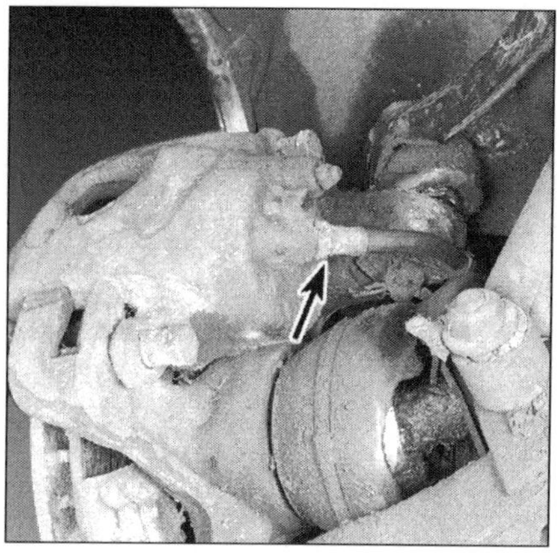

3.4a Brake hoses on early models are connected to the caliper by a conventional threaded tube-nut type fitting (arrow); be sure to use a new sealing washer when you install the fitting

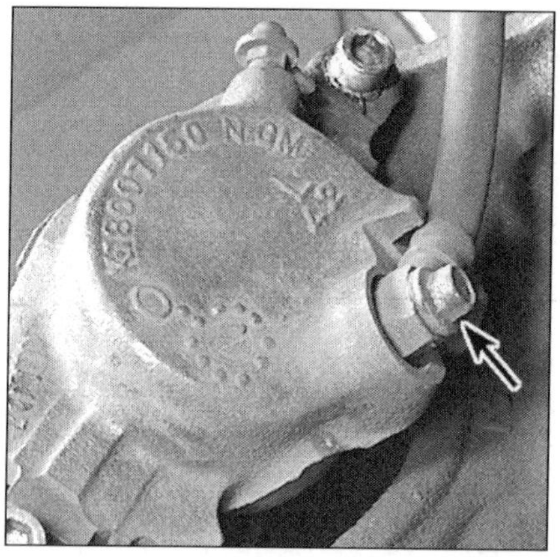

3.4b Later model calipers use a banjo-type brake hose fitting (arrow); be sure to use new sealing washers when installing the banjo bolt

3.8 With the caliper padded to catch the piston, use compressed air to force the piston out of the bore; make sure your fingers are not between the piston and the caliper!

3.9 When prying the dust boot out of the caliper, be very careful not to scratch the bore surface

3.10 Remove the piston seal with a wooden or plastic tool to avoid scratching the bore and seal groove (a pencil works nicely)

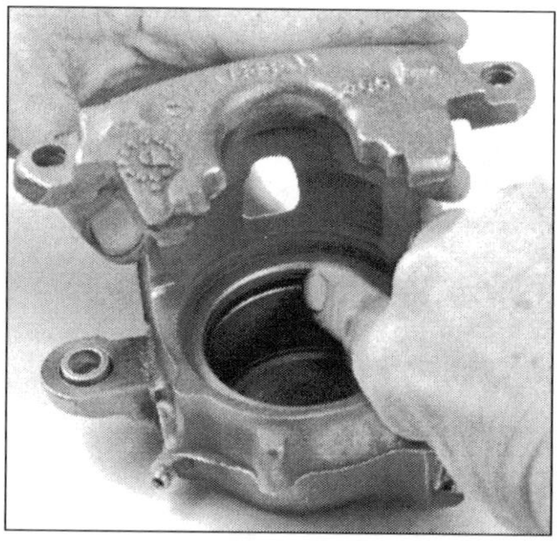

3.15 Position the seal in the caliper bore groove; make sure it isn't twisted

3 Disc brake caliper - removal, overhaul and installation

Warning: *Dust created by the brake system may contain asbestos, which is harmful to your health. Never blow it out with compressed air and don't inhale any of it. An approved filtering mask should be worn when working on the brakes. Do not, under any circumstances, use petroleum-based solvents to clean brake parts. Use brake system cleaner only!*

Note: *If an overhaul is indicated (usually because of fluid leakage) explore all options before beginning the job. New and factory rebuilt calipers are available on an exchange basis, which makes this job quite easy. If it's decided to rebuild the calipers, make sure a rebuild kit is available before proceeding. Always rebuild the calipers in pairs - never rebuild just one of them.*

Removal

Refer to illustrations 3.4a and 3.4b

1 Remove the cover from the brake fluid reservoir, siphon off two thirds of the fluid into a container and discard it.

2 Loosen the wheel lug nuts, raise the front of the vehicle and support it securely on jackstands.

3 Remove the front wheels.

4 Unscrew the brake hose fitting **(see accompanying illustrations and illustration 2.7a)** and detach the hose. Have a rag handy to catch spilled fluid and wrap a plastic bag tightly around the end of the hose to prevent fluid loss and contamination. **Note:** *If you're removing a front caliper to change the brake pads, rather than to overhaul it, do not disconnect the brake hose (the brake line must be disconnected to remove a rear caliper).*

5 Remove the two mounting bolts and detach the caliper from the vehicle (see Section 2).

Overhaul

6 Remove the brake pads from the caliper (see Section 2).

7 Clean the exterior of the caliper with brake system cleaner. Never use gasoline, kerosene or petroleum-based cleaning solvents. Place the caliper on a clean workbench.

Front caliper

Refer to illustrations 3.8, 3.9, 3.10, 3.15, 3.16, 3.17 and 3.18

8 Position a wood block or several shop rags in the caliper as a cushion, then use compressed air to remove the piston from the caliper **(see illustration)**. Use only enough air pressure to ease the piston out of the bore. If the piston is blown out, even with the cushion in place, it may be damaged. **Warning:** *Never place your fingers in front of the piston in an attempt to catch or protect it when applying compressed air, as serious injury could occur.*

9 Carefully pry the dust boot out of the caliper bore **(see illustration)**.

10 Using a wood or plastic tool, remove the piston seal from the groove in the caliper bore **(see illustration)**. Metal tools may cause bore damage.

11 Remove the caliper bleeder screw, then remove and discard the sleeves and bushings from the caliper ears. Discard all rubber parts.

3.16 Install the new dust boot in the piston groove

3.17 Install the piston squarely in the caliper bore and bottom it by pushing down evenly

3.18 Seat the boot in the counterbore (a seal driver is being used in this photo, but a drift punch will work if it's used carefully)

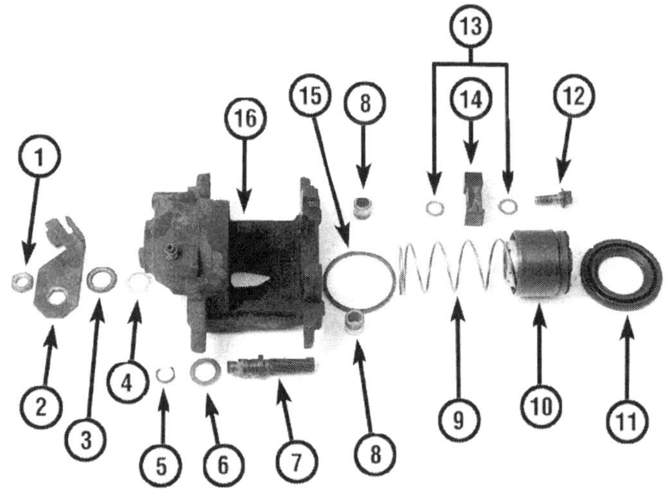

3.20 An exploded view of the rear caliper assembly

1 *Parking brake lever retaining nut*
2 *Parking brake lever*
3 *Parking brake lever seal*
4 *Nylon anti-friction washer*
5 *Actuator screw O-ring*
6 *Actuator screw thrust washer*
7 *Actuator screw*
8 *Caliper pin bushings*
9 *Piston return spring*
10 *Piston*
11 *Piston dust boot*
12 *Brake hose fitting banjo bolt*
13 *Banjo bolt sealing washers*
14 *Brake hose fitting*
15 *Piston seal*
16 *Caliper housing*

3.21a Remove the pad dampening spring

3.21b While pulling on the piston . . .

12 Clean the remaining parts with brake system cleaner then blow them dry with compressed air.
13 Carefully examine the piston for nicks and burrs and loss of plating. If surface defects are present, the parts must be replaced.
14 Check the caliper bore in a similar way. Light polishing with crocus cloth is permissible to remove light corrosion and stains. Discard the mounting bolts if they're corroded or damaged.
15 When assembling, lubricate the piston bores and seal with clean brake fluid. Position the seal in the caliper bore groove **(see illustration)**.
16 Lubricate the piston with clean brake fluid, then install a new boot in the piston groove with the fold toward the open end of the piston **(see illustration)**.
17 Insert the piston squarely into the caliper bore, then apply force to bottom it **(see illustration)**.
18 Position the dust boot in the caliper counterbore, then use a drift to drive it into position **(see illustration)**. Make sure the boot is recessed evenly below the caliper face.
19 Install new bushings in the mounting bolt holes and fill the area between the bushings with the silicone grease supplied in the rebuild kit. Push the sleeves into the mounting bolt holes. Install the bleeder screw, if removed.

Rear caliper

Refer to illustrations 3.20 and 3.21a through 3.21ii

20 Refer to the accompanying exploded view **(see illustration)**, if necessary, while rebuilding the rear caliper.
21 Follow the accompanying illustrations, beginning with **illustration 3.21a**, for the overhaul procedure. Be sure to stay in order and read the caption under each illustration.

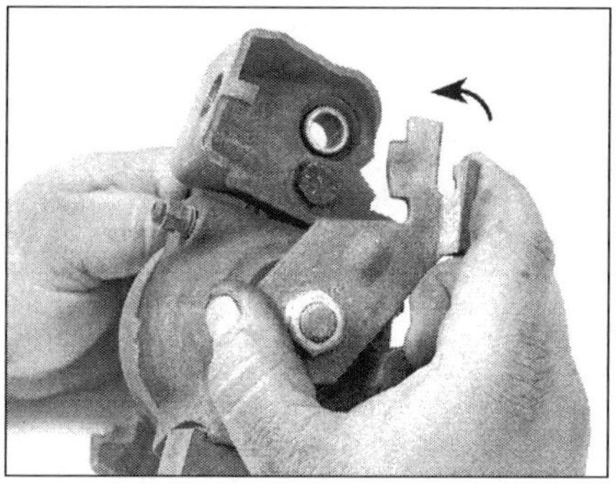

3.21c . . . ratchet the parking brake lever counterclockwise (towards the parking brake cable bracket); each time the parking brake lever reaches the limit of its travel, rotate it back in a clockwise direction (the piston will retract a little bit each time you rotate the lever clockwise but not as far as it comes out each time you ratchet the lever counterclockwise)

3.21d Remove the bolt that attaches the parking brake cable bracket to the caliper

3.21e Remove the piston and the spring from the caliper

3.21f Pry out the old piston dust boot

3.21g Remove the piston seal from its groove in the caliper bore

3.21h Remove the retaining nut from the parking brake lever

3.21i Remove the parking brake lever and the parking brake lever seal

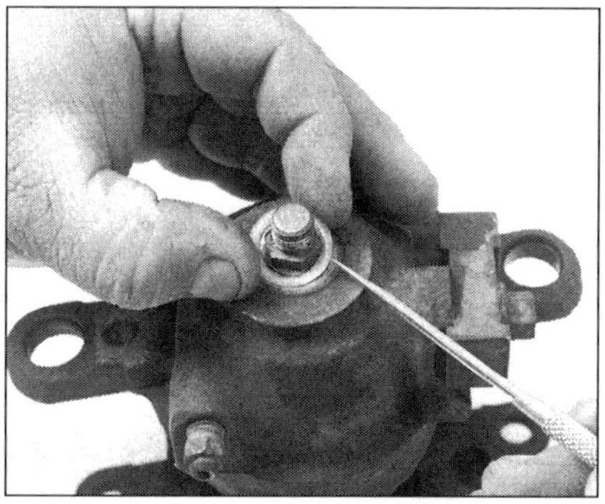

3.21j Remove the nylon anti-friction washer from the actuator screw

3.21k Carefully tap out the actuator screw

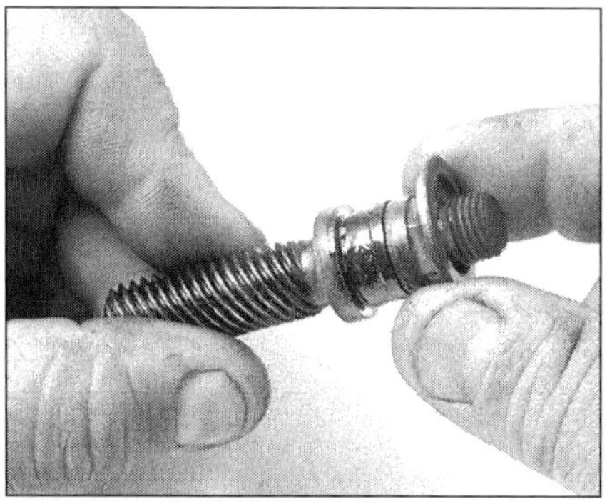

3.21l Remove the thrust washer from the actuator screw

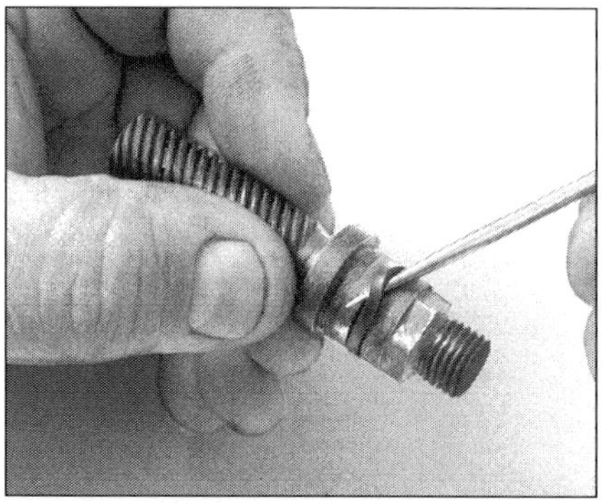

3.21m Remove the O-ring from the actuator screw

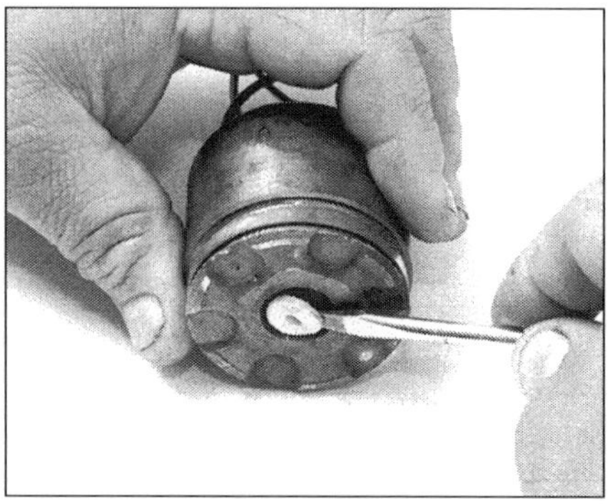

3.21n Remove the two-way check valve from the piston

3.21o Remove the bushings from the caliper ears

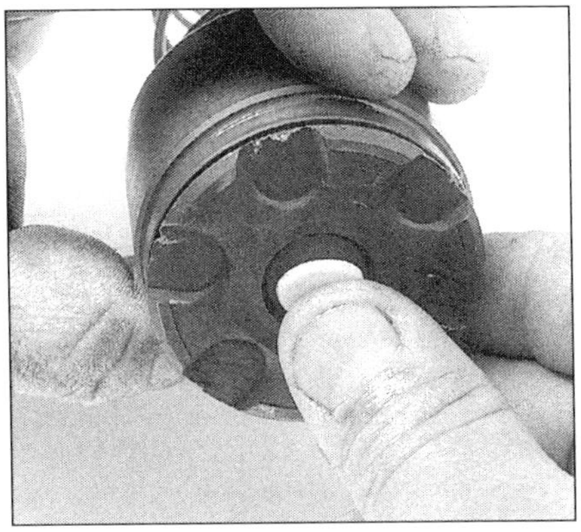

3.21p Install a new check valve in the piston

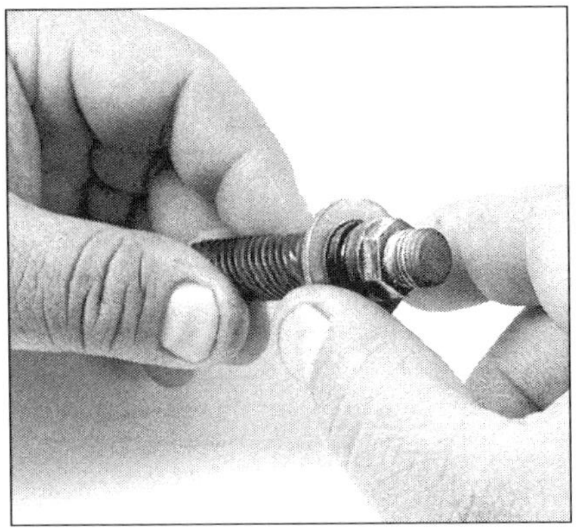

3.21q Install a new thrust washer on the actuator screw

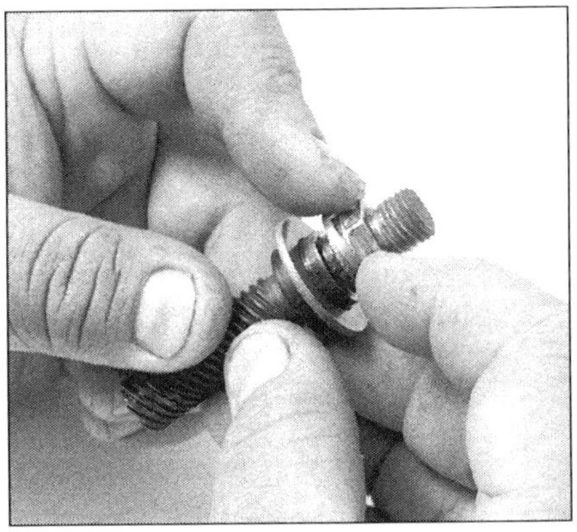

3.21r Coat the new O-ring with a little brake fluid and install it on the actuator screw

3.21s Install the actuator screw

3.21t Lubricate the piston seal with brake fluid and install it in its groove, making sure it isn't twisted

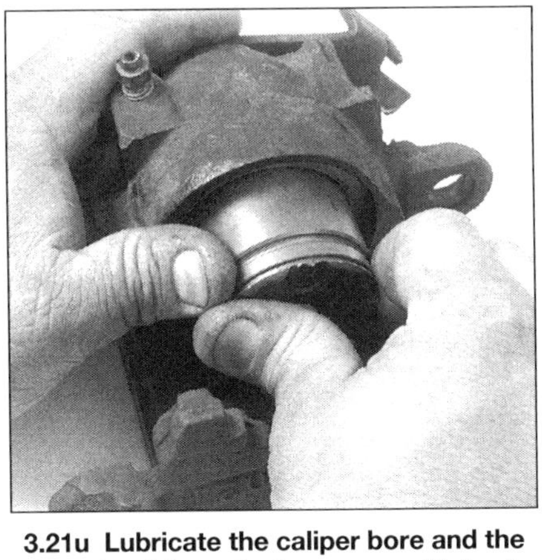

3.21u Lubricate the caliper bore and the threads of the actuator screw with fresh brake fluid, install the parking brake lever temporarily (to hold the actuator screw straight) and install the piston by placing it square to the bore and turning it slightly to start it on the actuator screw threads; once the piston is threaded onto the end of the actuator screw, remove the parking brake lever

3.21v Install the special tool, or a suitable equivalent, as shown, then slowly and carefully push the piston into the bore (as the piston is depressed, the actuator screw is threaded into the piston); do not remove the special tool until the parking brake lever has been installed

3.21w Install a new nylon anti-friction washer on the actuator screw

Installation

22 Inspect the caliper mounting bolts for corrosion. Replace as necessary.

23 Install the brake pads (see Section 2).

24 Place the caliper in position over the disc (see Section 2), install the caliper bolts and tighten them to the torque listed in this Chapter's Specifications.

25 Make sure the clearance between the caliper and the bracket stops is about 0.005 to 0.012-inch.

26 Reconnect the brake hose to the caliper. Be sure to use a new copper sealing washer, or washers, then tighten the brake hose threaded fitting securely.

27 Bleed the brakes (see Section 10).

28 Install the wheels and lower the vehicle.

29 After the job has been completed, firmly depress the brake pedal a few times to bring the pads into contact with the disc. **Note:** *If you're installing a rear caliper, this may require heavy pedal pressure, as the friction of the parking brake actuator screw must be overcome as the piston moves out towards the pads.*

30 Check brake operation before driving the vehicle in traffic.

3.21x Install a new parking brake lever seal on the actuator screw

3.21y Install the parking brake lever on the actuator screw so it's positioned as shown, up against the lever stop

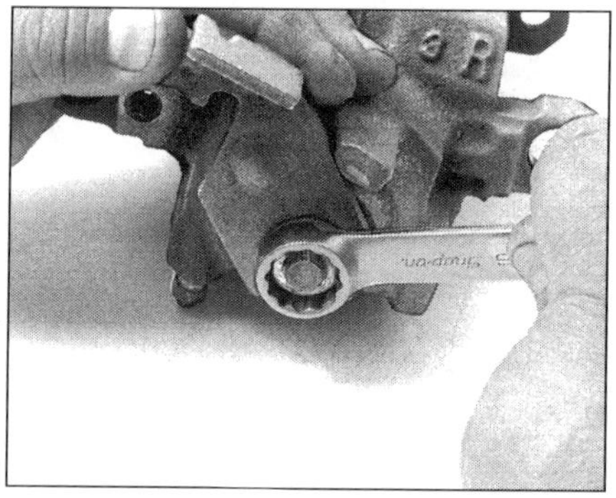

3.21z Install the lever retaining nut and, holding the lever against the stop, tighten the nut securely

3.21aa Slip the new dust boot over the piston . . .

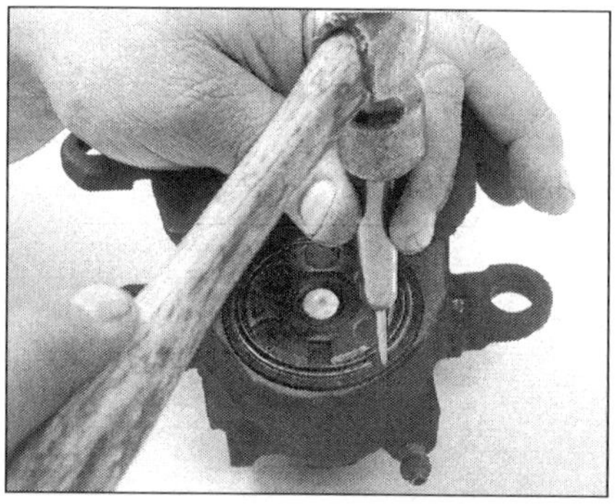

3.21bb . . . and carefully, very carefully, tap the outer edge of the boot into place with a small drift until it's fully seated into the outer shoulder in the caliper bore

3.21cc Using your thumbs as shown, carefully work the inner circumference of the dust boot into its groove in the piston

3.21dd Install a new pad dampening spring in its groove in the piston; make sure that both ends are at the top as shown

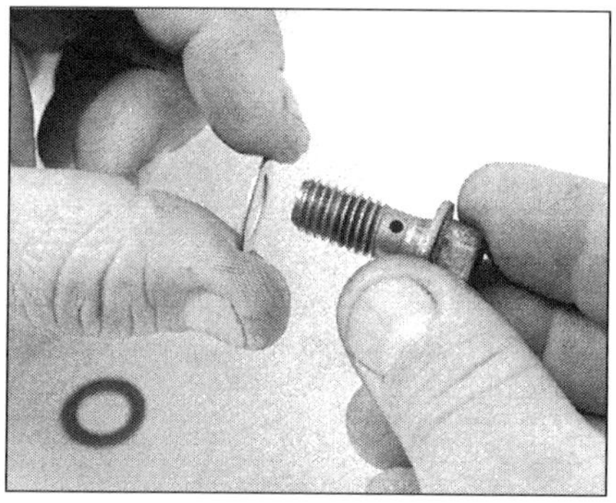

3.21ee Install a new copper sealing washer on the banjo bolt . . .

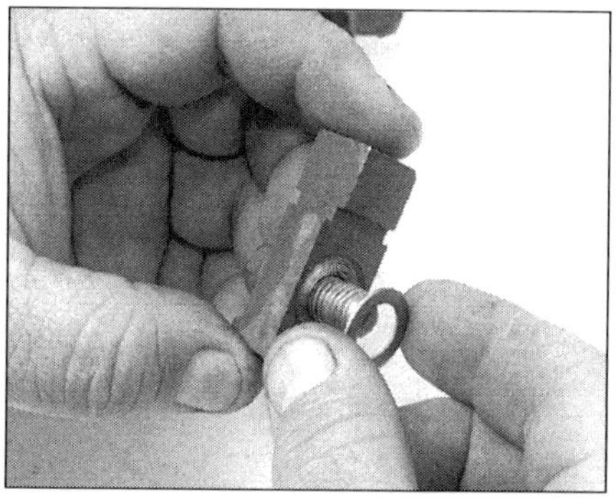

3.21ff . . . insert the banjo bolt through the fitting, install another new copper sealing washer on the banjo bolt . . .

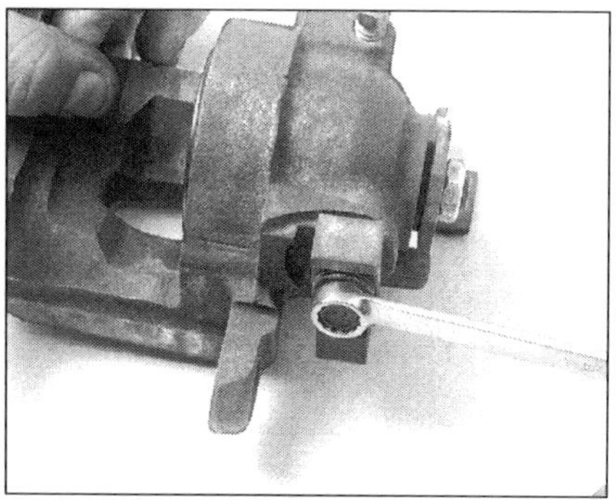

3.21gg . . . then install the fitting and tighten the banjo bolt to the torque listed in this Chapter's Specifications

3.21hh Install the bushings in the caliper ears; use new bushings if the old ones are damaged or worn

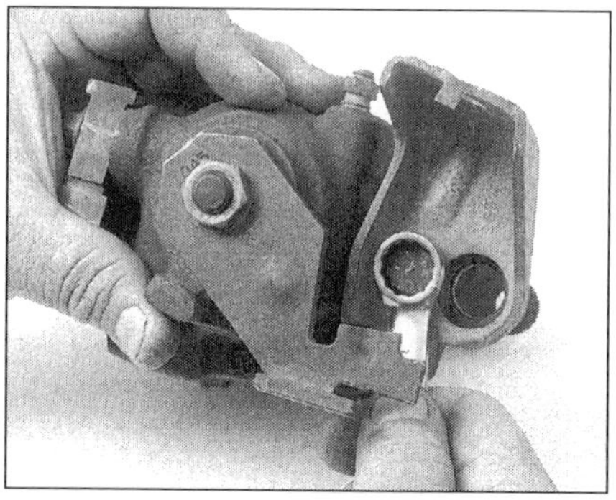

3.21ii Install the parking brake cable bracket and tighten the bolt securely

4.3 Check the disc for deep grooves and score marks (be sure to inspect both sides of the disc)

4.4a Check disc runout with a dial indicator; if the reading exceeds the maximum allowable runout, the disc will have to be resurfaced or replaced

4.4b Using a swirling motion, remove the glaze from the disc with emery cloth or sandpaper

4.5 Use a micrometer to measure disc thickness; note that the minimum thickness is also indicated on the disc itself

4.8 If the disc sticks to the hub, tap around the center portion with a hammer to break the rust bond

4 Brake disc - inspection, removal and installation

Inspection

Refer to illustrations 4.3, 4.4a, 4.4b, 4.5 and 4.8

1 Loosen the wheel lug nuts, raise the vehicle and support it securely on jackstands. Remove the wheel.

2 Remove the brake caliper as outlined in Section 2. It isn't necessary to disconnect the brake hose on front brakes. After removing the caliper bolts, suspend the caliper out of the way with a piece of wire. Don't let the caliper hang by the hose and don't stretch or twist the hose. Install three lug nuts with the flat sides against the disc to hold it in place during inspection.

3 Visually check the disc surface for score marks and other damage. Light scratches and shallow grooves are normal after use and may not always be detrimental to brake operation, but deep score marks - over 0.015-inch (0.38 mm) - require disc removal and refinishing by an automotive machine shop. Be sure to check both sides of the disc **(see illustration)**. If pulsating has been noticed during application of the brakes, suspect disc runout. Be sure to check the wheel bearings to make sure they're properly adjusted (front brakes).

4 To check disc runout, place a dial indicator at a point about 1/2-inch from the outer edge of the disc **(see illustration)**. Set the indicator to zero and turn the disc. The indicator reading should not exceed the specified allowable runout limit. If it does, the disc should be refinished by an automotive machine shop. **Note:** *Professionals recommend resurfacing of brake discs regardless of the dial indicator reading (to produce a smooth, flat surface that will eliminate brake pedal pulsations and other undesirable symptoms related to questionable discs). At the very least, if you elect not to have the discs resurfaced, deglaze them with emery cloth or sandpaper (use a swirling motion to ensure a nondirectional finish)* **(see illustration)**.

5 The disc must not be machined to a thickness less than the specified minimum thickness. The minimum wear (or discard) thickness is cast into the inside of the disc. The disc thickness can be checked with a micrometer **(see illustration)**.

Removal and installation

6 Remove the caliper, if you haven't already done so (see Sections 2 and 3).

7 The disc may be retained by a couple of factory-installed retainer washers. Cut these off with a pair of diagonal cutters and discard them.

8 Pull the disc straight off the hub. If it sticks, tap on the hub area with a hammer to break the bond **(see illustration)**. If it still won't come off, spray some penetrating oil into the areas where the hub and studs protrude (but if this is done, be sure to thoroughly clean the disc with brake system cleaner).

9 Installation is the reverse of removal.

10 Install the caliper and brake pad assembly (see Sections 2 and 3). Be sure to tighten the caliper bolts to the torque listed in this Chapter's Specifications.

11 Install the wheel, then lower the vehicle to the ground.

12 Depress the brake pedal a few times to bring the brake pads into contact with the disc.

13 Bleed the brake system, if the brake hose was disconnected (see Section 10).

5.4a Remove the brake drum

5.4b Wash off the drum brake assembly with brake system cleaner; do NOT use compressed air to blow the dust out (hub removed for clarity)

5.4c Disengage the primary shoe retracting spring from the anchor with a brake spring tool

5.4d Disengage the other end of the retracting spring from the primary shoe

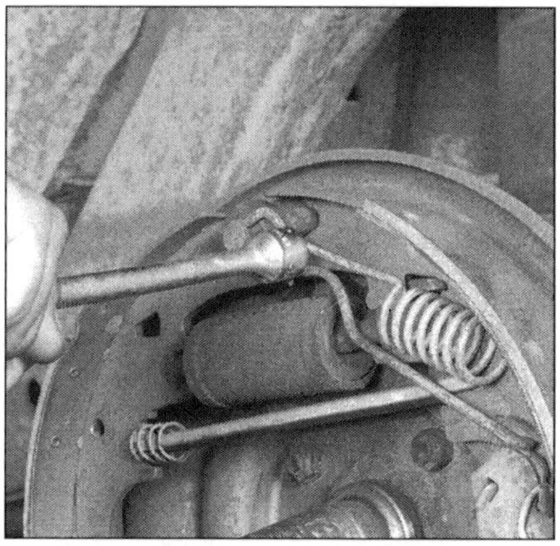

5.4e Disengage the secondary shoe retracting spring from the anchor with a brake spring tool

5.4f Disengage the retracting spring from the secondary shoe

5.4g To release the secondary shoe hold-down spring, depress it with a hold-down spring tool and rotate the tool 90-degrees . . .

5.4h . . . then remove the retainer, hold-down spring and seat

5.4i Remove the adjuster lever return spring

5 Drum brake shoes - replacement

Refer to illustrations 5.4a through 5.4hh

Warning: *Drum brake shoes must be replaced on both wheels at the same time - never replace the shoes on only one wheel. Also, the dust created by the brake system may contain asbestos, which is harmful to your health. Never blow it out with compressed air and don't inhale any of it. An approved filtering mask should be worn when working on the brakes. Do not, under any circumstances, use petroleum-based solvents to clean brake parts. Use brake system cleaner only!*

Caution: *Whenever the brake shoes are replaced, the retractor and hold-down springs should also be replaced. Due to the continuous heating/cooling cycle that the springs are subjected to, they lose their tension over a period of time and may allow the shoes to drag on the drum and wear at a much faster rate than normal.*

5.4j Disengage the actuating link from the anchor and the secondary shoe

5.4k Remove the primary shoe retainer, hold-down spring and seat

5.4l Remove the guide from the anchor

5.4m Disengage the strut from the primary shoe

5.4n Disengage the adjuster from the primary shoe and remove it

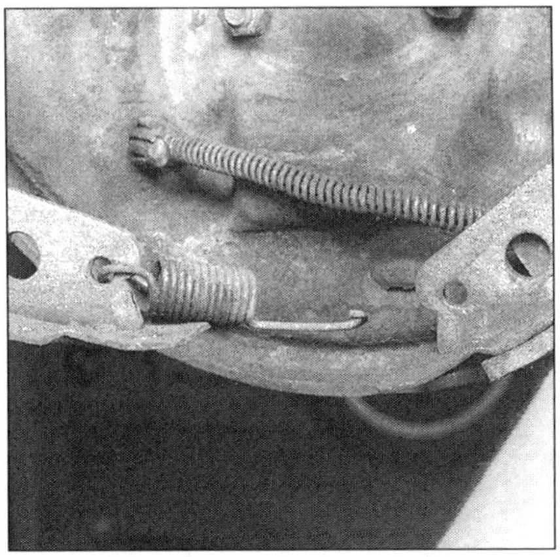

5.4o Disengage the lower return spring from both shoes (note how the front end of the spring is hooked into the front of the primary shoe and the rear end of the spring is hooked into the rear of the secondary shoe); remove the primary shoe

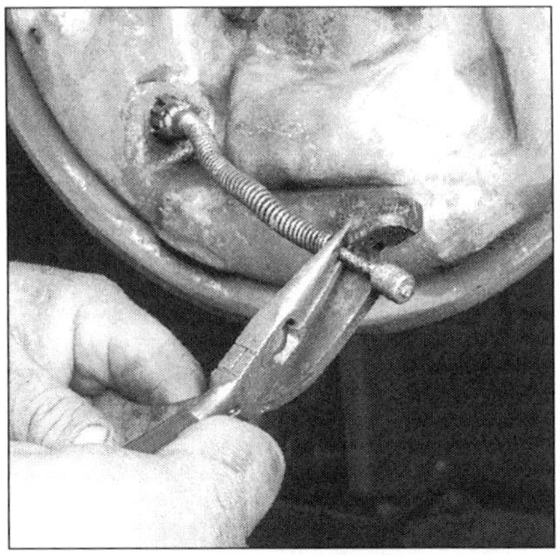

5.4p To remove the secondary shoe, flip it upside down and disengage the parking brake cable from the parking brake lever

5.4q Clean the shoe contact surfaces of the brake backing plate and lubricate them with high-temperature grease

1 Loosen the wheel lug nuts, raise the rear of the vehicle and support it securely on jackstands. Block the front wheels to keep the vehicle from rolling.

2 Release the parking brake.

3 Remove the wheel. **Note:** *All four rear brake shoes must be replaced at the same time, but to avoid mixing up parts, work on only one brake assembly at a time.*

4 Follow the accompanying photos **(illustrations 5.4a through 5.4hh)** for the inspection and replacement of the brake shoes. Be sure to stay in order and read the caption under each illustration. **Note:** *If the brake drum cannot be easily pulled off the axle and shoe assembly, make sure that the parking brake is completely released, then apply some penetrating oil at the hub-to-drum joint. Allow the oil to soak in and try to pull the drum off. If the drum still cannot be pulled off, the brake shoes will have to be retracted. This is accomplished by first removing the plug from the backing plate (or brake drum on early models). With the plug removed, pull the*

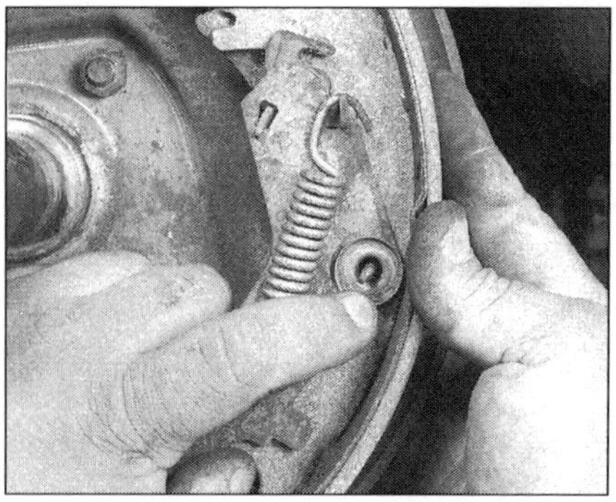

5.4r Using the hold-down pin as a centering device, place the secondary shoe and parking brake lever assembly in position, then place the adjuster lever and pawl assembly in position . . .

5.4s Install the hold-down spring and retainer . . .

5.4t . . . and lock the hold-down spring assembly into place with a hold-down tool

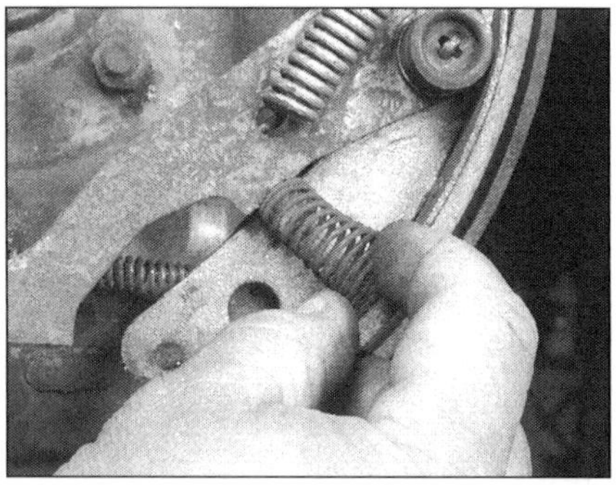

5.4u Install the adjuster lever return spring

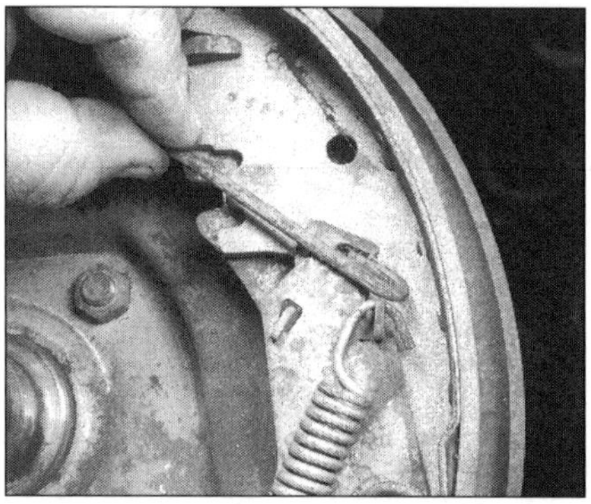

5.4v Engage the lower end of the actuating link with the notch in the top of the adjuster lever as shown . . .

5.4w . . . install the guide on the anchor pin . . .

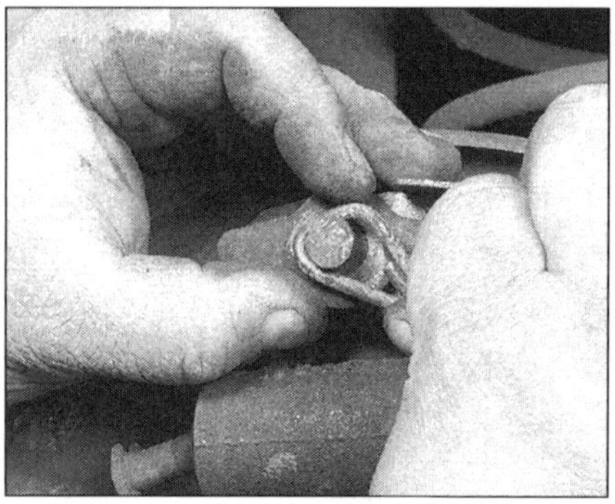

5.4x . . . and hook the upper end of the link over the anchor pin

5.4y Hook this end of the secondary shoe return spring into its hole in the secondary shoe . . .

5.4z . . . and, using a brake spring tool, hook the other end over the anchor pin

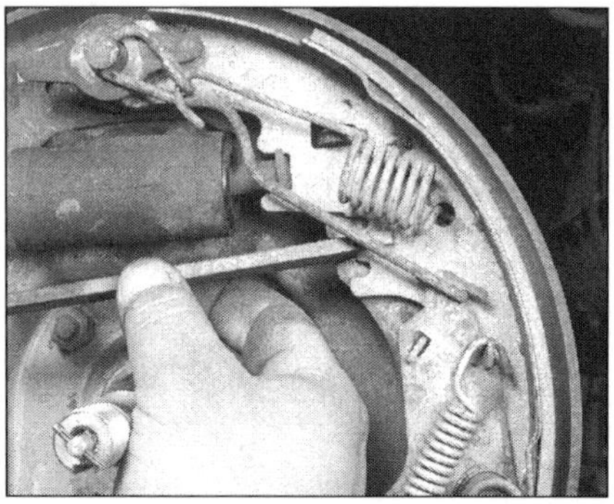

5.4aa Install the strut as shown (the small spring on the strut must be at the end of the strut not visible in this photo)

5.4bb Bring the primary shoe into position and engage the strut with the shoe as shown

5.4cc Install the primary shoe hold-down pin, seat, spring and retainer . . .

5.4dd . . . and lock the hold-down spring assembly into place with a hold-down tool

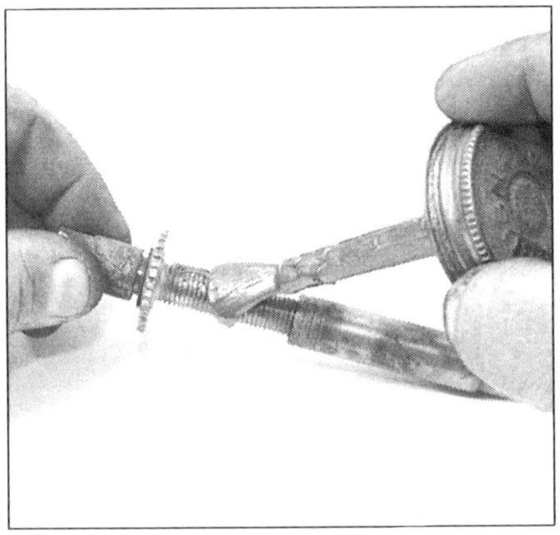

5.4gg Clean and lubricate the threads and the short, pivoting end of the adjuster screw with high-temperature grease. Install the lower return spring between the two shoes (see illustration 5.4o)

lever off the adjusting star wheel with one small screwdriver while turning the adjusting wheel with another small screwdriver, moving the shoes away from the drum. The drum should now come off.

5 Before reinstalling the drum it should be checked for cracks, score marks, deep scratches and hard spots, which will appear as small discolored areas. If the hard spots cannot be removed with fine emery cloth or if any of the other conditions listed above exist, the drum must be taken to an automotive machine shop to have it resurfaced. **Note:** *Professionals recommend resurfacing the drums whenever a brake job is done. Resurfacing will eliminate the possibility of out-of-round drums. If the drums are worn so much that they can't be resurfaced without exceeding the maximum allowable diameter (stamped into the drum), then new ones will be required. At the very least, if you elect not to have the drums resurfaced, remove the glazing from the surface with emery cloth or sandpaper using a swirling motion.*

6 Install the brake drum. Turn the brake adjuster until the shoes rub on the drum as the drum is turned, then back-off the adjuster until the shoes don't rub.

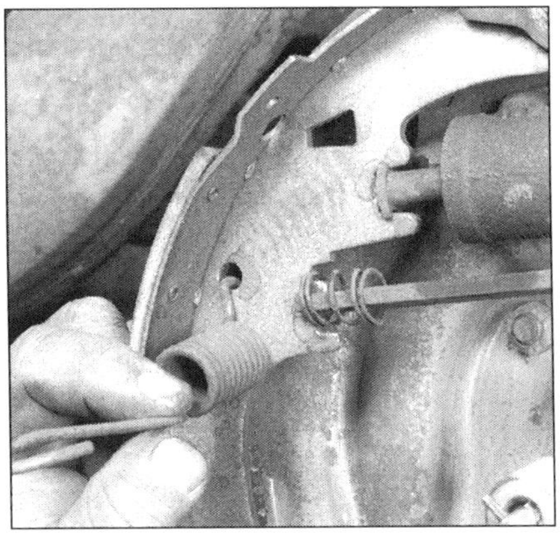

5.4ee Hook this end of the primary shoe return spring into its hole in the shoe . . .

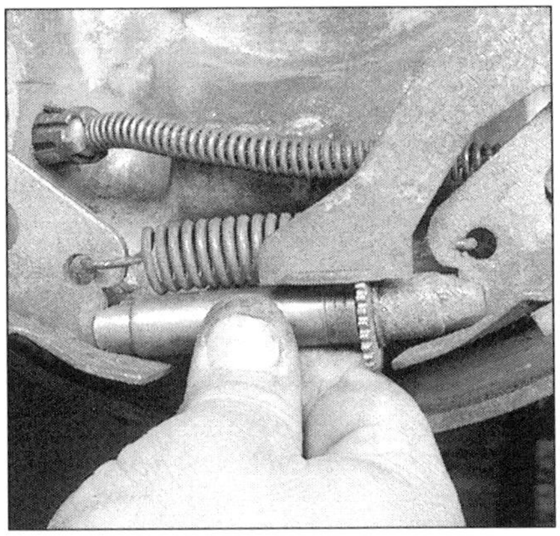

5.4hh . . . and install the adjuster assembly between the two shoes with the long end pointing forward; make sure both ends of the adjuster are properly engaged with the shoes

7 Mount the wheel, install the lug nuts, then lower the vehicle.

8 Make a number of forward and reverse stops to adjust the brakes until satisfactory pedal action is obtained.

9 Check brake operation before driving the vehicle in traffic.

6 Wheel cylinder - removal, overhaul and installation

Note: *If an overhaul is indicated (usually because of fluid leakage or sticky operation) explore all options before beginning the job. New wheel cylinders are available, which makes this job quite easy. If it's decided to rebuild the wheel cylinder, make sure that a rebuild kit is available before proceeding. Never overhaul only one wheel cylinder - always rebuild both of them.*

Removal

Refer to illustrations 6.2, 6.4 and 6.5

1 Loosen the rear wheel lug nuts, raise the rear of the vehicle and support it securely on jackstands. Block the front wheels to keep the vehicle from rolling. Remove the rear wheels.

5.4ff . . . and hook the other end over the anchor pin with a brake spring tool

6.2 To remove the links from the wheel cylinder, pull them straight out

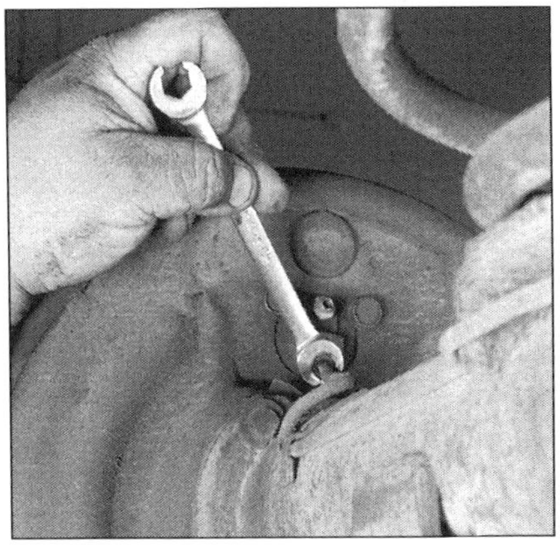

6.4 Use a flare-nut wrench to unscrew the brake line fitting from the wheel cylinder

2 Remove the brake shoe assembly (see Section 5). Remove the links from the wheel cylinder **(see illustration)**.

3 Remove all dirt and foreign material from around the wheel cylinder.

4 Unscrew the brake line fitting **(see illustration)**. Don't pull the brake line away from the wheel cylinder.

5 Remove the wheel cylinder mounting

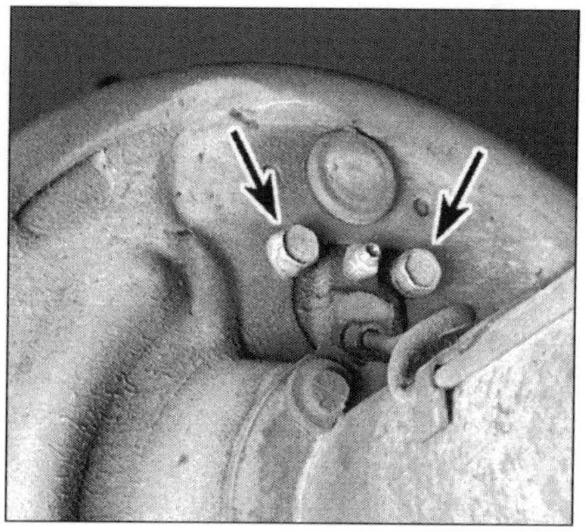

6.5 To detach the wheel cylinder from the brake backing plate, remove these bolts (arrows)

bolts **(see illustration)**.

6 Detach the wheel cylinder from the brake backing plate and place it on a clean workbench. Immediately plug the brake line to prevent fluid loss and contamination. **Note:** *If the brake shoe linings are contaminated with brake fluid, install new brake shoes (don't attempt to clean them).*

Overhaul

Refer to illustrations 6.7a, 6.7b, 6.10a and 6.10b

7 Remove the boots, pistons, cups and spring assembly from the wheel cylinder body **(see illustrations)**.

8 Clean the wheel cylinder with brake fluid, denatured alcohol or brake system cleaner. **Warning:** *Do not, under any circumstances, use petroleum based solvents to clean brake parts!*

9 Use compressed air to remove excess fluid from the wheel cylinder and to blow out the passages.

10 Inspect the cylinder bore for corrosion and score marks. Crocus cloth can be used to remove light corrosion and stains. The cylinder can also be lightly honed **(see illustrations)**, but the cylinder must be replaced with a new one if the defects cannot be removed easily, or if the bore is scored.

11 Lubricate the new cups with brake fluid.

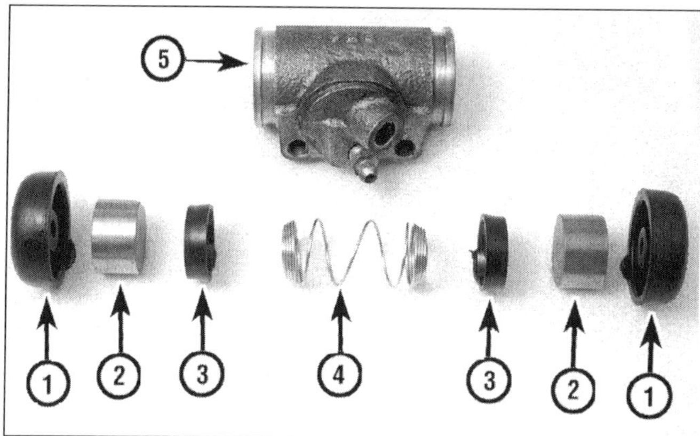

6.7a An exploded view of the wheel cylinder assembly

1. *Dust boot*
2. *Piston*
3. *Cup*
4. *Spring*
5. *Wheel cylinder housing*

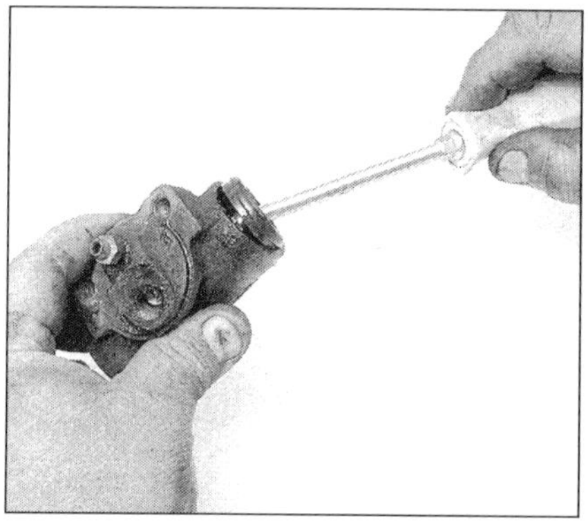

6.7b Pry out the dust boots with a screwdriver, but make sure you don't gouge or scratch the piston bore inside the wheel cylinder housing

12 Assemble the wheel cylinder components. Make sure the cup lips face in **(see illustration 6.7a)**.

Installation

13 Place the wheel cylinder in position and install the bolts and tighten them to the torque listed in this Chapter's Specifications.

14 Being careful not to cross-thread it, connect the brake line and tighten the fitting securely. Install the brake shoe assembly.

15 Bleed the brakes (see Section 10).

16 Check the operation of the brakes before driving the vehicle in traffic.

6.10a Insert the hone into the wheel cylinder bore as shown . . .

7 Master cylinder - removal, overhaul and installation

Removal

Refer to illustrations 7.2 and 7.4

Note: *Before deciding to overhaul the master cylinder, investigate the availability and cost of a new or factory rebuilt unit and also the availability of a rebuild kit.*

1 Place rags under the brake line fittings and prepare caps or plastic bags to cover the ends of the lines once they are disconnected. **Caution:** *Brake fluid will damage paint. Cover all body parts and be careful not to spill fluid*

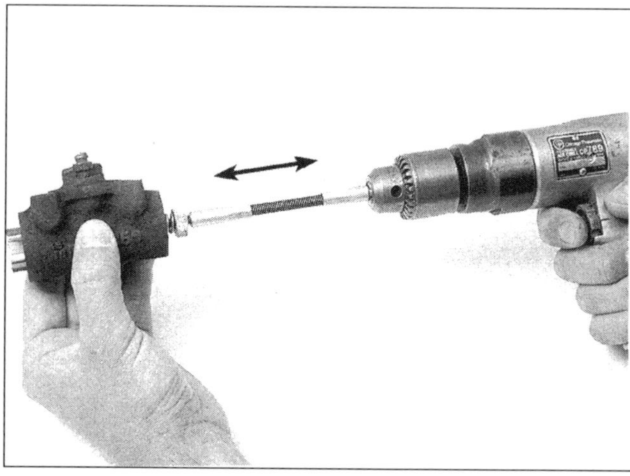

6.10b . . . and make several light passes up and down the bore; don't overdo it; stop and inspect your work. You're only trying to remove any glaze or small imperfections so the piston cups seal properly. If you take off too much material, the wheel cylinder won't seal well and will have to be replaced

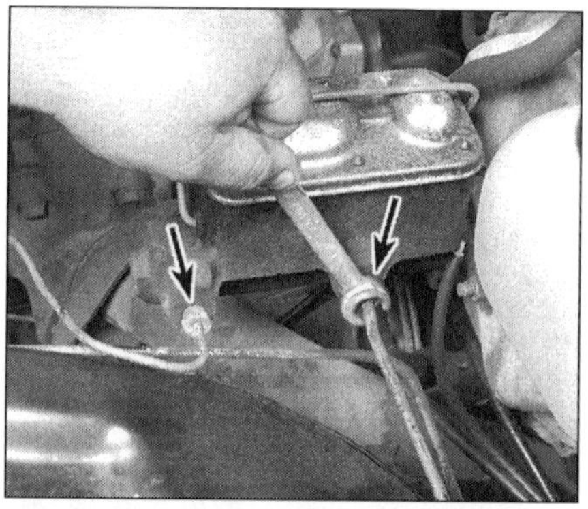

7.2 To disconnect the metal brake lines from the master cylinder, unscrew these threaded fittings with a flare-nut wrench

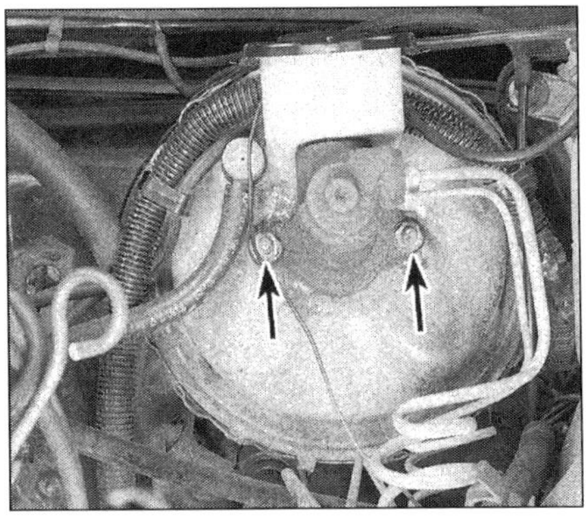

7.4 To detach the master cylinder from the power brake booster, remove these nuts (arrows)

7.7 Pry the reservoir out of the grommets

during this procedure.

2 Loosen the tube nuts at the ends of the brake lines where they enter the master cylinder. To prevent rounding off the flats on these nuts, a flare-nut wrench, which wraps around the nut, should be used **(see illustration)**.

3 Pull the brake lines away from the master cylinder slightly and plug the ends to prevent contamination.

4 Remove the two master cylinder mounting nuts **(see illustration)**. Remove the master cylinder from the engine compartment, being careful not to spill any brake fluid. If you do spill some fluid on the paint, rinse it off immediately with water, as brake fluid will damage the paint.

5 Remove the reservoir cover and reservoir diaphragm, then discard any fluid remaining in the reservoir.

Overhaul

Plastic reservoir master cylinder

Refer to illustrations 7.7a, 7.7b, 7.8, 7.9, 7.10, 7.14, 7.15a, 7.15b, 7.15c, 7.15d and 7.16

6 Mount the master cylinder in a vise. Be sure to line the vise jaws with blocks of wood to prevent damage to the cylinder body.

7 Carefully pry the reservoir from the cylinder body with a screwdriver **(see illustration)**. Remove the grommets.

8 Remove the primary piston lock ring by depressing the piston and prying the ring out with a screwdriver **(see illustrations)**.

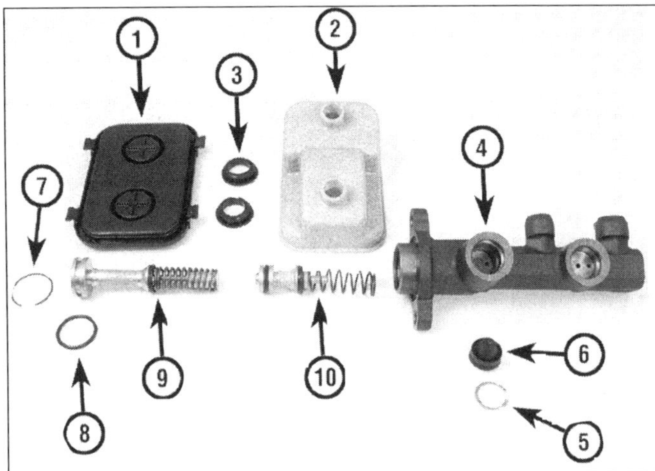

7.8a Exploded view of a later model master cylinder

1 *Reservoir cover and diaphragm*
2 *Reservoir*
3 *Reservoir grommets*
4 *Master cylinder body*
5 *Quick take-up valve circlip*
6 *Quick take-up valve*
7 *Lock ring*
8 *Primary piston O-ring*
9 *Primary piston assembly*
10 *Secondary piston assembly*

7.8b Push the primary piston in and remove the lock ring

7.10 To remove the secondary piston, tap the cylinder against a block of wood

9 Remove the primary piston assembly from the cylinder bore **(see illustration)**.

10 Remove the secondary piston assembly from the cylinder bore. It may be necessary to remove the master cylinder from the vise and invert it, carefully tapping it against a block of wood to expel the piston **(see illustration)**.

11 Do not attempt to remove the quick take-up valve from the master cylinder body - it isn't serviceable.

12 Inspect the cylinder bore for corrosion and damage. If any corrosion or damage is found, replace the master cylinder body with a new one, as abrasives cannot be used on the bore.

7.9 Pull the primary piston and spring assembly out of the bore

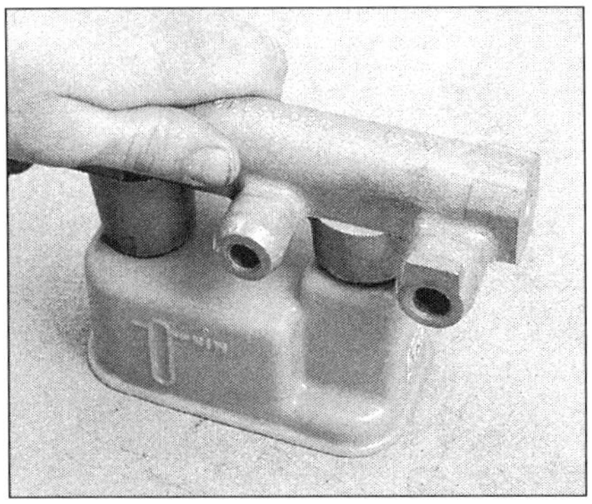

7.14 Lay the reservoir face down on the bench and push the master cylinder straight down over the reservoir tubes using a rocking motion

13 Lubricate the new reservoir grommets with silicone lubricant and press them into the master cylinder body. Make sure they're properly seated.

14 Lay the reservoir on a hard surface and

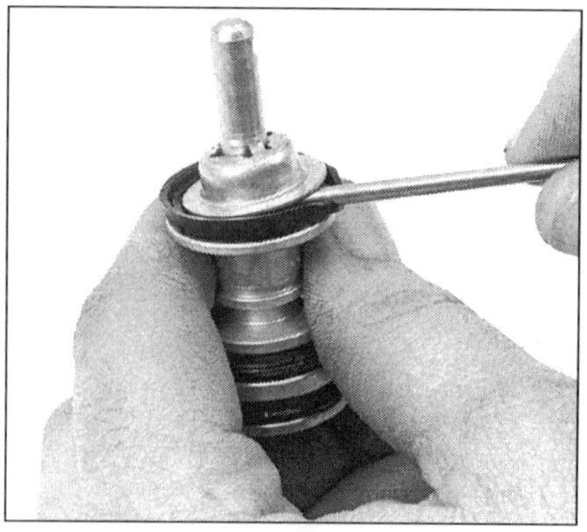

7.15a Pry the secondary piston spring retainer off with a small screwdriver, then remove the seal

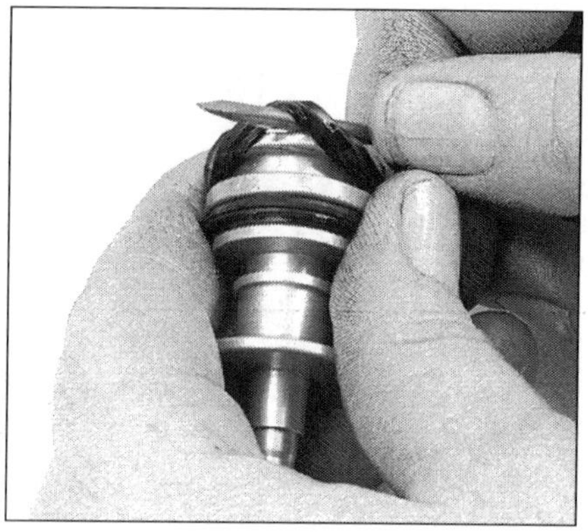

7.15b Remove the secondary seals from the piston (some models only have one seal)

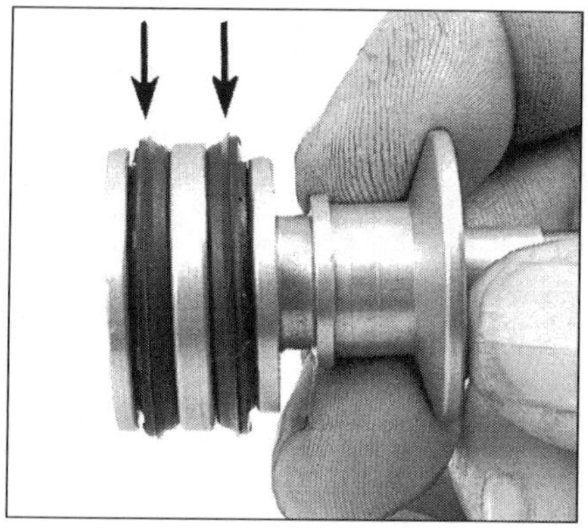

7.15c Install the secondary seals with the lips facing away from each other (on the single-seal design, the seal lip should face away from the center of the piston)

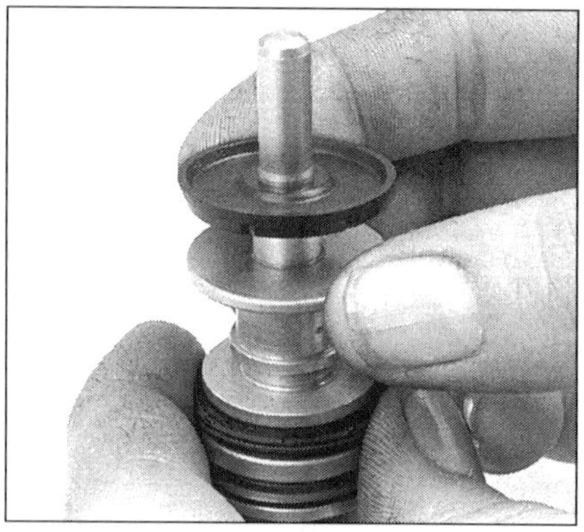

7.15d Install a new primary piston on the secondary piston with the seal lip facing in the direction shown

7.16 Install a new spring retainer over the end of the secondary piston and push it into place with a socket

7.22 Remove the secondary stop bolt

press the master cylinder body onto the reservoir, using a rocking motion **(see illustration)**.

15 Remove the old seals from the secondary piston assembly and install the new secondary seals with the lips facing away from each other **(see illustrations)**. The lip on the primary seal must face in **(see illustration)**.

16 Attach the spring retainer to the secondary piston assembly **(see illustration)**.

17 Lubricate the cylinder bore with clean brake fluid and install the spring and secondary piston assembly.

18 Install the primary piston assembly in the cylinder bore, depress it and install the lock ring.

19 Inspect the reservoir cover and diaphragm for cracks and deformation. Replace any damaged parts with new ones and attach the diaphragm to the cover.

20 **Note:** *Whenever the master cylinder is removed, the complete hydraulic system must be bled. The time required to bleed the system can be reduced if the master cylinder is filled with fluid and bench bled (refer to Steps 35 through 39) before the master cylinder is installed on the vehicle.*

7.23 Depress the piston and remove the retaining ring

7.26a If the line seats are damaged, thread a screw into them and pry them out

Cast iron master cylinder

Refer to illustrations 7.22, 7.23, 7.26a, 7.26b, 7.27, 7.29a, 7.29b and 7.30

21 Drain all fluid from the master cylinder and place the unit in a vise. Use wood blocks to cushion the jaws of the vise.

22 Remove the secondary stop bolt, if equipped, from the bottom of the front fluid reservoir or from the base of the master cylinder body **(see illustration)**.

23 Remove the retaining ring from the groove and take out the primary piston assembly **(see illustration)**. Following the primary piston out of the bore will be the secondary piston, spring and retainer. Tap the cylinder against a wood block to eject the secondary piston assembly.

24 Examine the inside surface of the master cylinder and the secondary piston. If there is evidence of scoring or "bright" wear areas, the entire master cylinder should be replaced with a new one.

25 If the components are in good condition, wash them in clean brake fluid or brake cleaner. Discard all the rubber components and the primary piston. Purchase a rebuild kit which will contain all the necessary parts for the overhaul.

26 Inspect the line seats which are located in the master cylinder body where the lines connect. If they appear damaged they should be replaced with new ones, which come in

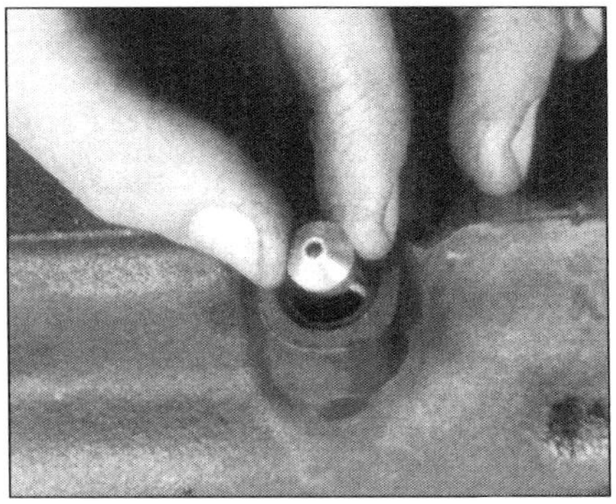

7.26b Install the new line seats with the cone-shaped ends facing up, then press them into place using a spare brake line end and tube nut

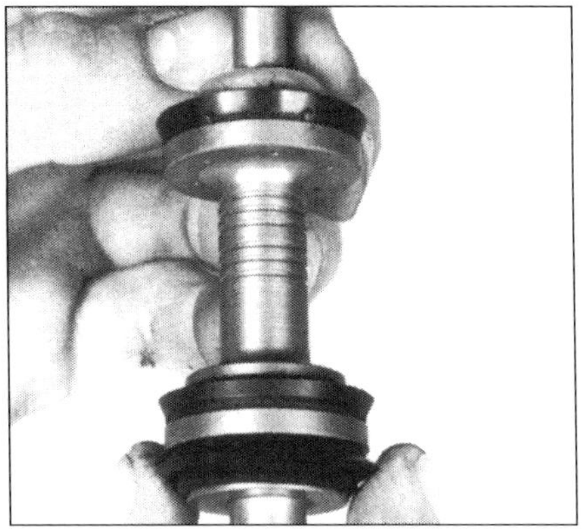

7.27 Install the seals on the piston as shown

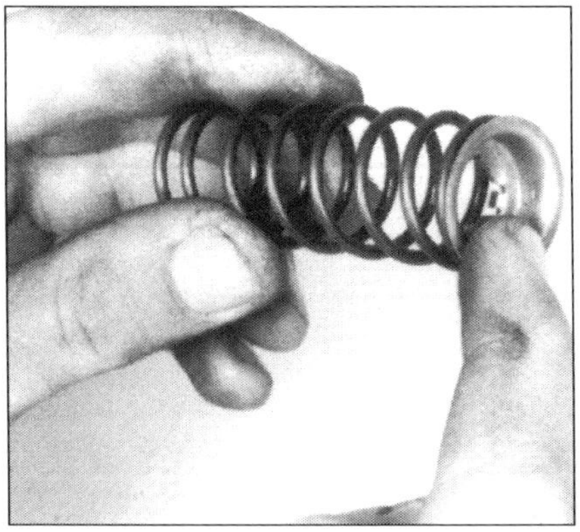

7.29a Assemble the retainer and spring

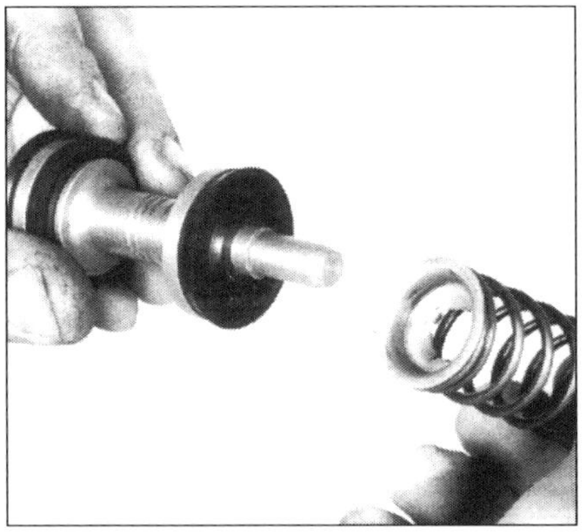

7.29b Assemble the spring and piston

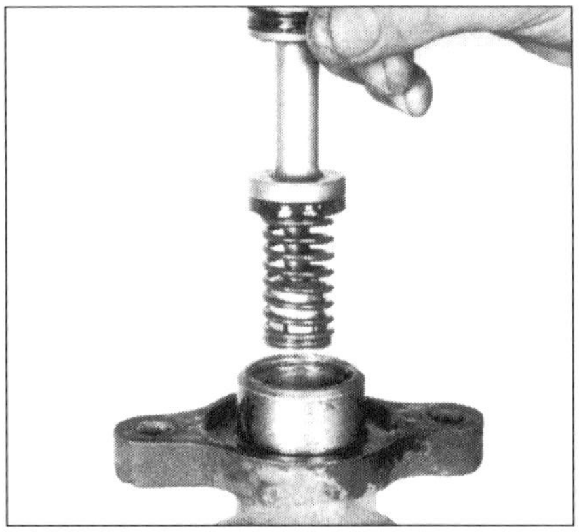

7.30 Install the piston and spring assembly into the master cylinder

the overhaul kit. They are forced out of the body by threading a screw into the seat and then prying out **(see illustration)**. The new ones are forced into place using a spare brake line and tube nut **(see illustration)**.

27 Place the new secondary seals in the grooves of the secondary piston **(see illustration)**.

28 Assemble the primary seals and seal protector over the end of the secondary piston.

29 Lubricate the cylinder bore and secondary piston with clean brake fluid. Insert the spring retainer into the spring then place the retainer and spring over the end of the secondary piston **(see illustrations)**. The retainer should locate inside the primary seal lips.

30 With the master cylinder vertical, push the secondary piston into the bore to seat its spring **(see illustration)**.

31 Coat the seals of the primary piston with brake fluid and fit it into the cylinder bore. Hold it down while the retaining ring is installed in the cylinder groove.

32 Continue to hold the piston down while the stop screw (if equipped) is installed.

33 Install the reservoir diaphragm into the reservoir cover plate, making sure it is fully collapsed inside the recess lid.

34 **Note:** *Whenever the master cylinder is removed, the complete hydraulic system must be bled. The time required to bleed the system can be reduced if the master cylinder is filled with fluid and bench bled (refer to Step 35 through 39) before the master cylinder is installed on the vehicle.*

Bench bleeding

35 Insert threaded plugs of the correct size into the cylinder outlet fittings and fill the reservoirs with brake fluid. The master cylinder should be supported in such a manner that brake fluid will not spill during the bench bleeding procedure.

36 Loosen one plug at a time and push the piston assembly into the bore to force air from the master cylinder. To prevent air from being drawn back into the cylinder, the appropriate plug must be replaced before allowing the piston to return to its original position.

37 Stroke the piston three or four times for each outlet to ensure that all air has been expelled.

38 Since high pressure is not involved in the bench bleeding procedure, an alternative to the removal and replacement of the plugs with each stroke of the piston assembly is available. Before pushing in on the piston assembly, remove one of the plugs completely. Before releasing the piston, however, instead of replacing the plug, simply put your finger tightly over the hole to keep air from being drawn back into the master cylinder. Wait several seconds for the brake fluid to be drawn from the reservoir to the piston bore, then repeat the procedure. When you push down on the piston it will force your finger off the hole, allowing the air inside to be expelled. When only brake fluid is being ejected from the hole, replace the plug and go on to the other port.

39 Refill the master cylinder reservoirs and install the diaphragm and cover assembly. **Note:** *The reservoirs should only be filled to the top of the reservoir divider to prevent overflowing when the cover is installed.*

Installation

40 Carefully install the master cylinder by reversing the removal steps, then bleed the brakes (see Section 10).

8 Combination valve - check and replacement

Check

Refer to illustration 8.1

1 Disconnect the wire from the pressure differential warning switch **(see illustration)**. **Note:** *When unplugging the connector, squeeze the side lock releases, moving the inside tabs away from the switch, then pull*

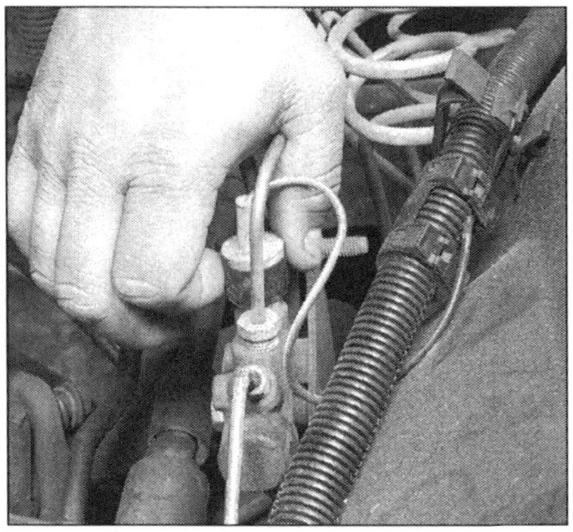

8.1 To unplug the electrical connector from the combination valve, squeeze the tangs on either side of the connector and pull up

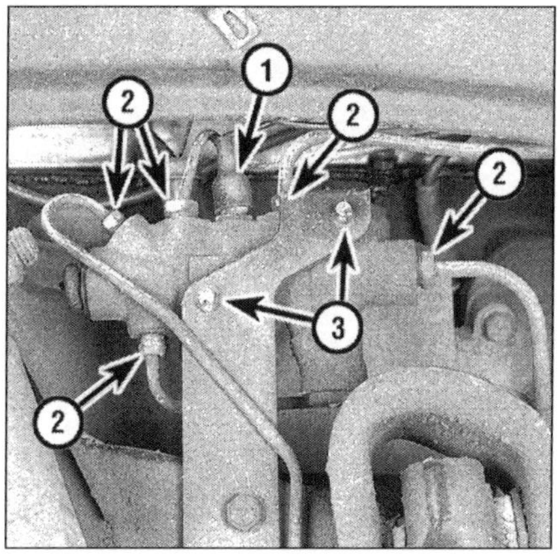

8.14 To remove the combination valve, unplug the electrical connector (1) for the pressure differential warning switch, unscrew the tube nuts (2) for all brake lines, and remove the mounting bolts (3) (bolt heads are on the engine side of the valve)

9.2 To disconnect a flexible brake hose from a metal brake line, loosen and back off the fitting on the male side (the metal line side) of the bracket as shown; if the bracket starts to bend or twist, put a back-up wrench on the female fitting (the flexible hose side)

9.3 Remove the U-clip from the hose fitting and detach the hose from the bracket; use a pair of pliers if you can; otherwise, push the clip off with a screwdriver

up. Pliers may be used as an aid if necessary.

2 Using a jumper wire, connect the switch wire to a good ground, such as the engine block.

3 Turn the ignition key to the On position. The warning light in the instrument panel should light.

4 If the warning light does not light, either the bulb is burned out or the electrical circuit is defective. Replace the bulb (see Chapter 12) or repair the electrical circuit as necessary.

5 When the warning light functions correctly, turn the ignition switch off, disconnect the jumper wire and reconnect the wire to the switch terminal.

6 Make sure the master cylinder reservoirs are full, then attach a bleeder hose to one of the rear wheel bleeder valves and immerse the other end of the hose in a container partially filled with clean brake fluid.

7 Turn the ignition switch On.

8 Open the bleeder valve while a helper applies moderate pressure to the brake pedal. The brake warning light on the instrument panel should light.

9 Close the bleeder valve before the helper releases the brake pedal.

10 Reapply the brake pedal with moderate to heavy pressure. The brake warning light should go out.

11 Attach the bleeder hose to one of the front brake bleeder valves and repeat Steps 8 through 10. The warning light should react in the same manner as in Steps 8 and 10.

12 Turn the ignition switch Off.

13 If the warning light did not come on in Steps 8 and 11, but does light when a jumper is connected to ground, the warning light switch portion of the combination valve is defective and the combination valve must be replaced with a new one since the components of the combination valve are not individually serviceable.

Replacement

Refer to illustration 8.14

14 Place a container under the combination valve and protect all painted surfaces with newspapers or rags.

15 Disconnect the hydraulic lines at the combination valve **(see illustration)**, then plug the lines to prevent further loss of fluid and to protect the lines from contamination.

16 Disconnect the electrical connector from the pressure differential warning switch.

17 Remove the bolts holding the valve to the mounting bracket and remove the valve from the vehicle.

18 Installation is the reverse of the removal procedure.

19 Bleed the entire brake system.

9 Brake hoses and lines - inspection and replacement

Inspection

1 About every six months, with the vehicle raised and supported securely on jackstands, the rubber hoses which connect the steel brake lines with the front and rear brake assemblies should be inspected for cracks, chafing of the outer cover, leaks, blisters and other damage. These are important and vulnerable parts of the brake system and inspection should be complete. A light and mirror will be helpful for a thorough check. If a hose exhibits any of the above conditions, replace it with a new one.

Replacement

Front brake hose

Refer to illustrations 9.2 and 9.3

2 Disconnect the brake line from the hose fitting, being careful not to bend the frame bracket or brake line **(see illustration)**. If the bracket starts to bend, use a back-up wrench on the female fitting (flexible hose side of the bracket).

3 Remove the U-clip from the female fitting at the bracket **(see illustration)**, then detach the hose from the bracket.

4 Unscrew the brake hose from the caliper. On earlier calipers without a fitting block, simply unscrew the hose from the caliper and discard the sealing washer. On later calipers with a fitting block, unscrew the hose from the fitting block and discard the sealing washer. Do not remove the fitting block bolt unless brake fluid is leaking out. If you do unbolt the fitting block, discard the sealing washer on either side of the fitting block bolt.

5 If you removed the fitting block, install a new sealing washer on the fitting block bolt, insert the bolt through the block, add another new sealing washer to the bolt and install the bolt/block assembly (see Section 3). Be sure to tighten the bolt to the torque listed in this Chapter's Specifications.

6 To install the brake hose, install a new copper sealing washer, lubricate the threads with clean brake fluid, screw it into the caliper or fitting block and tighten it securely.

7 Install the female fitting at the other end of the hose into the hose bracket. It will fit the bracket in only one position. Make sure the hose is neither twisted nor kinked.

8 Install the U-clip retaining the female fitting to the frame bracket.

9 Attach the brake line to the hose fitting. If the bracket starts to bend, use a back-up wrench on the female fitting.

10 When the brake hose installation is complete, there should be no kinks in the hose. Verify that the hose doesn't contact any part of the suspension by turning the wheels to the extreme left and right positions. If the hose makes contact, remove it and correct the installation as necessary. Bleed the system (see Section 10).

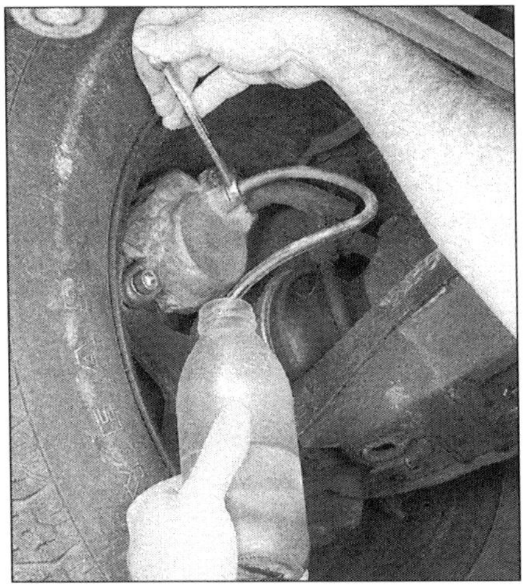

10.9 When bleeding the brakes, a hose is connected to the bleed screw at the caliper or wheel cylinder and then submerged in brake fluid - air will be seen as bubbles in the tube and container (all air must be expelled before moving to the next wheel)

Rear brake hose

11 Disconnect the hose at the frame bracket, being careful not to bend the bracket or steel lines. If the bracket starts to bend, use a back-up wrench on the female fitting (flexible hose side of the bracket).
12 Remove the U-clip with a pair of pliers and separate the female fitting from the bracket.
13 Disconnect the two hydraulic lines at the junction block, then unbolt and remove the hose.
14 Bolt the junction block to the axle housing and connect the lines, tightening them securely. Without twisting the hose, install the female end of the hose in the frame bracket.
15 Install the U-clips retaining the female end to the bracket.
16 Using a back-up wrench, attach the steel line fittings to the female fittings. Again, be careful not to bend the bracket or steel line.
17 Make sure the hose installation did not loosen the frame bracket. Tighten the bracket if necessary.
18 Fill the master cylinder reservoir and bleed the system (see Section 10).

Metal brake lines

19 When replacing brake lines, be sure to use the correct parts. NEVER use copper tubing for any brake system components. Purchase prefabricated steel brake lines, with the tube ends already flared and fittings installed, from a dealer parts department or auto parts store. These lines are also sometimes bent to the proper shapes, but if you purchase straight steel tubing, be sure to use a bending tool to make kink-free bends.
20 When installing the new line make sure it's well supported in the brackets and has plenty of clearance between moving or hot components.
21 After installation, check the master cylinder fluid level and add fluid as necessary. Bleed the brake system (see Section 10) and test the brakes carefully before placing the vehicle into normal operation.

10 Brake system bleeding

Refer to illustration 10.9

Warning: *Wear eye protection when bleeding the brake system. If the fluid comes in contact with your eyes, immediately rinse them with water and seek medical attention.*

Note: *Bleeding the hydraulic system is necessary to remove any air that manages to find its way into the system when it's been opened during removal and installation of a hose, line, caliper or master cylinder.*

1 It will probably be necessary to bleed the system at all four brakes if air has entered the system due to low fluid level, or if the brake lines have been disconnected at the master cylinder.
2 If a brake line was disconnected only at a wheel, then only that caliper or wheel cylinder must be bled.
3 If a brake line is disconnected at a fitting located between the master cylinder and any of the brakes, that part of the system served by the disconnected line must be bled.
4 Remove any residual vacuum from the brake power booster by applying the brake several times with the engine off.
5 Remove the master cylinder reservoir cover and fill the reservoir with brake fluid. Reinstall the cover. **Note:** *Check the fluid level often during the bleeding operation and add fluid as necessary to prevent the fluid level from falling low enough to allow air bubbles into the master cylinder.*
6 Have an assistant on hand, as well as a supply of new brake fluid, a clear container partially filled with clean brake fluid, a length of 3/16-inch plastic, rubber or vinyl tubing to fit over the bleeder valve and a wrench to open and close the bleeder valve.
7 On early models equipped with the Trackmaster ABS system, the modulator (located on top of the master cylinder) must be bled first, using the same procedure (with a hose connected to the bleeder valve and a container partially filled with brake fluid) as described below, before proceeding.
8 Beginning at the right rear wheel, loosen the bleeder valve slightly, then tighten it to a point where it is snug but can still be loosened quickly and easily.
9 Place one end of the tubing over the bleeder valve and submerge the other end in brake fluid in the container **(see illustration)**.
10 Have the assistant pump the brakes slowly a few times to build up pressure in the system, then hold the pedal firmly depressed.
11 While the pedal is held depressed, open the bleeder valve just enough to allow a flow of fluid to leave the valve. Watch for air bubbles to exit the submerged end of the tube. When the fluid flow slows after a couple of seconds, close the valve and have your assistant release the pedal.
12 Repeat Steps 10 and 11 until no more air is seen leaving the tube, then tighten the bleeder valve and proceed to the left rear wheel, the right front wheel and the left front wheel, in that order, and perform the same procedure. Be sure to check the fluid in the master cylinder reservoir frequently.
13 Never use old brake fluid. It contains moisture which will deteriorate the brake system components.
14 Refill the master cylinder with fluid at the end of the operation.
15 Check the operation of the brakes. The pedal should feel solid when depressed, with no sponginess. If necessary, repeat the entire process. **Warning:** *Do not operate the vehicle if you are in doubt about the effectiveness of the brake system.*

11 Parking brake - adjustment

Refer to illustration 11.3

1 The adjustment of the parking brake cable may be necessary whenever the rear brake cables have been disconnected or the parking brake cables have stretched due to age and stress.
2 On models equipped with rear drum brakes, depress the parking brake pedal two or three clicks. On models with rear disc brakes, the parking brake must be in the released position. Raise the car for access underneath, supporting it securely on jackstands.

Rear drum brake models

3 Tighten the adjusting nut **(see illustration)** until light drag is felt on either wheel when rotated in a forward direction.
4 Carefully release the parking brake pedal and verify that the wheel is able to rotate freely in either direction. It is important that there is no drag on the rear brakes with the pedal released.

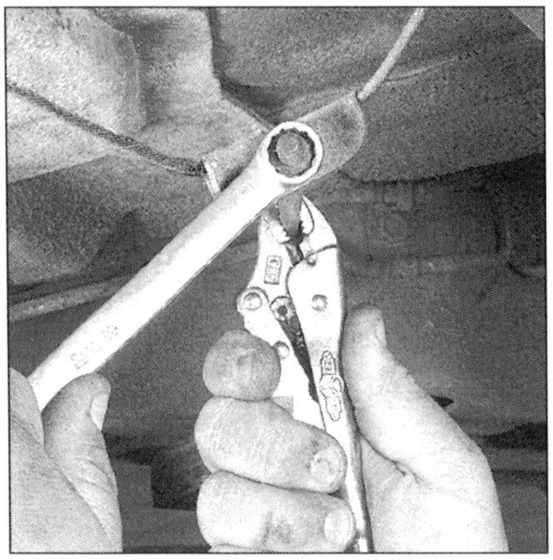

11.3 Adjust the parking brake by turning the nut at the equalizer

12.3 To release the parking brake cable from the backing plate of a rear drum brake, squeeze the cable housing retainer tangs together and pull the cable housing through the backing plate

Rear disc brake models

5 Tighten the adjusting nut **(see illustration 11.3)** until all slack is removed from the parking brake cables. The parking brake caliper levers must be in contact with their stops after adjustment. If they are off the stops, loosen the adjuster as necessary.

12 Parking brake cables - replacement

1 Loosen the wheel lug nuts, raise the vehicle and support it securely on jackstands. Remove the wheel(s).

Rear cables

Refer to illustrations 12.3, 12.5a, 12.5b, 12.5c and 12.5d

2 Loosen the equalizer nut (see Section 11) to slacken the cables, then disconnect the cable to be replaced from the equalizer.

3 On models with rear drum brakes, remove the brake drum and brake shoes, then disconnect the parking brake cable from the parking brake lever on (see Section 5). Depress the tangs on the cable housing retainer **(see illustration)** and push the housing and cable through the backing plate.

4 On models with rear disc brakes, disengage the rear end of the parking brake cable from the parking brake lever on the caliper **(see illustrations 2.7b, 2.7c and 2.7d)**.

5 Detach the parking brake cable from the underside of the vehicle **(see illustrations)**.

6 Installation is the reverse of removal. On models with rear drum brakes make sure that the cable is pulled through the backing plate far enough to allow the tangs on the cable housing retainer to lock against the backing plate. On models with rear disc brakes, make sure the rear end of the cable is properly connected to the parking brake lever.

7 Adjust the cable (see Section 11) when you're done.

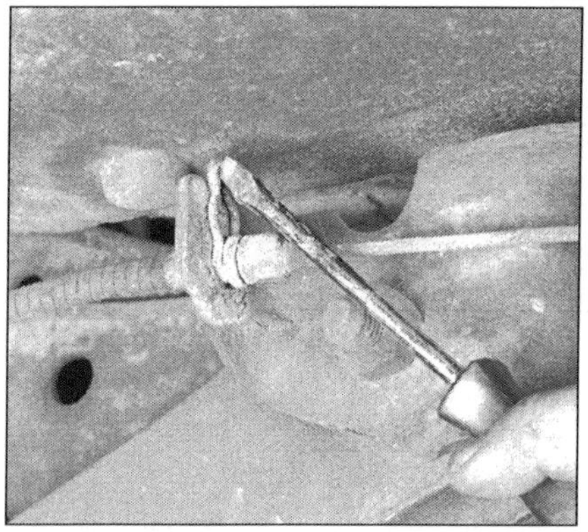

12.5a To detach a rear parking brake cable from the underside of an older model with rear drum brakes, remove this clip from the bracket at the forward end of the suspension link . . .

12.5b . . . and pull off this locking U-clip from the crossmember

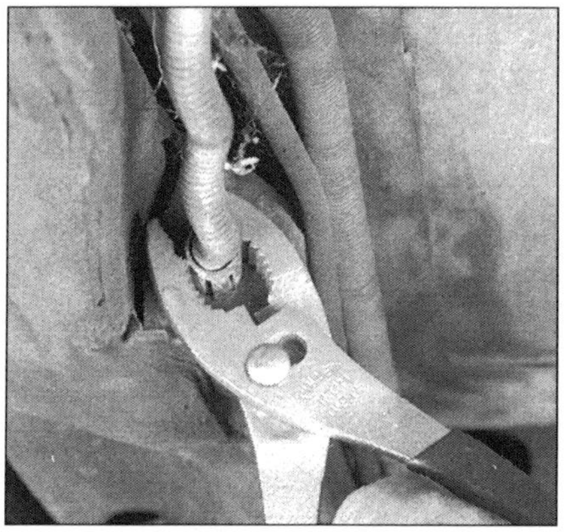

12.5c To detach the parking brake cable from the underside of a later model with rear disc brakes, squeeze together the tangs on the cable housing retainer at the frame rail . . .

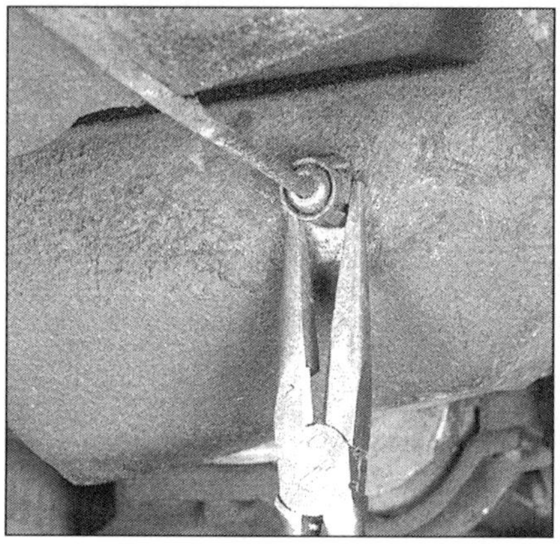

12.5d . . . and squeeze the tangs on the retainer at the crossmember

Front cable

Refer to illustrations 12.11a, 12.11b, 12.11c, 12.11d, 12.12a and 12.12b

8 Loosen the equalizer assembly (see Section 11) to provide slack in the cable.

9 Disconnect the front cable from the equalizer.

10 Remove the carpeting and sound insulation material from the kick panel area.

11 Unbolt the parking brake pedal assembly **(see illustrations)**.

12 Disengage the parking brake cable from the parking brake pedal assembly **(see illustrations)**.

12.11a To detach the parking brake pedal assembly, remove this bolt (arrow) from the lower rear corner of the pedal assembly . . .

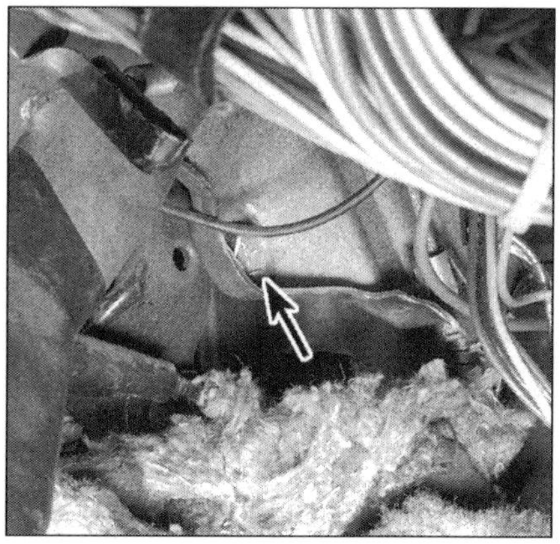

12.11b . . . remove this bolt (arrow) from the lower front part of the pedal assembly, and the upper front bolt (not visible in this photo) . . .

12.11c . . . pull the pedal assembly down far enough to unplug the electrical connector (arrow) for the parking brake warning light . . .

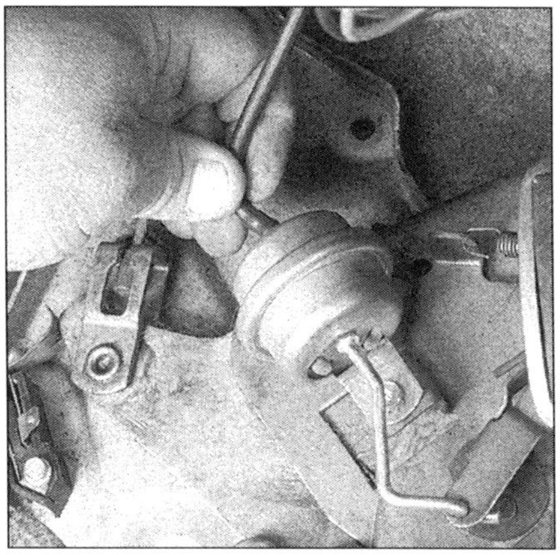

12.11d . . . and detach the vacuum line from the pedal release diaphragm (if equipped)

12.12a To disconnect the parking brake cable from the parking brake pedal, disengage the plug on the end of the cable from its slot . . .

12.12b . . . and squeeze the cable housing retainer tangs together to release the cable from the bracket

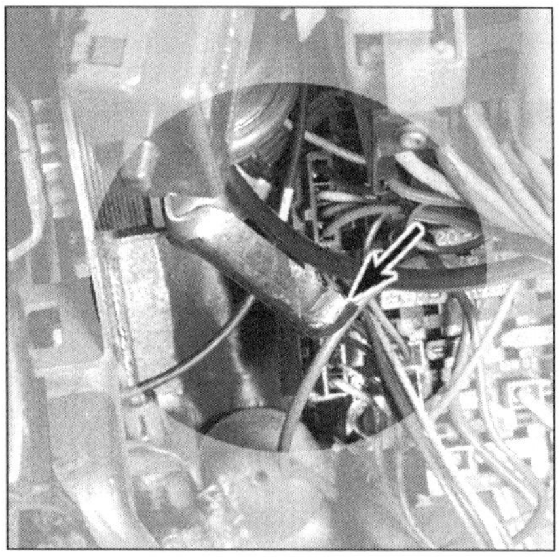

13.2 If the vacuum-operated parking brake pedal release system malfunctions, there's a manual override lever (arrow) just to the right of the hood release

13.3 To detach the release diaphragm from the parking brake pedal assembly, remove this mounting bracket bolt (arrow), pull the diaphragm down, disengage the link rod from the pedal ratchet mechanism and detach the vacuum line from the diaphragm

13 Free the cable from the routing clips and push the cable and grommet through the lower firewall.

14 Installation is the reverse of removal.

15 Adjust the cable when you're done (see Section 11).

13 Parking brake pedal release diaphragm - check

Refer to illustrations 13.2, 13.3 and 13.6

1 When the engine is started and the shift lever is moved out of the Park position, intake manifold vacuum is applied to a diaphragm on the parking brake pedal assembly. When the diaphragm moves, it pulls on a lever that releases the ratcheting mechanism on the parking brake pedal assembly, allowing the parking brake pedal to release.

2 If the parking brake pedal fails to release automatically when the shift lever is moved out of Park (with the engine running), you can release it manually with a small manual override lever on the parking brake pedal assembly **(see illustration)**.

3 If the parking brake pedal release diaphragm fails to operate as describe above, there are three possibilities: either the vacuum line between the intake manifold and the neutral start/back-up light switch, or the line between the neutral start switch and the parking brake pedal release diaphragm, is damaged or disconnected; or the vacuum switch on the backside of the neutral start switch is defective; or the parking brake pedal release diaphragm **(see illustration)** is torn.

4 First, make sure all vacuum lines are attached to the manifold and throttle body or carburetor.

5 Inside the vehicle, trace the vacuum line to the neutral start/back-up light switch on the steering column (see Chapter 8) and verify that the connection is good there. If it is, trace the vacuum line from the neutral start switch to the parking brake pedal release diaphragm and verify that it's in good shape and connected at both ends.

6 If the vacuum lines are in good shape and connected, the problem is either the neutral start switch (see Chapter 8) or the diaphragm. To check the diaphragm, discon-

13.6 To test a release diaphragm, apply some vacuum and note whether the diaphragm holds it or not; if the diaphragm won't hold any vacuum, the diaphragm is torn and must be replaced

nect the vacuum line from the diaphragm, hook up a hand-operated vacuum pump **(see illustration)** and apply some vacuum to the diaphragm chamber. If the diaphragm won't hold a vacuum, replace it.

7 To replace the diaphragm, unbolt the parking brake pedal assembly (see Section 12), unbolt the diaphragm **(see illustration 13.3)**, and unhook the link rod from the ratcheting mechanism.

8 Installation is the reverse of removal.

14 Power brake booster - inspection, removal and installation

1 The power brake booster unit requires no special maintenance apart from periodic inspection of the vacuum hose and the case.

2 Disassembly of the power unit requires special tools and is not ordinarily performed by the home mechanic. If a problem develops, it's recommended that a new or factory rebuilt unit be installed.

Operating check

3 Depress the brake pedal several times with the engine off and make sure that there is no change in the pedal reserve distance.

4 Depress the pedal and start the engine. If the pedal goes down slightly, operation is normal.

Airtightness check

5 Start the engine and turn it off after one or two minutes. Depress the brake pedal several times slowly. If the pedal goes down farther the first time but gradually rises after the second or third depression, the booster is airtight.

6 Depress the brake pedal while the engine is running, then stop the engine with the pedal depressed. If there is no change in the pedal reserve travel after holding the pedal for 30 seconds, the booster is airtight.

Removal and installation

7 Remove the nuts attaching the master cylinder to the booster and carefully pull the master cylinder forward until it clears the mounting studs. Don't bend or kink the brake lines.

8 Disconnect the vacuum hose where it attaches to the power brake booster.

9 From the passenger compartment, disconnect the pushrod from the brake pedal.

10 Also from this location, remove the nuts attaching the booster to the firewall.

11 Carefully lift the booster unit away from the firewall and out of the engine compartment.

12 To install, place the booster in position and tighten the nuts to the Specifications. Connect the brake pedal.

13 Install the master cylinder and vacuum hose.

14 Carefully test the operation of the brakes before placing the vehicle in normal service.

15 Brake light switch - check, adjustment and replacement

Refer to illustration 15.1

1 The brake light switch **(see illustration)** is located on a flange or bracket protruding from the brake pedal support.

2 With the brake pedal in the fully released position, the plunger of the switch should be fully pressed in. When the pedal is depressed, the plunger releases and sends electrical current to the brake lights at the rear of the car.

3 To check the brake light switch, simply note whether the brake lights come on when the pedal is depressed and go off when the pedal is released. If they don't, adjust the switch. To do this, depress the brake pedal about 1/2-inch, push the switch forward until the plunger contacts the brake pedal, then release the pedal. Lightly pull up on the pedal to its normal released position; it will push the switch into the proper position.

15.1 The brake light switch (arrow) is located at the top of the brake pedal; to remove it, simply unplug the electrical connectors and pull the switch out of its mounting bracket (those are serrations on the switch - not threads)

4 If the lights still don't come on, either the switch is not getting voltage, the switch itself is defective, or the circuit between the switch and the lights is defective. There is always the remote possibility that all of the brake light bulbs are burned out, but this is not very likely.

5 Use a voltmeter or test light to verify that there's voltage present at one side of the switch connector. If no voltage is present, troubleshoot the circuit from the switch to the fuse box. If there is voltage present, check for voltage on the other terminal when the brake pedal is depressed. If no voltage is present, replace the switch. If there is voltage present, troubleshoot the circuit from the switch to the brake lights (see the *Wiring diagrams* at the end of Chapter 12).

6 To replace a faulty switch, simply unplug the electrical connectors (one for the switch circuit, one for cruise control) and pull the switch out of its bracket. Installation is the reverse of removal. Be sure to adjust the switch as described in Step 2.

Chapter 10
Suspension and steering systems

Contents

Specifications

Torque specifications

Ft-lbs (unless otherwise indicated)

Front suspension

Hub and bearing retainer-to-knuckle bolts	
Buick	75
Cadillac	
1971 through 1973	35
1974 through 1978	30
1979 on	75
Oldsmobile	
1971 through 1978	40
1979 on	75
Lower balljoint stud-to-steering knuckle nut	
Buick	
1979 through 1983	65
1984 on	83
Cadillac	
1971	85
1972 on	80
Oldsmobile	
1971 through 1974	85
1975 through 1977	95
1978	83
1979 and 1980	65
1981	85
1982 and 1983	70
1984 on	83

Front suspension (continued)	**Ft-lbs** (unless otherwise indicated
Lower control arm-to-frame pivot bolt nut	
Buick	90
Cadillac	
1971	75
1972 through 1978	80
1979 on	90
Oldsmobile	
1971 through 1977	90
1978	80
1979 through 1983	90
1984 on	88
Shock absorber to frame bracket bolt/nut	
Buick	
1979 through 1983	95
1984 on	70
Cadillac	
1971 through 1978	75
1979 on	92
Oldsmobile	
1971 through 1977	90
1978	78
1979 and 1980	95
1981 through 1983	75
1984 on	70
Shock absorber-to-lower control arm stud nut	
Buick	
1979 through 1983	75
1984 on	92
Cadillac	
1971 through 1978	75
1979 through 1981	65
1982 on	92
Oldsmobile	
1971 through 1977	90
1978	78
1979	65
1980 through 1983	75
1984 on	92
Stabilizer bar bracket-to-frame bolts/nuts	
Buick	24
Cadillac	
1971 through 1978	35
1979 on	24
Oldsmobile	
1971 through 1974	30
1975 through 1977	28
1978 on	24
Stabilizer bar link nuts	156 in-lbs
Balljoint-to-control arm bolts/nuts (replacement balljoints)	
Buick	
1979 through 1983	96 in-lbs
1984 on	156 in-lbs
Cadillac	
1971 through 1978	
Lower balljoint	
Side bolts	25
Top nut	45
Upper balljoint	20
1979 on	96 in-lbs
Oldsmobile	
1971 through 1978	
Lower balljoint	
Side bolts	25
Top nut	45
Upper balljoint	20
1979 through 1982	96 in-lbs
1983 on	156 in-lbs

	Ft-lbs (unless otherwise indicated
Upper balljoint stud-to-steering knuckle nut	
Buick	
1979 through 1983	90
1984 on	55
Cadillac	
1971	85
1972 through 1978	60
1979 on	90
Oldsmobile	
1971 through 1974	50
1975 and 1976	60
1977	105
1978	50
1979 and 1980	90
1981	55
1982 and 1983	50
1984 on	55
Upper control arm-to-frame nuts	
Buick	70
Cadillac	
1971 through 1978	95
1979 on	70
Oldsmobile	
1971 through 1977	110
1978	98
1979 on	70

Rear suspension

Hub and bearing assembly-to-control arm bolts (1979 and later models)	
Buick	
1979 through 1981	32
1982 through 1984	37
1985	32
Cadillac	75
Oldsmobile	32
Rear control arm pivot bolt nuts (1979 and later models)	
Buick	
1979	100
1980 through 1984	75
1985	98
Cadillac	
1979 through 1981	98
1982 on	70
Oldsmobile	
1979	98
1980 on	75
Rear shock absorbers	
Lower nut	
Buick	65
Cadillac	
1971 through 1978	50
1979 on	65
Oldsmobile	
1971 through 1977	75
1978 on	65
Upper nut/bolt	
Buick	65
Cadillac	
1971 through 1978	144 in-lbs
1979 on	65
Oldsmobile	
1971 through 1977	25
1978	20
1979 on	65
Rear stabilizer bar (1979 and later models)	
Front link-to-control arm	63
Stabilizer-to-rear link	22
Stabilizer-to-rear link control arm bracket	30

Rear suspension (continued)	**Ft-lbs** (unless otherwise indicated
Rear suspension arms (1971 through 1978 models)	
Lower control arm bolts	
Cadillac	
1971 and 1972	100
1973 through 1976	145
1977 and 1978	142
Oldsmobile	
1971 through 1975	115
1976	
At axle	115
At frame	95
1977	95
1978	98
Upper control arm bolts	
Cadillac	
1971 and 1972	
At axle	75
At frame	100
1973 through 1978	
At axle	110
At frame	142
Oldsmobile	
1971 through 1974	
At axle	90
At frame	115
1975 and 1976	
At axle	85
At frame	95
1977	95
1978	98

Steering

Idler arm-to-center link nut	
Buick	
1979	52
1980	40
1981	50
1982 through 1985	60
Cadillac	
1971 through 1974	40
1976 on	60
Oldsmobile	
1971 through 1976	45
1977 through 1979	60
1980	40
1981 on	60
Idler arm-to-frame bolt/nut	
Buick	
1979	61
1980	60
1981 and 1982	50
1983 through 1985	60
Cadillac	
1971	35
1972 through 1982	95
1983 on	61
Oldsmobile	
1971 through 1977	110
1978	95
1979	130
1980 on	60
Pitman arm stud-to-center link nut	
Buick and Cadillac	60
Oldsmobile	
1971 through 1974	50
1975	85
1976 through 1979	60

Pitman arm stud-to-center link nut	
Oldsmobile	
1980	40
1981 on	50
Pitman arm-to-pitman shaft retaining nut	
Buick and Cadillac	185
Oldsmobile	
1971 through 1977	210
1978	180
1979 on	185
Steering damper-to-frame bolt	35
Steering damper-to-center link nut	50
Steering gear-to-frame bolts	80
Steering wheel-to-steering shaft nut	30
Tie-rod adjuster sleeve clamp nut	168 in-lbs
Tie-rod end-to-center link nut	60
Tie-rod end-to-steering knuckle nut	35

1 General information

Refer to illustrations 1.1a, 1.1b, 1.2 and 1.3

Caution: *Whenever any suspension or steering fasteners are loosened or removed they must be inspected and, if necessary, replaced with new ones of the same part number or of original equipment quality and design. Cotter pins, used extensively on steering components, should never be reused - always replace them with new ones. Torque specifications must be followed for proper reassembly and component retention. Never attempt to heat, straighten or weld any steering or suspension component. Always replace bent or damaged parts with new ones.*

The front suspension **(see illustrations)** consists of upper and lower control arms which position steering knuckles between them with upper and lower balljoints. The upper ends of the shock absorbers are connected to frame brackets, the lower ends to the lower control arms. A pair of longitudinal torsion bars are attached to the lower control arms up front and to a crossmember at the other end. A stabilizer bar is bolted to the frame rails by a pair of brackets and is attached to the lower control arms by links.

The semi-independent rear suspension **(see illustration)** on 1971 through 1978 models consists of a tube axle located by upper and lower control arms, with coil springs and shock absorbers supplying the suspension. Some models are equipped with a rear stabilizer bar as well. On many models,

1.1a Front suspension (1971 through 1978 models)

1 *Stabilizer bar*
2 *Stabilizer bar bracket*
3 *Stabilizer bar link*
4 *Lower control arm*
5 *Torsion bar*
6 *Adjuster sleeve*
7 *Adjuster sleeve clamp*
8 *Outer tie rod*
9 *Steering knuckle*

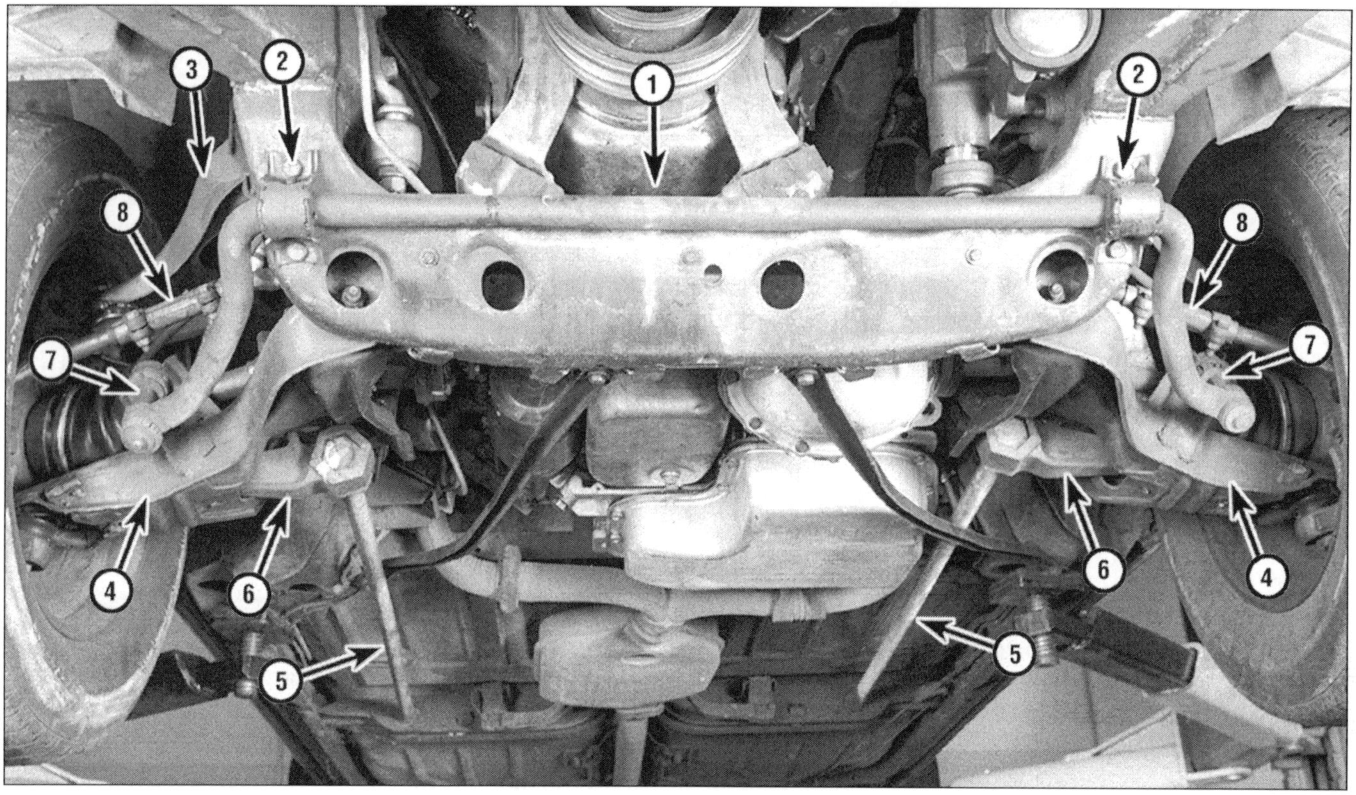

1.1b Front suspension (1979 and later models)

1 *Stabilizer bar*
2 *Stabilizer bar bracket*
3 *Upper control arm*
4 *Lower control arm*
5 *Torsion bar*
6 *Torsion bar forward arm*
7 *Stabilizer-to-lower arm link*
8 *Tie-rod assembly*

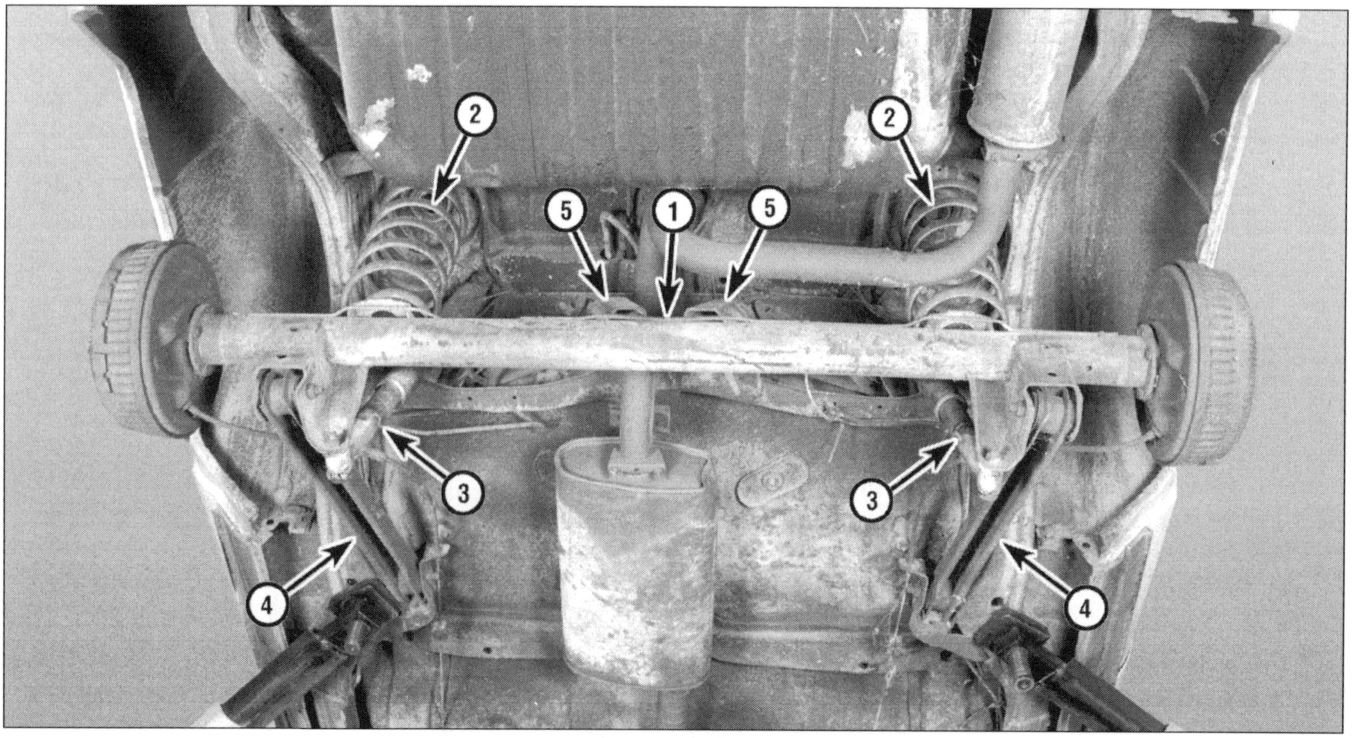

1.2 Rear suspension (1971 through 1978 models)

1 *Tube axle*
2 *Coil spring*
3 *Shock absorber*
4 *Lower suspension arm*
5 *Upper suspension arm*

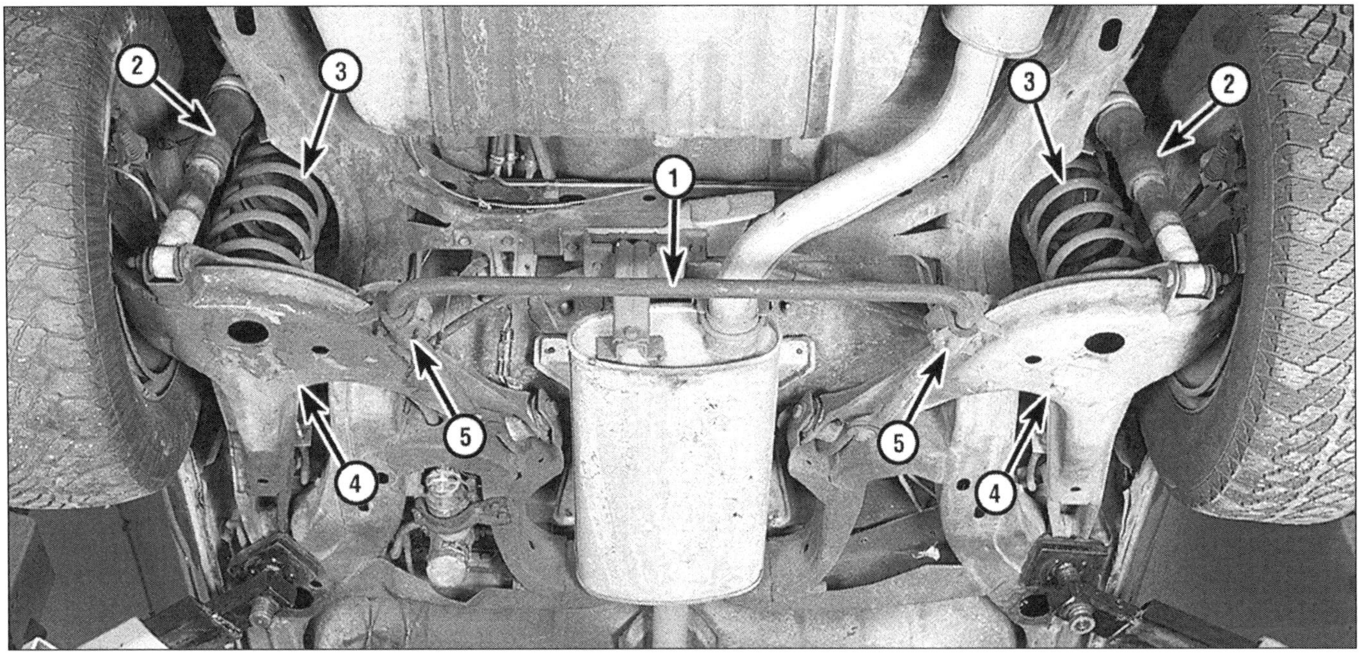

1.3 Rear suspension (1979 and later models)

1 Stabilizer bar
2 Shock absorber
3 Coil spring
4 Control arm
5 Stabilizer bar bushing bracket

the shocks are air-assisted to compensate for different loads.

The fully independent rear suspension **(see illustration)** on 1979 and later models consists of a pair of semi-trailing arms, coil springs and air shocks, and a stabilizer bar.

The steering system consists of a steering wheel and column (many of which are tilt), an articulated intermediate shaft, a recirculating ball steering gear and the steering linkage. Power steering is standard on all models.

Frequently, when working on the suspension or steering system components, you may come across fasteners which seem impossible to loosen. These fasteners on the underside of the vehicle are continually subjected to water, road grime, mud, etc., and can become rusted or "frozen," making them extremely difficult to remove. In order to unscrew these stubborn fasteners without damaging them (or other components), be sure to use lots of penetrating oil and allow it to soak in for a while. Using a wire brush to clean exposed threads will also ease removal of the nut or bolt and prevent damage to the threads. Sometimes a sharp blow with a hammer and punch is effective in breaking the bond between a nut and bolt threads, but care must be taken to prevent the punch from slipping off the fastener and ruining the threads. Heating the stuck fastener and surrounding area with a torch sometimes helps too, but isn't recommended because of the obvious dangers associated with fire. Long breaker bars and extension, or "cheater," pipes will increase leverage, but never use an extension pipe on a ratchet - the ratcheting mechanism could be damaged. Sometimes, turning the nut or bolt in the tightening (clockwise) direction first will help to break it loose. Fasteners that require drastic measures to unscrew should always be replaced with new ones.

Since most of the procedures that are dealt with in this chapter involve jacking up the vehicle and working underneath it, a good pair of jackstands will be needed. A hydraulic floor jack is the preferred type of jack to lift the vehicle, and it can also be used to support certain components during various operations. **Warning:** *Never, under any circumstances, rely on a jack to support the vehicle while working on it.*

2.2 To disconnect the stabilizer bar from the lower control arms, remove the link nuts and disassemble both links; note the order in which the bushings and washers are installed and which way they face

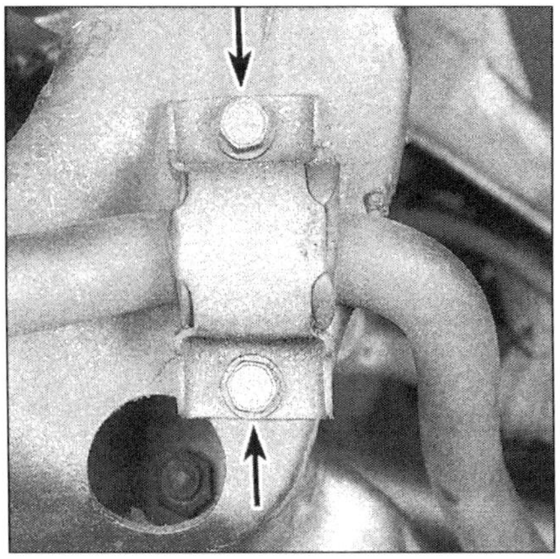

2.3 To detach the stabilizer bar from the frame, remove the bracket bolts (arrows) from both brackets

2 Stabilizer bar (front) - removal and installation

Removal

Refer to illustrations 2.2 and 2.3

1 Raise the vehicle and support it securely on jackstands. Apply the parking brake.

2 Remove the stabilizer bar link nuts, noting how the grommets and retainers are positioned **(see illustration)**.

3 Remove the stabilizer bar bracket bolts and detach the bar from the vehicle **(see illustration)**.

4 Pull the brackets off the stabilizer bar and inspect the bushings for cracks, hardening and other signs of deterioration. If the

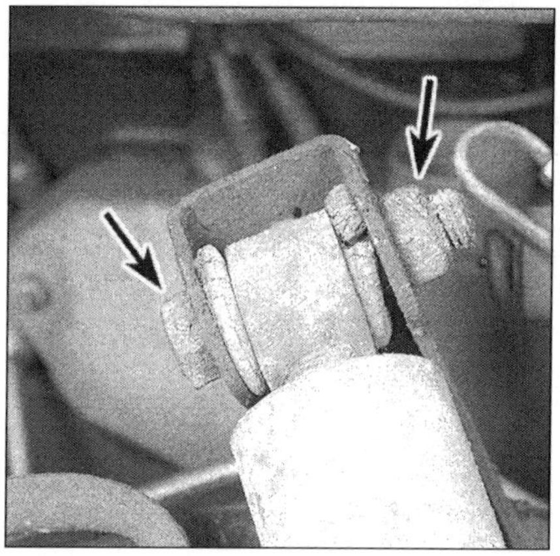

3.3 To detach the upper end of the shock absorber from the frame, remove this nut and bolt (arrows) (note the condition of the upper shock bushing on this vehicle - it's definitely a candidate for a new bushing!)

bushings are damaged, cut them from the bar and replace them.

Installation

5 Position the stabilizer bar bushings on the bar with the slits facing the front of the vehicle.

6 Push the brackets over the bushings and raise the bar up to the frame. Install the bracket bolts but don't tighten them completely at this time.

7 Install the stabilizer bar link nuts, washers and rubber bushings and tighten the nuts securely.

8 Tighten the bracket bolts.

3 Shock absorbers (front) - removal and installation

Refer to illustrations 3.3 and 3.4

1 Loosen the wheel lug nuts, raise the vehicle and support it securely on jackstands. Apply the parking brake. Remove the wheel.

2 Place a floor jack under the lower con-

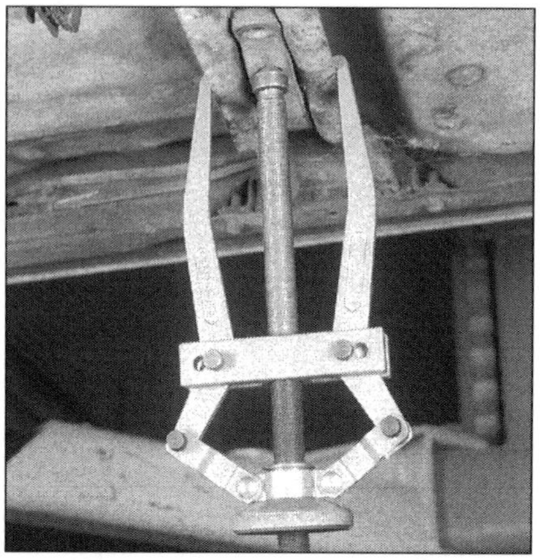

4.4a Use a heavy-duty, two-jaw puller to release tension on the adjusting arm

3.4 To detach the lower end of the shock absorber from the lower control arm, remove this nut (arrow)

trol arm and raise the arm slightly to take the load off the shock and to prevent the torsion bar from snapping the arm down when the shock is removed.

3 Remove the upper shock absorber nut and bolt **(see illustration)**.

4 Remove the lower nut from the stud on the lower control arm **(see illustration)**.

5 Tilt the upper end of the shock out (away from the vehicle), then slide the lower end off the stud on the lower control arm.

6 Installation is the reverse of removal. Be sure to tighten the lower nut and upper nut and bolt to the torque listed in this Chapter's Specifications.

4 Torsion bar - removal, installation and adjustment

Removal

Refer to illustrations 4.3, 4.4a, 4.4b, 4.5, 4.7a, 4.7b and 4.7c

1 Loosen the wheel lug nuts, raise the front of the vehicle and support it securely on jackstands positioned under the frame. **Note:** *Don't place jackstands under the control

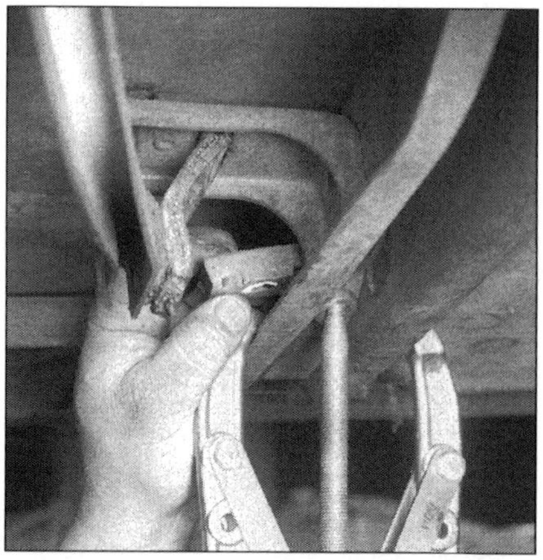

4.4b With the tension on the adjusting arm released, remove the adjusting nut

4.3 At the crossmember end of the torsion bar, remove the adjusting bolt from the adjusting nut

arms - put them under the frame. The front suspension must be in full rebound (under no load) for this procedure. Remove the front wheel.

2 Disconnect the stabilizer bar and the shock absorber from the lower control arm (see Sections 2 and 3, respectively). Support the lower control arm with a floor jack, then disconnect the steering knuckle from the lower control arm (see Section 5). Slowly lower the floor jack until it is no longer under pressure from the torsion bar. This removes some of the tension from the torsion bar adjusting arm.

3 Remove the adjusting bolt from the adjusting nut **(see illustration)**. Be sure to COUNT THE NUMBER OF TURNS required to remove the bolt. When you install the adjusting bolt again, tighten it exactly this many turns. Otherwise, the torsion bar will be out of adjustment.

4 Install a heavy-duty two-jaw puller on the crossmember and raise the torsion bar adjusting arm high enough to remove the adjusting nut **(see illustrations)**.

5 On 1971 through 1978 models, unbolt the rear end of the small diagonal brace **(see**

4.5 On 1971 through 1978 models with small diagonal braces, remove the rear bolt (shown), loosen the front bolt (not shown) and swing the brace out of the way

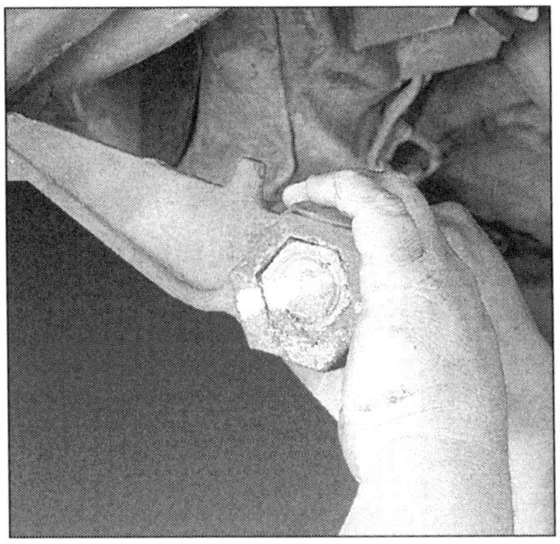

4.7a On 1979 and later models, remove the forward arm from the lower control arm . . .

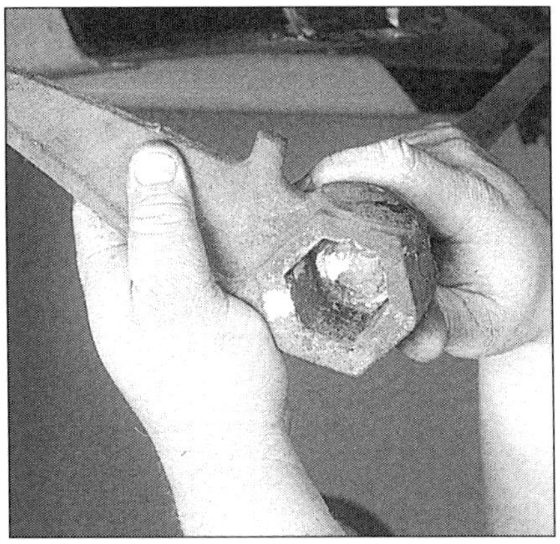

4.7b . . . remove the forward arm from the torsion bar (note that the relationship of the arm and bar is marked) . . .

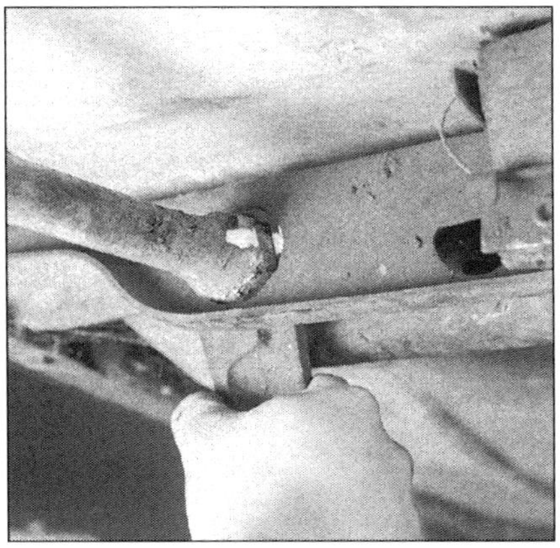

4.7c . . . pull the torsion bar forward, disengage it from the adjusting arm and pull the bar out of the crossmember

illustration), loosen the front end of the brace from the front lower crossmember, and push the brace out of the way for torsion bar removal.

6 On 1971 through 1978 models, remove the lower control arm (see Section 9). After detaching the lower control arm, mark the relationship of the torsion bar to the adjusting arm, pull forward on the torsion bar to disengage it from the adjusting arm and pull the torsion bar from the crossmember. Mark the relationship of the torsion bar to the lower control arm, then tap the torsion bar out of the arm with a brass or a plastic-tipped dead blow hammer. If the torsion bar is "frozen" in the control arm, apply a penetrant and try again. If you can't knock it loose, take the arm and torsion bar to an automotive machine shop and have the two components pressed apart.

7 On 1979 and later models, pull the forward torsion bar arm down from the lower control arm and remove it from the torsion bar **(see illustrations)**. Be sure to mark the relationship of the forward arm to the torsion bar to ensure proper alignment upon reassembly. Then mark the relationship of the torsion bar to the adjusting arm, pull forward on the torsion bar, disengage it from the adjusting arm **(see illustration)** and pull it out of the crossmember.

Installation

Refer to illustrations 4.10a and 4.10b

Note: *Before installing the torsion bar, check it carefully for nicks and hairline cracks, which could cause the torsion bar to break.*

8 Clean out the hex holes in the adjusting arm and in the lower control arm (1971 through 1978 models) or the forward arm (1979 and later models) with a wire brush, then put a little chassis grease in the holes and slide the torsion bar through the hole in the lower control arm (1971 through 1978 models) or the forward arm (1979 and later models). Make sure the bar is aligned with the marks you made before disassembly.

9 On 1971 through 1978 models, insert the torsion bar through the crossmember, install the adjusting arm, making sure the marks you made before disassembly are aligned, and install the lower control arm (see Section 9). Don't raise the lower control arm yet.

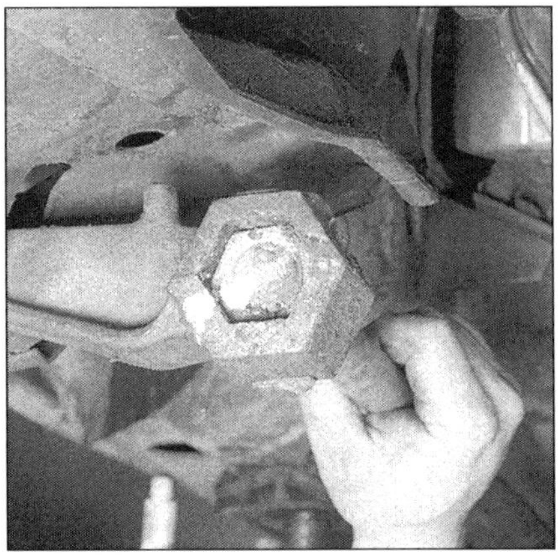

4.10a When installing the torsion bar on 1979 and later models, make sure the positioning pin on top of the forward arm is aligned with the hole in the underside of the lower control arm . . .

4.10b . . . and make sure that the outer tip of the forward arm is properly seated in its groove on the top of the lower control arm

10 On 1979 and later models, install the forward arm into the lower control arm with the positioning pin on the forward arm properly engaged with the hole in the underside of the lower control arm and with the outer tip of the forward arm properly seated in its groove in the top side of the lower control arm **(see illustrations)**.

11 Rotate the adjusting arm up into the crossmember as far as it will go, install the heavy-duty two-jaw puller and raise the adjusting arm high enough to install the adjusting nut. Release tension on the adjusting arm and remove the puller.

12 Place the floor jack under the lower control arm, raise it up into position and connect it to the steering knuckle (see Section 5). Attach the stabilizer bar and shock absorber to the lower control arm (see Sections 2 and 3, respectively). Remove the floor jack.

13 Install the adjusting bolt and tighten it the same number of turns to which it was tightened prior to disassembly.

14 On 1971 through 1978 models, install the small diagonal brace and tighten the bolts securely.

15 Install the wheel and snug the wheel lug nuts. Remove the jackstands and lower the vehicle. Tighten the wheel lug nuts to the torque listed in this Chapter's Specifications.

16 If you just remove the torsion bar from one side, measure the height of the vehicle on the opposite side (from a point such as the top of the wheel opening or from the rocker panel to the ground). Now take a measurement from the corresponding point on the other side of the vehicle. If this measurement is higher than the one taken on the other side, loosen the torsion bar adjusting bolt slightly, jounce the front of the vehicle to settle the suspension and recheck the height. If the measurement is lower, tighten the adjusting bolt slightly, jounce the suspension and recheck the ride height. Continue this procedure until the ride height on each side of the vehicle is equal.

17 Have the front wheel alignment and ride height checked and, if necessary, adjusted by an alignment shop.

5.7a Use a puller to separate the lower balljoint from the steering knuckle (note that the nut is loose but intact - this prevents the arm from jumping out of the knuckle when the ballstud pops loose)

5.7b Use a "picklefork" -type balljoint tool to separate the upper balljoint from the steering knuckle (again, note that the nut is loose but still threaded on); because of the close proximity of the driveaxle assembly, there's no room to get a puller on the upper balljoint stud

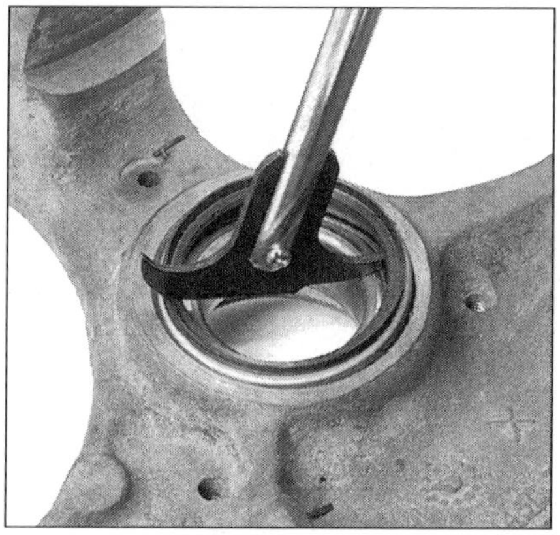

5.9a Use a seal removal tool to pry out the old seal

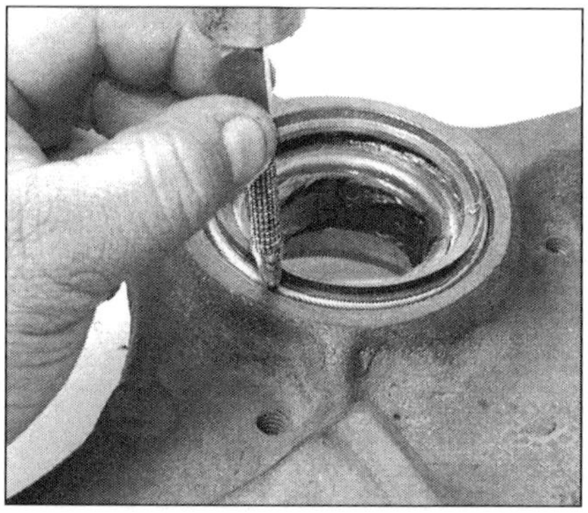

5.9b To install the seal, carefully tap it into place with a small drift until it's fully seated

5 Steering knuckle - removal and installation

Removal

Refer to illustrations 5.7a, 5.7b, 5.9a and 5.9b

1 Remove the cotter pin, nut lock, nut and washer from the driveaxle (see Chapter 8).

2 Loosen the wheel lug nuts, raise the vehicle and support it securely on jackstands placed under the frame. Apply the parking brake. Remove the wheel.

3 Remove the brake caliper and suspend it with a piece of wire (see Chapter 9). Do not let it hang by the brake hose! Remove the brake disc.

4 Separate the tie-rod end from the steering knuckle (see Section 20).

5 Position a floor jack under the lower control arm and raise it just enough to unload the torsion bar. **Caution:** *The jack must remain in this position throughout the entire procedure.*

6 Remove the cotter pins from the upper and lower balljoint studs and back off but do not remove the nuts.

7 Break the balljoints loose from the steering knuckle with a puller **(see illustrations)**. **Note:** *A "picklefork" -type balljoint separator will probably damage the balljoint dust boots, so don't use it unless you have to. In the case of the upper balljoint, try striking the steering knuckle in the vicinity of the balljoint stud - sometimes this will cause the balljoint and knuckle to separate. If that doesn't work, you'll have to use a picklefork because the driveaxle doesn't leave room for a puller.*

8 Remove the nuts from the balljoint studs, separate the control arms from the steering knuckle and remove the knuckle from the vehicle. If the knuckle gets stuck on the driveaxle splines, knock the driveaxle out with a brass hammer.

Installation

9 If you're planning to install a new steering knuckle or a new hub and bearing assembly, unbolt the hub and bearing assembly and brake shield from the knuckle and swap them as necessary (see Section 6). This is also a good time to replace, if necessary, the steering knuckle seal **(see illustrations)** and the upper and/or lower balljoints (see Section 7).

10 Lubricate the steering knuckle seal lip, slide the steering knuckle onto the driveaxle assembly and install the washer and nut hand tight (see Chapter 8).

11 Place the knuckle between the upper and lower control arms and insert the balljoint studs into the knuckle, beginning with the lower balljoint. Install the nuts and tighten them to the torque listed in this Chapter's Specifications. Install new cotter pins, tightening the nuts slightly to align the slots in the nuts with the holes in the balljoint studs, if necessary.

12 Connect the tie-rod end to the steering arm (see Section 20) and tighten the nut to the torque listed in this Chapter's Specifications. Be sure to use a new cotter pin.

13 Install the brake disc, caliper and brake pads (see Chapter 9).

14 Install the wheel and lug nuts. Lower the vehicle to the ground and tighten the wheel lug nuts to the torque listed in Chapter 1. Also tighten the driveaxle nut to the torque listed in the Chapter 8 Specifications, then install the nut lock and a new cotter pin.

15 Have the front end aligned by an alignment shop.

6 Hub and bearing assembly (front) removal and installation

Removal

Refer to illustration 6.4

1 Remove the cotter pin, lock nut and washer from the driveaxle (see Chapter 8).

2 Loosen the wheel lug nuts, raise the vehicle, support it securely on jackstands and remove the wheel.

3 Remove the brake caliper and suspend it with a piece of wire (see Chapter 9). Remove the brake disc.

4 Remove the three bolts retaining the hub and bearing assembly to the steering knuckle **(see illustration)**.

5 Using a slide hammer-type puller attached to the wheel studs, pull the hub and bearing assembly from the drive axle and spindle.

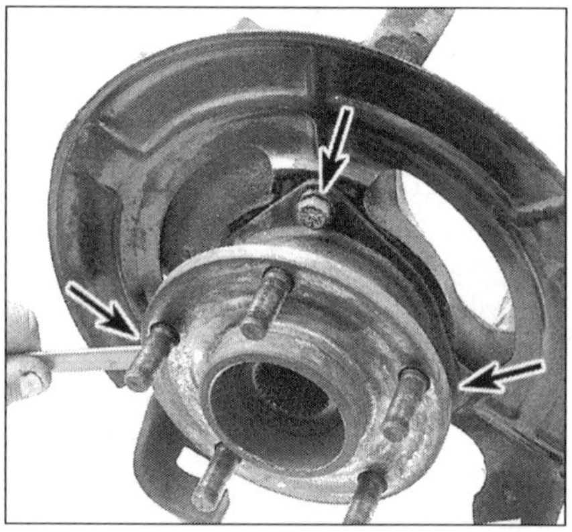

6.4 To remove the hub and bearing assembly and the brake shield from the steering knuckle, remove these three bolts (arrows)

7.5 Use progressively larger diameter drill bits to remove the balljoint rivet heads: start with a 1/8-inch bit, then proceed to a 1/4-inch, then use a 1/2-inch bit to drill off the heads

Installation

6 Lubricate the outside diameter of the bearing with multi-purpose grease. Install the brake shield and the hub and bearing assembly, aligning the driveaxle splines with the hub splines. Install the three mounting bolts and tighten them to the torque listed in this Chapter's Specifications.

7 Install the brake disc and caliper. Tighten the caliper mounting bolts to the torque listed in Chapter 9 Specifications.

8 Install the wheel and lug nuts. Lower the vehicle to the ground and tighten the wheel lug nuts to the torque listed in Chapter 1 Specifications. Install the driveaxle nut and washer, tighten the nut to the torque listed in Chapter 8 Specifications, and install the nut lock and a new cotter pin.

7 Balljoints - replacement

Upper balljoint

Refer to illustrations 7.5, 7.7a, 7.7b, 7.8a, 7.8b, 7.9a, 7.9b and 7.9c

1 Loosen the wheel lug nuts, raise the vehicle and support it securely on jackstands. Apply the parking brake. Remove the wheel.

7.7a Once the rivet heads are removed, use a punch to knock out the rivet shanks

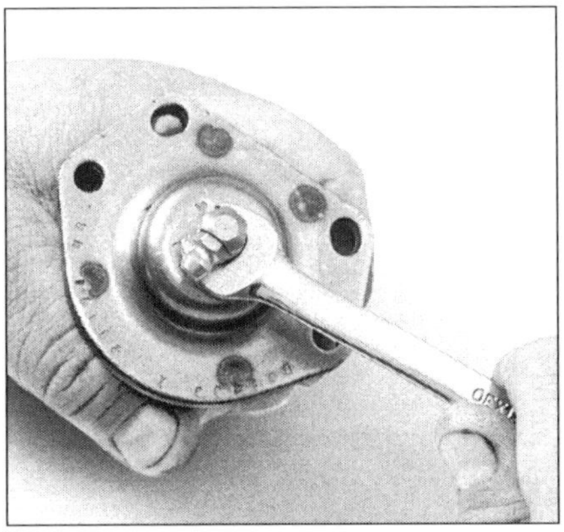

7.8a To assemble the new balljoint, install the grease fitting . . .

2 Place a floorjack under the lower control arm. Raise the jack just far enough to unload the torsion bar. **Caution:** *The jack must remain under the control arm during removal and installation of the balljoint to hold the control arm in position.*

3 Remove the cotter pin from the upper balljoint stud and back off the nut two turns.

4 Separate the balljoint from the steering knuckle **(see illustration 5.7b)**.

5 Using a 1/8-inch drill bit, drill a 1/4-inch deep hole in the center of each rivet head **(see illustration)**.

7.7b If any rivet material remains, the balljoint may not want to come off; use a chisel to knock it loose

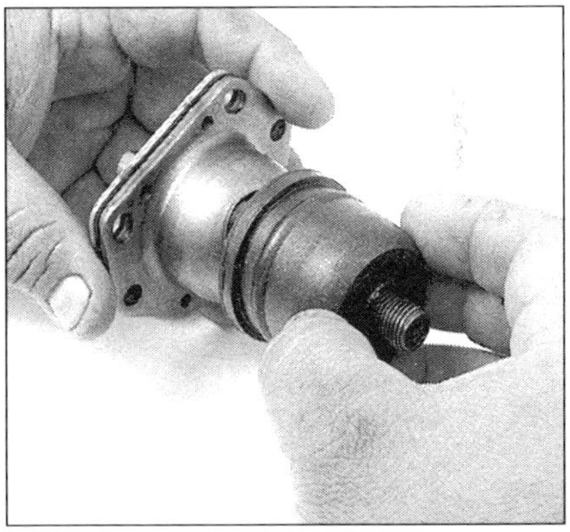

7.8b . . . and install the new dust boot

6 Using a 1/2-inch diameter drill bit, drill off the rivet heads, but don't drill through the balljoint retainer and into the control arm.

7 Use a punch to knock out the rivet shanks **(see illustration)**, then use a chisel to knock the old balljoint loose **(see illustration)**. Remove it from the control arm.

8 Assemble the new balljoint **(see illustrations)**.

9 Position the new balljoint on the control arm and install the bolts and nuts supplied in the kit **(see illustrations)**. Be sure to tighten the nuts to the torque specified on the

7.9a Install the balljoint in the upper control arm as shown . . .

7.9b . . . install the metal dust boot shield (if equipped) . . .

7.9c . . . and install the bolts and nuts

7.19a A grinder is the fastest way to remove the big rivets from a lower control arm balljoint on older models

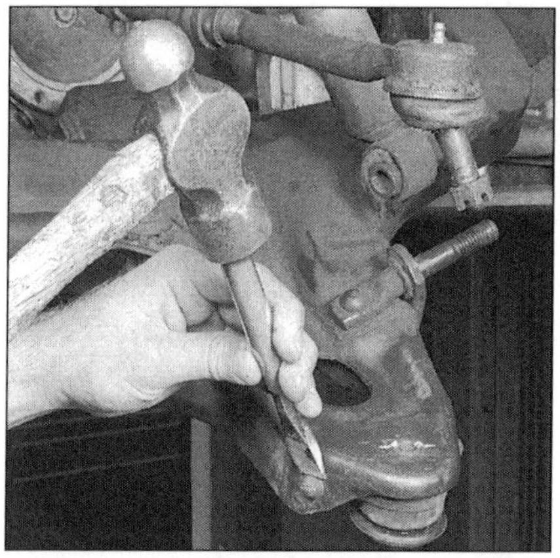

7.19b If you don't have a grinder, a big sharp chisel works well too

7.19c Once the rivet heads are completely removed, use a drill bit to remove the rivet material inside the holes in the control arm (be careful not to enlarge the holes)

balljoint kit instruction sheet. If no torque is provided, use the torque listed in this Chapter's Specifications.

10 Insert the balljoint stud into the steering knuckle, install the nut and tighten it to the torque listed in this Chapter's Specifications. Remove the floor jack from under the lower control arm.

11 Install a new cotter pin, tightening the nut slightly if necessary to align a slot in the nut with the hole in the balljoint stud. Pack the balljoint with grease.

12 Install the wheel and hand tighten the wheel lug nuts. Remove the jackstands and lower the vehicle. Tighten the wheel lugs nuts to the torque listed in this Chapter's Specifications.

13 Have the alignment check and, if necessary, adjusted by an alignment shop.

Lower balljoint

Refer to illustrations 7.19a, 7.19b, 7.19c, 7.19d and 7.20

14 There are two basic types of lower balljoints: 1971 through 1978 models use a balljoint with one large rivet in the top and two rivets on the side, one in front and one in back. The following procedure depicts the replacement of this earlier style balljoint. 1979 and later models use a riveted balljoint that's replaced the same way as the upper balljoint shown above.

15 Loosen the wheel lug nuts, raise the vehicle and support it securely on jackstands. Apply the parking brake. Remove the wheel.

16 Place a floorjack under the lower control arm. Raise the jack just far enough to unload the torsion bar. **Caution:** *The jack must remain under the control arm during removal and installation of the balljoint to hold the control arm in position.*

17 Remove the cotter pin from the lower balljoint stud and back off the nut two turns.

18 Separate the balljoint from the steering knuckle **(see illustration 5.7a)**.

19 Again, using progressively larger drill bits - 1/8-inch, then 1/4-inch, then 1/2-inch - will eventually remove the rivets. But these models use bigger rivets, so to speed things up, use a grinder **(see illustration)** once you've drilled out the rivet heads. If you don't have a grinder, use a large sharp chisel to knock off the heads **(see illustration)**. Once the heads are completely removed, use a big drill bit to drill out the material in the hole **(see illustration)**. Finally, use that big sharp chisel again to knock the balljoint loose **(see illustration)**.

7.19d Use the big chisel to knock the balljoint out of the lower control arm; the two side rivets can be a problem because until ALL the rivet material has been removed from them, the balljoint won't budge

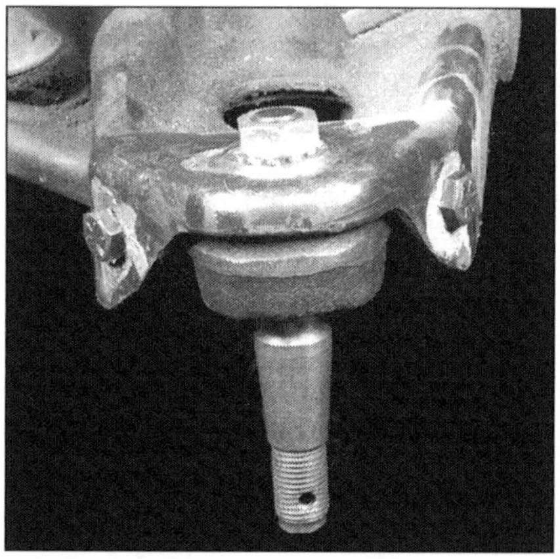

7.20 Install the new balljoint with the nuts and bolts supplied with the kit

20 Position the new balljoint on the control arm and install the bolts and nuts supplied in the kit **(see illustration)**. Be sure to tighten the nuts to the torque specified on the balljoint kit instruction sheet. If no torque is provided, use the torque listed in this Chapter's Specifications.

21 Insert the balljoint stud into the steering knuckle, install the nut and tighten it to the torque listed in this Chapter's Specifications. Remove the floor jack from under the lower control arm.

22 Install a new cotter pin, tightening the nut slightly if necessary to align a slot in the nut with the hole in the balljoint stud.

23 Pack the balljoint with grease.

24 Install the wheel and hand tighten the wheel lug nuts. Remove the jackstands and lower the vehicle. Tighten the wheel lugs nuts to the torque listed in this Chapter's Specifications.

25 Have the alignment check and, if necessary, adjusted by an alignment shop.

8 Upper control arm (front) - removal and installation

Removal

Refer to illustration 8.5

1 Loosen the wheel lug nuts, raise the front of the vehicle and support it securely on jackstands. Apply the parking brake. Remove the wheel.

2 Support the lower control arm with a floor jack. **Caution:** *The jack must remain under the control arm during removal and installation of the balljoint to hold the control arm in position.*

3 Disconnect the upper balljoint from the steering knuckle **(see illustration 5.7b)**.

4 Remove the upper shock absorber

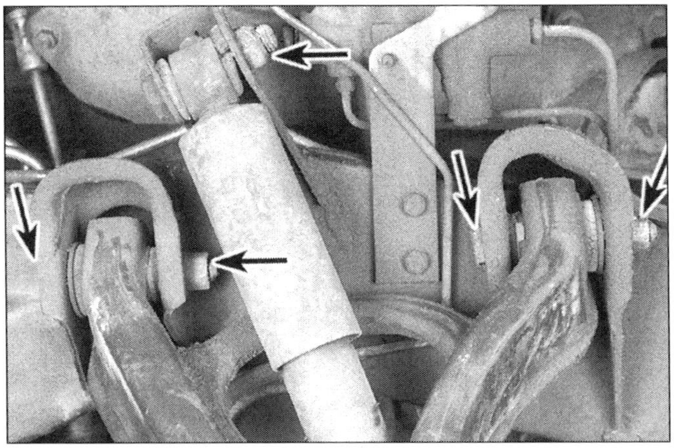

8.5 To detach the upper control arm from the frame, remove the indicated nuts and pivot bolts; to remove the arm, you'll also have to disconnect the upper end of the shock absorber

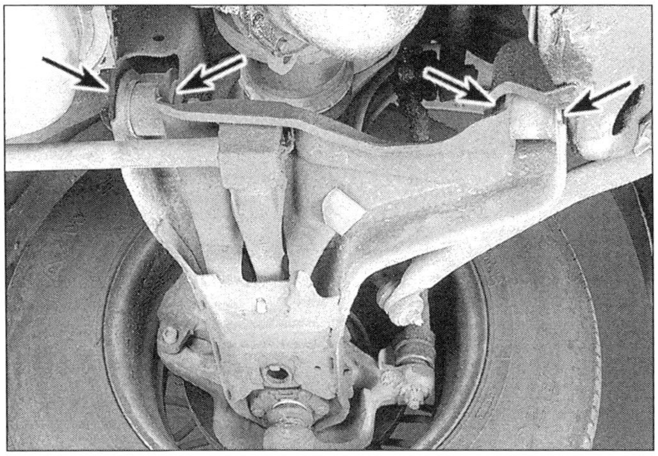

9.6a To detach the lower control arm from the frame brackets, remove these nuts and bolts (arrows)

mounting nut and bolt (see Section 3).

5 Mark the relationship of the cam bolts to the frame bracket. Remove the control arm-to-frame bracket nuts and bolts **(see illustration)**.

6 Detach the control arm from the vehicle. **Note:** *The control arm bushings are pressed into place and require special tools for removal and installation. If the bushings must be replaced, take the control arm to a dealer service department or an automotive machine shop to have the old bushings pressed out and the new ones pressed in.*

Installation

7 Position the control arm on the frame and install the bolts and nuts, lining up the marks made on the cam bolts and the frame brackets. **Note:** *The position of the cam bolts in relation to the frame brackets determines the camber and caster settings (that's why they were marked in Step 5). Make sure, however, that the bolt holes in the adjustment cams are offset towards the bottom (somewhere below the 3 and 9 o'clock positions).* Tighten the nuts to the torque listed in this Chapter's Specifications.

8 Insert the balljoint stud into the steering knuckle and tighten the nut to the torque listed in this Chapter's Specifications. Install a new cotter pin, tightening the nut slightly, if necessary, to align a slot in the nut with the hole in the balljoint stud.

9 Install the wheel and lug nuts and lower the vehicle. Tighten the lug nuts to the torque listed in the Chapter 1 Specifications.

10 Drive the vehicle to an alignment shop to have the front end alignment checked and, if necessary, adjusted.

9 Lower control arm (front) - removal and installation

Removal

Refer to illustrations 9.6a, 9.6b and 9.6c

1 Loosen the wheel lug nuts, raise the vehicle and support it securely on jackstands. Apply the parking brake. Remove the wheel.

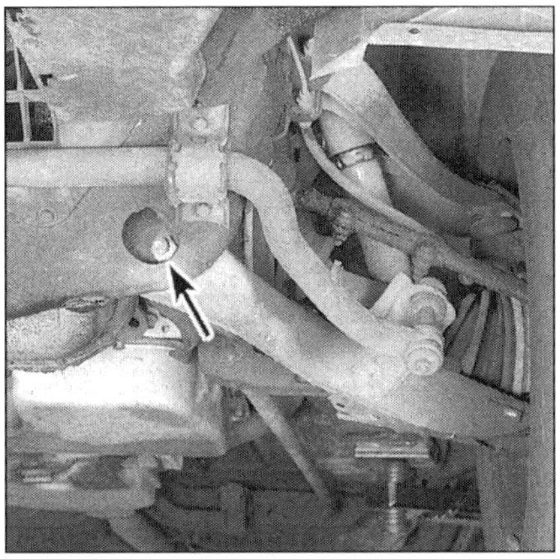

9.6b The front pivot bolt nut is inside this hole in the front lower crossmember

9.6c Use a back-up wrench on each bolt while breaking loose the nut

2 Unbolt the shock absorber from the lower control arm (see Section 3).

3 Disconnect the stabilizer bar from the lower control arm (see Section 2).

4 Remove the cotter pin and back off the lower control arm balljoint stud nut two turns. Separate the lower balljoint from the steering knuckle (see Section 5).

5 Disconnect the rear end of the torsion bar from the crossmember (see Section 4). On 1971 through 1978 models, the torsion bar must remain attached to the lower control arm for now. On 1979 and later models, detach the torsion bar from the lower control arm.

6 Remove the lower control arm bolts and nuts **(see illustrations)** and remove the control arm from the vehicle.

7 On 1971 through 1978 models, separate the torsion bar from the lower control arm. Be sure to mark the relationship of the bar to the arm before separating the two components.

8 Inspect the control arm bushings for cracks, tears and deterioration. If they're damaged or worn, replace them. **Note:** *The control arm bushings are pressed into place and require special tools for removal and installation. If the bushings must be replaced, take the control arm to a dealer service department or an automotive machine shop to have the old bushings pressed out and the new ones pressed in.*

Installation

9 On 1971 through 1978 models, clean out the hex hole in the lower control arm with a wire brush and install the torsion bar into the lower control arm. Make sure the marks you made prior to disassembly are aligned.

10 Install the control arm/torsion bar assembly (1971 through 1978 models) or control arm (1979 and later models). Install the front and rear pivot bolts and nuts. Make sure the bolts face in (heads toward each other) and the nuts face out. Tighten them to the torque listed in this Chapter's Specifications.

11 On 1971 through 1978 models, install the rear end of the torsion bar; on 1979 and later models, install the torsion bar assembly (see Section 4).

12 Raise the lower control arm with the floor jack, insert the balljoint stud into the steering knuckle (see Section 5), tighten the nut to the torque listed in this Chapter's

11.2 Unscrew and disconnect the air line fitting (arrow) before removing a rear shock absorber, then remove the upper mounting bolts (arrow)

11.4a To disconnect the lower end of the shock from the axle tube on a 1971 through 1978 model, remove this nut and bolt (arrow)

11.4b To disconnect the lower end of the shock absorber from the control arm on a 1979 and later model, remove this bolt (arrow)

Specifications and install a new cotter pin. If necessary, tighten the nut slightly to align a slot in the nut with the hole in the balljoint stud.

13 Connect the stabilizer bar to the lower control arm (see Section 2).

14 Attach the shock absorber to the lower control arm (see Section 3).

15 Install the wheel and lug nuts, remove the jackstands, lower the vehicle and tighten the lug nuts to the torque specified in Chapter 1. If necessary, adjust the torsion bar as described in Section 4.

16 Drive the vehicle to an alignment shop to have the front end alignment checked and, if necessary, adjusted.

10 Air suspension systems - general information

Both of the following systems automatically adjust the "trim," or ride, height in proportion to the load.

Automatic Level Control

Some 1971 through 1978 models are equipped with Automatic Level Control (ALC). The ALC system automatically adjusts the height of the rear of the vehicle, maintaining a preset height, regardless of load. The system consists of an air compressor, air reservoir and regulator located at the front of the vehicle; a height control sensor valve and leveling arm link connected to the rear suspension; and two air adjustable rear shock absorbers.

The system operates with the ignition On when weight is added or removed from the rear of the vehicle. The leveling arm moves with the suspension, turning the compressor on or off as necessary or releasing air from the shock absorbers to maintain a constant height.

Because of the special equipment and techniques required to work on this system, servicing should be performed by a dealer service department.

Electronic Level Control

Some 1979 and later models are equipped with an optional Electronic Level Control system which consists of an air compressor, a compressor relay, an air dryer, an exhaust solenoid, a height sensor, a pair of air adjustable rear shock absorbers and the air lines and fittings connecting the compressor to the shocks. Make sure the fittings at the shocks are tight and the link rod between the control arm and the height sensor is connected.

11 Shock absorbers (rear) - removal and installation

Refer to illustrations 11.2, 11.4a and 11.4b

1 Loosen the rear wheel lug nuts, raise the rear of the vehicle and support it securely on jackstands. Remove the rear wheels.

2 On models equipped with Automatic Level Control or Electronic Level Control, disconnect the air fitting(s) at the shock absorber **(see illustration)**.

3 Remove the upper shock absorber mounting bolts (1978 and earlier models) or the nut and bolt (1979 and later models).

4 Disconnect the lower end of the shock from the bracket on the axle tube (1971 through 1978 models) or from the control arm (1979 and later models) **(see illustrations)**.

5 Installation is the reverse of removal. Make sure that all shock mounting fasteners are tightened to the torque listed in this Chapter's Specifications. Also, make sure the air line fittings are secure (if equipped).

6 Start the engine after the vehicle is back on the ground and allow the compressor to fill the shocks to their normal pressure before driving anywhere.

12 Stabilizer bar (rear) - removal and installation

1 Loosen the rear wheel lug nuts, raise the rear of the vehicle and support it securely on jackstands. Remove the rear wheels.

1971 through 1978 models

Note: *Not all of these models are equipped with a rear stabilizer bar.*

2 Remove the four bolts (two on each side) which attach the stabilizer bar to the lower control arms.

3 Remove the stabilizer bar.

4 Installation is the reverse of removal.

1979 and later models

Refer to illustrations 12.5 and 12.6

5 Disconnect the forward ends of the stabilizer from the control arms **(see illustration)**.

6 Unbolt the stabilizer bushing brackets **(see illustration)**.

7 Inspect the bushings for cracks and tears. If they're worn or damaged, replace them.

8 Installation is the reverse of the removal procedure. Be sure to tighten all fasteners to the torque listed in this Chapter's Specifications.

12.5 To detach the forward ends of the stabilizer from the control arms, remove this bolt and washer from each control arm

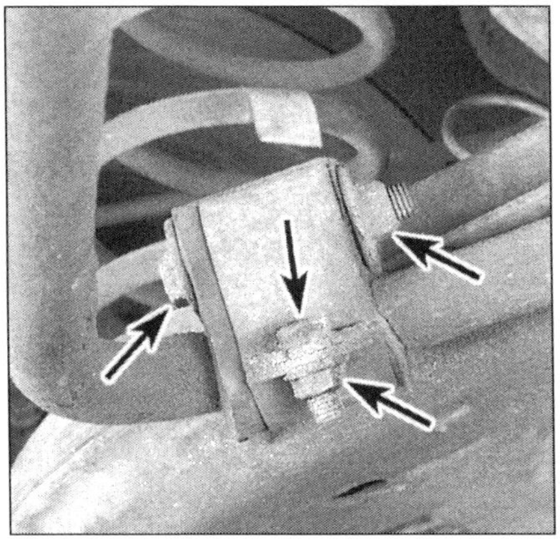

12.6 To detach the bushing brackets and the bushings from the control arms, remove these nuts and bolts (arrows) from each control arm

13.3 To remove a rear hub and bearing assembly, remove the four retaining bolts; use a back-up wrench to hold the nuts while breaking loose the bolts

14.5 To detach the rear end of an upper rear control arm from the axle tube, remove this nut and bolt (1971 through 1978 models)

13 Hub and bearing assembly (rear) - removal and installation

Refer to illustration 13.3

Note: *This procedure applies only to 1979 and later models; see Chapter 1 for 1978 and earlier model information.*

1 Loosen the rear wheel lug nuts, raise the vehicle and support it securely with jackstands. Remove the rear wheel.

2 Remove the rear drum brake or disc brake assembly (see Chapter 9).

3 Remove the four hub retaining bolts, using a back-up wrench on the nuts **(see illustration)**. On some models, these bolts are conventional hex head bolts; on others, they're Torx head bolts.

4 Installation is the reverse of removal. Be sure to use new bolts and nuts and tighten them to the torque listed in this Chapter's Specifications.

14 Rear suspension arms - removal and installation

1 Loosen the rear wheel lugs nuts, raise the vehicle and support it securely with jackstands. Remove the rear wheels. Support the rear axle tube with a floor jack.

1971 through 1978 models

Upper control arm

Refer to illustrations 14.5 and 14.6

2 If you're removing or replacing the right upper control arm an a model equipped with Automatic Level Control, disconnect the overtravel link from the overtravel lever and rotate the overtravel lever to its center position.

3 Disconnect the lower end of the shock absorber from the axle tube (see Section 11) and swing it out of the way.

4 Place a floor jack under the axle and raise the axle just enough to take the load off the upper control arm.

5 Unbolt the upper control arm from the axle tube **(see illustration)**.

6 Unbolt the upper control arm from the frame crossmember **(see illustration)**.

7 Remove the upper control arm.

8 Inspect the control arm bushings. If the front bushing is torn, cracked or worn out, replace the control arm (the front bushing is not removable). If the rear bushing is damaged, take the control arm to an automotive machine shop and have the bushing replaced.

9 Installation is the reverse of removal. Be sure to tighten the control arm fasteners to the torque listed in this Chapter's Specifications.

Lower control arm

Refer to illustration 14.11

10 Unbolt the lower control arm from the bracket on the axle tube.

11 Unbolt the lower control arm from the frame **(see illustration)**.

12 Inspect the control arm bushings. If either bushing is torn, cracked or worn out, replace the control arm (the lower control arm bushings are not removable).

13 Installation is the reverse of the removal procedure. Be sure to tighten the control arm fasteners to the torque listed in this Chapter's Specifications.

1979 and later models

Refer to illustrations 14.19a and 14.19b

14 Remove the drum brake or disc brake assembly (see Chapter 9).

15 Remove the hub and bearing assembly (see Section 13).

16 Support the control arm with a floor jack

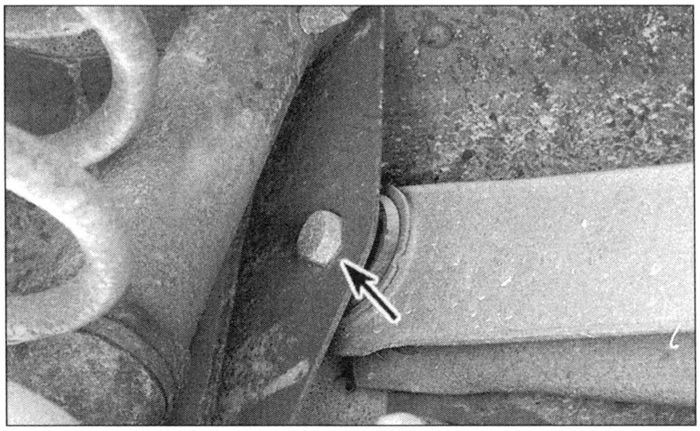

14.6 To detach the front end of an upper rear control arm from the crossmember, remove this bolt (arrow) and nut (1971 through 1978 models)

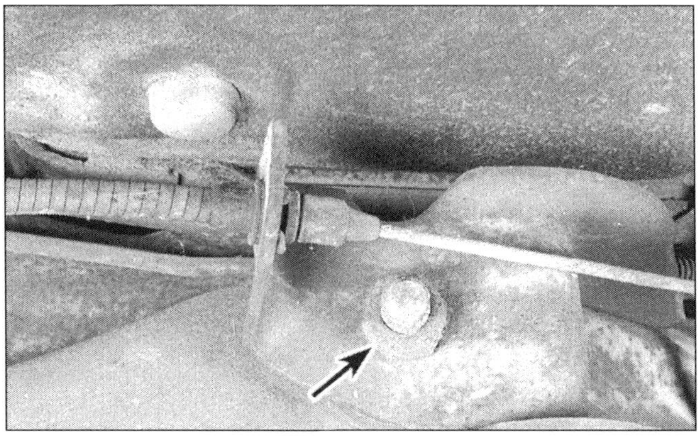

14.11 To detach the front end of the lower control arm from the frame, remove this nut and bolt (arrow) (1971 through 1978 models)

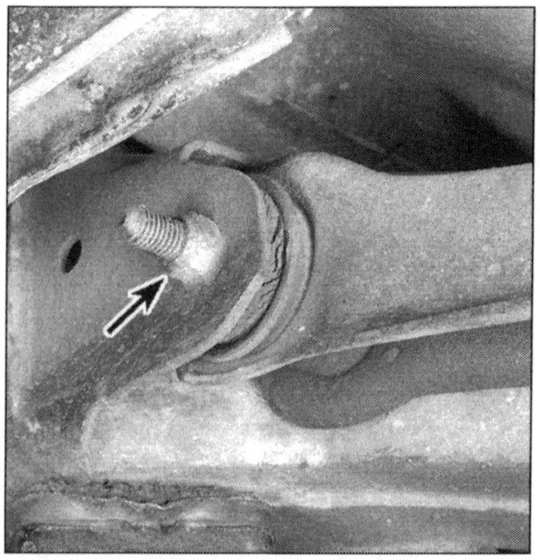

14.19a To unbolt a rear control arm from the frame on 1979 and later models, remove this nut and bolt (arrow) . . .

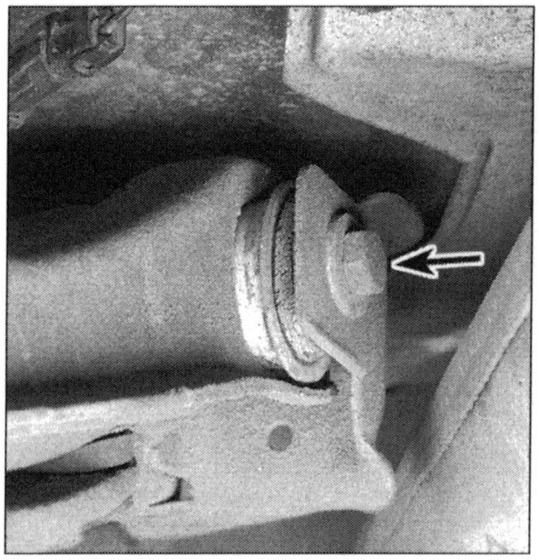

14.19b . . . and this bolt (arrow) and nut

and raise it just enough to take the load off the rear shock absorber. Unbolt the lower end of the rear shock absorber from the control arm **(see illustration 11.4b)**.

17 Unbolt the stabilizer from the control arm (see Section 12).

18 Slowly lower the jack and release spring tension. Remove the coil spring.

19 Unbolt the control arm from the frame **(see illustrations)**.

20 Installation is the reverse of removal. Be sure to tighten all fasteners to the torque listed in this Chapter's Specifications.

15 Rear coil springs - removal and installation

1 Loosen the rear wheel lug nuts, raise the rear of the vehicle and support it securely on jackstands. Remove the rear wheel.

2 Place a floor jack under the axle tube (1971 through 1978 models) or under the control arm (1979 and later models) and raise the axle tube or control arm just enough to support the axle or control arm. **Warning:** *Once the springs are removed, the floor jack will be the sole support for the axle tube or control arm, so make sure the jack is well positioned.*

3 On 1971 through 1978 models, disconnect the lower ends of both shock absorbers from the axle tube (see Section 11) and disconnect the rear ends of both upper control arms from the axle tube brackets (see Section 14). Wrap a chain through the coil spring and bolt the ends together (leaving enough slack in the chain to allow the coil springs to extend fully), then carefully lower the axle tube until spring tension is released. Unbolt the chain and remove the coil spring.

4 On 1979 and later models, disconnect the lower end of the shock absorber from each control arm (see Section 11) and detach the stabilizer bar from the control arm (see Section 12). Wrap a chain through the coil spring and bolt the ends together (leaving enough slack in the chain to allow the coil springs to extend fully, then slowly lower the control arm until spring tension is released. Remove the coil spring.

5 Inspect the lower spring insulators on the axle tube or control arms and the upper insulators installed between the upper ends of the springs and the vehicle underbody. If they're cracked, torn or deteriorated, replace them.

6 Installation is the reverse of removal. Be sure to tighten all fasteners to the torque listed in this Chapter's Specifications.

16 Spindle (1971 through 1978 models) - removal and installation

Refer to illustration 16.4

Note: *You'll need three special tools - slide hammer, slide hammer adapter and spindle adapter, available at most auto parts stores, to pull the spindle from the axle tube and to install it. If you don't have, or can't obtain, these tools, remove the axle tube and take it to an automotive machine shop to have the following procedure done.*

1 Loosen the rear wheel lug nuts, raise the rear of the vehicle and support it securely on jackstands. Remove the rear wheel.

2 Remove the rear brake assembly (see Chapter 9).

3 Remove the hub and bearing assembly (see Chapter 1).

4 Remove the four brake backing plate/spindle retaining nuts **(see illustration)**. After removing the brake backing plate, thread the nuts back onto the ends of the four studs (to prevent the spindle from suddenly popping out of the axle tube and causing injury when it's removed with the slide hammer).

5 Install the three special tools - slide hammer, slide hammer adapter and spindle adapter, to pull the spindle from the axle tube. Use the same tools to install the new spindle.

6 Installation is the reverse of removal.

17 Rear axle tube (1971 through 1978 models) - removal and installation

1 Loosen the rear wheel lug nuts, raise the rear of the vehicle and support it securely on jackstands. Remove the rear wheels.

2 If the vehicle is equipped with Automatic Level Control, disconnect all ALC lines from the axle.

3 Remove both rear brake assemblies (see Chapter 9). Disconnect all metal brake lines attached to the axle tube.

4 Remove the brake backing plates **(see illustration 16.4)** and - if you're planning to swap the spindles to another axle tube, or swap the axle tube to another set of spindles - remove the spindles (see Section 16).

5 Place a floor jack under the center of the axle tube and raise it just enough to take the load off the suspension.

6 Disconnect the lower ends of the shock absorbers from the axle tube (see Section 11).

7 Disconnect the stabilizer bar from the lower control arms (see Section 12).

8 Disconnect the rear ends of both pairs of upper and lower control arms from the axle tube (see Section 14).

9 Wrap chain through the coil springs and bolt the ends together (leaving enough slack in the chain to allow the coil springs to extend fully) to prevent them from popping out.

10 Carefully lower the axle tube assembly and remove it from under the vehicle.

11 Installation is the reverse of removal. Be sure to tighten all fasteners to the torque listed in this Chapter's Specifications and bleed the brakes (see Chapter 9).

16.4 To detach the brake backing plate and spindle from the rear axle tube, remove these four nuts; after removing the backing plate, install the nuts on the ends of the studs to prevent the spindle from suddenly flying out of the axle tube when you remove it with a slide hammer

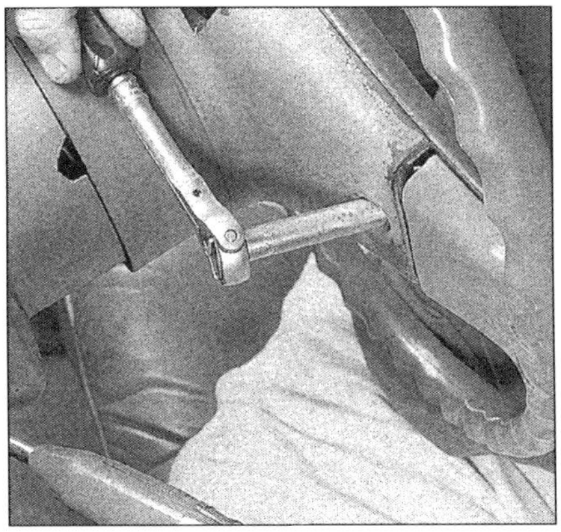

18.2a To detach the horn pad from most steering wheels, remove the two retaining screws located on the backside of the steering wheel

18.2b To disconnect the horn lead, push in on the black plastic connector (arrow) and turn it counterclockwise

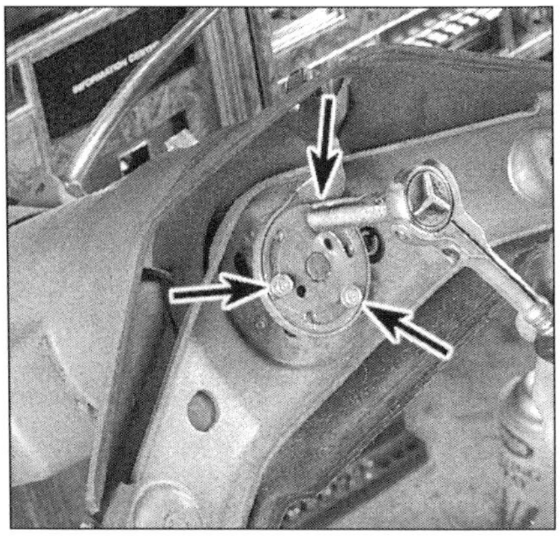

18.3a To detach the telescope locking lever assembly from the flange and screw assembly, remove these three screws . . .

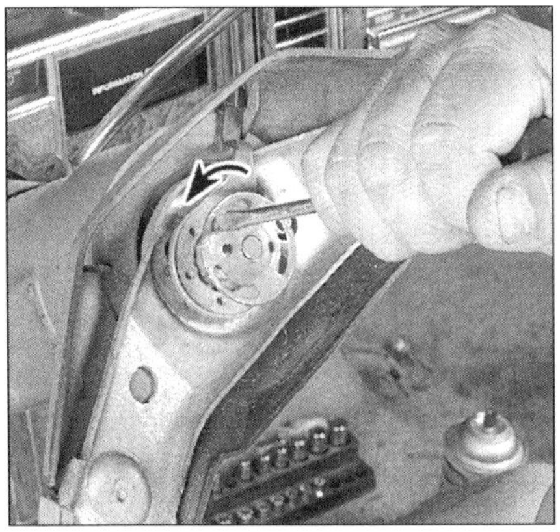

18.3b . . . then rotate the flange and screw assembly counterclockwise to remove it

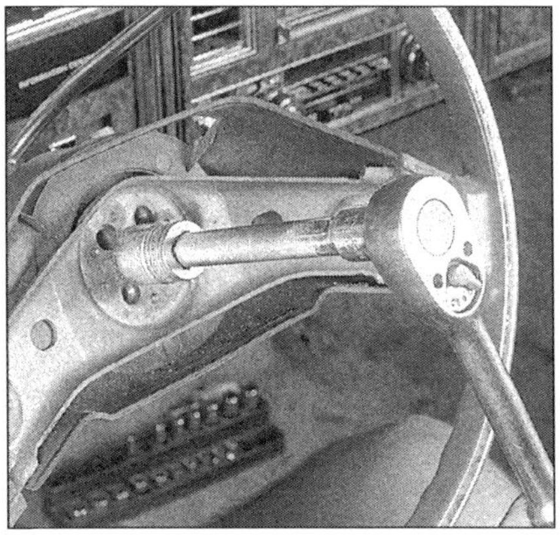

18.4a Remove the steering wheel nut . . .

18.4b . . . and mark the relationship of the steering wheel hub to the shaft

18 Steering wheel - removal and installation

Refer to illustrations 18.2a, 18.2b, 18.3a, 18.3b, 18.4a, 18.4b and 18.5

1 Disconnect the cable from the negative terminal of the battery.

2 Remove the horn pad from the steering wheel **(see illustration)**. Most pads are secured with screws which must be removed from the back of the steering wheel. Pull off the horn pad and disconnect the horn contact lead **(see illustration)**.

3 If the steering column is a tilt/telescopic unit, remove the three screws which attach the telescope locking lever assembly to the flange and screw assembly **(see illustrations)**.

4 Remove the steering wheel retaining nut, then mark the relationship of the steering shaft to the hub (if marks don't already exist or don't line up) to simplify installation and ensure steering wheel alignment **(see illustrations)**.

5 Use a puller to disconnect the steering wheel from the shaft **(see illustration)**. DON'T hammer on the shaft in an attempt to remove the wheel.

6 Installation is the reverse of removal. Be sure to align the mark on the steering wheel hub with the mark on the shaft. Tighten the steering wheel nut to the torque listed in this Chapter's Specifications.

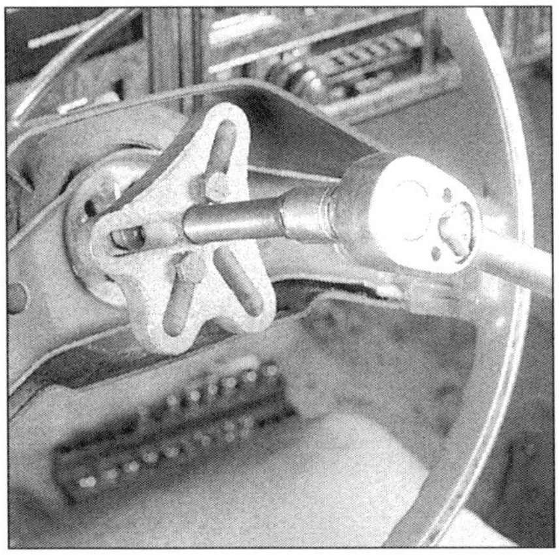

18.5 Use a steering wheel puller to remove the wheel

19 Tilt/telescopic steering column - repair

Refer to illustrations 19.4a through 19.4p

1 Disconnect the negative battery cable.

2 Remove the steering wheel (see Section 18).

3 Remove the turn signal switch and the key lock cylinder (see Chapter 12).

4 Follow the accompanying photo sequence **(see illustrations)**. Stay in order and read each caption carefully.

5 Installation is the reverse of removal.

19.4a Remove the turn signal switch lever. On some models this is accomplished by pulling straight out; on other models it's attached to the switch with a screw. Remove the turn signal switch

19.4b Remove the three screws (arrows) which retain the switch cover assembly

19.4c Remove the switch cover assembly and set it on the floor; be careful not to damage the cruise control wire

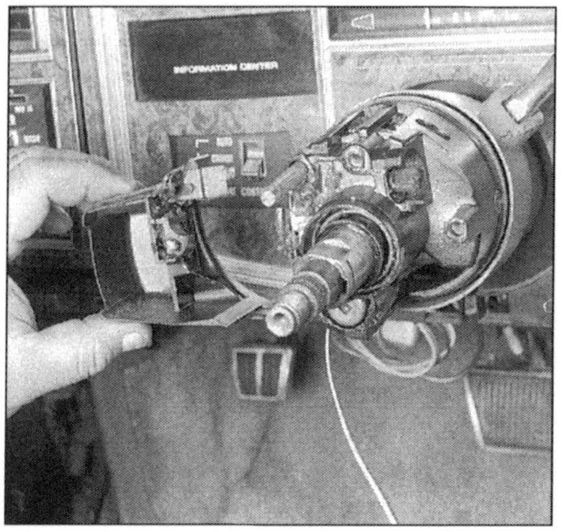

19.4d Remove the high-beam/turn signal switch actuator (if equipped);

19.4e To release the tilt mechanism retainer, push it in and turn it counterclockwise

19.4f The tilt pivot pins (arrow) are located on each side of the housing

19.4g A small slide hammer and an 8-32 machine screw . . .

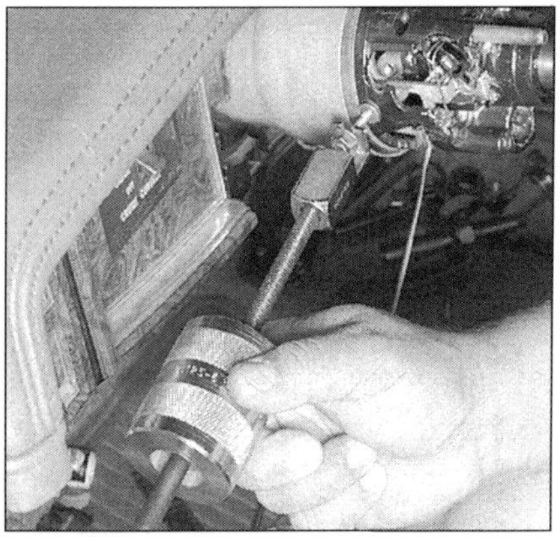

19.4h . . . is the best way to remove the pivot pins

19.4i If you don't have a small slide hammer, screw an 8-32 machine screw into each pin, clamp a pair of locking pliers onto the screw and use a large screwdriver to pry out the pins as shown

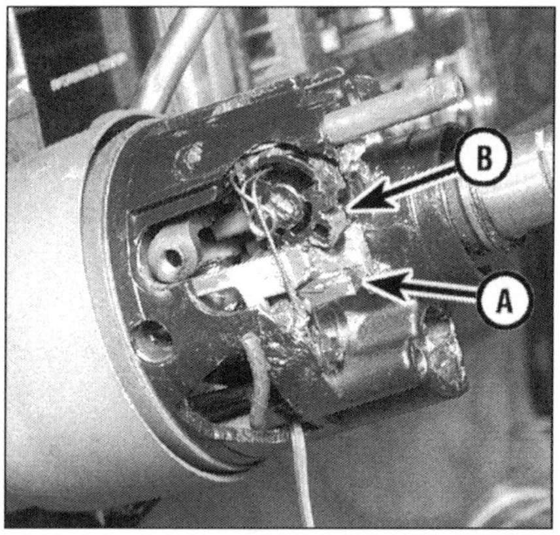

19.4j Before you remove the housing, pay very close attention to the relationship between the rack (A) and the sector (B); when the housing is installed again, this is how these two parts must fit together

20 Steering linkage - inspection, removal and installation

Warning: *Whenever any of the suspension or steering fasteners are loosened or removed they must be inspected and, if necessary, replaced with new ones of the same part number or of original equipment quality and design. Torque specifications must be followed for proper reassembly and component retention. Never attempt to heat, straighten or weld any suspension or steering component. Instead, replace any bent or damaged part with a new one.*

Caution: *DO NOT use a "picklefork" type separator when disconnecting the tie-rod ends or any other balljoint type steering linkage connections - it may damage the seals (however, if you're replacing components with new ones, it doesn't matter).*

Inspection

1 The steering linkage connects the steering gear to the front wheels and keeps the wheels in proper relation to each other. The

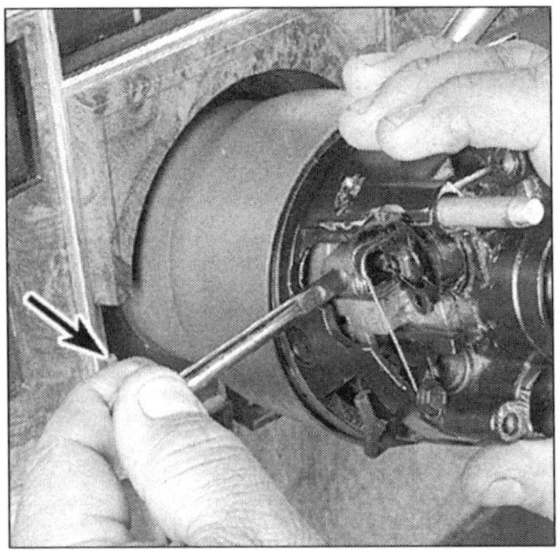

19.4k Temporarily install the tilt lever and pull toward you to release the tilt shoes from the shaft . . .

19.4l . . . and remove the housing (you will need to use this same procedure to install the housing

19.4m After disconnecting the cruise control lead down at the base of the column, carefully fish it out of the column and set the housing on the floor

19.4n Remove the rack; note how the rack is oriented - it must go back in exactly this way

19.4o Remove these four screws (arrows), apply some Loctite to the threads, install the screws and tighten them securely; this will eliminate the "sloppiness" in the steering column

19.4p Install the rack and housing and pass the cruise control harness through the column (remember to pull back on the tilt lever when installing the housing). To install the pivot pins, carefully tap them into place with a hammer. The remainder of installation is the reverse of removal

linkage consists of a Pitman arm which, when turned by the steering gear shaft, moves a center link back-and-forth. The Pitman arm is connected to the left (driver's side) end of the center link; an idler arm, which is anchored to the frame, is connected to the right end of the center link. The Pitman arm and idler arm support the center link and allow it to move back and forth. This back-and-forth motion is transmitted to the steering knuckles through a pair of tie-rod assemblies. Each tie-rod assembly consists of an inner and outer tie-rod end, a threaded adjuster tube and two clamps. Some models are also equipped with a shock absorber-like steering damper attached between the center link and the frame to cushion steering system shocks.

2 Set the wheels in the straight-ahead position and lock the steering wheel by turning the ignition key to the OFF position.

3 Raise one side of the vehicle until the tire is approximately 1-inch off the ground. Be sure the vehicle is supported securely.

4 Mount a dial indicator with the needle resting on the outside edge of the wheel, at the rear. Grasp the front and rear of the tire and, using light pressure, wiggle the wheel back-and-forth and note the dial indicator reading. The reading should be less than 0.108-inch. If the play in the steering system is more than specified, inspect each steering linkage pivot points (such as the tie-rod ends and idler arm) for looseness. Replace parts if necessary.

5 Raise the vehicle and support it on jackstands. Push up, then pull down on the end of the idler arm, exerting a force of approximately 25 pounds each way. Measure the total distance the end of the arm travels. If the play is greater than 1/4-inch, replace the idler arm.

6 Check for torn tie-rod end boots, oil leaking from the steering damper, frozen joints and bent or damaged linkage components.

Removal and installation

7 Loosen the wheel lug nuts, raise the vehicle and support it securely on jackstands. Apply the parking brake. Remove the wheel.

Tie-rod

Refer to illustrations 20.8a, 20.8b, 20.10 and 20.12

8 If you're planning to use the same tie-rod end, simply mark the point at which the

20.8a If you're planning to install the old tie-rod end, simply paint a mark on the threads where they meet the adjuster tube and screw it back in to this same point; to remove the tie-rod end from the adjuster tube, loosen the clamp nut

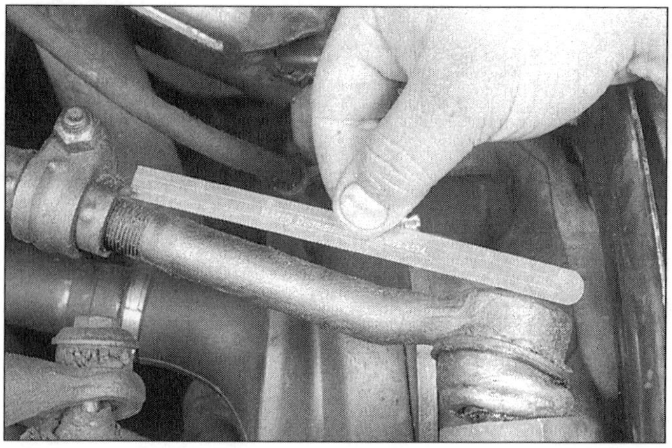

20.8b If you're installing a new tie-rod end, measure the distance between the end of the adjuster tube and the center of the ball stud and record this measurement for later use

20.10 A typical balljoint separator; note that the nut is loosened but not removed - this prevents the ball stud from popping out of its hole in the steering knuckle

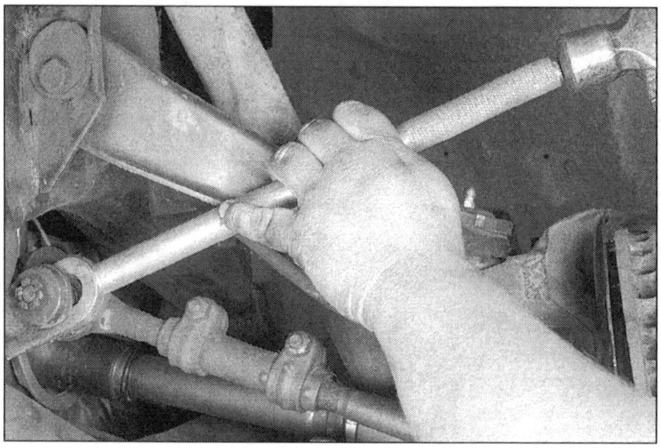

20.12 If possible, you want to use a balljoint separator on the inner tie-rod end too, but on some models, there's not enough room, so you'll have to resort to a picklefork tool

20.19 Use a two-jaw puller to separate the idler arm ballstud from the center link

threads meet the adjuster tube **(see illustration)**. If you're planning to install a new tie-rod end, measure the distance between the adjuster tube and the center of the tie-rod end **(see illustration)**.

9 Remove the cotter pin and loosen, but do not remove, the castellated nut from the ball stud.

10 Using a two-jaw puller, separate the tie-rod end from the steering knuckle **(see illustration)**. Remove the castle nut and pull the tie-rod end from the knuckle.

11 If you're just replacing the tie-rod end, loosen the adjuster tube clamp nuts and bolts, unscrew the old tie-rod end and screw in the new unit until the distance from the adjuster tube to the center of the new tie-rod end is the same as the distance you measured for the old unit (if you're installing the old tie-rod, lubricate the threads and screw it in until the paint mark is touching the adjuster tube again). Tighten the adjuster tube clamp nuts and bolts securely.

12 If you're replacing the entire tie-rod assembly (inner tie-rod end, adjuster tube and tie-rod end), remove the cotter pin and loosen the nut securing the inner tie-rod end to the center link rod. Separate the inner tie-rod end from the center link in the same manner as Step 10. On some models, it may be impossible to get a puller on this balljoint stud because of clearance problems. If necessary, use a picklefork tool **(see illustration)**.

13 If you're replacing the entire tie-rod assembly, loosen the adjuster tube clamp and screw the tie-rod end in or out until the distance between the adjuster tube and the center of the ball stud is the same length you measured on as the old unit.

14 Whether you're installing an entire tie-rod assembly or just a tie-rod end, the number of threads showing on the inner and outer tie-rod ends should be equal within three threads. Don't tighten the clamp nuts yet.

15 To connect the inner tie-rod to the center link, insert the ball stud until it's seated. Install the nut and tighten it to the torque listed in this Chapter's Specifications. If the ball stud spins when attempting to tighten the nut, force it into the tapered hole with a pair of large adjustable pliers.

16 Connect the outer tie-rod end to the steering knuckle and install the castle nut. Tighten the nut to the torque listed in this Chapter's Specifications and install a new cotter pin. If necessary, tighten the nut slightly to align a slot in the nut with the hole in the ball stud.

17 Tighten the clamp nuts. The center of the bolt should be nearly horizontal and the adjuster tube slot must not line up with the gap in the clamps.

18 Install the wheel and lug nuts, lower the vehicle and tighten the lug nuts to the torque listed in this Chapter's Specifications. Drive the vehicle to an alignment shop to have the front end alignment checked and, if necessary, adjusted.

Idler arm

Refer to illustrations 20.19 and 20.20

19 Loosen but do not remove the idler arm-to-center link nut. Separate the idler arm from the center link with a two-jaw puller **(see illustration)**. Remove the nut.

20 Remove the idler arm-to-frame bolt **(see illustration)**.

21 To install the idler arm, position it on the frame and install the bolt, tightening it to the torque listed in this Chapter's Specifications.

22 Insert the idler arm ball stud into the center link and install the nut. Tighten the nut to the torque listed in this Chapter's Specifications. If the ball stud spins when attempt-

20.20 The idler arm is bolted to the right front corner of the frame; to detach it, remove this bolt

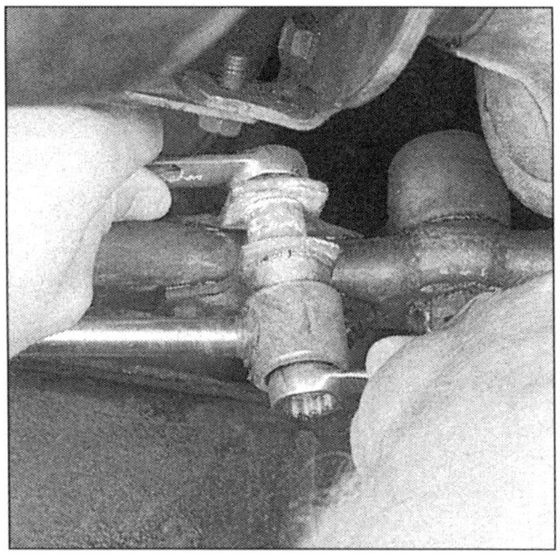

20.28a To disconnect the steering damper from the center link, remove the nut and bolt as shown, using a back-up wrench

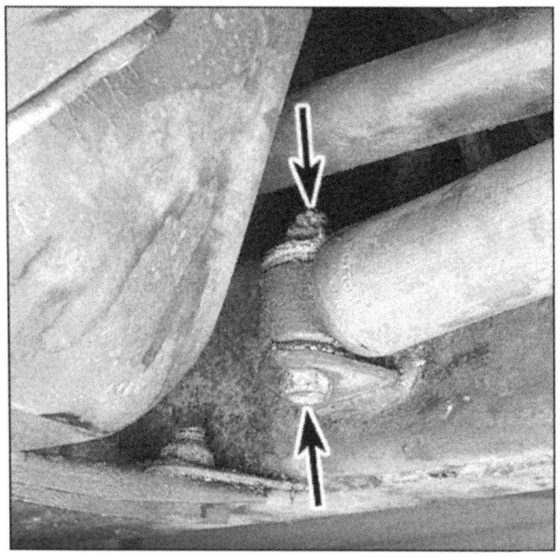

20.28b To detach the steering damper from the frame, remove this nut and bolt (arrows)

21.2a Disconnect the power steering pressure and return lines (left arrows) from the steering gear; before removing the pinch bolt (right arrow), be sure to mark the relationship of the U-joint to the steering gear

21.2b A "crow's foot" is a handy tool for loosening the power steering hose and line fittings from the steering gear

21.3 Turn the steering column so that the pinch bolt is facing straight up, then remove the bolt with a socket and long extension

ing to tighten the nut, force it into the tapered hole with a large pair of pliers.

Center link

23 Raise the vehicle and support it securely on jackstands. Apply the parking brake.
24 Separate the two inner tie-rod ends from the center link (see Step 12).
25 Separate the idler arm from the center link (see Steps 18 and 19).
26 Separate the Pitman arm from the center link the same way you would separate the idler arm.
27 Installation is the reverse of the removal procedure. If the ball studs spin when attempting to tighten the nuts, force them into the tapered holes with a large pair of pliers. Be sure to tighten all of the nuts to the torque listed in this Chapter's Specifications.

Steering damper

Refer to illustrations 20.28a and 20.28b

28 Remove the bolts and nuts and detach the damper from the steering linkage and frame mounting bracket **(see illustrations)**.
29 Installation is the reverse of removal. Be sure to tighten the fasteners to the torque listed in this Chapter's Specifications.

Pitman arm

30 To remove the Pitman arm, you'll have to remove the steering gear (see Section 21).

21 Steering gear - removal and installation

Refer to illustrations 21.2a, 21.2b, 21.3, 21.5, 21.6 and 21.7

1 Raise the front of the vehicle and support it securely on jackstands. Apply the parking brake.
2 Place a drain pan under the steering gear. Disconnect the power steering pressure and return lines **(see illustrations)** and cap the ends to prevent excessive fluid loss and contamination.
3 Mark the relationship of the lower intermediate shaft universal joint to the steering gear input shaft. Remove the lower intermediate shaft pinch bolt **(see illustration)**.
4 Disconnect the Pitman arm from the center link (see Section 20).
5 Support the steering gear and remove the steering gear-to-frame mounting bolts from inside the left wheel well **(see illustration)**. Lower the unit, separate the intermediate shaft from the steering gear input shaft and remove the steering gear from the vehi-

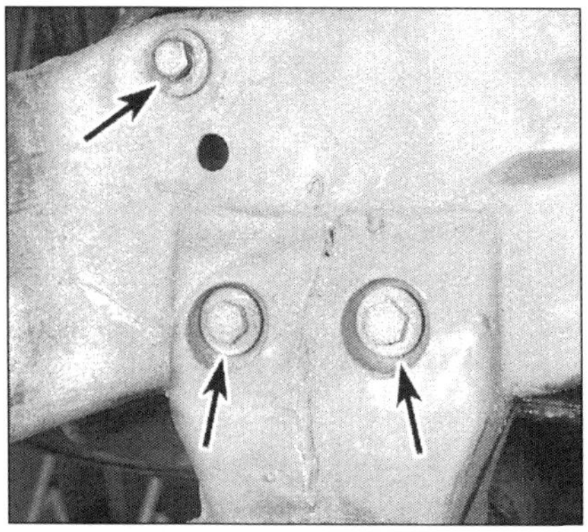

21.5 To detach the steering gear from the frame, remove these three bolts (arrows) from the frame inside the left wheel housing

21.6 With the steering gear in a bench vise, remove the Pitman arm retaining nut; you may need a breaker bar to loosen the nut, which is usually very tight; be sure to mark the relationship of the Pitman arm to the shaft before pulling off the arm

cle.

6 Place the steering gear in a vise. Remove the Pitman arm nut **(see illustration)** and washer. Before removing the Pitman arm, be sure to mark the relationship of the arm to the shaft so it can be installed in the same position.

7 Remove the Pitman arm from the shaft with a Pitman arm puller **(see illustration)**.

8 Installation is the reverse of removal. Be sure to align the marks you made before removing the Pitman arm and tighten all fasteners to the torque listed in this Chapter's Specifications.

22 Power steering pump - removal and installation

Refer to illustrations 22.1, 22.2a, 22.2b, 22.2c, 22.2d, 22.2e, 22.2f, 22.2g, 22.4 and 22.5

Note: *There are too many different power steering pump bracket arrangements to illustrate them all here. Three common setups are shown.*

21.7 Use a Pitman arm puller to pull off the Pitman arm!

22.2a To remove the power steering pump from an early big V8 (500 cubic inch shown, 425 and 368 similar), remove the bracket bolt (lower arrow) . . .

1 Disconnect the hydraulic lines from the pump **(see illustration)** and support them in a raised position to keep the fluid from draining. If you disconnect the lines at the pump, plug the fittings at the pump so the reservoir won't drain.

22.1 Detach the power steering pressure and return lines (arrows) from the power steering pump and either plug them or hang them up to prevent fluid from spilling

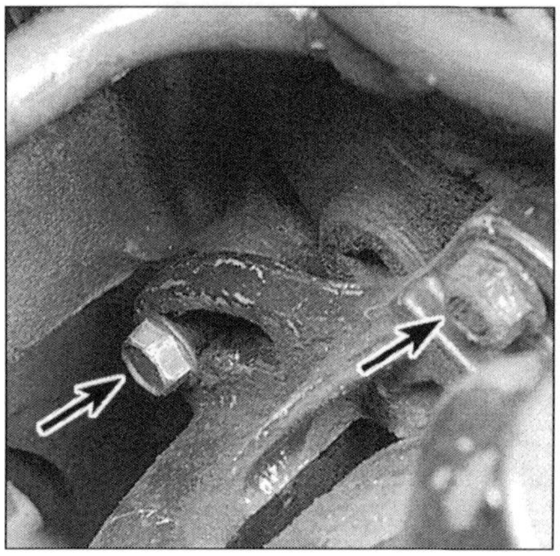

22.2b . . . the adjustment nut and bolts (arrows) . . .

2 Loosen the pump mounting bolts **(see illustrations)** and remove the drivebelt. On Cadillac models with the HT4100 engine, the pulley must be removed for access to the pump mounting bolts **(see illustration)**.

3 Remove the pump mounting bolts and braces and remove the pump and pulley.

4 Mount the pump in a vise, remove the

22.2c . . . and the bolt and nut underneath

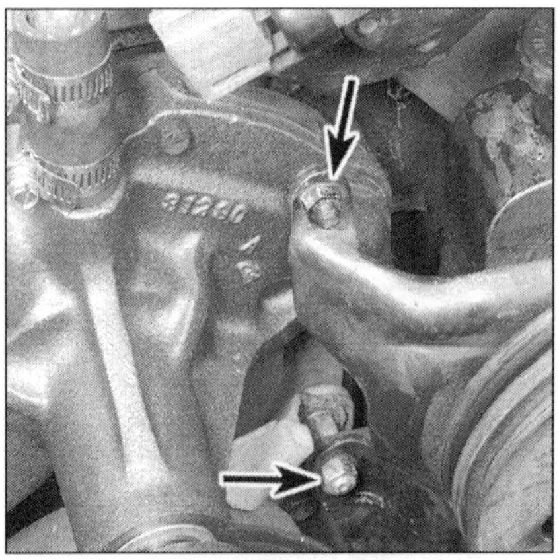

22.2d Typical power steering pump bracket and bolts (arrows) (Oldsmobile-built 350 cubic inch V8) . . .

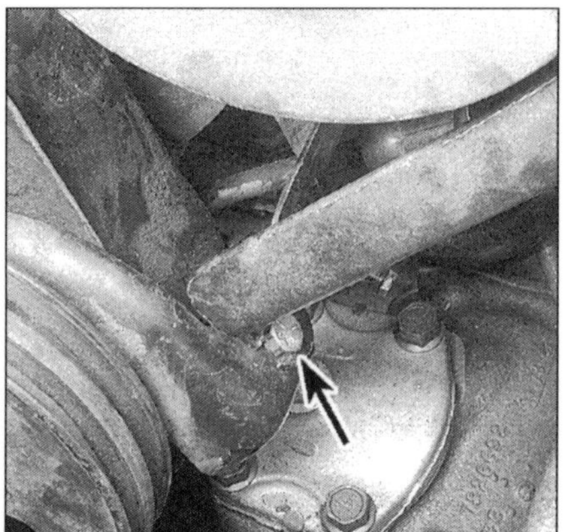

22.2e . . . there's also a bracket bolt on the other side of the pump

22.2f On models with the HT4100 engine, the pulley must be removed for access to the pump mounting bolts - a special pulley removal tool is required

22.2g Typical power steering pump bolts (arrows) (HT4100 engine)

22.4 On some models the power steering pump pulley is retained by a nut. To remove the pulley, remove the nut, using a back-up wrench to hold the pulley, then slide the pulley off the shaft (use a pulley removal tool if necessary)

22.5 To install the pulley on the shaft, use a long bolt with the same thread pitch as the internal threads of the power steering pump shaft, and a nut, washer and socket that's the same diameter as the pulley hub

pulley nut and remove the pulley **(see accompanying illustration and illustration 22.2f)**.

5 Installation is the reverse of removal. To install the pulley on models that don't have a nut retaining the pulley, press the pulley on with a pulley installation tool or an alternative fabricated from a long bolt, nut, washer and a socket of the same diameter as the pulley hub **(see illustration)**. Push the pulley onto the shaft until the front of the hub is flush with the shaft, but no further.

6 Before installing the drivebelt, prime the pump by filling the reservoir with fluid, then turn the pulley in the opposite direction of normal rotation until no more air bubbles are observed in the reservoir.

7 Install the drivebelt (see Chapter 1) and bleed the system (see Section 23).

23 Power steering system - bleeding

1 Following any operation in which the power steering fluid lines have been disconnected, the power steering system must be bled to remove all air and obtain proper steering performance.

2 With the front wheels in the straight ahead position, check the power steering fluid level and, if low, add fluid until it reaches the Cold mark on the dipstick.

3 Start the engine and allow it to run at fast idle. Recheck the fluid level and add more if necessary to reach the Cold mark on the dipstick.

4 Bleed the system by turning the wheels from side-to-side, without hitting the stops. This will work the air out of the system. Keep the reservoir full of fluid as this is done.

5 When the air is worked out of the system, return the wheels to the straight ahead position and leave the vehicle running for several more minutes before shutting it off.

6 Road test the vehicle to be sure the steering system is functioning normally and noise free.

7 Recheck the fluid level to be sure it is up to the Hot mark on the dipstick while the engine is at normal operating temperature. Add fluid if necessary (see Chapter 1).

24 Wheels and tires - general information

Most vehicles covered by this manual are equipped with metric-sized fiberglass or steel belted radial tires. Use of other size or type of tires may affect the ride and handling of the vehicle. Don't mix different types of tires, such as radials and bias belted, on the same vehicle as handling may be seriously affected. It's recommended that tires be replaced in pairs on the same axle, but if only one tire is being replaced, be sure it's the same size, structure and tread design as the other.

Because tire pressure has a substantial effect on handling and wear, the pressure of all tires should be checked at least once a month or before any extended trips (see Chapter 1).

Wheels must be replaced if they are bent, dented, leak air, have elongated bolt holes, are heavily rusted, out of vertical symmetry or if the lug nuts won't stay tight. Wheel repairs that use welding or peening are not recommended.

Tire and wheel balance is important in the overall handling, braking and performance of the vehicle. Unbalanced wheels can adversely affect handling and ride characteristics as well as tire life. Whenever a tire is installed on a wheel, the tire and wheel should be balanced by a shop with the proper equipment.

25 Front end alignment - general information

A front end alignment refers to the adjustments made to the front wheels so they are in proper angular relationship to the suspension and the ground. Front wheels that are out of proper alignment not only affect steering control, but also increase tire wear. The front end adjustments normally required are camber, caster and toe-in.

Getting the proper front wheel alignment is a very exacting process, one in which complicated and expensive machines are necessary to perform the job properly.

Because of this, you should have a technician with the proper equipment perform these tasks. We will, however, use this space to give you a basic idea of what is involved with front end alignment so you can better understand the process and deal intelligently with the shop that does the work.

Toe-in is the turning in of the front wheels. The purpose of a toe specification is to ensure the front wheels roll parallel with each other when the vehicle is in motion. In a vehicle with zero toe-in, the distance between the front edges of the wheels will be the same as the distance between the rear edges of the wheels. The amount that the wheels are toed-in is only a fraction of an inch. Toe-in adjustment is controlled by the tie-rod end position on the inner tie-rod. Incorrect toe-in will cause the tires to wear improperly by making them scrub against the road surface.

Camber is the tilting of the front wheels from the vertical when viewed from the front of the vehicle. When the wheels tilt out at the top, the camber is said to be positive (+). When the wheels tilt in at the top the camber is negative (-). The amount of tilt is measured in degrees from vertical and this measurement is called the camber angle. This angle affects the amount of tire tread which contacts the road and compensates for changes in the suspension geometry when the vehicle is cornering or traveling over an undulating surface. Camber is adjusted by turning the cam bolts securing the upper control arm to the frame.

Caster is the tilting of the top of the front steering axis from the vertical. A tilt toward the rear is positive caster and a tilt toward the front is negative caster. Caster is also adjusted by turning the upper control arm cam bolts.

Chapter 11 Body

Contents

1 General information

Warning: *Some models covered by this manual are equipped with a supplemental restraint system, more commonly known as an airbag. Always disable the airbag before any repair in the vicinity of the dash or removal of the instrument panel assembly. To disable the airbag system place the ignition key in the lock position and disconnect the negative battery cable.*

All models covered by this manual have a separate frame and body. Certain components are particularly vulnerable to accident damage and can be unbolted and repaired or replaced. Among these parts are the body moldings, bumpers, doors, fenders, hood, trunk lid and all glass.

Only general body maintenance practices and body panel repair procedures within the scope of the do-it-yourselfer are included in this Chapter.

2 Body - maintenance

1 The condition of your vehicle's body is very important, because the resale value depends a great deal on it. It's much more difficult to repair a neglected or damaged body than it is to repair mechanical components. The hidden areas of the body, such as the wheel wells, the frame and the engine compartment, are equally important, although they don't require as frequent attention as the rest of the body.

2 Once a year, or every 12,000 miles, it's a good idea to have the underside of the body steam cleaned. All traces of dirt and oil will be removed and the area can then be inspected carefully for rust, damaged brake lines, frayed electrical wires, damaged cables and other problems. The front suspension components should be greased after completion of this job.

3 At the same time, clean the engine and the engine compartment with a steam cleaner or water soluble degreaser.

4 The wheel wells should be given close attention, since undercoating can peel away and stones and dirt thrown up by the tires can cause the paint to chip and flake, allowing rust to set in. If rust is found, clean down to the bare metal and apply an anti-rust paint.

5 The body should be washed about once a week. Wet the vehicle thoroughly to soften the dirt, then wash it down with a soft sponge and plenty of clean soapy water. If the surplus dirt is not washed off very carefully, it can wear down the paint.

6 Spots of tar or asphalt thrown up from the road should be removed with a cloth soaked in solvent.

7 Once every six months, wax the body and chrome trim. If a chrome cleaner is used to remove rust from any of the vehicle's plated parts, remember that the cleaner also removes part of the chrome, so use it sparingly.

3 Vinyl trim - maintenance

Don't clean vinyl trim with detergents, caustic soap or petroleum-based cleaners. Plain soap and water works just fine, with a soft brush to clean dirt that may be ingrained. Wash the vinyl as frequently as the rest of the vehicle.

After cleaning, application of a high quality rubber and vinyl protectant will help prevent oxidation and cracks. The protectant can also be applied to weatherstripping, vacuum lines, rubber hoses, and to tires.

4 Upholstery and carpets - maintenance

1 Every three months remove the carpets or mats and clean the interior of the vehicle (more frequently if necessary). Vacuum the upholstery and carpets to remove loose dirt and dust.

2 Leather upholstery requires special care. Stains should be removed with warm water and a very mild soap solution. Use a clean, damp cloth to remove the soap, then wipe again with a dry cloth. Never use alcohol, gasoline, nail polish remover or thinner to clean leather upholstery.

3 After cleaning, regularly treat leather upholstery with a leather wax. Never use car wax on leather upholstery.

4 In areas where the interior of the vehicle is subject to bright sunlight, cover leather seats with a sheet if the vehicle is to be left out for any length of time.

5 Use of an interior-type windshield sun deflector is also recommended.

5 Body repair - minor damage

See photo sequence

Repair of minor scratches

1 If the scratch is superficial and does not penetrate to the metal of the body, repair is very simple. Lightly rub the scratched area with a fine rubbing compound to remove loose paint and built up wax. Rinse the area with clean water.

2 Apply touch-up paint to the scratch, using a small brush. Continue to apply thin layers of paint until the surface of the paint in the scratch is level with the surrounding paint. Allow the new paint at least two weeks

to harden, then blend it into the surrounding paint by rubbing with a very fine rubbing compound. Finally, apply a coat of wax to the scratch area.

3 If the scratch has penetrated the paint and exposed the metal of the body, causing the metal to rust, a different repair technique is required. Remove all loose rust from the bottom of the scratch with a pocket knife, then apply rust-inhibiting paint to prevent the formation of rust in the future. Using a rubber or nylon applicator, coat the scratched area with glaze-type filler. If required, the filler can be mixed with thinner to provide a very thin paste, which is ideal for filling narrow scratches. Before the glaze filler in the scratch hardens, wrap a piece of smooth cotton cloth around the tip of a finger. Dip the cloth in thinner and then quickly wipe it along the surface of the scratch. This will ensure that the surface of the filler is slightly hollow. The scratch can now be painted over as described earlier in this Section.

Repair of dents

4 When repairing dents, the first job is to pull the dent out until the affected area is as close as possible to its original shape. There is no point in trying to restore the original shape completely as the metal in the damaged area will have stretched on impact and cannot be restored to its original contours. It is better to bring the level of the dent up to a point which is about 1/8-inch below the level of the surrounding metal. In cases where the dent is very shallow, it is not worth trying to pull it out at all.

5 If the back side of the dent is accessible, it can be hammered out gently from behind using a soft-face hammer. While doing this, hold a block of wood firmly against the opposite side of the metal to absorb the hammer blows and prevent the metal from being stretched.

6 If the dent is in a section of the body which has double layers, or some other factor makes it inaccessible from behind, a different technique is required. Drill several small holes through the metal inside the damaged area, particularly in the deeper sections. Screw long, self-tapping screws into the holes just enough for them to get a good grip in the metal. Now the dent can be pulled out by pulling on the protruding heads of the screws with locking pliers.

7 The next stage of repair is the removal of paint from the damaged area and from an inch or so of the surrounding metal. This is easily done with a wire brush or sanding disk in a drill motor, although it can be done just as effectively by hand with sandpaper. To complete the preparation for filling, score the surface of the bare metal with a screwdriver or the tang of a file, or drill small holes in the affected area. This will provide a good grip for the filler material. To complete the repair, see the Section on filling and painting.

Repair of rust holes or gashes

8 Remove all paint from the affected area and from an inch or so of the surrounding metal using a sanding disk or wire brush mounted in a drill motor. If these are not available, a few sheets of sandpaper will do the job just as effectively.

9 With the paint removed, you will be able to determine the severity of the corrosion and decide whether to replace the whole panel, if possible, or repair the affected area. New body panels are not as expensive as most people think, and it is often quicker to install a new panel than to repair large areas of rust.

10 Remove all trim pieces from the affected area except those which will act as a guide to the original shape of the damaged body, such as headlight shells, etc. Using metal snips or a hacksaw blade, remove all loose metal and any other metal that is badly affected by rust. Hammer the edges of the hole inward to create a slight depression for the filler material.

11 Wire brush the affected area to remove the powdery rust from the surface of the metal. If the back of the rusted area is accessible, treat it with rust-inhibiting paint.

12 Before filling is done, block the hole in some way. This can be done with sheet metal riveted or screwed into place, or by stuffing the hole with wire mesh.

13 Once the hole is blocked off, the affected area can be filled and painted. See the following subsection on *filling and painting*.

Filling and painting

14 Many types of body fillers are available, but generally speaking, body repair kits which contain filler paste and a tube of resin hardener are best for this type of repair work. A wide, flexible plastic or nylon applicator will be necessary for imparting a smooth and contoured finish to the surface of the filler material. Mix up a small amount of filler on a clean piece of wood or cardboard (use the hardener sparingly). Follow the manufacturer's instructions on the package, otherwise the filler will set incorrectly.

15 Using the applicator, apply the filler paste to the prepared area. Draw the applicator across the surface of the filler to achieve the desired contour and to level the filler surface. As soon as a contour that approximates the original one is achieved, stop working the paste. If you continue, the paste will begin to stick to the applicator. Continue to add thin layers of paste at 20-minute intervals until the level of the filler is just above the surrounding metal.

16 Once the filler has hardened, the excess can be removed with a body file. From then on, progressively finer grades of sandpaper should be used, starting with a 180-grit paper and finishing with 600-grit wet-or-dry paper. Always wrap the sandpaper around a flat rubber or wooden block, otherwise the surface of the filler will not be completely flat. During the sanding of the filler surface, the wet-or-dry paper should be periodically rinsed in water. This will ensure that a very smooth finish is produced in the final stage.

17 At this point, the repair area should be surrounded by a ring of bare metal, which in turn should be encircled by the finely feathered edge of good paint. Rinse the repair area with clean water until all of the dust produced by the sanding operation is gone.

18 Spray the entire area with a light coat of primer. This will reveal any imperfections in the surface of the filler. Repair the imperfections with fresh filler paste or glaze filler and once more smooth the surface with sandpaper. Repeat this spray-and-repair procedure until you are satisfied that the surface of the filler and the feathered edge of the paint are perfect. Rinse the area with clean water and allow it to dry completely.

19 The repair area is now ready for painting. Spray painting must be carried out in a warm, dry, windless and dust-free atmosphere. These conditions can be created if you have access to a large indoor work area, but if you are forced to work in the open, you will have to pick the day very carefully. If you are working indoors, dousing the floor in the work area with water will help settle the dust which would otherwise be in the air. If the repair area is confined to one body panel, mask off the surrounding panels. This will help minimize the effects of a slight mismatch in paint color. Trim pieces such as chrome strips, door handles, etc., will also need to be masked off or removed. Use masking tape and several thicknesses of newspaper for the masking operations.

20 Before spraying, shake the paint can thoroughly, then spray a test area until the spray painting technique is mastered. Cover the repair area with a thick coat of primer. The thickness should be built up using several thin layers of primer rather than one thick one. Using 600-grit wet-or-dry sandpaper, rub down the surface of the primer until it is very smooth. While doing this, the work area should be thoroughly rinsed with water and the wet-or-dry sandpaper periodically rinsed as well. Allow the primer to dry before spraying additional coats.

21 Spray on the top coat, again building up the thickness by using several thin layers of paint. Begin spraying in the center of the repair area and then, using a circular motion, work out until the whole repair area and about two inches of the surrounding original paint is covered. Remove all masking material 10 to 15 minutes after spraying on the final coat of paint. Allow the new paint at least two weeks to harden, then use a very fine rubbing compound to blend the edges of the new paint into the existing paint. Finally, apply a coat of wax.

6 Body repair - major damage

1 Major damage must be repaired by a properly equipped auto body shop. These shops have the specialized equipment required to do the job properly.

2 If the damage is extensive, the body must be checked for proper alignment or the

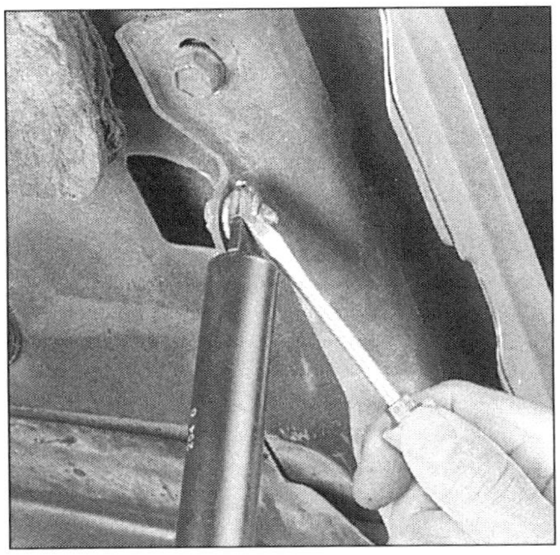

9.2 Use a small screwdriver to pry the clip out of its locking groove, then detach the end of the strut from the locating stud

vehicle's handling characteristics may be adversely affected and other components may wear at an accelerated rate.

3 Due to the fact that all of the major body components (hood, fenders, etc.) are separate and replaceable units, any seriously damaged components should be replaced rather than repaired. Sometimes the components can be found in a wrecking yard that specializes in used vehicle components, often at considerable savings over the cost of new parts.

7 Hinges and locks - maintenance

Once every 3000 miles, or every three months, the hinges and latch assemblies on the doors, hood and trunk should be given a few drops of light oil or lock lubricant. The door latch strikers should also be lubricated with a thin coat of grease to reduce wear and ensure free movement. Lubricate the door and trunk locks with spray-on graphite lubricant.

8 Windshield and fixed glass - replacement

Replacement of the windshield and fixed glass requires the use of special fast-setting adhesive/caulk materials and some specialized tools and techniques. These operations should be left to a dealer service department or a shop specializing in glass work.

9 Hood and trunk lid support struts - removal and installation

Refer to illustration 9.2

Note: *The hood and trunk lid are heavy and somewhat awkward to hold - at least two people should perform this procedure.*

1 Open the hood or trunk lid and support

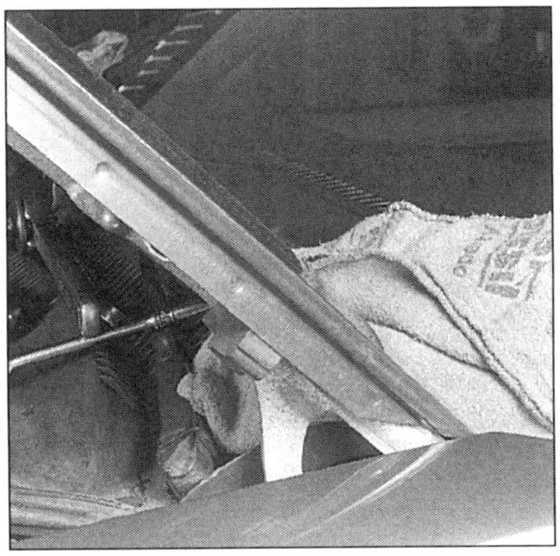

10.1 Pad the back corners of the hood with rags so the windshield won't be damaged if the hood accidentally swings rearward

it securely.

2 Using a small screwdriver, detach the retaining clips at both ends of the support strut, then pry or pull sharply to detach it from the posts **(see illustration)**. **Note:** *Be careful not to break or severely distort retaining clips. Replacement support struts might not come equipped with new retaining clips.*

3 Remove the retaining clips from the old support strut and install them on the replacement strut.

4 Installation is the reverse of the removal procedure.

10 Hood - removal, installation and adjustment

Note: *The hood is extremely heavy and somewhat awkward to remove and install - at least two people should perform this procedure.*

Removal and installation

Refer to illustration 10.1

1 Use blankets or pads to cover the fenders and rear of the hood **(see illustration)**. This will protect the windshield, body and paint as the hood is lifted off.

2 Use a felt-tip marker or white paint to make alignment marks around the bolt heads to insure proper alignment during installation.

3 Disconnect any cables or wire harnesses which will interfere with removal.

4 Have an assistant support the weight of the hood. Remove the hinge-to-hood nuts or bolts.

5 Lift off the hood.

6 Installation is the reverse of the removal procedure.

Adjustment

Refer to illustrations 10.10 and 10 11

7 Fore-and-aft and side-to-side adjustment of the hood is done by moving the hood in relation to the hinge plate after loosening

10.10 Loosen the bolts (arrows) and move the hood latch to adjust the hood closed position. **Note:** *Later models have only two mounting bolts.*

10.11 Screw the hood bumpers in or out to adjust the hood flush with the fenders

the bolts or nuts.

8 Scribe a line around the entire hinge plate so you can judge the amount of movement.

9 Loosen the bolts or nuts and move the hood into correct alignment. Move it only a little at a time. Tighten the hinge bolts or nuts and carefully lower the hood to check the alignment.

10 If necessary after installation, the entire hood latch assembly can be adjusted up and down as well as from side-to-side on the radiator support so the hood closes securely and is flush with the fenders. To do this, scribe a line around the hood latch mounting bolts to provide a reference point, then loosen the bolts and reposition the latch assembly as necessary **(see illustration).** Following adjustment, retighten the mounting bolts.

11 Finally, adjust the hood bumpers on the radiator support so the hood, when closed, is flush with the fenders **(see illustration).**

12 The hood latch assembly, as well as the hinges, should be periodically lubricated with white lithium-base grease to prevent sticking and wear.

These photos illustrate a method of repairing simple dents. They are intended to supplement *Body repair - minor damage* in this Chapter and should not be used as the sole instructions for body repair on these vehicles.

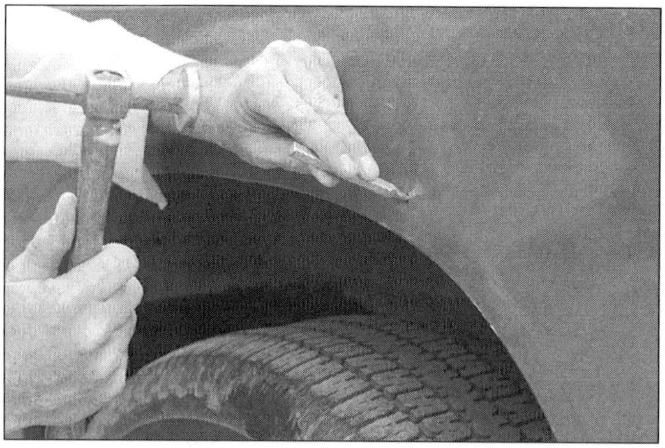

1 If you can't access the backside of the body panel to hammer out the dent, pull it out with a slide-hammer-type dent puller. In the deepest portion of the dent or along the crease line, drill or punch hole(s) at least one inch apart . . .

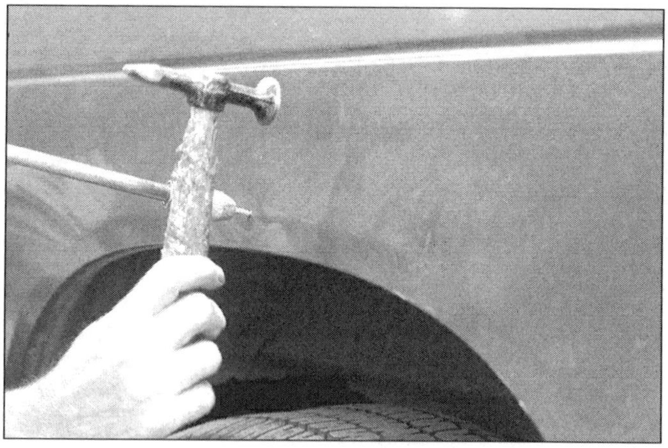

2 . . . then screw the slide-hammer into the hole and operate it. Tap with a hammer near the edge of the dent to help 'pop' the metal back to its original shape. When you're finished, the dent area should be close to its original contour and about 1/8-inch below the surface of the surrounding metal

3 Using coarse-grit sandpaper, remove the paint down to the bare metal. Hand sanding works fine, but the disc sander shown here makes the job faster. Use finer (about 320-grit) sandpaper to feather-edge the paint at least one inch around the dent area

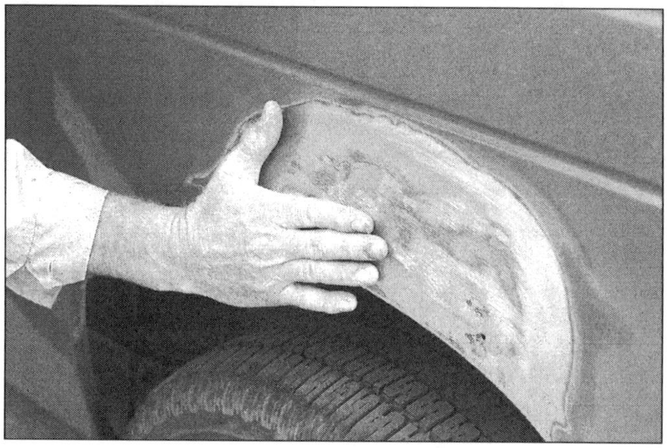

4 When the paint is removed, touch will probably be more helpful than sight for telling if the metal is straight. Hammer down the high spots or raise the low spots as necessary. Clean the repair area with wax/silicone remover

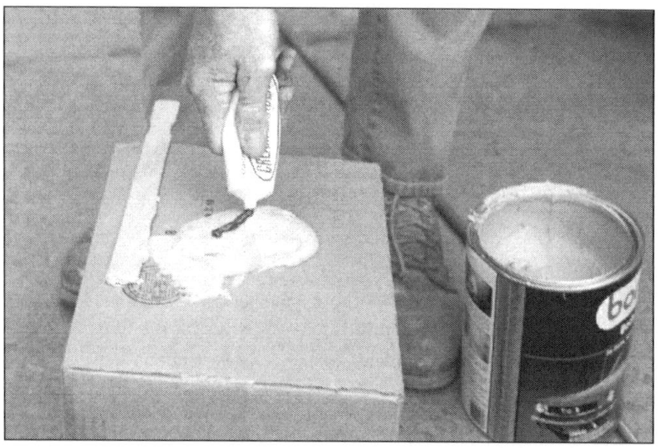

5 Following label instructions, mix up a batch of plastic filler and hardener. The ratio of filler to hardener is critical, and, if you mix it incorrectly, it will either not cure properly or cure too quickly (you won't have time to file and sand it into shape)

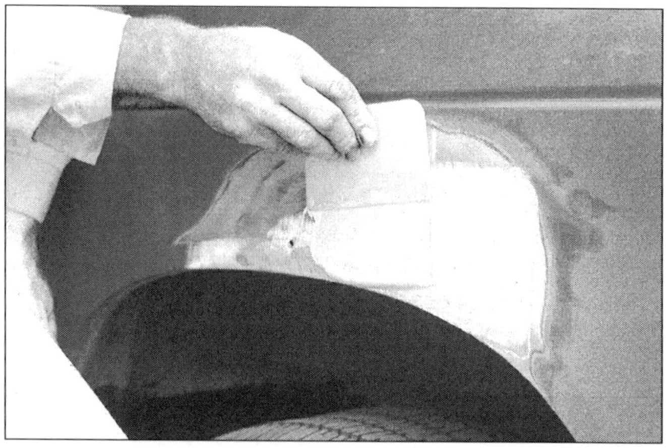

6 Working quickly so the filler doesn't harden, use a plastic applicator to press the body filler firmly into the metal, assuring it bonds completely. Work the filler until it matches the original contour and is slightly above the surrounding metal

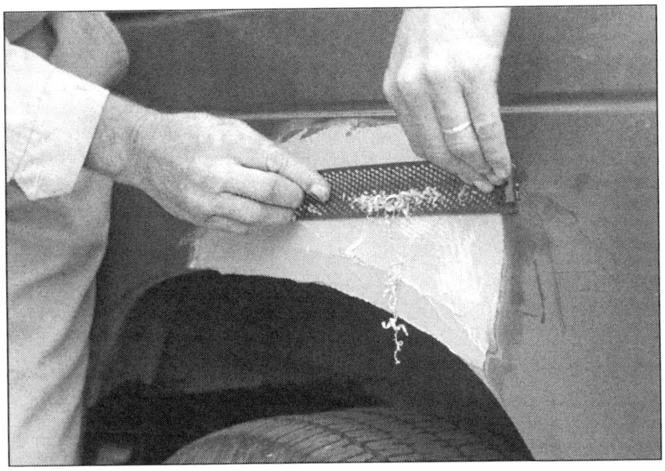

7 Let the filler harden until you can just dent it with your fingernail. Use a body file or Surform tool (shown here) to rough-shape the filler

8 Use coarse-grit sandpaper and a sanding board or block to work the filler down until it's smooth and even. Work down to finer grits of sandpaper - always using a board or block - ending up with 360 or 400 grit

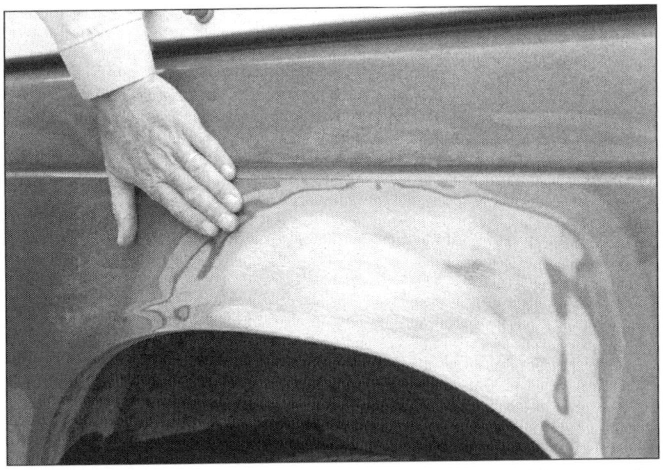

9 You shouldn't be able to feel any ridge at the transition from the filler to the bare metal or from the bare metal to the old paint. As soon as the repair is flat and uniform, remove the dust and mask off the adjacent panels or trim pieces

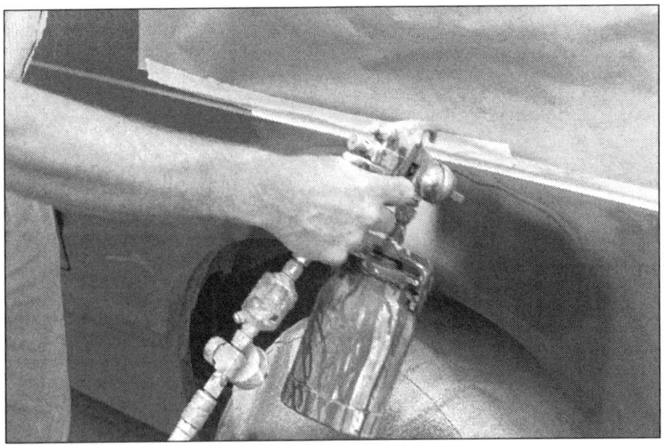

10 Apply several layers of primer to the area. Don't spray the primer on too heavy, so it sags or runs, and make sure each coat is dry before you spray on the next one. A professional-type spray gun is being used here, but aerosol spray primer is available inexpensively from auto parts stores

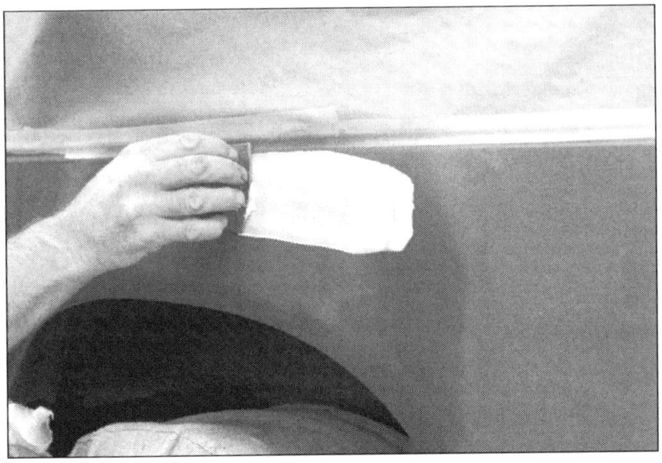

11 The primer will help reveal imperfections or scratches. Fill these with glazing compound. Follow the label instructions and sand it with 360 or 400-grit sandpaper until it's smooth. Repeat the glazing, sanding and respraying until the primer reveals a perfectly smooth surface

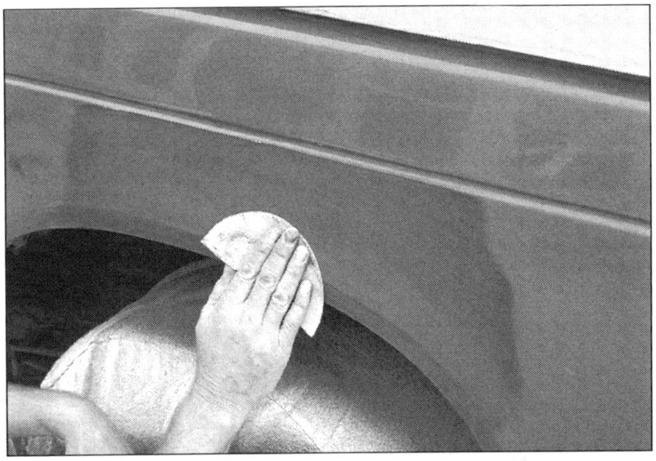

12 Finish sand the primer with very fine sandpaper (400 or 600-grit) to remove the primer overspray. Clean the area with water and allow it to dry. Use a tack rag to remove any dust, then apply the finish coat. Don't attempt to rub out or wax the repair area until the paint has dried completely (at least two weeks)

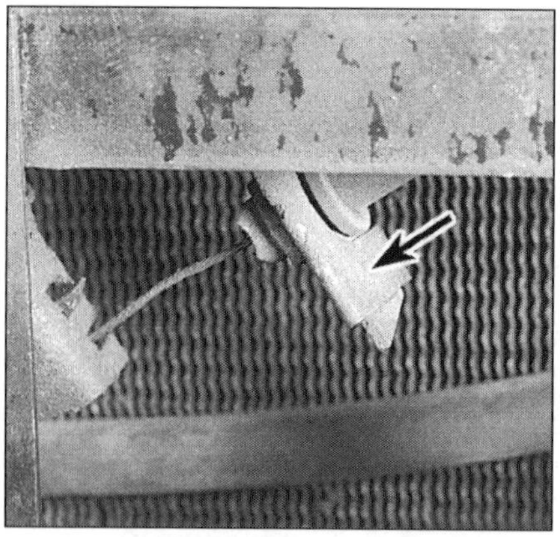

11.1 Using a small screwdriver pry off the retaining clip (arrow) and remove the cable from the latch assembly

11 Hood release latch and cable - removal and installation

Latch

Refer to illustrations 11.1 and 11.2

1 Disconnect the hood release cable by removing the cable retaining clip and disengaging the cable from the latch assembly **(see illustration).**

2 Scribe a line around the latch to aid alignment when installing, then remove the retaining bolts **(see illustration)**. Remove the latch.

3 Installation is the reverse of the removal procedure. **Note:** *Adjust the latch so the hood engages securely when closed and the hood bumpers are slightly compressed.*

Cable

4 Disconnect the hood release cable from the latch.

5 Attach a piece of thin wire or string to the end of the cable and unfasten all remaining cable retaining clips.

6 Working in the passenger compartment, remove the drivers side kick panel. Then remove the two release lever mounting bolts and detach the hood release lever.

7 Pull the cable and grommet rearward into the passenger compartment until you can see the wire or string. Ensure that the new cable has a grommet attached, then remove the old cable from the wire or string and replace it with the new cable.

8 Working in the engine compartment, pull the wire or string back through the firewall.

9 Installation is the reverse of the removal procedure. **Note:** *Push on the grommet with your fingers from inside the passenger compartment to seat the grommet in the firewall correctly.*

12 Trunk lid - removal, installation and adjustment

Note: *The trunk lid is heavy and somewhat awkward to remove and install - at least two people should perform this procedure.*

11.2 Remove the hood latch mounting bolts (arrows)

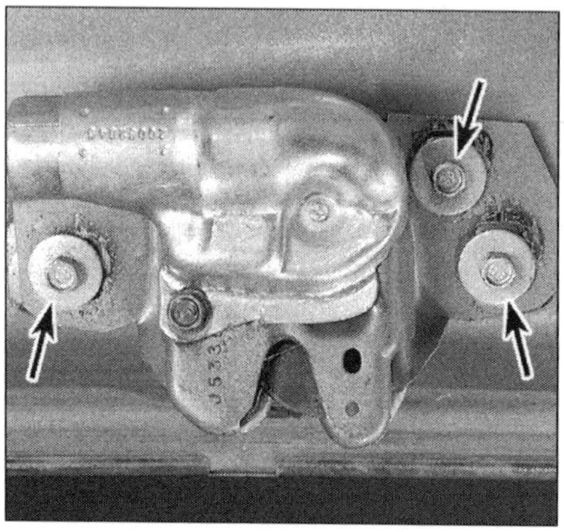

12.9 Loosen the bolts (arrows) and move the trunk latch assembly to adjust the closed position

Removal and installation

Refer to illustration 12.3

1 Open the trunk lid and cover the edges of the trunk compartment with pads or rags to protect the painted surfaces when the lid is removed.

2 Disconnect any cables or electrical connectors attached to the trunk lid that would interfere with removal. On some models it may be necessary to remove the bolts and detach the cover for access to the attaching bolts.

3 Use a felt-tip marker or scribe to make alignment marks around the trunk lid hinge **(see illustration)**.

4 While an assistant supports the lid, remove the hinge bolts from both sides and lift it off.

5 Installation is the reverse of the removal procedure. **Note:** *When reinstalling the trunk lid, align the hinge with the marks made during removal.*

Adjustment

Refer to illustration 12.9

6 Fore-and-aft and side-to-side adjustment of the trunk lid is done by moving the hood in relation to the hinge plate after loosening the bolts or nuts.

7 Scribe a line around the entire hinge

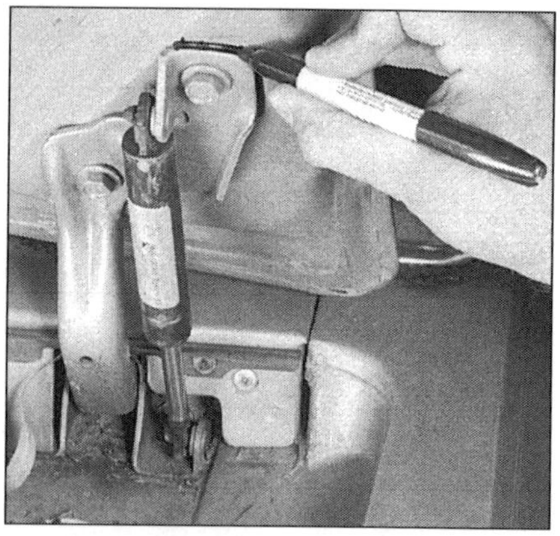

12.3 Use a felt tip marker or scribe to mark around the trunk lid hinge before loosening the bolts

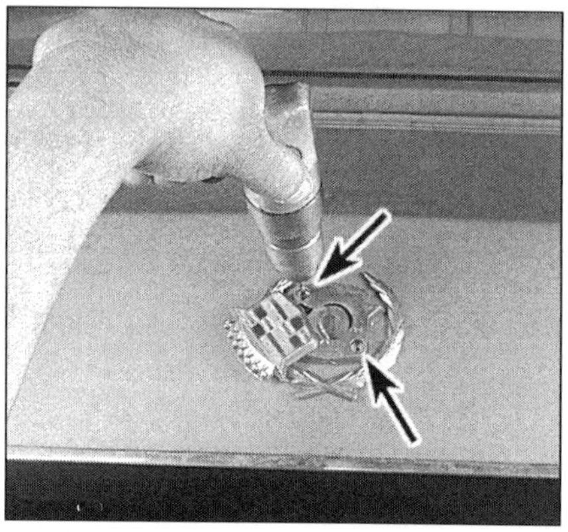

13.2 Drill out the two retaining rivets securing the emblem

plate as described earlier so you can judge the amount of movement.

8 Loosen the bolts or nuts and move the trunk lid into correct alignment. Move it only a little at a time. Tighten the hinge bolts or nuts and carefully lower the trunk lid to check the alignment.

9 If necessary after installation, the entire trunk lid latch assembly can be adjusted up and down as well as from side to side on the trunk lid so the lid closes securely and is flush with the rear quarter panels. To do this, scribe a line around the trunk lid latch mounting bolts to provide a reference point. Then loosen the bolts and reposition the latch assembly as necessary **(see illustration).** Following adjustment, retighten the mounting bolts.

10 The trunk lid latch assembly, as well as the hinges, should be periodically lubricated with white lithium-base grease to prevent sticking and wear.

13 Trunk lid lock cylinder - removal and installation

Refer to illustrations 13.2 and 13.3

1 Open the trunk. On older models with trunk lock emblems it will be necessary to remove the trunk latch for access to the

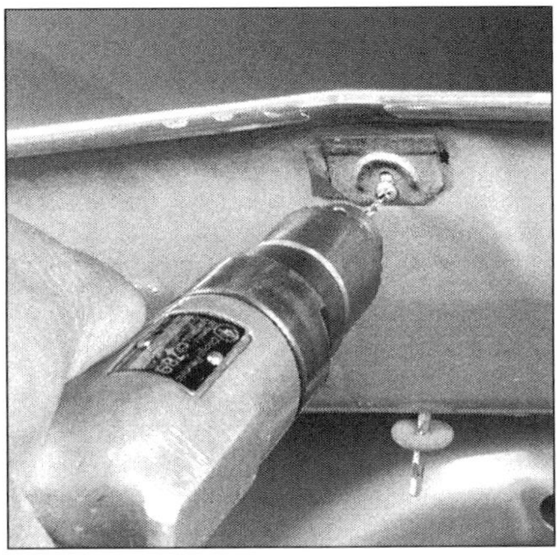

13.3 Drill out the rivet and remove the lock cylinder retaining clip

14.3a Locations of the automatic closing unit retaining bolts (arrows) - early models

14.3b Locations of the automatic closing unit retaining bolts (arrows) - later models

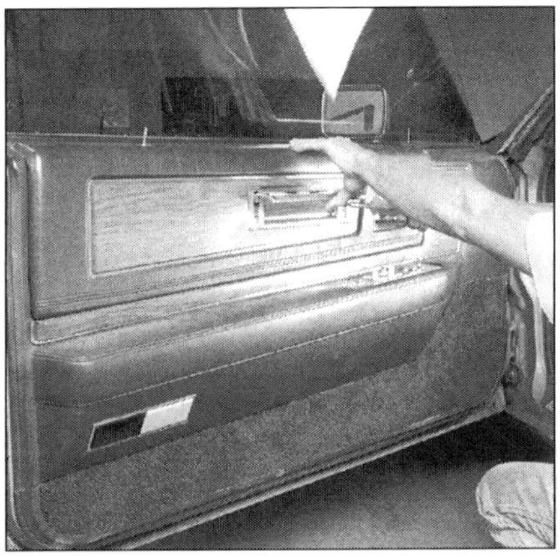

15.2 Remove all door handle and door pull trim plate screws

15.3a Lift out the switch control plate and unplug the connectors

15.3b Remove the door panel retaining screw in the switch opening

emblem retaining nuts.

2 Remove the emblem retaining rivets or nuts, then remove the emblem so the lock cylinder can be withdrawn **(see illustration)**.

3 Using a small drill bit, drill out the rivet securing the lock cylinder retaining clip **(see illustration)**, then pull the retaining clip off and remove the cylinder.

4 Installation is the reverse of the removal procedure.

14 Trunk lid latch and striker - removal and installation

Refer to illustrations 14.3a and 14.3b

1 On models with electrically operated automatic closing units, disconnect the negative cable from the battery. Unplug any electrical connectors and detach any cables from the latch assembly.

2 The trunk lid latch is retained by bolts which can readily be removed with a wrench **(see illustration 12.9)**. For adjustment procedures see Section 12.

3 On models with a manually operated trunk lid the striker is welded to the trunk and can not be adjusted. On models with an automatic closing unit the striker is retained with bolts **(see illustrations)**.

4 Disconnect all electrical connections, then detach the closing unit retaining bolts and remove the striker assembly from the vehicle.

5 Installation is the reverse of the removal procedure.

15 Door trim panel - removal and installation

Refer to illustrations 15.2, 15.3a, 15.3b, 15.5, 15.6a, 15.6b and 15.7

1 Lower the window all the way, then disconnect the negative cable from the battery.

2 Remove all door trim panel retaining screws, door handle cover plates and door pull/armrest assemblies **(see illustration)**, then unscrew the door lock knob.

3 Remove the retaining screw from the armrest switch plate, lift out the switch assembly and unplug it **(see illustration)**. Remove the retaining screw in the switch opening **(see illustration)**.

4 Early models have a two-piece door trim panel which requires lifting the upper half and detaching the electrical connector from the windshield wiper switch. After lifting the upper trim panel off, remove the lower trim panel retaining screws. **Note:** *These screws are sometimes hard to find, as they are often obscured by the carpet on the panel.*

5 Insert a putty knife or a trim panel removal tool between the trim panel and the door and disengage the retaining clips **(see illustration)**. Work around the outer edge until the panel is free. **Note:** *The trim panel retaining clips are approximately five to six*

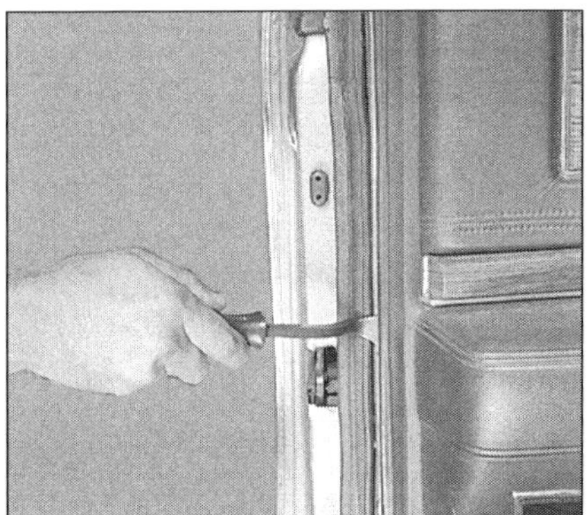

15.5 Insert a putty knife or trim tool between the door and the trim panel and carefully pry the clips out

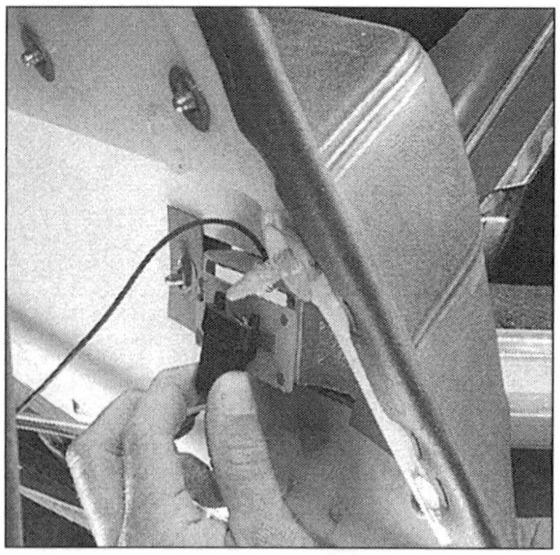

15.6a Lift the lower edge of the door trim panel, unplug the courtesy lamp electrical connector and fiber optic cable (if so equipped)

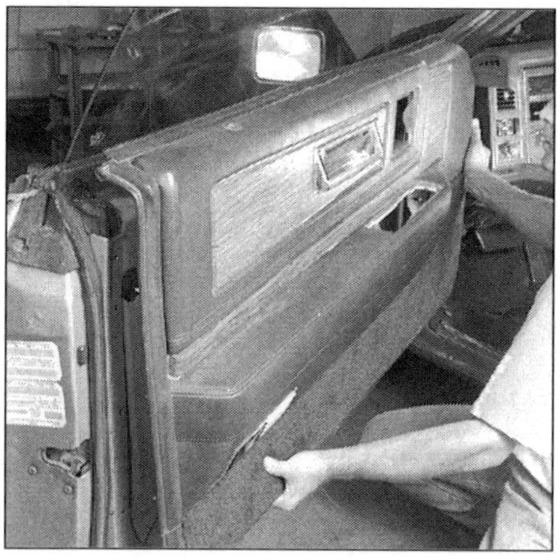

15.6b Lift up and away to remove the door trim panel

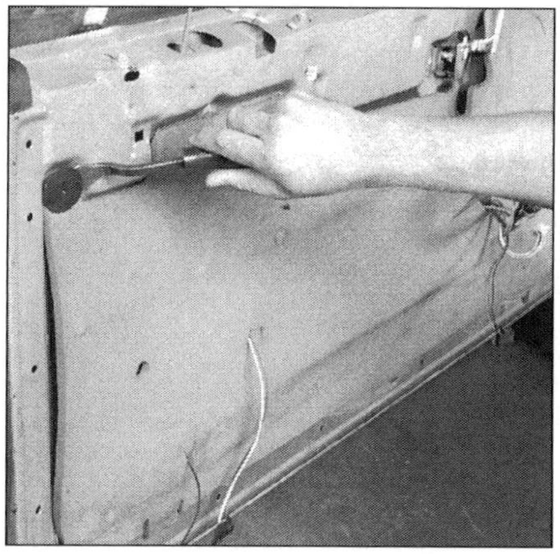

15.7 Pry out the retaining clips and carefully peel off the water deflector

inches apart - pry at the location of the clip only. Prying in between clips will result in a distorted or damaged door trim panel.

6 Once all of the clips are disengaged, detach the trim panel and unplug any electrical connectors **(see illustration).** To remove the door trim panel, lift up and away from the vehicle **(see illustration). Note:** *It may be necessary to gently hit the top of the panel with the heel of your hand to disengage the clips that secure the panel to the door sheetmetal.*

7 For access to the inner door, remove the water deflector either by prying out the retaining clips or carefully peeling back the plastic **(see illustration).**

8 Prior to installation of the door panel, be sure to reinstall any clips in the panel which may have come out during the removal procedure and remain in the door itself.

9 Installation is the reverse of the removal procedure. **Note:** *When installing door trim panel retaining clips, make sure the clips are lined up with their mating holes first, then gently tap in with the palm of your hand.*

16.4 To remove the latch assembly, unscrew the retaining screws (arrows) at the rear edge of the door. Note: In this photo the upper screw is obscured by the sticker

16 Door latch and lock cylinder assembly - removal and installation

Door latch

Refer to illustration 16.4

1 To remove the latch assembly, raise the window and remove the door trim panel and water deflector (see Section 15).

2 Working through the large access hole, disengage the inside door handle-to-latch rod and lock knob-to-latch rod.

3 On later models also disengage the outside door handle-to-latch rod and the door lock cylinder-to-latch rod. All of these rods are attached by either a spring clip or plastic clip. Spring clips can be removed by inserting a small screwdriver or pick to disengage the locating tang and then sliding the clip off. Plastic clips can be removed by unsnapping the portion engaging the connecting rod and then by pulling the rod out of its locating hole.

4 Remove the screws securing the latch to the door **(see illustration),** then remove the latch assembly from the door.

5 Installation is the reverse of the removal procedure.

Door lock cylinder

Refer to illustration 16.8

6 To remove the lock cylinder, raise the window, then remove the door trim panel and water deflector as described in Section 15.

7 Working through the large access hole, unplug the electrical or fiber optic connectors from the lock cylinder (If so equipped).

8 On later models also disengage the spring clip from the door lock cylinder-to-latch rod **(see illustration).**

9 Using a screwdriver, slide the lock cylinder retaining clip out of engagement and remove the lock cylinder from the door.

10 Installation is the reverse of the removal procedure.

17 Door handle - removal and installation

Outside handle

Refer to illustration 17.3

1 Different designs of outside door handles are used according to vehicle model and date of production, but removal is similar for all types.

2 Raise the window completely, remove the door trim panel (see Section 15) and peel away the upper corner of the water deflector.

3 Working through the large access hole, disengage the spring clip from the door handle-to-latch rod (later models only). Unscrew the mounting nuts or bolts to remove the

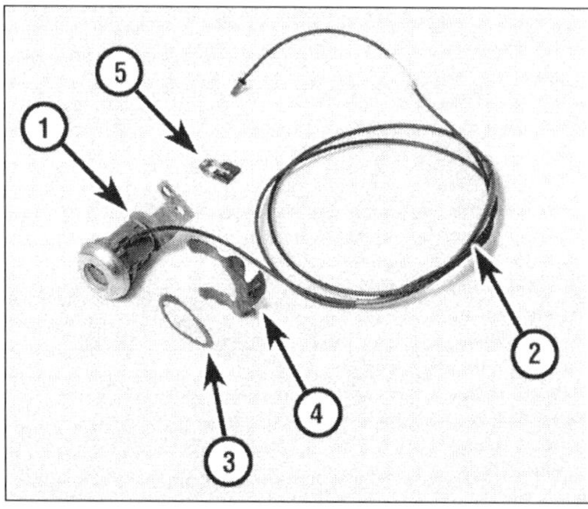

16.8 Typical door lock cylinder assembly

1 *Lock cylinder*
2 *Fiber optic cable*
3 *Body sealing gasket*
4 *Lock cylinder retaining clip*
5 *Lock rod retaining clip*

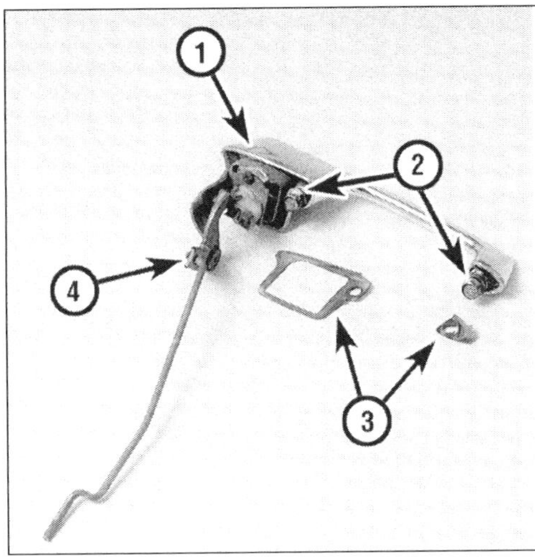

17.3 Typical outside door handle assembly

1 *Door handle*
2 *Mounting bolts*
3 *Body sealing gaskets*
4 *Spring clip*

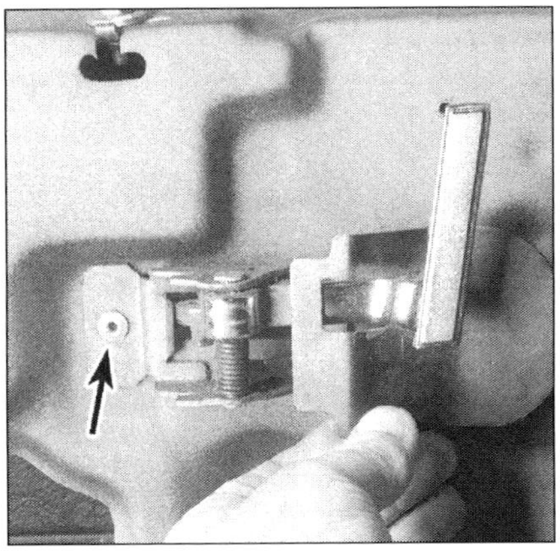

17.8 Drill out the rivet (arrow) then rotate the handle outward to gain access to the locking rod spring clip - on installation, install a new rivet with a hand-held riveting tool

handle and gaskets **(see illustration)**.

4 Installation is the reverse of the removal procedure.

Inside handle

Refer to illustration 17.8

5 Different designs of inside door handles are used according to vehicle model and date of production, but removal is similar for all types.

6 Raise the window completely, remove the door trim panel (see Section 15) and peel the water deflector down.

7 On early models remove the three door handle mounting bolts, then disengage the plastic clip from the door handle to latch rod and remove handle from the door.

8 On later models detach door handle air deflector and drill out the rivet securing the handle to the door frame, then disengage the spring clip from the door handle to latch rod and remove the handle **(see illustration)**.

9 Installation is the reverse of the removal procedure.

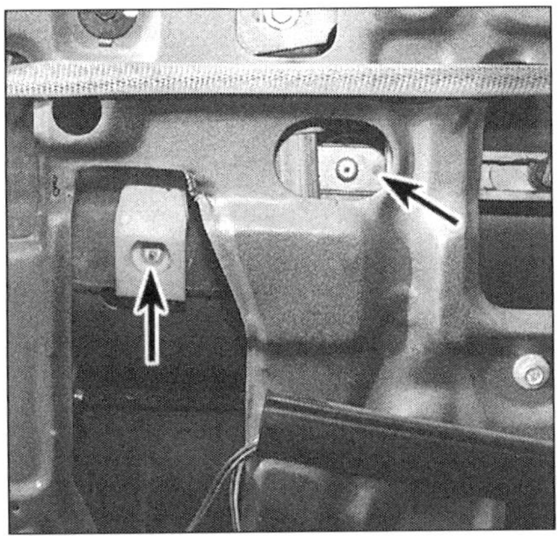

18.2a Drive out the center pins then drill out the rivets to detach the window from the regulator

18.2b Drill out the rivet from the front up-stop

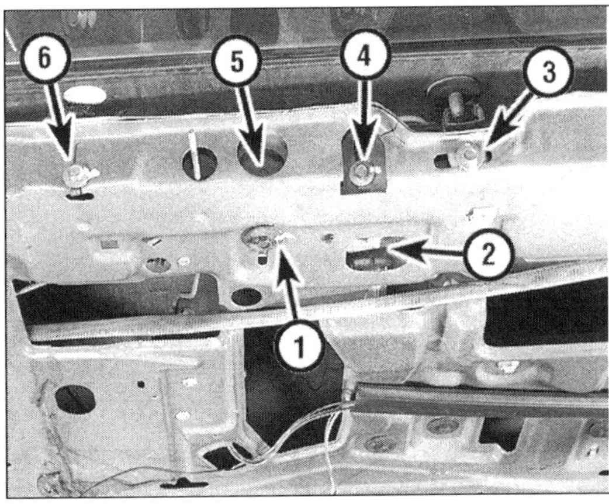

18.6 Typical door window glass adjustments

1 *Rear up-stop (up-and-down adjustment)*
2 *Rear vertical guide (side-to-side adjustment)*
3 *Front vertical guide (side-to-side adjustment)*
4 *Rear vertical guide (in-and-out adjustment)*
5 *Rear up stop (in-and-out adjustment)*
6 *Rear glass stabilizer adjustment*

18 Door window glass - removal, installation and adjustment

Removal and installation

Refer to illustrations 18.2a and 18.2b

1 Remove the door trim panel and water deflector (see Section 15).

2 Set the window to the half-raised position so the window retaining rivets or bolts are visible through the access holes in the door **(see illustrations)**.

3 Place a rag or towel over the window regulator to keep metal chips from entering the mechanism, then drill out the retaining rivets or remove the bolts.

4 Tilt the top of the glass until the rear roller is clear of the inner panel, then lift the glass from the door.

5 Installation is the reverse of the removal procedure. **Note:** *If you don't have a riveting tool, a bolt-on hardware package may be purchased. Do not install regular bolts, as glass breakage will occur.*

Adjustment

Refer to illustration 18.6

6 Adjust the channels, guides and stops as necessary to give smooth operation and proper closing before finally tightening their mounting nuts **(see illustration)**. It is sometimes easier to make these adjustments with the door closed. Make sure the door opens and closes properly and the window seats on the weatherstripping before installing the door trim panel.

19 Door window regulator - removal and installation

Refer to illustrations 19.3, 19.4a and 19.4b

1 Remove the door trim panel and water deflector (see Section 15).

2 Raise the window completely and prop it up in this position with two rubber

19.3 Mark the position of the inner panel cam bolts then remove the bolts and cam assembly

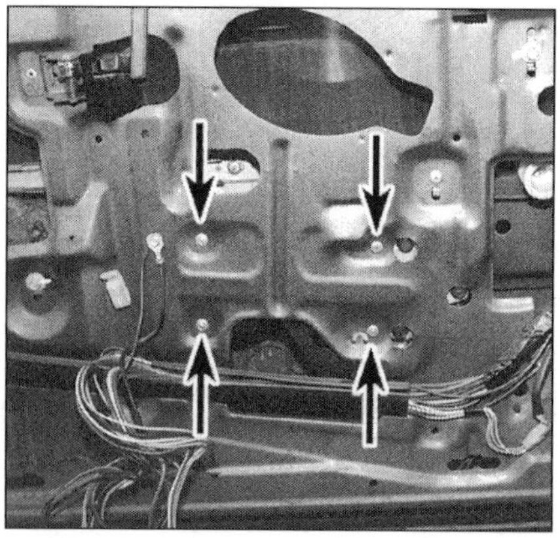

19.4a Locations of the window regulator retaining rivets (arrows) - 1979 and later models (except Seville)

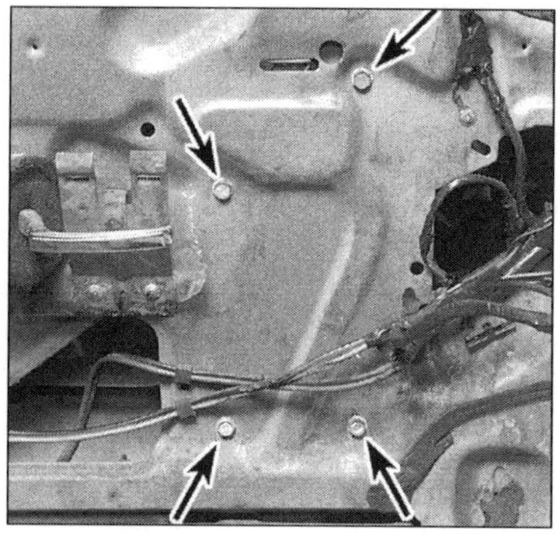

19.4b Locations of the window regulator retaining bolts (arrows) - 1978 and earlier models

doorstops wedged between the door opening and the glass. Do not proceed until you're sure the weight of the window is supported.

3 Use a felt-tip marker or white paint to make alignment marks around the bolt heads to insure proper alignment during installation, then remove the inner panel cam attaching bolts **(see illustration)** and remove the cam (this Step does not apply to Seville models).

4 Drill out the window regulator retaining rivets on later models or remove the bolts on early models **(see illustrations)**.

5 With electrically operated regulators, unplug the electrical connector from the motor.

6 On all models except Seville, slide the front upper arm from the sash, then slide the rear lift arm forward from the sash cam.

7 Slide the regulator to the rear of the door and withdraw it through the largest access hole.

8 On sector gear regulators, if the motor or regulator requires replacement, it is necessary to lock the sector gear to the regulator backplate. This can be done by fastening the sector gear to the backplate with a bolt and nut inserted through one of the holes in the backplate and sector gear. If none of the holes line up, drill a hole through the backplate and sector gear. **Warning:** *The regulator arms are under pressure and can cause serious injury if the motor is removed without locking the sector gear.* The motor and regulator can now safely be separated.

9 Installation is the reverse of the removal procedure.

20 Door - removal, installation and adjustment

Note: *The door is heavy and somewhat awkward to remove and install - at least two people should perform this procedure.*

Removal and installation

1 Lower the window completely in the door, then disconnect the negative cable from the battery.

20.11 Add or subtract washers so the striker has the proper depth to engage the latch correctly

2 Open the door all the way and support it on jacks or blocks covered with rags to prevent damaging the paint.

3 Remove the door trim panel and water deflector (see Section 15).

4 Unplug all electrical connections, ground wires and harness retaining clips from the door. **Note:** *It is a good idea to label all connections to aid the reassembly process.*

5 From the door side, detach the rubber conduit between the body and the door. Then pull the wiring harness through the conduit hole.

6 Mark around the door hinges with a pen or a scribe to facilitate realignment during reassembly.

7 Have an assistant hold the door, then remove the hinge to door bolts and lift the door off.

8 Installation is the reverse of the removal procedure.

Adjustment

Refer to illustrations 20.11 and 20.12

9 Having proper door to body alignment is a critical part of a well functioning door assembly. First check the door hinge pins and bushings for excessive play. **Note:** *If the door can be lifted 1/16-inch or more, the hinge pins and bushings should be replaced.*

20.12 Loosen the striker bolt and adjust it as necessary to provide positive latch engagement

10 Door to body alignment adjustments are made by loosening the hinge-to-body or hinge to door bolts and moving the door. Proper body alignment is achieved when the top of door is aligned with the top of front fender and rear quarter panel and the bottom of the door is aligned with the lower rocker panel. If these goals can't be reached by adjusting the hinge to body or hinge to door bolts, body alignment shims may have to be purchased and inserted behind the hinges to achieve correct alignment.

11 To adjust the door closed position, first check that the door latch is contacting the center of the latch striker bolt. If not, remove striker bolt and add or subtract washers to achieve correct alignment **(see illustration)**.

12 Finally, adjust latch striker bolt as necessary (up and down or sideways) to provide positive engagement with the latch mechanism **(see illustration)** and the door panel is flush with rear quarter panel.

21 Instrument cluster bezel - removal and installation

Warning: *Some models covered by this manual are equipped with a supplemental re-*

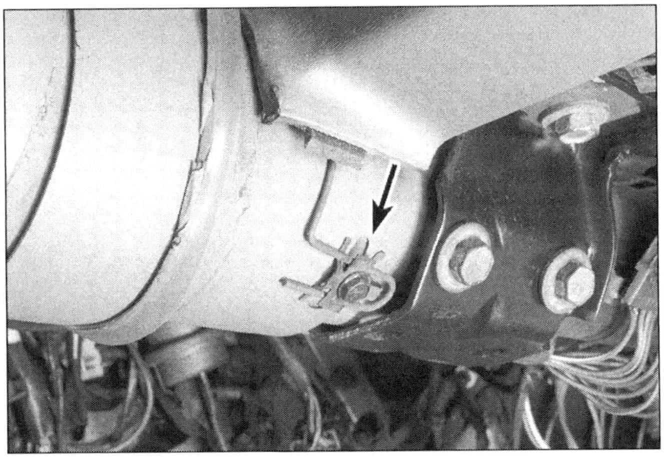

21.2 Loosen the bolt (arrow) and remove the shift indicating pointer

21.24 Unsnap the trim plate under the steering column, then remove the two screws along the top edge and two screws along the lower edge of the bezel

straint system, more commonly known as an airbag. Always disable the airbag before any repair in the vicinity of the dash or removal of the instrument panel assembly. To disable the airbag system place the ignition key in the lock position and disconnect the negative battery cable.

Caution: *Always disconnect negative battery cable before removing any electrical connections.*

1 Disconnect the cable from the negative terminal of the battery.

Eldorado (1971 through 1973 models)

Refer to illustration 21.2

Note: *The instrument cluster bezel on these models is a integral part of the dashboard assembly which requires removing the dash pad and the lower steering column trim panel (see Section 22).*

2 Working on the right-hand side of the steering column at the bottom of the bezel, detach the shift indicator retaining bolt and remove the shift indicating pointer **(see illustration)**. **Note:** *The radio, instrument cluster, climate control panel and other various accessory switches (headlight, cruise control, rear window defogger and convertible top switch, if equipped) must be removed through the dash pad area or lowered through the steering column area before instrument cluster bezel can be removed.*

3 After all the instruments and accessory switches have been removed detach the four steering column upper trim panel screws, then detach the remaining four bezel bolts located at each corner and remove the bezel.

4 Installation is the reverse of the removal procedure.

Toronado (1971 through 1973 models)

5 The instrument panel on these models has a three-piece design which consists of an instrument cluster bezel and a left and right control panel bezel.

6 The Toronado requires removing the instrument cluster (see Chapter 12) before the instrument cluster bezel can be removed.

7 After the instrument cluster has been removed detach the two bezel retaining screws located on the front side and two bezel retaining screws located on the back side, then remove the bezel from the instrument cluster.

8 To remove the left-hand control panel bezel, detach the lower steering column trim panel (see Section 22). Then pry out the flood lamp assemblies with a small screwdriver and remove the four control panel retaining screws.

9 Pull the control panel rearward, then disconnect all electrical connectors and air conditioning vent hoses and remove the bezel from the vehicle.

10 To remove the right-hand control panel bezel, detach the radio control knobs and remove the two hex nuts securing the radio. Then pry out the flood lamp assemblies with a small screwdriver and remove the four control panel retaining screws.

11 Looking up underneath the dash detach the screws securing the control panel-to-radio brace located on the right-hand side of the radio.

12 Pull the control panel rearward, then disconnect all electrical connectors and air conditioning vent hoses and remove the bezel from the vehicle.

13 Installation is the reverse of the removal procedure.

Eldorado (1974 through 1978 models)

14 The instrument panel on these models has a four-piece design which consists of a two-piece instrument cluster bezel and a left and right control panel bezel.

15 The Eldorado requires detaching six retaining screws on the instrument cluster bezel and removing the upper half of the bezel, then spread the steering column seal at the bottom and remove the lower half of the bezel.

16 To remove the left-hand control panel bezel detach the lower steering column trim panel (see Section 22) and four bezel retaining screws, then remove the bezel from the vehicle.

17 To remove the right-hand control panel bezel, detach the radio control knobs and remove the two hex nuts securing the radio. Working through the access hole located in the top of the glove compartment remove the remaining four retaining screws from the back side of the bezel.

18 Pull the control panel rearward, then disconnect all electrical connectors and remove the bezel from the vehicle.

19 Installation is the reverse of the removal procedure.

Toronado (1974 through 1978 models)

20 The instrument cluster bezel on these models has a one piece design which requires detaching three retaining screws from the lens, then pull the lens rearward and lift up and out to unlock the retaining tabs at the bottom of the lens.

21 Detach four more retaining screws from the bezel and lift it away from the instrument cluster.

22 Installation is the reverse of the removal procedure.

Eldorado and Seville (1979 through 1985 models)

Refer to illustrations 21.24, 21.25, 21.26 and 21.27

23 The instrument panel on these models has a three-piece design which consists of an instrument cluster bezel and a left and right control panel bezel.

24 The Eldorado and Seville require unsnapping the bezel trim plate directly below the steering column, then remove the four instrument cluster bezel retaining screws **(see illustration)**.

25 Move the tilt steering column to its lowest position and spread apart the rubber seal surrounding the steering column. Tilt the upper edge of the instrument cluster bezel

21.25 Tilt the top edge rearward then lift the bezel up and out

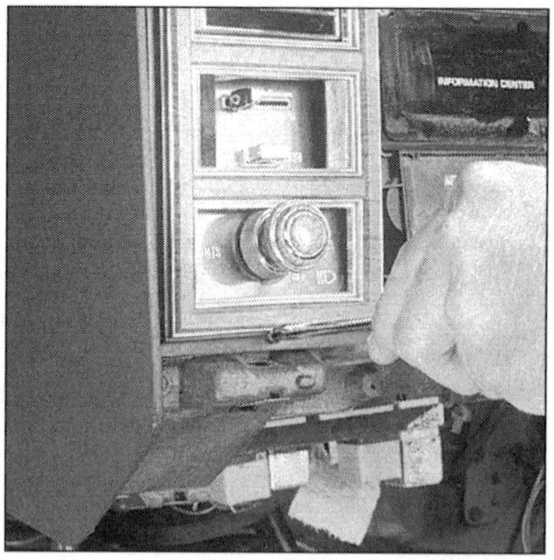

21.26 Remove the retaining screws along the top edge and the bottom edge

21.27 Remove the hex nuts (arrows) located behind the radio control knobs

rearward and lift it up and out **(see illustration)**.

26 To remove the left-hand control panel bezel, detach the two retaining screws and remove the bezel **(see illustration)**.

27 To remove the right-hand control panel bezel, detach the radio control knobs and remove the 5/8 inch hex nuts **(see illustration)**. Unscrew the two retaining screws along the upper edge and remove the bezel.

28 Installation is the reverse of the removal procedure.

Riviera (1979 through 1985 models)

29 The instrument panel on these models has a two piece design which consists of an instrument cluster bezel and a right control panel bezel.

30 The Riviera requires detaching two screws to remove the ALDL connector (if equipped) then detach four more retaining screws and remove the bezel trim plate directly below steering column.

31 Remove the headlight switch knob, then looking up at the bottom of the instrument cluster bezel remove the remaining four retaining screws.

32 Tilt the steering column to its lowest position, then pull the bottom of the bezel rearward while simultaneously unclipping the top of the bezel and remove it from the vehicle.

33 To remove the right-hand control panel bezel, detach the radio control knobs. Using both hands carefully pry off the right hand bezel and remove it from the vehicle.

34 Installation is the reverse of the removal procedure.

Toronado (1979 through 1985 models)

35 The instrument cluster bezel on these models has a one piece design which requires detaching two screws to remove the ALDL connector (if equipped) then detach four more retaining screws and remove the bezel trim plate directly below steering column.

36 Remove the headlight switch and radio control knobs. Looking up at the bottom of the instrument cluster bezel, remove the remaining four retaining screws.

37 Tilt the steering column to its lowest position, then pull the bottom of the bezel rearward while simultaneously unclipping the top of the bezel and remove from the vehicle.

38 Installation is the reverse of the removal procedure.

22 Dashboard trim panels and glove box- removal and installation

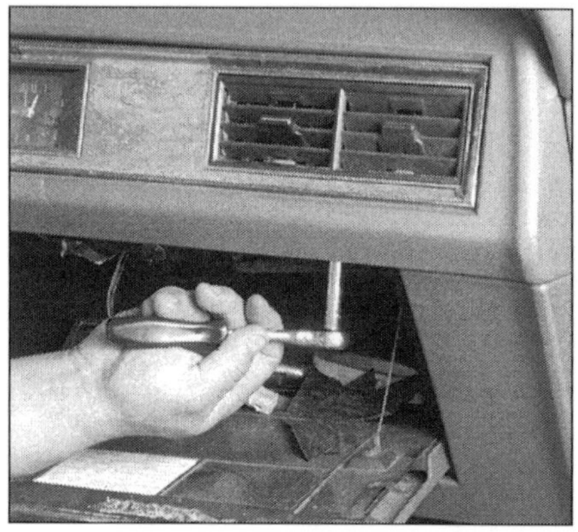

22.1 Remove the retaining screws along the top edge of the glove compartment

Warning: *Some models covered by this manual are equipped with a supplemental restraint system, more commonly known as an airbag. Always disable the airbag before any repair in the vicinity of the dash or removal of the instrument panel assembly. To disable the airbag system place the ignition key in the lock position and disconnect the negative battery cable.*

Eldorado (1971 through 1973 models)

Refer to illustrations 22.1, 22.2 and 22.3

1 Disconnect the cable from the negative terminal of the battery. To remove the dash

22.2 Disconnect all electrical connectors and lift the dash pad up and out

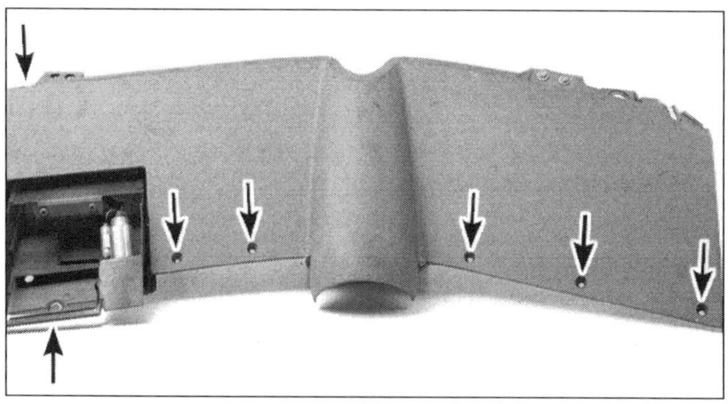

22.3 Remove the eight retaining screws (arrows) from the lower trim panel

22.26 Remove the dash pad retaining screws located in the defroster grilles

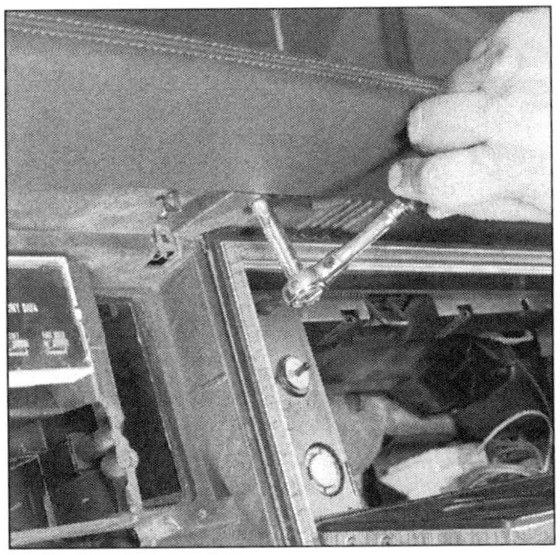
22.27 Unbolt the four screws on the bottom side of the dash pad

22.28 Lower the sound insulator panels and remove the courtesy lamp electrical connectors (arrow)

pad, detach the two retaining screws in the glove compartment **(see illustration)**, then remove four more retaining screws at the top of the instrument cluster bezel.

2 Tilt the steering column to its lowest position, then lift the leading edge of the dash pad, detach all electrical connections and remove the dash pad from the vehicle (**see illustration)**.

3 To remove the lower steering column trim panel, detach the ash tray trim cover and remove the ash tray, then detach the eight retaining screws securing the lower trim panel (**see illustration)**.

4 Disconnect all electrical connectors and remove the trim panel.

5 To remove the glove box detach the four door retaining screws and remove the door, then detach five more screws securing the glove box liner and remove liner through the door opening.

6 Installation is the reverse of the removal procedure.

Toronado (1971 through 1973 models)

7 Disconnect the cable from the negative terminal of the battery. The dash pad on these models is an integral part of the dashboard and requires removing every major component in the dash assembly, such as the instrument cluster and bezel (see Chapter 12), left and right-hand control panels (see Section 21), and the lower left and right-hand trim panels (below) to access the fasteners used to secure the dash pad.

8 Looking into the right-side air conditioning vents, detach the two retaining screws, then using both hands pull rearward to remove the clock bezel.

9 To remove the lower left-hand trim panel detach the five retaining screws, then pull the bezel rearward to detach the parking brake cable and remove the bezel from the vehicle.

10 To remove the lower right-hand trim panel, open the glove compartment and remove the ash tray. Detach the four retaining screws located at the upper edge of the glove box and one retaining screw at the far right-hand edge of the trim panel.

11 Looking up at the bottom of the lower trim panel detach five retaining screws, then detach the last two retaining screws above the ash tray and remove the trim panel and glove box assembly from the vehicle.

12 After all the major components and trim panels have been removed from the dashboard assembly, detach the eight dash pad retaining screws located along the lower edge. Working through the large access holes, detach six nuts from the backside of the dash pad and lift the dash pad up and out.

13 Installation is the reverse of the removal procedure.

Eldorado (1974 through 1978 models)

14 Disconnect the cable from the negative terminal of the battery. To remove the dash pad, detach the air conditioning vent grilles by compressing the release tabs and pulling outward, then remove the three nuts located in the vent openings.

15 Looking up at the bottom of the dash pad, remove five more retaining screws, then detach all electrical connections and remove the dash pad from the vehicle.

16 To remove the lower steering column trim panel, remove the eight retaining screws and remove trim panel from the dash.

17 To remove the glove box, detach the three door hinge retaining screws and the door stop cable retaining screw and remove the door assembly, then detach five more screws securing the glove box liner and remove the liner through the door opening.

18 Installation is the reverse of the removal procedure.

Toronado (1974 through 1978 models)

19 Disconnect the cable from the negative terminal of the battery. To remove the dash pad use a small screwdriver to pry out speaker grilles and remove the speakers, then detach the map light retaining screws and remove the map lights.

20 Detach three screws in the glove box compartment, two screws from the instrument cluster bezel, one screw from the lower left corner of dash pad and two more retaining screws in the speaker openings, then lift the dash pad up and out to remove it.

21 To remove the lower steering column trim panel detach two retaining screws at each end of the trim panel and lightly pull the upper trim panel covers off to access the lower trim panel retaining screws.

22 Looking up at the bottom of the lower trim panel, detach two retaining screws at each end of the panel, then detach eight more screws along the top edge of the trim panel.

23 Detach all electrical connections and the air conditioning vent hoses, then remove the trim panel from the vehicle.

24 To remove the glove box, detach the four door-hinge retaining screws. Lift the door upward to guide the door stops out and remove the door assembly.

25 Installation is the reverse of the removal procedure.

Eldorado and Seville (1979 through 1985 models)

Refer to illustrations 22.26, 22.27, 22.28 and 22.29

26 Disconnect the cable from the negative terminal of the battery. To remove the dash pad, unscrew the four retaining screws at the lower edge of the windshield (**see illustration)**.

27 Looking up at the bottom side of the dash pad, detach the remaining four screws, then remove the dash pad from the vehicle (**see illustration)**.

28 To remove the lower steering column trim panel, remove the screws from the driver and passenger side sound insulator panels located underneath the dashboard **(see illustration).**

29 Open the ash tray and disconnect the cigarette lighter electrical connector. Remove

22.29 Remove the retaining screws behind the ash tray

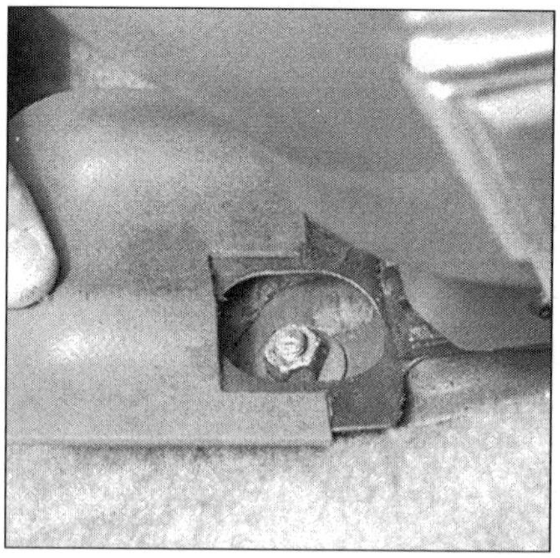

23.1 Remove the trim covers to access the seat mounting nuts

the two retaining screws behind the ash tray **(see illustration)** and the remaining screws from the lower trim panel, then lower the panel away from the dash.

30 To remove the glove box, detach the five screws securing the glove box liner and remove the liner, then detach the three screws from the glove box door hinge and remove the glove box door.

31 Installation is the reverse of the removal procedure.

Riviera and Toronado (1979 through 1985 models)

32 The dash pad on these models is an integral part of the dashboard which requires removing every major component in the dashboard assembly, such as the instrument cluster and bezel (see Chapter 12), instrument control panels (see Section 21), the radio (see Chapter 12), and the lower trim panels (below) to access the fasteners used to secure the dash pad.

33 Disconnect the cable from the negative terminal of the battery. To access the lower steering column trim panels, remove the screws from the driver and passenger side sound insulator panels located underneath the dashboard.

34 On Riviera models, open the ash tray and disconnect the cigarette lighter electrical connector. Remove the two retaining screws behind the ash tray and the remaining six screws from the lower trim panel, then lower the panel away from dashboard.

35 On Toronado models, remove the four screws from the lower steering column cover and remove the cover.

36 After all the major components and trim panels have been removed from the dashboard assembly, remove the dash pad retaining screws located along the lower edge of the windshield. Looking up underneath the dashboard remove the screws and lift the dash pad up and out to remove it from the vehicle.

37 To remove the glove box, open the door and remove the four retaining screws located at each corner, then remove the screw securing the lamp. Using both hands, pull the glove box assembly and trim panel rearward to remove them from the vehicle.

38 Installation is the reverse of the removal procedure.

23 Seats - removal and installation

Refer to illustration 23.1

Front seats

1 Remove the seat trim covers to access the front and rear mounting nuts **(see illustration)**.

2 Tilt the seat back enough to access the underside and disconnect the electrical connectors, then remove the seat.

3 Installation is the reverse of the removal procedure. **Note:** *Tighten the seat mounting nuts securely.*

Rear seat

4 Disengage the rear seat cushion by pushing the front edge rearward and lifting up, then remove the cushion from the vehicle.

5 Remove the retaining bolts at the lower edge of the seat back then lift the seat back upward and out to remove it from the vehicle.

6 Installation is the reverse of the removal procedure.

Chapter 12
Chassis electrical system

Contents

1 General information

The electrical system is a 12-volt, negative ground type. Power for the lights and all electrical accessories is supplied by a lead/acid-type battery which is charged by the alternator.

This Chapter covers repair and service procedures for the various electrical components not associated with the engine. Information on the battery, alternator, ignition system and starter motor can be found in Chapter 5. It should be noted that when portions of the electrical system are serviced, the negative battery cable should be disconnected from the battery to prevent electrical shorts and/or fires.

2 Electrical troubleshooting - general information

A typical electrical circuit consists of an electrical component, any switches, relays, motors, fuses, fusible links or circuit breakers related to that component and the wiring and electrical connectors that link the component to both the battery and the chassis. To help you pinpoint an electrical circuit problem, wiring diagrams are included at the end of this book.

Before tackling any troublesome electrical circuit, first study the appropriate wiring diagrams to get a complete understanding of what makes up that individual circuit. Trouble spots, for instance, can often be narrowed down by noting if other components related to the circuit are operating properly. If several components or circuits fail at one time, chances are the problem is in a fuse or ground connection, because several circuits are often routed through the same fuse and ground connections.

Electrical problems usually stem from simple causes, such as loose or corroded connections, a blown fuse, a melted fusible link or a bad relay. Visually inspect the condition of all fuses, wires and connections in a problem circuit before troubleshooting it.

If testing instruments are going to be utilized, use the diagrams to plan ahead of time where you will make the necessary connections in order to accurately pinpoint the trouble spot.

The basic tools needed for electrical troubleshooting include a circuit tester or voltmeter (a 12-volt bulb with a set of test leads can also be used), a continuity tester, which includes a bulb, battery and set of test leads, and a jumper wire, preferably with a circuit breaker incorporated, which can be used to bypass electrical components. Before attempting to locate a problem with test instruments, use the wiring diagram(s) to decide where to make the connections.

Voltage checks

Voltage checks should be performed if a circuit is not functioning properly. Connect one lead of a circuit tester to either the negative battery terminal or a known good ground. Connect the other lead to an electrical connector in the circuit being tested, preferably nearest to the battery or fuse. If the bulb of the tester lights, voltage is present, which means that the part of the circuit between the electrical connector and the battery is problem free. Continue checking the rest of the circuit in the same fashion. When you reach a point at which no voltage is present, the problem lies between that point and the last test point with voltage. Most of the time the problem can be traced to a loose connection. **Note:** *Keep in mind that some circuits receive voltage only when the ignition key is in the Accessory or Run position.*

Finding a short

One method of finding shorts in a circuit is to remove the fuse and connect a test light or voltmeter in its place to the fuse terminals. There should be no voltage present in the circuit. Move the wiring harness from side-to-side while watching the test light. If the bulb goes on, there is a short to ground somewhere in that area, probably where the insulation has rubbed through. The same test can be performed on each component in the circuit, even a switch.

Ground check

Perform a ground test to check whether a component is properly grounded. Disconnect the battery and connect one lead of a self-powered test light, known as a continuity tester, to a known good ground. Connect the other lead to the wire or ground connection being tested. If the bulb goes on, the ground is good. If the bulb does not go on, the ground is not good.

Continuity check

A continuity check is done to determine if there are any breaks in a circuit - if it is passing electricity properly. With the circuit off (no power in the circuit), a self-powered continuity tester can be used to check the circuit. Connect the test leads to both ends of the circuit (or to the "power" end and a good ground), and if the test light comes on the circuit is passing current properly. If the light

3.1 The fuse block is located under the left side of the instrument panel (later model with miniaturized fuses shown)

doesn't come on, there is a break somewhere in the circuit. The same procedure can be used to test a switch, by connecting the continuity tester to the switch terminals. With the switch turned On, the test light should come on.

Finding an open circuit

When diagnosing for possible open circuits, it is often difficult to locate them by sight because oxidation or terminal misalignment are hidden by the electrical connectors. Merely wiggling an electrical connector on a sensor or in the wiring harness may correct the open circuit condition. Remember this when an open circuit is indicated when troubleshooting a circuit. Intermittent problems may also be caused by oxidized or loose connections.

Electrical troubleshooting is simple if you keep in mind that all electrical circuits are basically electricity running from the battery, through the wires, switches, relays, fuses and fusible links to each electrical component (light bulb, motor, etc.) and to ground, from which it is passed back to the battery. Any electrical problem is an interruption in the flow of electricity to and from the battery.

3 Fuses - general information

Refer to illustrations 3.1 and 3.3

1 The electrical circuits of the vehicle are protected by a combination of fuses, circuit breakers and fusible links. The fuse block is located under the left side of the instrument panel, near the steering column **(see illustration)**.

2 Each of the fuses is designed to protect a specific circuit, and the various circuits are identified on the fuse panel itself.

3 Miniaturized fuses are employed in the fuse block on later models, while earlier models employ glass-tube-type fuses. These compact fuses, with blade terminal design, allow fingertip removal and replacement. Glass-tube-type fuses are easiest to remove with an inexpensive special tool that's available at most auto parts stores. If an electrical component fails, always check the fuse first. A blown fuse is easily identified through the clear plastic or glass body. Visually inspect the element for evidence of damage **(see illustration)**. If a continuity check is called for, check from terminal to terminal on glass-tube-type fuses. On miniaturized fuses, the blade terminal tips are exposed in the fuse body for easy continuity checks.

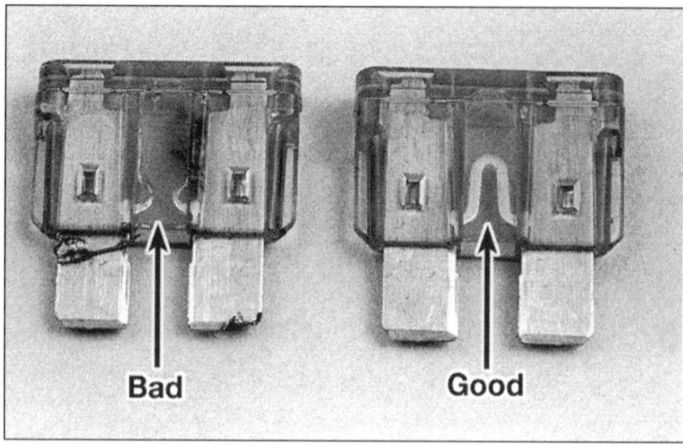

3.3 To check for a blown fuse, pull it out and inspect it visually - the fuse on the left is blown - the one on the right is good (miniaturized fuses shown)

4 Be sure to replace blown fuses with the correct type. Fuses of different ratings are physically interchangeable, but only fuses of the proper rating should be used. Replacing a fuse with one of a higher or lower value than specified is not recommended. Each electrical circuit needs a specific amount of protection. The amperage value of each fuse is molded into the fuse body. If the replacement fuse immediately fails, don't replace it again until the cause of the problem is isolated and corrected. In most cases, the cause will be a short circuit in the wiring caused by a broken or deteriorated wire.

4 Fusible links - general information

Some circuits are protected by fusible links. Fusible links are used in circuits which are not ordinarily fused, such as the ignition circuit.

Although the fusible links appear to be a heavier gauge than the wire they are protecting, the appearance is due to the thick insulation. All fusible links are four wire gauges smaller than the wire they are designed to protect.

Fusible links cannot be repaired, but a new link of the same size wire can be put in its place. The procedure is as follows:

a) Disconnect the negative cable from the battery.

b) Disconnect the fusible link from the wiring harness.

c) Cut the damaged fusible link out of the wiring just behind the electrical connector.

d) Strip the insulation back approximately 1/2-inch.

e) Position the electrical connector on the new fusible link and crimp it into place.

f) Use rosin core solder at each end of the new link to obtain a good solder joint.

g) Use plenty of electrical tape around the soldered joint. No wires should be exposed.

h) Connect the battery ground cable. Test the circuit for proper operation.

5 Circuit breakers - general information

Circuit breakers protect components such as power windows, power door locks and headlights.

On some models the circuit breaker resets itself automatically, so an electrical overload in a circuit breaker protected system will cause the circuit to fail momentarily, then come back on. If the circuit doesn't come back on, check it immediately. Once the condition is corrected, the circuit breaker will resume its normal function. Some circuit breakers must be reset manually.

6 Relays - general information and testing

General information

Several electrical accessories in the vehicle, such as the fuel injection system (models so equipped), power windows, power door locks, power seats, cruise control and air conditioning use relays to transmit the electrical signal to the component. Relays use a low-current signal (the control circuit, which is opened and closed by the circuit's switch) to turn the high-current flow in the main circuit on and off. If the relay is defective, that component will not operate properly.

The various relays are grouped together in several locations. Some relays are grouped together in the engine compartment.

If a faulty relay is suspected, it can be removed and tested using the procedure below or by a dealer service department or a repair shop. Defective relays must be replaced as a unit.

Testing

1 It's best to refer to the wiring diagram for the circuit to determine the proper hook-ups for the relay you're testing. However, if you're not able to determine the correct hook-up from the wiring diagrams, you may be able to determine the test hook-ups from the information that follows.

Relays with four terminals

2 On most relays with four terminals, two of the four terminals are for the relay's *control circuit* (they connect to the relay's coil which, when energized, closes the large contacts to complete the circuit). The other two terminals are for the relay's *power circuit* (they are connected together within the relay when the control-circuit coil is energized).

3 Relays are sometimes marked as an aid to help you figure out which two terminals are for the control circuit and which are for the power circuit. As a general rule, the two thicker wires connected to the relay are for the power circuit; the two thinner wires are for the control circuit.

4 Remove the relay from the vehicle and check for continuity between the relay's power circuit terminals. There should be no continuity.

5 Connect a fused jumper wire between one of the two control circuit terminals and the positive battery terminal. Connect another jumper wire between the other control circuit terminal and ground. When the connections are made, the relay should click. On some relays, polarity may be critical, so, if the relay doesn't click, try swapping the jumper wires on the control circuit terminals.

6 With the jumper wires connected, check for continuity between the power circuit terminals. Now there should be continuity.

7 If the relay fails any of the above tests, replace it.

Relays with three terminals

8 If the relay has three terminals, it's best to check the wiring diagram to determine which terminals connect to which of the relay's components. Most three-terminal relays are either case-grounded or externally grounded.

9 On a case-grounded relay, one side of the relay's control circuit grounds through the relay case, eliminating the need for the fourth terminal. This type of relay requires the case to be securely connected to a good chassis ground. Check this type of relay the same way you would a four-terminal relay, noting that one of the control circuit's terminals is actually the relay case.

10 On an externally grounded relay, one of the relay's terminals is connected to a positive power source. We'll call this the *battery power* terminal. Inside the relay, the battery power terminal is connected to one side of both the relay's power and control circuits. Another terminal is connected to the other side of the control circuit; the circuit is completed through a switch to ground. The third terminal is connected to the other side of the power circuit; it's grounded at the circuit's load component. This type of three-terminal relay is sometimes a plug-in type with no connection between the case and ground.

11 To check an externally grounded relay, remove it from the vehicle and check for continuity between the relay's battery power terminal and its power circuit terminal. There should be no continuity.

12 Connect a fused jumper wire between the battery power terminal and the positive battery terminal. Connect another jumper wire between the relay's control circuit terminal and ground. The relay should click.

13 With the jumper wires in place, connect a test light between the relay's power circuit terminal and ground. The test light should light. If the relay fails any of these tests, replace it.

7 Turn signal/hazard flasher - check and replacement

Refer to illustration 7.4

Turn signal flasher

1 The turn signal flasher, a small canister-shaped unit located under the dash in a clip near the steering column, flashes the turn signals.

2 When the flasher unit is functioning properly, an audible click can be heard during its operation. If the turn signals fail on one side or the other and the flasher unit does not make its characteristic clicking sound, a faulty turn signal bulb is indicated.

3 If both turn signals fail to blink, the problem may be due to a blown fuse, a faulty flasher unit, a broken switch or a loose or open connection. If a quick check of the fuse box indicates that the turn signal fuse has blown, check the wiring for a short before installing a new fuse.

4 To replace the flasher, simply unplug it and pull it out of the clip **(see illustration)**.

5 Make sure that the replacement unit is identical to the original. Compare the old one to the new one before installing it.

6 Installation is the reverse of removal.

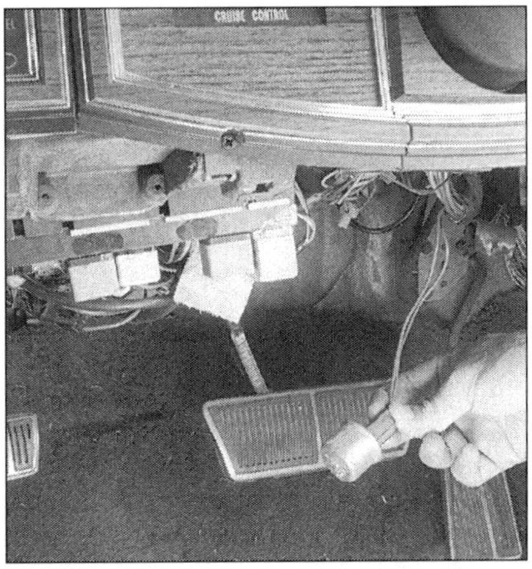

7.4 The turn signal flasher is located to the right side of the steering column - the knee bolster may have to be removed for access

Hazard flasher

7 The hazard flasher, a small canister-shaped unit, located in the fuse block, flashes all four turn signals simultaneously when activated.

8 The hazard flasher is checked in a fashion similar to the turn signal flasher (see Steps 2 and 3).

9 To replace the hazard flasher, reach under the dash and pull the flasher from the fuse block or clip.

10 Make sure the replacement unit is identical to the one it replaces. Compare the old one to the new one before installing it.

11 Installation is the reverse of removal.

8 Turn signal switch - removal and installation

Refer to illustrations 8.3a, 8.3b, 8.3c, 8.4, 8.5, 8.6a, 8.6b, 8.7a, and 8.7b

1 Disconnect the negative battery cable and remove the steering wheel (see Chapter 10).

2 Remove the steering column trim cover located below the dashboard.

3 The lockplate will now have to be removed from the steering column. This is held in place with a snap-ring or clip which fits into a groove in the steering shaft. The lockplate must be depressed to relieve pressure on the snap-ring clip. A special U-shaped tool which fits on the shaft should be used to depress the lockplate as the snap-ring is removed from its groove **(see illustrations)**.

8.3a Use a special tool (available at auto parts stores) to compress the lockplate for access to the retaining clip

8.3b With the lockplate compressed, remove the retaining clip

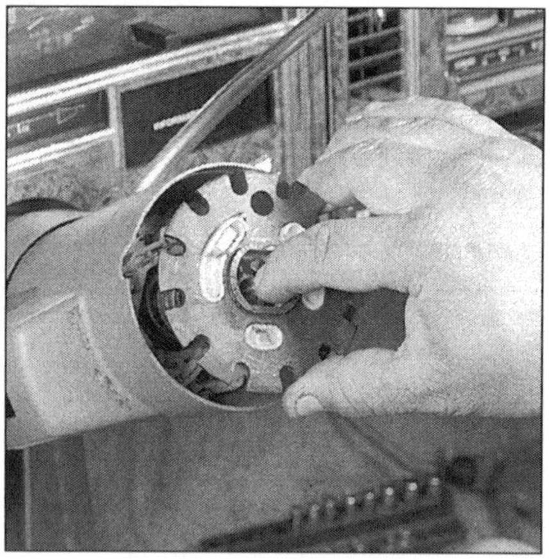

8.3c Lift the lockplate out

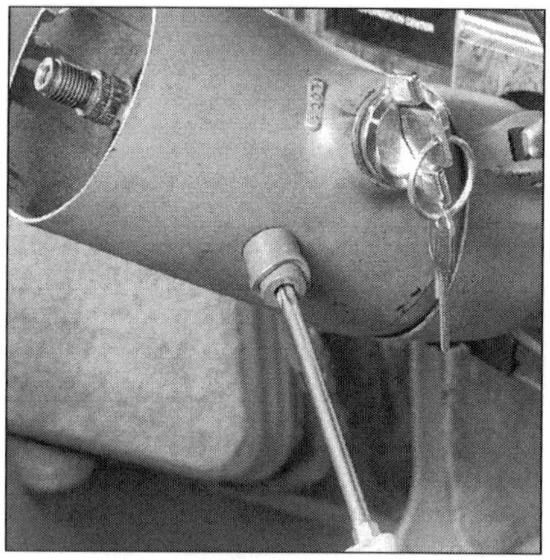

8.4 Remove the hazard warning knob screw and the knob

8.5 Remove the spring assembly

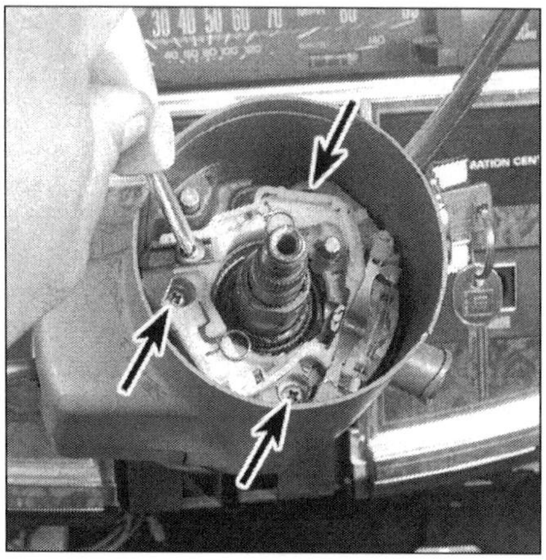

8.6a Remove the turn signal lever screw; the locations of the switch screws are shown by arrows - to get at the upper screw in this photo, the top of the switch must be rotated

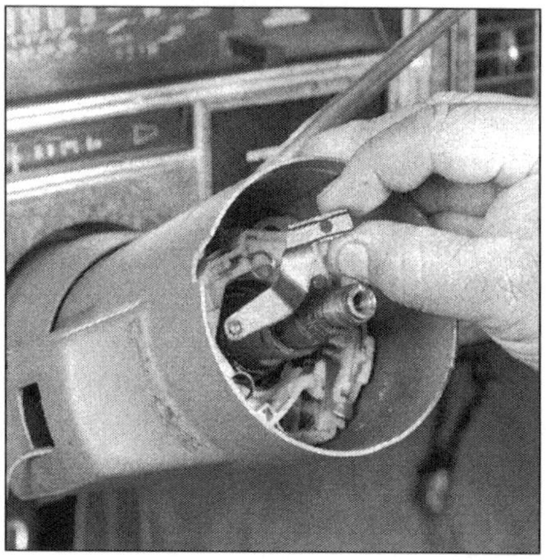

8.6b Lift out the turn signal internal lever

4 Use a Phillips-head screwdriver to unscrew the hazard warning knob **(see illustration)**.

5 Remove the upper bearing preload spring and thrust washer off the end of the shaft **(see illustration)**.

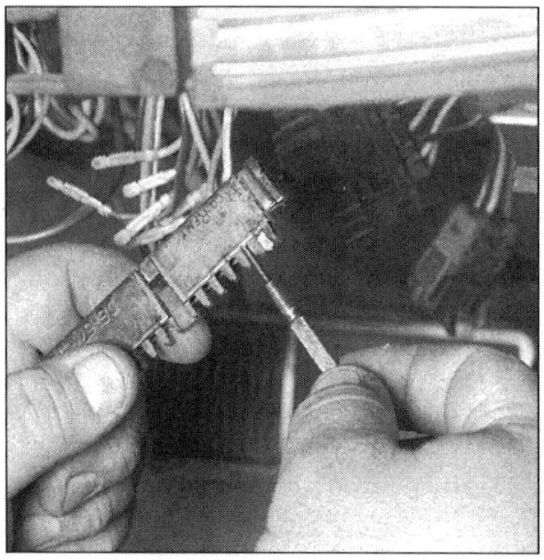

8.7a The turn signal switch electrical connector is located under the dash near the steering column - unplug it as shown and detach the turn signal switch wires (if necessary, mark them so they can be returned to the same locations on the connector)

6 Remove the screw that secures the turn-signal switch actuating lever and remove the lever **(see illustrations)**. Remove the three screws that secure the plastic turn signal switch assembly to the steering column bowl. It may be necessary to rotate the top portion of the switch to gain access to all the screws.

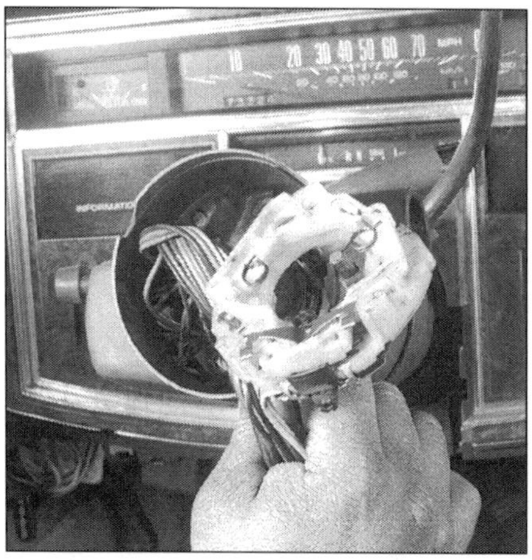

8.7b Pull the turn signal switch out, carefully drawing the wiring harness through the steering column

7 Pull the switch connector out of the bracket on the steering column jacket. Mark the locations of the wires at the switch connector, then use a small screwdriver to detach the connector terminals **(see illustration)**. Feed the wiring connector up through the column support bracket and pull the switch, wiring harness and connectors out the top of the steering column **(see illustration)**.

8 Installation is the reverse of removal. If using a new switch, try to feed the wiring harness through the steering column with the connector still attached.

9 Ignition switch/key lock cylinder - removal and installation

Refer to illustrations 9.3, 9.4 and 9.5

Lock cylinder

1 The lock cylinder is located on the upper right-hand side of the steering column. It should be removed only in the Run position,

9.3 **Lift off the buzzer switch and clip with needle-nose-pliers**

9.4 **The lock cylinder is held in place by a screw**

9.5 **Pull the lock cylinder straight out**

otherwise damage to the warning buzzer switch may occur.

2 Remove the steering wheel (Chapter 10) and turn signal switch (see Section 8). **Note:** *The turn signal switch need not be fully removed provided that it is pushed to the rear far enough for it to be slipped over the end of the shaft. Do not pull the harness out of the column.*

3 Insert the key and place the lock cylinder in the Run position, then use needle-nose pliers to remove the buzzer switch **(see illustration)**.

4 Remove the lock cylinder retaining screw **(see illustration)**.

5 Remove the lock cylinder by turning the key to the Start position, then pulling the assembly straight out **(see illustration)**.

6 To install, rotate the lock cylinder and align the cylinder key with the keyway in the steering column housing.

7 Push the lock all the way in and install the retaining screw.

8 Install the remaining components, referring to the appropriate Sections.

Ignition switch

Refer to illustrations 9.13 and 9.14

9 Disconnect the negative cable at the battery.

10 Place the ignition switch in the Lock position. If the key lock cylinder has been removed, pull the actuating rod up until a definite stop can be felt, then move it down one detent.

11 Remove the lower finish panel from beneath the steering column .

12 Remove the two nuts that secure the steering column to the lower edge of the dash assembly, then carefully lower the steering column down and rest the steering wheel on the seat.

13 Disconnect the electrical connector at the switch, then remove the ignition switch retaining screws **(see illustration)** and lift the switch out of the steering column jacket.

14 Prior to installation, make sure the ignition switch is in the Lock position **(see illustration).**

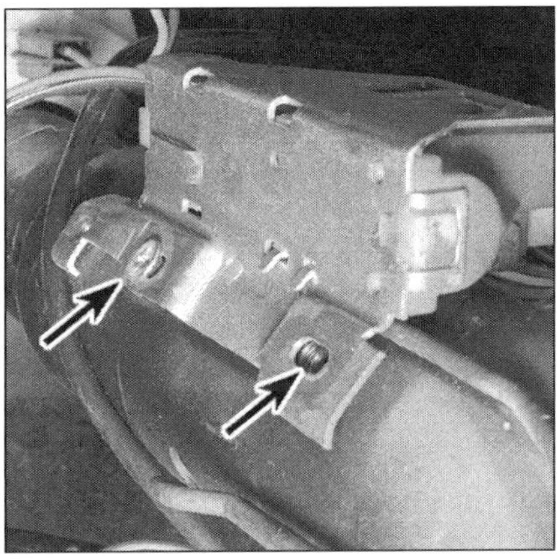

9.13 **The ignition switch is located on top of the lower end of the steering column - disconnect the electrical connector, remove these two screws (arrows) and lift it off**

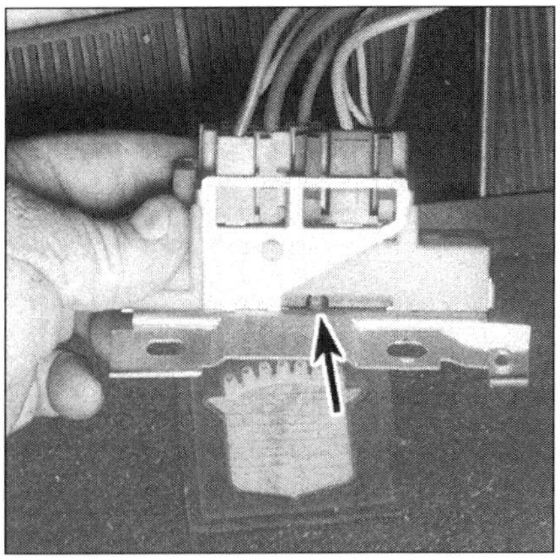

9.14 **The slot in the ignition switch slider (arrow) must be all the way forward when installing the switch so the actuating rod will engage it**

15 Connect the actuating rod to the switch.

16 Press the switch into position and install the screws.

17 Raise the steering column into position and install and tighten the nuts.

10 Headlight switch - check and replacement

Check

Refer to illustrations 10.3 and 10.4

Note: *The wiring diagrams in Chapter 12 may help with the following checks. Keep in mind that power wires are generally larger in diameter and brighter colors, where ground wires are usually smaller in diameter and darker colors. When checking for voltage, the probe of a grounded 12-volt test light may be touched to each terminal at a connector until it lights; this verifies voltage (power) at that terminal.*

1 Check the headlight circuit fuse first (see Section 3).

2 If the fuse is OK, disconnect the negative battery cable and remove the headlight switch (see below).

3 To check the interior lights dimmer switch function, connect an ohmmeter to the switch and rotate the switch handle to make sure the reading goes up and down smoothly **(see illustration)**. If there is no reading or the reading does not go up and down smoothly, replace the switch with a new one.

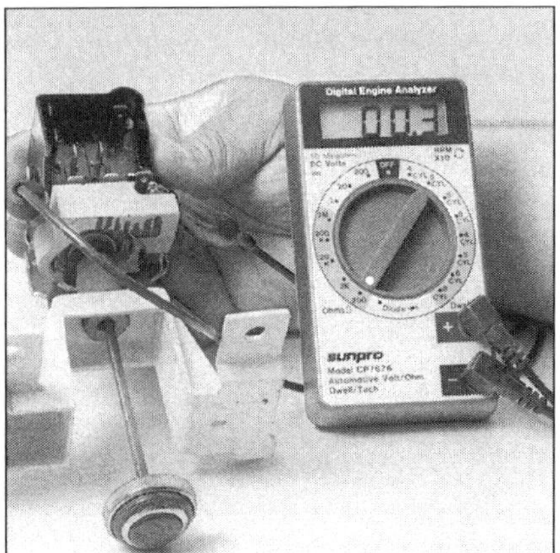

10.3 **Use an ohmmeter to check the interior lights dimmer switch for continuity**

10.4 With the electrical connector attached and the battery reconnected, check for voltage (power) to the switch and from the switch to the headlights/parking lights

4 To check the headlight/parking light on/off function, reconnect the headlight switch and battery and check for power into and out of the switch **(see illustration).** If there's power to the switch but no power out to the lights, replace the switch. If there's power into and out of the switch, the switch is probably good. If there's no power to the switch, there's a problem in the wiring harness to the switch.

Replacement

Earlier models

Refer to illustration 10.8

5 Remove the instrument panel bezel (see Chapter 11).

6 Unplug the switch electrical connector and illumination bulb.

7 Pull the headlight control knob to the On position.

8 Reach up under the instrument panel and depress the button that holds the knob and shaft in place, then slide the knob and shaft out of the switch **(see illustration).** Unscrew the escutcheon (retaining nut on the instrument panel, around the knob shaft).

9 Remove the retaining screw, lower the switch, disconnect the upper bulb, then remove the switch. Installation is the reverse of removal.

Later models

10 Remove the instrument panel bezel and left control panel bezel (see Chapter 11).

11 Remove the mounting screws, detach the switch and unplug the electrical connector.

12 Installation is the reverse of removal.

11 Windshield wiper/washer switch - check and replacement

Refer to illustration 11.4

Check

1 Checking the wiper switch is covered in

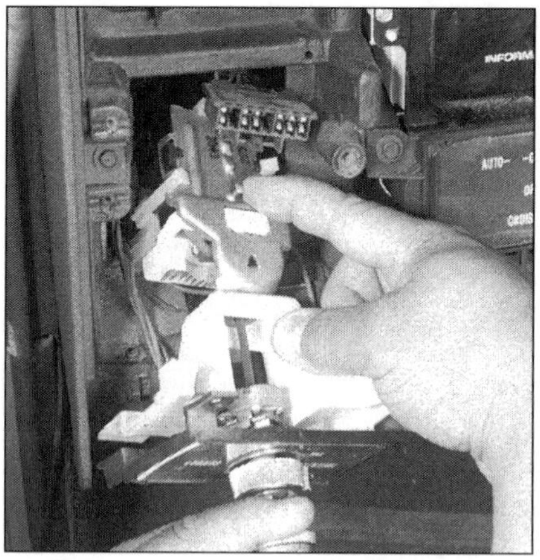

10.8 Reach up under the dash to depress the button and remove the headlight knob and shaft (switch shown removed for clarity)

Section 18 as part of the procedure for checking the wiper circuit.

Replacement

2 On early models with the switch mounted in the door panel, remove the upper door trim panel (see Chapter 11).

3 On all other models, remove the left control panel bezel from the instrument panel (see Chapter 11).

4 Remove the mounting screws, detach the switch and unplug the electrical connector **(see illustration).**

5 Installation is the reverse of removal.

12 Dimmer switch - check and replacement

1 Disconnect the negative battery cable.

Floor-mounted switch

Check

2 Pull back the carpet, remove the bolts and detach the switch.

3 Use an ohmmeter to check for continuity between the terminals. Connect one lead to the center terminal and the other lead to the low beam terminal. There should be continuity with the switch in either position. Repeat the test with the high beam terminal - it should only have continuity in one position. Replace the switch if it fails either test.

Replacement

4 Plug the electrical connector into the new switch, place the switch in position and install the bolts. Tighten the bolts securely.

Steering column mounted switch

Check

Refer to illustration 12.7

5 The dimmer switch is located on the

11.4 Remove the bolts, pull the wiper switch out, then detach the electrical connector

lower steering column and connected to the turn signal switch by an actuating rod. Remove the bolts that secure the steering column to the dash frame, then lower the steering column for access.

6 Unplug the electrical connector from the switch.

7 Use an ohmmeter to check for continuity between the terminals **(see illustration).** Connect one lead to the center terminal and the other to the low beam terminal. Repeat the test with the high beam terminal it should only have continuity in one position. If it doesn't, replace the switch.

Replacement

8 Remove the bolts, detach the switch from the steering column and unplug the electrical connector.

9 Place the new switch in position and install the bolts finger tight.

10 Move the switch as necessary to take up any slack in the actuator control rod, then tighten the bolts securely. Plug in the electrical connector and install the steering column bolts.

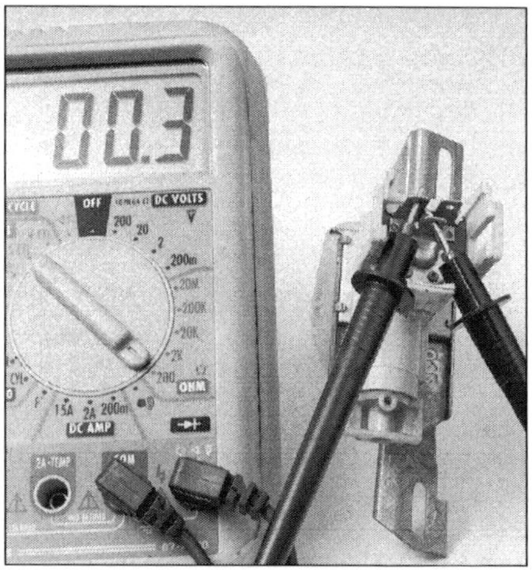

12.7 The dimmer switch can be checked with an ohmmeter, as described in the text

13.2 Use a Phillips-head screwdriver to remove each headlight bezel screw (arrow)

13.3 Remove the retaining screws (don't confuse them with the adjustment screws) and lift the headlight ring off (round headlight shown, rectangular headlight attaches the same way)

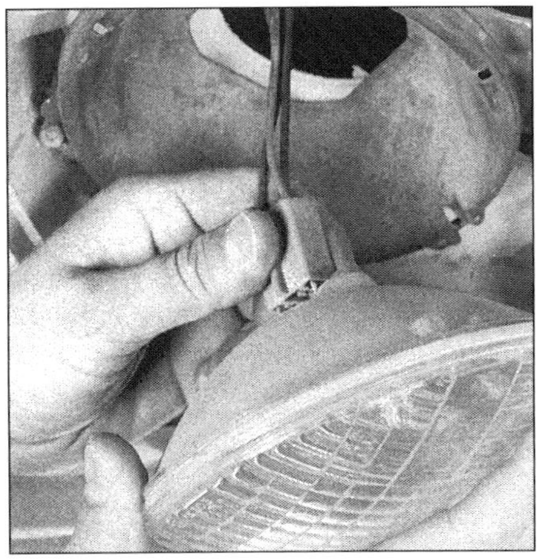

13.4 Pull the headlight forward and unplug the connector

13 Headlight - removal and installation

Refer to illustrations 13.2, 13.3 and 13.4

1 Whenever replacing a headlight, be careful not to turn the spring-loaded adjusting screws of the headlight, as this will alter the aim.

2 Remove the headlight bezel screws and remove the bezel **(see illustration)**.

3 Remove the screws which secure the retaining ring and withdraw the ring. Support the light as this is done **(see illustration)**.

4 Pull the headlight out slightly and disconnect the electrical connector from the rear of the light. Remove the light from the vehicle **(see illustration)**.

5 Position the new unit close enough to connect the electrical connector. Make sure that the numbers molded into the lens are at the top.

6 Install the retaining ring with its mounting screws and spring.

7 Install the bezel and check the headlights for proper operation and adjustment. If the adjusting screws were not altered, the new headlight will not need to have its aim adjusted.

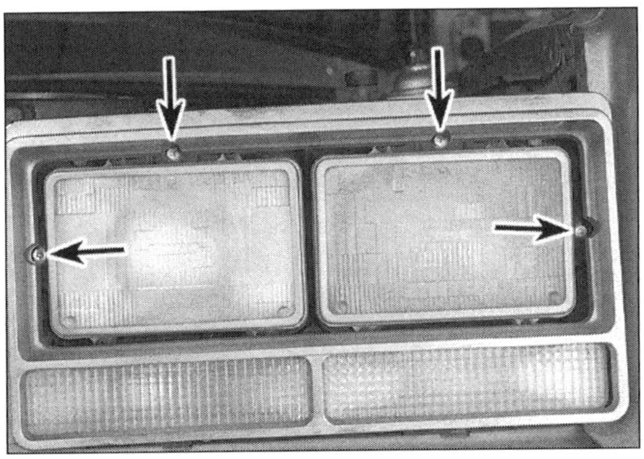

14.1 The headlight vertical adjustment screw is located at the top of the headlight and the horizontal screw is on the side of the headlight (arrows) (rectangular headlight shown, round headlight similar)

14 Headlights - adjustment

Refer to illustrations 14.1 and 14.2

Note: *The headlights must be aimed correctly. If adjusted incorrectly they could blind the driver of an oncoming vehicle and cause a serious accident or seriously reduce your ability to see the road. The headlights should be checked for proper aim every 12 months and any time a new headlight is installed or front end body work is performed. It should be emphasized that the following procedure is only an interim step which will provide temporary adjustment until the headlights can be adjusted by a properly equipped shop.*

1 Sealed beam headlights have two spring loaded adjusting screws, one on the top controlling up-and-down movement and one on the side controlling left-and-right movement **(see illustration)**.

2 There are several methods of adjusting the headlights. The simplest method requires a blank wall 25-feet in front of the vehicle and a level floor **(see illustration)**.

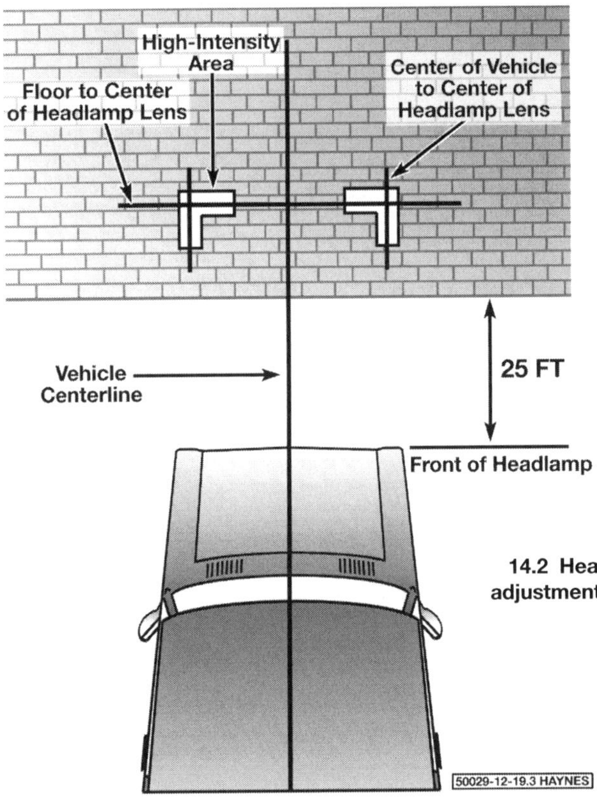

14.2 Headlight adjustment details

15.1a Some lenses are held in place by screws

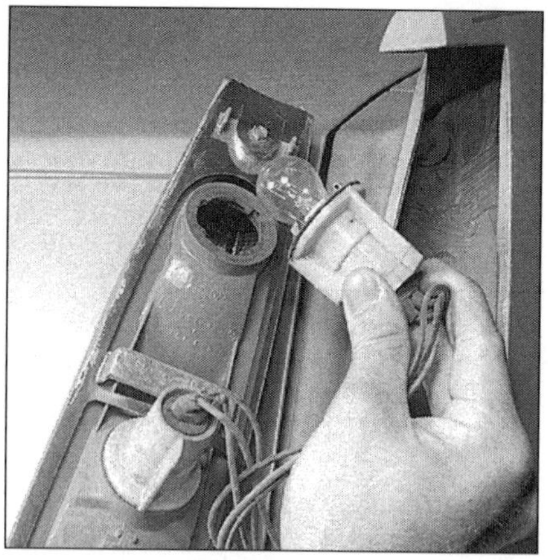

15.1b Pull out the housing/lens assembly, rotate the bulb holder and lift it out

15.2 Some lenses can be pried out with a small screwdriver

3 Position masking tape vertically on the wall in reference to the vehicle centerline and the centerlines of both headlights.

4 Position a horizontal tape line in reference to the centerline of all the headlights. **Note:** *It may be easier to position the tape on the wall with the vehicle parked only a few inches away.*

5 Adjustment should be made with the vehicle sitting level, the gas tank half-full and no unusually heavy load in the vehicle.

6 Starting with the low beam adjustment, position the high intensity zone so it's two inches below the horizontal line and two inches to the right of the headlight vertical line. Adjustment is made by turning the top adjusting screw clockwise to raise the beam and counterclockwise to lower the beam. The adjusting screw on the side should be used in the same manner to move the beam left or right.

7 With the high beams on, the high intensity zone should be vertically centered with the exact center just below the horizontal line. **Note:** *It may not be possible to position the headlight aim exactly for both high and low beams. If a compromise must be made, keep in mind that the low beams are the most used and have the greatest effect on driver safety.*

8 Have the headlights adjusted by a dealer service department or service station at the earliest opportunity.

15 Bulb replacement

Refer to illustrations 15.1a, 15.1b, 15.2, 15.3a, 15.3b and 15.5

1 The lenses of many lights are held in place by screws, which makes it a simple procedure to gain access to the bulbs **(see illustrations)**.

2 On some lights the lenses are held in place by clips. The lenses can be removed either by unsnapping them or by using a small screwdriver to pry them off **(see illustration)**.

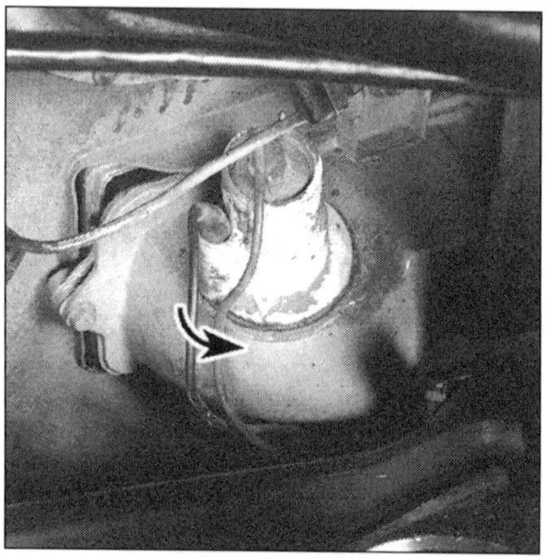

15.3a Rotate the bulb holder counterclockwise to remove it

15.3b Push in and rotate the bulb counterclockwise to remove it from the holder

3 Some bulb holders are removed by rotating and lifting them out of the back of the housing **(see illustrations)**.

4 Several types of bulbs are used. Some are removed by pushing in and turning them counterclockwise. Others can simply be unclipped from the terminals or pulled straight out of the socket.

5 To gain access to the instrument panel lights, the instrument cluster will have to be removed first **(see illustration)**.

16 Radio and speakers - removal and installation

Radio

Refer to illustrations 16.4 and 16.5

1 Disconnect the negative cable at the battery.

2 On earlier models, remove the control knobs and bezel. Use a deep socket to

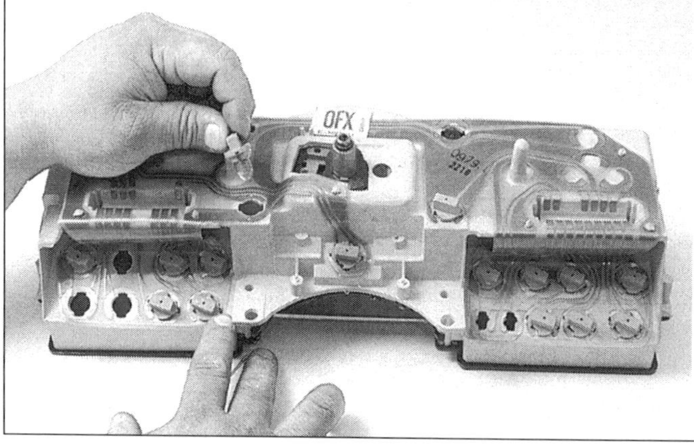

15.5 Remove the instrument cluster bulbs by rotating them 1/4-turn counterclockwise and pulling straight out

16.4 Remove the bolts securing the radio

remove the control shaft nuts and washers.

3 On later models, remove the radio trim cover (see Chapter 11).

4 Remove the mounting bolts and pull the radio from the instrument panel until the wiring can be reached and disconnected **(see illustration)**.

5 Lower the radio, unplug the connectors and remove it from the instrument panel **(see illustration)**.

6 Installation is the reverse of removal. Make sure all speaker leads, the antenna lead and any other connectors are plugged in before turning on the power to the radio.

Front speakers

Refer to illustration 16.8

7 Remove the instrument panel pad (see Chapter 11).

8 Remove the bolts and detach the speaker, then lift the speaker out and unplug the electrical connector **(see illustration)**.

9 Installation is the reverse of removal.

Rear speakers

10 Open the trunk, remove the retainers and detach the baffles for access to the rear speakers.

11 Unplug the connectors and remove the retaining nuts or unhook the retaining clips, then remove the speakers.

12 Installation is the reverse of removal.

17 Antenna - replacement

1 Lower the antenna. Disconnect the negative cable at the battery.

2 Block the rear wheels, raise the front of the vehicle and support it securely on jackstands.

3 Remove the front wheel. Remove the wheelhouse from the fender for access.

4 Use needle-nose pliers to unscrew the retaining nut securing the antenna to the fender. Pad the area around the antenna base so the pliers don't scratch the fender if they slip off.

5 Remove the radio and unplug the antenna wire, then attach a piece of thin wire or string, approximately four-feet long, to the wire and pull it through into the wheel well.

16.5 Pull the radio out, support it and unplug the connectors

6 Remove the bolts and guide the antenna and motor assembly out through the fenderwell.

7 Installation is the reverse of removal. Attach the string or wire to the new antenna mast, guide the assembly up into position and hold it before installing the bolts and retaining nut.

18 Windshield wiper motor and circuit - checking and motor replacement

Refer to illustrations 18.2, 18.9 and 18.11

Wiper motor circuit check

Note: *The wiring diagrams in Chapter 12 may help with the following checks. Keep in mind that power wires are generally larger in diameter and brighter colors, where ground wires are usually smaller in diameter and darker colors. When checking for voltage, the probe of a grounded 12-volt test light may be touched to each terminal at a connector until it lights; this verifies voltage (power) at the terminal.*

1 **If the wipers work slowly,** make sure the battery is in good condition and has a strong charge (see Chapter 1). If the battery is in good condition, remove the wiper motor (see below) and operate the wiper arms by hand. Check for binding linkage and pivots. Lubricate or repair the linkage or pivots as necessary. Reinstall the wiper motor. If the wipers still operate slowly, check for loose or corroded connections, especially the ground connection. If all connections look OK, replace the motor.

2 **If the wipers don't work at all**, check the fuse. If the fuse is OK, connect a jumper wire between the wiper motor and ground, then retest. If the motor works now, repair the ground connection. If the wipers still don't work, turn on the wipers and check for voltage at the motor **(see illustration).** If there's no voltage at the motor, remove the motor and check it off the vehicle with fused jumper wires from the battery. If the motor now works, check for binding linkage (see Step 1 above). If the motor still doesn't work, replace it. If there's no voltage at the motor, check for voltage at the switch. If there's no voltage at the switch, check the wiring between the switch and fuse panel for continuity. If the wiring is OK, the switch is probably bad.

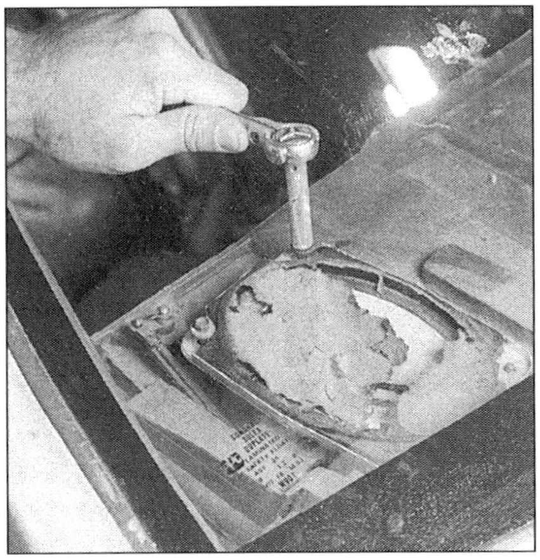

16.8 Remove the bolts, detach the speaker and unplug the electrical connector

3 **If the wipers only work on one speed,** check the continuity of the wires between the switch and motor. If the wires are OK, replace the switch.

4 **If the interval (delay) function is inoperative,** check the continuity of all the wiring between the switch and motor. If the wiring is OK, replace the interval module.

5 **If the wipers stop wherever they are when the switch is turned off (fail to park),** check for voltage at the wiper motor when the wiper switch is OFF but the ignition is ON. If voltage is present, the limit switch in the motor is malfunctioning. Replace the wiper motor. If no voltage is present, trace and repair the limit switch wiring between the fuse panel and wiper motor.

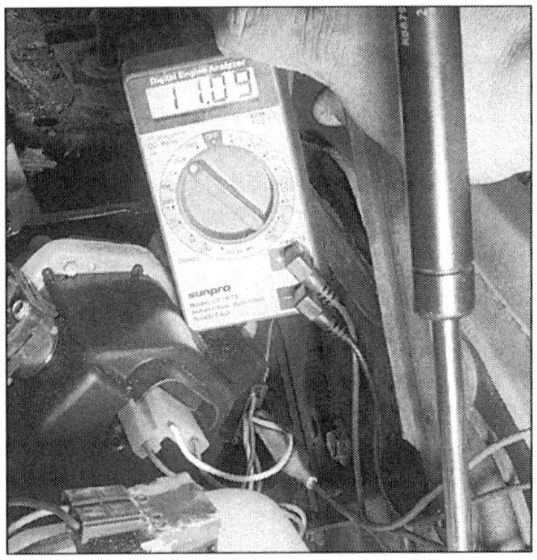

18.2 Use an voltmeter (shown here) or test light to check for power at the wiper motor

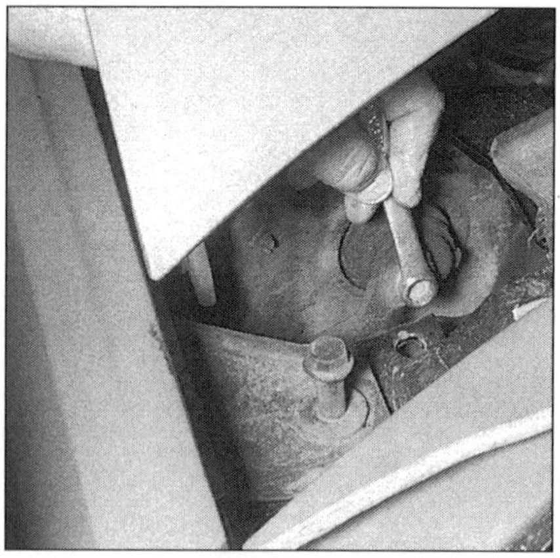

18.9 Remove the nut and detach the wiper arm from the motor

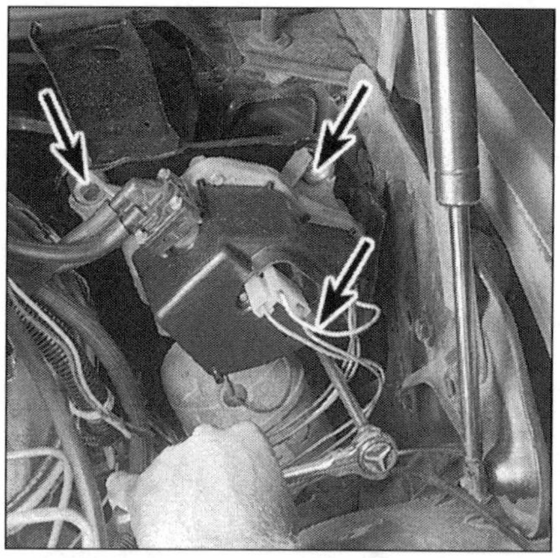

18.11 Remove the bolts (there are usually three, as shown by the arrows) and lift the windshield wiper motor assembly out

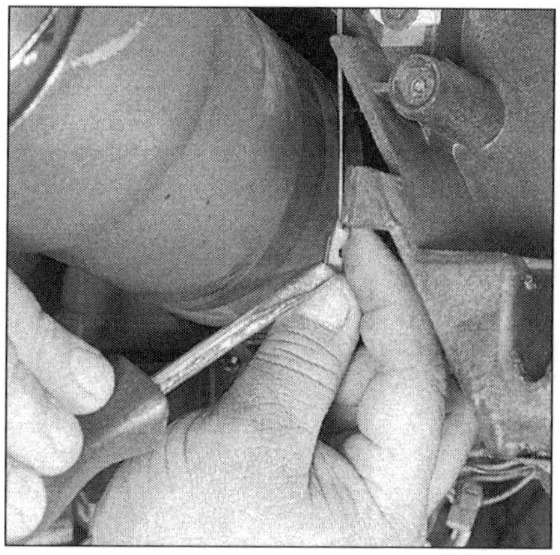

19.3 Use a screwdriver to detach the shift indicator cable

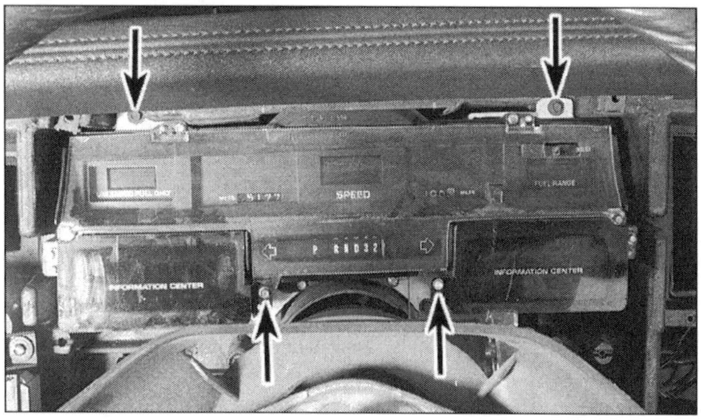

19.4a Remove the instrument cluster bolts (arrows)

19.4b Pull the cluster straight out

6 **If the wipers won't shut off unless the ignition is OFF,** disconnect the wiring from the wiper control switch. If the wipers stop, replace the switch. If the wipers keep running, there's a defective limit switch in the motor; replace the motor.

7 **If the wipers won't retract below the hoodline,** check for mechanical obstructions in the wiper linkage or on the vehicle's body which would prevent the wipers from retracting. If there are no obstructions, check the wiring between the switch and motor for continuity. If the wiring is OK, replace the wiper motor.

Wiper motor replacement

8 On firewall-mounted wiper motors, remove the cowl screen for access to the drive arms.

9 Remove the drive link-to-crank arm nut **(see illustration)**.

10 Detach the crank arm from the motor shaft.

11 Remove the motor mounting bolts **(see illustration)**.

12 Disconnect the wiring and the washer hoses and remove the motor.

13 Installation is the reverse of removal, but before connecting the drive arm, check that the motor is in Park.

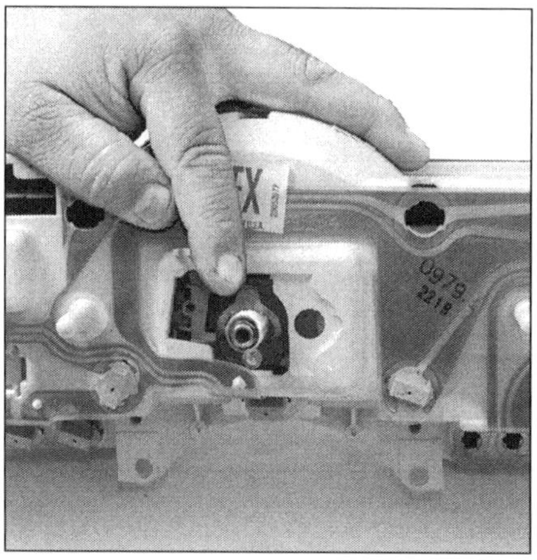

19.4c Reach behind the cluster and depress the clip to release the speedometer cable

19.5 Detach the electrical connectors from the back of the cluster

19 Instrument cluster - removal and installation

Refer to illustrations 19.3, 19.4a, 19.4b, 19.4c and 19.5

1 Disconnect the negative cable at the battery.

2 Remove the instrument cluster bezel (Chapter 11).

3 Apply the parking brake and block the wheels, then place the shift lever in Park. Detach the indicator cable **(see illustration)**.

4 Remove the cluster retaining bolts, pull the cluster out and disconnect the speedometer cable **(see illustrations)**.

5 Unplug any electrical connectors which would interfere with removal and detach the cluster from the instrument panel **(see illustration)**.

6 Installation is the reverse of removal.

20 Speedometer cable - replacement

Refer to illustrations 20.2 and 20.3

1 The instrument cluster must first be removed as described in Section 19.

2 Once the end of the speedometer drive cable is exposed, grip the inner cable with pliers and draw it out of the housing **(see illustration)**.

3 Lubricate the entire new cable. Use special speedometer cable lubricant, not oil, for this purpose **(see illustration)**.

4 Insert the cable into the housing using a twisting movement until the lower end is felt to engage with the pinion gear at the transmission. The remainder of installation is the reverse of removal.

20.2 Use pliers to pull the speedometer cable out

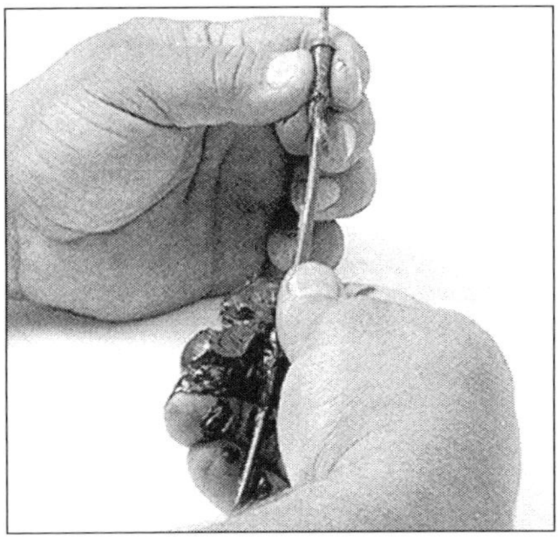

20.3 Coat the entire length of the cable with a lubricant designed for use on speedometer cables (available at auto parts stores)

21 Horn - check and replacement

Check

1 Check the horn circuit fuse (see Section 3). If it is bad, replace it.

2 If the fuse is OK, check the relay. When the horn button is depressed, you should hear a faint click if the relay is functioning. To verify the relay is operating properly, test it (see Section 6).

2 To test the horn, unplug its electrical connector. Connect battery voltage to the two electrical terminals on the horn with a pair of fused jumper wires. If the horn doesn't sound, the horn is bad; replace it.

3 If the horn sounds during this test but does not sound when the horn button is depressed, the problem lies in the wiring, connections or horn switch.

Replacement

4 To replace the horn, unplug the electrical connector and remove the bracket bolt.

5 Installation is the reverse of removal.

22 Electric rear view mirrors - description and check

Refer to illustration 22.7

1 Electric rear view mirrors use two motors to move the glass; one for up-and-down adjustments and one for left-to-right adjustments.

2 The control switch has a selector portion which sends voltage to the left or right side mirror. With the ignition ON but the engine OFF, roll down the windows and operate the mirror control switch through all functions (left-right and up-down) for both the left and right side mirrors.

3 Listen carefully for the sound of the electric motors running in the mirrors.

4 If the motors can be heard but the mirror glass doesn't move, there's probably a problem with the drive mechanism inside the mirror. Remove and disassemble the mirror to locate the problem.

5 If the mirrors don't operate and no sound comes from the mirrors, check the fuse (see Section 3).

6 If the fuse is OK, remove the mirror control switch from its mounting without disconnecting the wires attached to it. Turn the ignition ON and check for voltage at the switch. There should be voltage at one terminal. If there's no voltage at the switch, check for an open or short in the wiring between the fuse panel and the switch.

7 If there's voltage at the switch, disconnect it. Check the switch for continuity in all its operating positions **(see illustration)**. If the switch does not have continuity, replace it.

8 Re-connect the switch. Locate the wire going from the switch to ground. Leaving the switch connected, connect a jumper wire between this wire and ground. If the mirror works normally with this wire in place, repair the faulty ground connection.

9 If the mirror still doesn't work, remove the cover and check the wires at the mirror for voltage with a test light. Check with ignition ON and the mirror selector switch on the appropriate side. Operate the mirror switch in all its positions. There should be voltage at one of the switch-to-mirror wires in each switch position (except the neutral "off" position).

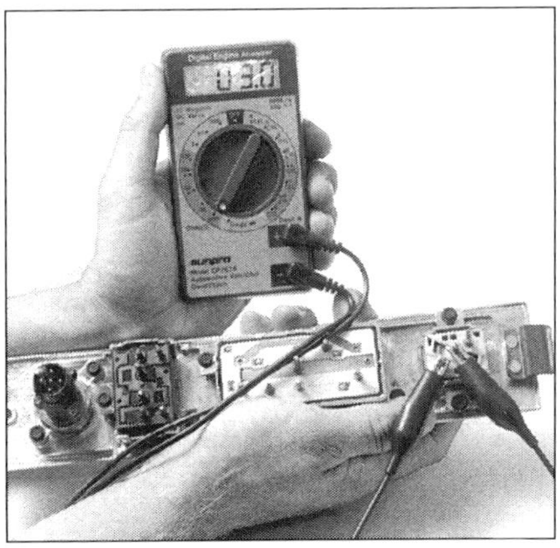

22.7 Use an ohmmeter to check the mirror switches for continuity

10 If there's not voltage in each switch position, check the wiring between the mirror and control switch for opens and shorts.

11 If there's voltage, remove the mirror and test it off the vehicle with jumper wires. Replace the mirror if it fails this test (see Chapter 11).

23 Cruise control system - description and check

1 The cruise control system maintains vehicle speed with a vacuum actuated servo motor located in the engine compartment, which is connected to the throttle linkage by a cable. The system consists of the servo, brake switch, control switches, a relay, the vehicle speed sensor and associated wiring. Listed below are some general procedures that may be used to locate common cruise control problems.

2 Locate and check the fuse (see Section 3).

3 Have an assistant operate the brake lights while you check their operation (voltage from the brake light switch deactivates the cruise control).

4 If the brake lights don't come on or don't shut off, correct the problem and retest the cruise control.

5 Inspect the cable linkage between the cruise control servo and the throttle linkage. The cruise control servo is mounted on the engine block.

6 Visually inspect the wires and vacuum hoses connected to the cruise control servo and check for damage and broken wires or hoses.

7 The vehicle speed sensor is located in the rear axle housing on 1971 through 1978 models or at the back of the speedometer on 1979 and later models. On earlier models, inspect the cable that runs from the left rear wheel to the sensor inside the axle and, if necessary, pull out the grommet and inspect the speed sensor inside the axle tube. On later models, remove the cluster and inspect

the speed sensor magnet and mirror. If the magnet is damaged or mirror is discolored or dark, replace the speed sensor assembly.

8 Test drive the vehicle to determine if the cruise control is now working. If it isn't, take it to a dealer service department or an automotive electrical specialist for further diagnosis and repair.

24 Power door lock system - description and check

1 Power door lock systems are operated by bi-directional solenoids located in the doors. The lock switches have two operating positions: Lock and Unlock. These switches activate a relay which in turn connects voltage to the door lock solenoids. Depending on which way the relay is activated, it reverses polarity, allowing the two sides of the circuit to be used alternately as the feed (positive) and ground side.

2 Always check the circuit protection first (see Section 3).

3 Operate the door lock switches in both directions (Lock and Unlock) with the engine off. Listen for the faint click of the relay operating.

4 If there's no click, check for voltage at the switches. If no voltage is present, check the wiring between the fuse panel and the switches for shorts and opens.

5 If voltage is present but no click is heard, test the switch for continuity. Replace it if there's not continuity in both switch positions.

6 If the switch has continuity but the relay doesn't click, check the wiring between the switch and relay for continuity. Repair the wiring if there's no continuity.

7 If the relay is receiving voltage from the switch but is not sending voltage to the solenoids, check for a bad ground at the relay case. If the relay case is grounding properly, replace the relay.

8 If all but one lock solenoid operates, remove the trim panel from the affected door (see Chapter 11). and check for voltage at the solenoid while the lock switch is operated. One of the wires should have voltage in the Lock position; the other should have voltage in the unlock position.

9 If the inoperative solenoid is receiving voltage, replace the solenoid.

10 If the inoperative solenoid isn't receiving voltage, check for an open or short in the wire between the lock solenoid and the relay. **Note:** *It's common for wires to break in the portion of the harness between the body and door (opening and closing the door fatigues and eventually breaks the wires).*

25 Power window system - description and check

1 The power window system consists of the control switches, the motors, glass mechanisms (regulators), and associated wiring.

2 Power windows are wired so they can be lowered and raised from the master control switch by the driver or by remote switches located at the individual windows. Each window has a separate motor which is reversible. The position of the control switch determines the polarity and therefore the direction of operation. The system is equipped with a relay that controls current flow to the motors.

3 The power window system operates when the ignition switch is ON. In addition, these models have a window lockout switch at the master control switch which, when activated, disables the switches at the rear windows and, sometimes, the switch at the passenger's window also. Always check these items before troubleshooting a window problem.

4 These procedures are general in nature, so if you can't find the problem using them, take the vehicle to a dealer service department or other qualified repair shop.

5 If the power windows don't work at all, check the fuse or circuit breaker.

6 If only the rear windows are inoperative, or if the windows only operate from the master control switch, check the rear window lockout switch for continuity in the unlocked position. Replace it if it doesn't have continuity.

7 Check the wiring between the switches and fuse panel for continuity. Repair the wiring, if necessary.

8 If only one window is inoperative from the master control switch, try the other control switch at the window. **Note:** *This doesn't apply to the drivers door window.*

9 If the same window works from one switch, but not the other, check the switch for continuity.

10 If the switch tests OK, check for a short or open in the wiring between the affected switch and the window motor.

11 If one window is inoperative from both switches, remove the trim panel from the affected door and check for voltage at the motor while the switch is operated.

12 If voltage is reaching the motor, disconnect the glass from the regulator (see Chapter 11). Move the window up and down by hand while checking for binding and damage. Also check for binding and damage to the regulator. If the regulator is not damaged and the window moves up and down smoothly, replace the motor (see Chapter 11). If there's binding or damage, lubricate, repair or replace parts, as necessary.

13 If voltage isn't reaching the motor, check the wiring in the circuit for continuity between the switches and motors. Check that the relay is grounded properly and receiving voltage from the switches. Also check that the relay sends voltage to the motor when the switch is turned on. If it doesn't, replace the relay.

14 Test the windows after you are done to confirm proper repairs.

26 Power seats - description and check

1 Power seats allow you to adjust the position of the seat with little effort. The optional power seats on these models adjust forward and backward, up and down and tilt forward and backward.

2 The power seat system consists of a motor, a switch on the seat and a relay and fuse in the engine compartment fuse block.

3 Look under the seat for any objects which may be preventing the seat from moving.

4 If the seat won't work at all, check the fuse (see Section 3).

5 With the engine off to reduce the noise level, operate the seat controls in all directions and listen for sound coming from the seat motor(s).

6 If the motor runs or clicks but the seat doesn't move, the integral the seat drive mechanism is damaged and the motor assembly must be replaced.

7 If the motor doesn't work or make noise, check for voltage at the motor while an assistant operates the switch.

8 If the motor is getting voltage but doesn't run, test it off the vehicle with jumper wires. If it still doesn't work, replace it.

9 If the motor isn't getting voltage, check for voltage at the switch. If there's no voltage at the switch, check the wiring between the fuse panel and the switch. If there's voltage at the switch, obtain the wiring diagrams for the vehicle and check the switch for continuity in all its operating positions. Replace the switch if there's no continuity.

10 If the switch is OK, check for a short or open in the wiring between the switch and motor. If there's a relay between the switch and motor, check that it's grounded properly and there's voltage to the relay. Also check that there's voltage going from the relay to the motor when the when the switch is operated. If there's not, and the relay is grounded properly, replace the relay.

11 Test the completed repairs.

27 Wiring diagrams - general information

Since it isn't possible to include all wiring diagrams for every year covered by this manual, the following diagrams are those that are typical and most commonly needed.

Prior to troubleshooting any circuit, check the fuse and circuit breakers (if equipped) to make sure they're in good condition. Make sure the battery is properly charged and check the cable connections (see Chapter 1).

When checking a circuit, make sure that all electrical connectors are clean, with no broken or loose terminals. When unplugging an electrical connector, do not pull on the wires. Pull only on the connector housings themselves.

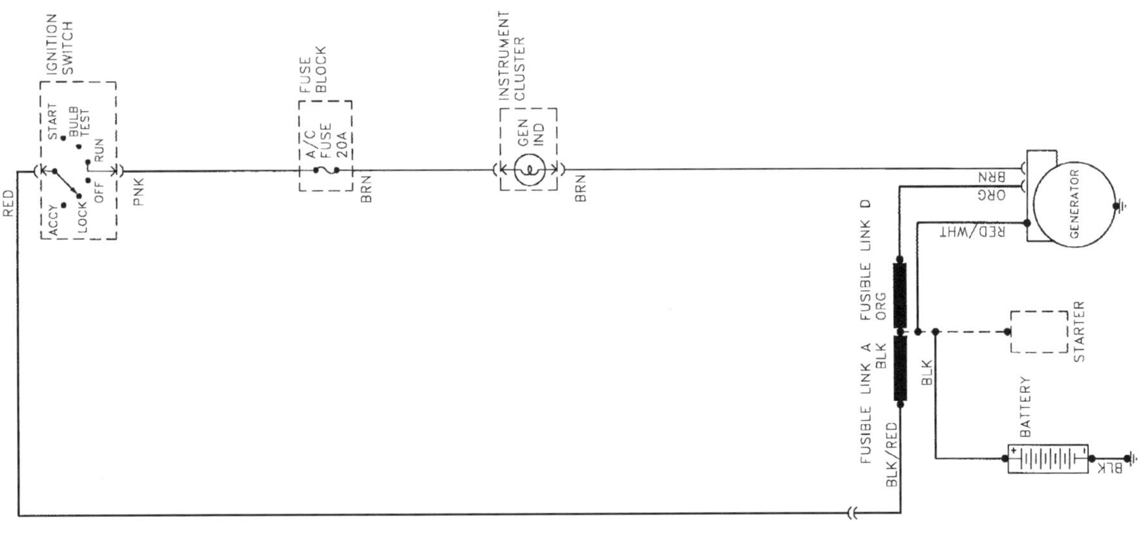

Typical 1979 through 1980 Eldorado/Seville and 1979 through 1981 Toronado/Riviera charging system

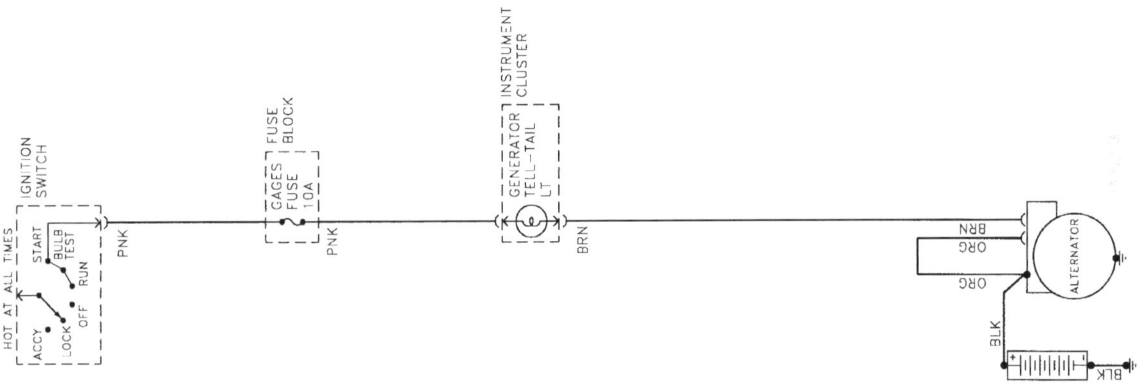

Typical 1974 through 1978 charging system

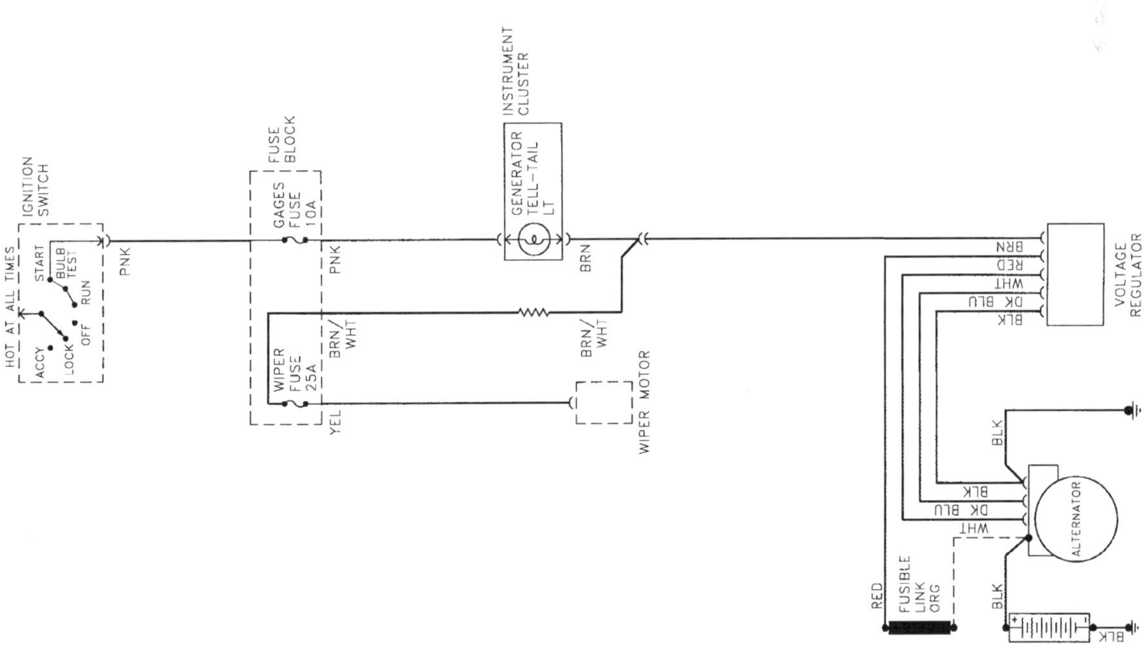

Typical 1973 and earlier charging system

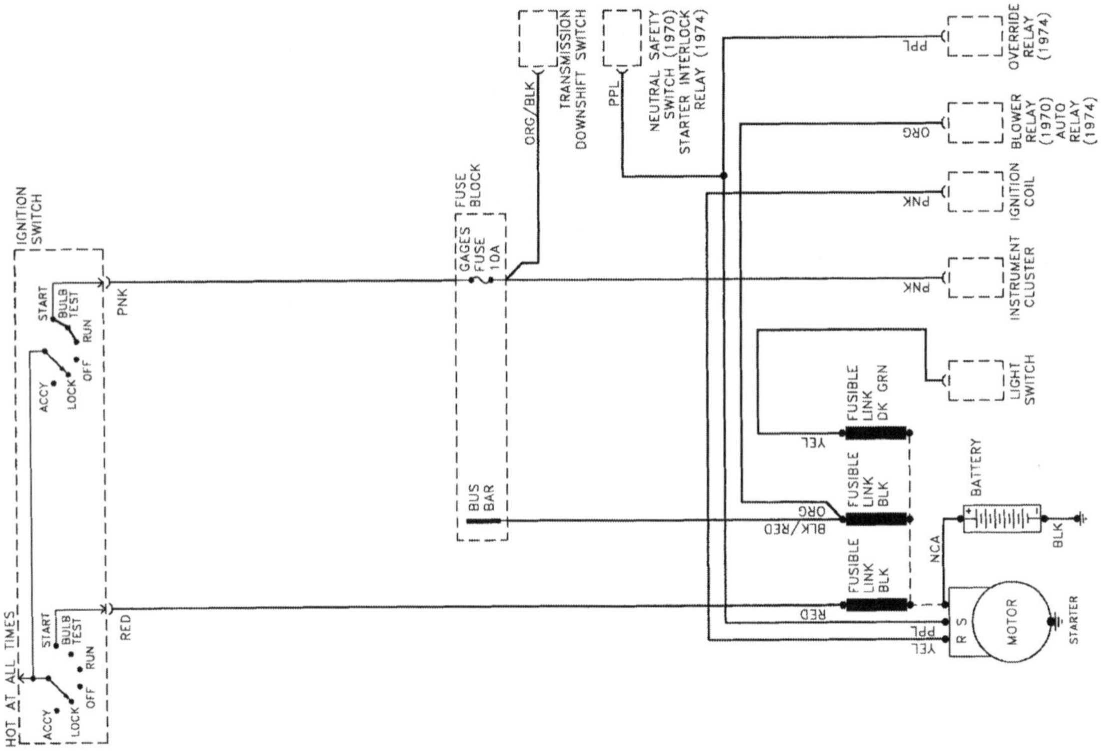

Typical 1978 and earlier starting system

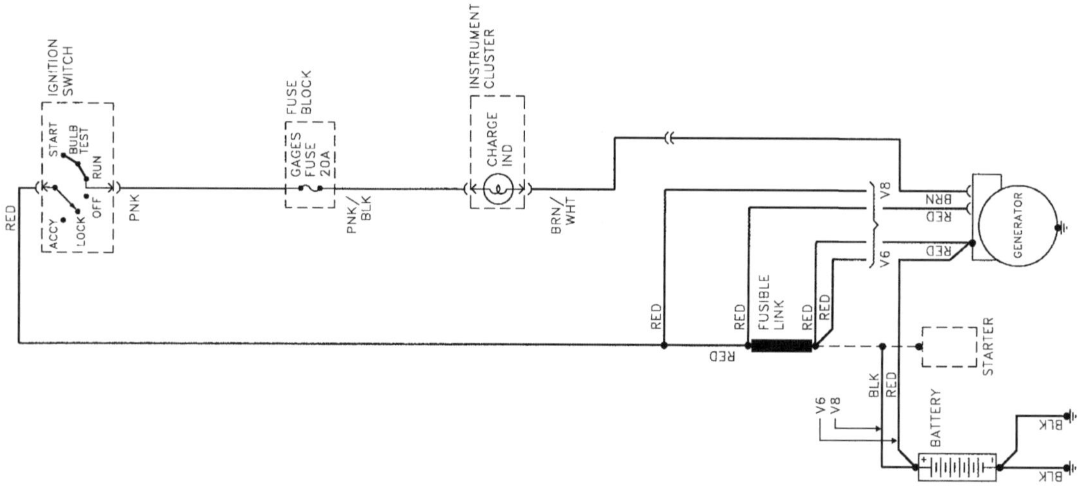

Typical 1982 and later Toronado/Riviera charging system

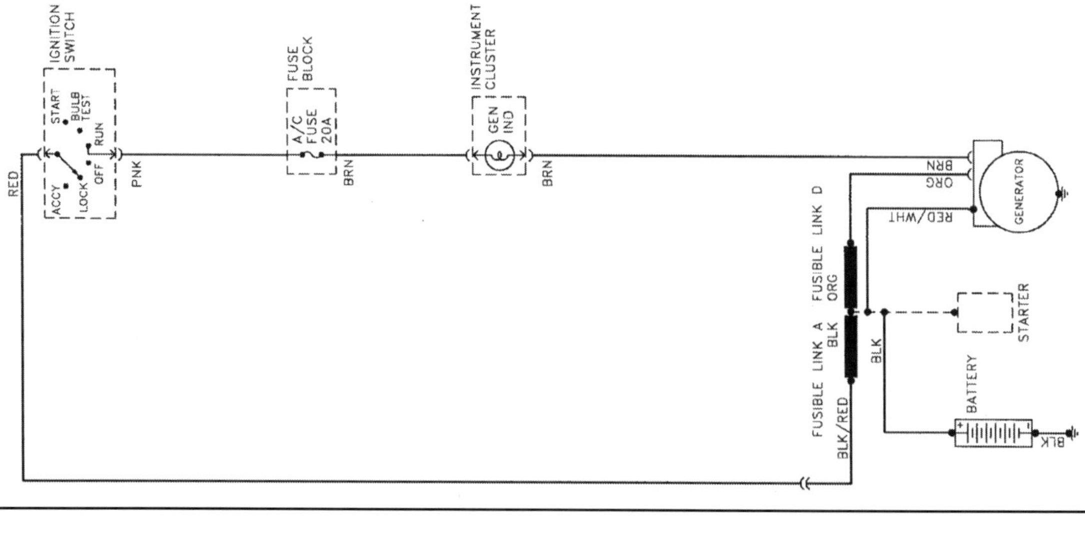

Typical 1981 and later Eldorado/Seville charging system

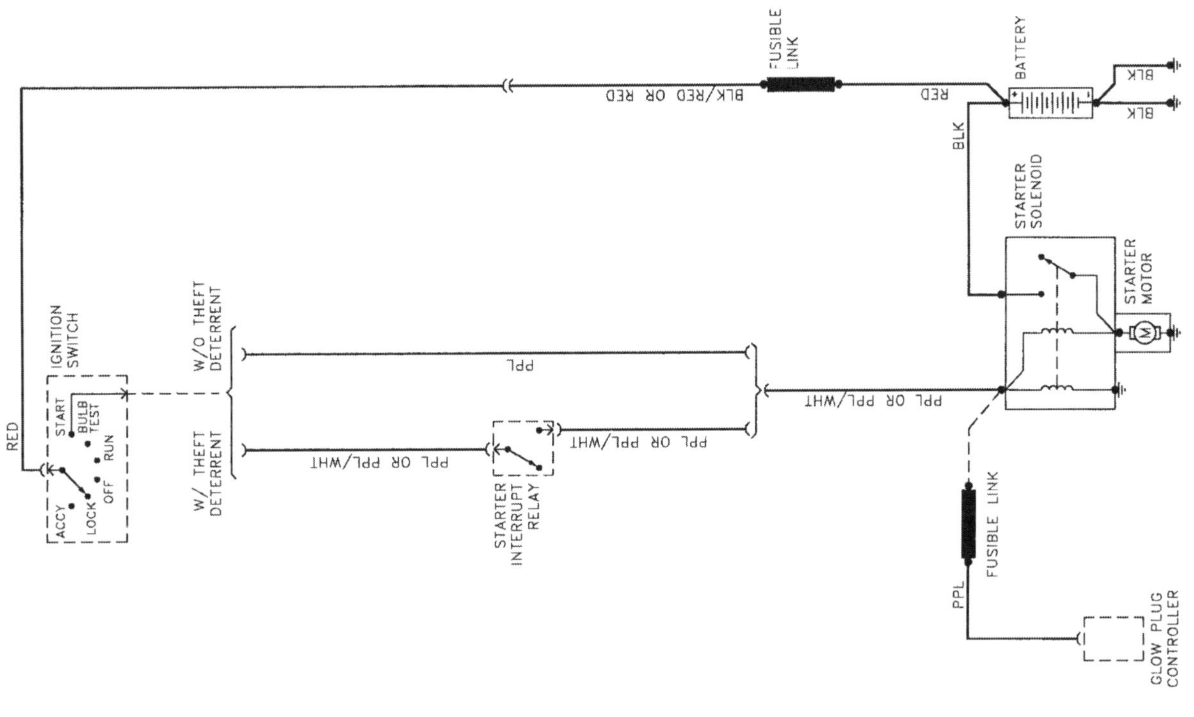

Typical 1985 Eldorado/Seville and 1983 and later Toronado/Riviera starting system

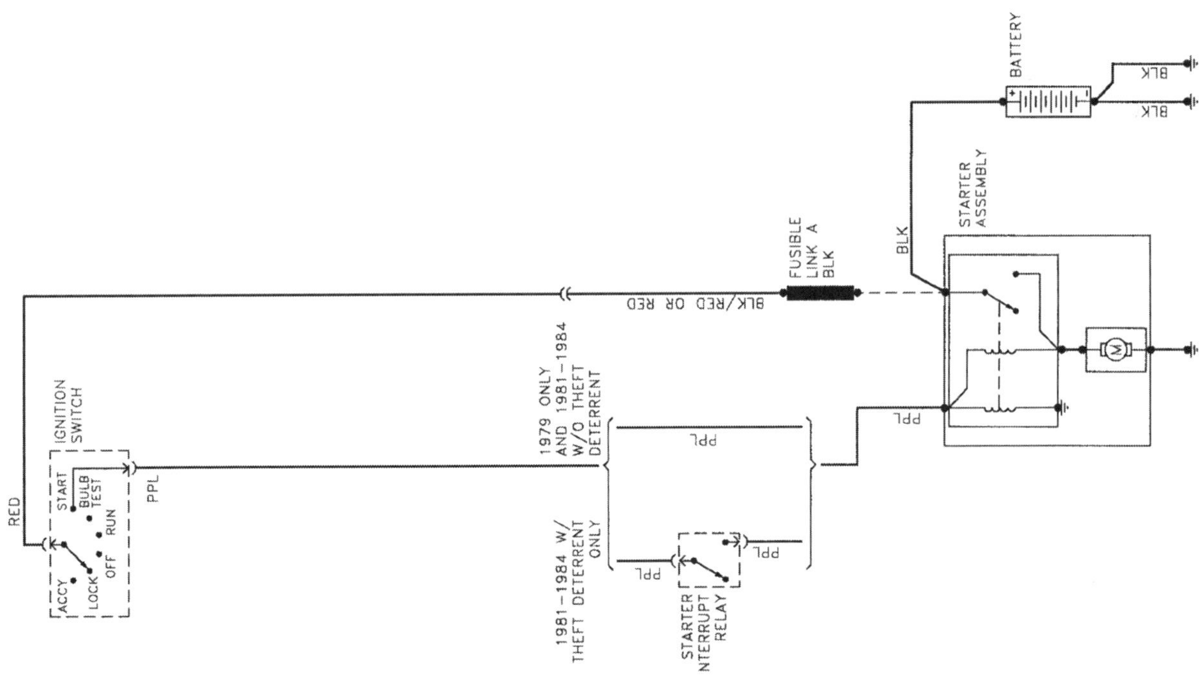

Typical 1979 through 1984 Eldorado/Seville and 1979 through 1982 Toronado/Riviera starting system

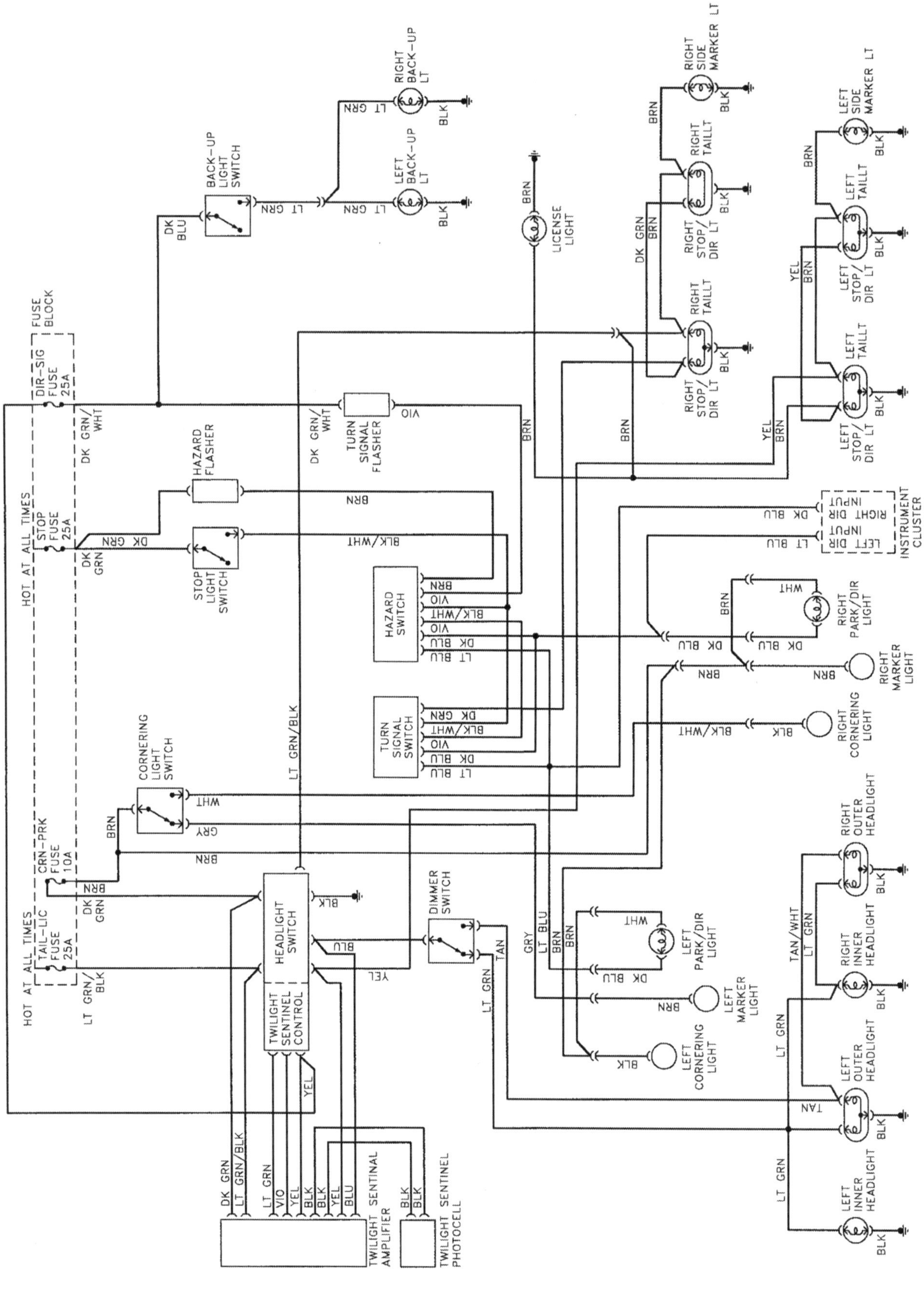

Typical 1978 and earlier exterior lighting system

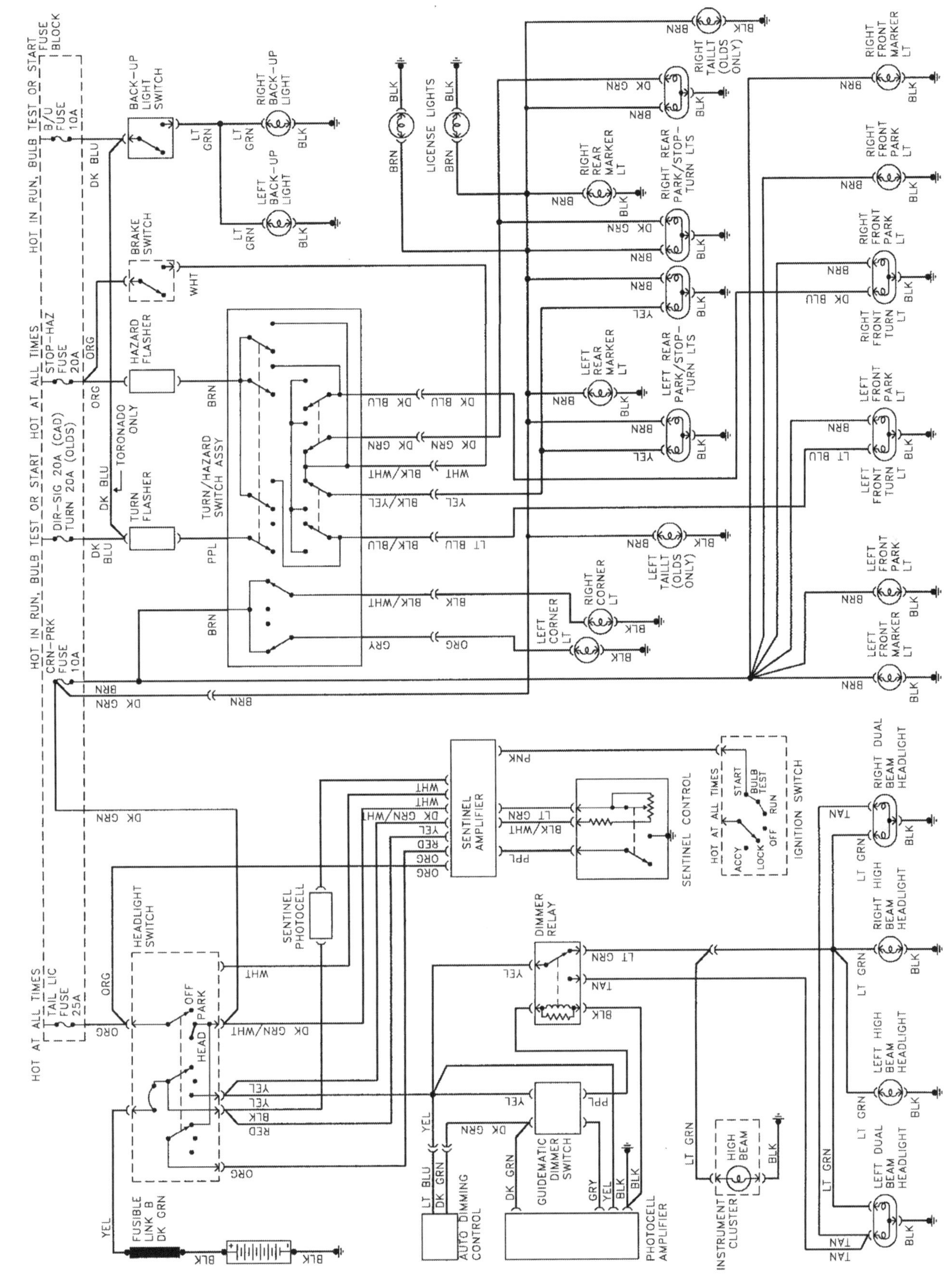

Typical 1979 and later Eldorado/Seville and 1982 and later Toronado exterior lighting system

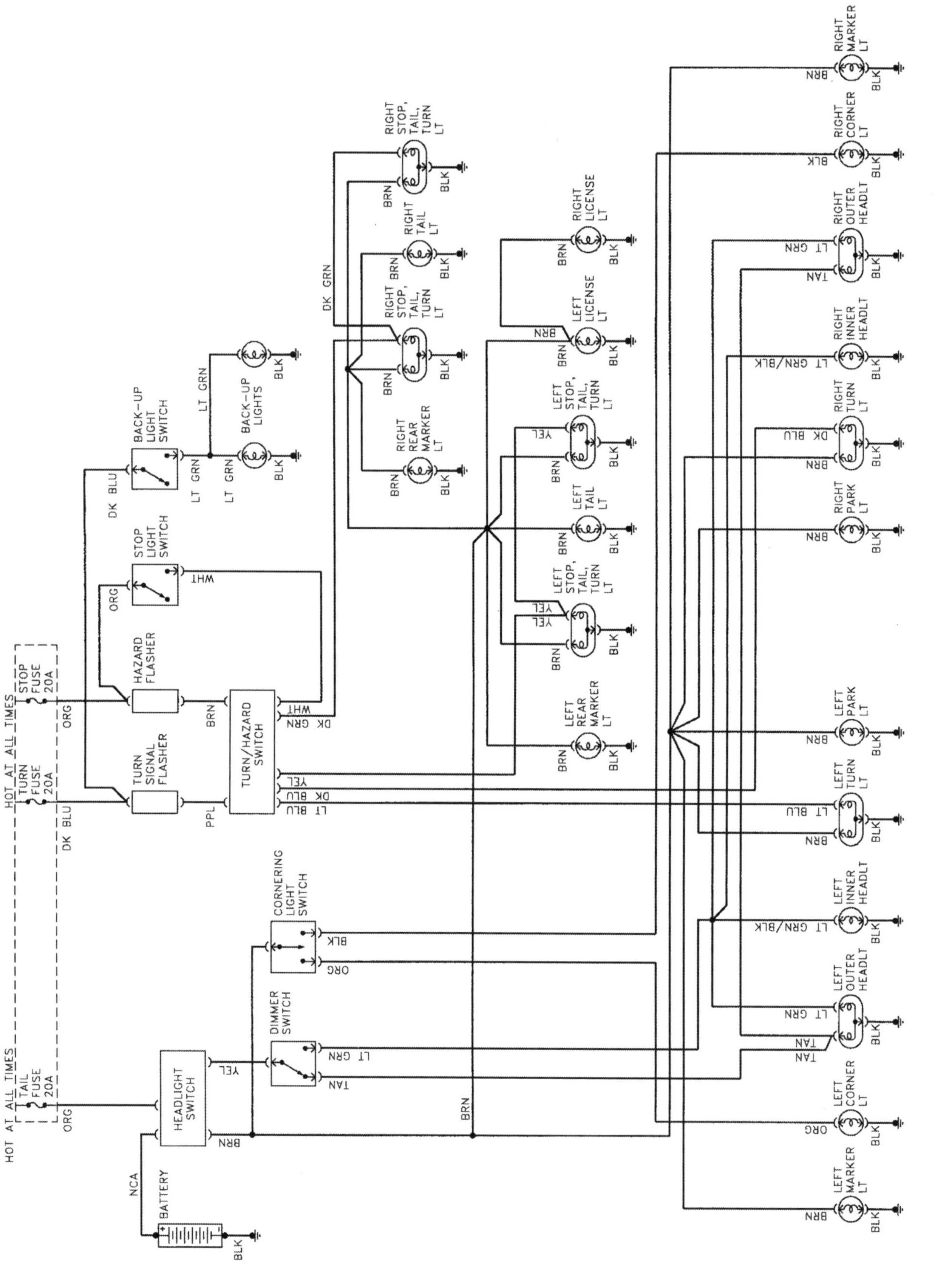

Typical 1979 through 1982 Riviera and 1979 through 1981 Toronado exterior lighting system

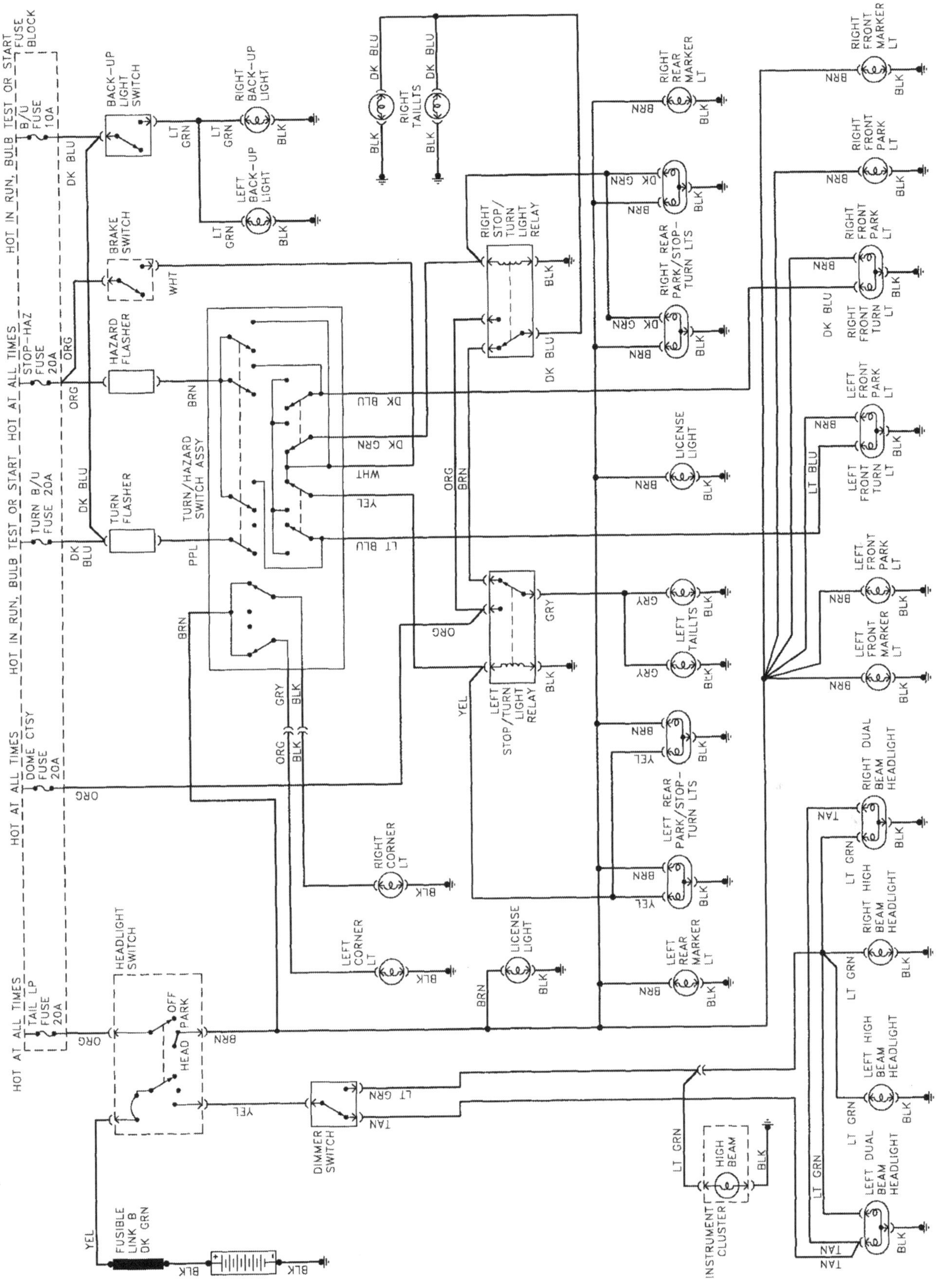

Typical 1983 and later Riviera exterior lighting system

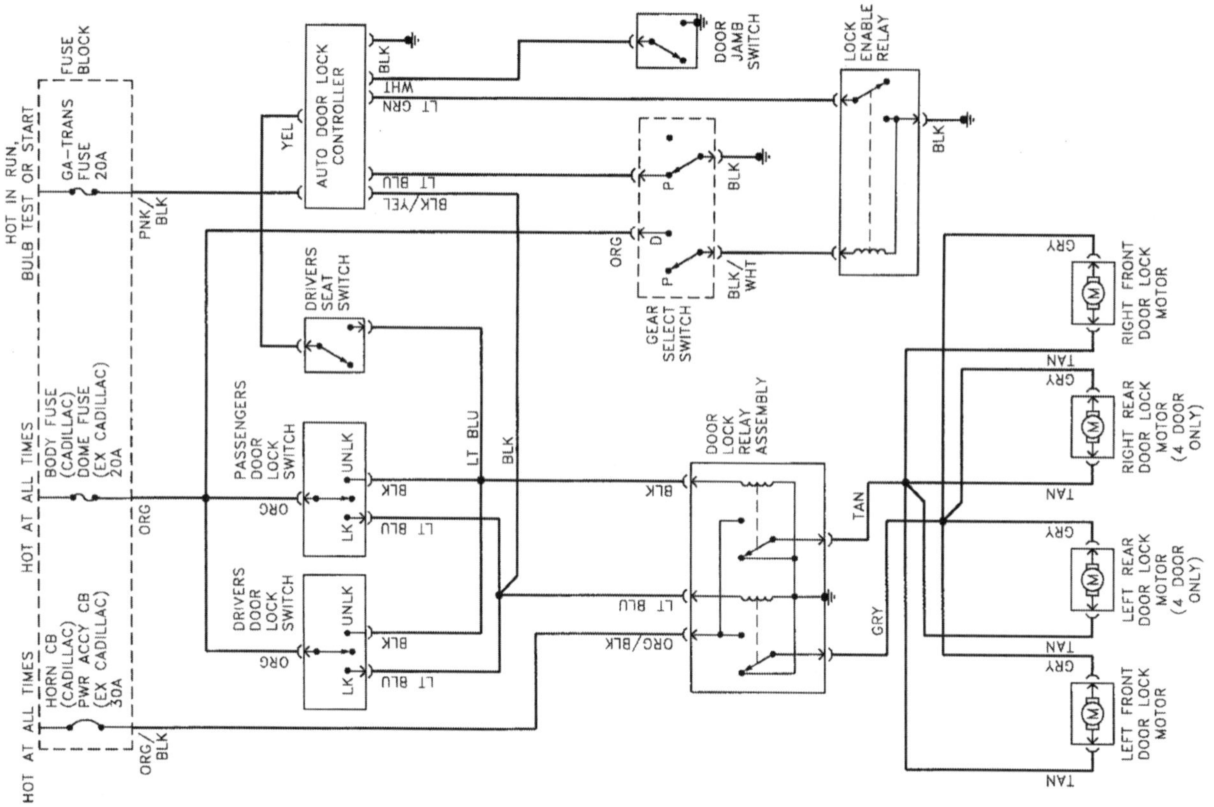

Typical 1979 and later power door lock system

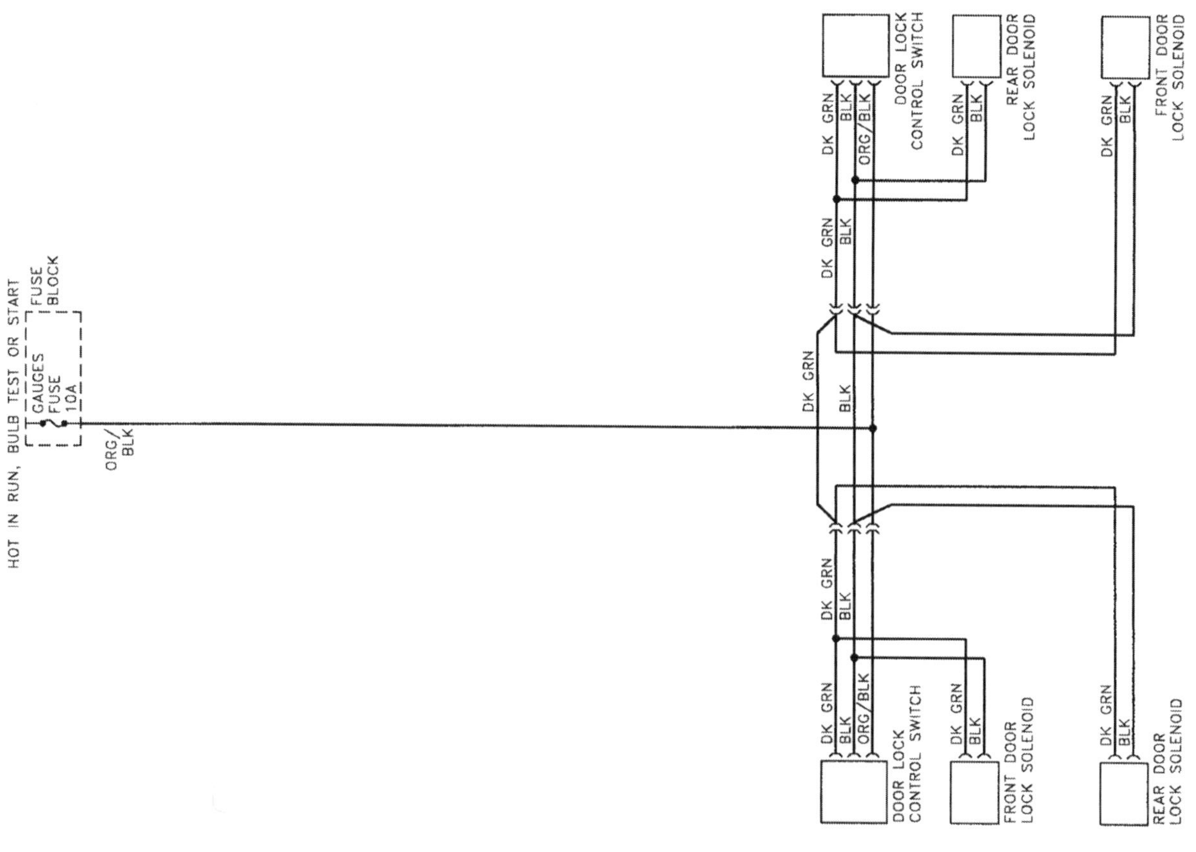

Typical 1978 and earlier power door lock system

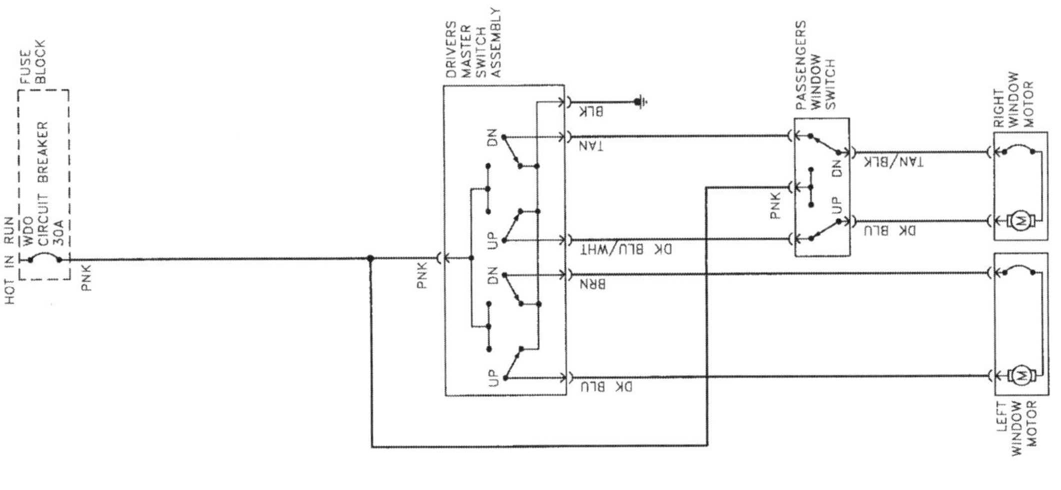

Typical 1979 and later power window system (coupe)

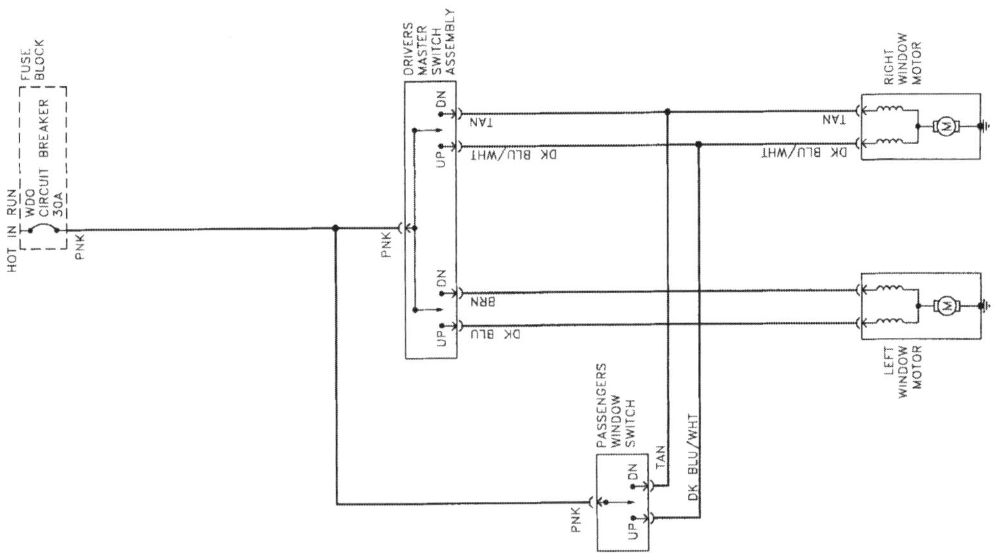

Typical 1979 early production Eldorado power window system

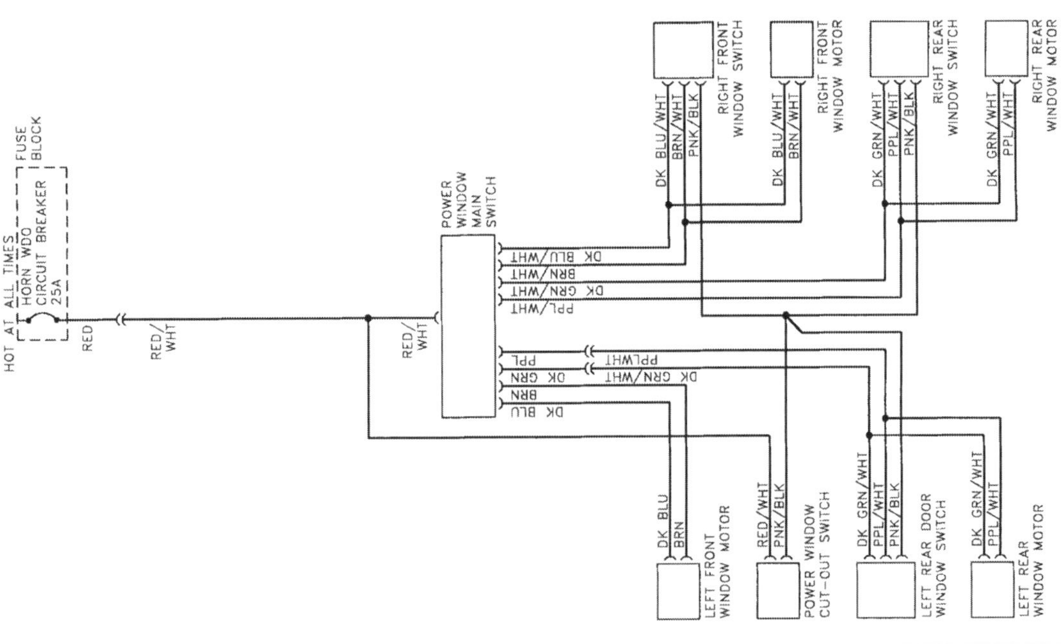

Typical 1978 and earlier power window system

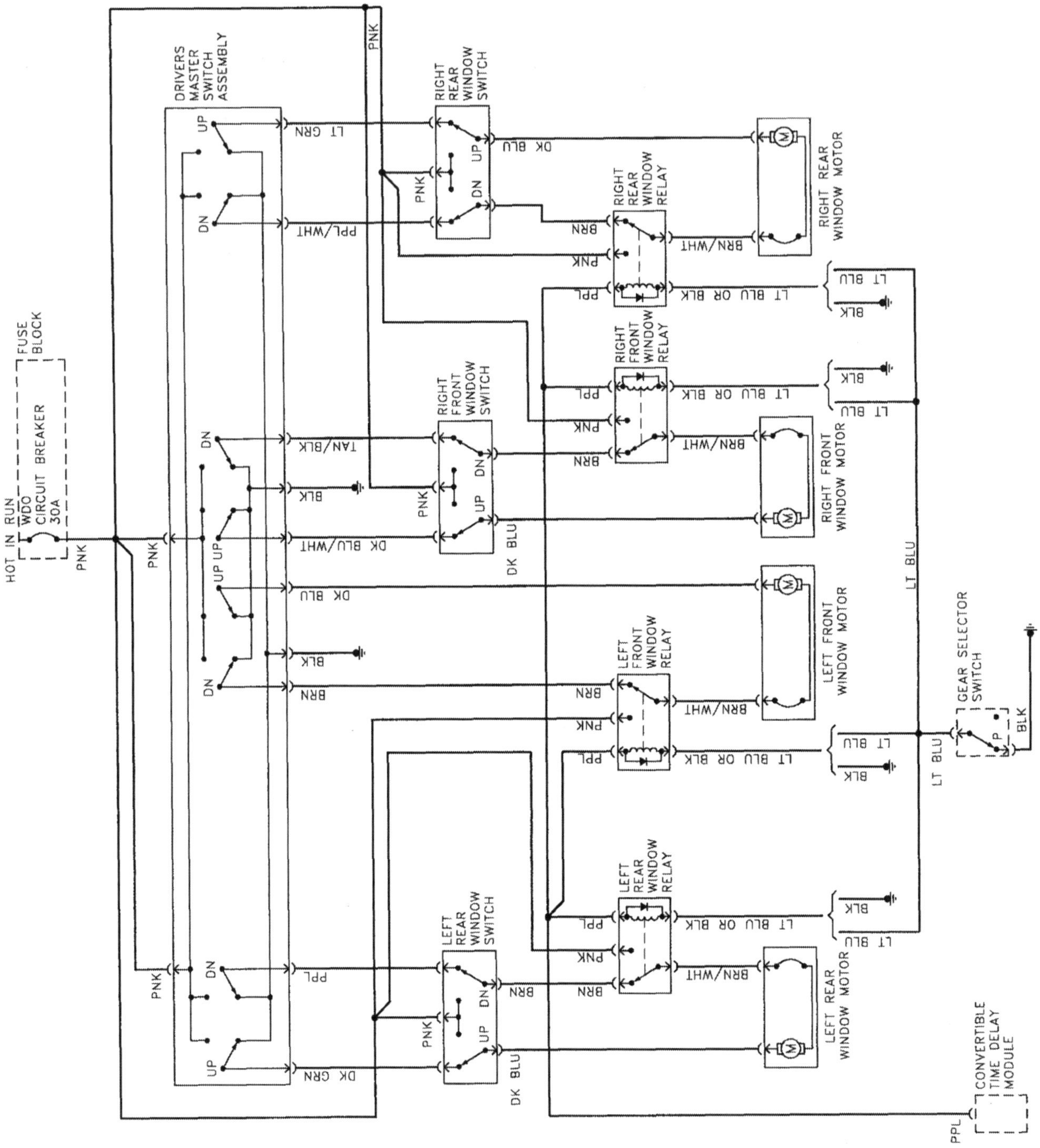

Typical 1979 and later power window system (convertible)

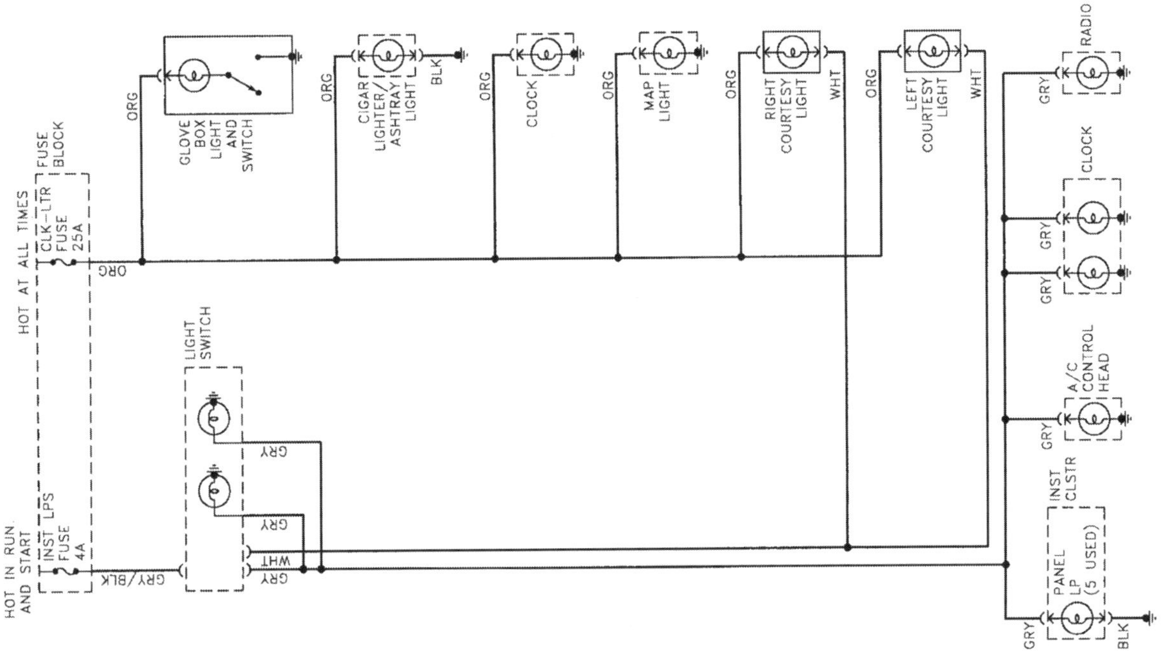

Typical 1978 and earlier interior lighting system

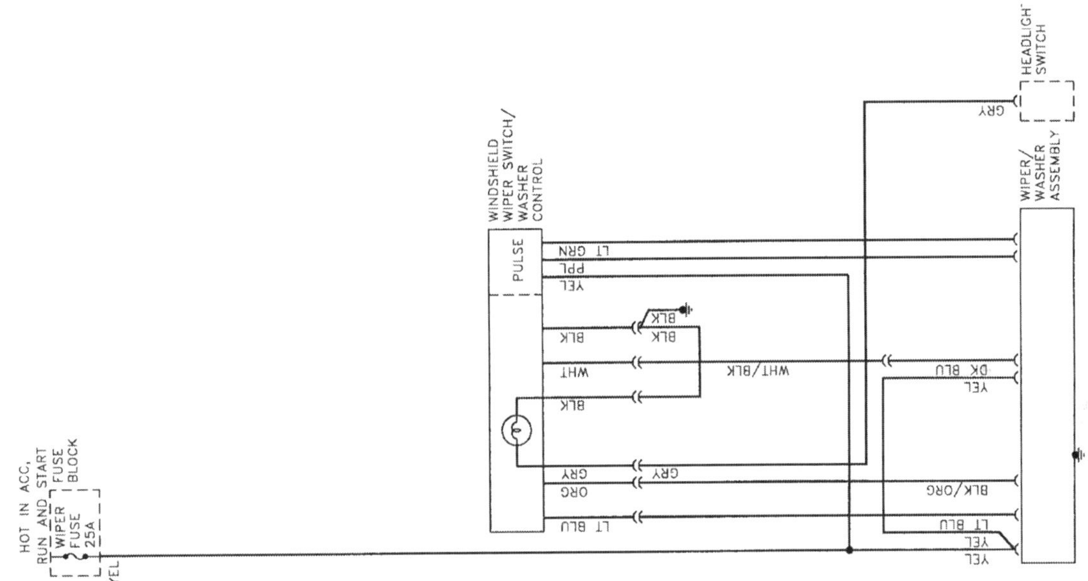

Typical 1974 through 1978 windshield wiper/washer system

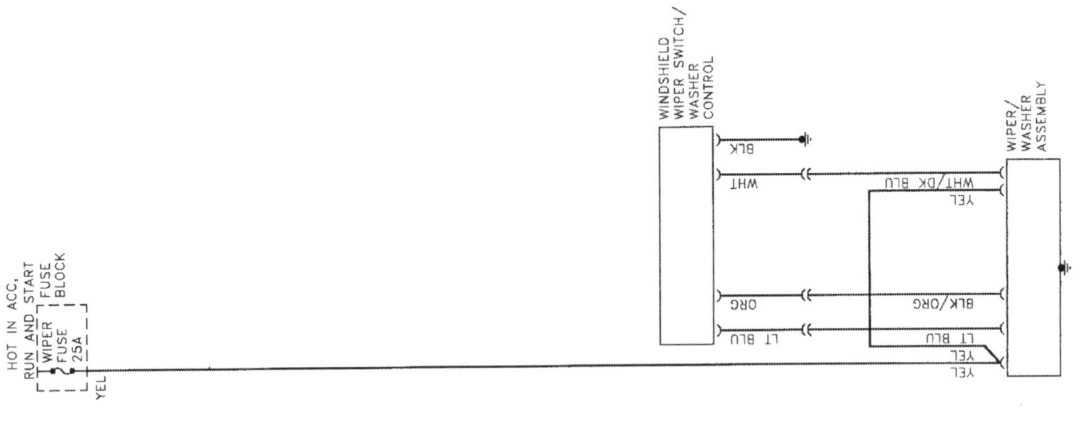

Typical 1973 and earlier windshield wiper/washer system

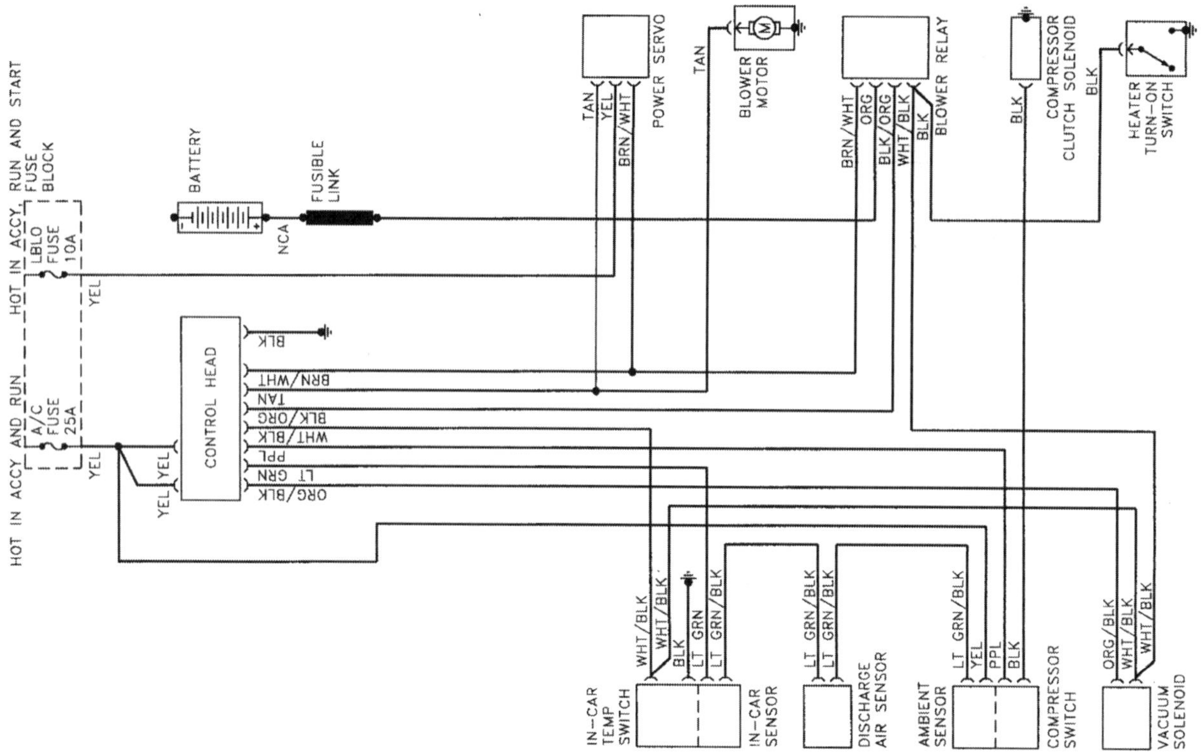

Typical 1978 and earlier air conditioning system

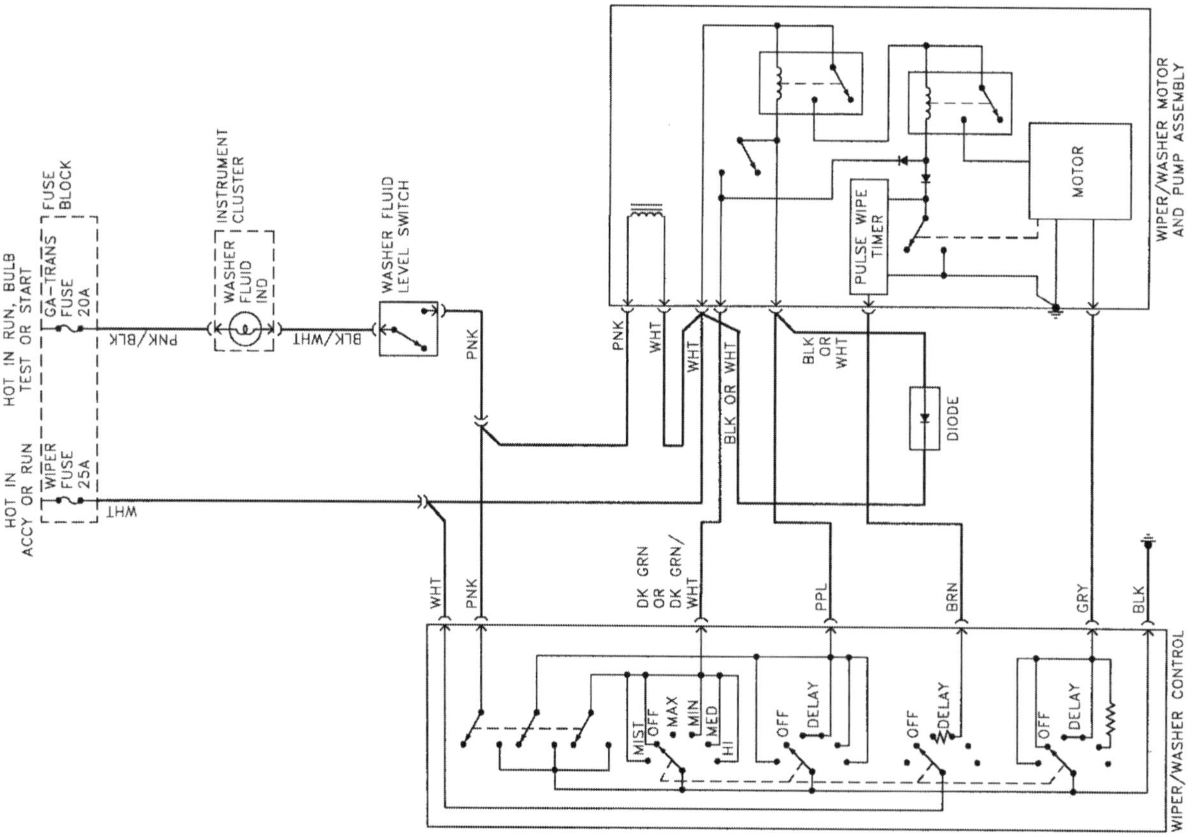

Typical 1979 and later windshield wiper/washer system

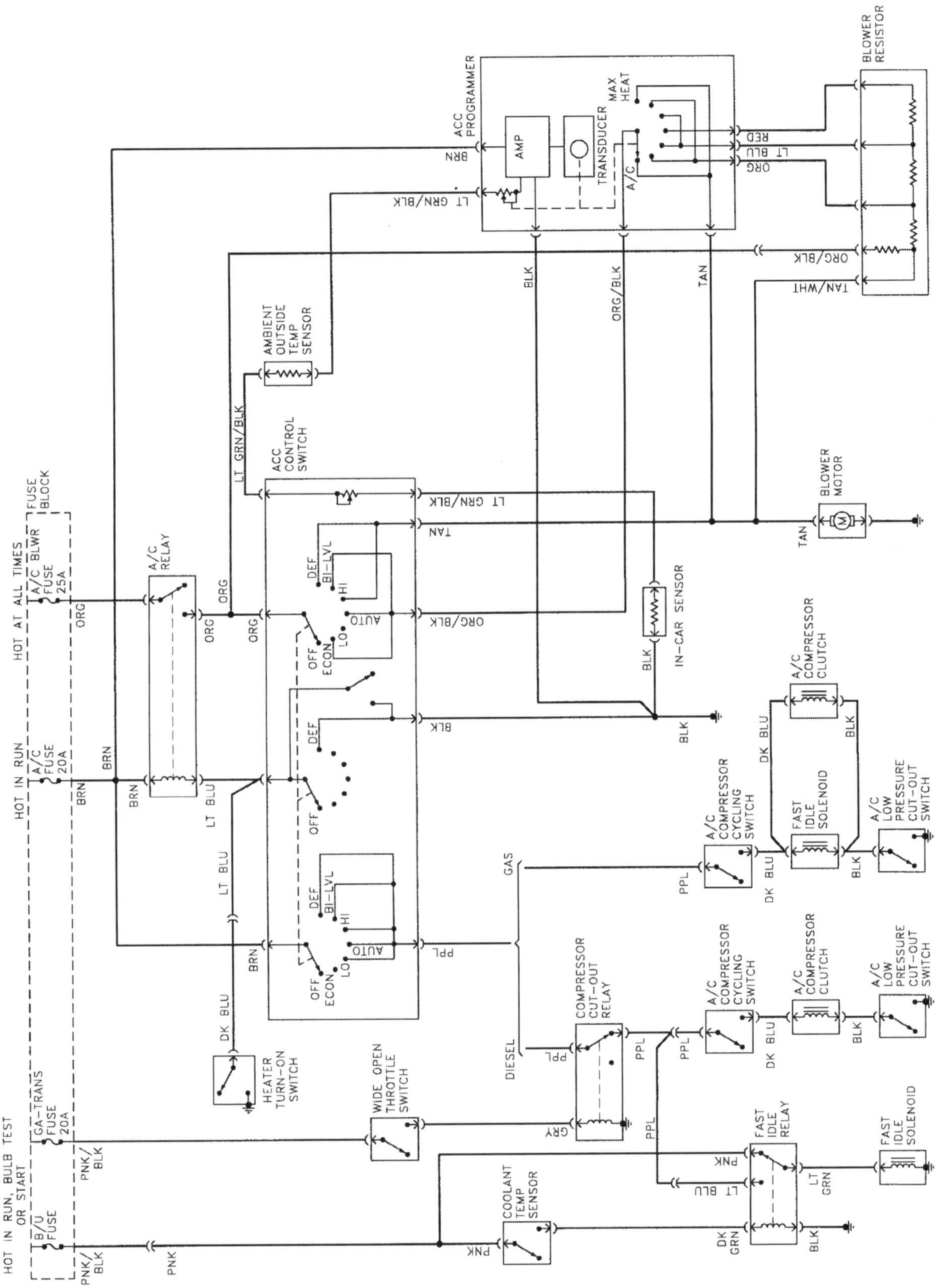

Typical 1979 and 1980 Eldorado/Seville air conditioning system

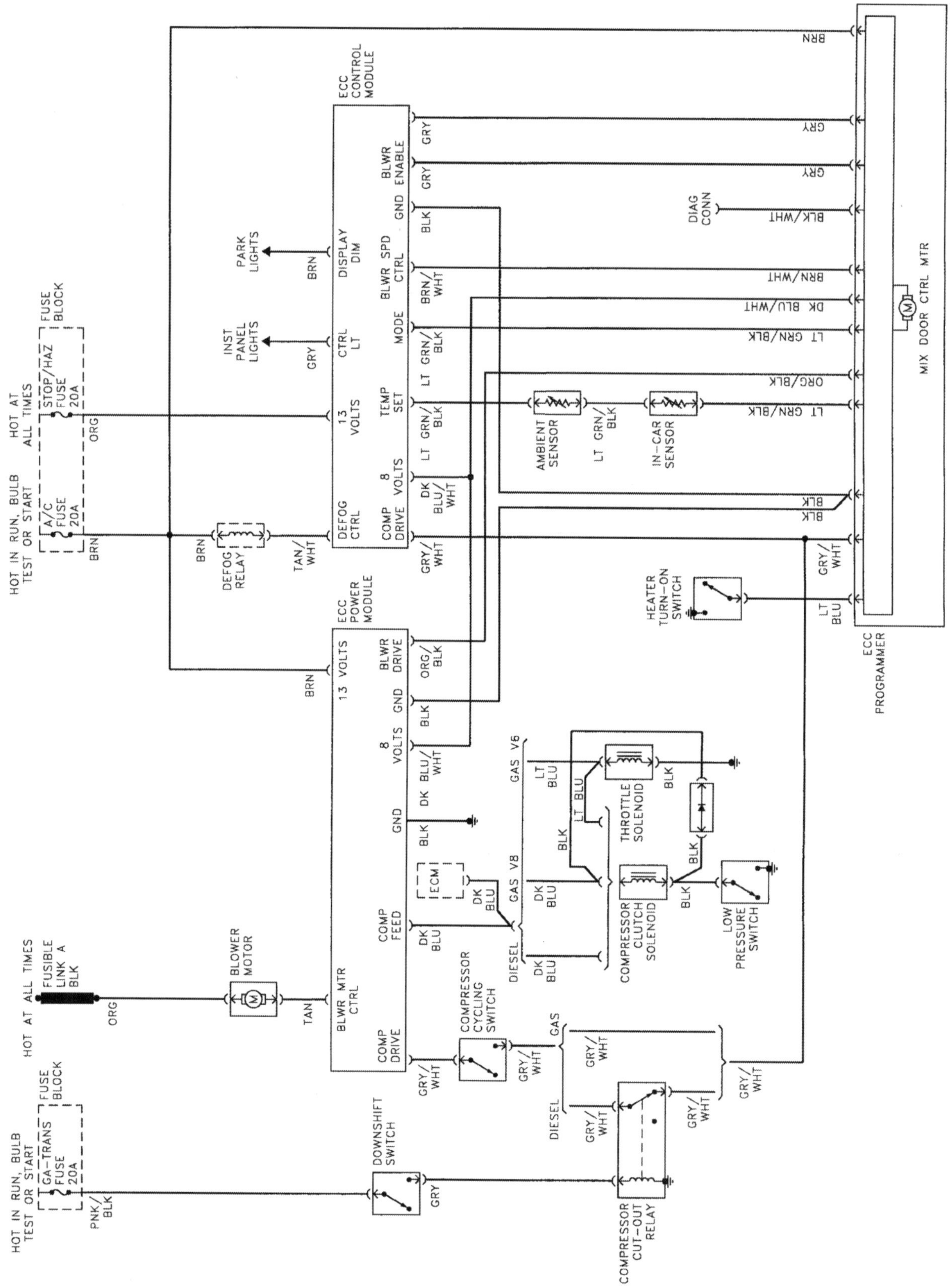

Typical 1981 Eldorado/Seville Electronic Climate Control system

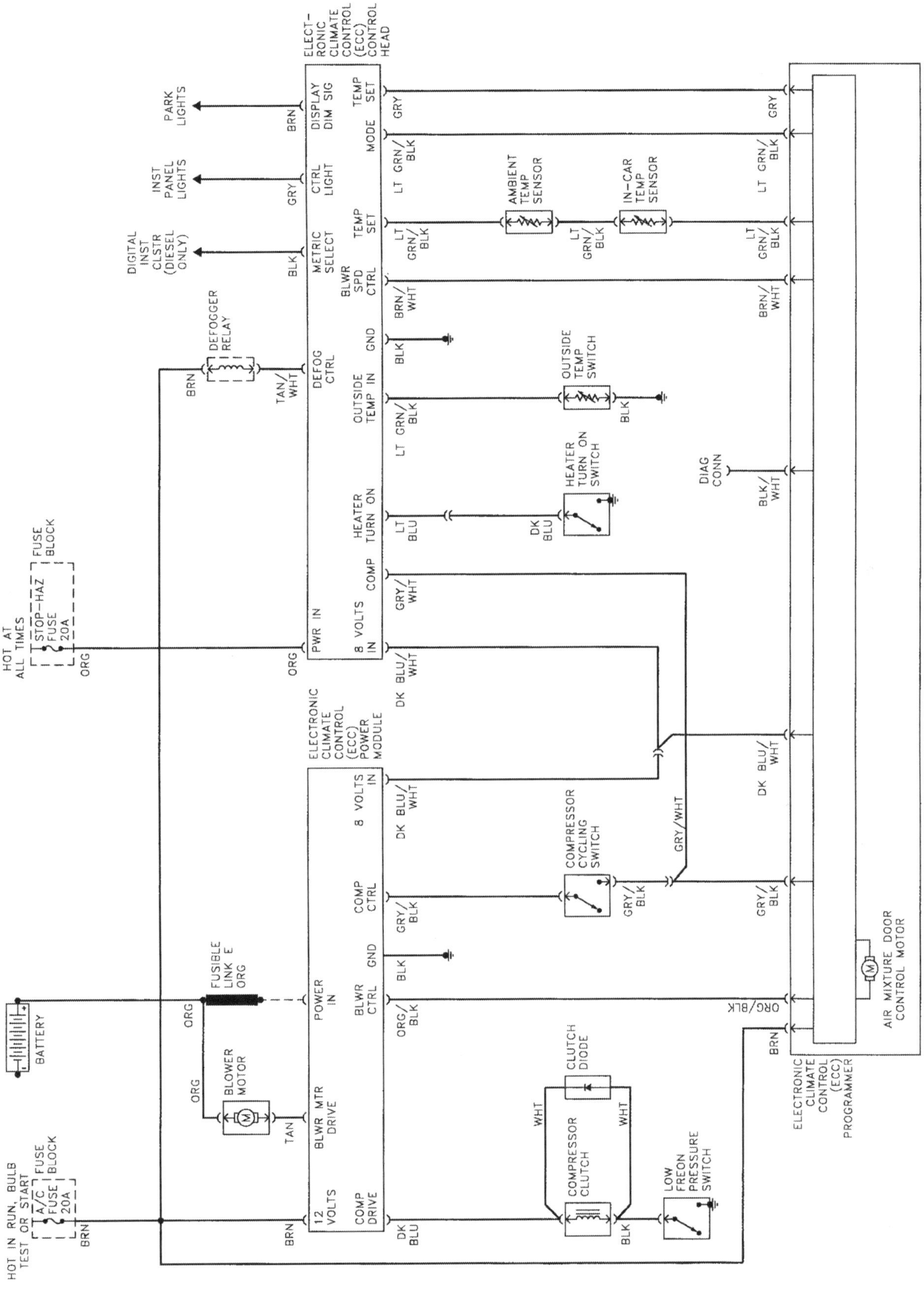

Typical 1982 and later Eldorado/Seville Electronic Climate Control system

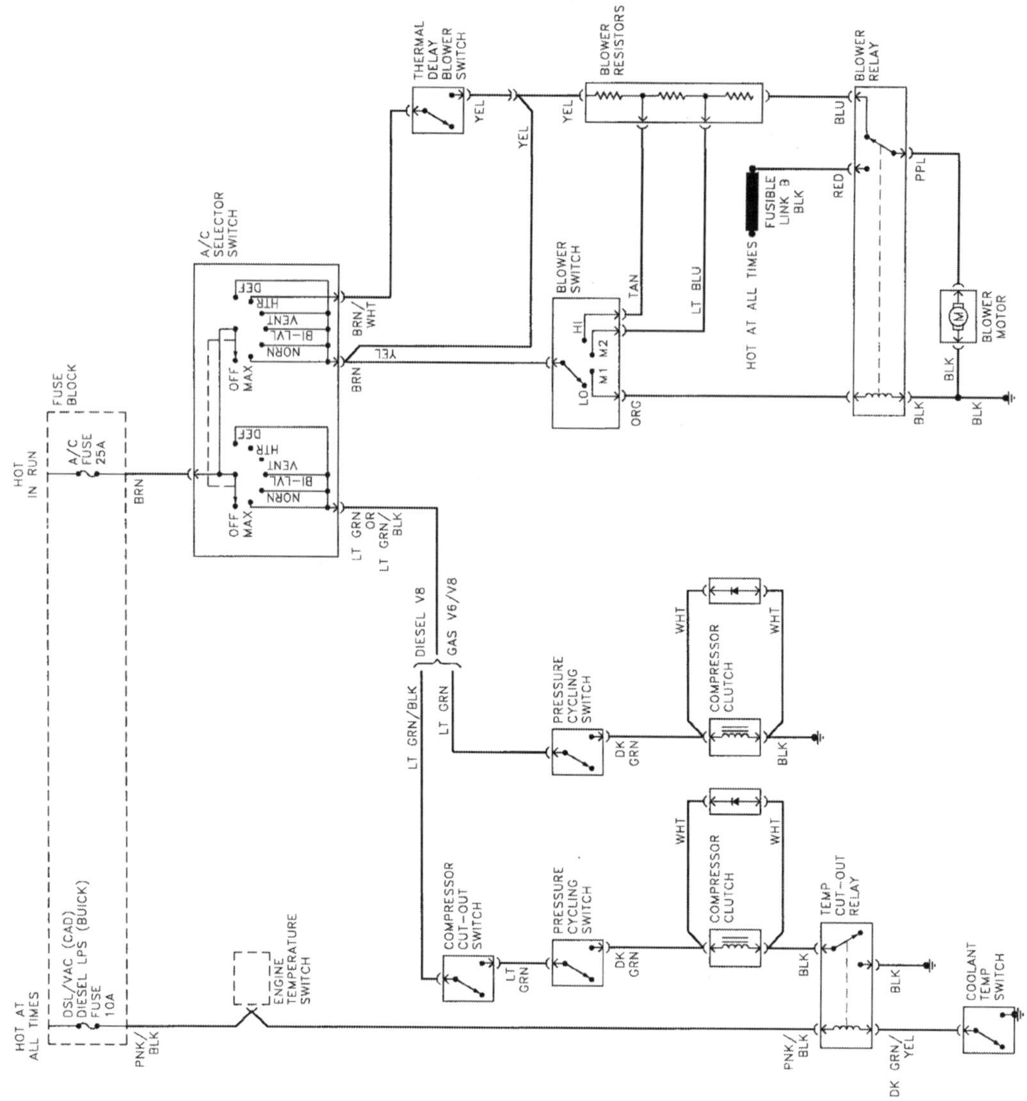

Typical 1982 through 1985 Toronado/Riviera air conditioning system (except Electronic Climate Control)

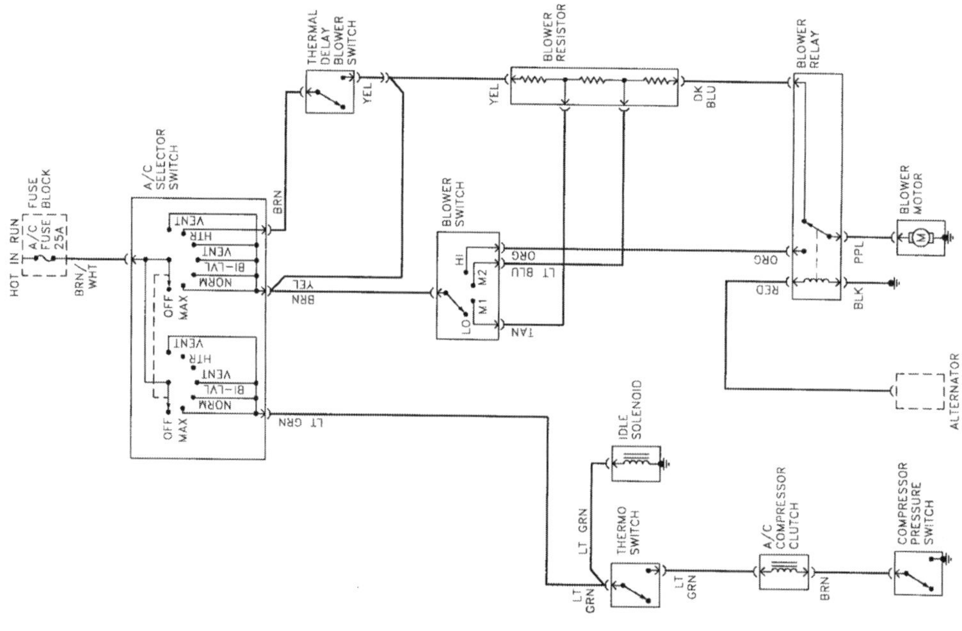

Typical 1979 through 1981 Toronado/Riviera air conditioning system

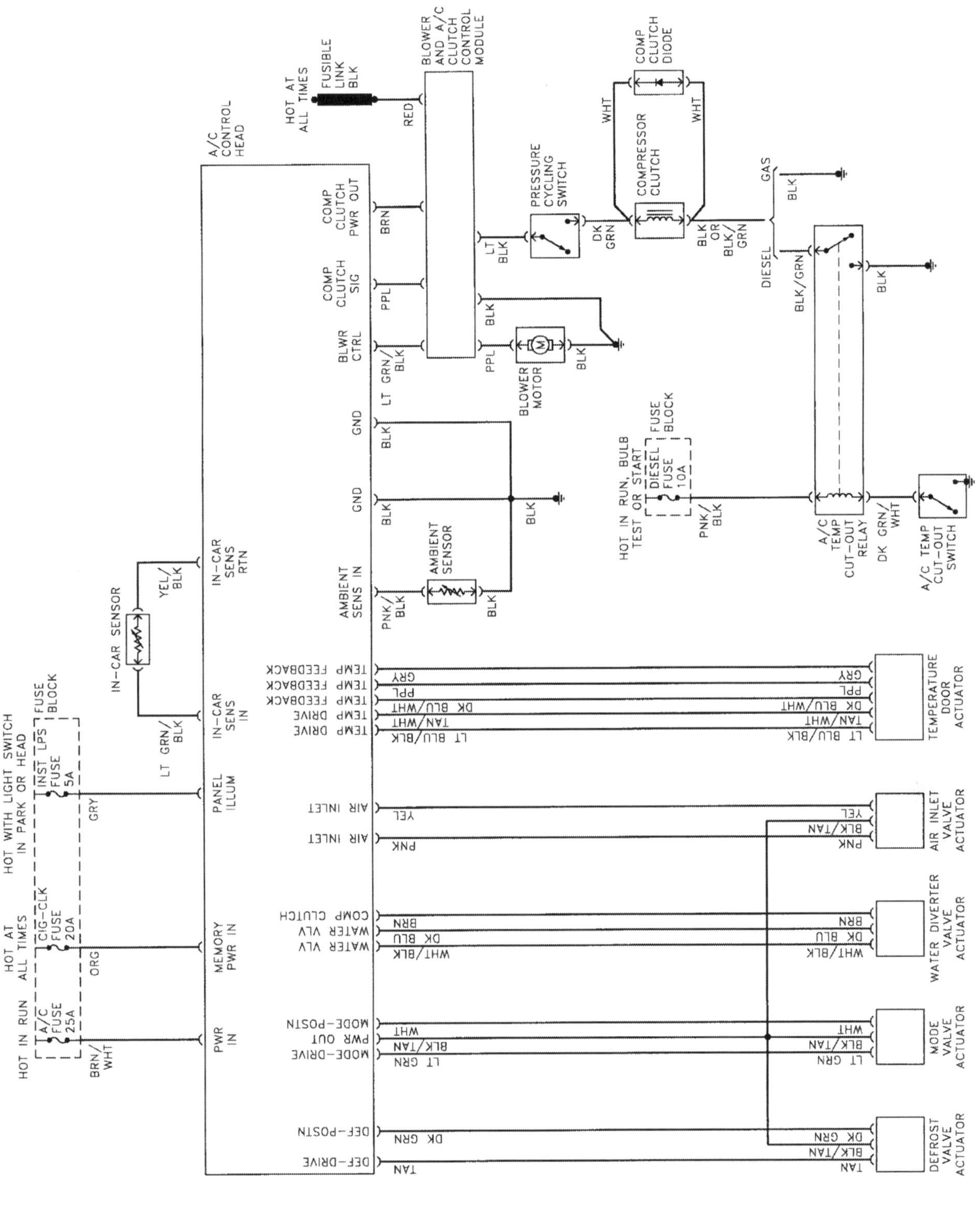

Typical 1983 and later Toronado/Riviera Electronic Climate Control system

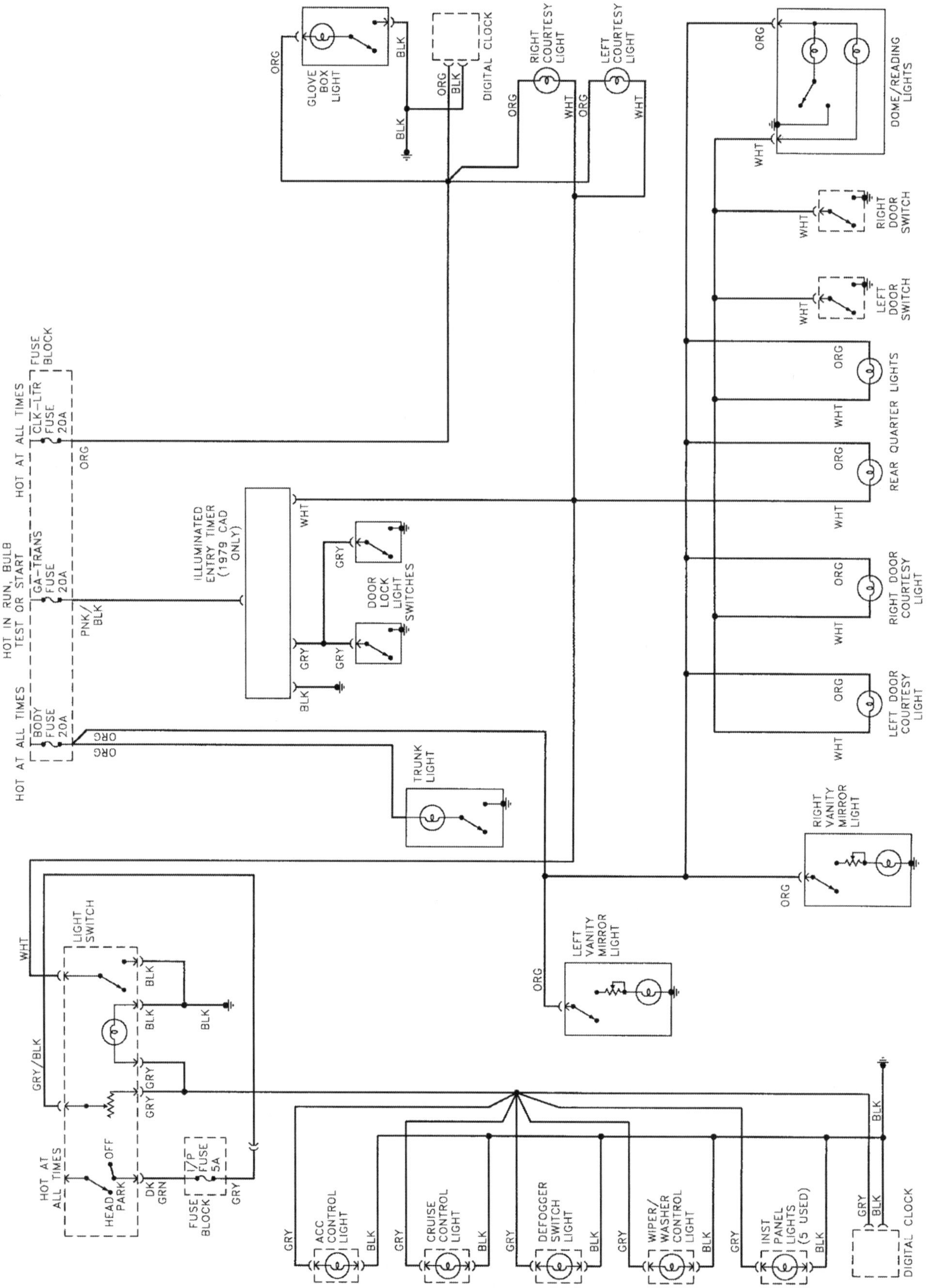

Typical 1979 and 1980 interior lighting system

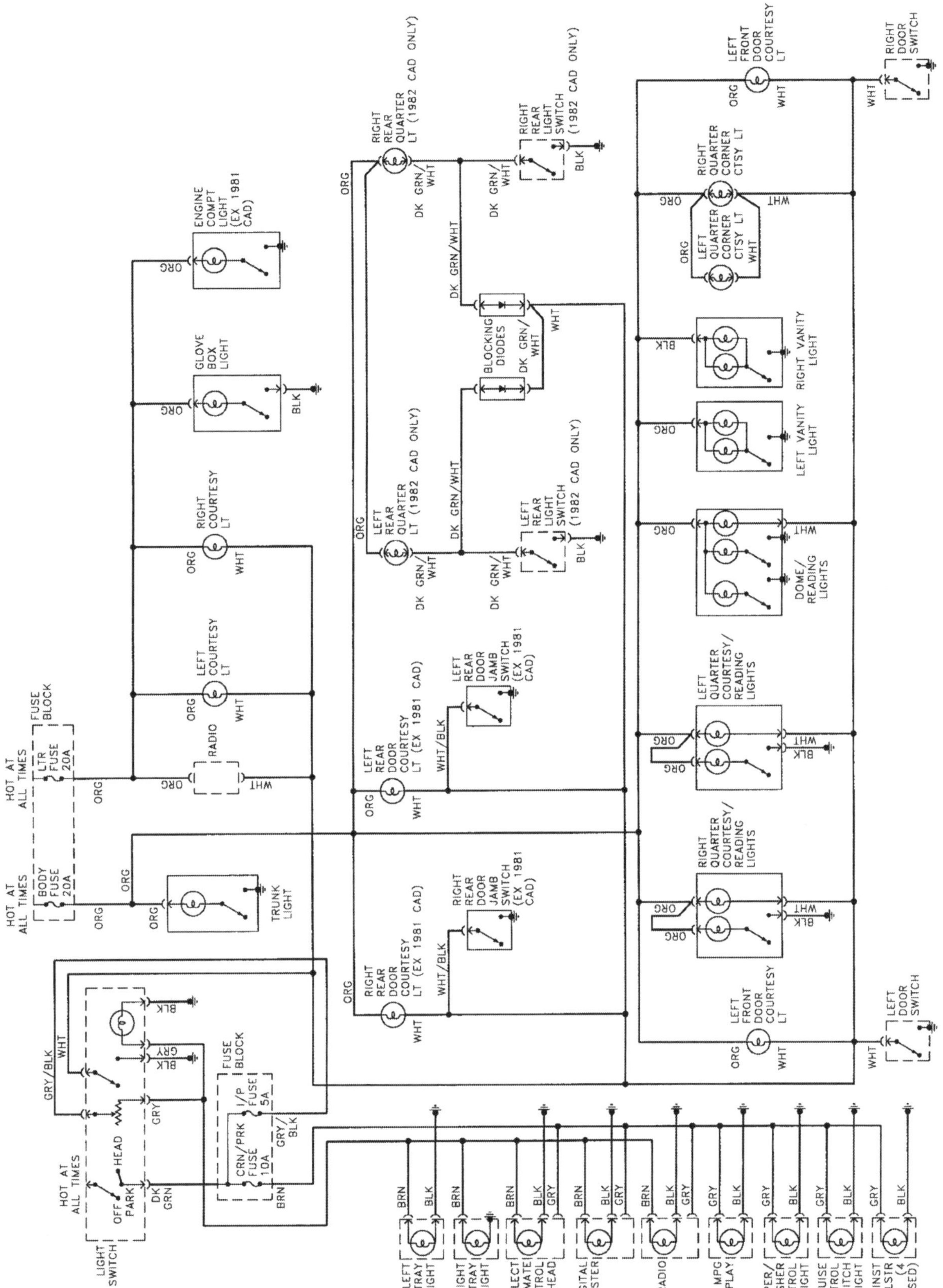

Typical 1981 and later interior lighting system

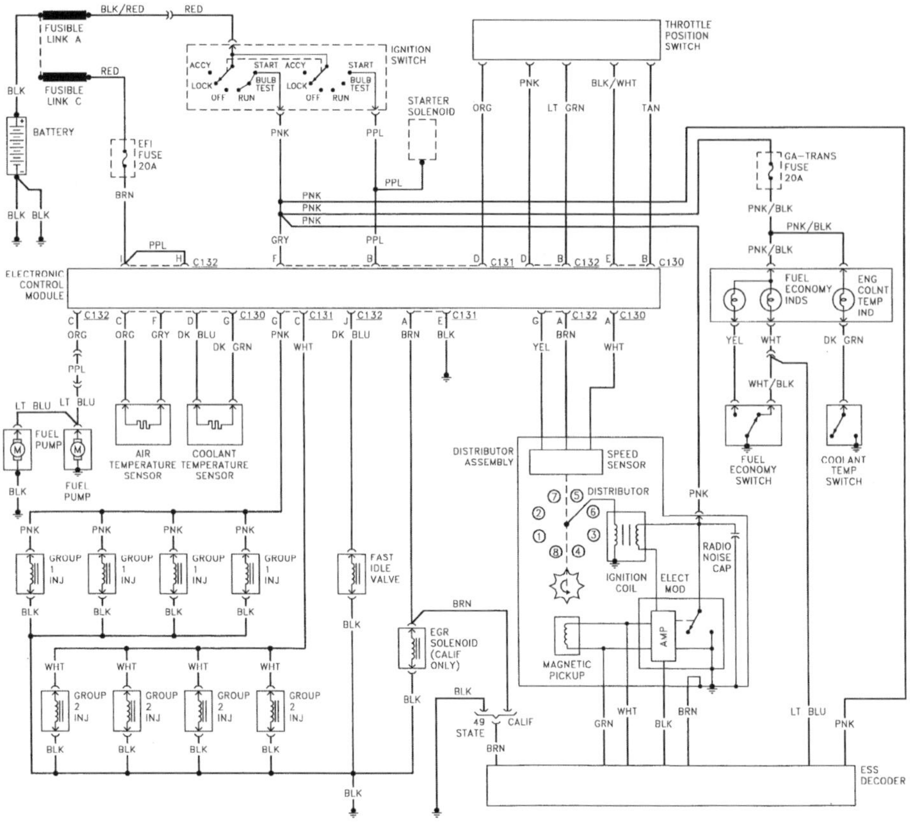

Typical Eldorado/Seville Electronic Fuel Injection engine management system (MPFI)

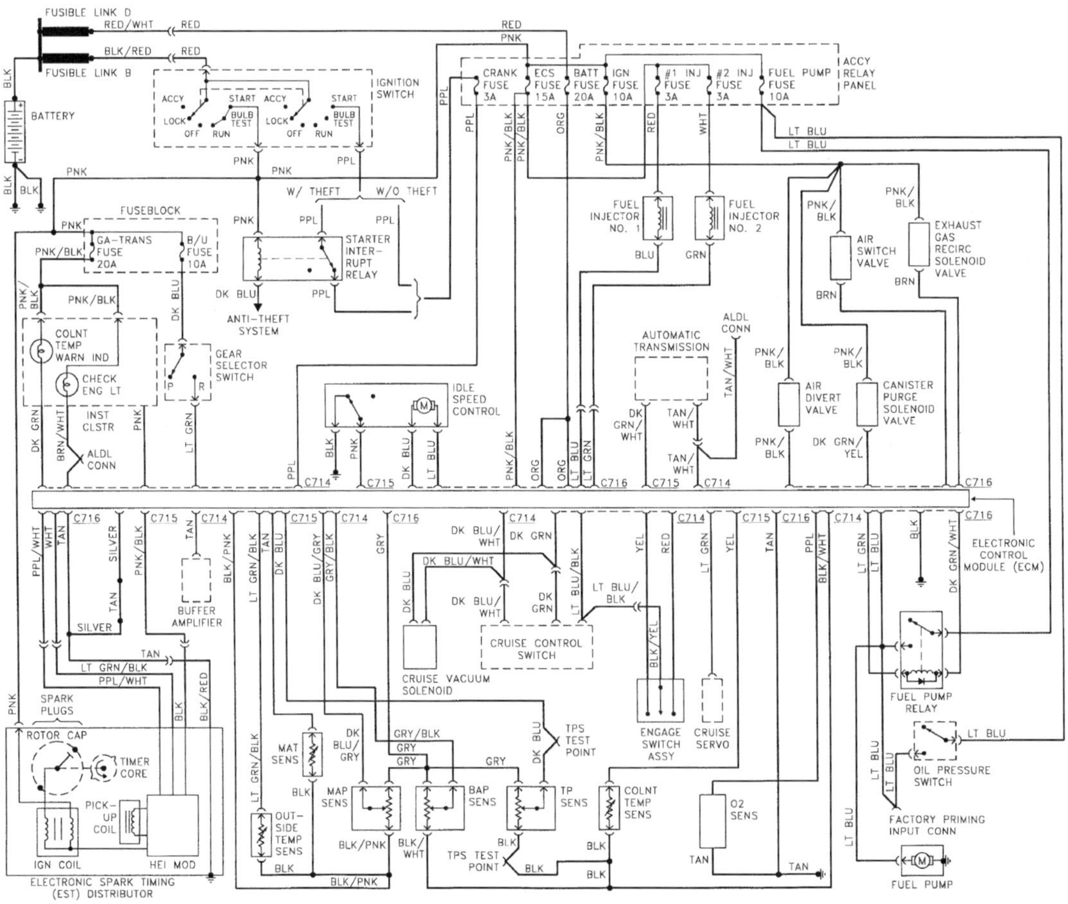

Typical Eldorado/Seville Digital Fuel Injection engine management system (TBI)

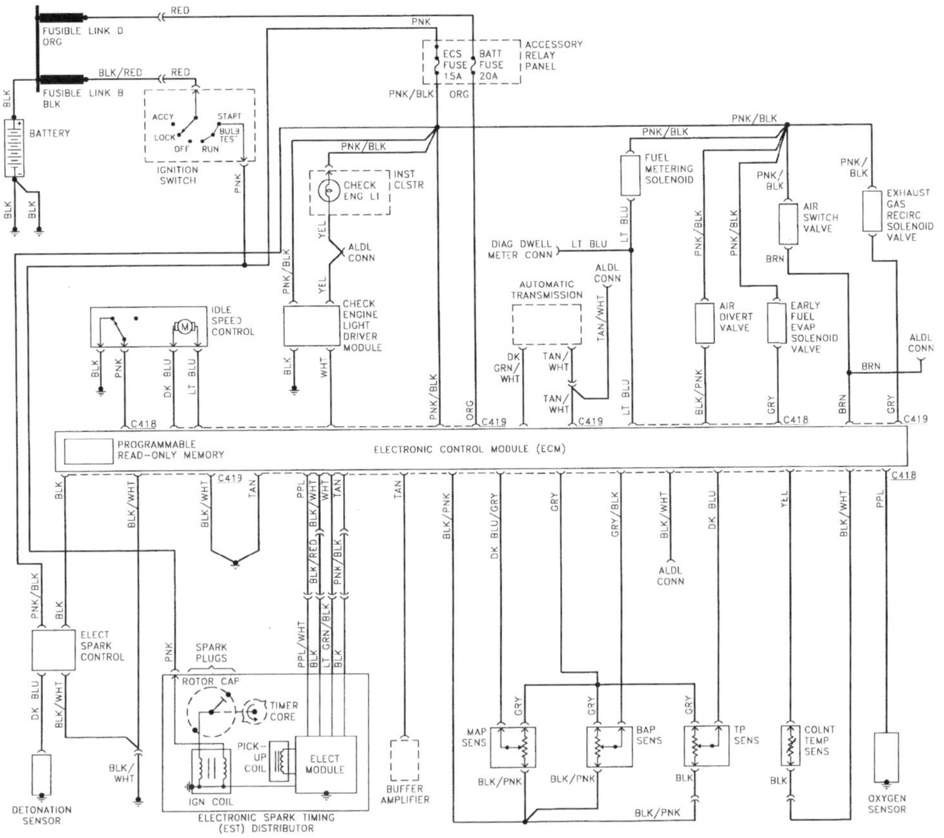

Typical Eldorado/Seville V6 engine management system (carbureted)

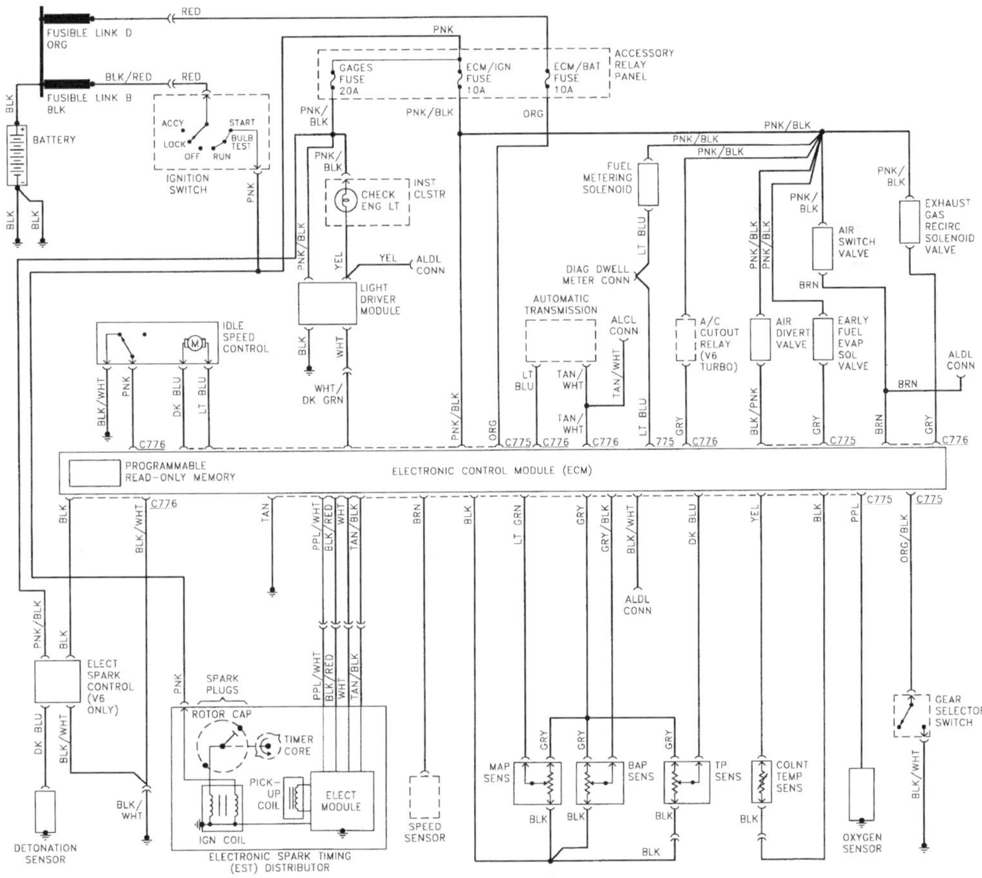

Typical 1983 and earlier Toronado/Riviera V6 and V8 engine management system

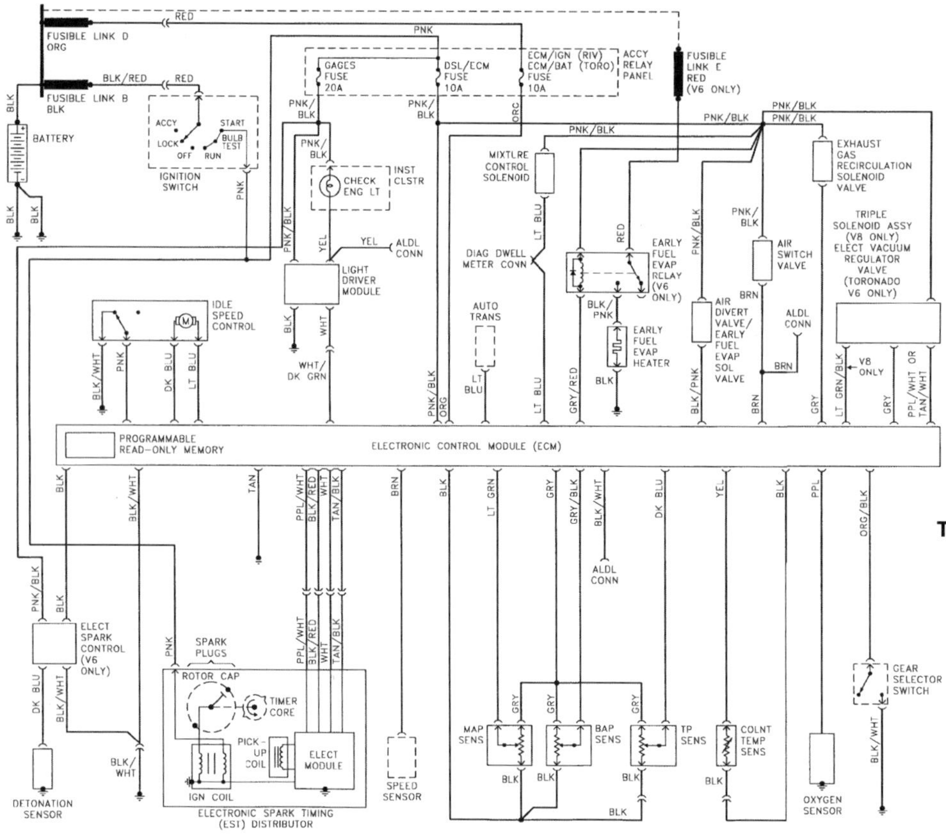

Typical 1984 Toronado/Riviera V6 and V8 engine management system

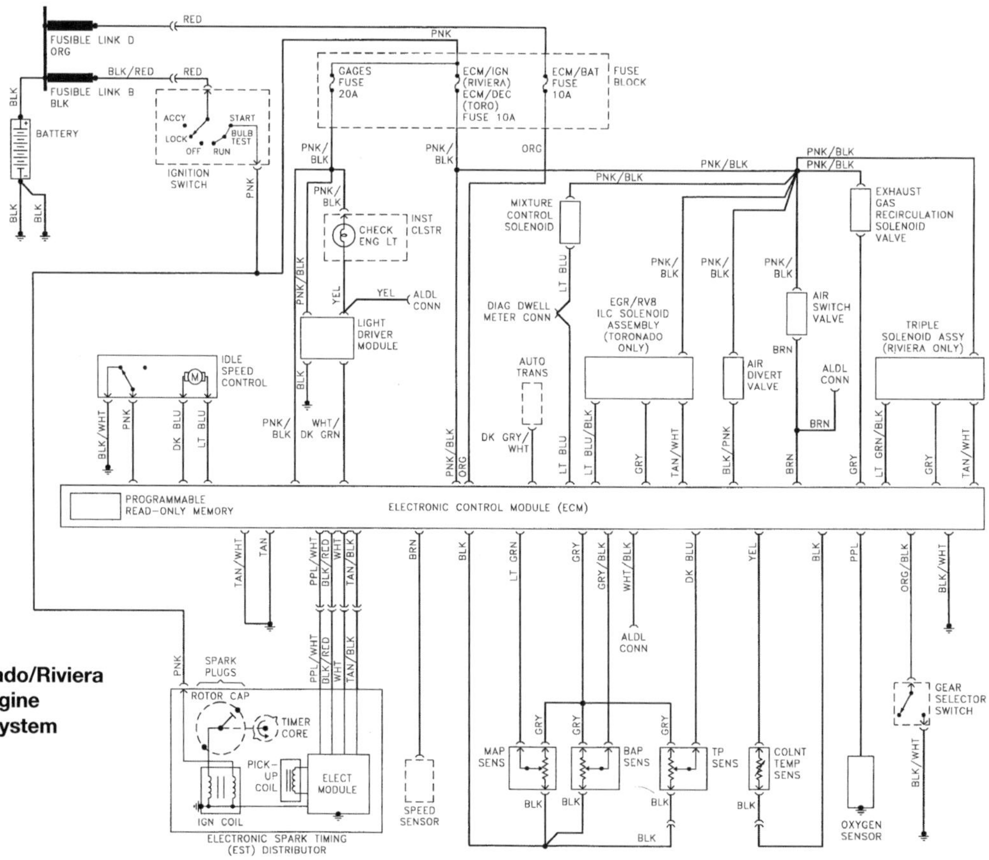

Typical 1985 Toronado/Riviera V6 and V8 engine management system

Index

F

G

H

I

J

L

M

N

O

P

R

S

T

U

V

W

Haynes Automotive Manuals

NOTE: If you do not see a listing for your vehicle, please visit **haynes.com** *for the latest product information and check out our* ***Online Manuals!***

ACURA
12020 **Integra** '86 thru '89 **& Legend** '86 thru '90
12021 **Integra** '90 thru '93 **& Legend** '91 thru '95
Integra '94 thru '00 - *see HONDA Civic (42025)*
MDX '01 thru '07 - *see HONDA Pilot (42037)*
12050 **Acura TL** all models '99 thru '08

AMC
14020 Concord/Hornet/Gremlin/Spirit '70 thru '83
14025 **(Renault) Alliance & Encore** '83 thru '87

AUDI
15020 **4000** all models '80 thru '87
15025 **5000** all models '77 thru '83
15026 **5000** all models '84 thru '88
Audi A4 '96 thru '01 - *see VW Passat (96023)*
15030 **Audi A4** '02 thru '08

AUSTIN-HEALEY
Sprite - *see MG Midget (66015)*

BMW
18020 **3/5 Series** '82 thru '92
18021 **3-Series** including Z3 models '92 thru '98
18022 **3-Series** including Z4 models '99 thru '05
18023 **3-Series** '06 thru '14
18025 **320i** all 4-cylinder models '75 thru '83
18050 **1500 thru 2002** except Turbo '59 thru '77

BUICK
19010 **Buick Century** '97 thru '05
Century (front-wheel drive) - *see GM (38005)*
19020 **Buick, Oldsmobile & Pontiac Full-size (Front wheel drive)** '85 thru '05
19025 **Buick, Oldsmobile & Pontiac Full-size (Rear wheel drive)** '70 thru '90
19027 **Buick LaCrosse** '05 thru '13
Regal - *see GENERAL MOTORS (38010)*
Skyhawk - *see GM (38015)*
Skylark - *see GM (38020, 38025)*
Somerset - *see GENERAL MOTORS (38025)*

CADILLAC
21015 **CTS & CTS-V** '03 thru '14
21030 **Cadillac Rear Wheel Drive** '70 thru '93
Cimarron, Eldorado & Seville - *see GM (38015, 38030, 38031)*

CHEVROLET
10305 **Chevrolet Engine Overhaul Manual**
24010 **Astro & GMC Safari Mini-vans** '85 thru '05
24015 **Camaro V8** all models '70 thru '81
24016 **Camaro** all models '82 thru '92
Cavalier - *see GM (38016)*
Celebrity - *see GM (38005)*
24017 **Camaro & Firebird** '93 thru '02
24018 **Camaro** '10 thru '15
24020 **Chevelle, Malibu, El Camino** '69 thru '87
24024 **Chevette & Pontiac T1000** '76 thru '87
Citation - *see GENERAL MOTORS (38020)*
24027 **Colorado & GMC Canyon** '04 thru '12
24032 **Corsica & Beretta** all models '87 thru '96
24040 **Corvette** all V8 models '68 thru '82
24041 **Corvette** all models '84 thru '96
24042 **Corvette** all models '97 thru '13
24044 **Cruze** '11 thru '19
24045 **Full-size Sedans** Caprice, Impala, Biscayne, Bel Air & Wagons '69 thru '90
24046 **Impala SS & Caprice and Buick Roadmaster** '91 thru '96
Impala '00 thru '05 - *see LUMINA (24048)*
24047 **Impala & Monte Carlo** all models '06 thru '11
Lumina '90 thru '94 - *see GM (38010)*
24048 **Lumina & Monte Carlo** '95 thru '05
Lumina APV - *see GM (38035)*
24050 **Luv Pick-up** all 2WD & 4WD '72 thru '82
24051 **Malibu** '13 thru '19
24055 **Monte Carlo** all models '70 thru '88
Monte Carlo '95 thru '01 - *see LUMINA (24048)*
24059 **Nova** all V8 models '69 thru '79
24060 **Nova/Geo Prizm** '85 thru '92
24064 **Pick-ups** '67 thru '87 - Chevrolet & GMC
24065 **Pick-ups** '88 thru '98 - Chevrolet & GMC
24066 **Pick-ups** '99 thru '06 - Chevrolet & GMC
24067 **Chevy Silverado & GMC Sierra** '07 thru '14
24068 **Chevy Silverado & GMC Sierra** '14 thru '19
24070 **S-10 & S-15 Pick-ups** '82 thru '93
24071 **S-10 & Sonoma Pick-ups** '94 thru '04
24072 **Chevrolet TrailBlazer, GMC Envoy & Oldsmobile Bravada** '02 thru '09
24075 **Sprint** '85 thru '88, **Geo Metro** '89 thru '01
24080 **Vans - Chevrolet & GMC** '68 thru '96
24081 **Chevrolet Express & GMC Savana** Full-size Vans '96 thru '19

CHRYSLER
10310 **Chrysler Engine Overhaul Manual**
25015 **Chrysler Cirrus, Dodge Stratus, Plymouth Breeze,** '95 thru '00
25020 **Full-size Front-Wheel Drive** '88 thru '93
K-Cars - *see DODGE Aries (30008)*
25025 **Chrysler LHS, Concorde & New Yorker, Dodge** Intrepid, **Eagle** Vision, '93 thru '97
25026 **Chrysler LHS, Concorde, 300M, Dodge** Intrepid '98 thru '04
25027 **Chrysler 300** '05 thru '18, **Dodge Charger** '06 thru '18, **Magnum** '05 thru '08 **& Challenger** '08 thru '18
25030 **Chrysler & Plymouth Mid-size** '82 thru '95
Rear-wheel Drive - *see DODGE (30050)*
25035 **PT Cruiser** all models '01 thru '10
25040 **Chrysler** Sebring '95 thru '06, **Dodge** Stratus '01 thru '06 **& Dodge** Avenger '95 thru '00
25041 **Chrysler Sebring** '07 thru '10, **200** '11 thru '17 **Dodge Avenger** '08 thru '14

DATSUN
28005 **200SX** all models '80 thru '83
28012 **240Z, 260Z & 280Z** Coupe '70 thru '78
28014 **280ZX** Coupe & 2+2 '79 thru '83
300ZX - *see NISSAN (72010)*
28018 **510 & PL521 Pick-up** '68 thru '73
28020 **510** all models '78 thru '81
28022 **620 Series Pick-up** all models '73 thru '79
720 Series Pick-up - *see NISSAN (72030)*

DODGE
30008 **Aries & Plymouth Reliant** '81 thru '89
30010 **Caravan & Plymouth Voyager** '84 thru '95
30011 **Caravan & Plymouth Voyager** '96 thru '02
30012 **Challenger & Plymouth Sapporro** '78 thru '83
30013 **Caravan, Chrysler Voyager & Town & Country** '03 thru '07
30014 **Grand Caravan & Chrysler Town & Country** '08 thru '18
30020 **Dakota Pick-ups** all models '87 thru '96
30021 **Durango** '98 & '99 **& Dakota** '97 thru '99
30022 **Durango** '00 thru '03 **& Dakota** '00 thru '04
30023 **Durango** '04 thru '09 **& Dakota** '05 thru '11
30025 **Dart, Challenger/Plymouth Barracuda & Valiant** 6-cylinder models '67 thru '76
30030 **Daytona & Chrysler Laser** '84 thru '89
Intrepid - *see Chrysler (25025, 25026)*
30034 **Neon** all models '95 thru '99
30035 **Omni & Plymouth Horizon** '78 thru '90
30036 **Dodge & Plymouth Neon** '00 thru '05
30040 **Pick-ups** full-size models '74 thru '93
30041 **Pick-ups** full-size models '94 thru '01
30042 **Pick-ups** full-size models '02 thru '08
30043 **Pick-ups** full-size models '09 thru '18
30045 **Ram 50/D50 Pick-ups & Raider and Plymouth Arrow Pick-ups** '79 thru '93
30050 **Dodge/Plymouth/Chrysler** RWD '71 thru '89
30055 **Shadow & Plymouth Sundance** '87 thru '94
30060 **Spirit & Plymouth Acclaim** '89 thru '95
30065 **Vans - Dodge & Plymouth** '71 thru '03

EAGLE
Talon - *see MITSUBISHI (68030, 68031)*
Vision - *see CHRYSLER (25025)*

FIAT
34010 **124 Sport Coupe & Spider** '68 thru '78
34025 **X1/9** all models '74 thru '80

FORD
10320 **Ford Engine Overhaul Manual**
10355 **Ford Automatic Transmission Overhaul**
11500 **Mustang '64-1/2 thru '70 Restoration Guide**
36004 **Aerostar Mini-vans** '86 thru '97
36006 **Contour & Mercury Mystique** '95 thru '00
36008 **Courier Pick-up** all models '72 thru '82
36012 **Crown Victoria & Mercury Grand Marquis** '88 thru '11
36016 **Escort & Mercury Lynx** '81 thru '90
36020 **Escort & Mercury Tracer** '91 thru '02
36022 **Escape** '01 thru '17, **Mazda Tribute** '01 thru '11 **& Mercury Mariner** '05 thru '11
36024 **Explorer & Mazda Navajo** '91 thru '01
36025 **Explorer & Mercury Mountaineer** '02 thru '10
36026 **Explorer** '11 thru '17
36028 **Fairmont & Mercury Zephyr** '78 thru '83
36030 **Festiva & Aspire** '88 thru '97
36032 **Fiesta** all models '77 thru '80
36034 **Focus** all models '00 thru '11
36035 **Focus** '12 thru '14
36045 **Ford Fusion** '06 thru '14 **& Mercury Milan** '06 thru '10
36048 **Mustang V8** all models '64-1/2 thru '73
36049 **Mustang II** 4-cylinder, V6 & V8 '74 thru '78
36050 **Mustang & Mercury Capri** '79 thru '93
36051 **Mustang** all models '94 thru '04
36052 **Mustang** '05 thru '14
36054 **Pick-ups and Bronco** '73 thru '79
36058 **Pick-ups and Bronco** '80 thru '96
36059 **F-150** '97 thru '03, **Expedition** '97 thru '17, **F-250** '97 thru '99, **F-150 Heritage** '04 **& Lincoln Navigator** '98 thru '17
36060 **Super Duty Pick-up & Excursion** '99 thru '10
36061 **F-150** full-size '04 thru '10
36062 **Pinto & Mercury Bobcat** '75 thru '80
36063 **F-150** full-size '15 thru '17
36064 **Super Duty Pick-ups** '11 thru '16
36066 **Probe** all models '89 thru '92
36070 **Ranger & Bronco II** gas models '83 thru '92
36071 **Ranger** '93 thru '11 **& Mazda Pick-ups** '94 thru '09
36074 **Taurus & Mercury Sable** '86 thru '95
36075 **Taurus & Mercury Sable** '96 thru '07
36076 **Taurus** '08 thru '14, **Five Hundred** '05 thru '07, **Mercury Montego** '05 thru '07 **& Sable** '08 thru '09
36078 **Tempo & Mercury Topaz** '84 thru '94
36082 **Thunderbird & Mercury Cougar** '83 thru '88
36086 **Thunderbird & Mercury Cougar** '89 thru '97
36090 **Vans** all V8 Econoline models '69 thru '91
36094 **Vans** full size '92 thru '14
36097 **Windstar** '95 thru '03, **Freestar & Mercury Monterey Mini-van** '04 thru '07

GENERAL MOTORS
10360 **GM Automatic Transmission Overhaul**
38005 **Buick Century, Chevrolet Celebrity, Olds Cutlass Ciera & Pontiac 6000** '82 thru '96
38010 **Buick Regal, Chevrolet Lumina, Oldsmobile Cutlass Supreme & Pontiac Grand Prix** front wheel drive '88 thru '07
38015 **Buick Skyhawk, Cadillac Cimarron, Chevrolet Cavalier, Oldsmobile Firenza Pontiac J-2000 & Sunbird** '82 thru '94
38016 **Chevrolet Cavalier/Pontiac Sunfire** '95 thru '05
38017 **Chevrolet Cobalt & Pontiac G5** '05 thru '11
38020 **Buick Skylark, Chevrolet Citation, Olds Omega, Pontiac Phoenix** '80 thru '85
38025 **Buick Skylark & Somerset, Olds Achieva, Calais & Pontiac Grand Am** '85 thru '98
38026 **Chevrolet Malibu, Olds Alero & Cutlass, Pontiac Grand Am** '97 thru '03
38027 **Chevrolet Malibu** '04 thru '12
38030 **Cadillac Eldorado, Seville, Oldsmobile Toronado & Buick Riviera** '71 thru '85
38031 **Cadillac Eldorado, Seville, DeVille, Fleetwood, Oldsmobile Toronado & Buick Riviera** '86 thru '93
38032 **Cadillac DeVille** '94 thru '05, **Seville** '92 thru '04 **& Cadillac DTS** '06 thru '10
38035 **Chevrolet Lumina APV, Olds Silhouette & Pontiac Trans Sport** all models '90 thru '96
38036 **Chevrolet Venture, Olds Silhouette, Pontiac Trans Sport & Montana** '97 thru '05
38040 **Chevrolet Equinox** '05 thru '17, **GMC Terrain** '10 thru '17 **& Pontiac Torrent** '06 thru '09

GEO
Metro - *see CHEVROLET Sprint (24075)*
Prizm - *'85 thru '92 see CHEVY (24060), '93 thru '02 see TOYOTA Corolla (92036)*
40030 **Storm** all models '90 thru '93
Tracker - *see SUZUKI Samurai (90010)*

GMC
Vans & Pick-ups - *see CHEVROLET*

HONDA
42010 **Accord CVCC** all models '76 thru '83
42011 **Accord** all models '84 thru '89
42012 **Accord** all models '90 thru '93
42013 **Accord** all models '94 thru '97
42014 **Accord** all models '98 thru '02
42015 **Accord** '03 thru '12 **& Crosstour** '10 thru '14
42016 **Accord** '13 thru '17
42020 **Civic 1200** all models '73 thru '79
42021 **Civic 1300 & 1500 CVCC** '80 thru '83
42022 **Civic 1500 CVCC** all models '75 thru '79
42023 **Civic** all models '84 thru '91
42024 **Civic & del Sol** '92 thru '95
42025 **Civic** '96 thru '00 **& CR-V** '97 thru '01 **& Acura Integra** '94 thru '00
42026 **Civic** '01 thru '11 **& CR-V** '02 thru '11
42027 **Civic** '12 thru '15 **& CR-V** '12 thru '16
42030 **Fit** '07 thru '13
42035 **Odyssey** models '99 thru '10
Passport - *see ISUZU Rodeo (47017)*
42037 **Honda Pilot** '03 thru '08, **Ridgeline** '06 thru '14 **& Acura MDX** '01 thru '07
42040 **Prelude CVCC** all models '79 thru '89

HYUNDAI
43010 **Elantra** all models '96 thru '19
43015 **Excel & Accent** all models '86 thru '13
43050 **Santa Fe** all models '01 thru '12
43055 **Sonata** all models '99 thru '14

INFINITI
G35 '03 thru '08 - *see NISSAN 350Z (72011)*

ISUZU
Hombre - *see CHEVROLET S-10 (24071)*
47017 **Rodeo** '91 thru '02, **Amigo** '89 thru '94 & '98 thru '02 **& Honda Passport** '95 thru '02
47020 **Trooper** '84 thru '91 **& Pick-up** '81 thru '93

JAGUAR
49010 **XJ6** all 6-cylinder models '68 thru '86
49011 **XJ6** all models '88 thru '94
49015 **XJ12 & XJS** all 12-cylinder models '72 thru '85

JEEP
50010 **Cherokee, Comanche & Wagoneer Limited** all models '84 thru '01
50011 **Cherokee** '14 thru '19
50020 **CJ** all models '49 thru '86
50025 **Grand Cherokee** all models '93 thru '04
50026 **Grand Cherokee** '05 thru '19 **& Dodge Durango** '11 thru '19
50029 **Grand Wagoneer & Pick-up** '72 thru '91
50030 **Wrangler** all models '87 thru '17
50035 **Liberty** '02 thru '12 **& Dodge Nitro** '07 thru '11
50050 **Patriot & Compass** '07 thru '17

KIA
54050 **Optima** '01 thru '10
54060 **Sedona** '02 thru '14
54070 **Sephia** '94 thru '01, **Spectra** '00 thru '09, **Sportage** '05 thru '20
54077 **Sorento** '03 thru '13

LEXUS
ES 300/330 - *see TOYOTA Camry (92007, 92008)*
RX 300/330/350 - *see TOYOTA Highlander (92095)*

LINCOLN
Navigator - *see FORD Pick-up (36059)*
59010 **Rear-Wheel Drive Continental** '70 thru '87, **Mark Series** '70 thru '92 **& Town Car** '81 thru '10

MAZDA
61010 **GLC (rear wheel drive)** '77 thru '83
61011 **GLC (front wheel drive)** '81 thru '85
61012 **Mazda3** '04 thru '11
61015 **323 & Protegé** '90 thru '03
61016 **MX-5 Miata** '90 thru '14
61020 **MPV** all models '89 thru '98
61030 **Pick-ups** '72 thru '93
Pick-ups '94 thru '09 - *see Ford (36071)*
61035 **RX-7** all models '79 thru '85
61036 **RX-7** all models '86 thru '91
61040 **626 (rear-wheel drive)** all models '79 thru '82
61041 **626 & MX-6 (front-wheel drive)** '83 thru '92
61042 **626** '93 thru '01 **& MX-6/Ford Probe** '93 thru '02
61043 **Mazda6** '03 thru '13

MERCEDES-BENZ
63012 **123 Series Diesel** '76 thru '85
63015 **190 Series** 4-cylinder gas models '84 thru '88
63020 **230, 250 & 280** 6-cylinder SOHC '68 thru '72
63025 **280 123 Series** gas models '77 thru '81
63030 **350 & 450** all models '71 thru '80
63040 **C-Class:** C230/C240/C280/C320/C350 '01 thru '07

MERCURY
64200 **Villager & Nissan Quest** '93 thru '01
All other titles, see FORD listing.

MG
66010 **MGB** Roadster & GT Coupe '62 thru '80
66015 **MG Midget & Austin Healey Sprite Roadster** '58 thru '80

MINI
67020 **Mini** '02 thru '13

MITSUBISHI
68020 **Cordia, Tredia, Galant, Precis & Mirage** '83 thru '93
68030 **Eclipse, Eagle Talon & Plymouth Laser** '90 thru '94
68031 **Eclipse** '95 thru '05 **& Eagle Talon** '95 thru '98
68035 **Galant** '94 thru '12
68040 **Pick-up** '83 thru '96 **& Montero** '83 thru '93

NISSAN
72010 **300ZX** all models incl. Turbo '84 thru '89
72011 **350Z & Infiniti G35** all models '03 thru '08
72015 **Altima** all models '93 thru '06
72016 **Altima** '07 thru '12
72020 **Maxima** all models '85 thru '92
72021 **Maxima** all models '93 thru '08
72025 **Murano** '03 thru '14
72030 **Pick-ups** '80 thru '97 **& Pathfinder** '87 thru '95
72031 **Frontier, Xterra & Pathfinder** '96 thru '04
72032 **Frontier & Xterra** '05 thru '14
72037 **Pathfinder** '05 thru '14
72040 **Pulsar** all models '83 thru '86
72042 **Roque** all models '08 thru '20
72050 **Sentra** all models '82 thru '94
72051 **Sentra & 200SX** all models '95 thru '06
72060 **Stanza** all models '82 thru '90
72070 **Titan pick-ups** '04 thru '10 **& Armada** '05 thru '10
72080 **Versa** all models '07 thru '19

OLDSMOBILE
73015 **Cutlass** V6 & V8 gas models'74 thru '88
For other OLDSMOBILE titles, see BUICK, CHEVROLET or GM listings.

PLYMOUTH
For PLYMOUTH titles, see DODGE.

PONTIAC
79008 **Fiero** all models '84 thru '88
79018 **Firebird** V8 models except Turbo '70 thru '81
79019 **Firebird** all models '82 thru '92
79025 **G6** all models '05 thru '09
79040 **Mid-size Rear-wheel Drive** '70 thru '87
Vibe '03 thru '10 - *see TOYOTA Corolla (92037)*
For other PONTIAC titles, see BUICK, CHEVROLET or GM listings.

PORSCHE
80020 **911** Coupe & Targa models '65 thru '89
80025 **914** all 4-cylinder models '69 thru '76
80030 **924** all models including Turbo '76 thru '82
80035 **944** all models including Turbo '83 thru '89

RENAULT
Alliance & Encore - *see AMC (14025)*

SAAB
84010 **900** all models including Turbo '79 thru '88

SATURN
87010 **Saturn** all S-series models '91 thru '02
Saturn Ion '03 thru '07- *see GM (38017)*
87020 **Saturn L-series** all models '00 thru '04
87040 **Saturn VUE** '02 thru '09

SUBARU
89002 **1100, 1300, 1400 & 1600** '71 thru '79
89003 **1600 & 1800** 2WD & 4WD '80 thru '94
89080 **Impreza** '02 thru '11, **WRX** '02 thru '14 **& WRX STI** '04 thru '14
89100 **Legacy** all models '90 thru '99
89101 **Legacy & Forester** '00 thru '09
89102 **Legacy** '10 thru '16 **& Forester** '12 thru '16

SUZUKI
90010 **Samurai/Sidekick & Geo Tracker** '86 thru '01

TOYOTA
92005 **Camry** all models '83 thru '91
92006 **Camry** '92 thru '96 **& Avalon** '95 thru '96
92007 **Camry, Avalon, Solara, Lexus ES 300** '97 thru '01
92008 **Camry, Avalon, Lexus ES 300/330** '02 thru '06 **& Solara** '02 thru '08
92009 **Camry, Avalon & Lexus ES 350** '07 thru '17
92015 **Celica Rear-wheel Drive** '71 thru '85
92020 **Celica Front-wheel Drive** '86 thru '99
92025 **Celica Supra** all models '79 thru '92
92030 **Corolla** all models '75 thru '79
92032 **Corolla** rear-wheel drive models '80 thru '87
92035 **Corolla** front-wheel drive models '84 thru '92
92036 **Corolla & Geo/Chevrolet Prizm** '93 thru '02
92037 **Corolla** '03 thru '19, **Matrix** '03 thru '14, **& Pontiac Vibe** '03 thru '10
92040 **Corolla Tercel** all models '80 thru '82
92045 **Corona** all models '74 thru '82
92050 **Cressida** all models '78 thru '82
92055 **Land Cruiser** FJ40/43/45/55 '68 thru '82
92056 **Land Cruiser** FJ60/62/80/FZJ80 '80 thru '96
92060 **Matrix** '03 thru '11 **& Pontiac Vibe** '03 thru '10
92065 **MR2** all models '85 thru '87
92070 **Pick-up** all models '69 thru '78
92075 **Pick-up** all models '79 thru '95
92076 **Tacoma** '95 thru '04, **4Runner** '96 thru '02 **& T100** '93 thru '08
92077 **Tacoma** all models '05 thru '18
92078 **Tundra** '00 thru '06, **Sequoia** '01 thru '07
92079 **4Runner** all models '03 thru '09
92080 **Previa** all models '91 thru '95
92081 **Prius** all models '01 thru '12
92082 **RAV4** all models '96 thru '12
92085 **Tercel** all models '87 thru '94
92090 **Sienna** all models '98 thru '10
92095 **Highlander** '01 thru '19 **& Lexus RX330/330/350** '99 thru '19
92179 **Tundra** '07 thru '19 **& Sequoia** '08 thru '19

TRIUMPH
94007 **Spitfire** all models '62 thru '81
94010 **TR7** all models '75 thru '81

VW
96008 **Beetle & Karmann Ghia** '54 thru '79
96009 **New Beetle** '98 thru '10
96016 **Rabbit, Jetta, Scirocco & Pick-up** gas models '75 thru '92 & Convertible '80 thru '92
96017 **Golf, GTI & Jetta** '93 thru '98, **Cabrio** '95 thru 02
96018 **Golf, GTI & Jetta** '98 thru '05
96019 **Jetta, Rabbit, GLI, GTI & Golf** '05 thru '11
96020 **Rabbit, Jetta, Pick-up** diesel '77 thru '84
96021 **Jetta** '11 thru '18 **& Golf** '15 thru '19
96023 **Passat** '98 thru '05, **Audi A4** '96 thru '01
96030 **Transporter 1600** all models '68 thru '79
96035 **Transporter 1700, 1800, 2000** '72 thru '79
96040 **Type 3 1500 & 1600** '63 thru '73
96045 **Vanagon Air-Cooled** all models '80 thru '83

VOLVO
97010 **120, 130 Series & 1800 Sports** '61 thru '73
97015 **140 Series** all models '66 thru '74
97020 **240 Series** all models '76 thru '93
97040 **740 & 760 Series** all models '82 thru '88
97050 **850 Series** all models '93 thru '97

TECHBOOK MANUALS
10205 **Automotive Computer Codes**
10206 **OBD-II & Electronic Engine Management**
10210 **Automotive Emissions Control Manual**
10215 **Fuel Injection Manual** '78 thru '85
10225 **Holley Carburetor Manual**
10230 **Rochester Carburetor Manual**
10305 **Chevrolet Engine Overhaul Manual**
10320 **Ford Engine Overhaul Manual**
10330 **GM and Ford Diesel Engine Repair Manual**
10331 **Duramax Diesel Engines** '01 thru '19
10332 **Cummins Diesel Engine Performance**
10333 **GM, Ford & Chrysler Engine Performance**
10334 **GM Engine Performance**
10340 **Small Engine Repair Manual,** 5 HP & Less
10341 **Small Engine Repair Manual,** 5.5 thru 20 HP
10345 **Suspension, Steering & Driveline Manual**
10355 **Ford Automatic Transmission Overhaul**
10360 **GM Automatic Transmission Overhaul**
10405 **Automotive Body Repair & Painting**
10410 **Automotive Brake Manual**
10411 **Automotive Anti-lock Brake (ABS) Systems**
10425 **Automotive Heating & Air Conditioning**
10435 **Automotive Tools Manual**
10445 **Welding Manual**

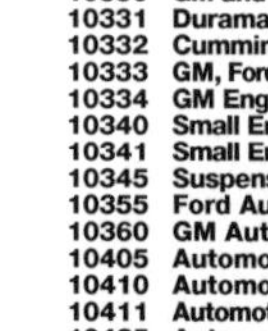

Over a 100 Haynes motorcycle manuals also available

10/22